Biology and

Comparative Physiology of

BIRDS

VOLUME II

AFRICAN WEAVER FINCHES

For explanation of these color photographs see page 168

Biology and
Comparative Physiology of
BIRDS

Edited by
A. J. MARSHALL

Monash University
Victoria, Australia

VOLUME II

1961

ACADEMIC PRESS
NEW YORK and LONDON

QL 673

ACADEMIC PRESS, INC.
111 Fifth Avenue, New York, New York 10003

United Kingdom Edition published by
ACADEMIC PRESS, INC. (LONDON) LTD.
Berkeley Square House, London W.1

LIBRARY OF CONGRESS CATALOG CARD NUMBER: 60-9073

Third Printing, 1969

PRINTED IN THE UNITED STATES OF AMERICA

Contributors to Volume II

R. H. J. Brown, *Department of Zoology, University of Cambridge, England*

Donald S. Farner, *Department of Zoophysiology, Washington State College, Pullman, Washington*

John A. Gibb, *Animal Ecology Section, Department of Scientific and Industrial Research, Wellington, New Zealand*

R. A. Hinde, *Department of Zoology, University of Cambridge, England*

E. Otto Höhn, *Department of Physiology and Pharmacology, University of Alberta, Edmonton, Alberta, Canada*

James R. King, *Department of Experimental Biology, University of Utah, Salt Lake City*

G. Kramer, *Max-Planck-Institute, Wilhelmschaffen, Germany*

A. J. Marshall, *Monash University, Victoria, Australia*

Adolf Portmann, *Department of Zoology, The University, Basle, Switzerland*

R. J. Pumphrey, f.r.s., *Department of Zoology, University of Liverpool, England*

Werner Stingelin, *Department of Zoology, The University, Basle, Switzerland*

Emil Witschi, *Department of Zoology, State University of Iowa, Iowa City*

Contents

Chapter XXI.   Breeding Seasons and Migration

A. J. MARSHALL

Chapter XXII.   Long-Distance Orientation

G. KRAMER

Chapter XXIII.   Behavior

R. A. HINDE

Chapter XXIV.   Bird Populations

JOHN A. GIBB

Contents of Volume I

CHAPTER XIII

The Central Nervous System

ADOLF PORTMANN and WERNER STINGELIN

I. The Brain

A. HISTORICAL

Our knowledge of the avian brain is the result of prolonged researches that fall into two main periods. The first, before 1900, was devoted essentially to macroscopic description. In the second period, studies were revolutionized by microscopical methods. Huber and Crosby (1929) must be consulted for a general survey of the bibliography.

The first precise neurological studies in this special field are those of Bumm (1883), Turner (1891), Herrick (1893), and Münzer and Wiener (1898). The first outstanding level is reached in the classical studies of Edinger and associates (1903). Edinger's work is the basis for all subsequent workers. We owe later experimental contributions to Kalischer (1905) and Rogers (1922); Rose (1914) and Dennler (1921) made advances in cytoarchitectural description. The publications of Lapicque and Girard (1905) and Küenzi (1918), mark important steps in the biometrical understanding of mass development in the different avian groups. The studies of Kappers (1921) on the comparative anatomy of the central nervous system are the starting point for every modern approach to avian brain structure. Kappers' original contributions made possible a thorough interpretation of the fundamental parts.

The results of contributions published since the work of Kappers, and significant modifications in the interpretation of the brain structure are discussed below.

B   1

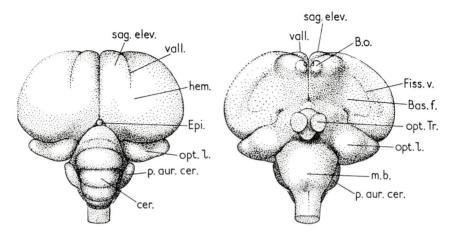

FIG. 1. Brain of bee eater (*Merops apiaster*), a typical avian brain of archaic character, dorsal (left) and ventral views. *Bas. f.*, Basal field; *B.o.*, bulbus olfactorius; *cer.*, Cerebellum; *Epi.*, epiphysis; *Fiss. v.*, fissura ventralis; *hem.*, hemisphere; *m.b.*, medullary bulb; *opt. l.*, optic lobe; *opt. Tr.*, optic tract; *p. aur. cer.*, pars auricularis cerebelli; *sag. elev.*, sagittal elevation; *vall.*, vallecula.

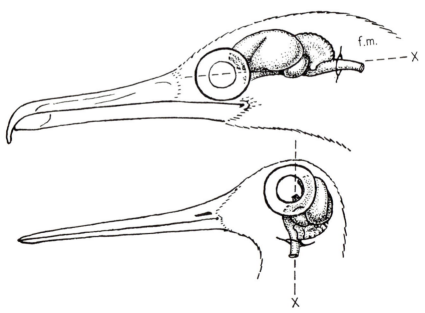

FIG. 2. Extreme differences in the relation of the brain axis to the axis of the bill: cormorant (*Phalacrocorax*) and snipe (*Capella*). *x*. Axis of the brainstem rest; *f.m.*, foramen magnum of the skull.

B. General Aspect and Situation in the Skull

The great vertebrate integration centers—the cerebral hemispheres, cerebellum, and optic lobes—determine the general aspect of the avian brain by their mass as well as by their relative positions (Figs. 1 and 3). The narrowness of the cranial cavity, filled by the cerebral hemispheres and the cerebellum, force the optic lobes into a ventral position between eyes and labyrinth. The eyes exercise a particular influence on the disposition of its parts, as well as on the brain as a whole. Figure 2 gives two extreme possibilities: The forebrain of snipe is drive so far back by

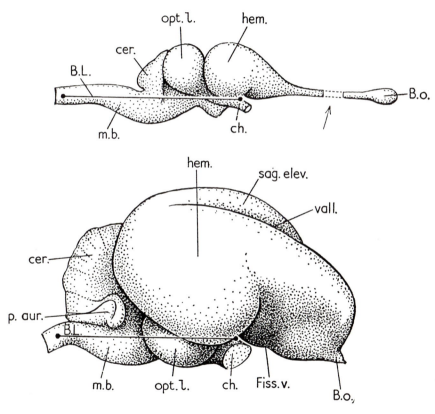

Fig. 3. Comparison of a reptile (*Varanus*) and a bird (*Ara*) shows the mass development of the integration centers, especially of the cerebral hemispheres and cerebellum. The brains of both are drawn to the same scale; the base line from the optic chiasma to the occipital limit of the skull is the unit of measure. *B.l.*, Base line; *B.o.*, bulbus olfactorius; *cer.*, cerebellum; *ch.*, chiasma; *Fiss. v.*, fissura ventralis; *hem.*, hemisphere; *m.b.*, medullary bulb; *opt. l.*, optic lobe; *p. aur.*, pars auricularis cerebelli; *sag. elev.*, sagittal elevation; *vall.*, vallecula.

the big eyeballs that its ventral surface is turned upward and backward compared to the axis of the bill; the ventral side is thus visible in dorsal view! In cormorants, on the other hand, the eyes are relatively small and the axis of brain and bill are nearly parallel.

If we compare a reptile and a bird of approximately the same body weight, the difference of the brain masses marks the new level of nervous organization attained by the Aves (Fig. 3). Even the lowest degree of brain organization found in birds requires a brain mass six to eleven times greater than that found in reptiles of the same proportions (Table I).

TABLE I

Comparison of Brain Weights of Reptiles and Birds
Having Approximately Equal Body Weights

Body weight (grams)	Reptiles		Birds	
	Species	Brain weight (grams)	Species	Brain weight (grams)
11.5	Sand lizard (*Lacerta agilis*)	0.05	Siskin (*Carduelis spinus*)	0.54
19	Green lizard (*Lacerta ocellata*)	0.09	Garden warbler (*Sylvia borin*)	0.58
80	Viper (*Vipera aspis*)	0.08	Quail (*Coturnix coturnix*)	0.73

The fossil record gives a partial answer to the question of how this evolution has come about. The brain of the Jurassic *Archaeopteryx* shows very definitely reptilian proportions (de Beer, 1954), whereas that of cretaceous forms resembles the modern condition (Edinger, 1951). Most of the important steps in brain evolution have taken place since the emergence of true birds; and the latest steps of this evolution are represented in the present fauna. If we consider some unrelated species we find that with about the same body weight (e.g. 80–90 gm.), the brain weights range as follows:

Quail (*Coturnix coturnix*)	0.73
Spotted crake (*Porzana porzana*)	1.1
European starling (*Sturnus vulgaris*)	1.8
Scops owl (*Otus scops*)	2.2
Great spotted woodpecker (*Dryobates major*)	2.7

The differences in brain weight of the unrelated species listed above indicate the scope of the evolution of the avian central nervous system.

C. Cerebral Hemispheres

1. *Development*

The hemispheres are formed as paired lateral evaginations of the unpaired embryonic forebrain. The material constituting this region corresponds to the sensitive part, the alar plate, of the primitive spinal cord. The hemispheres are linked together by the unpaired telencephalon and separated from the diencephalon in a conventional vertebrate manner by the dorsal transverse velum.

In an early stage, four longitudinal zones are already distinct in each hemisphere (Fig. 4). These are: the eminentia basalis in a medioventral situation; the basal ganglion (Paleostriatum, Neostriatum and Hyperstriatum ventrate) ventrally; the laterodorsal paleopallium in the upper region; and the archipallium mediodorsally. The archipallium touches ventrally the eminentia basalis. The most rostral part of each hemisphere is formed by the olfactory bulb, the primary center of smell.

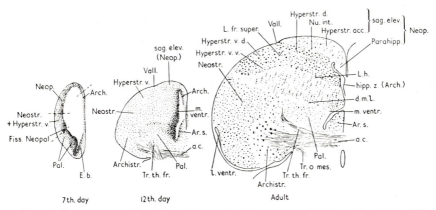

Fig. 4. Transverse sections through two development stades (seventh and twelfth day of incubation) and an adult forebrain of the budgerigar (*Melopsittacus undulatus*). The seventh-day stade shows the general characters of the vertebrate brain. In the twelfth-day stade the ventricle is narrowed to a median slit and the typical configuration of cell masses in birds is reached. Specific cell differentiation and mass development takes place after the twelfth day of incubation. After Haefelfinger (1958).

a.c., anterior commissure; *Arch.* archipallium; *Archistr.*, archistriatum; *Ar. s.*, area septalis; *d.m.l.*, dorsal medullary lamina; *E. b.*, eminentia basalis; *Fiss. Neopal.*, fissura neopaleostriatica; *hipp. z.*, hippocampal zone; *Hyperstr. d.*, hyperstriatum dorsale; *Hyperstr. v.*, hyperstriatum ventrale; *Hyperstr. v.d.*, hyperstriatum ventrodorsale; *Hyperstr. v.v.*, hyperstriatum ventroventrale; *L. fr. super.*, lamina frontalis superior; *L.h.*, lamina hyperstriatica; *l. ventr.*, lateral ventricle; *m. Ventr.*, medial ventricle; *Neop.*, neopallium; *Neostr.*, neostriatum; *Nu. int.*, nucleus intercalatus hyperstriati; *Pal.*, paleostriatum; *Parahipp.*, parahippocampal zone; *sag. elev.*, sagittal elevation; *Tr. th. fr.*, tractus thalamofrontalis; *Tr. o. mes.*, tractus occipitomesencephalicus; *Vall.*, vallecula.

In all Amniota a new region, the neopallium, is added to the four primary longitudinal zones. In reptiles this remains in a very rudimentary condition, whereas in birds and mammals it forms, by lateral and caudal extension, an important part of the hemisphere.

Whereas the neopallium of mammals develops as a surface structure, its growth in birds is massive; it becomes intimately connected with the basal striatal region. Laterally it forms the sagittal elevation and, in the medial zone, the parahippocampus. A cortical layer connects with the archipallium (= hippocampus) (Fig. 5).

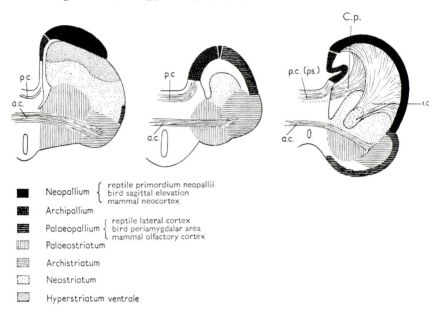

■	Neopallium	{ reptile primordium neopallii bird sagittal elevation mammal neocortex
▓	Archipallium	
☰	Palaeopallium	{ reptile lateral cortex bird periamygdalar area mammal olfactory cortex
▥	Palaeostriatum	
▤	Archistriatum	
▦	Neostriatum	
▨	Hyperstriatum ventrale	

Fig. 5. Comparative diagram of amniote hemispheres (transverse sections); *a.c.*, Anterior commissure; *C.p.*, corpus callosum; *i.c.*, interne capsule; *p.c.*, pallial commissure; *p.s.*, psalterium.
From left to right: bird, reptile, mammal.

Until the seventh day of embryonic life the hemispheres of birds present the general vertebrate structure. The differentiation of marked avian characters takes place from the seventh to the twelfth day (Haefelfinger, 1958) (Fig. 4). The central space, the ventricle, is narrowed to a small medial and caudolateral slit by the ventricular growth of the lateral wall. This massive development is produced by the corpus striatum, especially by the paleo- and the neostriatum in its basal part, and the hyperstriatum on the dorsal side. Compared with this huge mass, the cortical parts of the hemisphere remain in a reduced stage. In some groups (Psittaci and Passeres) the whole olfactory region is reduced (see page 14).

As early as the fifteenth day, while cellular differentiation is only beginning, the disposition of parts typical for orders and even families is appearing.

The two hatching types show marked differences in embryonic development. In a nidifugous bird, myelin sheaths are visible in the forebrain as early as the fifteenth day of incubation. A nidicolous species (e.g. the magpie) does not attain this stage until 3 days after hatching (total age 21 days) (Schifferli, 1948). The difference between the two types is particularly clear when we consider the postembryonic mass development of the hemispheres. The factor of mass growth is 3.23–6.49 in nidifugous birds and 8.79–37.42 in nidicolous species (Sutter, 1943; Portmann, 1947).

2. *Adult hemispheres*

All birds present typically reptilian structures: paleo-, archi-, and neostriatum in the corpus striatum; paleo-, archi-, and neopallium in the pallial region. Figure 5 shows the main differences between reptiles, birds, and mammals.

In birds the neostriatum constitutes by far the greatest part of the hemisphere. Covering the paleostriatum like a cap, it extends from the rostral to the caudal pole (Fig. 6). The uniform cellular structure of the neostriatum in reptiles is differentiated into at least two horizontal layers, partly separated by the lamina hyperstriatica. The true neostriatum forms the ventral part. The dorsal mass (the hyperstriatum ventrale) is often further subdivided into a ventroventral and a ventrodorsal zone (Huber and Crosby, 1929).

The limit of neo- and paleostriatum is marked by a fiber lamina (lamina medullaris dorsalis). A nucleus basalis is differentiated near this limit in a frontobasal position; the ectostriatum, genetically probably part of the neostriatum, lies on the dorsolateral side.

The archistriatum is uniform in the Reptilia, but in birds it is differentiated into several regions. It is surrounded by the neostriatum, excepting the parts limited by the paleostriatum and the basal surface of the hemisphere.

A fiber lamina extending from the dorsal angle of the ventricle laterally to the periphery, marks the dorsal limit of the striatal region. This, the lamina frontalis superior, develops more or less in correspondence with the dimensions of the sagittal elevation. On the dorsal surface the limit of neopallial and striatal structure is indicated by an important furrow, the vallecula. This varies from a flat groove to a deep incision.

Above the lamina frontalis superior the masses of neopallial structures are grouped in "onion sheets" from the bottom to the surface as follows: hyperstriatum dorsale, nucleus intercalatus hyperstriati (sometimes wanting), and hyperstriatum accessorium. The latter region

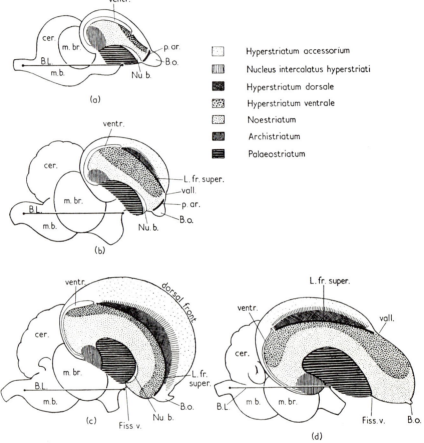

FIG. 6. Parasagittal section through: a, a hypothetical hemisphere intermediate between reptile and bird; b, a primitive avian hemisphere (pigeon); c and d, two evolved avian hemispheres (owl and parakeet). Sections show the structural evolution of the forebrain (a,b) and the two possible types of front formation (c,d): dorsal front formation in c (increased sagittal elevation) and basal front formation in d (increased frontal neostriatum and hyperstriatum ventrale.

B.l., base line (see Fig. 3); *B.o.*, bulbus olfactorius; *cer.*, cerebellum; *Fiss. v.*, fissura ventralis; *L. fr. super.*, lamina frontalis superior; *m.b.*, medullary bulb; *m.br.*, midbrain; *Nu. b.*, nucleus basalis; *p.ar.*, prepyriform area; *vall.*, vallecula; *ventr.*, ventricle.

is connected, without a sharp border, to the parahippocampus, the cortical part of the neopallium.

Parahippocampus and hippocampus enter in contact with the paleopallium in a laterocaudal region, the periamygdalar area. This area is reduced in highly evolved groups. In archaic forms like the Palaeognathae (especially the emu) it forms a cortical zone of considerable extent (Craigie, 1935, 1940).

In the reptilian brain a lateral cortex is found between the periamygdalar field and the prepyriform area (nucleus olfactorius anterior). This zone is generally absent in birds, but in the loon (*Gavia immer*) a very narrow cortical structure connects the two areas. This exceptional case proves that the rostral area prepyriformis and the caudal periamygdalar field are the remnants of the reptilian paleopallium (Craigie, 1940) (Fig. 7). The primitive continuity of these two fields can be detected also in the young cormorant, the grebe (Craigie, 1940), and in the newly hatched emu (Craigie, 1936).

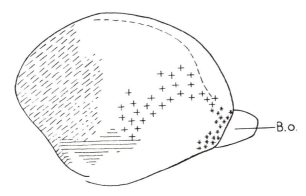

Fig. 7. Outlines of the lateral view of the cerebral hemisphere of a loon (*Gavia*). The widely spaced crosses indicate the more or less vestigial sheet connecting prepyriform and periamygdalar area. Vallecula: Broken line; parahippocampal field *d*: obliquely hatched; periamygdalar area: horizontally hatched; prepyriform area: crosses with double uprights; vestigial sheet: widely spaced crosses. After Craigie (1940).

The medioventral eminentia basalis gives rise in the hemispheres to the nucleus accumbens (ventrofrontal), the nuclei of the septum (ventral), the "bed nucleus" of the pallial commissure and the primordium hippocampi in the dorsal part.

Knowledge of the cytoarchitecture of the avian hemisphere is less precise than that of the mammalian brain. The layered structure of the mammalian cortex offers much more distinctive features than do the cellular masses of the avian brain nuclei. Archaic types present less regional difference than highly evolved groups (Stingelin, 1958). On the other hand, the cytological differences in the basal parts, paleostriatum and archistriatum, are relatively general, while those of the dorsal zones vary much more from one systematic group to the other. The nucleus intercalatus in the dorsal part shows a remarkably uniform texture of small cells.

As a high center of coordination the hemisphere contains big systems of fibers connecting the gray substance of the forebrain; first of all with diencephalic and midbrain centers, and, in a lower degree, with those of the cerebellum and the myelencephalon. There are no direct tracts from the hemispheres to the spinal cord comparable with the pyramidal tracts of mammals.

The transverse or commissural connections of the hemispheres correspond with those of reptiles and mammals but show considerable quantitative differences.

The archaic commissura anterior running in the lamina terminalis shows mainly archistriatal tracts (Fig. 5). The fibers connecting other regions have not been analyzed with certainty, but it is practically certain that they are not related to the neocortical fiber tracts as in the commissura anterior or in the corpus callosum of mammals. There is a commissura pallii, corresponding to the psalterium of mammals, which connects the archipallial parts of the two medial walls of the hemisphere. But this transverse fiber system is just as reduced as the hippocampus structures in birds. Another commissural fiber tract connecting neostriatal centers, the commissura supraoptica, is essentially located in the diencephalon. It is homologous with the commissure of Meynert in mammals.

The sagittal elevation gives rise to a strong tractus corticoseptomesencephalicus. This centrifugal tract is particularly strong in forms with a powerful development of the sagittal structures (e.g. owls) (Stingelin, 1956). Its neopallial fibers, accompanied by archipallial fibers from the hippocampus, end mainly in the diencephalon and in the roof of the midbrain. One branch can be traced as far as the bulb; this, the ramus basalis, perhaps corresponds to the fornix longus of mammals. Certainly it is not homologous with the pyramidal tracts (Huber and Crosby, 1929).

It is highly probable that centrifugal fibers from the sagittal elevation are present in the big striatal tracts known as the peduncles of the forebrain. The dorsal part of these tracts is considered to be mainly afferent, connecting secondary sensitive centers of the diencephalon (nucleus rotundus, nucleus anterior, and nucleus dorsalis) to the ecto- and neostriatum. The basal part is efferent, transmitting impulses from the paleostriatum (eventually the Neostriatum) to the ventral diencephalon and the basal midbrain. It carries fibers which assure the direct connection of the hemispheres with the motor nuclei of the eye muscles in the midbrain. Fibers of the tractus striocerebellaris pass directly to the cerebellum.

Important relations between different fields of the hemispheres are furnished by the four conspicuous horizontal laminas of fibers: lamina medullaris dorsalis, lamina hyperstriatica (tractus frontooccipitalis), lamina frontalis superior, and lamina frontalis suprema. A dense network of associative fibers is developed in the whole hemisphere.

Our knowledge concerning the function of the hemispheres is based essentially on extirpation studies in pigeons that have been carried out since the beginning of the nineteenth century. All these experiments show that sensory and motor activity in pigeons can continue in the absence of the hemispheres. Such pigeons can fly, run, peck, and avoid obstacles: vision, therefore, remains intact. They lack, however, all conditioned responses, as well as the faculty of forming new ones. The capacity to deal with objects in a more complicated manner and to relate objects to needs has been lost (Cate, 1936). Without hemispheres the ability to eat and drink is lost. However, Thauer and Peters (1938) kept a pigeon alive for two years without its hemispheres; it was neither blind, nor had it lost the spontaneity of reaction or the ability to take up food. The authors suppose that in earlier extirpation experiments the diencephalon was injured.

The extirpation of neo- and hyperstriatum leaves intact only the possibility of alimentation; this operation deprives the bird of any faculty of learning, pairing, or care of the offspring (Rogers, 1922).

The archistriatum is a principal center of sensory integration, involving optical impressions and those of other sense organs as well (Kalischer, 1905). The work of Erulkar (1955), with the use of the evoked potential technique, shows that a small region of the mediocaudal neostriatum is an area for the projection of both auditory and tactile sensations. The results of Erulkar and Kalischer thus confirm the general idea that the caudal part of the hemisphere is to be considered as a projection area for sensory stimulation. On the other hand, the experiments of Erulkar reveal considerable physiological differences in sensory projection between the striatum of birds and the cortex of mammals.

Coordination centers for drinking, eating, courtship, and social relations have been located in the lower part of the striatum, particularly in the paleostriatum. Neo- and hyperstriatum are indispensable for pairing, nest building, and parental care. Injuries to the foremost frontal parts of neo- and hyperstriatum, and extirpation of true cortical zones, have no notable consequences in bird behavior (Kalischer, 1905; Rogers, 1922).

3. *Variation in Cytoarchitecture and External Sculpture*

The experimental work so far dealt with has considered the avian hemisphere as a relatively uniform structure throughout the whole group. This is partly due to the lack of a broader comparative basis. During recent years, however, more knowledge has been gained concerning the differences between evolutionary levels and morphological variations. As experimental work of the near future must be based upon a more intimate knowledge of these facts, we will give attention to this aspect of brain morphology.

The cytoarchitectural centers in the hemispheres show important differences of proportions, sometimes from one species to another, and always from group to group. These variations are the expression of systematic differences in groups of the same cerebral level; or they are part of evolutionary changes leading to different cerebral levels. The considerable differences between the relative mass of different brain parts lead to a similar conclusion. In the following comparative section we will use the results of quantitative studies (Portmann, 1946, 1947). The methods will be presented below (page 31).

Evolution of the avian brain to higher degrees of complexity is always combined with a tendency to concentrate the mass of higher centers in the front part of the hemisphere (Stingelin, 1958) (Figs. 6 and 8). This general tendency is expressed in two different ways:

(1) The frontal development may be concentrated in the dorsal part on the sagittal elevation: in this case the primitive disposition of the olfactory bulb is preserved (= dorsal front formation) (Figs. 6c and 8).

(2) The frontal mass development is concentrated in the more basal parts of the higher centers and separates the olfactory bulb from the sagittal elevation; it thus forces the latter into a more caudal extension (basal front formation) (Figs. 6d and 8).

In either case, the dorsal zone (neostriatum, hyperstriatum ventrale, and sagittal elevation) is concerned in this mass development of the structural centers of most forms of complex behavior. The basal centers (paleo- and archistriatum) play a more passive role and are more or less compressed by the processes of frontal development.

In the two above-described trends of frontal development high hemispheric indexes are reached (see pages 32–33): dorsal front, 18–19 (*Corvus corax*); ventral front, 28 (*Ara ararauna*). The lower degrees of structural evolution never attain indexes higher than 5.5. It seems that the structural transformation of the hemisphere (leading to frontal development) was the primary condition for the successive mass development of the higher degrees of avian brain evolution.

The considerable variation in the olfactory bulbs of birds invites

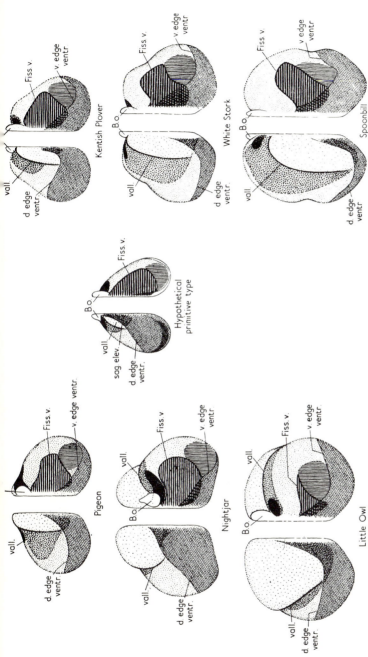

FIG. 8. Dorsal and ventral view of hemispheres of different levels of form evolution in two series of morphological differentiation. The surface extension of the cell zones is marked with different signs. From a hypothetical primitive cerebral hemisphere to the highest structural level, the *dorsal front formation* shows an increased sagittal elevation in contact with the bulbus olfactorius; the *basal front formation*, an increased neostriatum and hyperstriatum ventrale, with the sagittal elevation displaced caudally. Generally in the two trends, the dorsal cell masses (neostriatum, hyperstriatum ventrale, sagittal elevation) are increased, while the basal cell masses (paleostriatum, archistriatum) are compressed.

B.o., bulbus olfactorius; *d. edge ventr.*, dorsal edge of ventricle; *Fiss. v.*, fissura ventralis; *vall.*, vallecula; *v. edge ventr.*, ventral edge of ventricle. Prepyriform area: black; zone of ventricle: obliquely hatched; see also Fig. 6 legend.

special attention (Fig. 9). There occurs a marked decrease in the size of the bulb in higher evolutionary levels of the hemispheres. Where evolution has given rise to specialization, the olfactory bulbs are sometimes well developed, as in the ostrich and its allies. The maximum is reached, or perhaps retained (if we consider the primary condition as macrosmatic), in kiwis. The bulbs are relatively large in Galli, Laro-Limicolae, and Anseres but are extremely reduced in Psittaci, Passeres, and Accipitres. The Passeres, however, are far from being uniform as may be seen by comparing the magpie and flycatcher (Fig. 9): the two bulbs may be partially or completely fused in one unpaired structure.

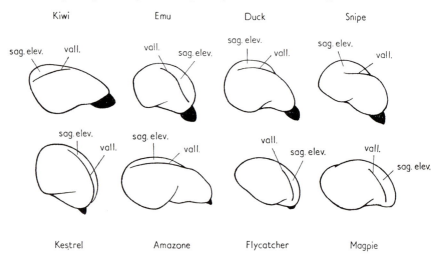

FIG. 9. Outlines of the lateral view of the cerebral hemispheres, demonstrating the difference in size of the olfactory bulb (black) in relatively macrosmatic and in extremely microsmatic birds. *sag. elev.*, Sagittal elevation; *vall.*, vallecula.

D. BETWEENBRAIN (DIENCEPHALON) and MIDBRAIN (MESENCEPHALON)

The high development of hemispheres and cerebellum in birds leads to important displacements in the region of both diencephalon and mesencephalon. The functional evolution of the higher centers involves corresponding mass development, and dislocation, in the lower centers. The mass of the hemispheres forces the two optic lobes and the midbrain into a lateral, and finally into a ventral, position and brings them into close contact with centers of the diencephalon.

These dislocations and changes do not, however, change the general plan, which conforms to the structure in other vertebrates. The limiting furrow (sulcus limitans) separating the dorsal or sensory alar from the ventral or motor basal plate divides the midbrain into a basal part (tegmentum) and a roof (tectum). In the diencephalon this furrow ends in the recessus preopticus directly in front of the optic chiasma. All parts of the diencephalon lying dorsally to the furrow (thalamus, epithalamus, and parietal structures) are derived from the alar plate. Only the relatively small hypothalamus, on the ventral side of the sulcus limitans, is a basal plate structure.

On the bottom of the diencephalon the chiasma of the optic tract forms a conspicuous structure. With few exceptions all the fibers of these tracts end in the two large optic lobes. These lobes are not only relatively bigger than the corresponding parts in reptiles and mammals: their structure, too, is much more complicated. We can (in agreement with Ramon y Cajal, 1891; Schüpbach, 1905) distinguish up to fifteen cortical layers, together constituting a highly developed apparatus of integration.

In all amniotes the nuclei of the dorsal thalamic region are greatly enlarged, as are the tracts connecting these centers with the hemisphere. In birds the most conspicuous of these nuclei are the nucleus rotundus and the nucleus dorsalis, the first in particular being much larger than in Reptilia (Fig. 10). It is related to the statoacoustical region, the cerebellum, the sensory midbrain nucleus of the trigeminus, and the tectum opticum. The same nucleus is connected with the neo- and hyperstriatum of the telencephalon by the tractus thalamofrontalis. We recall experimental work of Erulkar (1955) proving that the functional significance of this thalamic region is far from being elucidated. Figures 10 and 11 demonstrate that the contact of the smaller nuclei of the avian diencephalon with the midbrain centers and the tectum is more intimate than in reptiles (nucleus pretectalis, nucleus spiriformis, nucleus geniculatus laterale). This concentration of nuclei of midbrain and diencephalon is on the one hand an expression of neurobiotactic influences exerted from the midbrain on the diencephalon and, on the other hand, a consequence of the expansion of the cerebellum and the hemispheres.

Effector fibers of the tectum run to the diencephalic nucleus rotundus and nucleus geniculatus laterale, to the lower main center of the midbrain (the nucleus mesencephalicus laterale), and finally by the tectobulbar tract to the medullary bulb. The nucleus mesencephalicus laterale receives fibers from the sensory nucleus of the trigeminus and the statoacoustic zone. Special tracts correlate visual impulses and eye movements: such tracts run from the nucleus mesencephalicus laterale and the more ventral nucleus isthmi to the nuclei of the motor eye nerves oculomotorius and trochlearis.

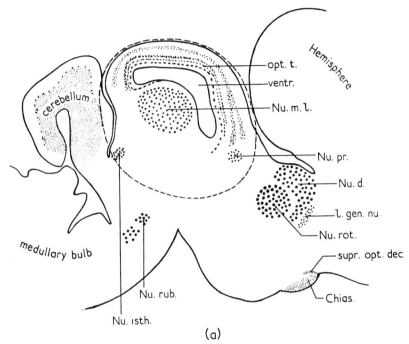

FIG. 10. Parasagittal sections through midbrain and betweenbrain of alligator (a) and budgerigar (b) showing the concentration of the nuclei, the ventral extension of the optic lobes (outlines stippled), the mighty chiasma, and the narrow ventricle in birds. In the budgerigar a lateral and a more medial section are combined and projected into one plane. The more lateral nuclei are indicated with stippled reference lines. a. After Huber and Crosby (1926).

The longitudinal fasciculus arising in the tegmentum is related to the motor nuclei of the eye, the nuclei of the posterior commissure, and the nucleus interstitialis. Near the median plan in the caudal tegmentum of the midbrain lies the nucleus ruber (the nucleus motorius tegmenti of lower vertebrates). This motor center of the midbrain is much more complex in birds than in reptiles, but not differentiated into micro- and macrocellular parts as in mammals. The brachium conjunctivum is the afferent pathway from the nucleus ruber to the cerebellum, while motor impulses from the nucleus ruber are conducted by the rubrospinal tract to the medullary bulb and perhaps even to the spinal cord.

Two commissural systems are located in the di- and mesencephalon: one rostroventral, the other, caudodorsal. The rostral supraoptical commissure connects regions of the forebrain (in its dorsal part), nuclei of the tegmentum (in the ventral part). The posterior commissure at the dorsal limit of di- and mesencephalon is in its dorsal pathways the

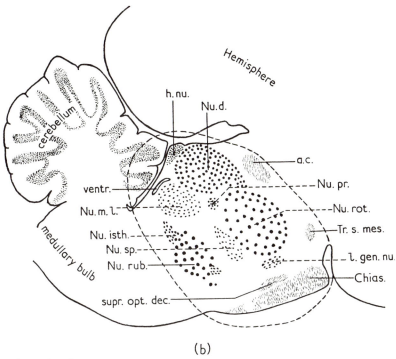

(b)

Fig. 10 (*continued*)

    a.c., Anterior commissure; *Chias.*, chiasma; *h. nu.*, habenular nucleus; *l. gen. nu.*, lateral geniculate nucleus; *Nu. pr.*, nucleus pretectalis; *Nu. rot.*, nucleus rotundus; *Nu. rub.*, nucleus ruber; *Nu. sp.*, nucleus spiriformis; *Nu. isth.*, nucleus isthmi; *Nu. m. l.*, nucleus mesencephalicus lateralis; *Nu. d.*, nucleus dorsalis; *opt. t.*, optic tectum; *supr. opt. dec.*, supraoptic decussation; *Tr. s. mes.*, tractus septomesencephalicus: *ventr.*, ventricle.

link between the nucleus pretectalis, the nucleus spiriformis, and the tectum of the two sides. In the ventral part it contains transverse fibers uniting the contralateral nuclei of the longitudinal fasciculus.

    The third ventricle of the lower vertebrates is, in its di- and mesencephalic parts, reduced to a narrow fissure with two small lateral recesses directed to the optic lobes (Figs. 10 and 11).

    In lower vertebrates, the midbrain correlates optic stimuli with those of general sensibility of static origin. The motor discharge runs through the nucleus motorius tegmenti (= nucleus ruber of birds) and through primary motor centers. In fishes and amphibians behavior depends in great part on midbrain centers; in reptiles, and much more in birds, it is guided by the hemispheres. But the mesencephalon of birds still remains a main sensory center of the fibers of the retina ending directly in the optic lobes. The combined sensory-motor actions (flying, running, avoidance of obstacles, etc.) of pigeons deprived of their hemispheres are particularly due to the action of the midbrain.

The thalamic region shows fiber connections between the hind part of the brain and the telencephalon. The important tracts from the thalamus to the neohyperstriatum are the basis for the complicated behavior of birds.

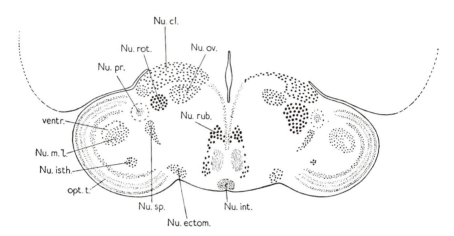

Fig. 11. Transverse section through betweenbrain and midbrain of the budgerigar. The pressure of the cerebral hemispheres and the cerebellum causes a far-ventral position of the optic lobes. We can therefore see several regions of betweenbrain and midbrain on the same section: in the lateral part, the tectum and the nucleus mesencephalicus lateralis; in the dorsal part, the nuclei of the dorsal thalamus; in the median part, the nucleus ruber of the midbrain tegmentum and ventrally the hypothalamic nucleus interpeduncularis.

Nu. ov., Nucleus ovoidalis; *Nu. ectom.*, nucleus ectomammilaris; *Nu. int.*, nucleus interpeduncularis; other abbreviations as in Fig. 10 legend.

The nerve structures of epi- and hypothalamus are part of the olfactory system of the forebrain. Two nuclei (nucleus preopticus and nucleus paraventricularis) form part of the neurohumoral system; they contain secretory cells, the products of which accumulate in the neurohypophysis.

Structural differences of diencephalon and of the tegmental part of the mesencephalon are found to be unimportant when we compare the systematic groups of birds. The same may be said of the structure of the tectum opticum. The relative growth, however, as well as the position of the optic lobes, varies considerably. The relative proportion of the centers of vision is obviously related to habit. The biggest optic lobes are found in falcons and their allies; they are less developed in flamingos and most cursorial birds (Fig. 12) (see cerebral indexes, Table II).

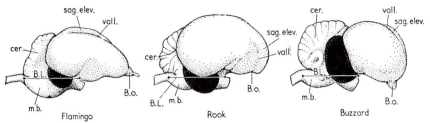

FIG. 12. Brains of flamingo, rook, and buzzard in lateral view. Relative mass development of the optic centers (in black) from a bird of low degree of visual orientation (flamingo) to a bird of high degree of optical activity (buzzard). The position of the optic lobes depends on the extension of the caudotemporal part of the cerebral hemisphere.

B.o., Bulbus olfactorius; *cer.*, cerebellum; *m.b.*, medullary bulb; *sag. elev.*, sagittal elevation; *vall.*, vallecula; *B.l.*, base line.

E. RHOMBENCEPHALON

The cerebellum (metencephalon) and the medullary bulb (myelencephalon) are so intimately related in ontogenesis that a common denomination imposes itself. The embryonic basal plates of these two regions fuse in one uniform structure. The following description must be limited to the general avian features of this part for a detailed comparison of the differences in the main groups has not yet been made.

1. *The Cerebellum*

The alar plates of the embryonic rhombencephalon fuse dorsally in their rostral parts and form a conspicuous suprasegmental structure of considerable dimensions in teleosts, birds, and mammals. This cerebellum is situated immediately behind the roof of the midbrain where the wide fourth ventricle of the medullary bulb narrows to form the isthmus.

In birds the cerebellum is much more differentiated than in any living reptile; nevertheless, it lacks the hemispheres of the mammalian metencephalon (Fig. 13). The base of the cerebellum corresponds to the archaic or auricular parts in the rhombencephalon of lower vertebrates. This part consists of three transverse thickenings: these are the lingula on the rostral side and, in the caudal part, the (basal) nodulus, and (more dorsal) the uvula. The uvula usually contains several folds. The nodulus continues laterally in the flocculus on each side, the uvula in the corresponding paraflocculus. There is strong evidence that these two lateral structures are homologous with the same parts in the mammalian brain. The main central part of the cerebellum corresponds to the vermis of mammals. Following Larsell (1948), we may distinguish an anterior and a posterior lobe separated by an important cleft, the fissura prima (fissura x). In addition to the folds of the lingula and the nodulus, the anterior, as well as the posterior lobe shows five primary transverse folds, some of which can be subdivided. In nightjars and hummingbirds the anterior lobe (particularly folds 2 and 3) is absent

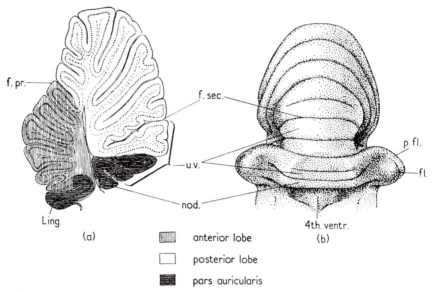

FIG. 13. Cerebellum of *Anas platyrhynchus*. a. Midsagittal plane. b. Posterior view. After Larsell (1948). *f.pr.*, Fissura prima; *f. sec.*, fissura secunda; *fl.*, flocculus; *p.fl.* paraflocculus; *Ling.*, lingula; *nod.*, nodulus; *uv.*, uvula; *4th ventr.*, fourth ventricle.

or rudimentary. Whitlock (1952) has shown that these reduced regions are projection centers of legs and tail.

Degeneration experiments (Brodal *et al.*, 1950) have made clear that in birds, as in mammals, the cerebellum contains pontine fibers ending in pontine nuclei situated ventrally in the medial and lateral part of the medullary bulb. The origin of these fibers lies in the lateral parts of posterior folds 6 to 8, as well as in the unfoliated cortex continuing these folia in a lateral direction. This leads to the conclusion that not only the unfolded parts, but also the lateral parts of posterior folds 6 to 8 correspond to the hemispheres of mammals.

The development of the avian cerebellum beyond the stage in reptiles consists in a multiplication of cortical folds as well as an augmentation of gray matter and fibers in the more central parts. The ventricle is reduced and four nuclear groups (Sanders, 1929) are clearly differentiated.

The cortical layer shows the granular, Purkinje, and molecular cells typical of all vertebrates, but it exhibits greater differentiation than in lower groups. The same is true of the ascending and descending fiber tracts. Ascending fibers to the cortex and cerebellar nuclei come from the static nerve, from the spinal cord (as far as the lumbar region), from the trigeminus and from midbrain centers and the paleostriatum. Descending fibers go to the vestibular nuclei and the medulla. In the rostral direction, cerebellar fibers end in the tegmentum of the midbrain.

The cerebellum is an important part of the motor apparatus of the brain. The fact that it is highly developed in groups with varied possibilities of motor behavior shows its role in the regulation of attitude and movements. The particular importance of the trigeminocerebellar connection seems to be the neural basis of the bill functions (Kappers, 1947). In contrast to the primary motor centers, the cerebellum cannot directly release movements: its influence is regulatory.

2. *Myelencephalon*

The general plan of the medullary bulb is the same as in all amniotes. The centers of this region present a high degree of differentiation. In general, the efferent nuclei and pathways of the reflex system seem to be particularly developed by comparison with the ascending fiber systems. The arrangement and the structure of the nuclei differ markedly from those in reptiles and mammals and are in large part related to the typical posture and structure of the head of birds. The differences concern particularly the static centers, the nuclei of vagus and hypoglossus nerves, and the region of the inferior olive intercalated in the spinocerebellar system. We may add, too, the pontine fibers and nuclei already mentioned. We consider individually these particular zones:

a. Vestibular region. The nucleus of Deiters, principal center of this region, is well developed in birds. Additional oral and dorsal vestibular nuclei are grouped with the main nucleus. The tractus vestibulospinalis, outgrowth of the nucleus of Deiters, is the principal pathway for motor impulses to the nuchal region, trunk, and members. The particular development of this tract and the corresponding nucleus is in clear relation to the importance of motor coordination in a flying organism.

b. Hypoglossus and vagus zone. In reptiles the hypoglossus nerve of the somatic tongue muscles has its own nucleus in the somatomotor zone of the medullary bulb. In birds, part of this nucleus detaches from the main mass in the direction of the vagus nucleus and forms a separate nucleus intermedius. The development of this special center depends on the importance of the tongue muscles: it is more conspicuous in the budgerigar than in the sparrow (Sanders, 1929).

In reptiles a nucleus of the vagus complex has already become displaced ventrolaterally. In birds this part is enlarged and is more independent from the dorsal main nucleus. In this dorsal nucleus Kosaka and Yagita (1903) and Moffie (1942) (both cited by Kappers, 1947) have found a group of larger cells claimed by Kosaka to be concerned with the innervation of the stomach, the musculature of which is particularly powerful in birds.

c. *Inferior olive.* This is considered to be derived from the reticular nuclei and probably has static functions. It is peculiar to homoiotherms, but never attains, in birds, the development found in mammals. The differences in birds are very marked: again the inferior olive is much more differentiated in the budgerigar than in the sparrow (Sanders, 1929).

d. *Pontine structures.* The medial and lateral pontine nuclei in the ventral part of the medullary bulb, between the fifth and the eighth nerve, are homologous with the pontine gray of mammals. The tracts from the cerebellum to these centers correspond with similar structures of mammals (Brodal *et al.*, 1950). This entire formation is therefore typical for all homoiotherms. The nucleus intermedius and the disposition of the vestibularis region are characteristic of birds only.

F. The Cranial Nerves

The twelve pairs of cranial nerves are conventionally classified by the Roman numerals I to XII, corresponding to their position in the medullary bulb. The nerves are better arranged in functional groups. Nerve I (olfactory) and nerve II (fasciculus opticus) are never true nerves but are in fact part of special sensory structures. The statoacoustic nerve (VIII) is to be dealt in connection with the inner ear. Nerve XII (hypoglossus) has a special character: it originates from the junction of the first somites of the spinal cord during ontogenesis of the head. Its territory is somatic trunk muscles which are included in head formation and which take part in the formation of the tongue. The hypoglossus nerve of birds, then, has lost the sensory dorsal roots typical for spinal nerves.

Three of the remaining brain nerves are attached to the true somatic head muscles forming the musculature of the eye: nervus oculomotorius

(III), trochlearis (IV), and abducens (VI). The regions of origin of this group are to be found in Fig. 14.

Nerves V, VII, IX, and X (including XI) are sometimes termed branchial nerves. They are, in fact, intimately related with embryonic visceral clefts, or with structures that are dependent on these clefts.

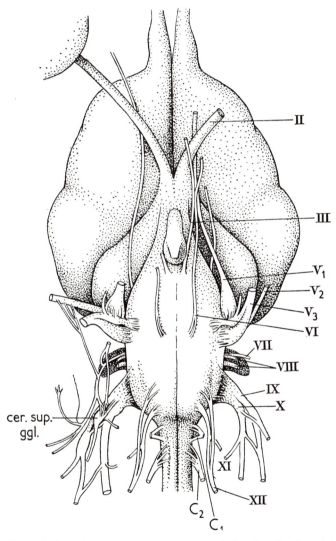

FIG. 14. Ventral view of the brain of a goose (*Anser*) showing the disposition of the brain nerves. *I–XII*, Brain nerves; *V 1,2,3*, branches of trigeminus; *C 1,2*, cervical nerves; *cer. sup. ggl.*, cervical superior ganglion. After Cords (1904).

They may be grouped according to their position relative to the stato-acoustic or octavus nerve in a preotic (V, VII) and a postotic (IX, X, XI) group. The sensory cells of each branchial nerve form a brain ganglion situated outside the brain but still within the bony brain case. The cells of the motor fibers of the branchial nerves are to be found in the medullary bulb. In striking contrast to the trunk nerves, ectoblastic cells of special epidermic placodes take part in the structure of the brain ganglia.

Nerve V (trigeminus) is the most conspicuous of the branchial group. After leaving the bulb it forms the ganglion of Gasser (or maxillomandibular ganglion) leaving the skull through two (sometimes three) foramina. The dorsal opening in the hind part of the orbit transmits the ophthalmic branch; the second, more ventral, opening, the mandibular and maxillary branch (Fig. 15). The ophthalmic and maxillary

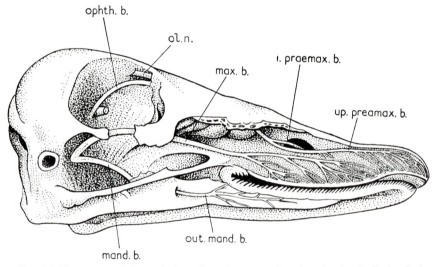

Fig. 15. The course of the main branches of nervus trigeminus in the skull of a duck (*Anas*). *i. praemax. b.*, Inner premaxillary branch; *mand. b.*, mandibular branch; *max. b.*, maxillary branch; *ol. n.*, olfactory nerve; *ophth. b.*, ophthalmic branch; *out. mand. b.*, outer mandibular branch; *up. praemax b.*, upper praemaxillary branch. After Cords (1904).

nerves contain mainly fibers of the somatic sensory system; the large mandibular branch is composed of sensory and motor fibers.

The VIIth (facial) nerve is much thinner than the trigeminus. Its roots are to be found rostrally from, and very near to the statoacoustic nerve. The ganglion geniculi of this nerve is not very marked. The tympanic chord, part of the hyomandibular branch of this nerve, runs in the tympanic cavity, along the quadratum to the mandibular articulation, where it enters the articular bone (Fig. 16).

The IXth (glossopharyngial) nerve forms the jugular ganglion immediately behind the statoacoustic nerve. Its strongest part is the senory nerve of the tongue.

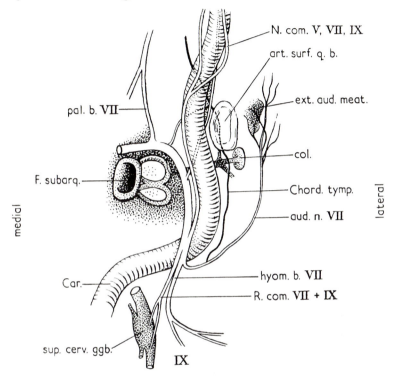

FIG. 16. The course of the right facial nerve in a duck (*Anas*) seen from the medial side. After Cords (1904). *art. surf. q. b.*, Articulation surface of quadrate bone; *aud. n. VII*, auditory nerve VII; *Car.*, carotid; *col.*, columella; *Chord. tymp.*, chorda tympani; *ext. aud. meat.*, external auditory meatus; *F. subarq.*, fossa subarquata; *hyom. b. VII*, hyomandibularis branch VII; *pal. b. VII*, palatine branch VII; *R. com. VII+IX*, ramus communicans VII and IX; *sup. cerv. ggl.*, superior cervical ganglion; *N. com. V, VII, IX*, nervus communicans V, VII, IX.

The Xth nerve (vagus) has from four to eight roots, all of which are collected into a single ganglion of the vagus nerve. It leaves the brain case by the same opening as the IXth nerve. The intestinal branch is the most massive nerve of the vagus system. It supplies heart, lungs, and stomach, and in it run parasympathetic fibers of the autonomic system. A thoracic ganglion in the region of the lungs is part of the sensory system of the vagus. The XIth nerve (the spinal accessory nerve of mammals) is in birds merely a side branch of the vagus.

II. Spinal Cord

The spinal cord of birds has the structure and position typical of the vertebrates as a whole. The presence of a central canal recalls its origin from the two medullary folds; it is enclosed by the neural arcs of the vertebral column. The nerves of the spinal cord are segmentally arranged. A dorsal pair of sensory nerves, with spinal ganglia and a ventral pair of motor nerves (without ganglia), constitute the spinal segment.

In mammalia and other vertebrates differential growth and suppression of caudal segments cause a shortening of the spinal cord relative to the vertebral column. In birds the two structures are very similar in growth: the spinal cord extends as far as the last free vertebra. The caudal regression, typical for mammals eliminates only the very last segments of the tail.

The structure of the spinal cord shows few differences when we compare birds with the other vertebrates. The cellular arrangement in birds presents a distinct resemblance to the mammalian condition, though on the whole we find a more primitive differentiation (Huber, 1936).

The tectospinal and the cerebellospinal tracts are more prominent than in reptiles. An afferent spinocerebellar tract begins in the lumbar region; other afferent tracts lead to the tectum of the midbrain and the medullary bulb.

In both reptiles and birds afferent fibers of the dorsal tracts run to the end of the spinal cord and to the medullary bulb, where they terminate in particularly large cells within the dorsal horns. Secondary fibers connect these cells with the thalamic region. The direct spino-thalamic tracts of mammals—a progressive character of this group—is absent in birds.

A peculiar marginal cell group, the nuclei of Hoffmann-Kölliker, present in all reptiles and birds, are conspicuous in the latter. These nuclei consist of great cells which are rich in glycogen. They are of ventral origin and form ventrolateral masses at the periphery of the cervical and lumbar regions. The peripheral ventral cells described by Retzius (1912) in the chick belong to the same system. The function of these two ventral cell types in unknown (Figs. 17 and 18).

In both cervical and lumbar regions there exist marked swellings associated with the powerful innervation of wings and hind limbs. The nerves of the wing form the brachial plexus in the region of the last four to six cervical vertebrae. The caudal swelling or intumescentia lumbalis is more complicated (Figs. 17 and 18). It is not, in fact, formed by the mass development of gray matter, as supposed by early observers; its origin is a peculiar dorsal transformation of the spinal cord found only in birds.

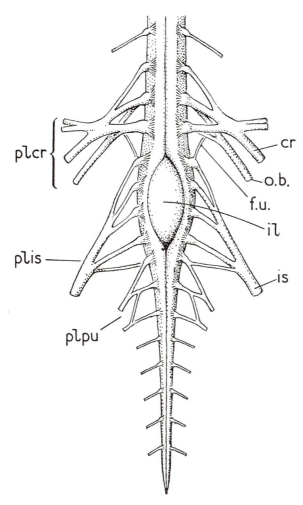

FIG. 17. Lumbosacral part of the spinal cord of a flamingo (*Phoenicopterus*) showing the three nerve plexuses and the intumescentia lumbalis. After Imhof (1905).

cr. Nervus cruralis; *fu.*, nervus furcalis; *il.*, intumescentia lumbalis; *is.*, nervus ischiadicus; *ob.*, nervus obturatorius; *plcr.*, plexus cruralis; *plis.*, plexus ischiadicus; *plpu.*, plexus pudendus.

At the level of the roots of the ischiadic (sciatic) nerve the dorsal tracts separate along a zone of six or seven segments and leave a cleft filled by a mass of large cells that are rich in glycogen. Both the origin and the special function of the sinus rhomboidalis is still obscure. It is supposed by some (Pruso, 1923; Kappers, 1924; both cited by Kappers, 1947) to be of meningeal origin and by others (Terni, 1924; cited by Kappers, 1947) to be a glial structure. Its glycogen content points to a role in the metabolism of the nervous system. Jelgersma (1951) has shown some striking parallels between this structure and that termed "status disraphicus" in human pathology.

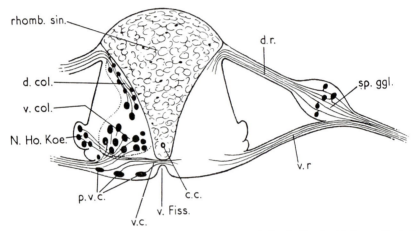

Fig. 18. Transverse section through the intumescentia lumbalis of a bird. *c.c.*, Central canal; *d.col.*, dorsal column; *d.r.*, dorsal root; *Nu. Ho. Koe.*, nuclei of Hoffmann-Kölliker; *p.v.c.*, peripheral ventral cells; *rhomb. sin.*, rhomboid sinus; *sp. ggl.*, spinal ganglion, *v.c.*, ventral commissure; *v.col.*, ventral column; *v.Fiss.*, ventral fissure; *v.r.*, ventral root.

III. The Autonomic Nervous System

The visceral or autonomic system consists of sympathetic and para-sympathetic parts (Fig. 19). It is not easy anatomically to separate the two components. Very often only the antagonistic reaction to pharma-cological influence gives a criterion for their separation.

The *sympathetic system* is the more important of the two parts. Its main components are a ganglionic chain on either side of the vertebral column near the dorsal wall of the coelomic cavity. The two chains join in a last unpaired ganglion of the cloacal region. The cranial part of this sympathetic system is connected with the cranial nerves; the thoracolumbar part, with the spinal nerves. The fiber connections with the central nervous system are distinguished as preganglionic fibers. The peripheral nerves originating in the ganglionic chain are post-ganglion.

In lower vertebrates, including reptiles, the postganglionic nerves run directly to their destination, the effector organs. In birds and mammals, these visceral nerves form a network with numerous ganglia.

The sympathetic fibers of the head form a great upper cervical ganglion, from which nerve fibers run rostrally up to the ganglion of the trigeminus. The cervical part consists of two tracts, the deeper one running in a channel formed by the transverse process of the cervical vertebra. The superficial tract follows the vagus in its course and reaches the thoracolumbar chain at the end of the cervical region. The thoracic part often has double internodal connections turning round on each side of the ribs. The abdominal system of the chain is more prominent in birds than the thoracic part. A sympathetic intestinal branch is a particular feature in birds. Only in Crocodilia has a similar branch been observed. This intestinal nerve leaves the sympathetic chain near the caudal pole of the kidney and runs along the intestine through the mesentery. Near the ovary this nerve comes in contact with parasympathetic fibers of the vagus.

The *parasympathetic components* of the autonomic system originate either in cranial nerves or in the spinal cord, and not in the ganglionic chain. In the cerebral part, parasympathetic fibers are to be found in the oculomotor, facial, and glossopharyngeal nerves and in the vagus. The vagus is the main conductor of parasympathetic fibers to the thoracic region and beyond into the abdominal zone, where branches of the vagus (as mentioned above) join the intestinal nerve of the sympathetic part.

The spinal cord furnishes what is sometimes called the sacral parasympathetic outflow: the pelvic nerves of cloaca, bursa Fabricii, and ureters. Again, fibers of the pelvic nerve join the intestinal branch of the sympathetic system (Pera, 1952).

IV. Cerebralization and Related Problems

The progressive mass development of the cerebral hemispheres demonstrated by the whole series of vertebrates from fishes to homoiothermic animals is one of the conspicuous phenomena of evolution. Cerebralization, as the fact has been termed, is understood here as the progressive development in mass of all higher centers of integration. It may be useful to designate by the term "telencephalization" the special fact that in mammals and birds the forebrain takes over functions of other centers of integration, e.g. the transfer of optical centers from the midbrain to the hemispheres.

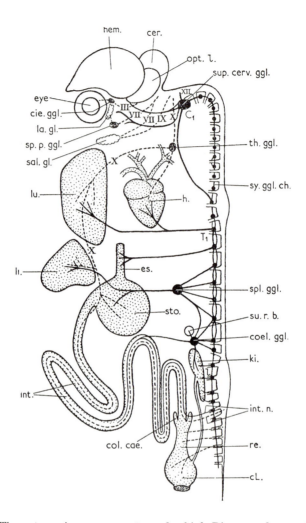

FIG. 19. The autonomic nervous system of a bird. Diagram of sympathetic fibers (drawn outlines) and parasympathetic fibers (broken lines) showing their course from the central nervous system to the viscera and to some head organs. Modified after Kappers (1947).

I–XII, Brain nerves; *C1*, cervical nerve 1; *T1*, thoracic nerve 1; *L1*, lumbal nerve 1; *cer.*, cerebellum; *cie. ggl.*, ciliary ganglion; *cl.*, cloaca; *coel. ggl.*, coeliac ganglion; *col. cae.*, colic ceca; *es.*, esophagus; *h.*, heart; *hem.*, hemisphere; *int.*, intestine; *int. n.*, intestinal nerve; *ki.*, kidney; *la. gl.*, lachrymal gland; *li.*, liver; *lu.*, lung; *opt. l,* optic lobe; *re.*, rectum; *sal. gl.*, salivary gland; *sp. p. ggl.*, sphenopalatine ganglion; *sto.*, stomach; *su.r.b.*, suprarenal body; *sup. cer. ggl.*, superior cervical ganglion; *sy. ggl. ch.*, sympathetic ganglion chain; *th. ggl.*, thoracic ganglion.

We have already pointed out the important differences of mass development and structure of the forebrain of birds. These differences have been underrated for a long time, those in mammals being far more impressive. However, the first attempts to make an exact determination [by the methods of E. Dubois (1897), followed by Lapicque and Girard (1905), and Lapicque (1909)] long ago gave convincing evidence of the scope of brain evolution in birds. These first measurements were based on the assumption that cerebral evolution was an exponential function with a constant relationship between body mass and brain weight. It was even thought that this relation was of the same degree in birds as in mammals. Sholl (1948) and Wirz (1950) in mammals, and Portmann (1946) in birds, have shown that the orders, and sometimes even families, have characteristic differences in body-brain relationship. As the so-called cephalization factor of Dubois was determined on the basis of a general body-brain relationship, this cephalization value had to be discarded.

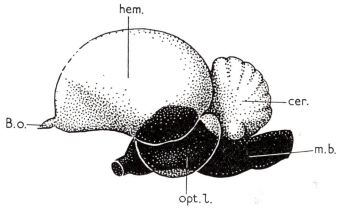

Fig. 20. Lateral view of the avian brain. The "brain stem rest" which serves for measuring the relative mass of the brain parts is drawn in black. *B.o.*, Bulbus olfactorius; *Cer.*, cerebellum; *hem.*, hemisphere; *m.b.*, medullary bulb; *opt.l.*, optic lobe.

We have followed another way and tried to determine intracerebral indexes for brain constituents. As a unit, we take a part of the brain of relatively elementary functions that is easy to prepare: the brain stem rest. This is smaller than the brain stem of neurologists; it is composed of the diencephalon, the tegmentum of the midbrain, and the medullary bulb. Figure 20 shows this part in black.

However, the brain stem rest in birds of the same body weight shows differences from 1 to 2.7 and thus proves to have its special evolution. We therefore determined which group of birds shows the smallest brain

TABLE II
CEREBRAL INDEXES

Order and species	Weight (grams)	Basic number	Stem rest	Indexes of brain parts Optic lobes	Cerebellum	Hemispheres	Total number
Struthiones							
Struthio camelus ♀	90,000	6.34	0.97	0.28	0.95	4.27	1
Casuarii							
Dromiceius novae-hollandiae	40,500	4.18	0.92	0.342	0.91	4.18	1
Sphenisci							
Spheniscus demersus	2,700	1.01	2.28	0.78	1.94	9.31	1
Podicipedes							
Podiceps cristatus	1,050	0.61	1.04	0.52	1.11	3.46	6
Gaviae							
Gavia stellatus	1,200	0.66	1.37	0.68	1.63	3.69	1
Steganopodes							
Phalacrocorax carbo	2,200	0.89	1.64	0.66	1.65	7.08	12
Accipitres							
Buteo buteo ♀	900	0.566	1.96	1.59	2.14	9.78	3
Gressores							
Ardea cinerea	1,500	0.74	1.56	1.01	1.35	6.73	10
Phoenicopteri							
Phoenicopterus roseus	3,000	1.35	1.08	0.29	1.35	5.46	9
Anseres							
Anas plytyrhyncha ♂	1,200	0.66	1.41	0.61	0.84	6.08	4
Cygnus olor ♂	11,000	2.10	1.16	0.27	1.03	5.16	4
Galli							
Coturnix coturnix	85	0.17	1	0.70	0.54	2.36	16
Pavo cristatus ♂	3,500	1.16	1	0.63	0.87	3.74	5
Cuculi							
Cuculus canorus	100	0.18	1.31	1.26	0.99	4.61	4
Grues							
Gruidae: Balearica pavonina	3,250	1.11	1.58	0.84	1.76	8.80	3
Rallidae: Fulica atra	410	0.37	1.41	0.80	1.09	5.57	15

(Continued)

CEREBRAL INDEXES

Order and Species	Weight (grams)	Basic number	Indexes of brain parts				Total number
			Stem rest	Optic lobes	Cerebellum	Hemispheres	
Laro-Limicolae							
Charadriidae: *Vanellus vanellus*	200	0.31	1.38	0.67	1.04	5.22	6
Laridae: *Larus ridibundus*	250	0.29	1.42	1.25	1.70	5.36	11
Alcidae: *Fratercula arctigrabae*	330	0.33	2.03	1.15	2.48	7.57	4
Columbae							
Columba palumbus	450	0.39	1.12	0.76	0.89	3.32	7
Psittaci							
Melopsittacus undulatus	37	0.10	1.28	0.76	1.14	7.40	11
Ara ararauna	850	0.55	2.66	0.99	2.38	28.02	2
Striges							
Athene noctua	165	0.23	1.58	1.00	1.28	12.9	6
Bubo bubo	2,000	0.85	2.15	0.88	1.59	15.07	7
Caprimulgi							
Caprimulgus europaeus	70	0.14	1.26	0.73	0.93	2.35	1
Coraciae							
Meropidae: *Merops apiaster*	60	0.14	1.38	0.87	1.13	3.03	2
Alcedinidae: *Alcedo atthis*	35	0.10	1.40	1.36	1.12	4.86	1
Upupidae: *Upupa epops*	55	0.13	1.14	0.72	1.28	6.27	4
Macrochires							
Micropus apus	38	0.11	1.06	0.65	1.02	3.43	14
Pici							
Jynginae: *Jynx torquilla*	37	0.10	1.21	0.82	0.86	4.62	4
Picinae: *Dryobates major*	80	0.16	1.85	1.04	1.76	12.35	7
Passeres							
Hirundinidae: *Hirundo rustica*	18.5	0.07	0.97	0.74	1.11	4.62	12
Fringillidae: *Carduelis carduelis*	14.5	0.06	1.22	0.76	1.07	6.47	13
Paridae: *Parus major*	17.5	0.07	1.44	1.17	1.09	8.92	7
Corvidae: *Corvus frugilegus*	430	0.383	1.75	1.24	1.67	15.68	8
Corvus corax ♂	1,250	0.67	1.66	1.17	1.70	18.95	7

D

stem rest for a given body weight. This group proved to be the Galli. Certain other groups fall in line with the Galli but none has lower values, not even the ostrich nor other flightless groups. Therefore, we took as our basic unit the mass of the brain stem rest of a gallinaceous bird of a given body weight. Measuring in relation to this unit, we obtained indexes for every part of a brain (including the stem rest itself). Table II gives examples of the considerable variety of the relative mass development.

These indexes are quantitative expressions of the relative mass development, and cannot therefore be taken as a measure of psychic complexity or intelligence. They give instead the first objective basis for any determination of the level of brain evolution and permit a deeper understanding of morphological and ethological considerations. Together with the morphological analysis, the index method allows an appreciation of evolutionary trends in different groups. If we compare the index of hemispheres in a wryneck (4.6) and in woodpeckers (11 to 19), and take into consideration the many differences of structure in these two groups, it is clear that the index is a significant expression of the evolution in Piciformes. The great differences of indexes in song birds (4 to 19) make it possible to distinguish between radiative adaptation and evolution to different levels.

The comparison of the index groups gives other significant results. In some groups all centers are well differentiated above the lowest level (Accipitres); in others only the hemispheres show this evolution.

In practically all groups the index of the hemispheres increases with the body weight. While this increase is not very striking in Galli, owls, and corvids, it is very great in parrots, woodpeckers, and steganopods. This fact poses many physiological and evolutionary problems.

An important hint to an understanding of bird evolution is given by the study of hemisphere indexes in relation to the hatching stage. The reptilian type of nidifugous young must be taken as the archaic condition from which the more primitive ontogenetic mode of birds has derived (groups like grebes, Galli, Anseres, plovers, the ostrich, etc., show this stage). If we compare the indexes of hemispheres, we see immediately that forms with a relatively low brain development already present the advanced nidifugous type of parental care. This highly dependent type of development must already have evolved in groups of low cerebral level. Only groups of this advanced ontogenetic type have evolved to the highest degrees of brain level. The corvids, woodpeckers, owls, and parrots (hemisphere indexes greater than 10) all have the secondary type of nidicolous development. Ontogenetic evolution seems to precede that of the hemispheres.

References

Brodal, A., Kristiansen, K., and Jansen, J. (1950). Experimental demonstration of a pontine homologue in birds. *J. Comp. Neurol.* **92**: 23–69.

Bumm, A. (1883). Das Grosshirn der Vögel. *Z. wiss. Zool.* **38**: 430–467.

Cate, J. ten (1936). Physiologie des Zentralnervensystems der Vögel. *Ergeb Biol.* **13**: 93–173.

Cords, E. (1904). Beiträge zur Lehre vom Kopfnervensystem der Vögel. *Anat. Hefte* **26**: 49–100.

Craigie, E. H. (1935). The hippocampal and parahippocampal cortex of the Emu (*Dromiceius*). *J. Comp. Neurol.* **61**: 563–591.

Craigie, E. H. (1936). Notes on cytoarchitectural features of the lateral cortex and related parts of the cerebral hemispheres in a series of reptiles and birds. *Trans. Roy. Soc. Can.* [3]*V*, **30**: 87–113.

Craigie, E. H. (1940). The cerebral cortex in Palaeognathine and Neognathine birds. *J. Comp. Neurol.* **73**: 179–234.

de Beer, G. (1954). Archaeopteryx lithographica. British Museum, London.

Dennler, G. (1921). Zur Morphologie des Vorderhirns der Vögel. Der Sagittalwulst. *Folia neuro-biol.* **12**: 342–362.

Dubois, E. (1897). Sur le rapport du poids de l'encéphale avec la grandeur du corps chez les mammifères. *Bull. soc. anthropol. Paris* [4] **8**: 337–376.

Edinger, L., Wallenberg, A., and Holmes, G. (1903). Untersuchungen über das Vorderhirn der Vögel. *Abhandl. senckenberg. naturforsch. Ges.* **20**: 341–426.

Edinger, T. (1951). The brains of the Odonthognathae. *Evolution* **5**: 6–24.

Erulkar, S. D. (1955). Tactile and auditory areas in the brain of the pigeon. An experimental study by means of evoked potentials. *J. Comp. Neurol.* **103**: 421–458.

Haefelfinger, H. R. (1958). "Beiträge zur vergleichenden Ontogenese des Vorderhirns bei Vögeln." Helbing & Lichtenhahn, Basel.

Herrick, C. J. (1893). Illustrations of the surface anatomy of the brains of certain birds. *J. Comp. Neurol.* **3**: 171–176.

Huber, J. F. (1936). Nerve roots and nuclear groups in the spinal cord of the pigeon. *J. Comp. Neurol.* **65**: 43–91.

Huber, G. C., and Crosby, E. C. (1926). On thalamic and tectal nuclei and fiber paths in the brain of the American Alligator. *J. Comp. Neurol.* **40**: 97–227.

Huber, G. C., and Crosby, E. C. (1929). The nuclei and fiber paths of the avian diencephalon, with consideration of the telencephalic and certain mesencephalic centers and connections. *J. Comp. Neurol.* **48**: 1–225.

Imhof, G. (1905). Anatomie und Entwicklungsgeschichte des Lumbalmarks bei den Vögeln. *Arch. mikroskop. Anat. u. Entwicklungsgeschichte.* **65**: 1–114.

Jelgersma, H. C. (1951). On the sinus lumbosacralis, spinabifida occulta, and status dysraphicus in birds. *Zool. Mededeel.* **31**: 95–106.

Kalischer, O. (1905). Das Grosshirn der Papageien in anatomischer und physiologischer Beziehung. *Abhandl. preuss. Akad. Wiss.* Abh. **IV**: 1–105.

Kappers, C. U. A. (1921). "Die vergleichende Anatomie des Nervensystems der Wirbeltiere und des Menschen," Band II. Haarlem de Erven F. Bohn.

Kappers, C. U. A. (1947). "Anatomie comparée du système nerveux." Masson, Paris.

Küenzi, W. (1918). Versuch einer systematischen Morphologie des Gehirns der Vögel. *Rev. suisse zool.* **26**: 17–112.

Lapicque, L. (1909). Le poids de l'encéphale dans les différents groupes d'oiseaux. *Bull. Muséum hist. nat. (Paris)* **15**: 408–412.

Lapicque, L., and Girard, P. (1905). Poids de l'encéphale en fonction du poids du corps chez les oiseaux. *Compt. rend. soc. biol.* **57**: 665–668.

Larsell, O. (1948). The development and subdivisions of the cerebellum of birds. *J. Comp. Neurol.* **89**: 123–190.

Münzer, E., and Wiener, H. (1898). Beiträge zur Anatomie und Physiologie des Centralnervensystems der Taube. *Monatsschr. Psychiat. Neurol.* **3**: 379–406.

Pera, L. (1952). La morfologia del nervo intestinale di Remak in *Passer Italiae. Atti Soc. toscana Sci. nat.* **59B**: 222–261.

Portmann, A. (1946–1947). Études sur la cérébralisation chez les oiseaux. I, II, III. *Alauda* **14**: 2–20; I, II, III **15**: 1–15, 161–171.

Ramon y Cajal, S. (1891). Sur la fine structure du lobe optique des oiseaux et sur l'origine réelle des nerfs optiques. *J. intern. Anat. Physiol.* **8**: 337–366.

Retzius, G. (1912). Zur Kenntnis der oberflächlichen ventralen Nervenzellen im Lendenmark der Vögel. *Biol. Untersuch.* [*N.F.*] **10**: 21–24.

Rogers, F. T. (1922). Studies of the brain stem. VI. An experimental study of the corpus striatum of the pigeon as related to various instinctive types of behavior. *J. Comp. Neurol.* **35**: 21–60.

Rogers, F. T. (1922). A note on the excitable areas of the cerebral hemispheres of the pigeon. *J. Comp. Neurol.* **35**: 61–65.

Rose, M. (1914). Ueber die cytoarchitektonische Gliederung des Vorderhirns der Vögel. *J. Psychol. u. Neurol.* **21**: 278–352.

Sanders, E. B. (1929). A consideration of certain bulbar, midbrain, and cerebellar centers and fiber tracts in birds. *J. Comp. Neurol.* **49**: 155–221.

Schifferli, A. (1948). Ueber Markscheidenbildung im Gehirn von Huhn und Star. *Rev. suisse zool.* **55**: 117–212.

Schüpbach, P. (1905). Beiträge zur Anatomie und Physiologie der Ganglienzellen im Zentralnervensystem der Taube. Inaugural Dissertation, Universität, Bern.

Sholl, D. (1948). The quantitative investigation of the vertebrate brain and the applicability of allometric formulae to its study. *Proc. Roy. Soc. London, Series B* **135**: 243–258.

Stingelin, W. (1956). Studien am Vorderhirn von Waldkauz (*Strix aluco*) und Turmfalk (*Falco tinnunculus* L.). *Rev. suisse zool.* **63**: 551–660.

Stingelin, W. (1958). "Vergleichend-morphologische Untersuchungen am Vorderhirn der Vögel auf cytologischer und cytoarchitektonischer Grundlage." Helbing & Lichtenhahn, Basel.

Sutter, E. (1943). Ueber das embryonale und postembryonale Hirnwachstum bei Hühnern und Sperlingsvögeln. *Denkschr. schweiz. naturforsch. Ges.* **75**: 1–110.

Thauer, R., and Peters, G. (1938). Sensibilität und Motorik bei lange überlebenden Zwischen-Mittelhirntauben. *Arch. ges. Physiol. Pflüger's* **240**: 503–526.

Turner, C. H. (1891). Morphology of the avian brain. *J. Comp. Neurol.* **1**: 39–92.

Whitlock, D. G. (1952). A neurohistological and neurophysiological study of afferent fiber tracts and receptive areas of the avian cerebellum. *J. Comp. Neurol.* **97**: 567–635.

Wirz, K. (1950). Zur quantitativen Bestimmung der Ranghöhe bei Säugetieren. *Acta Anat.* **9**: 134–196.

Part I. Sensory Organs: Skin, Taste and Olfaction

A. PORTMANN

I. Skin

The sensory cells of the central nervous system produce many different end-structures that act as receptors for stimuli in the skin and buccal cavity. These are termed *exteroceptors*. Others, the *interoceptors* are located in the interior organs. According to the sources of stimuli the *interoceptors* may be classified in two groups, *proprioceptors* in muscles, tendons and mesenteries and *visceroceptors* located in the intestine and in its glands.

Corresponding to the high evolutionary level of birds such structures are present in great variety. For functional interpretations there has been an almost complete dependence on studies on Man because only subjective answers enable correlation between the quality of a certain stimulus and the receptors revealed by morphological study. Even in Man almost all of the supposed correlations between specific end-organs and particular sensations have been highly hypothetical. This is even more so in the case of birds. The interpretation of structure and function depends further on the theoretical viewpoint of the observer. The controversy involving classical views (the neuron theory) as against the idea of a reticulate nervous continuum has not been settled (Boeke, 1926a, b; Schartau, 1938, Bauer, 1953).

A. FREE NERVE ENDINGS AND TERMINAL NETWORK

As in all vertebrates, the inner organs of birds are rich in free nerve endings which terminate in fine knobs, dendritic structures, simple loops or complicated clues. Several nerve cells can fuse to form a common network.

The skin is particularly rich in such sensory receptors. Dense networks extend in the zone of contact of epiderm and cutis. Other nets enter the basal layers of the epidermis (Botezat, 1906). Schartau (1938) considers the terminal network as part of the autonomic system (page 28), the central system being represented by the terminal-knobs and the more complicated sense organs. The functions of these networks are doubtful: it is impossible to separate efferent and afferent structures. Schartau has shown in the sympathetic system of birds the presence of subepidermal nerve-cells which give off rich terminal networks to the epidermal layer.

B. COMPOSITE SENSORY CORPUSCLES

The skin, as well as the buccal cavity and particularly the tongue, is rich in the supposed tactile *corpuscles of Merkel*. These are formed by the cup-shaped terminal network of a main nerve fiber entering into intimate contact with a special tactile cell. A fine network formed by a small nerve fiber, supposedly part of the autonomic system, surrounds the whole corpuscle. Similar structures may be built up by several tactile cells. They are always without connective sheath cells. Corpuscles with two rows of tactile cells have been shown by Botezat (1906).

Clusters of dense terminal nets combined with secondary sensory cells are found in the subepidermal papillae of the cutis. These are very similar to the mammalian corpuscles of Krause.

Two further sensory structures peculiar to birds have attracted the attention of many neurologists and will be described in some detail. These are the corpuscles of Grandry and Herbst.

C. GRANDRY CORPUSCLES

Few vertebrate skin receptors have been more thoroughly studied than these. About 50μ in length they are found in the tongue and palate of many species and especially in the dorsal skin of the bill of ducks (Botezat, 1906; Boeke, 1926; Klein, 1931–1932; Dijkstra, 1933). At the ending of the principal nerve fiber there is formed a flat disk which is compressed between two large secondary sensory cells that constitute the main body of the Grandry corpuscle (Fig. 1). This group is surrounded by satellite cells with large nuclei, and it is covered by connective tissue. Boeke has evidence that suggests the presence of a periterminal network connecting the neuro-fibrillar disk of the primary fiber with the protoplasm of the secondary cells.

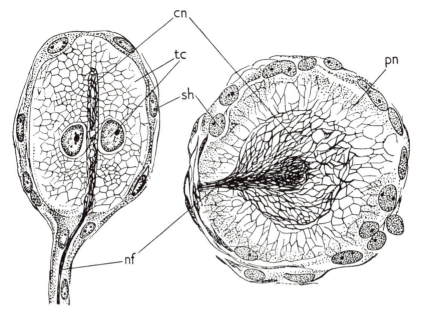

Fig. 1. Grandry Corpuscle in the skin of a Ducks bill; Longitudinal (at left) and horizontal section (after Boeke). *cn*, central net of neurofibrils; *nf*, nerve fiber; *pn*, peripheral net of neurofibrils; *sh*, sheath cells; *tc*. so-called tactile cells.

The terminal disks of the primary fibers lay parallel to the surface of the skin. The bigger corpuscles of this kind may contain up to five secondary cells and four corresponding disks produced by one nerve fiber. A pericorpuscular net of finest nerve fibers has been observed in many of these corpuscles.

D. HERBST'S LAMELLAR CORPUSCLES

The Vater-Pacini-corpuscles of mammals are found in birds as a specialization known as Herbst's Corpuscles (Botezat, 1906; Schumacher, 1911; Clara, 1925). The dorsal skin of the bill of snipe and the tongue of woodpeckers each contains a particularly large number. A lamellar capsule formed of connective tissue cells surrounds the inner corpuscle which is formed by a plasmodium with a double row of nuclei (Fig. 2). The nuclei are all arranged in a single plan. The protoplasm outside the nuclei may contain concentric lamellar structures (in snipe) or a more uniform plasmodium (in duck). In the center of this spindle the main nerve fiber terminates as a long fibrilla which sometimes gives off side-branches that penetrate into the surrounding protoplasm. A second nerve fiber has been described to enter the inner spindle to form an extremely thin fibrillar network surrounding the main nerve ending.

The outer lamellar structure has been interpreted to consist of a system of hemispheric double membranes. Each such pair encloses a space filled with fluid. Blood capillaries enter the lamellar part. The nuclei of the lamellar-cells occur in the smaller interlamellar spaces.

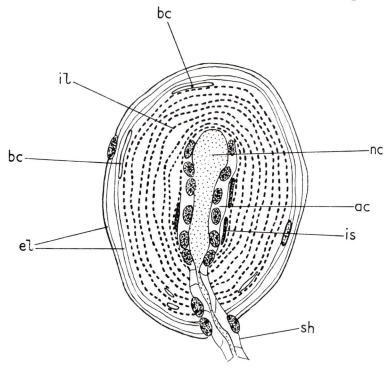

FIG. 2. Herbst-Corpuscle of the Ducks bill. Only the two innermost of the external lamellars are represented; until 12 may be present (slightly modified after Clara). *ac*, Axial cells; *bc*, blood-capillaries; *el*, external lamellar system; *il*, internal lamellar system; *is*, internal sheath-cells; *nc*. ending of the central nerve fiber; *sh*, sheath-cells of the nerve fiber.

The older interpretation of Herbst's corpuscles as tactile receptors has been rejected. They are sometimes supposed to react to variations of blood pressure and lesser fluids. Recently they have been considered as vibration receptors that are especially developed in birds. That the vibrational stimulus is independent of hearing has been shown by Schwartzkopf (1955). It is particularly efficient in the resting position on branches and the accumulation of a considerable number of corpuscles of Herbst between tibia and fibula is interpreted as a receptor system for vibrational stimuli.

II. Taste

The existence of special organs of taste has been known since the middle of the last century. In birds, however, the search for taste buds was unsuccessful until the beginning of the present century. Botezat (1904, 1910) and Bath (1906) finally found taste buds in the buccal cavity of many species and more especially in the basal part of the tongue and in the palatinal region. In birds taste buds have never been found on special papillae.

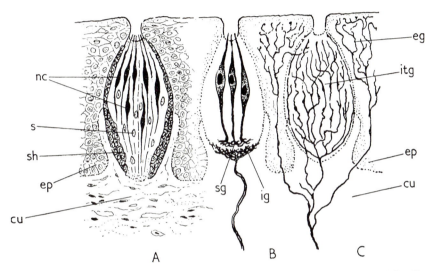

Fig. 3. Taste buds (diagrammatic) showing general structure (A), sensorial cells, subgemmal and infragemmal nerve supply (B), intra- and extragemmal nerves (C) (combined after Bath and Botezat). *cu*, Cutis; *eg*, extragemmal nerve fibers; *ep*, epidermal layer; *ig*, infragemmal plexus; *itg*, intragemmal nerve fibers; *nc*. sensorial cells; *s*, sustaining cells; *sg*, subgemmal plexus; *sh*, sheath-cells (or follicular cells);

These receptors are of the typical vertebrate pattern (Fig. 3). However, in many cases they are surrounded by follicular cells that do not occur in other vertebrates (Bath, 1906). In one type these follicular cells form a basal cup, leaving the external half of the bud free. In other cases the follicular cells form a complete cylindrical sheath; in parrots such sheath-cells are absent. Each species has taste buds of one type only. Bath estimates the number of sensory cells in one bud to be from 10 to 40. The lower number occurs in many Passeres. Pigeons possess from 25 to 40. About 40 have been found in parrots.

Taste buds are composed of indifferent cells and sensory elements. The nucleus of the sensory cells lies in the distal part; this is in contrast to its more basal situation in other vertebrates. The nerve supply to each bud has been studied by Botezat and corresponds to the general plan: a small basal or subgemmal network is formed by the sensory cells itself. The nerve fibers of central origin produce two different networks: a dense basal or infragemmal plexus and a larger intragemmal plexus that perhaps enters the sensory cells. Extragemmal fibers surround the bud as a whole.

Bath calculated the total number of buds to be from 50–75 in the pigeon, about 200 in starling and duck and from 300 to 400 in parrots. The detailed study of Moore and Elliot (1944) suggests that only from 27 to 59 buds occur on the pigeon's tongue.

The functional value of the taste buds is difficult to determine. Firstly, it is difficult to separate clearly choanal olfaction from taste sensation. Moreover, high mobility and alertness of birds, and the complexity of their behavior, constitute a serious handicap to the experimentalist as well as for the interpretation of the more anecdotical contributions that are constantly made. From many experiments Engelmann (1937) has concluded that not all of our sugars taste sweet to birds. Weischer (1953) believes that saccharine and dulcine lack the quality of "sweetness" for parrots. The general conclusion from scattered evidence is that birds probably distinguish the four primary gustative qualities typical in Man. The whole problem, however, needs much more rigorous study in relation to ethology.

III. Olfaction

A. GENERAL STRUCTURE OF NASAL ORGANS

The nasal region of birds follows the reptilian plan (Technau, 1936). The two elongated nasal chambers, separated by the nasal septum, lead from the external opening to the internal aperture or choana in the buccal cavity. Each cavity is divided into three successive regions. In general, each such region contains one concha or turbinal which is produced by its lateral wall (Fig. 4). In certain special cases the rostral part of the nasal cavity is bent backwards and the external opening lies at the posterior end near the orbit. In *Balaeniceps* and *Rhyticeros* this displaced opening is lateral; in *Rhamphastos* its position is dorsal. Whether the nasal condition found in Crocodilia, in which three nasal conchae are present, is truly homologous with that of birds is uncertain.

The first vestibule is separated from the main chamber by a transverse threshold, the development of which is in proportion to that of the nasal glands. Laterally, a large praeconcha is formed and supported by cartilage (Figs. 4 and 5). The epithelium of this structure has no special sensory function: the praeconcha is a simple lamella without scrolls and with its posterior end in contact with the transverse threshold. The structure is relatively enlarged in Galli and falcons, very small in storks, grebes, pterocles, penguins and the Tubinares. It is completely absent in cassowaries and Anhimae, as well as in *Opisthocomus*. One or two nasal glands open into the caudal part of the vestibule.

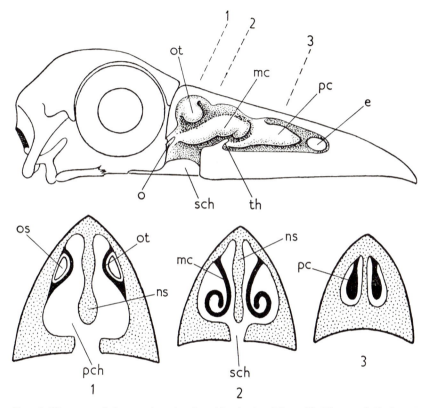

Fig. 4. Diagram of the nasal region (combined after Mangold, Plate and Technau). The lateral wall of the nasal cavity is seen in the longitudinal section, the broken lines indicate the position of the transverse sections 1, 2, and 3. *e.* External opening; *mc*, main concha; *ns*, nasal septum; *o*, opening of the orbital sinus; *os*, orbital sinus; *ot*, olfactory tubercle; *pc*, praeconcha; *pch*, primary choana; *sch*, secondary choana; *th*, threshold.

The second or main chamber extends from the threshold to the choana, by which it communicates with the buccal cavity. It contains the principal concha, homologous with that always present in Reptilia and to the maxilloturbinal in mammals. This concha is intensely scrolled and is covered with the same non-sensory ciliated epithelium as the vestibule. The naso-lacrymal duct opens under the principal concha. Where nasal glands are present, the secretion of the lacrymal glands flows out backwards through the choana. Where such glands are absent, the lacrymal secretion is directed to the external opening. The atrial threshold is in this case very low.

Behind and above lies the third, or olfactory, chamber. In general, its concha is a prominent tubercle which is the only region of the nasal

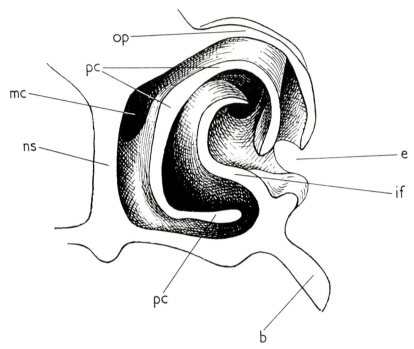

FIG. 5. Left nasal atrium of a Partridge (*Alectoris*) at the level of the external opening. *b*, External border of the bill; *e*, external opening; *if*, longitudinal fold; *mc*, entrance to the main cavity; *ns*, nasal septum; *op*, operculum; *pc*, praeconcha.

cavity covered with true olfactory epithelium. The tubercle contains part of the pneumatical system of the head: the orbital sinus connects with the nasal cavity through a small opening in the posterior wall of the main chamber (*o* in Fig. 4). Exceptionally this third concha may be developed in a turbinal system, especially in Tubinares (e.g. *Fulmarus*) and the New World vultures (Cathartidae) (Fig. 6). In the kiwis (Apteryx), where the olfactory system is particularly developed, the third concha presents about 5 transverse foldings and is enlarged by comparison with the respiratory parts (Fig. 7). The nasovomeral organ

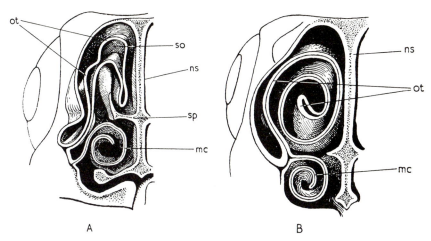

A   B

Fig. 6. Transverse section of the nasal cavity (olfactory region) of a Fulmar (*Fulmarus glacialis*) (A) and a New World Vulture (*Cathartes aura*) (B). In the latter case the olfactory tubercle forms a scroll. *mc*, Main concha; *ns*. nasal septum; *ot*, olfactory tubercle; *so*, orbital sinus; *sp*, septal processus separating main and olfactory cavity.

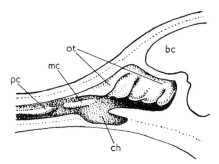

Fig. 7. Nasal cavity of a Kiwi (*Apteryx*) in sagittal section; showing the great development of the olfactory region (after Parker and Gurner). *bc*, Brain cavity; *ch*, choana; *mc*, main concha; *ot*, olfactory tubercle; *pc*. praeconcha.

(Organ of Jacobson) is absent in adult birds. A rudimentary naso-vomeral organ has been found in Anas and Gallus during early onto-genesis (Grewe, 1951).

The paired external nasal openings (nares) are situated near the basal part of the bill except in kiwis where they occur at the top of the very long probing bill. In many cases (e.g. Galli, Columbae) they are pro-tected by a horny operculum (Fig. 5). The external separation may be maintained in the interior (*nares imperviae*), or the septum may be suppressed (ducks, cranes, herons and others) and an unpaired atrium formed. In the Tubinares the nares are elongated tubes directed forward and dorsally placed. The two tubes are separated in albatrosses but fused into one in petrels. In the case of *Oceanites* the septum is incomplete and a single median nasal opening is formed.

In certain Galliformes (Fig. 5) each opening is partially divided by a wall, the anterior part leading to the nasal cavity, the posterior one into a special cavity behind the atrial concha. In Steganopodes (*Phaeton* excepted) the external openings are completely closed, or extremely narrow, and the nasal cavity lacks any turbinal structures. In such birds the choana establishes the only communication with the exterior. The two primary choanas open in an unpaired space which communicates with the buccal cavity by a single secondary choana.

B. Nasal Glands

One or two pairs of tubular nasal glands are variously situated. They may occur in front of the orbita, in the sinus orbitalis or in the sinus maxillaris, in the orbita itself or in special supraorbital grooves of the frontal bone (Technau, 1936; Marples, 1932). The openings of the ducts of these glands are relatively uniform in their situation in the hind part of the vestibule. There occur two pairs of apertures even when there is only a single gland on each side: a medial opening in the nasal septum and a lateral one on the under side of the praeconcha.

The stream of secretion is directed over the concha and the epithelium of the vestibulum. This secretion has a sanitary function. The respiration stream of air comes under its influence before entering the principal chamber. Further, it helps protect the nasal cavity of seabirds against the inflow of salt water. Comparison shows that sea-birds possess larger nasal glands than others; for example, the Greenland race of the Mallard has larger glands than other forms. In sea-birds kept away from salt water the nasal glands diminish. Those of freshwater ducks kept on sea-water enlarge. In extreme adaptation to freshwater habitat (as in *Cinclus*) the nasal glands are larger than in ordinary land forms.

C. Physiology of the Nasal Region

The combined structures of the nasal cavities serve several widely different functions. In general, an air current for respiration has to be conducted to the larynx and trachea and, at the same time, is the carrier of olfactory stimuli for orientation. Part of the turbinal structures help to cleanse the respiratory current. Another considerable part provides surface contact with capillaries, thus elevating the temperature of the current. In the Tubinares a special and remarkable function seems to be subserved in the nasal cavity. In the middle part, on each side of the nasal septum, there occurs a valvular structure, the triangular valve. This opens towards the tubular entrance (Technau, 1936). Fürst (cited by Mangold, 1946) has investigated this organ (Fig. 8) and shown that the air current fills the valve and exercises a strong pressure on the walls of the veil. Fürst and Mangold have suggested that this structure may function as an air pressure indicator during the peculiar dynamic sailing flight of petrels.

The physiological evidence for the function of the true olfactory structures is contradictory. It seems clear that in kiwis the sense of smell is well developed. Positive experimental results are given for

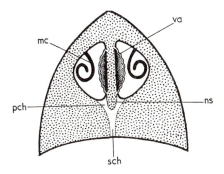

FIG. 8. Transverse section of the main nasal cavities of Tubinares showing the valve (after Mangold). *mc*, Main concha; *ns*. nasal septum; *pch*, primary choana; *sch*, secondary choana; *va*, valve.

ducks (*Turtur*) and many song-birds (Zahn, 1933; Wagner, 1939; Bajandurow and Larin, 1925). Observations of a strong sense of smell in *Catharistes urubu* have been made. The experimental work of Soudek (1927) and Walter (1943), however, leads to the opposite conclusion: both authors consider birds as completely anosmatic.

The unsettled state of current knowledge invites a re-examination of the whole problem. The wide, open secondary choana provides a special pathway for olfactory stimuli: choanal smell is probably a fact in many birds and particularly in groups where the external nasal openings are small or even closed. The role, and interaction, of vision and smell in orientation must be more carefully studied.

The morphological facts testify strongly against the simple conclusion that birds are completely anosmatic. The development of the olfactory part of the nasal cavity, and the well-marked variation in the proportion of the olfactory bulbs of the brain, are in favor of an opposite view.

References

Bajandurow, B. J., and Larin, E. F. (1925). Contributions to the physiology of the olfactory analysator in birds (in Russian). *Trudi Governm. Med. Inst. Tomsk.* **2**.

Bath, W. (1906). Die Geschmacksorgane der Vögel. Diss. Univ. Berlin. 1–46.

Bauer, K. F. (1953). Die Organisation des Nervengewebes und Neurencytiumstheorie. Urban und Schwarzenberg, München/Berlin: 1–166.

Boeke, J. (1926a). Die Beziehungen der Nervenfasern zu den Bindegewebselementen und Tastzellen. *Zs. f. mikros. anat. Forschung* **4**: 448–509.

Boeke, J. (1926b). Noch einmal das periterminale Netzwerk, die Struktur der motorischen Endplatte und die Bedeutung der Neurofibrillae. *Zs. f. mikr. anat. Forschung* **7**: 95–120.

Botezat, E. (1904). Geschmacksorgane und andere nervöse Endapparate im Schnabel der Vögel. *Biol. Centralblatt* **24**.

Botezat, E. (1906). Die Nervenendapparate in den Mundteilen der Vögel . . . *Zs. f. wiss. Zoologie* **84**: 205–360.

Botezat, E. (1910). Morphologie, Physiologie und phylogenetische Bedeutung der Geschmacksorgane der Vögel. *Anat. Anzeiger* **36**: 428–461.

Clara, M. (1925). Ueber den Bau des Schnabels der Waldschnepfe. *Zs. f. mikr. anat. Forschung* **3**: 1–108.

Dijkstra, C. (1933). De- und Regeneration der sensiblen Endkörperchen des Entenschnabels. *Zs. f. mikr. anat. Forschung* **34**: 75–158.

Engelmann, C. (1950). Ueber den Geschmackssinn des Huhnes. IX & X. *Zs. f. Tierpsychol.* **7**: 84–121, 240–264.

Grewe, F. J. (1951). Nuwe Gegewens aangaande die Ontogenese van die Neuskliere, die Organ van Jacobson en die Dekbene van die Skedel by die Genus Anas. *Ann. Univers. van Stellenbosch.* Jaarg. **27**, A, 69–99.

Klein, M. (1931–1932). Sur la différenciation d'éléments tactiles dans le névrone d'amputation des nerfs du bec de Canard. *Arch. Anat. Hist. and Embr.* Strasbourg **14**: 267–300.

Mangold, O. (1946). Die Nase der segelnden Vögel, ein Organ des Strömungssinnes? *Die Naturwissenschaften* **33**: 19–23.

Marples, B. J. (1932). Structure and Development of the Nasal Glands of Birds. *Proc. Zool. Soc. London* **IV**: 829–844.

Moore, C. A., and Elliott, R. E. (1946). Numerical and regional distribution of taste buds on the tongue of the bird. *J. comp. Neurol. Philadelphia* **84**: 119–131.

Schartau, O. (1938). Die periphere Innervation der Vogelhaut. *Zoologica* (Stuttgart) **95**: 1–17.

Schumacher, S. v. (1911). Beiträge zur Kenntnis des Baues und der Funktion der Lamellenkörperchen. *Arch. f. mikr. Anat.* (Abt. I & II.) **77**: 157–193.

Schwartzkopff, J. (1955). Schallsinnesorgane bei Vögeln. *Acta XI Congr. Int. Ornith.* Basel 1954. 189–208.

Technau, G. (1936). Die Nasendrüse der Vögel. *Journ. f. Ornith.* **84**: 511–617.

Wagner, H. O. (1939). Untersuchungen über Geruchsreaktionen bei Vögeln. *Journ. f. Ornith.* **87**: 1–9.

Weischer, B. (1953). Untersuchungen über das Verhalten von Eidechsen und Vögeln gegenüber "süssen" Stoffen. *Zs. vergl. Physiol.* **35/4**: 267–299.

Zahn, W. (1933). Ueber den Geruchssinn einiger Vögel. *Zs. f. vergl. Physiologie* **19**.

Part II.   Sensory Organs: Equilibration

A. PORTMANN

I. General Structure

The inner ear may be divided in two parts. The pars superior comprises the utricle with three semi-circular canals opening into it. The pars inferior is composed of the saccule, the ductus and saccus endolymphaticus and the cochlea and lagena. The present description deals with the structure of the labyrinth; the cochlea, the special organ of hearing, is considered in Chapter XV, Part II.

The membranous labyrinth develops very early in ontogenesis; its parts are formed at the seventh incubation day and grow rapidly to the definitive dimensions. It is surrounded by three centers of ossification: the petrosum, mastoid and epiotic bones. All these are very soon fused into a single osseous mass at the caudal basis of the skull (Freye, 1952–1953).

The walls of the membranous part are formed by an outer layer of flat cells (the *tunica propria*) and an inner layer of epithelium. This basic structure is modified in the sensory parts. The whole membranous labyrinth is surrounded by a basal membrane and is filled with endolymph secreted by glandular cells of the ampullae, the utricle and the saccule (Amerlink, 1930).

The shape of the osseous labyrinth is an exact reproduction of the membranous structure. At three points it permits the connection of the inner ear with the surrounding head-parts:

1. The connection with the middle ear is assured by the lateral fenestra ovalis. This is sometimes more triangular than oval.

2. On the internal side an opening, the aquaeductus vestibuli, gives passage to the endolymphatic duct on its way to brain case.

3. Also on the internal side there occurs another opening (*meatus acusticus internus*) surrounding the stato-acoustic nerve. This is closed

E

near the labyrinth, and five small pores transmit four branches of the vestibular nerve and, in addition, the cochlear or acoustic nerve.

Connective tissue extends between the tunica propria of the membranous part and the endosteum of the osseous formation. This space is filled with perilymph. The connective tissue is absent in the cochlear region where transmission of external stimuli takes place.

In general, the longitudinal axis of the labyrinth is inclined to the vertical, the upper end turned caudally, the lower pole in rostral direction. In smaller birds the two posterior semicircular canals may approach the mid-sagittal plane to a distance of a few millimetres. Sometimes the osseous labyrinth develops a communication between the two systems, a *foramen intercanaliculare* which is always closed by connective tissue. The various positions of the inner ear in the skull present one relatively constant character: the horizontal semicircular canal shows a clear tendency towards a horizontal position during the attitude of general alertness of the bird (not in the position of rest). A comparison of the normal alert head posture in an ostrich, heron, stork, raven, snipe or a cormorant shows the importance of this apparently insignificant detail. It is difficult to attribute an exact functional significance to the posture, but the generality of the fact is established (Duijm, 1951). It may be noted that the ampulla of the horizontal canal differs in structure of the two others.

The pars superior. The utricle may be taken as the central part of this region. In its anterior and lower part it forms a recessus containing the sensory structure, the *macula utriculi*, which is strictly horizontal in its position.

All semicircular canals are connected with the utricle, where they begin with an enlargement, the ampulla, bearing the sensory crest (*crista acustica*). The anterior canal, in general the longest of the three and bearing the largest ampulla, is situated roughly in the sagittal plane. The posterior canal is vertical like the first one, but on a plane perpendicular to it. Its ampulla is situated at the caudal end of the utricle. The difference in length may be considerable: in the pigeon, for example, the anterior canal measures 14 mm., the posterior 7.3 mm. only. Related to this difference the anterior canal joins the common utricle from behind and the posterior canal from the rostral side—a disposition particular to birds. The third—the lateral or horizontal canal—has an anterior ampulla. The horizontal canal is phylogenetically the last: it develops later in ontogenesis, and differs in the structure of its crista. Woodpeckers are exceptional in that the horizontal canal is the longest of the three.

Near the two anterior ampullae occurs another utricular sensory spot, the *macula neglecta*. Present in all reptiles, it is much reduced in birds and absent in mammals. In structure it corresponds to the crests of the ampullae.

The pars inferior. From the floor of the utricle a small utriculo-saccular opening leads to the saccule, which contains a sensory spot, the *macula sacculi*. Its position is inclined, forming (in the domestic fowl) an angle of about 40° with the vertical plane, the highest point lying inwards.

The small endolymphatic duct is given off at the inner side of the sacculus. It enters the brain case, passes through the dura mater and enlarges into an endolymphatic sack which, on the pigeon, is about 3 mm. of diameter. At the posterior end of the saccule a ductus reuniens (or *canalis sacculo-cochlearis*) runs in a ventral direction to the large cochlea and the lagena. The latter is part of the static structures; it is typical in all the more primitive vertebrates and absent in mammals. It forms the slightly enlarged end of the cochlea and contains the third of the great sensory spots, the *macula lagenae*. This macula is cup-shaped, following the form of the lagena. It has a vertical position, perpendicular to the plane of the macula utriculi.

II. Sensory Structures and Their Nerves

The labyrinth contains two different forms of sensory apparatus of static function: the cupula type, present in the three ampullae and in the macula neglecta of the utricle (Fig. 9), and the macula-type in the main sensory areas of utricle, saccule and lagena. In either of these types the basic structure is the same: the epithelium lining the labyrinth walls is thickened in the sensory areas by the differentiation of the cells and by an ingrowth of nerve fibers (Fig. 10). The sensory spots are formed by a layer of basal cells; a second row of nuclei occurs in the supporting cells. The outer layer consists of sensory cells with hairlike processes. These sensory elements are surrounded by connective tissue. The nerve fibers originating from the vestibular ganglion enter the sensory patch and surround the epithelial sensory cells with terminal network. Such sensory patches are covered by two types of additional structures (Satoh, 1917) as follows:

A. The Cupulae

The sensory part of the wall forms a crest (*crista statica*), the epithelium being folded and the fold filled with connective tissue. The hairlike processes of the epithelium of the static crest are enclosed in a gelatinous mass secreted by the epithelium. This material is difficult to

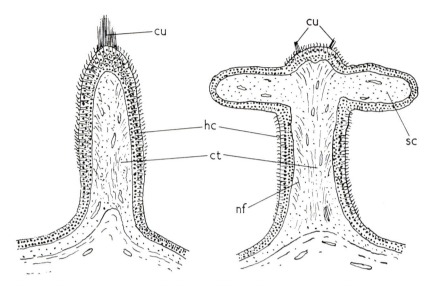

Fig. 9. Semicircular canals of a Parrot (*Chrysotis*); transverse sections of the static crest in the external ampulla (left) and in the posterior ampulla (after Satoh). *ct*, Connective tissue; *cu*, hair cells connected with the covering cupula; *hc*, hair cells; *nf*, nerve fibers; *sc*, septum cruciatum.

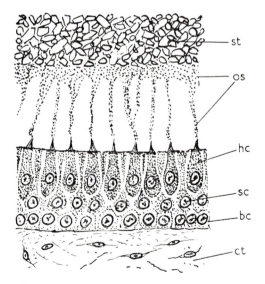

Fig. 10. Section of the sensorial patch of the utricle (combined after Satoh and Werner). *bc*, Basal cells; *ct*, connective tissue; *hc*. sensorial or hair cells; *os*, organic structure of the statolith; *sc*, sustaining cells; *st*, cristalline mass (statoconies).

preserve in fixed preparations. The secretion is non-crystalline. The ampullary crest of the horizontal canal remains as a simple fold similar to the condition of the cristae of mammals. The two other crests are of a structure peculiar to birds: near the culminating ridge a new fold (the septum cruciatum), without sensory epithelium, is formed on each side. This separates the sensory zone into three parts. This differentiation is certainly related to the important role of the static organization in birds. It is, however, impossible to attribute a particular function to these peculiar paired vertical canals (Fig. 9, right).

B. The Maculae

Each macula is covered by a gelatinous secretion, of fibrous consistency, on its border and more particularly in the marginal zone where the whole mass is attached to the sensory patch (Werner, 1939). The formation of this mass starts at the seventh day of incubation in the domestic fowl chick. At the same time it begins filling with statoconies. These crystalline contents are mostly calcium carbonate, but some Ca. phosphate is also present (Fig. 10). In none of the maculae the statoconies fuse to form a true statolith. The largest of the three is the utricular statolith.

C. The Vestibular Nerves

The static part of the stato-acoustic nerve (or *nervus octavus*) has its cellular center in the vestibular ganglion in the brain case of the skull and the acoustic part has separate cochlear ganglions. Three branches are given off by the vestibular ganglion. In turn these give off three smaller nerves to the ampullae (and to the macula neglecta), and three others to the maculae.

III. Regulation of Somatic Musculature

The most obvious function of the static part of the labyrinth is the reflex regulation of the movements of the whole of the somatic musculature. Such movements are obviously extremely variable and complicated in an organism with the wide range of locomotory behavior such as occurs in birds (Groebbels, 1926, 1927; Huizinga, 1931). It has been demonstrated experimentally that one special role of the macula sacculi is in relation to the rotation of the eye (Benjamin and Huizinga). The macula lagenae is not involved in reflex regulation.

The pars superior of the labyrinth provides continuous stimulation to the somatic musculature. Thus it is probably an important agent in

E*

the production of the general *tonus* necessary for the normal functioning of antagonitic muscles. It is specially controlled by the semicircular canals, whose function seems to be more important than in mammals. The utricle seems to be responsible for the body musculature.

References

Amerlinck, A. (1930). Nouvelles recherches sur l'histogénèse et la structure du labyrinthe membraneux de l'oreille des Oiseaux. *Arch. de Biol.* **40**: 19–56.

Benjamins, C. E., and Huizinga, E. (1926). Die Raddrehung wird bei den Tauben von den Sacculolithen ausgelöst. *Zs. f. Hals-Nasen-Ohrenheilk.* **15**: Part II.

Duijm, M. (1951). On the Head Posture in Birds and its relation to some anatomical features. I & II. *Proc. Koninkl. Nederl. Akad. v. Wetensch.* Ser. C. **54**: 3–24.

Freye, H.-A. (1952–1953). Das Gehörorgan der Vögel. *Wiss. Zeitschrf. d. Martin-Luther-Univ. Halle-Wittenberg* **2**: 267–297.

Groebbels, Fr. (1926). Die Lage und Bewegungsreflexe der Vögel III-VIII. *Pflüger's Archiv.* 214, 216, 217, 218 (1927).

Huizinga, E. (1931). Teilweise Entfernung der Pars superior labyrinthi bei der Taube. *Pflüger's Archiv.* 229.

Satoh, N. (1917). Der histologische Bau der Vogelschnecke. Basel 1–48.

Werner, Cl. F. (1939). Die Otolithen im Labyrinth der Vögel, besonders beim Star und der Taube. *Journ. f. Ornith.* **87**: 10–23.

Part I.   Sensory Organs: Vision

R. J. PUMPHREY

I. Introduction

Good general accounts of the structure of the avian eye are available (see Franz, 1934; Walls, 1942; Rochon-Duvigneaud, 1943), and it will be most useful here to limit attention to those features which are specially characteristic of birds.

The mammalian eyeball is usually nearly spherical—a shape which is mechanically strong and facilitates rotation of the eye in its orbit—but inevitably a considerable part of the volume is optically wasted. In birds the eyeball as a whole is far from spherical, though the retina usually closely follows a segment of a spherical surface centered on the posterior nodal point. The concavity around the cornea (Fig. 1) results

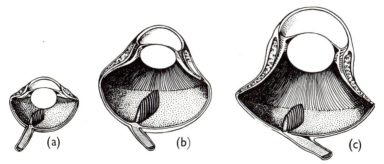

(a)   (b)   (c)

FIG. 1. Bird eyes, showing characteristic shapes. After Walls. (Each drawing shows the ventral half of the left eyeball; the nasal side is to the right; the plane of the ora terminalis retinae has been placed horizontally to bring out the nasal asymmetry which is present to some degree in the eyes of all birds.) a, Commonest, "flat" type (in a swan, *Cygnus olor*); b, "globose" type (in an eagle, *Aquila chrysaëtos*); c, "tubular" type (in an owl, *Bubo bubo*).

in a considerable saving of space and weight with no corresponding loss in optical efficiency; what would otherwise be a line of mechanical weakness is stiffened by the scleral ossicles which also provide a firm origin for the striated and rapidly acting muscles of accommodation. It is commonly believed that the shape and, even more, the fact that the eyeballs are so large in proportion to the rest of the head that they are almost in contact in the mid-line, have the effect of reducing eye movements to a very small compass. But, though the eyes of owls are incapable of any movement at all in their sockets, most birds are capable of forward convergence toward the tip of the beak: as is well known, the bittern can direct its eyes almost vertically downward (in the morphological sense) so that an intruder may be scrutinized with both eyes when the bird is in its characteristic cryptic posture with the beak pointing toward the zenith.

II. The Retina

Apart from the presence of specialized regions (*areae* and *foveae*) the retina of diurnal birds is characterized by the very high densities of cones. Rods may be absent altogether or scarce or confined to restricted regions. The density of cones in the fundus of *Motacilla* is 120,000 per square millimeter (Franz, 1934); and the density of nuclei in the ganglion-cell layer (100,000 per square millimeter), indicates that nearly

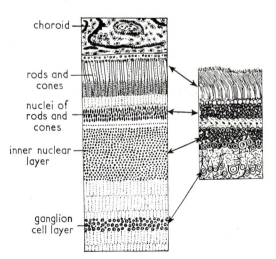

choroid

rods and cones

nuclei of rods and cones

inner nuclear layer

ganglion cell layer

FIG. 2. Semi-diagrammatic sections of retina distant from area or fovea: left, plover (*Charadrius*) after Rochon-Duvigneaud, right, primate (*Macacus*) after Polyak (approximately to scale). Note that in the bird both the ganglion-cell layer and the inner nuclear layer are 4–5 times as thick as in the monkey.

every visual cell is individually represented in the optic nerve. In man, by contrast, the cone density at a distance of 3 mm. from the fovea has already fallen to about 10,000 per square millimeter and the ganglion cells are thinly scattered, instead of being densely packed in a layer many cells deep as in birds (see Fig. 2).

It is an inevitable inference that the avian and human eyes are used in different ways and that a comparison of their efficiencies based on tests appropriate to human practice is likely to be misleading. For example, it is often categorically asserted that the visual acuity of birds in general is of a higher order than that of mankind. The evidence quoted in support of this assertion is that hawks, kites, and vultures come to objects which would, it is alleged, be quite invisible to a man in the bird's position and that insect-eating birds support themselves by picking up insects which a human observer cannot even see. Neither argument has substance. If, in the second case, the human observer had retained the power of accommodation which he had when he was 2 years old and so could get his eye as close to the prey as an insectivorous bird habitually does, he would have no difficulty in seeing it and, if he were sufficiently knowledgeable, identifying it. The ability of soaring birds to see "invisible" objects on the ground also becomes less remarkable on critical examination. Human acuity at its best is reckoned to be about 0.5 minutes of arc. A man should therefore be able to see an antelope or its shadow, to distinguish it from neighboring objects, and to determine whether it is stationary or moving when he is looking vertically down on it from a height of 10,000 feet, *if his attention is accurately directed to it.* He should be able to see a running herd as a collection of moving but unidentifiable points and to note if one point had ceased to move at a height much greater still. What he could *not* do (because his good acuity is restricted to the small angle of 2.5° subtended by his fovea) is to keep an adequate watch on all the antelopes in perhaps forty square miles of territory.

All the available evidence tends to support the belief that the acuity of birds is of the same order as that of men, but that the *rate* of assimilation of detail in the visual field is very much higher in birds. In other words the vision of birds as a whole is no sharper but a great deal faster than that of men. Donner (1951) has shown that the visual acuity actually realized by a number of small passerines is about $1\frac{1}{2}$ minutes of arc or about three times worse than human acuity. And he demonstrated, moreover, that there was in each case very good agreement between the acuity found and that computed from measurements of the cone density and the posterior nodal distance. Applying this basis of calculation to the larger birds, we may plausibly conclude that large hawks, eagles, and vultures may exceed man in optical acuity by a factor of 2 or 3, but certainly not much more. A bird with a single glance lasting perhaps a second takes in a picture which a man could accumulate only by laboriously scanning the whole field piece by piece with the most accurate portion of his retina. It must, however, be pointed out that the bird's picture is flat and that, in his slow binocular search, man acquires information about relative distances which is not immediately available to the bird, but which has to be built up from a succession of glances from *different* places. This use of parallax is conspicuous in the feeding of many birds; and the rapid lateral and sometimes vertical oscillations of the heads of owls confronted suddenly with an attractive or puzzling object may be presumed to be a subterfuge by which stereoscopic vision is achieved in spite of eyes incapable of convergence.

The probability that visual information is taken in by birds at a high rate and simultaneously over the greater part of the visual field has been increased by recent studies of bird navigation (Matthews, 1955, Chapter IX and *passim*). The only theory of navigation consistent with the evidence implies that birds can assess not only the elevation of the sun but also its rate of change of elevation and of azimuth with high accuracy. The human eye is, for the reasons already given, incapable of estimating large angles accurately without accessory apparatus such as a sextant: to the human eye, sun, moon, and planets appear to be stationary and their movements can be reliably inferred only from a comparison of their positions at quite long intervals. If any one doubts this, let him watch the setting sun as it touches the horizon and try to estimate (without calculation or reference to previous experience) how long it will take to disappear.

It would seem that in order for birds to navigate as well as they have been shown to do, their eyes must be capable of high resolution over a visual angle of 70–80° in order to ascertain the instantaneous *position* of the sun with the necessary accuracy: and to ascertain its *direction* of movement in the sky with the required accuracy seems further to imply a much lower threshold for movement than that of the human eye. To put it loosely, it is as if a bird could ascertain that a clock was going by looking at the hour hand in as short a time as a man could make the same discovery by looking at the minute hand from the same distance.

A. AREAE AND FOVEAE

Despite the high concentration of cones everywhere in the retina, there are usually, in the eyes of diurnal birds, one or more regions where the cone density is still higher. In such a region, or *area*, the number of cells in the nuclear layers is also higher and there is 1:1 correspondence between cones and ganglion cells. In consequence the retina is inevitably thicker in the *area* which appears as a low mound when seen ophthalmoscopically. Within the area, there is usually a *fovea*, a depression with

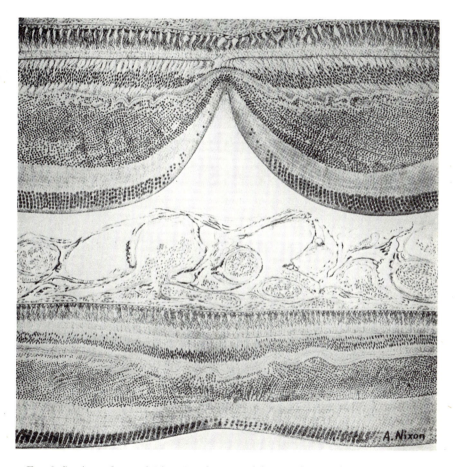

Fig. 3. Sections of central (above) and temporal foveae of the eagle, *Aquila chrysaetos* (from Polyak, 1957).

steeply sloping sides; and at the bottom of this the cones attain their closest packing (1,000,000/mm.^{2} in the larger hawks) (see Fig. 3). An area is doubtless a place of maximum optical resolution. The function of the (central) fovea is less obvious, but it has been argued (Pumphrey, 1948b) that, because of the refraction which must result from its steeply sloping sides, it is a device for enabling the eye to be "locked" to a given object and for increasing its sensitivity to movements of that object. (It should be noted that the fovea of primates does not have steep sides and that man is notoriously deficient in his ability to keep his eye on a small visual object for any length of time.)

It appears from the investigations of Wood (1917) and Duijm (1958) that there are three principal types of area-fovea arrangement in the

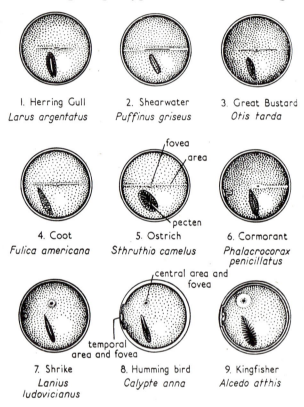

FIG. 4. Ophthalmoscopic appearance of the inner aspect of the retina as seen through the pupil, showing position and extent of area and fovea. (After Wood, 1917.)

eyes of birds (Fig. 4). In many graminivorous birds there is a single area, which may or may not be foveate, lying close to the optic axis and called an *area centralis*. In many water birds and in some which live in open plains the area is extended into a horizontal band and in some cases the fovea also is extended into a trough running along the area. Thirdly, there are in falconiform birds, in birds such as swifts and swallows which habitually take insects on the wing, in kingfishers, and in hummingbirds two areas, each foveate. The central fovea in these cases is close to the optic axis and the other, the *fovea temporalis*, is so disposed that the image of an object ahead can with a slight degree of convergence be formed on the temporal foveae of both eyes simultaneously. It seems certain that temporal foveae, where they occur, are used in the binocular stereoscopic vision without which the pursuit of prey in active flight would have little likelihood of success; the temporal fovea is always more open and less steep sided than the central fovea of the same eye, and in this it comes much closer to the fovea of the binocular primates on which stereoscopic vision is certainly dependent. It would seem that *for this purpose* the advantages of a steep-sided fovea are outweighed by the disadvantages. On the other hand the extended areae of the water birds suggests a device for accurately fixating the horizon as a datum to which other objects in the visual field can be referred.

B. THE PECTEN

As might perhaps be expected of an eye which is capable of high resolution over a large part of the visual field, the retina of the bird's eye is completely free of the rich vascularization which characterizes

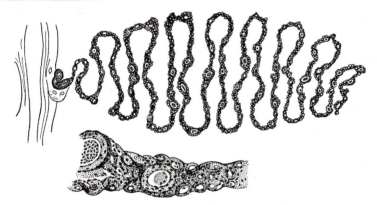

FIG. 5. Section through a pecten of the gannet, *Sula bassana*. Below, a portion at higher magnification. (Redrawn after Rochon-Duvigneaud.)

the retina of the mammal. It is generally accepted that nutrient substances and oxygen reach the retinal cells by diffusion through the vitreous humor and that their source is the *pecten*, a roughly conical object based on the blind spot at the entry of the optic nerve and having its apex directed toward the center of the lens (Fig. 5). The pecten is very vascular and (unlike the pecten of most reptiles, which is a simple peg) its surface is folded in a way calculated, one may suppose, to assist the diffusion of metabolites to and from the vitreous humor. As the visual cells are more numerous, the retina thicker, and the metabolic rate higher in birds than in most reptiles, a greater elaboration of the pecten in the former is only to be expected, and it remains highly probable that the nutrition of the retina is its primitive and principal function.

Menner (1938), however, pointed out a previously unsuspected relation between the form of the pecten and the habits of its owner. Using

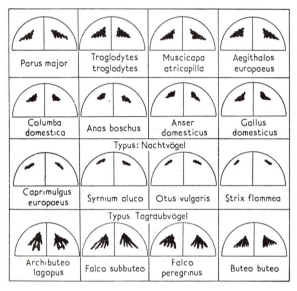

Fig. 6. A selection of tracings of the pecten shadow upon the retina. (From Menner, 1938.)

a special perimeter he plotted out for a variety of birds the region of the retina shadowed by the pecten from different points in the visual field. Some of his results are represented in Fig. 6, and they do not on the whole support the contention that the size and obstructiveness of the pecten is simply proportional to the number of visual cells requiring nourishment. Menner concluded that the pecten has an optical as well as a trophic function and that this optical function is the enhancement of the sensitivity of the eye to movements of objects in the visual field. Moreover he carried out the experiment of making an artificial eye—a camera, with a ground-glass screen, into which a cardboard model of a pecten could be inserted—and he claimed that when the camera was directed at some swifts wheeling high in the sky, their barely detectable

images became more prominent when the cardboard pecten was introduced. This experiment is not as easy to repeat as it might appear, and
I have not fully satisfied myself one way or the other that it works: nor
do I fully understand why it should. Crozier and Wolff (1943a, b),
however, have discussed the theory of the pecten and adduced further
evidence: so Menner's conclusion may be regarded as sound.

III. Color Vision

No one who has had anything to do with diurnal birds has ever
doubted that their perception of color is as good as ours, if not better:
and this common-sense conclusion has been confirmed by the careful
studies of Watson (1915) and Lashley (1916) and in even more detail
by Hamilton and Coleman (1933), who have shown that the curve
relating the least perceptible change of wavelength ($\Delta\lambda$) to the wavelength (λ) has exactly the same form for the pigeon as for man—a
finding which strongly suggests that the fundamental mechanism for
discriminating pure colors is the same in both.

It is possible, however, that in discriminating mixed or pigmentary
colors, birds may be able to improve on man's performance. Schultze's
(1866) observation that many of the cones of birds contain colored oil
droplets, red, orange, and yellow, has been confirmed and extended by
Walls and Judd (1933). It is easy to make up different mixtures of
spectral colors which appear identical to man's unaided vision, but
which can immediately be distinguished if the observer is allowed to
use extraocular color filters. It must be presumed that the colored oil
droplets are intraocular color filters which could continually give to
birds the same power of discrimination as man can achieve only with
external aids.

There is no satisfactory evidence that birds make use of extraspectral
frequencies at either end of the spectrum. Vanderplank's (1934) contention, that owls are sensitive (like pit vipers) to infrared rays and that
they are thus enabled to find their prey in the dark, was decisively
disproved by Matthews and Matthews (1939), who showed that the
dioptric system is quite opaque to infrared light. If owls can detect it, it
is not by means of their eyes.

Polaroid spectacles have proved so useful to anglers that it is not
surprising that it should have been suggested that herons, kingfishers,
and other birds which have to seek their prey through a water surface
are provided with internal polaroid spectacles of their own. So far as I
am aware there is no evidence in favor of this suggestion other than
the birds' success; but there is no doubt that if either the dioptric system
or the visual cells were polarized so that most of the reflected light from

a water surface was rejected it would be a great advantage to the birds: and the recently demonstrated use of plane-polarized light by arthropods, though in a different connection, emphasizes the technical possibility. It is known that migrating birds do not use sky polarization when the sun is obscured (as do bees), but it should be appreciated that sky polarization is an inappropriate reference for birds: even with the best instrumentation man cannot obtain as accurate information from sky polarization as he can get from a simple sextant observation of the sun. The fact that birds do not make use of polarization in circumstances where its usefulness would be doubtful is no evidence that some of them cannot do so in circumstances where the gain would be unquestionable.

IV. Nocturnality

The ability of owls to find their way and their prey in what appears to us to be almost total darkness has long presented an unsolved puzzle. Even if, as now seems likely, they depend heavily on their ears to find their prey, to fly without injury in near darkness through scrub and

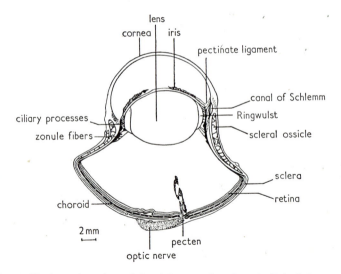

Fig. 7. Horizontal section of the right eye of eagle-owl, *Bubo bubo*.

under trees still seems an almost miraculous achievement, and it cannot be said that the structure of their eyes offers any immediate explanation. The human retina, when it is fully dark-adapted, is almost as sensitive as is theoretically possible (Pirenne, 1948) when allowance is made for the aperture of the eye and the absorption and reflection of light by the dioptric apparatus. This sensitivity is gained in a considerable degree by the sacrifice of resolution, since all the rods in quite large areas of the retina act as one unit for the purpose of collecting light energy, and their messages converge to a single ganglion cell.

The owl's eye is in many respects a typical nocturnal eye (see Fig. 7). Its pupil is enormous when fully extended, its focal length is short, and the visual field is restricted. It is not at all easy to see reflections from either surface of the lens, and it seems probable that the losses from reflection, absorption, and scattering may be much less than in the human eye. The visual receptor cells are almost exclusively rods, and

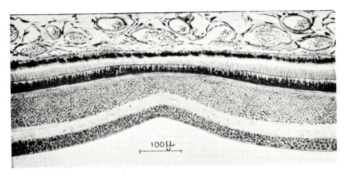

FIG. 8. Section of fovea of scops owl. *Otus scops*. Note the remarkable density of the ganglion-cell layer.

their terminal segments are proportionately very long and very full of rhodopsin; it seems likely that less light passes through them to be wasted in the pigment layers and sclera than in the human eye. But when all allowance is made, it is improbable that more than 100 times as much light is absorbed from a given faint source as would be absorbed by a fully dark-adapted human eye in the same position: and it does not seem likely that this advantage is great enough to account for the owl's performance. Moreover, the density of the ganglion-cell layers in the owl's retina is much greater than it is in the most sensitive part of the human retina, and presumably the degree of summation of rods into a single sensitive unit is correspondingly less. Although the visual cells of owls are predominantly rods, there is a fovea (so placed that the image of an object ahead falls on the foveae of both eyes) (Fig. 8). One must conclude that the resolving power of owls in near darkness approaches that of diurnal birds in daylight, but no plausible suggestion has been made as to how this is achieved without a corresponding loss in sensitivity.

F

V. Accommodation

Although the muscles of accommodation are much reduced in nocturnal birds, in which the focal length is for all practical purposes fixed, they are well developed and active in diurnal birds. The lateral compression of the lens which shortens its focal length does not depend, as in man, on the mere slackening of tension in the zonal fibers and on the residual elasticity of the lens capsule; the margin of the lens (*Ringwulst*) is in firm contact with the ciliary body and the latter is positively driven toward the axis of the eye principally by the contraction of Brücke's muscle (Fig. 10). In addition, though it is not established that

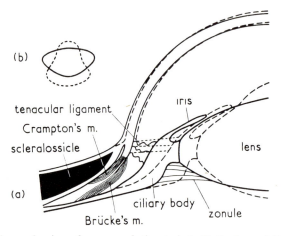

Fig. 9. (*a*) The mechanism of accommodation (orig.); (*b*) the lens of the cormorant's eye at rest (full line) and fully accommodated (dotted). (From Franz, after Hess, 1910.)

any change in the shape of the cornea accompanies accommodation, the disposition of Crampton's muscle suggests that its contraction would have the effect of pulling down the margin of the cornea toward the fundus, and so increasing the curvature at its center. The relative parts played in accommodation by changes in the radii of the lens surfaces (and of the corneal surface, if any) is not certainly known, but the most cursory observation of small birds is enough to show that the shortening in focus which results is rapid and ample. The redirection of attention from the horizon to an object 2 or 3 cm. from the eye seems to be complete in the time taken to move the head. Such observation also demonstrates that the act of accommodation is accompanied by a rapid and strong, though sometimes transient, pupillary contraction which, though it does not normally shorten the focus of the eye, does considerably increase its depth of focus. The muscles of accommodation and the *sphincter iridis*, which contracts the pupil, are therefore functionally synergic: and this helps to explain the curious situation which was found by Hess in the cormorant (*Phalacrocorax carbo*) and which is perhaps general in diving birds. Under water the cornea ceases to play an appreciable part in the refraction of the eye, and the sudden need for an additional 20 diopters or so of refraction over and above the normal requirements of accommodation is met by the compression of the anterior part of the lens by the *sphincter iridis* (Fig. 9). Crampton's muscle is said to be degenerate in diving birds, which is perhaps an additional reason for believing that its principal normal function is changing the corneal curvature.

VI. Size

Reference has been made at the beginning of this chapter to the probable importance to flying birds of the saving in weight achieved by departure from a spherical shape for the eyeball, but this is perhaps a misleading way of putting it. Birds of necessity are eye-dominated and eye-dependent to a greater extent than any mammal, even than the higher primates and man. Lorenz (1952) has commented on the deeply rooted inhibition which prevents corvines from attacking eyes with their beaks—an inhibition which makes even the raven safe to handle. My own more limited experience with owls, guillemots, and domestic poultry is similar: though I have usually worn spectacles as a precaution, my eyes have never been attacked even by agitated birds which were quite ready to draw blood at other points. I believe that Lorenz is right in finding the explanation of this inhibition in its selective value for the mutual protection of eyes among nestlings, and I believe, too, that it is general in Aves. It is possible, perhaps it is even likely, that this inhibition provides in its turn the explanation of the effectiveness of eyespot patterns as a defence by insects against the attacks of avian predators (see Blest, 1957).

The presence of such behavioral protective devices in addition to the mechanical devices of eyelids and a universally present and active nictitating membrane underlines the overriding importance of vision for birds, which is evident from the disproportionate size of their eyes. An ostrich which is the height of a man, though much lighter in body, has eyes that are five times as massive as human eyes; and in smaller birds the disproportion is greater. In starlings, as in man, the weight of the head is about one-tenth of the total body weight; but in man the weight of the eyes is less than 1% of the weight of the head; in the starling it is about 15%. It would perhaps be truer to regard all flying birds as having eyes as heavy as is aerodynamically practicable, and to suppose that the nonspherical eyeball is less a device for weight saving than for achieving the maximum efficiency consistent with a given weight.

References

Blest, A. D. (1957). The function of the eyespot patterns in the Lepidoptera. *Behaviour*, **11**: 210–254.

Crozier, W. J., and Wolff, E. (1943a). Modifications of the flicker response contour and the significance of the avian pecten. *J. Gen. Physiol.* **27**: 287–313.

Crozier, W. J., and Wolff, E. (1943b). Flicker response contours for the sparrow and the theory of the avian pecten. *J. Gen. Physiol.* **27**: 315–324.

Donner, K. O. (1951). The visual acuity of some passerine birds. *Acta Zool. Fennica* **66**: 1–40.

Duijm, M. (1958). On the position of a ribbon-like central area in the eyes of some birds. *Arch. Néerl. Zool.* **13**: 128–145.

Franz, V. (1934). Höhere Sinnesorgane (Auge). *In* "Handbuch der vergleichenden Anatomie der Wirbeltiere" (L. Bolk, E. Göppert, E. Kallius, and W. Lubosch, eds.), Vol. 2, Pt. 2, pp. 989–1292. Urban and Schwarzenberg, Berlin and Vienna.

Hamilton, W. F., and Coleman, T. B. (1933). Trichromatic vision in the pigeon as illustrated by the spectral line discrimination curve. *J. Comp. Psychol.* **15**: 183–191.

Hess, C. (1912). Vergleichende Physiologie des Gesichtsinnes. Gustav Fischer, Jena.

Lashley, K. S. (1916). The Colour vision of birds. I. The spectrum of the domestic fowl. *Animal Behaviour* **6**: 1–126.

Lorenz, K. Z. (1952). "King Solomon's Ring." Methuen, London.

Matthews, G. V. T. (1955). "Bird Navigation." Cambridge Univ. Press, London and New York.

Matthews, L. H., and Matthews, B. H. C. (1939). Owls and infra-red radiation. *Nature*, **143**: 983.

Menner, E. (1938). Die Bedeutung des Pecten im Auge des Vogels für die Wahrnehmung von Bewegungen. *Zool. Jahrb. Abt. Allgem. Zool. Physiol. Tiere* **58**: 481–538.

Pirenne, M. H. (1948). "Vision and the Eye." Pilot Press, London.

Pumphrey, R. J. (1948a). The theory of the fovea. *J. Exptl. Biol.* **25**: 299–312.

Pumphrey, R. J. (1948b). The sense organs of birds. *Ibis* **90**: 171–190: Annual Report *Smithsonian Inst.* 305–330.

Rochon-Duvigneaud, A. (1943). "Les yeux et la vision des Vertébrés." Masson, Paris.

Schultze, M. (1866). Zur Anatomie und Physiologie der Retina. *Arch. mikr. Anatomie* **2**: 175.

Vanderplank, F. L. (1934). The effect of infra-red waves on tawny owls (*Strix aluco*). *Proc. Zool. Soc. London*, 505–507.

Walls, G. L. (1942). "The Vertebrate Eye." Cranbrook Inst. Sci., Michigan.

Walls, G. L., and Judd, H. D. (1933). The intraocular colour filters of vertebrates. *Brit. Jour. Ophthalmol.* **17,** 641–675, 705–725.

Watson, J. B. (1915). Studies on the spectral sensitivity of birds. Pap. Dep. Marine Biol., Carnegie Inst., Wash. **7**: 87–104.

Wood, C. A. (1917). "The Fundus Oculi of Birds." Lakeside Press, Chicago, Illinois.

Part II. Sensory Organs: Hearing

R. J. PUMPHREY

I. Introduction

Since Helmholtz took note of Hasse's (1867) observation that Corti's rods are absent from the avian ear, it has been appreciated that there are substantial differences between the ear of the bird and that of the mammal. But, while Helmholtz was led by this discovery to seek a physiological basis for frequency analysis in the structures common to both, others less gifted have tacitly concluded that the differences do not matter much, and it seems probable that only a minority of zoologists and ornithologists today have any clear idea of what they are. Yet it is certain that birds and mammals are respectively the warm-blooded contemporary representatives of two lines of descent which separated not later than the Upper Carboniferous (250 million years ago) and which have been evolving independently ever since; it would indeed be surprising if the similarity of their auditory receptors extended beyond the requirements of the basic design which was inherited from the common ancestor. Although it is generally agreed that both birds and mammals have outstripped other animals in the excellence of their hearing, it by no means follows that this excellence is attained in the same way or even that it is of quite the same kind in the two classes. It is true, as Helmholtz believed, that in both classes the excellence depends in part on a peripheral process of frequency analysis which in turn is reflected in part in the psychophysical ability to discriminate pitch. But, as has been pointed out in this connection (Gold and Pumphrey, 1948), any practical frequency analysis is necessarily a compromise. The more detailed the analysis the longer it takes, the more out of date is the information finally available, and the less is the certainty of the moment at which the sound being analyzed actually occurred. Within the last few years circumstantial evidence has accumulated that the compromises adopted by birds and mammals, respectively, are different, and that the difference is in the direction which the differences in the structure of their ears would lead one to expect.

II. Structure of the Ear

The diagrams (Figs. 1–3) illustrate the relations of the principal parts of a bird's ear. The *external auditory meatus* in some species is open to the atmosphere, but in most is covered over with feathers, so as to be invisible externally. The middle-ear cavity, separated from the meatus by the tympanic membrane (eardrum) is also air-filled and is in communication with the atmosphere by way of the Eustachian tube and the mouth: the average pressure on each face of the eardrum is therefore

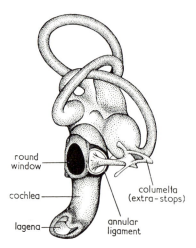

FIG. 1. Bony labyrinth. Bullfinch (*Pyrrhula*). (Modified after Schwartzkopf.)

normally the same, but rapid changes in pressure in the atmosphere, such as sounds, reach the eardrum almost entirely through the meatus, and the consequent displacements of the eardrum are communicated to the fluid of the inner ear by the *columella*, of which the footplate nearly fills the oval window (*fenestra ovalis*). The footplate is held in position by an impervious but flexible *annular ligament* which links its edges to those of the oval window; and its inner aspect is in contact with the perilymph of the *scala vestibuli*. The bony cochlea is a fingerlike tube down the center of which lies the cochlear duct or *scala media*. This is a outgrowth of the membranous labyrinth and contains endolymph. It is held in position by two cartilaginous shelves projecting inward from the

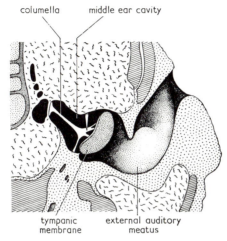

Fig. 2. Middle and outer ear. Ostrich (*Struthio*). (Modified after Grassé.)

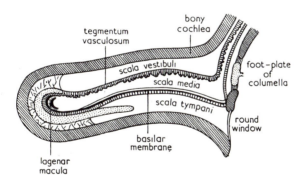

Fig. 3. Cochlea. Diagrammatic longitudinal section of cochlea. (Modified after Grassé.)

bony cochlea; its floor is the *basilar membrane* and its roof, the *tegmental membrane* (tegmentum vasculosum); at its blind end is the *macula lagenae*, a group of sensory hair cells provided with otoconia. The cavities above and below the scala media are filled with perilymph and are known as the *scala vestibuli* and the *scala tympani*, respectively. Near the basal end of the scala tympani is another aperture in the bony wall which elsewhere separates the inner from the middle ear. This aperture, the round window (*fenestra rotunda*), is covered by a thin, flexible membrane which separates the perilymph of the scala tympani from the air of the middle ear. It will be seen that, since perilymph is very much less compressible than air, a displacement of the columella into the scala vestibuli will be compensated by an equivalent displacement of the round-window membrane toward the middle ear and that, at the same time, the tegmental and basilar membranes will undergo displacement in the same sense; and vice versa. It is the displacement of the basilar membrane and the consequent deformation of its hair cells which is the immediate cause of the excitation of cochlear nerve fibers and ultimately of the sensation of hearing. The basilar membrane, hair cells, accessory supporting cells, nerve fibers, and the tectorial membrane

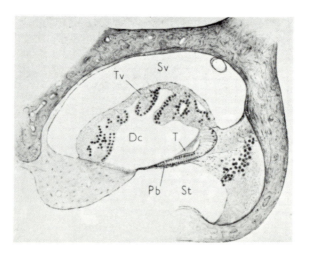

Fig. 4. Cochlea. Transverse section near base. Duck (*Anas*). Dc, *ductus cochlearis*; Pb, basilar membrane; St, *scala tympani*; Sv, *scala vestibuli*; T, tectorial membrane; Tv, tegmental membrane. (From Grassé, after Satoh.)

are often collectively referred to as the *organ of Corti*. The basilar membrane itself is strengthened by transverse fibers of which the ends are firmly anchored to the cartilaginous shelves referred to above (see Fig. 4). These fibers number between one and two thousand, and, except at the ends of the basilar membrane where it tapers fairly sharply, they increase progressively in length from the basal to the apical end: the increase is not very marked (about 25 %). Lying on and supported by the fibers are the hair cells, so disposed that thirty to fifty can be counted in a transverse section; the nerve fibers from the cochlear nerve penetrate the anterior cartilaginous shelf and ramify among them; and their hairs are embedded in the tectorial membrane, which is closely applied over the whole surface of the hair cell layer and anchored on the anterior side to the cartilaginous shelf.

Although there is a certain similarity in the disposition of the homologous parts, the differences between the mammalian and avian ears

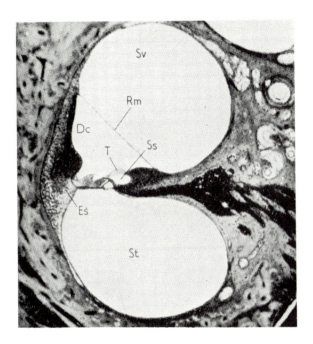

Fig. 5. Cochlea of cat. For comparison with Fig. 4: transverse section of middle section. Dc, *ductus cochlearis* or *scala media*; Es, external spiral ligament; Rm, Reissner's membrane; Ss, *spiral suleus*; St, *scala tympani*; Sv, *scala vestibuli*; T, tectorial membranes.

are evidently substantial and deserve detailed consideration. Among mammals only the egg-laying monotremes resemble birds in possessing a cochlea which is relatively short and uncoiled and which terminates in a *macula lagenae*. In all other mammals the cochlea is coiled in a tight spiral of two to four turns, the lagena is absent, and, at the apical end of the basilar membrane, the scala vestibuli is joined to the scala tympani by an opening, the *helicotrema*. In birds the lagenar macula is adherent to cartilage which in turn is anchored by trabeculae to the bony cochlea; the scalae appear to end blindly and there is no definite helicotrema.

There is no experimental evidence of the function of the lagena in birds (or reptiles or monotremes). In favor of the presumption of an auditory function are the facts (1) that in birds its afferent nerve fibers, which are very numerous, enter the medulla in company with those from the cochlea and, unlike the majority of the saccular fibers, are believed to enter the cochlear nuclei and not the vestibular (Kappers *et al.*, 1936) and (2) that it unquestionably is auditory in some fish. Against it is the fact that the cochlear architecture appears designed to ensure that the endolymph in the vicinity of the lagenar macula is stagnant and unaffected by perilymph movements originating from the columella. It is still, however, likely that the hair cells of the lagena could be excited by bone-conducted sounds, especially those of low frequency. The persistence of the lagena in egg-laying mammals as well as in birds is probably coincidental, but it is to be noted that birds at least display a certain capacity for auditory responses while still in the egg at a time when the middle ear is presumably liquid-filled and the columella functionless; in these circumstances all effective acoustic stimuli must be "bone-conducted" and the lagena would seem to be a more appropriate receptor than the cochlea. In the present state of knowledge it is probably safest to regard the lagenar macula as a relict which, in the adult at least, is either functionless or of secondary importance. It is, without doubt, the cochlea proper which is the principal auditory receptor in both birds and mammals (Fig. 5).

A. The Cochlea

Anyone who is willing to take the trouble to examine and compare the structures of the avian and mammalian cochleas can convince himself that though the specifications to which each is constructed may be equally strict they are very far from being identical. The basilar membrane of the bird is proportionately broader and very much shorter than that of the mammal. In the latter the lengths of the transverse fibers increase from base to apex in an exact and regular manner over a range (in man) of $160\mu–520\mu$; and the geometry and apparent strength of the external spiral ligament (Fig. 4) and of the internal bony lamina between which the fibers are stretched suggest that, even if these fibers are not normally under tension, the maintenance of an exact length is of functional importance, particularly at the basal (high-frequency) end. In birds there are no comparable supporting structures, the cartilaginous shelves show no special indications of strength and, though the transverse fibers of the membrane do increase in length toward the apex, the increase is less than two to one compared with a fourfold change in mammals. The absolute length of the basilar membrane in birds is about 3 mm. (*Columba*) compared with 35 mm. in man. The number of transverse fibers is probably between 10,000 and 20,000 in most mammals and about 1200 in *Columba*. Neglecting the tapering ends of the basilar membrane, these fibers range in the pigeon from 450μ to 570μ in length (Retzius, 1884) and are thus substantially longer than any but the apical fibers of the human ear.

One of the most impressive features of the mammalian cochlea is the cleanness and spaciousness of the design. The inner surfaces of the scalae are smooth and free from projections and re-entrant angles. Reissner's membrane which divides the scala vestibuli from the scala media is extremely thin and perfectly flat. In well-fixed preparations (Fig. 5) it can be seen that the tectorial membrane is a delicate arch springing from a firm base on the bony lamina and touching the basilar membrane only along the narrow band where the hairs of the hair cells of the inner and outer rows project and where Corti's arch gives it perhaps some support. Apart from this narrow band of contact, Corti's organ appears to have been designed to minimize obstruction to the free movement of liquid in the neighborhood of the hair cells. They and their supporting cells (Deiters' cells) are separated by spaces (the spaces of Nuel); and these and the tunnel of Corti's arch are obstructed only by extremely fine nerve fibers; on either side, the scala media and the internal sulcus beneath the arch of the tectorial membrane are completely free of obstruction.

In the bird's cochlea the contrast is striking. The sulcus is reduced or absent and the tectorial membrane[1] spreads like a blanket over the hair cells, which are densely packed and occupy nearly the full width of the basilar membrane. The tegmental membrane, which corresponds to Reissner's membrane in the mammal, is massive and full of blood vessels and apparently glandular in places; lobed processes project into and obstruct the scala media. It is reasonable to suppose that this membrane, like the stria vascularis of the mammalian cochlea, has a trophic function. If, as seems likely (Gold, 1948), Corti's organ behaves as a regenerative power amplifier, a continuous and adequate supply of fuel for it would be necessary, but, as this end is achieved in the mammal without obstructing the scala media, it is difficult to resist the conclusion that obstruction does not matter, or matters much less, in the ear of the bird. In addition to the vascularization of the tegmental

---

[1] Comparison of Satoh's figures with those of Retzius (1884) suggests that in the former, illustrated in Fig. 4, the tectorial membrane has shriveled very much in the course of fixation (as happens in all but the very best preparations of the mammalian cochlea).

membrane some blood vessels lie freely in the perilymph of the scala vestibuli and scala tympani, a state of affairs never to my knowledge recorded in mammals.

It has already been remarked that, though the basilar membrane of birds is only about one-tenth of the length of that of mammals, about ten times as many hair cells are visible in a transverse section. The number of primary sense cells in the organ of Corti is therefore about the same in the two classes. In default of evidence to the contrary, this suggests that the avian and mammalian ears may have a similar over-all figure of merit, but the difference of disposition suggests that the figure of merit is differently achieved in the two classes. It is therefore necessary to consider briefly what is the significance of the distribution in mammals.

Despite some persistent objectors the evidence is overwhelming that different frequencies of incident sound excite different regions of the basilar membrane and that, as the frequency of the stimulus falls from the highest audible frequency to the lowest, the point of maximum stimulation moves from the base of the cochlea to the apex. A long basilar membrane may therefore be held to imply either a wide auditory spectrum or good frequency discrimination or, of course, both. Moreover, a greater length of basilar membrane is required to deal with high frequencies than with low. In man, and in the few other mammals for which information is available, nearly three-quarters of the length of the basilar membrane is devoted to the five audible octaves above 1000 cycles per second, while the remaining apical quarter accommodates the five or six audible octaves below 1000 cycles per second. The relative shortness of the avian basilar membrane, considered by itself, may therefore indicate (1) an auditory spectrum which is restricted in comparison with typical mammals, particularly at the high frequency end, and (2) poorer frequency discrimination.

This inference must however be qualified by the consideration that there are many more hair cells per unit length of basilar membrane in the bird than in the mammal. In mammals, as has been said, only four or five hair cells can usually be seen in a thin transverse section of the basilar membrane: three (or sometimes four) just outside Corti's arch and one just inside. There is evidence that sounds of sufficiently low intensity excite only the outer hair cells for which there is a considerable degree of summation (a number of hair cells being innervated by a single nerve fiber) and that the hair cells of the inner row, which mostly have a nerve fiber to themselves or share one with a neighbor, come into play only when the sound intensity is far above the threshold. It is noteworthy that although the range of intensities over which the human ear is responsive is very great—a just tolerable noise is more than a million million times as intense as one which is just detectable—the number of detectable steps in loudness within this range is very small. There are only about 300 such steps in the middle of the audible-frequency band and less than 50 at extreme frequencies. By contrast, although the highest audible tone is only about one thousand times the frequency of the lowest, the number of detectable steps in pitch is over 1500. If it is permissible to assume, as the evidence seems to suggest, that the greater number of hair cells per unit length of basilar membrane in the avian ear is indicative of a comparably greater power of intensity discrimination compared with mammals, a number of apparent difficulties of interpretation vanish. In particular it becomes possible to account for the good frequency discrimination of birds (see page 82) without recourse to unsubstantiated and inherently improbable hypotheses of central analysis. [For a discussion of the interdependence of frequency and intensity discrimination, see Gold and Pumphrey (1948).]

Briefly to sum up the conclusions of the foregoing comparison of the avian and mammalian cochleas: (1) The general design of the former indicates that the minimization of viscous and turbulent resistance to the moving parts is of much less importance than in the mammal. (2) The shortness of (and the small numbers of transverse fibers in) the basilar membrane suggests that the range of frequencies to which birds are sensitive is less than in mammals. (3) The larger number of hair cells per unit length suggests that birds have a lower differential threshold for intensity. So far as this comparison is capable of quantitative expression it is approximately true that the avian basilar membrane is one-tenth the length of the mammalian with one-tenth the number of transverse fibers and with ten times as many hair cells per transverse row. The implications of this comparison are quite far reaching. If the avian cochlea is, in fact, ten times as sensitive to changes in amplitude as the mammalian, it is theoretically possible for the same degree of frequency discrimination over a given band of frequencies to be achieved with one-tenth of the number of frequency sensitive "elements"[1]; and each element need be only one-tenth as selective and consequently *may respond ten times as fast.* Common sense suggests that a price must be paid for the advantages of simplicity, ruggedness, and speed which the avian cochlea appears to gain over the mammalian

---

[1] This conclusion follows from elementary physical considerations and is quite independent of the particular mechanism of frequency discrimination which is assumed. For example, it applies with equal force to artificial frequency analyzers of whatever kind.

and, from theory, it is evident that the price is a tenfold decrease in signal-noise ratio, i.e. that the absolute threshold theoretically attainable is 10 decibels higher for the bird's cochlea than for the mammal's. It is not useful to comment on the relative importance of the limits of sensitivity of the cochleas in the two classes without data, which are not as yet available, on the relative efficiencies of the outer and middle ears. It may, however, be relevant to point out that, while some human ears appear to approach the theoretical limit of sensitivity, the average human is a long way from it; and any large sample of young men and women with allegedly normal hearing shows a scatter of thresholds greatly exceeding the 10-decibel difference postulated between mammal and bird (Dadson and King, 1952).

B. The Middle Ear

The morphology of the middle ear of birds has been described in standard texts (Stresemann, 1934; Portmann, 1950). Its acoustic functions are the transfer of sound power from the eardrum to the oval window and, presumably, the dissipation of power radiated into it at the round window. In this dissipation the extensive trabeculated air cavities opening into the middle ear doubtless play an important part: they have been supposed to be resonant, but there is no evidence of this and their structure is that of an efficient attenuator.

Although the mechanics of the transfer of sound power from the eardrum to the cochlea are apparently simpler in birds than in mammals, they are little understood. It has been customary to discuss them on the assumption that the eardrum and the footplate are massless free pistons linked by a massless rigid rod, the columella, normal to both. And on this assumption the transformation ratio would be simply equal to the ratio of the areas of the eardrum and footplate, and the sound pressures in the scale vestibuli and in the auditory meatus would be in this ratio. Schwartzkopf (1955) has compiled a valuable list of measurements of these areas (Table I).

The most important oversimplification in this analysis is the assumption that the columella is a rigid rod normal to the eardrum. Being composed partly of bone (stapes) and partly of cartilage (extrastapes), it is far from being a rigid unit; and in many, perhaps in all, birds, it is inserted at a substantial angle to the eardrum. The effect of this oblique insertion is that displacement of the eardrum necessarily induces a rocking movement of the columella. It acts as a lever whose fulcrum is one edge of the oval window and whose short and long arms are the radius of the footplate and the whole length of the columella, respectively. This lever evidently introduces an additional and important transformation factor which becomes predominant when the angle of incidence of the columella on the eardrum is very high, as it is in owls (perhaps 60–70°). In owls, as Schwartzkopf has pointed out, the inner aspect of the footplate is approximately hemispherical, and he suggests that this form is less apt to produce turbulence (and consequent loss of power in the perilymph of the scala vestibuli) when the movement of the footplate is principally a rotation in the plane of the stapes about a point in the annular ligament.

It is probably safe to assume that Schwartzkopf's table gives a

TABLE I

Areas of body surface, ear drum (movable part), and footplate and their ratios in some birds (from Schwartzkopf, 1955)

Species	Body surface (=weight$^{\frac{2}{3}}$) cm^2	Relative size of ear drum (Ear drum/ body surface)	Ear drum area cm^2	Columella base area cm^2	Area Ratio Ear drum/ Foot plate
Phylloscopus collybita	4.0	0.020	0.078	0.0036	22
Phylloscopus trochilus	4.5	0.021	0.094	0.0034	28
Parus communis	5.0	0.018	0.089	0.0039	23
Parus caeruleus	5.1	0.016	0.084	0.0032	26
Hippolais icterina	5.7	0.015	0.086	0.0030	29
Sylvia atricapilla	6.6	0.019	0.126	0.0044	29
Hirundo rustica	7.4	0.010	0.071	0.0038	19
Fringilla coelebs	7.9	0.015	0.114	0.0041	28
Parus major	7.9	0.013	0.104	0.0042	25
Pyrrhula pyrrhula	9.0	0.013	0.117	0.0048	24
Passer domesticus	9.6	0.0094	0.091	0.0042	22
Turdus merula	20.9	0.0077	0.160	0.0073	22
Pica pica	35.5	0.0075	0.265	0.0116	23
Corvus corone	65.5	0.0053	0.347	0.0151	23
Asio otus	44.9	0.0107	0.480	0.0120	40
Strix aluco	66.4	0.0089	0.593	0.0198	30
Columba livia	47.8	0.0043	0.204	0.0116	14
Gallinula chloropus	41.7	0.0032	0.132	0.0078	16
Fulica atra	84.0	0.0025	0.209	0.0106	19
Anas platyrhynchos	82.5	0.0034	0.285	0.0109	26
juv. 10d	15.2	0.0054	0.082	0.0055	15
Buteo buteo	86.1	0.0039	0.330	0.0180	18
Podiceps cristatus	86.0	0.0016	0.140	0.0095	16
Phasianus colchicus	113.0	0.0033	0.368	0.0133	28
Gallus domesticus	153.0	0.0019	0.291	0.0133	22
juv. 40d	27.6	0.0052	0.144	0.0083	17
juv. 1d	10.5	0.0066	0.069	0.0060	11
Grus grus	245.0	0.0017	0.418	0.0169	25

satisfactory qualitative indication of the variation of the middle-ear transformation ratio in birds, though, owing to differences in the incidence of the columella on the eardrum, the actual range is probably much greater than the table suggests.

The relative immunity of birds to either physical or psychological trauma consequent on exposure to loud noises is noteworthy. It seems likely that the oblique insertion of the columella and the ability of the cartilaginous extrastapes to yield by flexure to excessive pressure on the eardrum before the annular ligament is overstrained is an important element in this immunity.

C. THE OUTER EAR

The external auditory meatus of the mammal is characteristically extended by the *pinna*, a fleshy "horn" often of complex shape and substantial size, and usually supplied with an extrinsic musculature such that the left and right pinnae are capable of a considerable range of movement both conjugately and independently. The mammalian pinna has at least three distinct functions: (1) It increases the area over which acoustic energy is abstracted and so improves sensitivity. (2) It gives the ear directional properties which may be very sharp for a particular band of frequencies. (3) It prevents masking of wanted signals by wind-excited noise in the external auditory meatus. The importance of the first two functions is obvious, but that of the third is not always appreciated. Yet if a human subject, with reduced and immobile pinnae, stands facing directly into a strong breeze the wind-excited noise is often enough to make a companion's speech unintelligible. Intelligibility is easily restored by turning the head enough to shield one ear from the wind or, with a slight loss in sensitivity, by wearing a woolly cap over both ears, which makes the turbulence in the ears negligible at ordinary wind speeds.

Since birds have no pinnae and commonly fly at a speed equivalent to a strong breeze, the importance of the almost universal covering of feathers over the meatus for reducing both the drag due to turbulence and the auditory masking is clear enough, though it is equally clear that these advantages must be obtained at some sacrifice of absolute and of directional sensitivity, compared with a typical mammal. It is worth noting that in the bats, an ancient group of mammals which have been strong fliers since the Eocene, the pinnae have been retained and have probably increased in size in spite of their aerodynamic disadvantages.

There are exceptions to the rule that the external auditory meatus in birds is a simple, short, feather-covered tube. No general examination of the ears of the Strigiformes has been made, but Pycraft pointed out in 1898 that in some owls not only is the outer ear an extensive cavity spreading over almost the whole side of the head, but also the form of the cavity is different on the right and left sides. A possible functional explanation of this asymmetry has been suggested (Pumphrey, 1948), but it remains without experimental verification.

III. The Performance of the Bird's Ear

One long-standing mystery has recently been dispelled by Schwartz-kopf (1949). The remarkable and well-authenticated sensitivity of birds to distant explosions is in all probability due not to the ears at all but to the excitation of groups of sensory end organs (corpuscles of Herbst) in the legs by sound transmitted through the ground.

Determination of the true auditory threshold is a matter of considerable technical difficulty even in man. Measurements by indirect methods in other animals cannot yet be considered reliable even when there is a very fair agreement between estimates based on training and on direct measurement of the cochlear potential. But, though determinations both of the absolute sensitivity in the middle of the auditory band and of the upper and lower frequency limits of the response to sound cannot yet be regarded as more than guesses, there is no reason to doubt that measurements such as those of Schwartzkopf of the cochlear potential in the bullfinch (*Pyrrhula pyrrhula minor*) give a qualitatively satisfactory picture (Fig. 6), and these show that the band of maximum

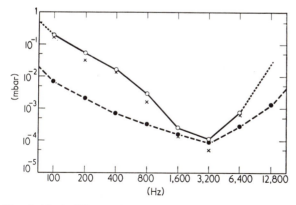

Fig. 6. Threshold at different frequencies of *Pyrrhula* (bullfinch) computed from measurement of the cochlear potential, 0—0; human threshold for comparison, ● – – – ●. x Represents the estimated threshold of an exceptionally sensitive bullfinch. From Schwartzkopf (1955).

sensitivity lies (as in man) between 2000 and 4000 cycles per second and that sensitivity decreases toward extreme frequencies in the same sort of way as in man, but more steeply. Many of the assessments of the upper limit of frequency response are suspect because they have been made with a Galton whistle, which generates a broad spectrum of noise superimposed on its computed frequency. It is legitimate to doubt whether there is any useful sensitivity above 10 kilocycles per second in birds other than owls and perhaps parrots.

A. Frequency Discrimination

Knecht (1940), by a training method, has demonstrated for *Loxia* and *Melopsittacus* an ability to discriminate frequencies differing by as little as 0.3–0.7%, *"ebenso fein oder besser als der Mensch."* Actually a very good human ear has distinguished frequencies differing by as little as 0.1%, but even so the performance of these birds is very remarkable and of quite a different order from the elementary frequency discrimination of about a 10% interval attributed to fish. It must be regarded as strong evidence of the existence of a peripheral analyzer of high quality, for no mechanism has ever been suggested by which so fine a discrimination could take place in the central nervous system.

B. Directional Sensitivity

The directionality of the ear of the bullfinch has been measured by Schwartzkopf (1955) (Fig. 7). The ability of birds to detect the direction of a sound does not, however, depend only on such directional properties

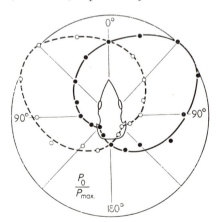

Fig. 7. Polar diagram showing the change in sensitivity of the bullfinch's ear with the direction of incidence of the sound (3.2 kilocycles); ●—●, right ear, 0 – – – 0, left ear; based on measurements of the cochlear potential.

which ensure that a source not in the sagittal plane produces a different intensity at each ear. It is also dependent (as in man) on the ability to recognize the later time of arrival of sounds at the more distant ear. This is doubtless the reason for the discrepancy between the results of Granit (1941), who used a source of pure tones as a stimulus, and the older observations of Englemann (1928), who used a natural source (the chirping of chicks). The latter found a discrimination of direction about ten times better than the former. Man, too, is very much better at estimating the direction of a source when the sound is full of transients (a rattle or, better still, human speech) than when it is a pure tone, but he appears to be no better than a bird, though the separation of the ears and consequently the time interval to be discriminated is less for the latter.

Marler (1955) has recently pointed out the significant difference between the songs of passerines, which are full of transients and accurately locatable both by man and other birds, and the interspecific hawk alarm call, which to man (and presumably to birds also) is almost uncannily lacking in any directional attributes. Analysis has shown that this call is in fact almost a pure tone with a gradual beginning and ending so that there is no element in it on which a true time comparison can be based.

C.   Time Discrimination

In addition to the evidence from directional sensitivity, there are two other valid reasons for inferring that the avian ear is capable of a more rapid response than the human. Griffin (1953) has shown that the oilbird (*Steatornis*), which roosts in dark caves, finds its way through them safely by a form of echo location resembling that which, as is now well known, is used by bats. When flying in the dark it utters continually a stream of short pulses of sound and from the delay in the echo locates, and so avoids, the walls of the cave. The significant difference from the bats is that the central frequency of the pulses is about 7 kilocycles, whereas in bats it is about 70 kilocycles. The pulse repetition rate is high in *Steatornis*, so that the silent interval between pulses is only 2–3 milliseconds: in order to obtain a comparable discrimination of the delay of an echo, the receptive elements in the oilbird's ear would need to be about ten times as highly damped as in the bat's ear, and evidently the speed of response must be very much higher than that of which the human ear is capable.

The second reason arises from the analysis of bird song. It is only recently that the development of recording frequency-analyzers of short time-constant has given any useful insight into the structure of the song and has incidentally demonstrated how inappropriate an instrument the human ear is for the purpose. The first published records (Potter *et al.*, 1947) showed a variation of frequency and intensity in bird song at a rate much faster than could be appreciated by the human ear. Their book is principally concerned with the analysis of

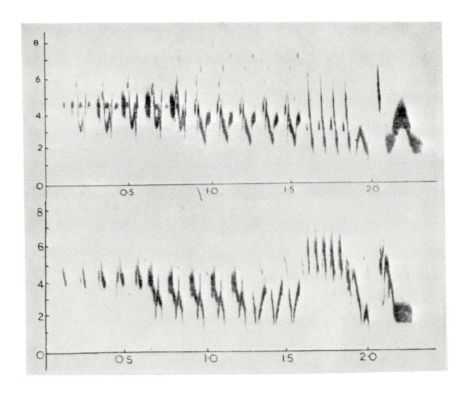

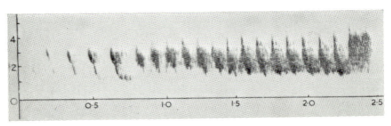

FIG. 8. Sonograms of chaffinch song. Upper records, normal song. Bottom record, song of bird deprived of opportunity to learn. (From Thorpe, 1956.)

human speech, in which frequency and intensity vary about as fast as the human ear can adequately appreciate them; the contrast between their records of speech and of bird song is very striking. It remained, however, a possibility that the rapid fluctuations of bird song were a consequence and, as it were, an accidental by-product of the structure of the syrinx and that the birds themselves did not appreciate them either. This possibility was finally dispelled by Thorpe (1954), who showed that in the chaffinch the fine structure was learned at a very early age and did not appear in the song of untaught birds (Fig. 4). This fine structure is quite unnoticed by a human auditor in normal circumstances, and it is certainly not fully resolved by him when the song is recorded and played back at quarter speed. Still lower playback speeds are not helpful because of the accompanying fall in pitch, but a comparison with the rate of variation of frequency in human speech (e.g. in diphthongs) suggests that the chaffinch song would need to be slowed up at least ten times before the human ear could fully resolve the detail which the young chaffinch hears and remembers well enough to reproduce it.

IV. Conclusion

Physiological and behavioral studies confirm the belief based on anatomical considerations that the cochlea of a bird is designed to have a speed of response about ten times as high as that of the human ear. The band of frequencies to which it is sensitive is more restricted than in mammals. It probably lies within the limits of 200 cycles and 10 kilocycles except in owls and parrots, where it may well extend an octave or two higher. [In these birds the cochlea is substantially longer than average (Retzius, 1884; Gray, 1907).] Pitch discrimination at least in passerines and parrots is extremely good, approaching the human capacity in the middle of the auditory band; and the ability of birds to determine the direction of a sound is comparable with man's and appears to be determined and limited by the physical nature of the sound in the same sort of way.

References

Dadson, R. S., and King, J. H. (1952). A determination of the normal threshold of hearing and its relation to the standardization of audiometers. *J. Laryngol. and Otol.* **66** (8): 366–377.

Englemann, W. (1928). Untersuchungen über die Schalllokalisation bei Tieren. *Z. Psychol. Physiol. Sinnesorg.* **105**: 317–370.

Gold, T. (1948). Hearing. II. The physical basis of the action of the cochlea. *Proc. Roy. Soc.* **B135**: 492–498.

G*

Gold, T. and Pumphrey, R. J. (1948). Hearing. I. The cochlea as a frequency analyser. *Proc. Roy. Soc.* **B135**: 462–491.

Granit, O. (1941). Beiträge zur Kenntniss des Gehörsinnes der Vögel. *Ornis. Fennica* **18**: 49–71.

Gray, A. A. (1907). "The Labyrinth of Animals." J. and A. Churchill, London.

Griffin, D. R. (1953). Acoustic orientation in the oil bird, *Steatornis. Proc. Nat. Acad. Sci. U.S.* **39**: 884–893.

Hasse, C. (1867). Die Schnecke der Vögel. *Z. wiss. Zoöl.* **17**: 56–104.

Helmholtz, H. L. F. (1877). "Tonempfindung," 4th ed. Vieweg, Brunschweig.

Kappers, C. U. A., Crosby, E. C., and Huber, G. C. (1936). Comparative anatomy of the nervous system of vertebrates, Macmillan, N.Y.

Knecht, S. (1940). Über den Gehörsinn und die Musikalität der Vögel. *Z. vergleich. Physiol.* **27**: 169–232.

Marler, P. (1955). Characteristics of some animal calls. *Nature* **176**: 6–8.

Portmann, A. (1950). Les organes des sens. *In* "Traité de zoologie" (P. P. Grassé, ed.), Vol. 15. Masson, Paris.

Potter, R. K., Kopp, G. A., and Green, H. C. (1947). "Visible Speech." *Van Nostrand,* New York.

Pumphrey, R. J. (1948). The sense organs of birds. *Ibis* **90**: 171–199: reprinted with some additions (1948). Annual Report Smithsonian Inst.: 305–330.

Pycraft, W. P. (1898). A contribution towards our knowledge of the morphology of owls. *Trans. Linnean Soc.* **7**: 223–275.

Retzius, G. (1884). "Das Gehörorgan der Wirbelthiere." Stockholm.

Satoh, N. (1917). Der Histologie und Bau der Vogelschnecke und ihre Schädigung durch Akustische Reize und durch Detonation, Basel.

Schwartzkopf, J. (1949). Über den Sitz und Leistung von Gehör und Vibrationssinn bei Vögeln. *Z. vergleich. Physiol.* **31**: 529–608.

Schwartzkopf, J. (1955). Schallsinnesorgane, ihre Funktion und biologische Bedeutung bei Vögeln. *Acta 11th Congr. Intern. Ornithol.* 1954, pp. 189–208.

Stresemann, E. (1934). Aves. *In* "Kükenthal's Handbuch der Zoologie," Vol. 7(2). De Gruyter, Berlin and Leipzig.

Thorpe, W. H. (1954). The process of song-learning in the Chaffinch as studied by means of the sound-spectrograph. *Nature* **173**: 465.

Thorpe, W. H. (1956). "Learning and Instinct in Animals." Methuen, London.

CHAPTER XVI

Endocrine Glands, Thymus and Pineal Body

E. OTTO HÖHN

I. Introduction

The endocrine glands, or glands of internal secretion, are collections of epithelial cells richly supplied with blood vessels but lacking ducts to drain their secretions. Instead, the secretion enters the blood stream to be carried all over the body, exerting effects, however, only on particular tissues. The active agents thus secreted are termed "hormones," and the tissues on which they act are their "target organs." In general, hormones can cause rapid growth of particular tissues or they can stimulate or inhibit chemical processes in various parts of the body. Precisely how hormones bring about their effects is still obscure, but in the case of the thyroid hormone, at least, there is evidence that it increases the concentration of certain intracellular enzymes, themselves the catalysts of particular chemical reactions.

Hormone action is often complicated when the target organ of a hormone itself is an endocrine gland. This "secondary" gland may be influenced to increase or decrease secretion of its own hormone with consequent effects on the target organs of the "secondary" hormone. Often there is a "negative feedback" type of inhibition of secretion of the first hormone. Such a relationship between the thyroid-stimulating

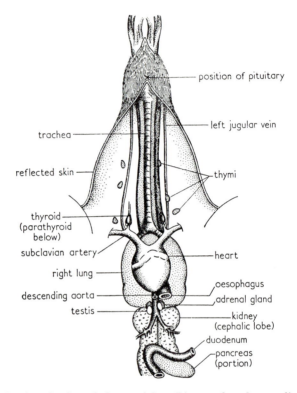

FIG. 1. Endocrine glands and thymus lobes. Diagram based on a dissection of an adult male white-winged (velvet) scoter (*Melanitta deglandi*). Ventral view, with most of alimentary tract removed. The bird was shot in October (autumn). The testes are small.

hormone of the pituitary and the thyroid hormone is briefly discussed in Section III.

The hormone-producing glands are essentially similar in all vertebrates and they secrete chemically identical, or at least very closely related, hormones in representatives of different classes. Moreover, hormones have, in the main, identical actions in widely different animals. Hormones are also produced in invertebrates, but these do not correspond in general to the vertebrate hormones. Chemically the thyroid and adrenal medullary hormones are relatively simple derivatives of the amino acid, tyrosine. The interrenal tissue of the adrenal and the gonads produce steroid hormones, while the pituitary, parathyroid, and pancreatic hormones are proteins. These last, being chemically complex, are most likely to show some structural differences in different vertebrate groups.

The endocrine glands of birds (cf. Fig. 1) are the pituitary, thyroids, parathyroids, adrenals, pancreas (in part), and the gonads (Chapter V). In addition to hormone-producing cells, the latter have elements which give rise to the reproductive cells or gametes. The pancreas is a gland of external secretion, producing a digestive juice, in which are embedded hormone-secreting islets. Gonads and pancreas are dealt with in other chapters. It has been suggested that the thymus and pineal produce hormones, but this is not yet established. In mammals at least, certain hormones which regulate digestive secretions and intestinal movements are also secreted into the blood by various portions of the digestive tract. These will probably also be found in birds. With the exception of the thyroid hormone the natural hormones are ineffective when given by mouth or beak, being destroyed by digestive enzymes; to produce experimental results they must therefore either be injected or implanted into the tissues, thence to be absorbed. Some hormones are as potent as any drugs known and can produce measurable effects in doses of a few millionths of a gram (micrograms).

Regulatory functions of specific chemical processes in the body, essential to life, are performed by the pancreatic hormone, one of the adrenal cortical hormones, and the parathyroid hormone. In birds the pituitary is virtually essential for survival, probably not because of the role of any one of its hormones but because of the total functions performed by several of them.

Hormones are involved in body growth, feather growth, and molting and in many cases in feather pigmentation. In sexually dimorphic species, the female plumage in some groups (domestic ducks, fowls, and pheasants) is dependent on the female sex hormone, the male plumage being genetically determined. In certain African weaver finches the male breeding plumage is induced by a pituitary hormone. Again certain adult plumages which show no sexual differentiation—as that of the herring gull (*Larus argentatus*), breeding plumage of black-headed gull (*Larus ridibundus*) and black-crowned night heron (*Nicticorax nicticorax*)— are dependent on the male sex hormone or androgen. Beaks which undergo a color change in the breeding season are also influenced by androgens in certain species.

Hormones exert a profound effect on behavior. They do not in general release specific individual responses, but rather by their action on the central nervous system make a whole range of responses possible and even facilitate them. Thus androgens are responsible in this sense for sexual behavior in male birds. This includes not merely courtship and copulatory behavior but also aggressive behavior including territorialism and song. Female sex behavior is more difficult to elicit with female sex hormones. It is indeed possible that female sex behavior, with the possible exception of the act of inviting copulation, is dependent on male sex hormones which are definitely produced in the female gonad in addition to the female sex hormone (Collias, 1950; Bullough, 1945).

Prolactin is responsible for broodiness, possibly also for nest building, and at least partially for maternal behavior. There is little doubt that the predisposition to migration is a hormone-induced state involving probably a complex of several hormones.

II. The Pituitary or Hypophysis

A. Position, Structure, and Development

The pituitary is situated in a rounded depression (sella turcica) of the sphenoid bone in the floor of the skull and connected to the midbrain just behind the optic chiasma (cf. Fig. 2). The gland consists of two portions which develop independently: the large anterior lobe and the pass tuberalis develop from the pharyngeal ectoderm and ultimately lose connection with the latter; the smaller neural or posterior lobe develops as a downgrowth from the midbrain. The two portions remain separated by a connective tissue barrier. A pars intermedia, also of pharyngeal origin, such as is seen in mammals, is absent in birds. In the anterior lobe, epithelial cells are arranged in cords separated by blood sinuses and these cords consist of chromophobe cells (which may be resting chromophiles) and granular chromophile cells of basophile or acidophile type. In twenty species of birds studied by Rahn and Painter (1941) and in representatives of about fifty genera examined by Wingstrand (1951) a caudal and a cephalic region are apparent in the anterior lobe (cf. Fig. 2). The caudal region has "A1" acidophiles resembling those of the mammalian pituitary, which stain red or orange-red with acid fuchsin; the "A2" acidophils of the cephalic region are smaller and less granular and stain scarlet with acid fuchsin; the basophiles in the cephalic region are smaller and more numerous than in the posterior or caudal region.

During broodiness in chickens, basophiles almost disappear and are replaced by small acidophiles. Castration increases the number of basophiles but does not in birds produce the peculiar basophiles— castration cells—seen in mammals. It is believed that the basophiles secrete the gonadotropic hormones. Degranulation of basophiles suggesting hormone discharge can be induced by exposure to light. An apparent decrease in basophile number probably due to degranulation is seen at the height of gonadal development in the mallard (Höhn, unpublished observation).

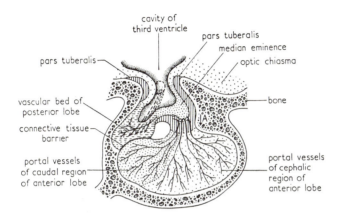

FIG. 2. Pituitary gland. A diagrammatic mid-line longitudinal section through the gland in a duck to show the component parts and their connections with the mid-brain, the principal nerve tract linking the hypothalamus to posterior lobe, and the hypophysial portal vessels running from the median eminence into the anterior lobe. The arrow ("A") indicates the direction of blood flow. (After various authors.)

The acidophiles secrete prolactin (Yasuda, 1953) and perhaps a growth hormone and probably also the thyroid-stimulating hormone and the adrenocorticotropic hormone.

The pars tuberalis contains mainly chromophobes but may in some species contain chromophilic cells.

An important nerve tract passes from the hypothalamus to the posterior lobe (cf. Fig. 2). An equally important system of "portal" blood vessels connects the median eminence via the tuberalis to the anterior lobe (Benoit and Assenmacher, 1951, 1952). In mammals these vessels run instead along the stalk of the posterior lobe. There is evidence that liberation of some chemical substance into these vessels, in the hypothalamic region, which is then transported by them, stimulates gonadotropic secretions from the anterior lobe and that the gonad-stimulating effect of light or of psychic factors like the mere sight of a conspecific bird, as in the domestic pigeon, is mediated by this pathway.

Recently "secretomotor" nerve endings supplying the gland cells of the anterior lobe have been described in domestic ducks and geese (Metzusals, 1956).

B. The Anterior Lobe

1. *Functions; and Effects of Removal*

The following hormones have been isolated from avian pituitaries:

Gonadotropins: (a) *Follicle-stimulating hormone* (FSH) stimulates ovarian follicles and in the male stimulates spermatogenesis in the testicular tubules. (b) *Luteinizing hormone* (LH), so named because in mammals it converts ovarian follicles into corpora lutea, which probably stimulates the interstitial cells of the testes, though some stipulate a separate *interstitial cell-stimulating hormone* (ICSH. It has been isolated in chickens and demonstrated in the pheasant pituitary.

Adrenocorticotropic hormone (ACTH) stimulates the adrenal inter-renal tissue, corresponding to the adrenal cortex of mammals; it has been extracted in the domestic fowl.

Thyroid-stimulating hormone (TSH) isolated from chicken pituitaries.

Prolactin or *Luteotropic hormone,* isolated in the domestic fowl.

The existence in birds of a pituitary hormone stimulating pancreatic islet cells is uncertain, as is that of a parathyroid-stimulating hormone.

A separate growth hormone has not been proved to exist in birds. Growth is deficient in hypophysectomized birds, but it can be restored by prolactin. Mammalian growth hormone has little growth effect on young domestic fowl although it depresses egg laying and induces a molt in older birds (Carter *et al.*, 1955).

A number of metabolic effects can be produced by anterior pituitary extracts, but these do not appear to be due to the existence of additional hormones but rather to be associated with one or other of the hormones listed above. In particular, the association of an insulin-antagonizing or diabetogenic effect with prolactin is well established in the pigeon. Although a pars intermedia is absent in birds, intermedin, the hormone secreted by this portion of the gland in other vertebrates, has been extracted from the anterior lobe of the pituitary of fowl. Though it is effective in causing expansion of pigment-carrying melanophores in amphibia and reptiles, it does not affect avian chromatophores. These are instead influenced by the thyroid hormone and in some cases by female sex hormones or the pituitary luteinizing hormone.

The existence of hormones which stimulate the secretions of several other endocrine glands confers on the pituitary the role of a master gland among the endocrines. However, with the possible exception of the gonads the glands acted upon are not entirely dependent on the appropriate pituitary "tropic" hormone. Thyroid and adrenocortical function continue, though at a reduced level, after hypophysectomy. Furthermore, in every case the secretion of the responding gland (target organ of the pituitary hormone) seems to inhibit further secretion of the pituitary tropic hormone. This relationship can be illustrated in the case of the pituitary and thyroid as follows:

Secretion of TSH ———→ stimulates thyroid
                               ↓
inhibits ←————————— thyroid hormone
TSH secretion

Hypophysectomy has been performed in chickens, ducks, and pigeons with the following effects: reduction of growth and resting metabolic rate; atrophy of thyroid, adrenals, and gonads; weight reduction of small intestine, liver, pancreas, and crop sac in pigeons; fall of body temperature; reduced general activity and food and water consumption; precipitation of a molt. The effects are almost without exception explicable on the basis of lack of the pituitary hormones listed above. In general, where it is not definitely fatal, the effects of pituitary removal are more serious than in mammals. (See also Chapter XVIII.)

The effects of light in increasing pituitary gonadotropin production and the actions of gonadotropic hormones are discussed in Chapters XVIII and XXI.

The actions of the thyrotropic or thyroid-stimulating hormone and the adrenocorticotropic hormone are described below in the section dealing with the glands on which they exert their principal action. It may be mentioned here that TSH, which is responsible for pathological eyeball protrusion (exophthalmos) in mammals as a direct (not thyroid-mediated) effect has also been shown to produce exophthalmos in ducklings. ACTH, which in mammals reduces the adrenocortical ascorbic acid (vitamin C) content while causing adrenocortical secretion does not in birds (domestic fowl, bob-white quail (*Collinus virginianus*), domestic ducks) decrease adrenal ascorbic acid (Zarrow and Zarrow, 1950).

2. *Prolactin*

This hormone has been isolated from hen pituitaries. In mammals it stimulates milk secretion from mammary glands previously developed by the action of sex hormones. In pigeons it stimulates growth and secretion of an organ of analogous function, the crop sac, which, largely by desquamation of degenerating cells, produces the pigeon's milk. The crop sac of pigeons of both sexes provides in fact a highly sensitive method of measurement (bioassay) of locally applied prolactin. Prolactin has an antigonadal effect in fowl and pigeons of both sexes which is due to suppression of gonadotropin secretion. An antigonadal effect has also been shown in house sparrows (*Passer domesticus*) and certain finches. Prolactin may well be involved in the normal postbreeding gonadal regression. It causes broodiness not only in pigeons but also in hens. The abrupt loss of interest in sexual matters often shown by birds once incubation has begun may be attributed to this antigonadal action of prolactin. The prolactin content of hen pituitaries rises just as incubation begins, and the raised level is maintained until hatching (Saeki *et al.*, 1956). While prolactin is required for broodiness, maternal behavior toward the young apparently does not require prolactin (Yamashima, 1952). In pigeons prolactin prevents the molt and raises the blood sugar (Kobayashi, 1953). It can also increase the weight of liver, pancreas, and intestine and raise the metabolic rate even after thyroidectomy. Some would attribute some of these effects to a separate growth hormone, always closely associated with prolactin in mammals. Pituitary prolactin secretion is apparently inhibited by estrogens while testosterone, progesterone, and deoxycorticosterone acetate induce prolactin release and can thus bring on broodiness in domestic hens and doves.

An important study by Bailey (1952) has shown that development of the incubation patch in passerine birds requires prolactin plus estrogen action. In normal females estrogens cause formation of an incubation patch in the nonbreeding season, but the hypophysectomized bird requires in addition prolactin. Formation of the incubation patch entails three phases of development: defeathering due to a local molt, increased local blood supply, and finally skin swelling due to hyperemia and edema. Bailey also showed that the pituitary prolactin content of breeding California gulls (*Larus californicus*) of both sexes (both sexes incubate) was higher than that of birds collected before or after incubation. Endocrine requirements for development of the avian incubation patch are strikingly similar to those of the mammary gland in mammals which, however, also requires progesterone.

It may be speculated that female redhead ducks (*Aythya americana*) which lay in the nests of other ducks (often of other species) and which develop no incubation patches (unpublished information from the Delta Waterfowl Research Station, Manitoba, Canada) lack prolactin, since they clearly do not lack estrogens. The parasitic habits of cuckoos and the North American cowbird (*Molothrus ater*) may quite possibly be explicable as a hereditary failure of prolactin secretion. Finally, the explanation of species differences in the part played by the two sexes (including the unusual case of the phalaropes) in incubation will probably also be shown to be due to differences in prolactin production.

C. The Posterior Lobe

This appears to produce the same hormones in birds as in other vertebrates: vasopressin, oxytocin, and an antidiuretic substance have been extracted from hen pituitary posterior lobes. It is generally stated that posterior lobe extracts depress the blood pressure in fowl (while they raise it in mammals). A recent study, however, shows that while oxytocin is always depressor, causing vasodilatation, vasopressin lowers the blood pressure if it is high initially but raises it, if it is initially low. It is always pressor if the bird shows no vascular response to oxytocin (Strahan and Waring, 1954). Oxytocin is also depressor in ducks. Neither hormone is believed to play a role in normal blood pressure regulation. Oxytocin which induces uterine contraction in mammals causes contraction of the analogous part of the avian oviduct in hens and pigeons leading to premature expulsion of eggs, even of soft-shelled eggs, if given before shell formation is completed.

The antidiuretic hormone reduces the urine volume so as to conserve body water in time of need, probably by increasing the resorption of water from pre-urine into the blood stream in the kidney tubules and by reducing blood filtration at the kidney glomeruli. In agreement with this, selective posterior lobe destruction in hens leads to excessive urine secretion with excessive thirst, a condition which could be relieved with posterior pituitary extract (Shirley and Nalbandov, 1956). Varying antidiuretic hormone production can thus regulate the amount of water lost in the urine according to varying body needs as in mammals (cf. Heller, 1950).

III. The Thyroid

A. Position, Structure, and Development

The avian thyroid develops as a mid-line outgrowth from the ventral pharyngeal wall at the level of the first and second branchial pouches of the embryo. Its connection with the pharynx is soon lost and it becomes separated into two lobes. The small, glistening, dark-red ovoid bodies are generally easily recognized and are situated low in the neck, each close to the angle formed by the union of the subclavian and the common carotid arteries (see Fig. 1). Thyroid weight relative to body weight shows marked species differences. Some examples of thyroid weight as percentages of body weight are: domestic fowl, 0.006%;

domestic pigeon, 0.01–0.025%; mallard, 0.01%; house sparrow, 0.033%.

Structurally the avian thyroid resembles that of other vertebrates (see Fig. 3). A connective tissue capsule encloses a mass of roughly spherical bladders or vesicles, each lined by a single layer of epithelial cells and containing a more or less homogenous fluid, the thyroid colloid. Walls of adjacent follicles are separated by connective tissue, richly permeated with blood vessels. The epithelial cells take up iodine from the blood stream far more actively than do other tissues and combine it as in mammals with the amino acid tyrosine, leading to the

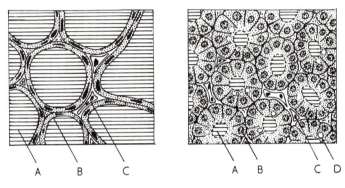

Fig. 3. Thyroid gland. Microscopic structures (× 500). *Left* resting; *Right* active. A = colloid within vesicle; B = epithelial lining of vesicle; C = inter-vesicular capillary and contained (nucleated) red cell; D = intra-cellular prosecretion droplets and vacuoles. The changes in the thyroid from the condition shown on the left to that shown on the right can occur in the same bird firstly, as part of a spontaneous seasonal cycle, related to climate or the molt; and secondly, experimentally as a result of (a) TSH administration, (b) exposure to cold, (c) following administration of thiourea anti-thyroid preparations which reduce formation of thyroid hormone by the gland but do not prevent a cellular response to the bird's own TSH.

formation of iodine tyrosine compounds, two molecules of which are eventually condensed to form one molecule of the hormone, thyroxine. The recently discovered highly active hormone, triiodothyronine, found in mammals in much smaller quantities than thyroxine, has not yet been isolated in birds. Thyroxine is finally combined with a protein to form thyroglobulin, in which form it is stored in the colloid. Thyroxine release depends on enzymatic decomposition of thyroglobulin, setting free thyroxine which is then passed through the ephithelial cells which originally formed it into the blood. In highly active thyroid glands (Fig. 3A), vesicles are small as the colloid is constantly being used up.

Epithelial cells are high and have pale, rounded nuclei. In inactive glands, vesicles are large and the epithelial cells are flattened, with dense flattened nuclei (Fig. 3B). Gland weight is not a reliable indication of activity for, though it tends to be raised by increased activity, it may rise even more in a resting gland owing to colloid accumulation. As in other animals, dietary iodine lack leads to a compensatory thyroid enlargement—goiter—at least in fowl. Thiouracil and related compounds do not reduce the iodine uptake of the gland but prevent incorporation of iodine into the hormone precursor. They cause a powerful inhibition of thyroid hormone production accompanied by a hyperplasia of the gland with the histological picture normally associated with increased activity. Thyroid function is normally controlled by the thyrotropic hormone (TSH) of the anterior lobe of the pituitary. This explains thyroid atrophy following hypophysectomy and thyroid hypertrophy following pituitary injections, in ducks and fowl. Thyroid stimulation following administration of pituitary preparations has also been obtained in the house sparrow (*Passer domesticus*), greenfinch (*Chloris chloris*), pigeon, and quail. Apparently, as in mammals, the response of the thyroid, a raised blood thyroxine level, in turn depresses production of pituitary TSH. The hyperplasia following thiouracil is thus explained as due to excessive TSH production.

B. Seasonal Changes

In temperate and cold climates thyroid activity is increased during the cooler periods of the year when an increase of metabolism (brought about by thyroid hormone) is desirable in view of increased temperature loss to the environment. Marked seasonal changes, shown mainly by the histological pattern of activity noted above, in autumn and winter as compared to a general picture of thyroid inactivity in spring and summer, have been observed in house sparrows [several observers, particularly Davis and Davis (1954)], crows (*Corvus* spp.), pigeons, domestic fowl, and mallards (*Anas platyrhynchos*). Moreover, experimental exposure of house sparrows to low temperatures can cause thyroid stimulation and a raised metabolic rate. This effect is almost certainly mediated by changes in pituitary TSH secretion. In fact, TSH content of hen pituitaries is higher in winter than in summer. Another period of increased thyroid activity occurs during warmer weather in association with, but preceding, the annual molt. This has been observed in the house sparrow (several observers), tree sparrow (*Passer montanus*), robin (*Erithacus rubecula*), and yellowhammer (*Emberiza citrinella*) and is indicated by raised metabolism before the molt in chickens. The association is particularly convincing in the mallard, where increased

H

thyroid activity occurs about one month earlier in males than in females [which have their main molt about a month later than the males (Höhn, 1949)].

C. General Effects of Thyroid Hormone

As in other vertebrates, the thyroid hormone produces a general stimulation of metabolism (over-all chemical activity) and, probably associated with this, it is required for normal growth and development, particularly sexual development. Thus, thyroidectomized hens and mallards show reduced growth and are generally somewhat obese. In hens, the reproductive system remains juvenile and comb growth is reduced. Metabolism is reduced by thyroidectomy, and the liver in ducks at least is markedly enlarged. Thyroidectomy also raises the cholesterol, fatty acid, and phospholipid content of the blood in ducks, due no doubt to decreased metabolic consumption of these substances. Thyroid hormone raises the blood sugar and red cell number and accelerates the heart in domestic fowls.

D. The Thyroid and Migration

A possible connection between increased thyroid activity and migration is suggested by the obvious need for raised metabolism during the exertion of migration and the restlessness of migrants, which recalls the nervousness associated with hyperthyroid states in man. It may be noted that the well-known increased deposition of body fat *before* migration of certain species speaks against increased thyroid activity at this period. The obvious experiment, effect of thyroidectomy on migration, is unlikely to be helpful in deciding the question, since thyroidectomized birds are so apathetic that suppression of migration could be due to general depression rather than to the absence of a specific role normally played by the thyroid gland. Nevertheless, the effect of moderate hypothyroidism (induced by thiouracil) on migration would be worth investigating. The information now available relating thyroid activity to migration is merely strongly suggestive. It has recently been reviewed by Farner (1955). Küchler (1935) reported a period of increased thyroid activity during the spring and autumn migratory periods in the robin, yellowhammer, and tree sparrow, though the resident house sparrow, according to him, also shows raised thyroid activity at these seasons. Others have reported some correlation between migration and thyroid activity in certain limicoline birds.

The restlessness, particularly nocturnal, of caged birds during the normal migratory periods, *"Zugunruhe,"* has been produced artificially by thyroxine injections in certain thrushes, the robin, and the white-throat (*Sylvia communis*). It seems that small doses produce this effect, whereas larger doses, such as might cause a molt, suppress "*Zugunruhe.*"

The thyroid of the migratory mourning dove (*Zenaidura macroura*) fails to respond to cold weather, whereas that of a resident species of pigeon does; this may be associated with the necessity to migrate to a milder wintering area in the first species.

E. The Thyroid-Gonad Relationship

The fact that the normal sexual development associated with matura-tion does not occur after thyroidectomy has already been mentioned, but even in mature birds, gonadal function is dependent on normal thyroid activity. Sexually mature young domestic fowls show gonadal atrophy after thyroidectomy and a reduction in comb and wattle size. Thyroid hormone stimulates testicular development in male ducks, domestic fowl, and the mallard. The mechanism of this effect has been shown, at least in the domestic duck, to be due to stimulation of release of pituitary gonadotropin.

There is also some evidence that thyroid hormone can increase egg production in hens and that thyroidectomy decreases it and causes the formation of calcium-deficient egg shells (Maqsood, 1952). In both cockerels and ducks, increased testicular activity suppresses the thyro-tropic activity of the pituitary. The estrogen-induced rise of plasma lipids, calcium, and plasma proteins can be prevented both by thyroxine and by thiouracil in hens. In pigeons, on the other hand, thyroidectomy does not suppress this estrogen effect, whereas in ducks it does reduce the blood calcium response to estrogen, which can then be restored if thyroxine is given. Moreover, as noted below (Section F.) excessive thyroid hormone has a gonad-depressing effect, particularly in chickens.

Finally, while in domestic fowl thyroidectomy leads to gonadal dysfunction, even in mature birds, Woitkewitsch (1940) found that in thyroidectomized starlings, the gonads of both sexes remained perma-nently in almost the breeding condition and that the bills retained their (androgen-induced) yellow color after the breeding season. This phenomenon should be confirmed in this or other species. It is quite possible that species with periodic gonadal activity respond in different manner in this respect than birds, like domestic fowl, which have lost a cyclical pattern.

Thyroid activity may in fact be causally related to normal gonadal regression after the breeding season, since this regression occurs even when increases of daylight are artificially produced beyond the normal period.

F. The Thyroid in Relation to Feather Growth, Feather Pigmentation, and the Molt

There is general agreement that thyroidectomy reduces the growth rate of feathers and that new feathers which grow thereafter are abnormal in structure. Such feathers are abnormally elongated and narrowed and loose in texture owing to a suppression of barbule formation. This observation has been made in several breeds of domestic fowl, the domestic pigeon, the mallard, and the magpie (*Pica pica*). Thyroxine can reverse these effects and in normal birds can cause shorter, wider, more rounded and less fringed feathers. The effect of the thyroid hormone on feather pigmentation shows more species variation. In pigeons, thyroidectomy did not affect feather color. In domestic fowl there is a general replacement of black pigment (melanin) by a reddish-brown pigment, whereas thyroxine can cause darkening of feathers. Similar effects have been observed in the mallard. In domestic fowl, thyroidectomy or thiouracil also influence another epidermal structure, namely the spurs, which show some atrophy and looseness of attachment at the tarsometatarsal bone.

The physiological process of molting in some birds, e.g. the ptarmigan, is a complex series of events, but in the majority of Northern Hemisphere birds at least, there is a main annual postnuptial molt. This fact alone suggests that the control mechanism, itself undoubtedly complex, is in the main hormonal and related to cyclic fluctuations in gonadal hormone production. But the picture is complicated by the fact that thyroid administration in certain birds can bring about a striking unseasonal molt. The association of periods of increased thyroid activity with the molt has already been noted above (Section B.). Considerable experimental work has been done, particularly in the last few years, on the hormonal factors which can induce molting out of season in domestic fowl. The main facts relating to this species are as follows:

(1) *Thyroid* hormone injected, given in the feed in the form of thyroid gland powder, or following stimulation of the thyroid by administration of pituitary TSH produces a striking molt. This is generally accompanied by signs of gonadal depression such as reduced egg laying and atrophy of combs and wattles (see Sturkie, 1954).

(2) *Progesterone* injections precipitate a molt and simultaneously depress the gonads as shown by reduced egg production and absence of "squatting," the female posture which expresses readiness for copulation (Adams, 1956; Shaffner, 1955).

(3) The substance *Enheptin* (2-amino-*m*, 5-nitrothiazole) which inhibits the secretion of gonadotropins by the pituitary but does not

interfere with pituitary TSH secretion (Pino *et al.*, 1954); brings on a molt with gonadal regression.

(4) *Hypophysectomy* in fowls brings on an unseasonal molt (Hill *et al.*, 1934).

(5) Injections of *mammalian pituitary growth hormone* in hens causes a marked depression of egg laying with a molt in most birds [incidentally, very little growth stimulation was noted in either young or adults (Carter *et al.*, 1955)].

(6) Complete *thyroidectomy* abolishes subsequent molts in domestic fowl.

(7) *Castration* of brown Leghorns also followed by irregular shedding of feathers instead of the regular annual molt shown by normal males (Parkes and Emmens, 1944).

These facts suggest a common factor, namely, inhibition or reduction of pituitary gonadotropic hormone secretion. This can be brought about by thyroid hormone (in fairly high doses), Enheptin, growth hormone, and progesterone (though this agent may act by direct antagonism with gonadal hormones) and by prolactin which, at least in pigeons, postpones the molt while inhibiting the gonads. The same effect is brought about more drastically by hypophysectomy.

On this hypothesis the role of the thyroid would be twofold.

(a) At rather high levels it inhibits pituitary gonadotropic activity as above.

(b) It is required for the stimulation of growth of new feathers, an essential factor in the molting mechanism. For this, lower levels of the hormone are probably sufficient. As will be seen below, in species other than fowl and pigeons the first function is apparently not important. A priming of the organism by the previous action of sex hormones may also be an essential factor.

The above hypothesis is a tentative but permissible synthesis of the main facts. Some of the hormonal factors considered above as inhibiting pituitary gonadotropic secretion or action may be shown later to act in part (in some cases even principally) by antagonism with the gonadal hormones, as indicated above in connection with progesterone.

The hypothesis appears to account also for the main facts relating to experimentally induced molts in other species, but it must be remembered that a modified mechanism is probably involved in prenuptial molts such as occur in the ducks and in juvenile molts, etc. (see Collias, 1950). The principal experimental results for species other than the chicken may be summarized as follows:

(1) Thyroid or TSH administration precipitates a molt in the quail and greenfinch but not in the mallard or domestic duck, house sparrow, crow, and herring gull (*Larus argentatus*).

(2) Thyroidectomy can suppress subsequent molts in the canary, domestic pigeon (though only in some, not all, of a group of experimental birds), starling, magpie, and quail. In mallard ducklings one observer reported molt suppression, two others working with older mallards found no clear-cut evidence of molt repression (cf. Höhn, 1949).

(3) Pituitary gonadotropins induce a molt in the mallard, while castration has been reported to suppress subsequent molting (Chu, 1940).

(4) In the herring gull androgens can precipitate a premature molt from the juvenile into the adult plumage (Boss, 1943). Unpublished findings of Boss (personal communication) in the common tern (*Sterna hirundo*) are similar.

(5) Unseasonal molts can be brought about by exposure to increased or decreased daily periods of illumination (which indirectly cause gonadal stimulation or regression) in juncos (*Junco* spp.), white-crowned sparrow (*Zonotrichia leucophrys*) and white-throated sparrow (*Z. albicollis*), greenfinch, starling (*Sturnus vulgaris*), mallard, and willow ptarmigan (*Lagopus lagopus*) (Collias, 1950). At least in some species light may induce changes in thyroid function. Increased illumination has been shown to stimulate thyroid activity in hens, though in ducks Benoit and Assenmacher (1953) have shown that light increases secretion of gonadotropin by the pituitary but does not increase TSH or ACTH production.

If, as suggested above, a reduction of gonadal hormone secretion, generally brought about by pituitary inhibition, is involved in the main summer molt, its timing, until reproduction is completed, may be due to the molt suppressing effect of prolactin secreted during the period of brooding eggs or young.

IV. The Adrenal Glands

A. Position, Structure, and Development

The adrenals are a pair of oval bodies, generally of a bright yellow or orange color, which lie anterior to the cephalic lobe of the kidney, one on each side (Fig. 1). The gland consists of two distinct elements which, in mammals, are arranged as an outer layer, the cortex, and the medulla or core, consisting of chromaffin tissue. In birds the two elements are intermingled, the tissue corresponding to the mammalian cortex is best termed interrenal, it being homologous with the interrenal gland of fishes. That corresponding to the medulla may be referred to as chromaffin or "medullary" tissue. The term chromaffin denotes the marked affinity of the cells for chromic acid, due to the presence of adrenalin (epinephrine) or noradrenalin (norepinephrine)—though a few related substances also give a color with chromic acid. Smaller aggregations of chromaffin tissue are found also outside the adrenal, e.g. the ultimobranchial body. The interrenal tissue arises from the coelomic epithelium just anterior to the genital ridge in which the gonads develop. The medulla arises from an ectodermal mass which also gives rise to the sympathetic nerve trunks and which later invades the interrenal tissue. Chromaffin cells show no definite pattern of cell arrangement. The interrenal tissue in the vast majority of species is arranged as thin strands, appearing in sections as double rows of cells (Fig. 4). Hartman and Albertin (1951), who have examined the adrenals of over 400 species of wild birds, point out that these strands are actually solid cords of cells arranged radially with their inner portions, containing the nuclei, wedge-shaped. The amount and pattern of distribution of the chromaffin tissue shows great variation from species to species. Only in the brown pelican (*Pelecanus occidentalis*), which has a very high proportion of interrenal tissue (Knouff and Hartman, 1951), was interrenal tissue found in cell masses arranged in zones corresponding to those found in the mammalian adrenal cortex.

There is some evidence that the interrenal tissue undergoes seasonal changes related to the gonadal cycle. In the brown pelican, it was noted that the largest glands were taken from males in breeding condition and ovulating females and that the zona fasciculata was most pronounced in these birds. In the mallard, though there is no obvious seasonal trend in gland weights, the ratio of interrenal volume to total gland volume increased during the breeding season in females (Höhn, 1947a).

An unpublished study by J. C. Busheikin on the house sparrow showed that the percentage volume occupied by interrenal tissue changed from 75% in the nonbreeding season to 90% in the course of natural gonadal recrudescence and also in birds brought into breeding condition by artificial illumination. There were histological signs of increased activity, particularly an intensification of osmic acid staining, indicating increased intracellular lipids.

In female pigeons, an adrenal enlargement before and during ovulation, followed by a return to normal, has been observed, and large doses of estrogens can cause adrenal enlargement in domestic fowl.

B. The Interrenal Tissue

A number of steroids, not all having biological activity, have been isolated from the mammalian adrenal cortex. Some of these are, no doubt, intermediate products in the formation of the final hormones. The cortical hormones fall into three main groups:

(1) *Mineralocorticoids*, e.g. aldosterone. The main action is the promotion of resorption of sodium and decrease of resorption of potassium in the kidney from the glomerular filtrate which is about to be converted into urine. The synthetic substance, deoxycorticosterone, has this type of action and its acetate (Doca or DCA) has been used a great deal experimentally. Loss of the sodium-retaining power results in death in the adrenalectomized animal. Secretion of vital mineralocorticoids is also performed by the bird adrenal, and adrenalectomy is fatal in ducks, fowl, and pigeons. Moreover, the provision of extra sodium (as sodium chloride) can considerably prolong survival after adrenalectomy, as can adrenal cortical extracts or DCA.

(2) *Gonadoids*. Estrogens and androgens, apparently of little biological importance under normal conditions since adrenal gonadoid secretion does not prevent the effect of sex hormone withdrawal following gonadectomy. The formation of gonadoids under certain conditions in the avian adrenal is shown by the masculinizing effects of interrenal tumors of the adrenal, reported in hens.

(3) *Glucocorticoids*, e.g. Cortisone, hydrocortisone and corticosterone. A *glucocorticoid* effect (action on carbohydrate metabolism) can be observed in birds; thus hydrocortisone raise the blood sugar in fowl and cortical extracts and pigeons and favor glycogen deposition in the liver of the pigeon.

As in the mammal, normal development and function of the interrenal tissue is dependent on a pituitary hormone, adrenocorticotropic hormone, hence hypophysectomy leads to a marked shrinkage of the interrenal tissue in ducks and pigeons (Fig. 4) and ACTH can cause interrenal enlargement in pigeons. The control of the avian interrenal tissue and its principal functions thus appear to be much the same as those of the mammalian adrenal cortex. In addition, certain differences have been noted and there is a considerable array of other observations, the importance of which it is difficult to assess at present.

In mammals, various forms of physical, chemical or even emotional stress, e.g. exposure to cold or the action of certain toxic substances, result in adrenal cortical hypertrophy with increased secretion of cortical hormones. This effect is mediated by increased ACTH secretion. Of substances which have this effect in mammals, thyroxine, insulin, Doca, $CuSO_4$, KCl formaldehyde, and adrenaline, only formaldehyde and adrenaline are active on the fowl adrenal, and the formaldehyde effect is apparently not mediated by the pituitary since it is only slightly less in hypophysectomized chicks. Insulin produced a pituitary-mediated adrenal enlargement in pigeons. Certain infections, which probably also act as stress agents, cause adrenal enlargement in pigeons and fowl. Thus there is evidence of adrenal enlargement in response to stress in birds though the array of effective stress agents may differ markedly from that listed in mammals and there appear also to be marked species differences. Wild birds lead more stressful lives than domesticated ones. It is therefore not surprising that wild North American turkeys (*Meleagris gallopava*) have larger adrenals than domestic breeds (Leopold, reference in Collias, 1950), particularly as there is a similar difference in the adrenals of wild and laboratory rats (*Rattus norvegicus*).

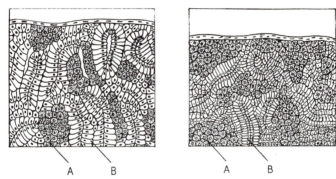

Fig. 4. Adrenal gland. Microscopic structures in typical avian adrenal (duck) showing a segment of the periphery from *Left* a normal bird, and *Right* a hypophysectomized bird. In the latter the number and appearance of chromoffin (medullary) cells (A) remain unaffected but the gland as a whole is shrunken due to decrease and degeneration of interrenal cells (B). (Based partly on photomicrographs by Benoit.)

In mammals, adrenocortical extracts cause marked atrophy of lymphoid tissues and thymus and a decrease of lymphocytes and eosiniphiles in the blood. In domestic fowl, though lymphocytes are decreased, eosiniphiles are unchanged and heterophiles (corresponding to mammalian neutrophiles) are increased. In mature hens both cortisone and Doca caused atrophy of the thymus (Höhn unpublished).

The interrenal steroids also have some effect on the gonads; thus, adrenalectomy in castrated cockerels maintained on extra salt causes testicular shrinkage with comb atrophy; cortisone causes testicular enlargement with increased androgen secretion. Probably an entirely different adrenal gonad relationship is the basis of the observation of Bülbring (1940) that adrenalectomized ducks needed a greater dose of adrenal extract to ensure a standard period of survival when operated on at the time of testicular growth than during gonadal quiescence.

Androgen injections did not reproduce these effects. The greater adrenal extract requirement may have been a reflection of a seasonal increase of interrenal activity suggested above, to which the body has become adapted; or it may be a direct result of rapid testicular growth.

C. The Chromaffin Tissue

Unlike the interrenal tissue, the chromaffin tissue of the adrenal is not under pituitary control. In mammals, secretion from the chromaffin cells is controlled by sympathetic nerve fibers. Since the embryological association of the chromaffin tissue and the sympathetic system is as close in birds as in mammals (see above) the sympathetic control of chromaffin tissue activity almost certainly applies in both. This is supported by the finding of nerve fibers which enter chromaffin cells, but not the interrenal cells, in bird adrenals. In mammals, the chromaffin cells secrete adrenalin and noradrenalin. In birds, these two hormones have so far been isolated only from the adrenal of the fowl and pigeon (West, 1951), but the staining reactions of the chromaffin tissue of other species suggest that they also produce one or both of these hormones. Adrenalin and noradrenalin have essentially similar actions, but noradrenalin constricts blood vessels in all parts of the body. Adrenalin, while constricting most vessels, actually dilates vessels in certain regions, particularly the skeletal muscles and heart. Both have an unusually short duration of action—a few minutes only—due to rapid destruction by enzymes.

The effects of adrenalin in birds appear to be essentially identical to those observed in mammals. Blood pressure is raised in the chicken mainly owing to contraction of the walls of small blood vessels—vasoconstriction. Whether adrenalin in birds, while causing, in general, constriction, also has the opposite effect of dilatation in the vessels of particular regions as in mammals, is unknown. The heart rate is raised in chickens by small doses; larger doses slow the heart. This apparent paradox is probably explained, as in mammals, by the fact that doses which raise blood pressure considerably, owing to the vascular constriction mentioned above, stimulate blood pressure-regulating mechanisms which slow the heart via nervous pathways—the direct effect of adrenalin on the heart being always one of acceleration.

Blood sugar is raised in ducks, geese, and fowl, and for the chicken at least it has been shown that this rise is brought about as in mammals by the decomposition of liver glycogen into glucose which enters the blood stream. Insulin, which itself lowers the blood sugar, leads to a release of noradrenalin from the chicken adrenal and a release of both chromaffin hormones in the pigeon (West, 1951).

Intestinal muscle is inhibited, e.g. the fowl cecum is relaxed by adrenalin and gizzard contractions are slowed down, and the ureter is constricted.

In ducks, adrenalin injections cause adrenal hypertrophy, possibly by stimulating increased ACTH secretion from the pituitary.

It is generally believed that secretion from the adrenal chromaffin tissue in mammals under resting conditions is at a slight, almost ineffective, level but that it is greatly increased in emergency states such as anger, which may precede fighting, or fear, which may precede flight. Both responses entail violent muscular exertion. The actions of adrenalin on blood flow, through its effect on heart rate and blood pressure and on blood glucose, providing a ready fuel for muscle energy, are such as to facilitate violent exercise. This "emergency theory" of adrenal function is probably applicable to birds. The fact that the excitement presumably entailed by handling did not raise the blood glucose level in domestic ducks (Sprague and Ivy, 1936) does not necessarily indicate that excitement did not cause adrenalin release, since these authors found that, compared to the mammal, rather large doses of adrenalin were required to raise the blood sugar level.

Perry (1941) observed that daily intramuscular injections of adrenaline into house sparrows (of both sexes) could suppress the development of the gonad and of accessory and secondary sex characters (bill color in the male) of the normal breeding cycle or that induced by exposure to light or following injections of gonadotropins. Wheeler *et al.* (1942) confirmed these effects in male domestic fowl, with doses of adrenalin corresponding to those used by Perry, with regard to gonadal development, semen volume, and sperm concentration. However, they point out that the adrenalin injections caused a 38% reduction in food consumption of the experimental birds. Since adverse conditions and noxious agents readily depress gonadal development, the antigonadal effect of adrenalin is probably nonspecific and its role in the normal bird is doubtful.

Perry, on the basis of his experiments, produced an entirely novel hypothesis to explain the avian gonadal cycle. He suggests that increased daylight in the spring increases physiological activity in the bird, This diminishes the available adrenalin in the blood and as it falls below its gonad-antagonizing value, the anterior pituitary gonadotropic mechanism is then allowed to function. When physiological activity diminishes with decreasing daylight, adrenalin again reaches a value at which it can antagonize the pituitary-gonad mechanism. While accepting the antigonadal effect of adrenalin in what are probably unphysiological high doses, the gonadal cycle is more reasonably attributed to seasonal variations in pituitary gonadotropin production (see Chapter XVIII). Moreover, it would appear that increased "physiological activity" would raise rather than lower the blood adrenalin level.

V. The Parathyroid Glands

The parathyroids arise from the third and fourth branchial pouches of the embryo, so that typically two glands are formed on each side which lie close to the posterior pole of the thyroid. This is the case in the pigeon, duck, and fowl. In the domestic fowl, the two lobes of one side are usually fused, and there are indications that in some other species there may appear to be only one parathyroid on each side. The weight of the gland is about 10 mg. per kilogram body weight in the species so far investigated. The microscopic structure is simple: cells of epithelial type—chief cells—are arranged in cords separated by thin strands of connective tissue and blood vessels. Oxyphile cells of unknown function, found among the chief cells in the mammalian parathyroid, are absent in birds. In mammals the hormone secreted by the chief cells—parathormone—is a protein, and presumably this is also the case in birds. Its principal function is to maintain the blood calcium level by stimulating the liberation of calcium from the mineral constituents of bone (principally calcium salts). It also promotes the excretion of phosphorus in the kidney. The maintenance of normal blood calcium level is of vital importance since blood calcium deficiency so increases the excitability of nerves and muscles that spontaneous muscular spasms occur, a condition called tetany. Tetanic convulsions, if unrelieved, lead to death. On the other hand, excessive calcium levels depress the nervous system and muscles. It must, however, be pointed out that while the above effects of calcium (as calcium ions) on nerve and muscle excitability are generally accepted, there is some doubt that tetany following parathyroid removal is always due to an abnormally low blood calcium level.

Up to the present, experimental work on the avian parathyroid has been carried out only in pigeons, ducks, and fowl. The results obtained, even in these few species, are not in agreement in certain important respects. An attempt to give an account of parathyroid functions in birds in general is therefore premature.

Removal of the parathyroids in ducks and pigeons results in tetany, which is fatal in about 24 hours; blood calcium is decreased and blood phosphorus increased, these changes being attributable to loss of the two functions of the parathyroid hormone cited above. In the fowl, parathyroidectomy has been reported by some to result in tetany, while in the hands of others it did not. However, accessory parathyroid tissue (in the thymus) has been found in this species, and cases of failure to induce tetany by parathyroidectomy in fowl may well be due to incomplete removal of parathyroid tissue. It is highly probable that the parathyroid is essential for life in all birds.

Parathormone injections can prevent the fall of blood calcium following parathyroid removal in ducks and pigeons. Injections of the hormone also raise the blood calcium in normal pigeons but have little effect in normal ducks and rather variable effects in fowl. A recent report (Polin *et al.*, 1957) indicates that mammalian parathormone consistently raises the blood calcium of domestic fowl (both sexes). As pointed out by Benoit, lack of response in some birds may also be due to the fact that parathyroid hormone of mammalian origin was used in these experiments. Avian parathormone, particularly from the species on which it is tested, might well be consistently effective in all birds.

Little is known about the factors which regulate the release of parathyroid hormone in birds. Hypophysectomy has been reported to lead to a temporary regression in parathyroid size and arrest of cell multiplication in ducks. This would suggest some degree of pituitary control. Probably, however, the main regulatory factor of parathyroid function is, as in mammals, the level of blood calcium—a calcium decrease acting as a stimulus to parathormone release whereas high calcium levels exert an inhibitory influence.

Interesting changes in calcium metabolism occur in female birds in connection with egg laying; these are brought about by estrogenic hormones. There is deposition of extra bone along the shaft cavities of long bones (medullary bone) which may be regarded as a calcium reservoir for use when the eggshell is formed. Blood calcium and phosphorus are raised considerably. Whether these effects of estrogens are generally brought about through stimulation of the parathyroid is, however, not clear. In ducks, but not fowl, estrogens cause parathyroid enlargement. In ducks, estrogens do not elevate the blood calcium after parathyroidectomy and the medullary bone laid down under estrogenic influence remains uncalcified in the parathyroidectomized bird (Benoit, 1950). On the other hand, in pigeons of both sexes, estrogens elevate blood calcium and phosphorus after parathyroidectonomy, just as in normal birds. Clearly, the estrogen-induced blood calcium changes related to ovulation appear to be dependent on the parathyroid in the duck but not in pigeons (Riddle *et al.*, 1945).

Seasonal changes in the parathyroid more or less in parallel with the gonadal cycle have been reported in pigeons and ducks. In fowl, ducks, and pigeons deprived of ultraviolet light or vitamin D, or with reduced calcium absorption in the intestine, or on calcium-deficient diets; there is marked parathyroid hypertrophy, generally followed by a return of the parathyroid to normal size after some time. The hypertrophy, under these conditions probably represents a compensatory attempt to maintain a normal blood calcium level by increased parathormone production.

VI. The Thymus and Pineal

There is as yet no generally accepted evidence that the thymus or the pineal have endocrine functions in any vertebrate.

A. THE THYMUS

The avian thymus, like the lymph nodes and the cloacal bursa Fabricii, consists predominantly of lymphoid tissue. However, in the thymus there are also reticular and epithelioid cells. The latter are arranged, generally in mammals and at least in some of the larger birds, into multicellular bodies known as Hassall's corpuscles. Thymus and bursa both undergo a fairly rapid involution as sexual maturity approaches. The bursa does not recover from this involution, so that "absence" of the bursa (on naked eye internal inspection of the dead bird, or on suitable probing through the cloaca on sizable live birds) can be used to determine whether the bird is immature (pre first sexual cycle) or has reached sexual maturity. Thus, in surface-feeding ducks an "absent" bursa indicates a bird which has reached its first or later breeding seasons, i.e. a bird about 9 or 10 months old or older. Larger water fowl, e.g. snow geese, do not reach sexual maturity until they are 2 years old and have large bursae and thymi until their first breeding season approaches. It was shown fairly recently (Höhn, 1947b, 1956) that the thymus (but not the bursa) of a variety of birds re-enlarges and also recovers its original, juvenile type of microscopic structure for some weeks following the first, and possibly also later, sexual cycles. An essentially similar thymus cycle has since been described in the mule deer (Browman and Sears, 1956). A number of observers have reported that complete thymectomy in birds (fowl and pigeons) is not fatal and that no consistent obvious effects follow thymus removal, this also applies to mammals. It must therefore be accepted that in postnatal life the avian thymus performs no vital function. However, there are recent observations in man and mammals which suggest strongly that it performs some specific, probably hormonal, function in addition to the obvious function of lymphocyte formation which it shares with other lymphoid tissue (Wilson and Wilson, 1955; Comsa, 1951).

If such a hormonal function is performed by the avian thymus it still remains to be demonstrated, but the seasonal re-enlargement of thymic tissue in sexually mature birds makes its existence likely.

The avian thymus develops from the first and third branchial pouches, and the single elongated body originally formed on each side of the neck soon divides into several lobes. In the fully fledged bird the

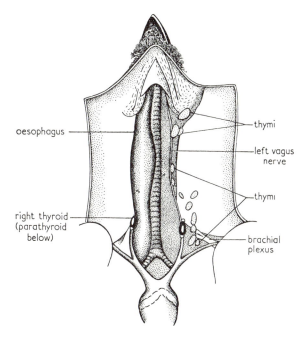

FIG. 5. Thymus "glands". Position in the passerine house sparrow (*Passer domesticus*). The bird was immature and taken in January (winter). It is seen from below with the gullet pulled to one side to show the left thymi and nearby structures. (Compare with Fig. 1.)

largest thymus lobes are found in the base of the neck, as in fowl (cf. the often-reproduced illustration of Nonidez and Goodale, 1927) and wild Galliformes as well as Laro-Limicolae, Colymbi, and Anseres (see Fig. 1). In passerine birds and *Falco* (two species of the latter examined), the largest thymic lobes are found just beneath the angle of the jaw (Fig. 5).

In mammals a rapid involution of the thymus in juveniles or adults occurs in response to stress. This involution is attributed to a hyper-secretion of adrenal glucocorticoids. Some forms of stress at least (e.g. infectious diseases) also cause thymic atrophy in birds; but the precise hormones responsible for this are still unknown. Some recent unpublished experiments (Höhn) indicate that thyroxine can cause enlargement, while cortisone (a glucocorticoid) and Doca bring on thymic atrophy, in fowl, oestrone and testosterone had no effect on the thymus in fowl nor was testosterone active on the mallard's thymus, contrary to findings in mammals where both cause thymic atrophy.

B. The Pineal

There appears to be no recent experimental work on the avian pineal. For a résumé of earlier results (which suggest that it may play a role as an endocrine organ) the reader is referred to Benoit (1950).

References

Adams, J. L. (1956). A comparison of different methods of progesterone administration to the fowl in affecting egg production and molt. *Poultry Sci.* **35**: 323–326.

Bailey, R. E. (1952). The incubation patch of passerine birds. *Condor* **54**: 121–136.

Benoit, J. (1950). Les glandes endocrines. *In* "Traité de Zoologie" (P. P. Grassé, ed.), Vol. 15, pp. 290–310, 314–329. Masson, Paris.

Benoit, J., and Assenmacher, I. (1951). Circulation porte tuberopréhypophysaire chez le canard domestique. *Compt. rend. soc. biol.* **145**: 112–115.

Benoit, J., and Assenmacher, I. (1952). La vascularization du complex hypophysaire chez le canard domestique. *Arch. anat. microscop. et morphol. exptl.* **41**: 69–105.

Benoit, J., and Assenmacher, I. (1953). Rapport entre la stimulation sexuelle préhypophysaire et la neurosécrétion chez les oiseaux. *Arch. anat. microscop. et morphol. exptl.* **42**: 334–386.

Boss, W. R. (1943). Hormonal determination of adult characters and sex behavior in herring gulls (*Larus argentatus*). *J. Exptl. Zool.* **94**: 181–203.

Bülbring, E. (1940). The relation between cortical hormone and the size of the testes in the drake with some observations on the effect of oils as solvents and on D.C.A. *J. Pharmacol. Exptl. Therap.* **69**: 52–63.

Bullough, W. S. (1945). Endocrinological aspects of bird behavior. *Biol. Revs. Cambridge Phil. Soc.* **8**: 89–99.

Browman, L. G., and Sears, H. S. (1956). Cyclic variation in the mule deer thymus. *Proc. Soc. Exptl. Biol. Med.* **93**: 161–162.

Carter, R. D., Risner, R. N., and Yacowitz, H. (1955). Some effects of growth hormone preparations in pullets and mature hens. *Poultry Sci.* **34**: 1407–1414.

Chu, J. P. (1940). The production of eclipse plumage in the mallard by injection of anterior pituitary extract and dehydroandrosterone. *J. Genet.* **39**: 517–524.

Collias, N. E. (1950). Hormones and behavior with special reference to birds and the mechanisms of hormone action. *Symposium on Steroid Hormones* **1950**: 277–329.

Comsa, J. (1951). Utilization of anti-thyroid action test for bioassay of thymus hormone. *Am. J. Physiol.* **166**: 550–554.

Davis, J., and Davis, B. S. (1954). The annual genod and thyroid cycles of the English Sparrow in Southern California. *Condor* **56**: 328–345.

Farner, D. S. (1955). The annual stimulus for migration: experimental and physiological aspects. *In* "Recent Advances in Avian Biology" (A. Wolfson, ed.), pp. 198–237. Univ. Illinois Press, Urbana, Illinois.

Hartman, F. A., and Albertin, R. H. (1951). A preliminary study of the avian adrenal. *Auk* **68**: 202–209.

Heller, H. (1950). The comparative physiology of the neurohypophysis. *Experientia* **6**: 368–376.

Hill, R. T., Corkill, A. B., and Parkes, A. S. (1934). Hypophysectomy of birds. 2. General effects of hypophysectomy of birds. *Proc. Roy. Soc.* **B116**: 208–220.

Höhn, E. O. (1947a). Sexual behaviour and seasonal changes in the gonads and adrenals of the Mallard. *Proc. Zool. Soc. Lond.* (A) **117**: 281–304.

Höhn, E. O. (1947b). Seasonal cyclical changes in the thymus of the Mallard. *J. Exptl. Biol.* **24**: 184–191.

Höhn, E. O. (1949). Seasonal changes in the thyroid gland and the effects of thyroidectomy in the Mallard, in relation to molt. *Am. J. Physiol.* **158**: 337–344.

Höhn. E. O. (1956). Seasonal recrudescence of the thymus in sexually mature birds. *Can. J. Biochem. and Physiol.* **34**: 90–101.

Knouff, R. A., and Hartman, F. A. (1951). A microscopic study of the adrenal of the Brown Pelican. *Anat. Record* **109**: 161–178.

Kobayashi, H. (1953). Inhibitory effect of lactogen on molting. *Japan. J. Zoöl.* **11**: 21–26.

Küchler, W. J. (1935). Jahreszyklische Veränderungen im histologischen Bau der Vogelschilddrüse. *J. Ornithol.* **83**: 414–461.

Maqsood, M. (1952). Thyroid function in relation to reproduction in mammals and birds. *Biol. Revs. Cambridge Phil. Soc.* **27**: 281–319.

Metzusals, J. (1956). The innervation of the adenohypophysis in the duck. *J. Endocrinol.* **14**: 87–94.

Nonidez, J. F., and Goodale, H. D. (1927). Histological studies on the endocrines of chickens deprived of ultraviolet light. (Fig. 1, p. 325). *Am. J. Anat.* **38**: 319–341.

Parkes, A. S., and Emmens, C. W. (1944). Effect of androgens and estrogens on birds. *Vitamins and Hormones* **2**: 361–408.

Perry, J. C. (1941). The antagonistic action of adrenalin on the reproductive cycle of the English Sparrow. *Anat. Record* **79**: 57–78.

Pino, J. A. (1954). Forced molting (interruption of egg laying) in white leghorns by the use of Enheptin (2-Amino, 5-Nitrothiazole). *Poultry Sci.* **34**: 540–546.

Pino, J. A., Rosenblatt, L. S., and Hudson, C. B. (1954). Inhibition of the pituitary gonadotrophic hormone secretion by Enheptin. *Proc. Soc. Exptl. Biol. Med.* **87**: 201–207.

Polin, D., Sturkie, P. D., and Hunsaker, W. (1957). The blood calcium response of the chicken to parathyroid extracts. *Endocrinology* **60**: 1–5.

Rahn, H., and Painter, B. T. (1941). The comparative histology of the bird pituitary. *Anat. Record* **79**: 297–312.

Riddle, O., Rauch, V. M., and Smith, G. C. (1945). Action of oestrogen on plasma calcium and endosteol bone formation in parathyroidectomized pigeons. *Endocrinology* **36**: 41–47.

Saeki, Y., Himeno, K., Tanabe, Y., and Katsugari, T. (1956). Comparative gonadotrophic potency of anterior pituitaries from cocks, laying hens and non-laying hens in molt. *Endocrinol. Japon.* **3**: 87–91.

Shaffner, C. S. (1955). Progesterone induced molt. *Poultry Sci.* **34**: 840–842.

Shirley, H. V., Jr., and Nalbandov, A. V. (1956). Effects of Neurohypophysectomy in domestic chickens. *Endocrinology* **58**: 477–483.

Sprague, R., and Ivy, A. C. (1936). Studies in avian carbohydrate metabolism. *Am. J. Physiol.* **115**: 389–394.

Strahan, R., and Waring, H. (1954). The effect of pituitary posterior lobe extracts on the blood pressure of the fowl. *Australian J. Exptl. Biol. Med. Sci.* **32**: 192–205.

Sturkie, P. D. (1954). "Avian Physiology." Comstock Publ. (Cornell Univ. Press), Ithaca, New York.

*Turner, C. D. (1955). "General Endocrinology." Saunders, Philadelphia and London.

West, G. B. (1951). The nature of avian and amphibian sympathin. *J. Pharm. and Pharmacol.* **3**: 400–408.

Wheeler, N. C., Search, G. L., Andrews, F. N. (1942). The effect of epinephrine on semen production in the domestic fowl. *Endocrinology* **30**: 369–374.

Wilson, A., and Wilson, H. (1955). The thymus in myasthenia gravis. *Am. J. Med.* **19**: 697–702.

Wingstrand, G. K. (1951). "The structure and development of the avian pituitary from a comparative and functional viewpoint." C.W.K. Gleevig, Lund.

Witschi, E. (1955). Vertebrate gonadotrophins. *Mem. Soc. Endocrinol. No.* **4**: 149–163.

Woitkewitsch, A. A. (1940). Dependence of seasonal periodicity in gonadal changes on the thyroid gland in *Sturnus vulgaris* L. *Compt. rend. acad. sci. U.R.S.S.* **27**: 741–745.

Yamashima, Y. (1952). Notes on experimental brooding induced by prolactin injections in the domestic cock. *Annotationes Zool. Japon.* **25**: 135–142.

Yasuda, M. (1953). Cytological studies of the anterior pituitary, in the broody fowl. *Proc. Japan. Acad.* **29**: 586–593.

Zarrow, M. X., and Zarrow, I. G. (1950). Ascorbic acid in the adrenal gland of the duck. *Anat. Record* **108**: 600–601.

* This book gives a concise account of certain avian studies in relation to general endocrinology.

Chapter XVII

Sex and Secondary Sexual Characters

EMIL WITSCHI

I. Genetic Sex and Sex Differentiation

A. Basic Sex Ratio

The immediate impression of equality as regards the number of individuals of each sex in birds at the time of hatching is so convincing that few pertaining data were collected and made available in the ornithologic literature. However, animal geneticists have published extensive accounts on sex ratios in domestic fowl. Moseley and Landauer (1949) relate data about the chicken which are summarized in Table I. They give also some figures from Asmundson for the brown turkey. In over 12,000 hatched, the percentage of males is 49.2. Prehatching

TABLE I

Sex Ratio in the Domestic Fowl[a]

Authority	No. of chicks hatched	Males (%)	No. of fetuses not hatched	Males (%)
Landauer and Landauer (1931)	67,993	48.8	—	—
Crew (1938)[b]	2,216,051	51.4	—	—
Crew (1938)[c]	515.976	50.3	8,565	51.0
Asmundson (1941)	114,536	49.4	35,513	48.7

[a] Compiled after Moseley and Landauer, 1949.
[b] Sexed by cloacal examination.
[c] Sexed on the basis of sex-linked plumage characters.

mortality seems to be higher in males. In fetuses dead before the 20th day the percentage of males is 55.3 (515 fetuses), but the figure falls to 51.5 for 6867 that died between the 20th and the 28th day. The impressive material establishes a basic $1\male{:}1\female$ ratio for chickens and turkeys. Slight deviations at the time of hatching are usually traceable to selective mortality during the incubation period. Other factors may also be operating. Claims of a relationship between egg size (or caloric value) and sex have often been made: best known is the work by Riddle (1917) on pigeons and doves. When mortality is very high, one sex may be more affected than the other. Thus, in pigeon-dove hybrids Painter and Cole (1943) explain the great prevalence of males (97%) by an excessive mortality of female embryos during the first week of incubation.

Field collections usually show a preponderance of one or the other, but most often of the male, sex. Hicks (1934) finds among 2173 starlings collected in Ohio, U.S.A., 1487 males (68%); from a total of 786 birds of the same species taken in England, Bullough (1942) reports 559 males (71%). Marshall and Baker (1940), collecting in the New Hebrides 2193 birds belonging to twenty different species, identify 59% as of male sex. Differences in longevity as well as in behavior are probably responsible for this imbalance.

B. SEX CHROMOSOMES AND SEX-LINKED INHERITANCE

In the course of the first half of this century the problem of the mechanism assuring maintenance of the balanced sex ratio found a satisfactory solution through the discovery of sex chromosomes and of sex-linked inheritance.

1. *Avian Chromosomes*

The *cytologic analysis* is rendered difficult by the high number of chromosomes. In diploid sets of the chicken, as for instance in spermatogonial metaphase plates, one counts from eleven to twelve large and fifty to seventy medium-size and small elements. The true chromosome character of the latter has been placed in doubt. Newcomer (1957) recognizes only twelve true chromosomes in the male (eleven in the female) and relegates all smaller chromatin particles to a status of *chromosomoids*. Luckily, the large chromosomes are well individualized, and by arranging them in pairs it becomes evident that in the female one element lacks an equivalent partner. Recent investigators (see Makino, 1951) agree that in most species this is the fifth chromosome of the haploid set (Fig. 1), though it is said to be the fourth in pigeons, doves

(Painter and Cole, 1943; Makino *et al.*, 1956), and sparrows (Riley, 1938) (Fig. 2). Actually the fourth and the fifth are of nearly the same size, but the special chromosome is of a characteristic V shape. In keeping with prevailing usage the sex chromosomes are designated with the letter Z. The assumption, that Z in the female has no small partner (W), was confirmed by the study of meiotic divisions in the spermatocytes of

Fig. 1. Large chromosomes of the fowl (*Gallus gallus*). Above: male diploid and haploid sets from spermatogonial and first spermatocyte metaphases of a cock. Below: female diploid and haploid sets from the testis of a sex-reversed hen. From Miller (1938).

Fig. 2. Large chromosomes of the house sparrow (*Passer domesticus*). Upper row, male set (ZZ); lower row, female set (ZO). From Riley (1938).

a sex-reversed hen (Miller, 1938). A single Z moves ahead of other elements to one pole of the first meiotic spindle; it has no partner going to the opposite side (Fig. 3).

Obviously the constitution of the male in regard to sex chromosomes is ZZ and that of the female is ZO. Genetic interpretation leads to the assumption that each Z chromosome carries a male-determining gene or gene complex (M), which is quantitatively balanced against female-determining genes (FF) in another chromosome pair in such a way that ZZ (2M) assures male differentiation, ZO (1M) female differentiation.

2. Sex-Linkage

All genes related to somatic characters which also are located in sex chromosomes follow the same course of inheritance as the M gene. Such sex-linked inheritance (Fig. 4) has early caught the attention of bird breeders, the reason being that often it is evinced by showy color variations. Several important factors regulating melanin production are carried by the Z chromosome. Complete absence of pigments results in albinism of the plumage and red eyes. More frequently seen are mutants of dilution or partial suppression of the wild type melanin patterns with blue or brown eyes. Sex-linked color variations have been reported for the domestic fowl and the turkey (Hutt, 1949), ring doves and pigeons (Cole and Hollander, 1950), ducks (Jaap, 1934), and geese (Jerome, 1953).

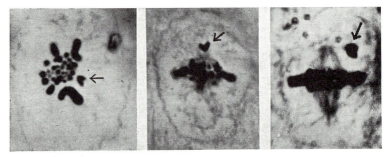

Fɪɢ. 3. The sex chromosome (arrow) in the first spermatocyte division in the testis of a sex-reversed hen. From Miller (1938).

Several yellow and white commercial varieties of the canary (Dunker, 1928) and the parakeet (Steiner, 1932) are analogous mutations. Other sex-linked characters such as *barred* and *silver* sometimes are used in the "auto-sexing" of chicks at hatching. On the basis of crossing-over data, maps have been constructed showing the relative locations of several factors in the Z chromosomes of the pigeon and the domestic fowl (Fig. 5).

3. Gynandromorphism

The literature contains at least a dozen well-authenticated reports on lateral gynandromorphism. In a majority of cases an ovary is found on the left and a testis on the right side (Fig. 6). Specimens with the reverse sex distribution have been reported, but unfortunately their internal anatomy has never been adequately described. Body size and skeleton conform with the sex, i.e. they are larger (cock size) on the testicular than on the ovarian side (hen size). In several finches also the plumages show the same correlation (Fig. 6). In fowls and other birds with hormonal control of feather dimorphism, plumage differences are not recognizable unless a sex-linked color factor happens to be involved.

The known facts indicate that one side of gynanders has a male, the other a female, chromosomal constitution. Sex composites of this type

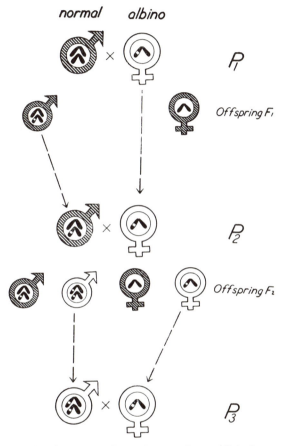

FIG. 4. Diagram showing mode of inheritance of a sex-linked recessive character (e.g. albinism) and development of a pure-breeding strain.

are known to become established in insects by loss of one sex chromosome during a cleavage division or by double fertilization of eggs containing two pronuclei. Conceivably one of these mechanisms may operate in the production of gynandric birds, though other irregularities of chromosomal distribution such as triploidy and nondisjunction have also been suggested. An interesting theory of "bipaternity," recently proposed by Hollander (1949) for somatic mosaics in pigeons, may be applicable to some cases of gynandromorphism. In several instances, daughters of males heterozygous for a sex-linked color factor showed areas of the dominant, as well as areas of the recessive, character. It is well known that at fertilization several sperms enter the avian egg, though only one fuses with its pronucleus. The supernumerary sperm

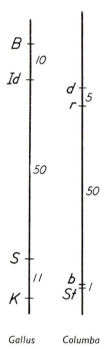

Gallus   Columba

Fig. 5. Map of sex chromosomes of fowl and pigeon based on linkage and crossing over of four mutant genes each. B, black; Id, inhibitor of melanin; S, silver; K, slow feathering; d, dilute; r, reduced; b, brown; St, almond. Data by courtesy of W. F. Hollander.

pronuclei divide and form so-called merocytes which, as a rule, degenerate. Hollander's assumption that merocytes occasionally survive and contribute, like a graft, to embryo formation may provide a satisfactory explanation not only for the analyzed pigeon mosaics but also for some domestic fowl gynanders recorded in the literature.

C. Development of the Sex Glands

1. Formation of Indifferent Gonads

The three major components of the gonads arise from separate embryonic sources. The core or *medulla* is formed by strands of blastema cells proliferating from the median edge of the mesonephric cords. The *cortex* or covering epithelium of the primitive gonadal ridge is a thickened part of the peritoneum adjacent to the coelomic angles along the root of the dorsal mesentery. The *germ cells* first occupy a crescent-shaped area in the upper yolk-sac endoderm. Before the establishment of blood circulation they begin to migrate into the splanchnic mesoderm. They

Fig. 6. Gynandromorph bullfinch (*Pyrrhula pyrrhula*).

then proceed through the just-forming mesentery and finally locate themselves in the gonadal folds. Originally distributed symmetrically, they move preferentially toward the left side after having reached the dorsal root of the mesentery (Fig. 7). Exceptions from this rule are found notably in some hawks. While in fowls and passerine birds the

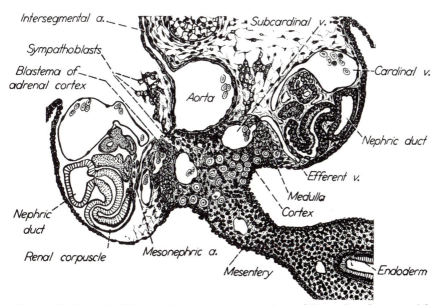

Fig. 7. Redwing blackbird (*Agelaius phoeniceus*) embryo of 38 somites. Large gonial cells occur at dorsal root of mesentery. From Witschi (1935a). Magnification: × 160.

left: right ratio of total numbers of germ cells in newly organized indifferent gonads is from 4:1 to 5:1, in the marsh hawk (*Circus hudsonius*)
it is near 1:1 (Witschi, 1935a; Stanley, 1937; Stanley and Witschi,
1940). Counting separately the gonia in cortex and medulla—temporarily
a few get lodged in the intervening albuginea—one perceives that in
cases of asymmetry the supply of the cortex of the right side is
particularly deficient.

In a sparrow embryo preserved early in the fifth day of incubation,
and in a hawk embryo of similar developmental stage, distribution of
gonia was as follows:

House Sparrow (*Passer domesticus*)

Right Gonad			Left Gonad		
Cortex	Albuginea	Medulla	Cortex	Albuginea	Medulla
180	57	187	1423	86	500

Marsh Hawk

Right Gonad			Left Gonad		
Cortex	Albuginea	Medulla	Cortex	Albuginea	Medulla
1751	208	560	2126	210	522

2. Differentiation of Testes and Ovaries

Sexual differentiation begins in the domestic fowl and song birds in
the course of the fifth day. In hawks, with their relatively slow rate of
development, corresponding changes occur on the eleventh day of
incubation. Characteristic for testicular differentiation are the prevalence of medullary development and the reduction and eventual disappearance of the cortex. On the other hand, in ovarial differentiation
the cortex is the leading element. In a few hawks (*Circus hudsonius*,
some accipiters) two ovaries of nearly equal size are formed, but in most
species the right gonad of females is small or vestigial (Figs. 11, 16a)
and sometimes not ovarian in structure. The early development of large
egg follicles, giving the surface of ovaries a rough, granulated appearance, is the most conspicuous feature of female differentiation. Medullary
remnants persist in various structural forms on both sides (Witschi,
1935b). Under certain circumstances they may later enlarge and become
the source of hermaphrodite development and sex reversal (see Sections
I, E and I, F, 1).

The gonads of male fetuses may, temporarily, exhibit an ambisexual
character, both testes of hawks and at least the left one of many other
birds being covered by more or less extensive cortical crusts (Figs. 8,
9 and 10). Ordinarily, these remnants disappear before hatching.
Testicular development is particularly characterized by the differentiation of medullary seminal tubules (Fig. 9). The development of a

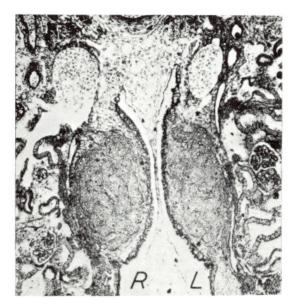

FIG. 8. Marsh hawk (*Circus hudsonius*) embryo of 15 mm. Both testes are covered with a cortex. Courtesy of A. J. Stanley. Magnification: × 100.

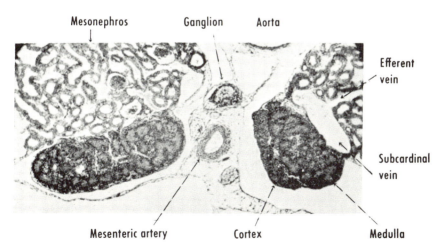

FIG. 9. House sparrow (*Passer domesticus*) embryo at 8 days, with considerable cortical remnant in left testis. From Witschi (1935b). Magnification: × 60.

fibrous tunic, the albuginea, gives the surface of the testis a smooth appearance.

Maturity with completion of egg and sperm production exceptionally may occur within the same breeding season, but in most species it is attained only in the second or third year. Hereafter seasonal breeding cycles become established with an alternation of eclipse and nuptial phases. During the periodic recrudescence and regression of the sex glands, testes and ovaries gain and lose from 200 to 500 times their weights (Figs. 18, 21; Tables III, IV).

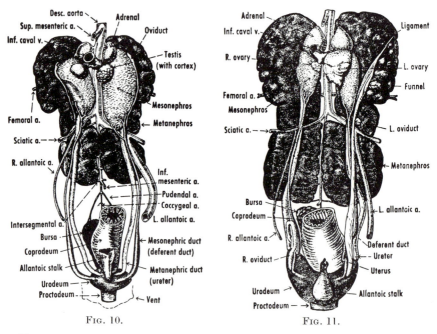

FIG. 10.   FIG. 11.

FIG. 10. Male urogenital organ of fetal redwing blackbird at 11 days. From Witschi (1956). Magnification: × 10.

FIG. 11. Female organ of fetal redwing blackbird at 11 days. From Witschi (1956). Magnification: × 10.

D. ACCESSORY SEX ORGANS

1. *Sperm Ducts*

The male gonaducts develop from the mesonephric system. At early fetal stages (eleventh day in passerines, somewhat later in the chick) the urinary functions are taken over by the adult kidneys (metanephric system). The mesonephros then transforms into an *epididymis* and the mesonephric duct becomes the *deferent duct*. The changes are essentially the same in both sexes (Figs. 10, 11); male gonaducts persist also in the adult female, even though they remain smaller and obviously have no functional value.

In the later development the ducts gain excessively in length, becoming folded and coiled until each forms a large body serving as a storage organ, the glomus. The very end becomes a thick-walled ejaculatory duct which enters the lower cloaca through its ventrolateral wall (Figs. 18, 21).

Two pairs of retractor muscles attaching the ventral wall of the cloaca just below the entrance of the ejaculatory ducts, one to the pelvis (synsacrum), the other to the skin of the tail, are possibly of importance for the mechanics of copulation and seminal discharge, though their occurrence in both sexes suggests that they serve also other functions (Figs. 18, 21).

2. Oviducts

In passerines and in the chick a pair of oviducal fields, consisting of thickened peritoneal epithelium, become organized during the fourth day of incubation. They are located at the level of transition from the pronephric vestiges to the first mesonephric tubules. Presently each forms a pit, then a funnel, and during subsequent days the oviducts arise by downgrowth alongside the mesonephric ducts (Fig. 12). This progressive phase ends shortly after the ducts have attained full length and their tips approach the cloaca. So far development had been symmetric and similar for both sexes; but now follows a period of regression and sexual differentiation that leads to complete disappearance of both ducts in the male (Figs. 10, 18) and to relative reduction of the right duct in the female (Figs. 11, 21). The timing of these events in five representative species is indicated in Table II. Figures 10 and 11 represent late stages of this differential reduction. In males the funnel parts disappear last. For a recent analysis of these developments see the paper by Scheib-Pfleger (1955).

Through the juvenal stages the oviducts remain closed tubes with lower ends only superficially attached to the cloacal wall. The left one gains an opening only at the approach of the first laying season (Greenwood, 1935).

3. Cloacal Differentiation

It is probable that all ancestral birds had penislike copulatory organs; but of recent forms only relatively few, particularly ostriches, tinamous, ducks, and geese, develop a phallus of considerable size. In the duck at early fetal stages a genital tubercle appears on the ventral circumference of the cloaca, in both sexes. It remains rudimentary in the females, while in the males it grows to considerable size, even before hatching (Fig. 13).

In most other birds the phallus persists only as a very small vestige or disappears completely. In the domestic fowl a small genital tubercle forms about the twelfth day in incubation. In female chicks it usually has disappeared at hatching time, while in males the rudiment persists

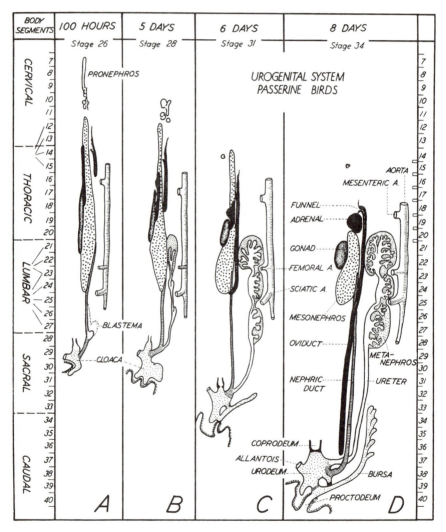

FIG. 12. Development of urogenital organs and cloaca in passerine birds during incubation age. From Witschi (1956).

TABLE II

OVIDUCT DEVELOPMENT IN FIVE SPECIES OF BIRDS[a,b]

Species	Progressive, indifferent period (day)	Regressive, differentiating period			
		Female: right duct only			Male: both ducts (days)
		Start (day)	Half length (day)	Vestige (day)	
House sparrow	5–8	$8\frac{1}{3}$	9	12	8 –(13)[c]
Redwing blackbird	5–8	$8\frac{1}{3}$	$9\frac{1}{2}$	12	8 –(13)
Domestic fowl	5–8½	9	12	16	8½–(15)
Domestic turkey	6–10	11	15	22	10 –(16)
Red-tailed hawk	9–18	20	28	32	18 –(26)
Stage:	26–34a	34a	34b	35	34 –(35)

[a] Witschi (1956).
[b] In this table *days* indicate incubation ages.
[c] In parentheses: day when remnants still are found in about half of the male fetuses.

and may even slightly enlarge. This dimorphism makes it possible to "sex" hatching chicks with an accuracy of 95–100%.

E. HERMAPHRODISM AND SPONTANEOUS SEX REVERSAL

The concept of sex determination by genic balance and the described ambisexual composition of the primordial gonads together furnish a basis for formal interpretation of the not too infrequent occurrences of intersexuality. In fact, normal fetal testes and ovaries often exhibit conditions that might be classified as rudimentary hermaphrodism. Yet more strictly the term hermaphrodism is reserved for conditions of higher than usual degrees of bisexuality.

Two entirely different types of true hermaphrodism have been reported. The first is the case of *hereditary hermaphrodism in male pigeons* (Lahr and Riddle, 1945; Riddle *et al.*, 1945). In a certain breed more than 80% of adult males show hermaphrodite features. In the extreme cases the left gonad is an ovotestis with small and medium-size ovocytes; a complete left oviduct is present. In cases with two testes the left one may be smaller than the right, which is an indication that an extensive left cortex had persisted for a considerable period. Left oviducts are nearly complete or show various degrees of reduction. Evidently, in all males of this race the cortical element of left gonads persists longer than in normal races (Fig. 14). Under its influence the oviducts do not disappear but assume a more or less female pattern in proportion to the status maintained by the cortex during the regression phase. The situation resembles that of so-called undifferentiated sex races of frogs (Witschi, 1929); however, in the pigeon the juvenile

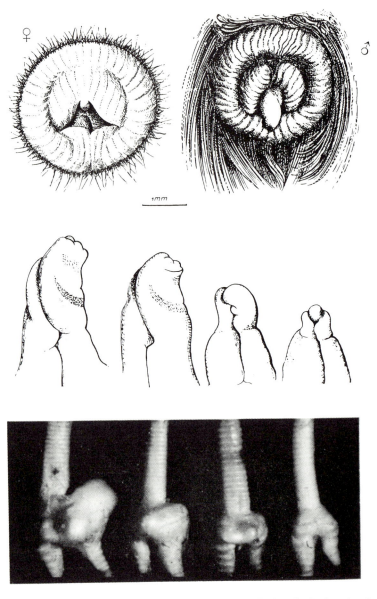

FIG. 13. Accessory sex organs of duck fetuses. Top row, left: female, 20 days incubated; external aspect of vent with small phallic tubercle. Right: male, 22 days incubated; with large phallus. From Em. Wolff (1950). Second row, phallus; from left: male, castrate, partially castrated female, female; all at 17 days. Third row: syrinx on the 17th day of incubation. From left: castrate (male type), three partially castrated females, the last one an almost normal female type. From Wolff and Wolff (1949).

hermaphrodism of the male is not primitive but results from a recent mutation in the sex-determining gene complex.

The second type is represented by *genetic females suffering sex reversal after pathologic regression of the ovarian cortex*. So far it has been reported only for the domestic fowl. In two instances hens that had been laying eggs changed into cocks, each one fathering two offspring

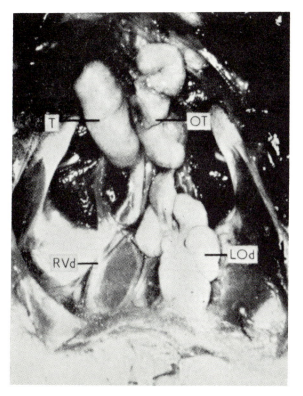

Fig. 14. Hermaphrodite domestic pigeon. From Riddle *et al.* (1945). LOd, left oviduct; OT, ovotestis; RVd, right vas deferens; T, testis.

before their death (Crew, 1923; Arnsdorf, 1947). It is assumed that the inversion is brought about by infective or cancerous destruction of the ovarian cortex and consequent compensatory hypertrophy of the medullary components on both the left and the right side.

F. EXPERIMENTAL MODIFICATION OF SEX DIFFERENTIATION

1. *Female to Male*

In the same year that Crew described the just-mentioned case of spontaneous sex reversal, Benoit (1923) published a first report on ovariectomy in hens, with results that essentially duplicate nature's experiment. The removal of the left ovary is followed by a compensatory hypertrophy of the right rudiment (Domm, 1939). In a few poulards a small ovary develops; but in more than 90% the nodule is of testicular structure, with about one out of ten cases showing active spermatogenesis (Fig. 15). Results evidently depend on condition and composition of the right rudiment at the time of the operation. If all germ cells have disappeared, only a sterile testis may develop. Hence, poults ovariectomized soon after hatching yield the highest percentage of fertile

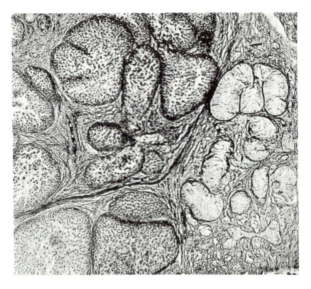

Fig. 15. Histologic detail from testislike right gonad of an ovariectomized hen showing fertile and sterile seminal tubules.

testes. In a few instances incomplete ovariectomy has resulted in testis formation also on the left side (Domm, 1939).

The behavior of the chromosomes during *female spermatogenesis* was described above (Fig. 3). The meiotic spindle of the primary spermatocyte, showing the Z element on its way to one pole only, provides a good picture of chromosomal distribution as it must normally occur in the seldom seen first polar spindle of the egg. Attempts at obtaining offspring from matings of masculinized poulards with normal hens so far have not yielded any results, probably because no connections were established between testicular nodes and deferent ducts. However, since female birds retain the rudiments of deferent ducts and epididymides, one may well expect that eventually some fertile sex-reversed poulards will be found.

Cavazza (1938) observed testicular development of the right rudiment also among a small number of ovariectomized ducks. In similarly operated adult passerines no corresponding changes have been encountered. Under the influence of injected gonadotropins the right rudiment of an ovariectomized *Quelea quelea* has been seen to develop into a functional ovary (Witschi, 1936a).

The reported experiments are of considerable theoretic interest. They reveal a persistent *antagonism between cortex and medulla*, not only within one gonad but also between the cortex of the left ovary and the medullary rudiment representing the right gonad. The epistasis of the female sex, based on a favorable genic balance, becomes nullified if only the medullary components of one or both gonads remain intact. We can further conclude that genic constitution controls sex differentiation not directly but by means of a pair of inductors: *cortex and medulla*. Ovariectomy in no way changes the potencies of sex-determining genes, but it reverses the relationship within the corticomedullary effector system.

The endocrine character and potentialities of the *female testes* of sex-reversed hens will be discussed below in Section II, C (Plumages).

2. *Male to Female*

As soon as, in the early 1930's, purified steroid hormones became available for experimentation, various groups of investigators independently began studying their effects on sex differentiation in incubating hen's eggs. Following a first announcement by Kozelka and Gallagher (1934), it became widely established that *all estrogens* produce a temporary feminization of gonad differentiation in genetically male embryos (see references in Dantchakoff, 1941; Willier, 1942; Et. Wolff, 1950). At hatching, optimally responding male (ZZ) chicks may have an ovarylike left gonad barely distinguishable from that of true (ZO) females. The right gonad retains a more obviously testicular character but usually is smaller than the right testis of control males. However, as Madame Dantchakoff (1936) dramatically describes in her "history of a cock," even the most promising appearing cases revert to the male sex within the first year after hatching. This does not mean that the treatment with female hormones would not leave some lasting imprints. Contrary to normal proportions the left testis often is considerably smaller than the right. Spermatogenesis shows great irregularities, and the reproductive value of these cocks is low. Domm and Davis (1948) report that many feminized cocks have intermediate or completely hen-type plumages even in the second year. Accordingly, their sexual behavior varies from normal male to inactive neutral. This indicates that the estrogen treatments may affect not only the generative, but also the endocrine component of the male sex glands.

Male hormones likewise produce incomplete feminization effects, sometimes alongside partial masculinization. An extensive study by Wolff *et al.* (1949) of sixteen steroids usually classified as *androgens* revealed that none exclusively supports testicular differentiation. Moreover, the acetate and the propionate of testosterone, which come nearest to producing a female-to-male shift, induce this reaction only on administration of very high, subtoxic doses. No attempts at rearing thus treated animals to reproductive age have been made or reported.

By far the most extensive work on hormonal sex reversion was done with chickens, and it is still carried on by poultry breeders in the hope of getting results of practical value. Investigations have also been extended to other species. Lewis (1946) reports on partial feminization of male *duck* embryos with estrogens, but injections of testosterone (2.5 mg.) produced no visible effects. In the *herring gull* (*Larus argentatus*) the male was found to be highly responsive to injections of the synthetic estrogen, stilbestrol (Boss, 1943; Boss and Witschi, 1947). The low dose of 2.5 µg. changed sex differentiation to such an extent that at laparotomy, one month after hatching, all gonads appeared to be of female type. However, in the course of the first year, while low dose injections were continued, the males became recognizable by their typically larger body size. At the age of two years laparotomy revealed that they had two testes, both partly covered with ovarian cortex (Fig. 16c). At about 4 years, i.e. two years after the last injection, the situation was still the same. Cortical patches contained egg follicles and loops of abnormal seminal tubules (Figs. 16d, 17). Much larger amounts of testosterone propionate (2.5 mg.) failed to affect sex differentiation perceptibly.

3. *Accessory Sex Organs*

Under this heading shall be comprised mainly the oviducts. The sperm ducts require no special consideration since they develop only minor degrees of sexual dimorphism at prepuberal levels. However, an introductory summary of the work by Em. Wolff (1950) and Wolff and Wolff (1949) on the development of *the genital tubercle and the syrinx of the duck* will assist in the analysis of the more complex case of the oviducts. In the early development of both these organs (8–18 days of incubation) the male conformation represents the neutral type. It develops in early castrates of either sex (Fig. 13). Even rudiments grown

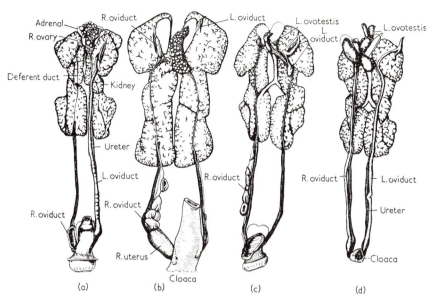

Fig. 16. Urogenital organs of herring gull (*Larus argentatus*). a, Control female (22 months); b, female (22 months) injected with 2.5 μg. stilbestrol on sixth day of incubation; c, male (2 years) injected with 2.5 μg. stilbestrol on ninth day of incubation; d, male (4 years, 1 month) injected with 2.5 μg. stilbestrol on sixth day of incubation. Left ovotestis was torn in three parts when biopsied at 2 years. From Boss and Witschi (1947).

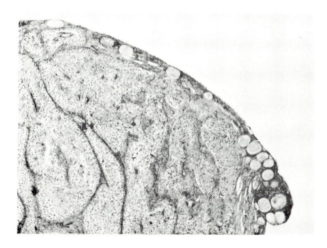

Fig. 17. Section through ovotestis of specimen shown in Fig. 16b. Magnification: ×55. From Boss and Witschi (1947).

in vitro, removed before the ninth day from all possible gonadal influences, assume the male-type characteristics. Addition of estrogens to the culture media results in the development of the female types (Wolff, 1952). Accordingly, estrogens injected into eggs on the tenth day of incubation or earlier also cause the male fetuses to develop female-type syrinx and penis organs. It is remarkable that in both instances the larger and more diversified alternative should be the neutral, self-differentiating form. During the period of embryonic segregation, presence of testes and administration of androgenic hormones exert no modifying influence.

The situation regarding differentiation of the *oviducts* is similar in principle but complicated by the fact that both the male and the female types deviate from the neutral form. By a precise technique of localized radiation Wolff and Wolff (1951) were able to sterilize chick embryos early in the third day of incubation—without destroying the incipient oviduct fields which are located at a higher somitic level (compare Fig. 12a, a later stage, but still showing the primitive localizations). Complete castrates of both genetic sexes—assured by sex-linked characters—developed and retained both oviducts. The fact that in normal males and females of the chicken this condition persists only up to the end of the eighth day (Table II) suggests that the differentiation of either testes or ovaries determines the character of the regressive processes: complete degeneration and resorption of both oviducts in the male (Figs. 10, 18), inhibition of further growth of the right oviduct in the female (Figs. 11, 16a, 21). By culture *in vitro* of pieces of oviducts, Wolff found that, irrespective of sex of the donor, those taken before the eighth day survive, as also do pieces taken from females 9 or 10 days old. On the contrary, those from males of over 8 days carry a principle of necrosis and disappear within a short time. That this latter condition has been induced by the testicles during the eighth day is quite evident. It is equally assured that the presence of an ovary causes an arrest in the growth of the right oviduct. Et. Wolff (1950) reports that in unilaterally X-ray sterilized females the right gonad alone, as well as the left one, can sustain the female type of differentiation. This is partly rendered understandable by a consideration of the hereditary pigeon hybrids. The report by Riddle *et al.* (1945), shows that the simultaneous presence, at the critical regression phase (eighth to twelfth day), of active cortical (ovarian) and medullary (testicular) parts results in persistence of female-type oviducts. Obviously, in case of competition the ovarian influence tends to prevail.

In cases of intersexuality produced by hormone injections, the picture of gonadal inductions is obscured by direct actions of the estrogens and androgens on the ducts. They are of double nature. As first described for amphibians (Foote, 1940) and then recognized likewise in experiments with birds (Boss and Witschi, 1947; Stoll, 1950), these hormones can stop the downgrowth of the oviducts at any stage of the progressive period. If administered very early, and in sufficiently large dosages, only funnel segments or no ducts at all differentiate. Apparently the hormones change the character of the embryonic blastema cells, rendering them incapable of proliferation and continued duct production. Such complete or partial agenesis is entirely different from secondary regression. Furthermore, the hormones cause a premature presecretory transformation of primitive duct cells, resulting in a type of epithelium which resists regression. By the later growth of the embryonic body the ducts become dislocated and often separate into several tubular or vesicular pieces. Together with variables of time and dosages, this explains sufficiently the irregularities as observed by all investigators. The same variations of response are observed in male and in female specimens (compare Figs. 16b and c). Occasionally, as in the case of the male gull shown in Fig. 16c, a small dose of stilbestrol may not interfere at the progressive phase but may entirely block regressive changes. As a result two full-length oviducts persist; this is similar to the effect of early castration. No decision can be made on the basis of these experiments about the nature of the substances involved in the normal coordination of the type of oviduct differentiation with the sex of the gonads. While the facts known about syrinx and genital tubercle in ducks may be explained satisfactorily by the assumption of estrogen secretion from fetal ovaries, the more complex mechanisms of control of oviduct differentiation remain in need of further elucidation.

II. Secondary Sex Characters

Nature seldom fits smoothly into systems of classification. Boundaries and the very nature of primary and secondary sex characters seem to change according to whether they are viewed from genetic, endocrine, or anatomic standpoints. The present chapter pledges no adherence to any strict and exclusive definition of secondary sex character. Its basic subject is the problem of correlation, at the adult level, of diverse expressions of sexual differentiation among each other but particularly with the gonadal sex. The relationship, if at all recognizable, will usually be of the nature either of cause and effect or of a common cause.

A. Functional Development of the Accessory Sex Organs

In the adult bird, oviducts and sperm ducts enlarge and regress in

harmony with the breeding and eclipse seasons. In midwestern North
America sparrow and starling testes are smallest in September and
October and attain maximal dimensions in April and May, enlarging
from 300 to 500 times (Fig. 18). By the end of May and in early June
the testes of starlings rapidly regress and return to the eclipse condition.
In the sparrow, which raises two, three, or even more broods, maximal
testicular size and spermatogenic activity continue until July (Keck,
1934).

Increase and decrease of the *sperm ducts* obviously follow rise and fall
of androgen production by the testes (Table III). After ablation of the

TABLE III

SEASONAL VARIATION OF GONADUCTS IN MALE STARLINGS AND SPARROWS[a,b]

Season	Testis (mg.)[c]	Deferent duct (mg.)[c]	Testosterone substitution (μg./day)
Eclipse: September–November	3(0.8)	5(0.4)	—
Prenuptial: December	5(3)	5(1)	1(0.2)
Prenuptial: January	8(4)	6(2)	20(4)
Prenuptial: March	500(160)	40(16)	100(20)
Nuptial: April	1000(300)	150(25)[d]	250(50)

[a] Partly after Witschi and Fugo (1940).
[b] The last column indicates the amount of testosterone propionate that must be injected into castrate males
to stimulate and maintain deferent ducts at the seasonal level. Values for sparrows are set in parentheses.
Weight of deferent duct refers only to the part between metanephros and cloaca.
[c] Round weights of fresh organs.
[d] Filled with seminal fluid, which may account for three-fourths of this weight.

testes they assume and retain a minimal size throughout the year.
Estrogenic steroid hormones do not noticeably change this castrate
condition (Fig. 19a), but injections of testosterone or androsterone
induce their growth to full breeding condition (Fig. 19b). Naturally,
stimulated ducts of castrates are empty while those of normal breeding
males may be inflated by quantities of seminal fluid. At the height of the
reproductive season the latter increases the total weight often as much
as four or five times. Unilateral castrates are best suited to illustrate the
difference of hormone-induced growth and of total seasonal enlargement
(Fig. 19c). Similar asymmetries occur in wild birds with unilateral
partial or complete testicular agenesis, or with obstructions in one of the
sperm ducts (Riddle, 1927; Witschi, 1945). The last column of Table III
shows daily amounts of testosterone that must be injected into castrated
male starlings to maintain the sperm ducts at the characteristic level of
four active seasonal periods. One may assume that the natural output
by the testes has a more economical mode of action and therefore totals
somewhat lower, at each level, than have the administered equivalents.

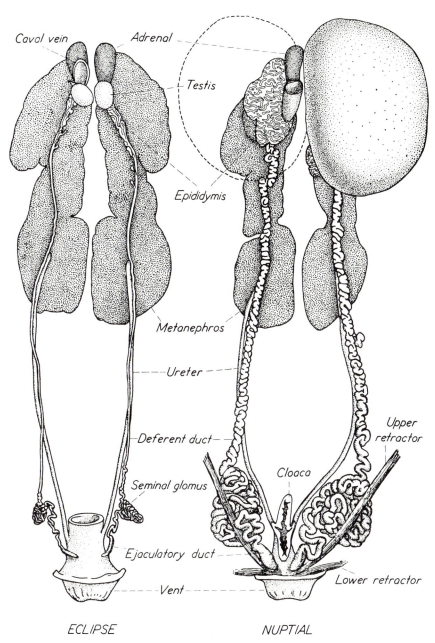

FIG. 18. Male urogenital organs of house sparrow in eclipse and nuptial condition. The latter condition was induced out of season by seventeen daily injections of 0.1 cc. pregnant mare serum. Retractor muscles are not represented in left figure. After Witschi (1935c).

Seasonal changes in the size and histologic character of the male gonaducts occur only in birds with distinct breeding cycles. In the domestic cock, testes and deferent ducts are in stimulated condition throughout the year (Domm, 1939). It does not seem that epididymis

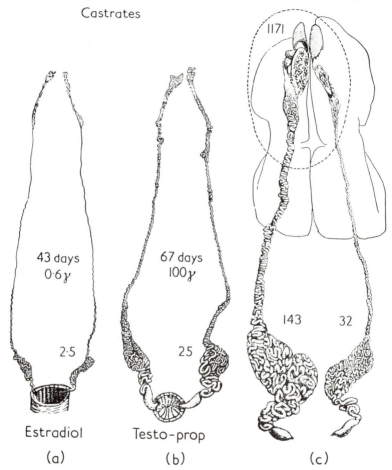

Castrates

43 days
0·6γ

67 days
100γ

1171

2·5

25

143   32

Estradiol   Testo-prop

(a)   (b)   (c)

Fig. 19. Accessory sex organs of *Sturnus vulgaris*. Males: a and b are castrates injected; c is a unilateral castrate. Testo-prop, testosterone propionate. Weights of seminal glomera and testis in mg. After Witschi (1945).

and sperm duct of gallinaceous birds are so important as storage organs for seminal fluid as they are in passerines. Although the deferent ducts are convoluted, they do not actually form glomera.

The prepuberal *phallic organ* of the male duckling—embryologically developed through absence of ovarial inhibition (see above)—at puberty becomes a large penis under the influence of testicular hormones (Fig. 20). Different from the gonaducts, it does not regress to near juvenal proportions during subsequent eclipse seasons or after castration, but retains a nearly constant adult size (Benoit, 1936).

In the female bird not only the *oviduct* but also the *sperm ducts* follow the seasonal cycle (Fig. 21). In the starling, while the oviduct increases from an average eclipse weight of about 20–2500 mg. in April and May (more than doubling this weight again during actual ovulation),

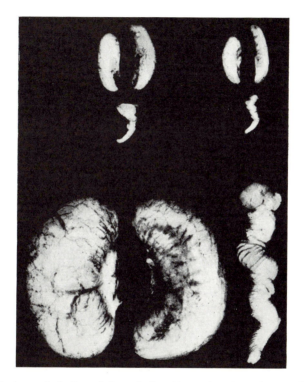

Fig. 20. Testes and phailus of three ducks. Above: two immature control animals. Below: light-stimulated animal of same age. After Benoit (1936).

the lower deferent ducts grow approximately from 2 mg. to 8 or 10 mg. Injection experiments (Witschi and Fugo, 1940) prove that estrogens stimulate only the oviducts while androgens cause an enlargement of both male and female ducts (Table IV). Daily injections of 500 μg. of estrone cause the oviduct of female castrates to attain a size characteristic of the breeding season; similarly, 100 μg. of testosterone propionate establish the characteristic size of the deferent ducts of the

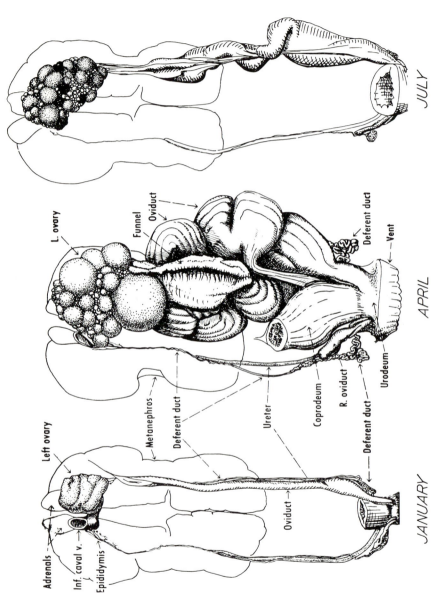

Fɪɢ. 21. Female urogenital organs of house sparrow. *January*: eclipse condition; *April*: early nuptial condition (note enlargement of seminal ducts and right oviduct); *July*: incubating female taken from nest on July 27th containing regressed ovary with several empty follicles and degenerating eggs.

breeding female. It must be assumed that the ovary is hormonally a bisexual gland. Even the possibility that testosterone normally contributes to the functional growth of the oviducts seems to be indicated by the reciprocally augmenting effect produced by injection of a mixture of estrone (50 μg.) and testosterone propionate (1000 μg.). The ambisexual effects induced by testosterone are the more remarkable as progesterone alone or in combination with estrogens does not elicit detectable responses in either male or female gonaducts. The artificial hormone, stilbestrol, is about as highly gynogenic as estradiol and at least ten times as efficient as estrone.

TABLE IV

CASTRATED FEMALE STARLINGS: HORMONAL STIMULATION OF GONADUCTS

Hormone	dose/day (μg.)	Oviduct		Vas deferens[a] (right)	
		Weight (mg.)	Type[b]	Weight (mg.)	Type[b]
Control	—	12	0	1.3	0
Estrone	50	180	I–II	1.3	0
Estrone	500	1680	III	1.6	0
Testosterone propionate	100	16	0	8	II
Testosterone propionate	1250	250	II	13	III
Testosterone propionate + estrone	1000 ⎱ 50 ⎰	940	II–III	10	III

[a] Only the part between metanephros and cloaca was weighed.
[b] Ovarian fresh weights in normal females: type 0, 10 mg. (eclipse season); type I, 20 mg. (prenuptial season); type II, 60–100 mg. (prenuptial season); type III, 300–1200 mg. (breeding season).

B. BILLS, COMBS, AND WATTLES

Some ornamental sex characters of the head have been studied with considerable accuracy because they are of use in the bioassay of hormones, particularly the androgenic steroids. The rudiments of *comb and wattles* of a newly hatched chick normally do not enlarge much during the first few weeks, but if daily doses of about 5 mg. of testosterone are injected into the breast muscle these head furnishings grow rapidly to puberal male proportions and turgescence, irrespective of the sex of the chick. Similarly, also the very small comb of a capon can be stimulated (Fig. 22). By local application directly to the comb, even the small dose of 1 μg. of testosterone produces a noticeable reaction (Gallagher and Koch, 1935).

Bills are of interest because of the great variety of their colors, and of *color-control mechanisms*. Surprisingly, "bird books" usually give only incomplete and often unreliable descriptions of the bills and of their sexual and seasonal variations. Bill pigments are mainly of two types: melanins and carotenoids. Brown and black *melanins* are produced in *melanophores* of the usual rhizoid- or neuronlike shape. They become injected into epidermal cells which are moving out of the proliferating layer (Fig. 23). The granular pigment becomes deposited as a cap over the outer surfaces of the nuclei. With the progress of proliferation and cornification the nuclei degenerate and the pigment caps become compressed into thin flakes that remain embedded in the horny scales which compose the sheath of the bill (Witschi and Woods, 1936).

Fig. 22. The capons: comb and wattles of the left one have been restored to the normal condition (right) by eighteen daily injections of androgenic hormone. From Koch (1938).

Yellow, orange, and red *carotenoids* are not synthesized by the bird but absorbed together with food stuffs and usually stored in considerable quantity in the liver and in egg yolks (Kritzler, 1942). It is not known by what mechanisms they become selectively acquired by certain structures —bills, feathers, scales of feet—and not by others. The following few examples probably still give only an incomplete listing of hormonal control types for seasonally changing, sex-dimorphic bill colors.

In the *house sparrow* (*Passer domesticus*) the bills of both sexes are a light brown during the eclipse season, particularly in September. In October and November many males develop blue or black bills which in December may bleach out again. This we consider an expression of an autumnal *mock breeding condition* which manifests itself also in increased activity and playfulness of the birds. In late December, but even more so in January, melanin production becomes copious. By February the bills have become jet black, almost without exception. This condition is maintained throughout the breeding season and may last until early August. Then a whitish ring appears around the base of upper and lower bills and within 2 weeks also the more heavily cornified parts toward the tip wear off their pigmented layer and the newer, unpigmented

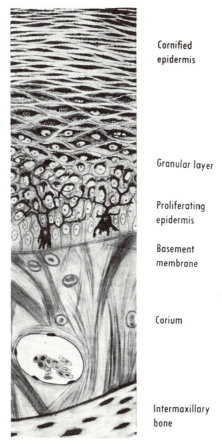

Cornified epidermis

Granular layer

Proliferating epidermis

Basement membrane

Corium

Intermaxillary bone

FIG. 23. Bill structure: Part of section through bill of house sparrow showing two melanophores supplying epidermis cells with melanin. From Witschi and Woods (1936).

stratum reaches the surface. Castration immediately stops pigment deposition and the bills assume permanently a light-ivory color (Keck, 1934). Injection of testosterone, androsterone, or dehydroandrosterone at adequate dosages promptly induces resumption of melanin production, even in birds that had been castrated as long as two years. On the other hand, progesterone and all natural and artificial estrogens produce no effects. This is of interest since also most females acquire blue or nearly black bills during the height of the breeding season and after androgen injections. The degree of reaction seems to depend on the relative abundance or scarcity of melanophores in the germinative layer. Their number is variable, but always below that of male bills. For assay purposes only males should be used (see Fig. 34).

African weaver finches of the genus *Euplectes* display an analogous seasonal sex dimorphism (Witschi, 1935c, 1955) (Frontispiece 2a, 2b, show the same male in breeding and eclipse seasons). It also is controlled by androgens, bills of castrates being white (Frontispiece 5a) and turning blue and black after injections of androgens (Frontispiece 5, b–d). The bill of females never was seen to turn darker than a light-brown horn color (Frontispiece 1c, 1d) except after injections of androgens.

In the *American indigo bunting* (*Passerina cyanea*) the bills of both males and females are about wheat color during their eclipse; castrates retain this color permanently. During the breeding season, or after injection of androgens in eclipse males, the upper bill turns black while the lower one becomes clear white except for a black center line. Male castrates, and to some extent also females, respond similarly. The obvious limitation of melanophore activity by androgens—here leading to pattern formation in the lower bill—becomes the main feature in some other instances. In the combassou (*Hypochera chalybeata*) the bill is brown in females and in males during eclipse, but white in males while in breeding condition. Castrates always have brown bills (Levi, 1936).

In the *common starling* (*Sturnus vulgaris*) the bills of both sexes are black during the eclipse and bright orange-yellow during the breeding season, though the females assume the yellow color almost a full month later than the males. Castration in both sexes leads to permanently black bills. Injections of androgens cause them to change to the yellow color, while progesterone, deoxycorticosterone, and all estrogens do not produce any effects. The yellow color is a carotenoid. Extractions show that it is present the year round, though yields are highest during the breeding season. In the starling the horn sheath of the bill grows rapidly from the base toward the tip. Consequently, assumption or disappearance of a new coloration always progresses in this same direction (Fig. 24).

A comparison of characteristic hormonal reactions of gonaducts and bills reveals some interesting features (Table V). Remarkable is the responsiveness of the oviducts to both estrogens and androgens and their failure to react on progesterone, whether administered alone or in combination with estrogens. The sparrow bill melanophore reaction seems to be the most sensitive biologic indicator for presence of traces of androgenic hormones.

Bill colors in *gulls* (*Larus ridibundus*: van Oordt and Junge, 1933; and *L. argentatus*: Boss, 1943) follow a pattern similar to that of the starling, seasonally as well as in their change from the juvenal to the adult condition.

The *masked weaver* (*Quelea quelea*) presents the only well-studied instance of control of seasonal bill colors by estrogenic hormones. Bills of males, castrates, and females in eclipse condition are blood-red (Frontispiece 4b). In females this color changes to a light yellow during the breeding season (Frontispiece 4a). The case is of particular interest because males never show the slightest tendency to change toward yellow. This sustains the impression, gained also from many other observations, that male birds produce only androgenic hormones, in

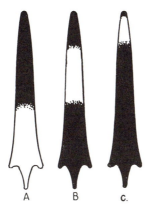

Fig. 24. Bill of female starling castrated on February 5th (northern hemisphere). a, distribution of black and yellow at time of operation; b, 47 days later; c, 80 days after castration. From Witschi and Miller (1938).

contrast to the females, which on study have always been found hormonally ambisexual.

Finally in the *paradise wydah* (*Steganura paradisea*) the bill colors show identical seasonal changes as in *Pyromelana*; however, the controlling hormone is not a steroid, but the luteinizing hormone (LH) of the pituitary (Witschi, 1955). The castrate male exhibits the same seasonal color changes as the intact. Injections of preparations containing the LH factor cause melanin production and darkening of bills in the eclipse season. The reactions of female bills have not yet been studied; they are bound to depend on the number of melanophores present and probably will show the same general type as in the male.

TABLE V

GONADUCTS AND BILLS OF SPARROWS AND STARLINGS:[a]
RESPONSE TO STEROID HORMONES[b]

Sex character	Testosterone propionate (μg.)	Estradiol (μg.)	Progesterone or deoxycorticosterone
Oviduct	60 (200)	0.03(0.1)	—
Vas deferens	5 (20)	—	—
Bill	0.2(1)	—	—

[a] Values for starlings in parentheses.
[b] Minimal dosages for positive reactions by systemic injections.

C. PLUMAGES

The possibilities of ornamental development of epidermal structures have been more abundantly exploited in birds than in any other class of vertebrates. Bird feathers have an artistic appeal so fascinating that they are borrowed for human adornment by fastidious fashion designers no less than by primitive savages. This appreciation has also affected the thinking of some biologists who tried to evaluate the survival value of the gorgeous displays in color and structure in Darwinian manner. The problem is still awaiting experimental investigation. The following

TABLE VI

BIRDS WITHOUT OBVIOUS SEASONAL CHANGE OF ADULT PLUMAGE TYPES

Species[a]	Male[b]	Female[b]
(1a) Chicken hawk (*Accipiter cooperi*)	H	H
(1b) Song sparrow (*Melospiza melodia*)	H	H
(7a) Leghorn fowl (*Gallus gallus*)	C	H
(7b) Hen-feathered chickens	H	H
(9) House sparrow (*Passer domesticus*)	C	H
(10) Pheasant (*Phasianus* sp.)	C	H
(11) Javanese quail (*Turnix pugnax*)	H	C
(4) Herring gull (*Larus argentatus*)	C	C
(12) Blue jay (*Cyanocitta cristata*)	C	C

[a] Numbers in parentheses indicate the sequence of discussion in Section II, C of text.
[b] H, hen plumage; C, cock plumage.

discussion attempts merely a classification of the many plumage types on the basis of known or assumed causal relationships.

Probably the modest *hen plumages* of brown, buff, and black which are essentially the same in the females of a great many birds, accipitrines, galli, anseres, and passerines (Frontispiece 1c, 3, 4a), represent the ancient prototype. On the other hand, the disparity of ornamental *cock plumages* even within closely related groups or single species (e.g. the ruff) discloses their relative evolutionary novelty.

Adherence to the terminology used here is mainly based on convention: hen and cock of the domestic chicken are, respectively, symbols of modesty and exuberance. However, exceptions and contradictions are legion. Even in chicken breeds such as Campines and Sebrights the male is "henfeathered." In many species both sexes wear hen plumages, in others both appear in cock plumages. Plumage types also may change seasonally. In the Tables VI and VII only the most characteristic distribution types are listed, omitting many minor variants; the left-hand numbers in parentheses indicate the sequence in which the various types are presented below.

TABLE VII

BIRDS WITH SEASONAL CHANGE OF ADULT PLUMAGES

Species[a]	Male[b]	Female[b]
(2) Ruff (*Philomachus pugnax*)	Ch	Hh
(3) Blackheaded gull (*Larus ridibundus*)	Ch	Ch
(5) Phalarope (*Phalaropus fulicarius*)	Hh	Ch
(6) Orange and yellow weaver finches (*Euplectes* spp.)	Ch	Hh
(8) Mallard duck (*Anas platyrhynchos*)	Hc	Hh

[a] Numbers in parentheses indicate the sequence of discussion in Section II, C of text.
[b] C and H designate nuptial cock and hen plumages; c and h, the eclipse plumages.

1a. Chicken hawk

The plumages of the adults are of the same pattern as that of juvenal birds. Most feathers are light brown or gray with dark streaks and bars. The same modest hen plumage is worn by all young, and most female, hawks. In some species the adult male shows a prevalence of slate gray and white. This is particularly the case in the marsh hawk (*Circus hudsonius*), possibly the most dimorphic member of the hawk family.

1b. Song sparrow

Juvenal and adult plumages are almost identical and of a very general hen type. Within the same genus *Melospiza*, the swamp sparrow (*M. georgiana*) acquires a somewhat more distinctive adult plumage, which is identical in both sexes.

Nothing is known about control mechanisms of these plumages. They remain the same throughout the entire year except for minor changes due to wear of the tips of some feathers. It is noteworthy that even the

Fig. 25. Juvenile plumages in hen and cock herring gulls, a, Control female (aged 90 days), in hen-type first summer plumage; b, male aged 46 days, injected with testosterone, changes prematurely to incomplete cock plumage (head),

slight beginnings of cock type differentiation may appear either in both or in one only of the sexes.

2. Ruff

This European bird of the family of snipes and sandpipers wears in the eclipse season an inconspicuous hen plumage. After the spring molt the male dons a very ornamental and fairly colorful plumage of which the "ruff" of long pectoral feathers is most spectacular. Castration in early winter prevents the assumption of the male plumage (van Oordt

FIG. 25 (*continued*). c, Control male herring gull at beginning of third year in transitory plumage; d, female, aged 2 years, injected with testosterone which has assumed adult (cock) plumage precociously. From Boss (1943).

and Junge, 1936). Therefore it is probable that testicular hormones, androgenic steroids, control its development. Considering that evidence of androgen production by ovaries of birds has already been observed in several species, it is noteworthy that also the female—the so-called reeve—puts on a rudimentary cock-type nuptial plumage. No ruff is formed, but neck and back assume colors similar to those of the male.

3. *Blackheaded gull*

Several species of gulls have a dark head during the breeding season, which changes to white after the fall molt. Even though the eclipse plumage is not exactly of hen type, it certainly is less ornamental than the nuptial garb and insofar it may be justified to speak of an alternation of cock and hen plumages. Van Oordt and Junge (1933) have shown also in this case that after castration of the male the cock plumage will no longer develop. No females were included in the experimental series, but the Dutch investigators believe that ovariectomy would similarly prevent cock plumage development in females.

4. *Herring gull*

In the experiments mentioned under 2 and 3, no hormone injections were included. Therefore the inference that androgenic steroids were inducing the assumption of cock plumages by the ruff and the laughing gull still lacks direct evidence. This, however, is available to some degree in the case of the herring gull. In this species the young for as long as three years wear hen-type juvenal plumages (Fig. 25) which are not caused to change by castration or by continuous injections of estrogenic steroids. However, administration of androgens induces the precocious assumption of the characteristic white and silver-gray adult plumages. It is not known whether castration would permanently prevent the development of a full adult plumage. Obviously, age factors, particularly changes of thyroid functions and metabolic rates, enter the picture; but certainly in this case a change from hen- to cock-type plumage is induced by androgenic hormones.

5. *Phalarope*

A strict counterpart to the ruff is played by the phalarope. Only females don bright cock plumages during the nuptial season. The males show but a minor seasonal change. The mechanism governing this change is unknown.

6. *Orange and yellow weaver finches*

While in cases of the ruff, blackheaded gull, and herring gull, the obvious relationship between gonadal recrudescence and the assumption of cock plumages apparently rests on the elaboration of androgenic hormones by the sex glands, the weavers exemplify an entirely different control mechanism.

Kept in the same laboratory with northern birds and under uniform feeding, the weavers get into breeding condition several months later, i.e. during the second half of the year (Fig. 26). This might seem to agree with the reported fact that in their tropical homelands they breed during or following the rainy season (Delacour and Edmond-Blanc.

1933; Chapin, 1954; Disney and Marshall, 1956) when cloudiness is apt to decrease intensity of illumination and day length. However, just as sparrows begin to show signs of activation in November and early December, when day length still declines, so weavers may regenerate nuptial-type feathers already early in June, before the days have reached maximal length. Obviously we are dealing with a complex but very characteristic situation pertaining to all weaver finch species observed

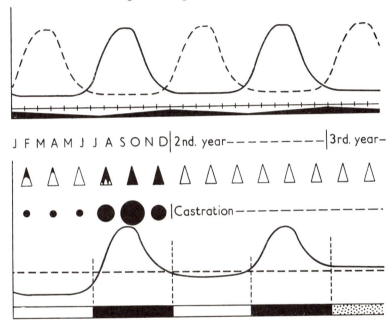

Fig. 26. Seasonal cycles of weaver finches in captivity at the Iowa Laboratories. *Upper graph*: Contrast of African (solid curve) and native (broken curve) behavior; under base line are indicated the respective changes in length of night and day. *Lower graph*: History of a male that was castrated at the end of the first year. From top to bottom are represented the changes in: bill color, testicular size, gonadotropin level, plumage (white-eclipse, black-nuptial).

in our laboratory. The gonads usually attain maximal size in September and October. The only egg spontaneously laid by an orange weaver was found on December 8, 1941. Usually ovaries regress in December without reaching the ovulation level of development. [On the other hand, some tropical birds adapt to the northern seasons. A Javanese quail (directly imported more than a year earlier) produced an egg on the 12th of May.] Considering that in the homeland of the weaver finches day lengths through the year vary only in terms of a few minutes, the conditions under which our birds were kept are distinctly atypical.

Experiments with varied factors like those started by Marshall and Disney (1957) will certainly serve to resolve the problem of factors controlling the reproductive periodicity of these birds. For the study of plumage cycles the relative time location of nuptial and eclipse seasons is irrelevant, since they are synchronized with the gonadal periodicity (Fig. 26).

In these finches the females constantly wear a typical hen plumage (Frontispiece 1c). It is molted once a year, at the end of the breeding season. The male changes seasonally between a nuptial cock plumage (Frontispiece 1a, 2a) and an ecliptic hen plumage (Frontispiece 1b, 2b). This necessitates a double molt. In addition to the complete postnuptial feather change, the males renew their "small plumage," i.e. practically

Fig. 27 Ovariectomized weaver (*Euplectes franciscanus*) which, since the operation, has changed plumages like a male. The bill, always white, indicates absence of androgens. This picture, taken twenty months after the operation, shows the bird in its second nuptial plumage.

all but the large feathers of wings and tail, also at the start of the breeding season, even preceding noticeable enlargement of the testes.

Castration does not alter the cycle of plumage changes of the males (Frontispiece 5a; Fig. 26). On the contrary, the same periodicity is also established in ovariectomized females (Fig. 27) (Witschi, 1935c; Levi, 1936). As in other birds, molting becomes irregular and almost continual after castration, but this does not interfere with the change between cock- and hen-feather production. Such facts suggested an interpretation which later was sustained by injection experiments. Since gonadal cycles themselves only reflect a primary hypophyseal periodicity, it was assumed that the plumages of the males and the castrates change in direct response to hypophyseal hormones. Apparently, in the normal female, development of a cock plumage is prevented by the early release of ovarian estrogens. Indeed estradiol and other gynogenic steroids, if injected into males while they should be putting on the plumage of the breeding season, prevent the differentiation of the cock plumage (Fig. 28). Later it was found that also androgens, in sufficiently large dosages, suppress the differentiation of cock-type plumages (Frontispiece 5b, c). These are not direct effects of the steroid hormones, for simultaneous injections of gonadotropin still result in typical breeding plumages (Frontispiece 5d). One must assume that the steroid hormones suppress the part of hypophyseal functions which induces cock feathering.

FIG. 28. Feathers of a male *Euplectes franciscanus*. During the breeding season the injection of estradiol for 6 days inhibits the cock-type dark pigmentation; the first feather had started regeneration before injection; the next five feathers during injections of the last two after injections. From Witschi (1936b).

From such experiences, what conclusions can be derived regarding the nature of the particular hypophyseal hormone that controls the appearance of the cock plumage? The fact that as little as one rat unit of pregnant mare serum produces the effect rules out any but the gonadotropins, particularly the thyrotropin (Witschi, 1955). Pregnant mare serum contains three biologically distinguishable gonad-stimulating principles: FSH, ICSH, and LH. Of these the follicle-stimulating hormone (FSH) is prevalent. However, it cannot be the determining factor since its production and release is blocked by estrogens only if they have reached a high concentration in the blood. Moreover, FSH is an essential factor for ovocyte growth and must be present in both sexes throughout the breeding season. Similarly the interstitial cell-stimulating hormone (ICSH), which is not a very potent fraction of pregnant mare serum, normally gives evidence of its presence in both sexes. By itself, or in combination with FSH, it does not induce the cock plumage reaction [extracts of men's urine (Segal, 1957)]. This points toward a third gonadotropin, namely the hormone that induces ovulation and, in mammals, luteinization of the ovarian follicles (LH). Often it appears closely combined with ICSH and the thyrotropic hormone (TSH), from both of which it is difficult to separate by biochemical means. Though its final characterization must await further biochemical work, it is quite clear that in the weaver finch the cock plumage is controlled by this third gonadotropin, probably LH, as defined above.

Castration, as is usual in birds, upsets the clear periodicity of molts; castrates almost always have incomplete plumages, some feather germs and half-grown feathers. Consequently their plumages often appear mixed, but the seasonal periodicity appears very clearly if one keeps a record of cock- and hen-type sprouting feathers. The injection of male hormones over periods of 10 days or longer restores a regular molt with replacement of a good plumage. As mentioned above, the latter is of the hen type; however, the male hormone has a mobilizing effect on the carotenoid stores in the liver and the new plumages are more or less brightly, but diffusely, dyed orange or red (Frontispiece 5b, c).

The *Euplectes* type of plumage control is widespread also among other finches, but only relatively few genera have been studied experimentally. At the Iowa laboratories the American indigo bunting (*Passerina cyanea*), the masked weaver or dioch (*Quelea quelea*; Frontispiece 4a, b) and the paradise wydah (*Steganura paradisea*; Frontispiece 3) have been examined in similar ways. Investigations bearing on the last-named species call for special caution since the bill color is controlled by the gonadotropin LH. Completeness of castration must therefore be ascertained at the end of an experiment by serial sectioning of upper kidney lobes. During the breeding season also the deferent ducts may be checked for eventual enlargement.

Indications of double cycles within one year have already been referred to. One usually is abortive ("mock breeding season"). Under the conditions in our Iowa laboratories some males of the large orange weaver (*Euplectes orix*) and particularly of the combassou (*Hypochera chalybeata*) assume again partial cock plumages after the postnuptial molt. Even first-year combassous that arrived in the juvenal hen plumage (brown bills) will after the first full nuptial cock plumage (white bills) acquire a mottled, only 40–60% hen-type, plumage. The first feathers changed may be brown (hen) colored, but soon dark-blue cock feathers appear again and the bills are mottled white and brown. Testes are largest in September and remain small during the incomplete eclipse (March–April).

Castration usually does not noticeably change the plumage reaction type, though it is among castrate *E. orix* that we have a few records of almost permanent cock plumages. On the other hand, in the paradise wydah the two longest tail feathers of the cock plumage often do not attain full length in complete castrates. This may be a consequence of the upset molting schedule rather than an indication of lowered hypophyseal activity.

The color of the feathers of the lower breast of *Euplectes* or of the subtail feathers of the paradise wydah is white in the hen plumage and black in the cock plumage (Fig. 29). The melanin responsible for the

FIG. 29. Subtail feathers of the paradise wydah (*Steganura paradisea*). The first (black) is the cock-nuptial type; the last (white) the eclipse and hen type. The four in the middle show the effect of two injections of pregnant mare serum (4 days apart) on regenerating hen-type feathers. From Witschi (1958).

latter is produced by epidermal melanophores. They are always present in the barbule-producing zone of the feather papilla (Fig. 30), but actively synthesize and inject melanin only if stimulated by LH. Since the reaction is elicited by very small injections, it serves to identify and quantitatively assay the luteinizing hormone in the so-called weaver

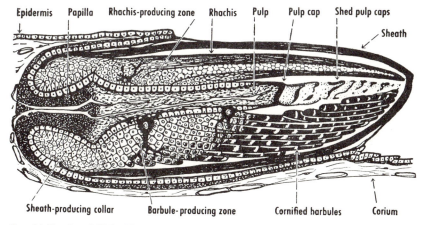

FIG. 30. Feather follicle. Three melnophores are supplying melanin to epidermal cells.

finch test. Feathers are plucked, and if on the fourth or fifth following day the test substance is injected into the breast muscle, it will produce a black or dark-brown bar across the regenerating feathers if LH in sufficient quantity was introduced. The white tips and bases serve as controls. In the wydah two bars may be produced by repeated injections (Fig. 29).

7a. Leghorn chicken

Even though the original red jungle fowl has a distinct but relatively short breeding season in spring, the male wears the cock plumage throughout the year. The domesticated Brown Leghorn race quite faithfully maintains the original plumage character. For centuries castration in both sexes has been practiced for commercial purposes, and the essential consequences were described and pictured in the *historia animalum* of 1555 by Konrad Gesner. However, scientific analysis dates only from the monographic publication of Goodale (1916). After complete castration the cock plumage is worn by poulards as well as by capons. Implantation of ovaries or injection of estrogens (Freud *et al.*, 1930; Juhn and Gustavson, 1930) into cocks and castrates causes hen feathering. Some seemingly not conforming responses eventually find their explanation on the same common basis. Ovariectomy after an initial period of cock feathering is often followed by reassumption of the hen plumage. In such cases examination of the gonad site reveals a compensatory growth of the right rudiment and sometimes also of remnants of the left ovary. While these nodules usually are of testicular type, the fact that in addition to androgens they produce also estrogens is indicated by the stimulated condition of the oviducts. Moreover, after complete removal of the gonadal regenerates, these poulards once more and now permanently don cock plumages (Domm, 1929). Another irregularity is exhibited by capons which were feminized by the implantation of ovaries. Complete hen plumages usually last only about one year. Then follows a gradual return to intermediate and finally completely cock-type plumages. This change is a consequence of the relative regression of cortical elements of the graft with consequent diminution of estrogen output. This in itself explains the plumage situation. The further observation that implanted capons usually have enlarged combs furnishes new evidence for androgenic activity of avian ovaries. It is of interest that even sterile seminal tubules may be found in the ovarian grafts (Benoit, 1926).

On the basis of these experiments investigators have usually considered the cock plumage as the neutral form and the hen plumage as its hormone (estrogen)-controlled variant. The weaver finch experiments (case 6, above) suggest another, possibly more adequate interpretation. All facts in both cases being the same except for the noncyclic nature of cock plumages in the leghorn, a single assumption will suffice to explain both on the same principles. If the chicken hypophysis has the tendency of releasing gonadotropin LH throughout the year in sufficient amounts to produce cock feathering, the hen plumage should form only whenever estrogens suppress the LH output. Complete ovariectomy, removing the source of estrogens, creates an unopposed LH condition with induction of cock plumages. That gonadotropic activity of the hypophysis has a tendency to spread over the entire year is evident in the prolonged periods of sexual activity and egg laying in commercial races.

FIG. 31. Effect of hypophysectomy on feather development in the brown leghorn male. a, normal breast feather; b, regenerated after operation. From Hill and Parkes (1935).

Hypophysectomy, which suggests itself as a crucial experiment, has not yet furnished a decisive answer. Its prevailing effect, so far as plumage is concerned, is one of hypothyroidism (Hill and Parkes, 1935). In other words, the effects on the plumage are very similar to those produced by thyroidectomy (Greenwood and Blyth, 1929; Blivaiss, 1947) or by administration of thiouracil (Domm and Blivaiss, 1948). In both sexes the melanin reaches only a red phase, barbule formation is deficient, and most feathers acquire a long, pointed and fringed shape (Fig. 31). Since hyperthyroidism produces exactly the opposite effects, namely increase of black colors, barbule formation, and blunt shape of feathers (Lillie and Juhn, 1932), it is evident that experiments on the determination of cock and hen feathering should be performed on animals with undisturbed or quantitatively restored thyroid function.

7b. Hen-feathered chickens

In fancy breeds of chickens a gene has appeared which prevents the development of the cock plumage in normal males. Originally it seems to have been associated with some small races, particularly Sebright bantams and Campines, but it can easily be bred into Leghorn and other races. Essentially the condition is brought about by a single dominant gene, though other genes may either enhance or dilute the effect. After castration both males and females of purebred hen-feathered stock assume the cock plumage (Morgan, 1919; Elliot, 1928; Fig. 32).

Fig. 32. Sebright cock (left) and Sebright capon (right). From Morgan (1919).

This effect is, however, reduced again to hen feathering through injections of either estrogens or androgens (Gallagher et al., 1933). The similarity of these reactions with those reported for castrated weaver finches in the breeding season (page 152) is quite obvious (Frontispiece 5b). The nature of the hen-feathering gene was fully elucidated by the skin-transplantation tests of Danforth (1930). Skin patches of hen-feathered males or females transplanted on a cock-feathered male still produce hen feathers; conversely, skin of cock-feathered males or females transplanted on a hen-feathered male regenerate cock feathers. Obviously the genetic difference concerns the threshold value of feather germs to react to the androgen level of cocks. Independent of genetic sex, the feather germs of mutant gene stock produce only hen feathers when under identical conditions feather germs of normal stock develop into cock feathers. The experiment also shows that the androgen levels in males of the two types of breeds are not essentially different. This latter point was confirmed by exchange transplantation of testes between Leghorn and Sebright bantam cockerels (Roxas, 1926). The plumage types remained unchanged, the endocrine potentialities of the two breeds being not noticeably different.

8. *Mallard duck*

Ducks are a most diverse group in regard to sexual plumages. Some species are dull-colored (hen type) in both sexes throughout the year; others have bright cock plumages in both sexes. Only the case of the mallard duck has been experimentally investigated. But conditions in this species are so peculiar that more work is still needed to complete the analysis. The female wears a hen-type plumage except for a bright white and blue *speculum*, which is a feature also of the cock plumage. Like all other ducks the mallard has two molts. The male or drake puts on the cock plumage after the postnuptial molt (September), when the testes already have regressed. This is therefore an eclipse plumage and is worn for about eight months. Then, at the height of the breeding season, there occurs the molt of the small plumage and the drake becomes hen-feathered. As Caridroit (1938) in one of his last studies has shown, the outside appearance is somewhat deceiving because the molts are delayed in regard to the underlying physiologic conditions that determine the plumage character. By systematic plucking and registry of the regenerating feathers it becomes clear that the hen plumage is hormonally induced by testes in full activity (Fig. 33). Like the Sebright cock, the mallard drake at the height of the breeding season is a hen-feathered male owing to testicular hormone production. However, in the drake the steroid output is seasonally limited and during an eight-month eclipse season does not check the hypophyseal component—probably LH—responsible for cock feathering.

Since these relationships were misunderstood before the work of Caridroit, the hen plumage of the drake is usually (even by Caridroit) designated as the eclipse plumage. This necessarily leads to confusion. Eclipse and breeding (or nuptial) seasons in the strict sense refer to the condition of sexual development, not necessarily to plumage character. A nuptial plumage may be either of cock type (weaver finches) or of hen type (Sebright, mallard).

Castration of male and female mallards leads to the permanent assumption of cock plumages. Caridroit was able to feminize presumptive male plumages by injections of estrogens, but not by androgens. These experiments will have to be extended, and the phenomenon of delayed response to testicular feminization deserves further study. If drakes are castrated in February or March, i.e. close to the breeding season, feathers will first begin to regenerate cock type, but later a transitory period of hen feathering may occur. Its onset is usually somewhat delayed in comparison with the hen-feathering period of intact males. In following years the same individuals will permanently produce cock feathers. It would seem that in the first year of castration a conditioning of the hypothalamic centers by testicular hormones may lead to specific reactions after a time lapse of one to three months.

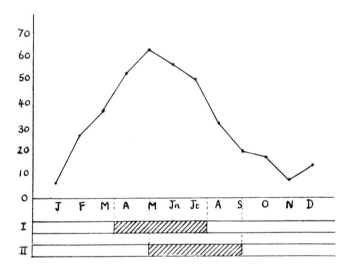

Fig. 33. Seasonal cycle of the male wild mallard duck. Curve of testicular weights. Below base line: I. Epoch during which regenerating feathers are of hen type; II. Normal hen-feather season, between first and second molts. From Caridroit (1938).

9. *House sparrow*

The female always wears a rather drab costume of gray and olive-brown. The male is more distinctive with slate-gray crown, black throat and lores, white cheeks and reddish-brown scapulars. The new winter plumage is relatively dull because many feathers, particularly those of the breast, have buff tips. When these wear off toward the breeding season, the plumage appears more resplendent. Keck (1934) has shown that these plumages cannot be modified by either castration or injection of steroid and hypophyseal hormones (Fig. 34). The sexual type of the feather is directly linked with hereditary constitution, ZO and ZZ, respectively. Nowikow has published similar results of castration experiments with the bullfinch (Nowikow, 1936) and the chaffinch (Nowikow,

1937) which are of particular interest because of the gynanders which were found in these species (Fig. 6). Unfortunately no observations on live gynanders are yet available. It should be desirable to follow them through their molts in the full course of a year. The Australian bower birds, which according to the descriptions of Marshall (1954) seem to have an extreme plumage dimorphism without seasonal change, and even the birds of paradise, may belong to this same group.

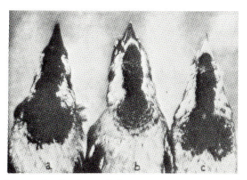

FIG. 34. Effect of castration in the male house sparrow. a, Normal control in breeding season; b, three weeks castrated; c, four months castrated.

FIG. 35. House sparrow. Throat feathers. From left: female, worn male (spring), new male (winter), and male regenerated during thyroxine administration. From Miller (1935).

Although sex hormones are without influence on the character of regenerating male and female feathers of the sparrow, thyroxine injections cause a radical change (Miller, 1939). Regenerating feathers of the male revert to the juvenal, which is close to the hen type (Fig. 35). Since Miller also showed that the thyroid-controlled metabolism of the sparrow male is not essentially different from that of the female (slightly higher in the breeding season), her observations do not explain the sexual dimorphism but probably bear on the interpretation of juvenal plumages.

M

10. Pheasants

The plumages of these birds seem to develop on the basis of a combination of principles that direct differentiations in the groups 6, 7 and 9. In weaver finches and in the domestic chicken the sexual dimorphism is entirely hormone-determined. After interchange of skin from homologous body regions between male and female chickens, the feathers of the graft assume fully the sex character of the host. Quite to the contrary, in the domestic sparrow and the bullfinch the dimorphism is determined by the genic sex constitution; hormones are unable to change the inherited sex type. The pheasants hold an intermediary position between these two clear-cut types. Danforth (1937), working with

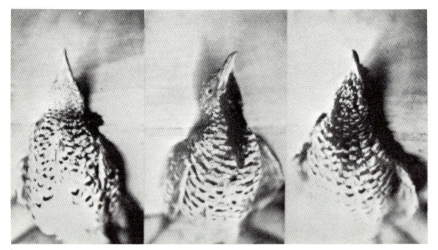

FIG. 36. Javanese quail (*Turnix pugnax*). From left: male, female in breeding season (worn tips of throat feathers), female entering breeding season (only partially worn tips).

various species of the genus *Phasianus* as well as with *Syrmaticus reevesi* (Reeve's pheasant), exchanged skin grafts between males and females and found that on the transplant grew feathers of two new, intermediary types. Collateral hormonal tests helped to bear out the conclusion that sex dimorphism in pheasant plumages is basically determined by the hereditary (chromosomal) sex constitution, but in part also by modifying endocrine factors. Estrogenic as well as androgenic hormones have a partially feminizing effect on the feather pattern (Koch, 1939). Other hormones obviously are also playing some role.

11. Javanese fighting quail

The female wears the cock plumage which is characterized by a black throat and upper breast (Fig. 36). The new feathers coming in after a molt have a broad buff fringe which wears off toward the breeding season. Otherwise neither female nor male plumages show any seasonal changes. Our limited observations and experiments seem to indicate that the control of the sexual difference is genetic, following the same pattern as in the domestic sparrow—except with sexes reversed.

12. *Blue jay*

In this bird culminates the evolutionary tendency of replacing the modest hen plumage with an ornamental garb. Not only both adult sexes but even the nestlings, as they acquire their first plumage, wear the same, i.e. the cock, plumage. Neither castration nor hormonal injections had a modifying influence (unpublished work by C. G. Danforth).

D. General Considerations

Our survey of types and control mechanisms of the dimorphism in secondary sex characters may at first sight present a confusing picture. However, the manifold correlations can be reduced by rational classification. Above all one can distinguish *perennial and seasonal sex characters*. Examples of the former are contained in Table VI. It is evident that among them are the species with full genic plumage control. By its very nature genic control extends over both eclipse and nuptial seasons. Occasionally, a semblance of seasonal change is secondarily established without involving a molt, simply by the discard of buff edges or spots by wear. Eclipse sparrow males and *Turnix* females appear almost as modest as their respective sex partners (Fig. 36). Without passing through a molt, in their old garb they appear more resplendent than ever at the approach of the breeding season. The case is even more striking for the starling, where both sexes acquire buff-tipped feathers after the postnuptial molt. Except for the color difference in the irises, sexes are barely distinguishable during fall and winter. In spring both lose the buff tips, but now the remaining base of the feathers is of a much more intense metallic luster in the male than in the female. Concordance between gonadal sex and dimorphic characteristics of this group rests on the common primary cause which is the *genic sex constitution*.

Turning now to the *seasonal sex characters*, one perceives that they are hormonally controlled. Again two types can be distinguished. One involves control by steroid hormones and depends on gonadal activity. The other type is controlled by *hypophyseal hormones* and therefore develops on a parallel track with the gonads, both depending on the seasonal activation of the hypophysis.

The phasianids might not seem to fit properly into the adopted classification. However, the Leghorn chicken, according to the above-proposed interpretation, is similar to the weaver finch type (6) except that its nuptial season extends over the entire year. Its plumages are hormonally controlled. The ancestral jungle fowl has not been sufficiently studied to provide desirable information concerning possible changes that may occur during the extended eclipse season. As to pheasants proper, which have a considerable gonadal rest or eclipse period, the work of Danforth makes it quite clear that this group is moving from hormonal toward genic control. Viewed this way it appears that hormonal control of seasonally developing secondary sex characters represents a relatively ancient evolutionary state and that direct genic determination is the stable type of control mechanism toward which further developments are moving.

The fact that hypophyseal cycles are controlled by way of the hypothalamus from tracts of the central nervous system opens up the way for one other type of control that works entirely at the neurophysiologic level. In a recent paper (Witschi, 1959), the probability was pointed out of such *associative control* in the release of some behaviorisms and particularly of the seasonal migrations to and from the breeding grounds.

References

Arnsdorf, R. E. (1947). Hen into rooster. *J. Heredity* **38**: 320.

Asmundson, V. S. (1941). Note on the sex ratio and mortality in turkeys. *Am. Naturalist* **75**: 389–393.

Benoit, J. (1923). Transformation expérimentale du sexe par ovariotomie précoce chez la poule domestique. *Compt. rend.* **177**: 1074–1077.

Benoit, J. (1926). Origine des cordons sexuels d'aspect male apparus dans des régénérats et des greffons ovariens chez la poule. *Compt. rend. soc. biol.* **94**: 875–877.

Benoit, J. (1936). Stimulation par la lumière de l'activité sexuelle chez le Canard et la Cane domestiques. *Bull. biol. France et Belg.* **70**: 487–533.

Blivaiss, B. B. (1947). Interrelations of thyroid and gonad in the development of plumage and other sex characters in brown leghorn roosters. *Physiol. Zoöl.* **20**: 67–107.

Boss, W. R. (1943). Hormonal determination of adult characters and sex behavior in herring gulls (*Larus argentatus*). *J. Exptl. Zool.* **94**: 181–209.

Boss, W. R., and Witschi, E. (1947). The permanent effects of early stilbestrol injections on the sex organs of the herring gull (*Larus argentatus*). *J. Exptl. Zool.* **105**: 61–77.

Bullough, W. S. (1942). The reproductive cycles of the British and continental races of the starling. *Phil. Trans. Roy. Soc. London* **B231**: 165–246.

Caridroit, F. (1938). Recherches expérimentales sur les rapports entre testicules, plumage d'éclipse et mues chez le Canard sauvage. *Sta. Zool. Wimereux* **13**: 47–67.

Cavazza, F. (1938). Ricerche sperimentali sui caratteri sessuali secondari ed il dimorfismo stagionale di *Anas boscas* L. *Arch. zool. exptl. et gen.* **79**: 409–461.

Chapin, J. P. (1954). "The Birds of the Belgian Congo," Pt. 4, ix, 846 pp. American Museum of Natural History, New York.

Cole, L. J., and Hollander, W. F. (1950). Hybrids of pigeon by ring dove. *Am. Naturalist* **84**: 275–307.

Crew, F. A. E. (1923). Sex reversal in the fowl. *Proc. Roy. Soc.* **95**: 256–278.

Crew, F. A. E. (1938). The sex ratio of the domestic fowl and its bearing upon the sex-linked lethal theory of differential mortality. *Proc. Roy. Soc. Edinburgh* **58**: 73–79.

Danforth, C. H. (1930). The nature of racial and sexual dimorphism in the plumage of campines and leghorns. *Biol. Generalis* **6**: 99–108.

Danforth, C. H. (1937). Artificial gynandromorphism and plumage in *Phasianus*. *J. Genet.* **34**: 497–505.

Dantchakoff, V. (1936). Histoire d'un coq. *Actualités sci. et ind.* **370** (VI): 1–42.

Dantchakoff, V. (1941). "Der Aufbau des Geschlechts beim hoeheren Wirbeltier." Fischer, Jena.

Delacour, J., and Edmond-Blanc, F. (1933). Monographie des veuves (revision des genres *Euplectes* et *Vidua*). *Oiseau: Rev. Fr. Ornith.* **3**: 519–562.

Disney, H. J. de S., and Marshall, A. J. (1956). A contribution to the breeding biology of the weaver finch *Quelea quelea* (Linnaeus) in East Africa. *Proc. Zool. Soc. London* **127**: 379–387.

Domm, L. V. (1929). The effects of bilateral ovariotomy in the brown leghorn fowl. *Biol. Bull.* **56**: 459–497.

Domm, L. V. (1939). Modifications in sex and secondary sexual characters in birds. *In* "Sex and Internal Secretions" (E. Allen, C. H. Danforth, and E. A. Doisy, eds.), 2nd ed., pp. 227–327. Williams & Wilkins, Baltimore, Maryland.

Domm, L. V., and Blivaiss, B. B. (1948). Plumage and other sex characters in thiouracil-treated brown leghorn fowl. *Am. J. Anat.* **82**: 167–202.

Domm, L. V., and Davis, D. E. (1948). The sexual behavior of intersexual domestic fowl. *Physiol. Zoöl.* **21**: 14–31.

Dunker, H. (1928). Genetik der Kanarienvoegel. *Bibliographia Genet.* **4**: 37–140.

Eliot, T. S. (1928). The influence of the gonads on the plumage of sebright bantams. *Physiol. Zoöl.* **1**: 286–324.

Foote. C. L. (1940). Influence of sex hormones on development and differentiation of gonads in *Ambystoma*. *Anat. Record (Suppl.)* **76**, 88.

Freud, J., de Jongh, S. E., and Laqueur, E. (1930). Über den Einfluss des weiblichen Sexualhormons Menformon auf das Federkleid der Vögel. *Arch. ges. Physiol. Pflüger's* **225**: 742–768.

Gallagher, T. F., and Koch, F. C. (1935). The quantitative assay for the testicular hormone by the comb-growth reaction; second communication. *J. Pharmacol. Exptl. Therap.* **55**: 97–117.

Gallagher, T. F., Domm, L. V., and Koch, F. C. (1933). The problem of hen-feathering in sebright cocks. *Proc. Am. Soc. Biol. Chem.* **8**: 47.

Goodale, H. D. (1916). Gonadectomy in relation to the secondary sexual characters of some domestic birds. Carnegie Inst. Wash., 52 pp.

Greenwood, A. W. (1935). Perforation of the oviduct in the domestic fowl. *Trans. Dynamics Develop.* **10**: 81–90.

Greenwood, A. W., and Blyth, J. S. S. (1929). An experimental analysis of the plumage of the brown leghorn fowl. *Proc. Roy. Soc. Edinburgh* **49**: 313–355.

Hicks, L. E. (1934). Individual and sexual variations in the European starling. *Bird-Banding* **5**: 103–118.

Hill, R. T., and Parkes, A. S. (1935). Hypophysectomy of birds. IV. Plumage changes in hypophysectomized fowls. V. Effect of replacement therapy on the gonads, accessory

M*

organs and secondary sexual characters of hypophysectomized fowls. *Proc. Roy. Soc.* **117**: 202–218.

Hollander, W. F. (1949). Bipaternity in pigeons. *J. Heredity* **40**: 271–277.

Hutt, F. B. (1949). "Genetics of the Fowl," xi and 590 pp. McGraw-Hill, New York.

Jaap, R. G. (1934). Alleles of the mallard plumage pattern in ducks. *Genetics* **19**: 310–322.

Jerome, F. N. (1953). Color inheritance in geese. *Poultry Sci.* **32**: 159–165.

Juhn, M., and Gustavson, R. G. (1930). The production of female genital subsidiary characters and plumage sex characters by injection of human placental hormone in fowl. *J. Exptl. Zool.* **56**: 31–61.

Keck, W. N. (1934). The control of the secondary sex characters in the English sparrow, *Passer domesticus* (Linnaeus). *J. Exptl. Zool.* **67**: 315–347.

Koch, E. L. (1939). Zur Frage der Beeinflussbarkeit der Gefiederfarben der Vögel. *Z. wiss. Zool.* (*A*) **152**: 27–82.

Koch, F. C. (1938). The chemistry and biology of male sex hormones. *Harvey Lectures Ser.* **33**: 205–236.

Kozelka, A. W., and Gallagher, T. F. (1934). Effect of male hormone extracts, theelin and theelol, on the chick embryo. *Proc. Soc. Exptl. Biol. Med.* **31**: 1143–1144.

Kritzler, H. (1942). The carotenoids of the display plumages of African bishop birds. *Anat. Record (Suppl.)* **84**: 78.

Lahr, E. L., and Riddle, O. (1945). Intersexuality in male embryos of pigeons. *Anat. Record* **92**: 425–431.

Landauer, W., and Landauer, A. B. (1931). Chick mortality and sex-ratio in the domestic fowl. *Am. Naturalist* **65**: 492–501.

Levi, G. (1936). Ricerche sperimentali sul determinismo dei caratteri sessuali secondari in passeracei dei gen. *Vidua* e *Euplectes*. *Riv. biol.* (*Perugia*) **20**: 61–79.

Lewis, L. B. (1946). A study of some effects of sex hormones upon the embryonic reproductive system of the white Pekin duck. *Physiol. Zoöl.* **19**: 282–329.

Lillie, F. R., and Juhn, M. (1932). Growth-rate and pattern in the individual feather. *Physiol. Zoöl.* **5**: 124–184.

Makino, S. (1951). "An Atlas of the Chromosome Numbers in Animals," 2nd ed., xxviii and 290 pp. Iowa State College Press, Ames, Iowa.

Makino, S., Udagawa, T., and Yamashina, Y. (1956). Karyotype studies in birds. 2: a comparative study of chromosomes in the *Columbidae*. *Caryologia* **8**: 275–293.

Marshall, A. J. (1954). "Bower-birds: their Displays and Breeding Cycles," x and 208 pp. Oxford Univ. Press, London and New York.

Marshall, A. J., and Baker, J. R. (1940). The sex-ratio in the wild animal populations of the New Hebrides. *Proc. Linnean Soc. N.S.Wales* **65**: 565–567.

Marshall, A. J., and Disney, H. J. de S. (1957). Experimental induction of the breeding season in a xerophilous bird. *Nature* **180**: 647–649.

Miller, D. S. (1935). Effects of thyroxin on plumage of the English sparrow, *Passer domesticus* (Linnaeus). *J. Exptl. Zool.* **71**: 293–309.

Miller, D. S. (1939). A study of the physiology of the sparrow thyroid. *J. Exptl. Zool.* **80**: 259–285.

Miller, R. A. (1938). Spermatogenesis in a sex-reversed female and in normal males of the domestic fowl. *Anat. Record* **70**: 155–189.

Morgan, T. H. (1919). The genetic and the operative evidence relating to secondary sexual characters. *Carnegie Inst. Wash. Publ. No.* **285**: 108 pp.

Moseley, H. R., and Landauer, W. (1949). Genetics and physiology of embryonic development. *In* "Fertility and Hatchability of Chicken and Turkey Eggs" (L. W. Taylor, ed.), pp. 244–337.

Newcomer, E. H. (1957). The mitotic chromosomes of the domestic fowl. *J. Heredity* 48: 227–234.

Nowikow, B. G. (1936). Die Analyse des Geschlechtsdimorphismus bei den Sperlingsvögeln (*Passeres*). II. *Biol. Zentr.* 56: 415–428.

Nowikow, B. G. (1937). Die Analyse des Geschlechtsdimorphismus bei den Sperlingsvögeln (*Passeres*). IV. *Acta Zool.* 18: 447–458.

Painter, T. S., and Cole, L. J. (1943). The genetic sex of pigeon-ring dove hybrids as determined by their sex chromosomes. *J. Morphol.* 72: 411–439.

Riddle, O. (1917). The theory of sex as stated in terms of results of studies on pigeons. *Science* 46: 19–24.

Riddle, O. (1927). The cyclical growth of the vesicula seminalis in birds is hormone controlled. *Anat. Record* 37: 1–11.

Riddle, O., Hollander, W. F., and Schooley, J. P. (1945). A race of hermaphrodite-producing pigeons. *Anat. Record* 92: 401–423.

Riley, G. M. (1938). Cytological studies on spermatogenesis in the house sparrow, *Passer domesticus*. *Cytologia* 9: 165–176.

Roxas, H. A. (1926). Gonad cross-transplantation in sebright and leghorn fowls. *J. Exptl. Zool.* 46: 63–117.

Scheib-Pfleger, D. (1955). Contribution biochimique à l'étude des processus de différenciation des canaux de Müller chez l'embryon de poulet. *Bull. biol. France et Belg.* 89: 403–490.

Segal, S. J. (1957). Response of weaver finch to chorionic gonadotrophin and hypophysial luteinizing hormone. *Science* 126: 1242–1243.

Stanley, A. J. (1937). Sexual dimorphism in North American hawks. *J. Morphol.* 61: 321–349.

Stanley, A. J., and Witschi, E. (1940). Germ cell migration in relation to asymmetry in the sex glands of hawks. *Anat. Record* 76: 329–342.

Steiner, H. (1932). Vererbungsstudien am Wellensittich Melopsittacus undulatus. *Arch. Julius Klaus-Stift. Vererbungsforsch. Sozialanthropol. u. Rassenhyg.* 7: 37–202.

Stoll, R. (1950). Sur la différenciation sexuelle de l'embryon de poulet. *Arch. anat. microscop. et morphol. exptl.* 39: 415–425.

van Oordt, G. J., and Junge, G. C. A. (1933). Der Einfluss der Kastration bei männlichen Lachmöwen (*Larus ridibundus* L.) *Wilhelm Roux' Arch. Entwicklungsmech. Organ.* 128: 165–180.

van Oordt, G. J., and Junge, G. C. A. (1936). Der Einfluss der Kastration auf männliche Kampfläufer (*Philomachus pugnax*). *Wilhelm Roux' Arch. Entwicklungsmech. Organ.* 134: 112–121.

Willier, B. H. (1942). Hormonal control of embryonic differentiation in birds. *Cold Spring Harbor Symposia Quant. Biol.* 10: 135–144.

Witschi, E. (1929). Rudimentary hermaphroditism and Y chromosome in *Rana temporaria*. *J. Exptl. Zool.* 54: 157–223.

Witschi, E. (1935a). Origin of asymmetry in the reproductive systems of birds. *Am. J. Anat.* 56: 119–141.

Witschi, E. (1935b). Die Amphisexualitaet der embryonalen Keimdrusen des Haussperlings *Passer domesticus* (Linnaeus). *Biol. Zentr.* 55: 168–174.

Witschi, E. (1935c). Seasonal sex characters in birds and their hormonal control. *Wilson Bull.* 47: 177–188.

Witschi, E. (1936a). Secondary sex characters in birds and their bearing on the theory of evolution. *Scientia* 60: 262–270.

Witschi, E. (1936b). Effect of gonadotropic and estrogenic hormones on regenerating feathers of weaver finches (*Pyromelana franciscana*). *Proc. Soc. Exptl. Biol. Med.* **35**: 484–489.

Witschi, E. (1945). Quantitative studies on the seasonal development of the deferent ducts in passerine birds. *J. Exptl. Zool.* **100**: 549–564.

Witschi, E. (1955). Vertebrate gonadotrophins. *Mem. Soc. Endocrinol.* **4**: 149–165.

Witschi, E. (1956). "Development of Vertebrates," xvi and 588 pp. Saunders, Philadelphia.

Witschi, E. (1959). Endocrine basis of reproductive adaptations in birds. I. Seasonal cycles. *In* "Comparative Endocrinology" (A. Gorbman, ed.) pp. 517–523. John Wiley and Sons, New York.

Witschi, E., and Fugo, N. W. (1940). Response of sex characters of the adult female starling to synthetic hormones. *Proc. Soc. Exptl. Biol. Med.* **45**: 10–14.

Witschi, E., and Miller, R. A. (1938). Ambisexuality in the female starling. *J. Exptl. Zool.* **79**: 475–487.

Witschi, E., and Woods, R. P. (1936). The bill of the sparrow as an indicator for the male sex hormone. II. Structural basis. *J. Exptl. Zool.* **73**: 445–459.

Wolff, Em. (1950). La différenciation sexuelle normale et le conditionnement hormonal des caractères sexuels somatiques précoces, tubercule génital et syrinx, chez l'embryon de Canard. *Bull. biol. France et Belg.* **84**: 119–193.

Wolff, Et. (1950). Le rôle des hormones embryonnaires dans la différenciation sexuelle des oiseaux. *Arch. anat. microscop. et morphol. exptl.* **39**: 426–450.

Wolff, Et. (1952). La culture d'organes embryonnaires *in vitro*. *Rev. sci.* **90**: 189–198.

Wolff, Et., and Wolff, Em. (1949). Application de la méthode de castration à l'embryon de canard: sur deux tests de l'activité précoce des gonades embryonnaires, la syrinx et le tubercule génital. *Compt. rend. soc. biol.* **143**: 529–531.

Wolff, Et., and Wolff, Em. (1951). The effects of castration on bird embryos. *J. Exptl. Zool.* **116**: 59–98.

Wolff, Et., Strudel, G., and Wolff, Em. (1949). L'action des hormones androgènes sur la différenciation sexuelle des embryons de poulets. *Arch. anat. histol. et embryol.* **31**: 237–310.

Explanation of Frontispiece

FIG. 1. Skins of *Euplectes pyromelana*. *a*, Male in September (cock plumage, black bill); *b*, male in February (hen plumage, light bill); *c*, female; *d*, female with positive LH reaction on regenerated left breast feathers, after injection of 15 mg bull hypophysis.

FIG. 2. Male of *Euplectes afra*. *a*, in July (cock plumage); *b*, in January (hen plumage).

FIG. 3. *Steganura paradisea*. Below: female, light bill; centre: male in cock plumage, black bill (August); top: male 2 years after total castration, in second cock plumage (black bill) after operation (photographed in December).

FIG. 4. Females of *Quelea quelea*. *a*, Control during breeding season, in hen plumage and with yellow bill; *b*, ovariectomized female during breeding season, in cock plumage, with red bill.

FIG. 5. Castrated males of *Euplectes pyromelana* photographed during the breeding season (fall); *a*, untreated, with new cock plumage and white bill; *b*, *c*, injected with testosterone and androsterone respectively, with black bills but new hen plumage (more carotenoid pigment than usual); *d*, injected with testosterone and pregnant mare's serum; new cock plumage and black bill.

CHAPTER XVIII

Reproduction

A. J. MARSHALL

I. Introduction

The reproductive system of birds repeats the basic vertebrate pattern of neuroendocrine relationships between the environment, central nervous system, adenohypophysis, and the gonads and the other target organs. Likewise, the primary organs of sex, the testes and the generally unilateral ovary, subserve the dual functions of gametogenesis and sex hormone production first seen, among living animals, in the jawless Agnatha, a fishlike stock that probably first appeared in Ordovician time, which ended some 330 million years ago.

With an increase in size, and the accompanying elaboration of the nervous and blood vascular systems in the earlier provertebrate, there came the specialization of suitably placed tissues into secretory components and the concomitant evolution of tissue products which began to flow through the blood stream as hormones. The evolution of the endocrine system has involved the differentiation of chemical substances and special means of producing them on the one hand, and specific tissue responses on the other. The evolution of birds, and the production of display and recognition plumes, wattles, elaborate behavior patterns (as well as the calcium-shelled avian egg), led to further extensions of the functions of the reproduction hormones. However, it must not be thought that the hormone is simply a "key" to "unlock" a response.

Many tissue reactions require a plurality of hormonal influences. Further, alien substances will sometimes bring about endocrine effects, e.g. the advent of comb growth and spermatogenesis after the administration of sulfonamide in chicken disease (Asplin and Boyland, 1947).

Brief discussions concerning the ontogeny and phylogenetic variations of the testicular network and gonoducts will be found in Goodrich (1930), Grassé (1950), and other authors. The internal network of testicular structures is basically, but by no means exactly, the same in all vertebrates. For internal variations, see Hoar (1957). In birds the anterior end of the Wolffian or mesonephric duct, and the contiguous mesonephros, together contribute to the formation of the epididymis, and the lower parts of the duct become the vas deferens (page 198).

In the female, the right ovary almost always remains vestigial in all families except Raptores. Birds fall into the general tetrapod pattern in which the Müllerian ducts persist and function as oviducts. The ovarian eggs are extruded into the splanchnocoele and pass from there into the wide anterior ostium abdominale or Müllerian funnel. In birds the left oviduct becomes remarkably diversified in correspondence with the plurality of functions associated with the final stages of the formation of the complicated avian egg (see page 203). The gonoducts of both sexes (as well as the alimentary canal) discharge into the cloaca, the terminal chamber that is retained by the jawless Agnatha and all gnathostomes (jawed vertebrates) except a few specialized bony fishes and "higher" mammals. Unlike those of mammals, the remaining accessory genitalia are otherwise relatively simple, though what may be a scrotal analog occurs in at least some groups (page 201). Each vas deferens transmits spermatozoa into the urodael chamber of the cloaca through an erectile papilla situated near the minute opening of the ureter of that particular side (see Fig. 6, page 342, Volume I).

In the ectoderm of the ventral wall of the cloaca there arises during embryonic life a genital tubercle. This becomes vestigial in most species: it persists long enough in newly hatched male domestic chicks to permit "sexing" with an accuracy of about 95%. The tubercle develops as a functional intromittent structure in Anseriformes and the so-called "ratites." In these, the organ consists of an upper corpus spongiosum and a lower corpus fibrosum. Together these form a substantial thickening in which a dorsal groove serves for the transmission of spermatozoa. The distal end is invaginated, in the position of rest, by an elastic ligament. The structure is very like that of crocodilians and turtles, and in both running birds and ducks there persists the female homolog, the clitorus.

Insemination in all birds is brought about by the eversion and apposition of the proctodea: the spermatozoa are discharged directly into the female urodeum and thence find their way through the genital papilla into the left oviduct. It is interesting, and not surprising, that the Aves, the only essentially volant chordate group, are likewise the only jawed animals in which viviparity has apparently never arisen.

II. The Anterior Pituitary

A. General Structure

The hypophysis, both neural and epithelial in origin, lies below the hypothalamus, with which it is connected by a prominent hypophyseal portal system (Fig. 2, and Fig. 2, Chapter XVI, page 91). The blood flows from brain to gland. It is no fortuitous happening that a gland of such diverse regulatory function has arisen in this particular situation. The pituitary is ideally sited to receive stimuli—both neural and humoral—from the central nervous system. The morphology of the neuroglandular relationships in birds has been described in detail by Rahn and Painter (1941) and Wingstrand (1951); and Benoit and associates (e.g. Benoit and Assenmacher, 1951, 1953, 1955) and Oksche, et al. (1959) have made lengthy physiological contributions to the subject (see also Chapter XVI). Pickford and Atz (1957) have given a comprehensive account of the region in the "lower" vertebrates.

B. Control of the Anterior Pituitary

Experimental work with birds appears to substantiate the concept of Green and Harris (1947), and Harris (1948), who, working with other groups, suggested that a hypothalamic neurohumour flowed down the hypophyseal portal system and activated the secretory elements of the adenohypophysis. Benoit and Assenmacher (1953) have summarized much of the early work concerning birds. More recently, Shirley and Nalbandov (1956) have described the complete transection of the hypophyseal stalk of laying domestic hens and a resultant quick loss of body weight and complete atrophy of ovary, oviduct, and comb. Thus, in regard to gonad function, a condition closely resembling that resulting from hypophysectomy was produced. However, stalk section did not significantly alter the secretory rate of either thyrotropic or adrenotropic hormones (as judged by the normal histology and weight of the relevant target glands) such as occurs after hypophysectomy. Shirley and Nalbandov's data tend to support the contention that the rate of secretion and release of gonadotropins is governed by neurosecretions transmitted by the hypophyseal portal system.

Nevertheless, the extent to which the release of gonadotropins is controlled by neural and hormonal influences is still undecided. Among wild birds the onset of unpropitious environmental circumstances may reflexly stop ovulation even after the first eggs of a clutch have been laid (Chapter XXI). In the domestic hen, too, ovulation is reflexly inhibited. Thus it was shown by Huston and Nalbandov (1953) that the presence of an irritant (such as a loop of thread) in the oviduct of laying birds suppressed ovulation in the great majority of cases. Yet there was no reduction in ovarian, oviducal, or comb dimensions for as long as 25 days. Further, when progesterone, or gonadotropin containing the luteinizing hormone (LH), was injected into such hens, ovulations occurred for the duration of the treatment. It was suggested therefore, that the presence of such an irritant prevents the secretion of amounts of LH sufficient to cause ovulation, but does not depress secretion to a level that is insufficient to assure normal androgen secretion from the ovary. Further, the above-mentioned authors suggested that the presence of the loop does not prevent the secretion of normal amounts of follicle-stimulating hormone (FSH), since the ovary remained of normal size. For approximately 25 days the ovary contained follicles of ovulatory size (30 mm. or over) and in the same numbers that would be present in intact hens. Such follicles continue to secrete estrogen at normal levels: thus the oviduct in operated hens did not hypotrophy and was still capable of secreting albumen. Such a neurogenic system as that suggested above may serve to synchronize ovulation with the other events of the cycle.

The possibility that the neural mechanism which excites the anterior pituitary to secretory activity may be influenced by an ovarian hormone has been suggested (see Fraps, 1955). Fraps believes that an "excitation hormone," possibly a progestin, from the maturing follicle may initiate the ultimate release of an ovulation-inducing hormone (OIH) from the anterior lobe.

Recent discussions have led to doubt concerning the validity of the traditional concept of adenohypophyseal *inhibition* by secreted sex hormones. Thus, Jungck *et al.* (1947) believe that *physiological* amounts of sex hormones do not in fact suppress gonadotropin output. These authors suggested that the increase in gonadotropins after castration is due to the absence of the target organ (and consequent metabolic failure) and to the accumulation of gonadotropin in the adenohypophysis. Breneman (1955) produced data in partial support of this view.

There is little doubt that tactile impressions from the ventral surface of the sitting female are influential in the determination of clutch size by way of the central nervous system and anterior pituitary (Taibel,

1928; F. H. A. Marshall, 1936; and see also page 178 in regard to visual impressions and prolactin secretion.)

It has sometimes been suggested that the anterior pituitary may function rhythmically and independently of environmental stimuli. There is no evidence whatever that such is the case. There is unequivocal evidence of the existence of an internal rhythm of reproduction (see Chapter XXI). In this the respective roles of the central nervous system and adenohypophysis in this cycle have not been determined; but in any case, when birds are removed from their natural environment, the normal seasonal cyclical peaks of gonad development drift out of phase (Benoit et al., 1956) and, in at least one wild species, full gametogenesis will not always occur (Marshall and Serventy, 1959). In wild birds the environment is vitally important as the ultimate breeding regulator.

C. Secretory Components and Their Products

The avian pars distalis appears to be bipartite, containing a cephalic "lobe" and a caudal "lobe." The posterior lobe is said to be influential in the processes of ovulation. No pars intermedia (Rahn and Painter, 1941; Wingstrand (1951)) occurs, but it may be mentioned that the pars distalis (and especially its cephalic, as opposed to its caudal, part) elaborates an intermedin-like substance capable of causing melanophore expansion in the hypophysectomized lizard *Anolis* (Kleinholtz and Rahn, 1940).

Rahn and Painter demonstrated two distinct areas of the avian adenohypophysis in eighteen different species. For two species only, the domestic fowl and pigeon, is detailed cytological information available. As would be expected, the two show a close similarity. Like the mammalian pituitary, the avian organ contains chromophobe and chromophile ("acidophile" and "basophile") cells. It seems to be established that the basophiles secrete gonadotropins (Schooley and Riddle, 1938). Payne has carried out a long series of painstaking fundamental investigations on pituitary cytology. Payne (1946) described two sorts of acidophiles (α^1 and α^2). Of the two principal acidophiles, α^1 cells occupy the caudal part of the lobe and α^2 cells the cephalic region. The former are said to resemble the α cells of mammals. A type with basophilic properties is the T cell of Payne (1944) which is possibly concerned with thyroid function. During the period of broodiness there is a striking reduction in alpha and beta (basophile) cells together with an extraordinary upsurge of another type, the 'broody cell' (Payne, 1943). This is distinct from both basophiles and acidophiles.

It is perhaps still uncertain which cell type elaborates prolactin.

Schooley and Riddle (1938) showed that a rapid increase in body weight (probably under the influence of prolactin, see page 178) occurred in pigeons at an early stage when pituitary eosinophiles are differentiated and seemingly active, but before the basophiles (generally held to secrete gonadotropins) are mature. The eosinophiles (held probably to produce prolactin) differentiate during the last part of embryonic life, and prolactin is demonstrably present in the anterior lobe at an age when gonadotropins cannot be detected by implantation techniques. Payne (1943) however has suggested that, in the female chick, apparently functional basophiles occur at 10 days and that in males they are even more prolific. Payne appeared to have localized eosinophilic components ("broody cells") as the source of prolactin. When hens periodically become broody, basophiles almost disappear and large numbers of small acidophilic "broody cells" (of Payne) arise. Yasuda (1953), however, has since claimed that prolactin is elaborated by carminophilic eosinophiles and that the broody cells of Payne are chromophobes and unconnected with such a function.

Breneman (1944) has shown that in domestic fowl the anterior pituitary weight increased more than nine times, and the testicular weight by more than eighty times between the date of hatching and an age of 90 days. Breneman believed that pituitary secretion is initiated perhaps as early as the fifth day and certainly by the fifteenth day after hatching. Thus, it would seem that at a very early age there arises the *potential* for gonadotropic stimulation. This is in agreement with the numerous reports of sexual precocity in young birds of widely unrelated groups.

There is a general similarity between avian and mammalian gonadotropins. Nevertheless, Nalbandov *et al.* (1951) have suggested that there occurs an avian interstitial cell-stimulating hormone (ICSH or LH) which is appreciably different from its mammalian homolog, or that an additional "avian ICSH" occurs in domestic fowl. They produced results suggesting that an avian LH may possess properties not shared by its mammalian homolog. Again there is some evidence that the avian seminiferous tubules do not respond well to pregnant mares' serum even though, of course, this contains the principles (FSH and LH) that have been proved to be present in birds (Witschi, 1935, 1937; Benoit, 1937; and Leonard, 1937).

Further evidence of an apparent difference between avian and mammalian gonadotropins has been obtained from experiments with embryos. The right ovary of the domestic fowl stops growing at about the ninth day of incubation. Sex differentiation is then about complete. The right gonad now regresses and only a vestige remains at hatching time. Hypophysectomy depresses the weight and secretory capacity of hypertrophied testicular rudiments. It would seem that hypophyseal gonadotropins are capable of stimulating the rudiments. Kornfield and Nalbandov (1954), however, failed to accelerate the growth of compensatory gonads, or to maintain them in hypophysectomized poulards by the use of mammalian gonadotropins. Avian gonadotropins, on the other hand, are effective.

Das and Nalbandov (1955), too, showed that follicle (as distinct from medullary) growth in females is obtainable after the administration of avian pituitary extracts, but not by the use of mammalian gonadotropin. In pullets nearing sexual maturity, however, exogenous mammalian gonadotropins did induce follicle development. On the other hand, both avian and mammalian gonadotropins activated the ovarian medulla and produced an increase of total ovarian weight and comb growth. The evidence suggested a relative inadequacy in the mammalian homolog to induce follicle maturation. Again there appeared to be a distinct qualitative difference between the avian and mammalian gonadotropic complexes.

1. *Hypophysectomy and Its Effects*

Parkes and Marshall (1960) have reviewed briefly the early attempts to hypophysectomize birds and the reported results. Probably the most successful technique is the parapharyngeal approach developed by Schooley (1939). This avoids the Eustachian tubes and gives access to both "lobes," either of which can be removed (without injury to the brain) by aspiration with a fine cannula. Schooley reported an operative mortality of less than 2%, but there followed a decrease in food and fluid intake, loss of weight and sometimes convulsions resembling those arising from hypoglycemic shock. Sick birds are best treated with an injection of whole anterior pituitary extract. Generally the operated birds live for more than a year. For anesthetization Schooley recommends Nembutal introduced intravenously (radial vein) at a level of 25 mg. per kilogram body weight.

Hill and Parkes (1934) found that hypophysectomized domestic cockerels suffered rapid testis hypotrophy, the maximum drop in weight occurring at the end of the fifth week. Within 2 weeks the tubules lacked spermatozoa and by the end of 5 weeks contained only spermatogonia and a few Sertoli cells. These changes were accompanied by a marked increase in the amount of intertubular tissue. Comparable results have been obtained in other species. As would be expected, there was a concurrent decrease in the size of the accessory reproductive organs and changes in the dependent secondary sexual characters. The vasa deferentia were atrophic 5 weeks after the operation and the comb and wattles showed a continuous decline that started within a few days and continued until the comb was the size of that of a bird caponized when adult. When the rate of comb atrophy after castration and hypophysectomy are compared, there is a clear suggestion that the endocrine activity of the testis stops immediately on removal of the pituitary. Benoit (1938) showed that removal of the pituitary of domestic drakes prevented the customary response to artificial illumination. Several others have described the gross effects of hypophysectomy on gonad weight and gametogenesis.

It is of particular interest that hypophysectomy abruptly provokes a testicular response that occurs naturally at the end of the spermatogenetic cycle of seasonally breeding birds. Thus, the removal from the cockerel or pigeon (Coombs and Marshall, 1956; Lofts and Marshall, 1958) of the adenohypophysis leads to a testis metamorphosis, including tubule steatogenesis and accompanying cholesterol production comparable with that occurring sharply and naturally at the conclusion of the breeding season (and spermatogenesis) in wild birds (Fig. 6, page 185).

Meanwhile, a new interstitium rhythmically arises. There is, of course, no suggestion that the new interstitium can *secrete* fully in the absence of gonadotropin. On the other hand, the cholesterol-positive tubule lipids gradually disappear in their absence. Thus, at about 60 days after hypophysectomy the "postnuptial" cholesterol begins to disappear from the tubules of hypophysectomized domestic cockerels. This process is hastened by the administration of FSH.

In general, removal of the anterior pituitary reduces behavioral reactions associated with androgen and estrogen secretion, but Collias (1944) has reported that hypophysectomized male pigeons sometimes remain extremely aggressive. It will be recalled, too, that combat occurs between male pigeons congenitally devoid of testes. In regard to the female, Hill and Parkes (1934) found that the ovary, oviduct, and comb of hypophysectomized laying hens reduced to a condition similar to that found in nonlaying birds.

2. *Gonadotropins*

The avian anterior pituitary secretes both FSH and LH (ICSH) (Domm and van Dyke, 1932; Witschi, 1935, 1937; Benoit, 1937; Leonard, 1937). The injection of either estrogen or androgen reduces their secretion (Kumaran and Turner, 1949; Nalbandov and Baum, 1948).

In regard to the testis, Pfeiffer and Kirschbaum (1943) showed that administration of pregnant mare serum (PMS) to males caused the advancement of both tubules and interstitium. In domestic chicks there was a marked response to PMS in the interstitium, and in the ovary luteinized "interstitial cells" arose. The Leydig cells of chicks injected by Taber (1949) with PMS, FSH, and LH developed a granular cytoplasm while those of controls, during the first month, retained cells filled with "large lipoidal droplets". Thus Leydig hyperplasia was accompanied by comb growth which was not primarily correlated with testis weight or with the degree of tubule advancement. Of the principles injected, LH had the least effect on the tubules and on testicular weight. Comb growth was stimulated to a less degree by FSH than by LH and PMS. Domm and van Dyke (1932) found that male domestic chicks injected with anterior pituitary extracts began to crow when 9 days old and exhibited the treading reflex when 13 days old. There is abundant evidence then, that birds follow the general vertebrate pattern (in so far as the various classes have been investigated) of dual stimulation of the gametogenetic and endocrine elements of the testis by FSH and LH (ICSH), respectively.

That greater gonadotropic stimulation is required for the ovaries than for the testes was suggested by the work of Kirschbaum *et al.* (1939) on the house sparrow (*Passer domesticus*). Under a photoperiod at which ovaries remained comparatively inactive, immature testes implanted into the same birds produced spermatozoa within a couple of weeks although the oocytes stayed relatively small. Witschi (1935) observed that the ovary of juveniles does not respond strongly to the administration of gonadotropin. He showed, too, that although in adults the ovary would respond throughout the year, the reaction was more profound close to the period of reproduction. Certainly, under natural conditions, male birds quickly outstrip females in gametogenetic development, even though both sexes of at least some species *begin* their seasonal cycle under the same day length (Marshall, 1952a, 1955). Environmental factors (other than day length) provide the end stimuli that finally accelerate the female cycle and so bring the two sexes into synchronization and allow actual reproduction (see Chapter XXI). The experimental administration of an anterior pituitary preparation causes the deposition of premigratory fat in passerine birds, as does the implantation of testosterone (Schildmacher and Steubing, 1952).

3. *Prolactin*

The pioneer work of Riddle and his associates directed a great deal of attention to the adenohypophyseal lactogenic hormone prolactin. In hypophysectomized pigeons, prolactin administration produces a generalized tropic response (Schooley *et al.*, 1941; Riddle, 1947). A specific somatotropic hormone has not been proved to exist in birds. Removal of the anterior pituitary stops the growth of young birds, and injections of purified prolactin leads to the development of a "super normal" (by 20 to 35%) body weight.

Prolactin bioassay methods based on the growth response of the crop gland have been discussed by Riddle and Bates (1939). In both sexes prolactin is responsible for a plurality of vital reproductive processes. If the ovary is in active condition, prolactin injections lead to broodiness. Pigeons become broody naturally when the second egg is laid and ovulation ceases. Collias (1946, 1950) has shown that if domestic hens are put with *chicks* they become broody, but only if they had previously laid or were injected with sex hormone.

In fowls, gonadotropins and thyrotropins do not induce broodiness (Riddle *et al.*, 1935), nor does estrone (Riddle and Lahr, 1944). Small quantities of androgen prevent the broodiness that otherwise follows prolactin administration (Nalbandov, 1945). On the other hand, Riddle and Lahr found that birds treated with progesterone, deoxycorticosterone acetate, and testosterone propionate became broody in 43 of 62 tests. Such treatment was ineffectual in young, isolated, and unpaired birds. The suggestion was made that the implants induced a release of prolactin from the birds' own anterior pituitary gland.

Prolactin is primarily responsible for the proliferation of the specialized epithelium that produces "pigeon's-milk," a proteinaceous (13.3–18.8%) and fatty (6.9–12.7%) material (see Needham, 1950) on which the squabs of pigeons and doves are fed (Riddle *et al.*, 1932, 1933; and others). During the second half of the incubation period the crop of both sexes enlarges. Crop milk and cast-off epithelial cells are available for discharge and consumption by the time the squabs appear. The female dove produces more "milk" than the male (Meites and Turner, 1947) and is said to spend about three times longer than the male in incubation and brooding activity (Lehrman, 1955). As small an amount as 0.1 mg. of prolactin, injected intracutaneously in the crop sac area, produces a pronounced reaction within 48 hours (Lyons and Page, 1935). As would be expected, hypophysectomy prevents the development of the crop gland; and sex hormones do not re-establish epithelial activity (Collias, 1946). Remarkable evidence of neural and hormonal integration in the production of pigeons' milk (see also later remarks concerning the onset of broodiness) is presented by Cole (1933) and Patel (1936). These authors showed that male doves separated from females produce "milk" only if they are allowed to *see* brooding females.

The injection of prolactin is followed by the appearance of certain forms of behavior and the suppression of others. For example the administration of prolactin inhibits cooing, an aspect of courtship behavior (Lehrman, 1955). It seems probable that the inhibition of sexual behavior of various kinds is due to suppression of gonadal activity by prolactin rather than a direct effect. Riddle (1935) showed that prolactin inhibited egg laying and often led to incubation. Riddle *et al.* (1935) reported that prolactin induced broodiness and maternal behavior only in the actively ovulating female, although incomplete activity was produced in sexually inactive females and cocks. Burrows and Byerly (1936) implanted single fowl pituitaries over the crop glands of 8–10-weeks-old pigeons and reported a prolactin-like reaction in many birds. Pituitaries from broody hens caused a greater crop gland reaction than those of laying females. Pituitaries from cocks stimulated a reaction about equal to, or slightly less than, those from laying hens. Nalbandov (1945) induced maternal tendencies, including broodiness, in cocks by the injection of prolactin, but prolactin plus androgen failed to effect such behavior. Broodiness can in fact be produced in cocks, but the response is less than is normal to naturally broody hens (Riddle *et al.*, 1935).

The regurgitation feeding characteristic of pigeons and doves appears to be yet another behaviorism that is partly under the control of prolactin. This can be induced in doves that are still sexually inactive (Lehrman, 1955).

That the injection of prolactin somehow retards spermatogenesis and causes testis collapse was first reported by Riddle and Bates (1933). Breneman (1942a) subsequently observed the same effect in domestic cockerels, and Bailey (1950) inhibited the light-induced testis response of North American passerine white-crowned "sparrows" (*Zonotrichia leucophrys*) by the same means. (Prolactin, incidentally, has no appreciable effect on the seminiferous tubules of the mouse.) The "regression" effects described by the above-mentioned authors were studied in detail by Lofts and Marshall (1956), who showed them to be identical with the events that accompany the normal postnuptial metamorphosis in seasonal wild birds (see page 185). Bates *et al.* (1935) likewise showed that prolactin inhibits ovarian activity. There now seems little doubt that prolactin does not directly affect ovaries and testes but in fact acts indirectly by inhibiting the production of gonadotropin by the adenohypophysis.

Prolactin is partly responsible for the production of the naked vascular brood patches that occur on the ventral surface in one or both sexes of most avian species. These "brood spots" were described by Faber as long ago as 1826. He saw that they allowed a closer contact between maternal warmth and the hatching eggs. Faber believed that the female plucked her own breast, or that the depluming was caused by the abrasive action of eggs and nest and the abdominal concentration of animal heat during incubation. For about a century it was generally thought that the sitting bird removed ventral down with the bill. This belief was refuted by Lange's (1928) observation that in a nonbreeding immature gull (*Larus ridibundus*) a special molt was responsible.

Bailey (1952) has shown that prolactin operates synergistically with estrogen in the seasonal production of brood patches of which the initial (depluming) stage occurs several days before the first egg is laid. Bailey found that in more than 125 specimens of 12 families no significant variations in structure existed in the single large passerine incubation patch that is located in the ventral apterium. He reported in detail the waxing and waning of the brood patch of passerine birds and correlated the various stages with phases of the nesting cycle as follows:

(1) *Defeatherization stage:* All the down from the ventral apterium is lost several days before ovulation.

(2) *Vascularization stage:* The size and number of the blood vessels in the dermis increase immediately after depluming. The skin becomes slightly thickened by dermal edema and the feather papillae disappear. The epidermis undergoes rapid cell division. This stage lasts until the start of incubation.

(3) *Edematous stage:* The brood patch becomes increasingly edematous and vascular and the dermal muscles disappear. This stage lasts throughout incubation and during the initial care of the young.

(4) *Recovery stage:* The edema and vascularity gradually subside. By the time the young fly, the skin has returned to normal. (If another clutch is laid, the cycle is repeated.) Repluming of the patch occurs during the postnuptial molt.

Bailey produced experimentally an incubation patch in nonbreeding birds by continuous estradiol administration, but in hypophysectomized individuals such treatment led only to increased vascularity. When both estradiol and prolactin were given to hypophysectomized birds, the complete patch developed. Prolactin alone had no effect. Nor was testosterone effective—either alone or in combination with other hormones. In the Fringillidae, prolactin plus estrogen produced a brood patch in males of species in which only the females normally produce one, perhaps indicating that the apparatus is a very primitive character.

At least within the "advanced" order of passerines, there seems to be little correlation between the incubation habit by the male and his possession of a brood patch. The incubating males of some species lack it, and the nonincubating cocks of certain others possess it (Skutch, 1957). This further suggests that the brood patch is a primitive passerine attribute and that behavioral deviations have subsequently arisen.

Assays of the prolactin content of the pituitary of California gulls (*Larus californicus*) by the pigeon crop sac method indicated that gulls of both sexes with incubation patches possess more prolactin than those without. A single implanted pituitary gave a recognizable crop sac response. This work is in agreement with that of Byerly and Burrows (1936) on domestic hens.

As previously mentioned, experimentally administered prolactin suppresses various vital physiological and behavioral functions that normally precede the above-described phenomena. Thus it extinguishes some forms of courtship behavior (e.g. bowing and cooing in pigeons). It inhibits (probably by the partial depression of anterior pituitary function) ovarian activity and causes testis alterations characteristic of the normal postnuptial metamorphosis (page 185). It is probably significant that when Bates *et al.* (1937) injected FSH and prolactin simultaneously, the customary effects of the latter did not occur. Prolactin administered alone suppresses gametogenesis in both sexes, but not after the injection of FSH. Collias (1946) showed that prolactin-induced broodiness can be suppressed by estrogen. These experiments tend to suggest that FSH production and gonad activity stops when full prolactin secretion occurs under natural conditions. Bailey (1950), too, showed that prolactin inhibited even light-induced gonadal development in the white-crowned "sparrow." Lofts and Marshall (1956) found that the prolactin-induced changes in the testes were similar to those occurring after hypophysectomy. It seems possible that after the clutch is complete, tactile and other neural influences sharply influence the adenohypophysis toward greater prolactin production, with the consequent establishment of broodiness and, in Columbiiformes, the synthesis and regurgitation of crop milk for the young.

III. The Testis

A. GENERAL STRUCTURE

The testis (Fig. 1) is the essential male organ of two primary functions. These are: (1) the original one, phylogenetically speaking, which is the production of spermatozoa; and (2) the elaboration and discharge of reproductive hormones. The very name of the organ comes from an ancient appreciation of its function as the testament of the individual. For many years the ovary was known as the female testis.

N*

The testes and immediately contiguous ducts are supplied by the
spermatic arteries. The left organ is usually the larger. If one testis is
removed, there is a compensatory hypertrophy of the other (Domm and
Juhn, 1927). Each testis is a generally ovoid, encapsulated body, the
shape and volume of which varies with season and sexual condition.
(Nevertheless, the testes are said to be vermiform in *Cypcelus*.) Internally each is composed primarily of long, coiled seminiferous tubules

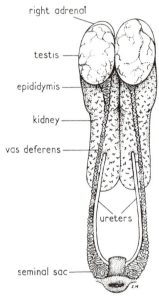

right adrenal

testis

epididymis

kidney

vas deferens

ureters

seminal sac

FIG. 1. Male reproductive system and associated structures in a seasonal passerine
bird (satin-bower bird, *Ptilonorhynchus violaceus*) near the height of breeding season.

which, unlike those of mammalia, are anastomotic and not restricted
by septa. From the tubule epithelia arise the male generative cells or
spermatozoa. The primary germ cells divide mitotically, and with the
waxing of the breeding season there arise successively the secondary
spermatogonia, primary and secondary spermatocytes, spermatids and
spermatozoa. Occasionally giant cells arise (Fig. 13). For avian chromosomes, see Chapter XVII, p. 116. It is generally considered that the
peripheral, probably syncitial, Sertoli cells possess a nutritive function
in relation to the maturing spermatids which aggregate in their vicinity.
They may possess additionally an endocrine function as well (p. 188).
    The mature spermatozoa, the shape of which varies greatly from
group to group, become centrally aggregated in bunches toward the
height of the sexual season. At this period the central regions of the

tubules become faintly lipoidal and cholesterol positive. These materials probably arise in the granules of von Ebner that are said to be part of spermatid protoplasm that becomes detached during the end phases of spermatogenesis. The slight appearance of such lipids (lipophanerosis) is not to be confused with the massive steatogenesis, which is more powerfully positive for cholesterol, that occurs after the cessation of hypophyseal influences of the termination of the breeding season (page 310).

The avian spermatozoon, like that of other vertebrates, consists essentially of the sperm head (with an apical cap above the acrosome containing the chromatic material), a mid-piece (or body) and a long lashing tail of propulsive function. The spermatozoa break away in millions and move through the anastomosing seminiferous, and next rete, tubules to the efferent ducts from which they pass to the convoluted epididymis which gives way to a relatively straight deferent duct or vas deferens. This discharges into the seminal sacs ("seminal vesicles") from which the spermatozoa are finally ejaculated into the urodeum (pages 170, 202).

The testis may increase at least 360-fold in size (e.g. *Fringilla montefringilla*) during the breeding season. The annual cyclical changes that occur in the testis of a wild bird are illustrated in Figs. 3–9. Certain less usual phenomena are shown in Figs. 10–13. The tunica propria bounding each seminiferous tubule, and the substantial tunica albuginea of the testis capsule and its fragile serous outer sheath, the tunica vaginalis, are grossly stretched. In some passerines the individual tubules can now be seen with the naked eye. In seasonal birds the old outer tunics are renewed annually as an upsurge of fibroblasts rebuilds the capsule from below. It is possible that this seasonal renewal is somehow initiated by the collapse of the old tunic and is part of an intrinsic regenerating mechanism operating within the individual organ. Occasionally, in birds living under abnormal climatic, or captive, conditions the testes may collapse, with concomitant formation of a new tunic, even though reproduction has not occurred and the tubules are still packed with bunched (now compressed) sperms (Keast and Marshall, 1954; Marshall and Serventy, 1957). Often, when a male fails to breed, an invasion of phagocytes destroys the unexpended Leydig lipids.

Not infrequently, sections of seminiferous tubules (including postnuptial lipids), or odd endocrine Leydig interstitial cells (see below), are incorporated in the new tunic. Microscopic sections of testis during the immediate postnuptial period will often show pieces of the old tunic peeling away from the rehabilitated organ.

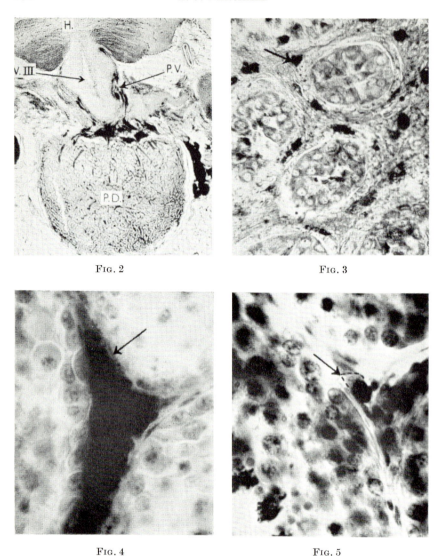

FIG. 2

FIG. 3

FIG. 4

FIG. 5

FIG. 2. Hypophyseal portal system in a passerine bird (adult rook, *Corvus frugilegus*). H: hypothalamus; V. III: third ventricle; P.V: portal vessels; P.D: pars distalis.

FIG. 3. Inactive seminiferous tubules and aggregations of rehabilitated lipoidal interstitial Leydig cells (arrowed) during winter (adult Australian "magpie", *Gymnorhina dorsalis*).

FIG. 4. Active seminiferous tubules and secretory interstitium (arrowed) during spring (adult *Corvus frugilegus*).

FIG. 5. Seminiferous tubules approaching height of spermatogenesis (note bunched spermatozoa). The interstitial cells (arrowed) have been largely dispersed by tubule expansion and much of their lipid content has been exhausted (adult *Corvus frugilegus*).

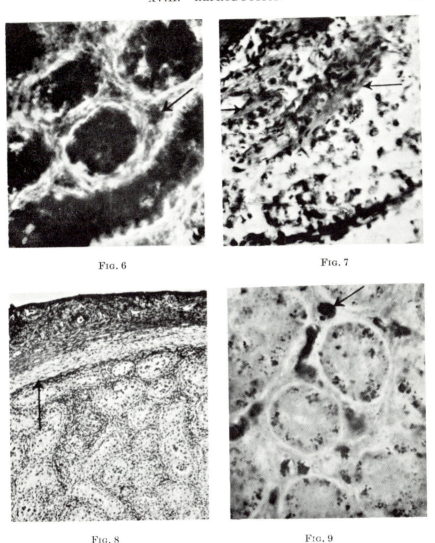

FIG. 6

FIG. 7

FIG. 8

FIG. 9

FIG. 6. Post-spermatogenetic steatogenesis and collapse of the seminiferous tubules, with beginnings of newly regenerated interstitium (arrowed) (adult rook, *Corvus frugilegus*).

FIG. 7. Fibroblasts (arrowed) are appearing (some inside the tubule walls) and are in the process of building a new tunica albuginea. This specimen is in the same condition as that shown in Fig. 6 (adult *Corvus frugilegus*).

FIG. 8. A new testis tunic (arrowed) has arisen inside the old one. The gonads are now rehabilitated. Nevertheless, as regards the general reproduction rhythm, the animal is still in its regenerative or "refractory" phase (see chapter XXI). (Adult Australian "Magpie", *Gymnorhina dorsalis*.)

FIG. 9. The new Leydig cells have become heavily lipoidal and grouped into a typical interstitium (arrowed) which is now readily susceptible to emergent hypophyseal influences. Only the last remnants of tubule lipids remain. These will be quickly dispersed at the very beginning of the next spermatogenesis (adult *Gymnorhina dorsalis*).

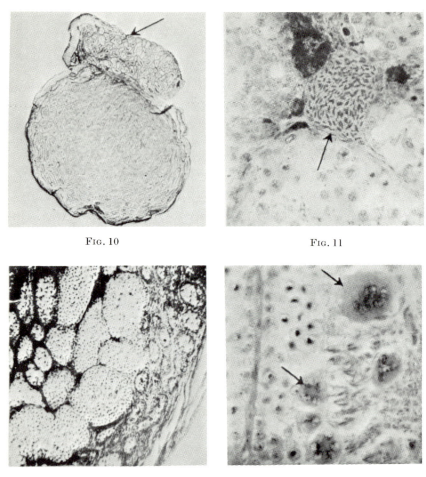

FIG. 10   FIG. 11

FIG. 12   FIG. 13

FIG. 10. An unusual non-breeding condition involving testis collapse and the renewal of the tunica without the lipoidal tubule metamorphosis shown in Fig. 6. The tubule network (containing bunched spermatozoa) is collectively constricted into a tight ball. Note relative great size of the epididymis (arrowed) which is abnormally filled with unshed spermatozoa (spotted bower-bird, *Chlamydera maculata*).

FIG. 11. A less unusual non-breeding condition involving partial spermatogenesis after which there arises in the unspent interstitium large sinusoidal vessels (arrowed) engorged with lymphocytes which appear to destroy the inactive Leydig cells nearby. (Parrot, *Barnardius macgillivravi*.) The specimen was taken after rainfall which was nevertheless inadequate to produce all the external effects necessary for successful reproduction.

FIG. 12. Asymmetric autumnal spermatogenesis of spring-breeder. This condition occurs in 10–15% of the Cornwall rook (*Corvus frugilegus*) population, but only rarely does full spermatogenesis, ovulation and reproduction take place.

FIG. 13. Giant cells (arrowed) with apparently normal primary spermatocytes and spermatozoa nearby (short-tailed shearwater, *Puffinus tenuirostris*), in September (Spring).

The interstices of the tubules are packed with areolar connective tissue, capillaries, and, much less obviously, of course, lymph vessels and nervous tissue. In some species (e.g. *Sturnus vulgaris*) great numbers of melanoblasts occur. These impart to the organ in its reduced condition a dense black pigmentation: occasionally one small collapsed testis is jet black and the other white, so erratic may be the distribution of melanoblasts. As the seasonal spermatogenesis proceeds, the organ becomes larger and the dispersion of the pigment cells allows it to appear gray and finally pearl white. Likewise, the rehabilitated (yet still small) testes of other (but by no means all) species may appear yellow or even orange in color. This is due to the rapid postnuptial proliferation of lipids in the cytoplasm of the connective tissue cells that develop postnuptially into endocrine Leydig cells. Subsequently, as the next season's spermatogenesis proceeds, the interstitial Leydig cells will be dispersed and the organ will become pearl white (Serventy and Marshall, 1956). The expanded gonad is usually heavily veined with tunica capillaries.

B. Secretory Components and Their Products

The first experimental evidence of endocrine function of the testis was obtained as long ago as 1762 when John Hunter described the transplantation of the testis of a domestic cock. Nearly a century later Berthold (1849) performed both autotransplantation and homotransplantation by "seeding" pieces of testis into the abdominal cavity of newly castrated birds. In so doing Berthold appears to have been the first actually to assign an endocrine function to an organ. He thus anticipated Claude Bernard.

Much work has been carried out on the interstitial cells of the avian testis, including especially observations on the relative amounts at different periods of sexual activity. A number of authors concluded that interstitial cells are of no physiological importance. Such views are of historical interest only.

There is no evidence that an interstitium occurs in any protochordate, but the typically vertebrate apparatus has made its appearance in the Agnatha. The evolution of such glandular cells in direct proximity to the gametogenetic machinery rather than elsewhere might suggest that one element influences the other (see page 171 in regard to the situation of the pituitary). In fact, under experimental conditions at least, it has been shown in at least some classes of vertebrates that androgens are concerned with spermatogenesis (see Dodd, 1955; Leatham and Wolf, 1955; Aron and Aron, 1957).

Most of the people who believed that the interstitium is without endocrine significance did so because at the height of the sexual season (as indicated by spermatogenesis, plumage condition, and behavior) they found a minimum number of Leydig cells in the interstitium. This is, in fact, true of seasonal birds. As a result, an inverse relationship between sexuality and interstitial activity was sometimes claimed (see e.g. Oslund, 1928); this, of course, is not true (Marshall, 1955). Actually, at the height of spermatogenesis in birds the Leydig cells are inevitably dispersed by tubule expansion. Therefore, there are very few in any given section. Cytological observations, however, make it clear that as such cells secrete, their cholesterol-positive lipids are gradually utilized, probably by conversion to androgens. Then the cells pass into a nonlipoidal and finally vacuolated, end phase (Fig. 5). Ultimately most of them disintegrate. Thus they become increasingly rare at the end of the sexual season, and most of them have disappeared by the period during which the effects of their secretions are most evident (Marshall, 1949, 1955). This cardinal fact was appreciated by Nonidez (1925). He observed lipid cells in the interstitium and concluded correctly that they disintegrated at the time of spermatogenesis.

Thus, by means of various techniques two apparently different kinds of Leydig cells can be readily shown: (1) a lipoidal, cholesterol-positive cell; and (2) one which has little or no lipid material or cholesterol but is highly fuchsinophile. Benoit (1927, 1929) described a transformation from the lipid to fuchsinophile cell, but a difference of opinion arose after work by Sluiter and van Oordt (1947, 1949), who called the fuchsinophile cell (which has a vacuolated end phase) the "secretory cell" and declared that it manufactures the sex hormone. It seems established, however, that the fuchsinophile cell is a lipid cell in its end phase that is about to disintegrate or to give rise to another generation of juvenile Leydig cells at the termination of the breeding season.

There is some evidence that a second and estrogenic secretory component is the sudanophilic Sertoli cell (Teilum, 1950). Further, Siller (1956) has described a distinctly feminized Brown Leghorn capon that suffered from Sertoli cell tumors which had developed in the gonadal area. The Sertoli cells of vertebrates contain cytoplasmic lipids that sometimes contain cholesterol. There is some evidence that the massive quantities of postnuptial cholesterol-positive lipids that arise in the testes may be at least partly derived from the syncitial Sertoli cytoplasm.

1. *Androgens*

The artificial administration of male sex hormones has been claimed to increase growth in domestic fowl and turkeys, but the data are conflicting (Wilckins and Fleischmann, 1946; Turner, 1948; Fraps *et al.*,

1951). Conversely, it has often been claimed that castrates grow bigger than intact cocks. This impression has not been substantiated, even though castrates often become fatter.

Some evidence has been found that castration in birds affects the length of the long bones (as in certain mammals, e.g. man) (Hutt, 1929). Temperament is altered by castration in birds (like mammals) in that activity and pugnacity are decreased. All observers have reported the relative lack of pugnacity in domestic capons. Castrated male satin bowerbirds (*Ptilonorhynchus violaceus*) lose the pronounced aggression for which the species is notable (Marshall, 1954). Australian "magpies" (*Gymnorhina* spp.) may become so savage toward the height of the breeding season that old males are sometimes shot for the protection of merely passing, not nest-robbing, children.

The capon-comb test was the first test regularly used for the demonstration of androgenic activity. Later, Callow and Parkes (1935) found that daily administration of 2.5 mg. rising to 5.0 mg. of androsterone into the pectoral muscle of a caponized domestic fowl restored its comb almost to normal size after 3 weeks. After 5 weeks it was indistinguishable from that of the intact bird. Emmens (1938) showed that tablets of testosterone propionate, averaging 11 mg. in weight, caused a rapid and extensive comb growth in capons. The combs of all birds became indistinguishable from those of normal cocks within 5 weeks of implantation. Wattles and ear lobes, too, are quickly restored to normality by androgens.

Crowing and sexual behavior can be re-established in castrates by the administration of androgenic crude extracts of testis or urine, or of crystalline androgenic substances. Beach (1948), Bullough (1945), and Collias (1950) have assembled many important data on hormones and behavior. Leonard (1939) and Shoemaker (1939b) caused female canaries to sing by injecting them with androgens. Testis extracts induce crowing and aggression in domestic hens. Noble and Wurm (1940a) found that the administration of testosterone propionate led to the renewal of breeding calls and other sexual behavior in laughing gulls (*Larus atricilla*), and Boss (1943) obtained similar results with the herring gull (*L. argentatus*).

When fowls' eggs are injected with male sex hormone, the mesonephric elements and the Wolffian ducts undergo great hypertrophy in embryos of both sexes. After comparable treatment, combs, too, are found to be considerably developed at the time of hatching (Dantchakoff and Kinderis, 1937). Such experiments may induce premature attempts to crow a few days after hatching (Dantchakoff, 1937a, b). Herring gull embryos, too, were found by Boss and Witschi (1941,

1942) to react to testosterone propionate. After the injection of eggs, the chicks assumed adult plumage when between 27 and 90 days old. The adult voice was attained at an age of 45 days. In Chapter XVII, Witschi refers to the remarkable modern work by Wolff and others concerning endocrine influences during development.

Allee *et al.* (1939) injected domestic hens with testosterone propionate and observed masculine courtship display which was lost at the end of such treatment. Domm *et al.* (1942) stimulated circling, "waltzing," and crowing in young domestic hens by means of testosterone. In a testosterone-implanted hen Zitrin (1942) produced waltzing, crowing, and treading. This behavior ceased after several months, when fertile eggs were laid. Noble and Zitrin (1942) obtained crowing at 4 days and treading at 15 days when testosterone propionate was injected from the time of hatching. Among wild species, month-old black-crowned herons (*Nicticorax nicticorax*) developed gutteral adult voices, territory consciousness, and nest-building, copulation, and brooding behavior after treatment with testosterone propionate (Noble and Wurm, 1938, 1940b).

At the same time, precocious sexual behavior has been recorded in untreated juvenile birds of various species (Craig, 1909; Watson, 1908; White, 1941; Williamson, 1941). How much such activity is due to androgen liberation is unknown. Certainly the Leydig cytoplasm of nesting British rooks (*Corvus frugilegus*) contains cholesterol-positive lipid droplets and is therefore potentially secretory.

That the seasonal development of wattles in the male wild turkey *Meleagris* is under the control of testicular androgens was proved by Leopold (1944). Again, Salomonsen (1939) demonstrated that the seasonal development of facial "roses" in the rock ptarmigan (*Lagopus mutus*), and the prominent "eyebrows" of the Hungarian partridge (*Perdix perdix*) and prairie chicken (*Tympanuchus cupido*), are controlled by testicular hormones. Juhn and Gustavson (1930) and Juhn *et al.* (1932) showed that the comb of the female domestic chick responds as well as that of the male chick to injections of androgenic extracts.

The influence of androgens on the social hierarchy or "peck order" was studied by Schjelderup-Ebbe (1935). In social hierarchy the species differences are remarkable. In the silver pheasant (*Gennaeus nycthemerus*) and the turkey (*Meleagris gallopavo*) the male is dominant; in certain other species the opposite is the case. Allee (1936) and Masure and Allee (1934) reported that although the male budgerygah (*Melopsittacus undulatus*) is dominant during the breeding season the roles are reversed at other times. Shoemaker (1939a) found that during the nonsexual season there was little suggestion of a peck order. During the reproductive period the female became dominant. Shoemaker was unable to improve the status of ovariectomized or nonbreeding females by injections of estrogen and suggested that the female secreted androgen during the breeding season (see page 197). Bennet's (1940) results with the ring dove, and those of Hamilton and Golden (1939) with domestic fowl chicks indicate that androgen administration elevates birds in the peck order.

The crowing hen, famous in legend and superstition, so commonly arises because, when the functional left ovary is pathologically damaged, the potentially testicular medullary tissue of the opposite organ responds to gonadotropins. Sometimes an ovotestis arises. At the next molt, deficiency of estrogen may allow plumage reversal to the asexual male feathering. Meanwhile, newly secreted androgens become responsible for a phenomenon that has excited interest, and often fear, since the time of Aristotle (see Forbes, 1947).

The couplet
> "A whistling maid and a crowing hen
> Are fit for neither Gods nor men"

is echoed in several European languages as, for example,
> "Poule qui chante, Prêtre qui danse,
> Et Femme qui parle latin,
> N'arrivent jamais à belle fin."

Up to medieval times, and after, the crowing hen has been regarded as a portent of awesome events, and there exist scattered records of such birds (and particularly those that laid eggs) which have been executed with or without the benefit of formal trial. It is probable that the so-called egg-laying cock is a genetic hen that, although changing sex and already indulging in androgen-induced male behavior, has nevertheless retained sufficient ovarian function to produce the odd egg, the chalaza of which sometimes becomes twisted into a somewhat serpentine form on the journey down the hypotropic oviduct. So, apparently, arose the legend of the cockatrice and the basilisk mentioned in the Bible and other ancient writings.

Masculinization has been reported in a variety of nonraptorial groups, and in one now celebrated case described by Crew (1923) a hen, reputedly a former mother, underwent such changes that allowed it to sire offspring. Riddle (1924), too, records a pigeon that had laid eggs and yet was found, after indulging in masculine behavior, to contain testes.

2. *Estrogens*

There exists scattered evidence that the male gonad may produce female sex hormone under both normal and pathological conditions.

As regards birds, Greenwood and Blyth (1938) reported the assumption of typical female plumage in a domestic cockerel after the injection of testis extract. The sudanophilic Sertoli cells have been thought possibly to be estrogenic (Teilum, 1950); and when Siller (1956) dissected a feminized domestic capon he found Sertoli cell tumors.

Full or even partial sex reversal from male toward the female condition is much rarer in nature than the phenomena described above. Marshall and Serventy (1956b) described a remarkable case of intersexuality in a wild, phenotypically male, Australian "magpie" (*Gymnorhina dorsalis*). The right testis was normal, but the left gonad was an irregularly shaped ovotestis. About three-quarters of this organ was made up of ovarian follicles. A considerable amount of blood, some in sinusoidal vessels and some extravasated, occurred in fibrous connective tissue investing the "female" area. The remaining quarter of the ovotestis was occupied by apparently normal seminiferous tubules in which mitotic figures occurred. Apart from its left gonad, the bird differed from normal lean males of the autumn season (April) only in possessing considerable quantities of subperitoneal depot fat. In this respect it approached the seasonal condition of true females (see also Greenwood and Blyth, 1932).

3. *Progestins*

Progesterone or a closely allied substance has been demonstrated in the plasma of cocks, but not in that of capons (Fraps *et al.*, 1949). It was suggested by Marshall and Serventy (1956a) that the postnuptial, cholesterol-positive lipids that appear seasonally in quantities in the seminiferous tubules of wild birds may be involved in the synthesis of a progestin (see Fig. 6). Lofts and Marshall (1959), by means of chromatography and the Hooker-Forbes (1949) bioassay method, have produced supporting evidence.

IV. The Ovary

A. GENERAL STRUCTURE

The female sex organ, like that of the male, has both gametogenetic and endocrine functions. First, it produces female sex cells (oogenesis), ova, and secondly, estrogens (female sex hormones) and, almost certainly, androgens (male sex hormones) as well. A progesterone-like material also occurs in birds and is probably of ovarian origin.

The ovary is an irregularly shaped whitish organ lying closely apposed to the kidneys (Fig. 14). It is supplied by the ovarian artery and is anchored to the dorsal peritoneum by a substantial ligament, the mesovarium. In most avian groups only the left ovary and oviduct reach functional development. Among Raptores, however, both left and right gonads (and associated oviducts) may become fully functional. In some nonraptorial species in which asymmetry is usual the primitive bilateral condition not infrequently arises. Chappelier (1913) reported an extraordinary such case in which a domestic duck laid two eggs daily (see also Romanoff and Romanoff, 1949).

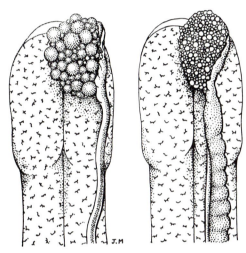

FIG. 14. Seasonal changes in the ovary and oviduct of a passerine bird. *Left:* Ovary (with beginning of seasonal development of oocytes) and oviduct at time of initial bower-building and display in satin bower-bird (*Ptilonorhynchus violaceus*). *Right:* Ovary (with regressed oocytes) and oviduct still distended by seasonal hormonal influences and the passage of eggs some two months before.

The ovary consists essentially of an outer cortex containing ova which surrounds a highly vascular medulla composed primarily of connective tissue. At the periphery of the cortex is the germinal epithelium which is made up of primordial germ cells that become enclosed follicles: first as primary, and next as secondary, oocytes. The number of ovarian follicles has been variously estimated in thousands, or even millions (Hutt, 1949). Of these, only a minute proportion mature sufficiently to ensure the extrusion of their egg. For details of the maturation of the ovarian egg, Romanoff and Romanoff (1949) should be consulted.

B. Secretory Components and Their Products

As each follicle develops, some of the cells of its newly arisen connective tissue thecal layers become lipoidal, cholesterol-positive, and

o

obviously secretory. Within each follicle there accumulates an estrogen-containing liquor folliculi. Like all endocrine elements every individual follicle is richly vascularized. This is to be expected when we reflect that follicle maturation is under the control of blood-borne hormones

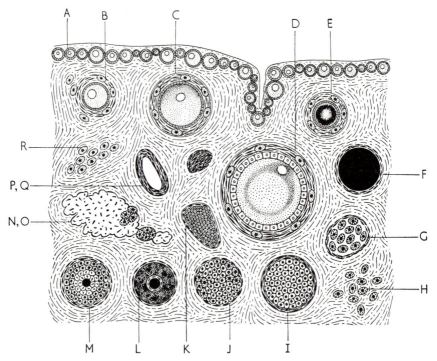

FIG. 15. Diagrammatic representation (not to scale) of some prominent structures in the avian ovary (rook, *Corvus frugilegus*). A: Oogonium; B: Developing follicle at time of the genesis and incorporation of its thecal gland-cells; C: Developing follicle at later stage; D: Follicle showing faint beginnings of lipoidal atresia; E: Younger follicle show-ing pronounced lipoidal atresia; F: Follicle in total atresia; G: Cholesterol-positive lipid cells—presumptive *ex-follicular cells*—that arise in atretic follicles. H: Ex-follicular gland cells, free in the ovarian stroma; I: Follicle that has undergone an essentially non-lipoidal atresia; J: As I, except that some cells are becoming lipoidal; K: Sinusoidal blood vessel; L: A type of atresia in which an amorphous clot of fat is expressed into the follicle centre and isolated by a wall of fibroblasts; M: An atresia in which lipoidal cells nearest the central clot discharge their cholesterol and become pycnotic, with distorted nuclei; N: Hyaline, sometimes lobate, mass of pycnotic cells that resembles the mammalian *corpus albicans*; O: Restricted area of a hyaline scar that has become glandular; P: Scars from a discharged follicle (these occasionally hold depot fat that does not contain cholesterol), and behind is Q, a scar from a discharged follicle that has been invaded by fibroblasts; R: Group of glandular cells that have arisen from connective tissue cells *in the stroma* and are therefore probably homologous with male interstitial (Leydig) cells.

and, conversely, the estrogen in the follicular fluid no doubt drains outward to exert characteristic effects. The follicles which only partly mature, generally undergo a fatty atresia. The formed lipid is heavily positive for cholesterol, which is almost certainly the precursor of steroid hormones. After the extrusion of the ripe egg there is a rapid compensatory production of fibroblasts which invade the cavity. No permanent corpus luteum is formed. A single exovular cavity can be bridged rapidly by connective tissue and converted into at least two scars. It is therefore impossible accurately to estimate the age of birds by scar count (Marshall and Coombs, 1957).

Figure 15 shows some of the remarkable diversity of minute structures within the avian ovary. That the stroma contains secretory cells has been clearly shown by the work of Fell (1923, 1924), Benoit (1926), Domm (1929), Pfeiffer and Kirschbaum (1943), and others. By studying their mode of origin, Marshall and Coombs (1957) were able to distinguish two different sorts of "female interstitial cells" in the ovary of the European rook (*Corvus frugilegus*). One type, the exfollicular cell, arises from atretic follicles. The other develops from stromal connective tissue cells (Fig. 15). The latter is therefore apparently homologous with the androgenic interstitial Leydig cells of the testis.

Although there is little doubt that the ovary produces both estrogen and androgen, there is little evidence concerning the specific site of interstitial origin. Unfortunately, no one has yet been able to distinguish between the two sorts of stromal secretory cells except at the time of their formation. The work of Taber (1951) strongly suggests that a stromal cell is responsible for androgen production. The comb of the domestic fowl is in both sexes under androgenic control, and, when Taber stopped administering exogenous gonadotropins to hens, comb regression (indicating decreased androgen output) occurred accompanied by the "reappearance of foamy, lipoid-filled interstitial cells" in the ovarian medulla. It may be that, in the absence of gonadotropic stimulation, these interstitial cells ceased to secrete, and so stored cholesterol-positive lipids, and therefore became more prominent.

1. *Estrogens*

Estrogens, whatever be their precise cellular origins, produce a wide variety of somatic and behavioral responses. In the red-billed dioch (*Quelea quelea*) and the budgerygah (*Melopsittacus undulatus*) (loosely called "the parakeet" in North America) the beak of the female changes color after the administration of female sex hormone (Witschi, 1935). In at least some breeds of domestic fowl castration does not affect male display plumage: sex dimorphism in these (and other species) is dependent on the presence of the *female* sex hormone (see Witschi, Chapter XVII, for various forms of plumage control). Lehrman and Brody (1957) and Lehrman (1959) have established that estrogen stimulates nest-building activity. The injection of estrogen, on the other hand, stops broodiness in females (possibly by the suppression of adenohypophyseal influences) and will generally eliminate crowing and other forms of sexual activity in cockerels (Ceni, 1927; Davis and Domm, 1941). Although castrated males sometimes continue to exhibit masculine behavior patterns after estrogen injections (Goodale, 1916, 1918; Davis and Domm, 1941, 1943), there is much evidence that the administration of estrogen generally leads to the assumption of female behavior. When Goodale implanted ovarian tissue into capons they exhibited feminine behavior, including the care and protection of chicks. When bilaterally ovariectomized pigeons were injected with estrogen they adopted a squatting reflex and received the male (Davis and Domm, 1941, 1943). Some individuals, however, did not do so in a study carried out by Allee and Collias (1940). These authors showed also that in domestic hens estrogen administration tended to reduce social status (see page 191). The gull *Larus atricilla*, when similarly treated, will adopt the food-begging and stooping activities characteristic of the female while mating. However, both in castrated males injected with estrogen, and ovariectomized females injected with testosterone, innate mechanisms will sometimes continue to express themselves (Davis and Domm, 1941, 1943).

Estrogen is vitally influential in the seasonal preparation of the oviduct and its role in the deposition of calcium in the marrow cavities of the long bones just before the formation of egg shell seems well established. If the ovaries of pigeons possess follicles 10 mm. or more in diameter, the marrow cavities always contain spicules of bone (Kyes and Potter, 1934). Seasonal hyperossification of the skeletal system of pigeons and house sparrows can be directly correlated with periodic ovarian activity (Pfeiffer and Gardner, 1938; Kirschbaum *et al.*, 1939). The formation of such medullary bone can be stimulated in both male and nonovulatory female pigeons by the injection of estrogen. Although much of the calcium needed for shell formation comes from exogenous material, that ingested is nevertheless insufficient to meet the heavy seasonal needs. Perhaps 35–40% of the required amount is withdrawn from body deposits (Driggers and Comar, 1949; Comar and Driggers, 1949). Calcium is not stored in the reproductive tract, but the accummulation in medullary bone is probably sufficient for the formation of about six eggs in the domestic hen. Such bone is said to hold a greater ratio of calcium to phosphorus than ordinary bone (Common, 1938).

Associated with the above-mentioned phenomenon is the fact that both blood calcium and phosphorus increase in amount during the period of ovulation in pigeons, hens, and ducks (McDonald and Riddle, 1945; Fleischmann and Fried, 1945; Common *et al.*, 1948). Estrogen injections raise the blood calcium level in pigeons after excision of the parathyroids (Riddle *et al.*, 1945; Riddle and McDonald, 1945).

There is evidence, too, that the increase in blood lipids is at the same time under the control of estrogen (Lorenz, 1938; Entenman *et al.*, 1940) and that in migratory birds estrogen, like androgen, is concerned with the increase in the amount of depot fat that accumulates in specific subcutaneous and intraperitoneal areas (Thayer *et al.*, 1945).

2. *Androgens*

There is unequivocal evidence that comb growth in the domestic hen is under androgenic control, and it is highly probable that ovarian androgens are responsible. In regard to behavior, the females of many species spasmodically, and in some species regularly, display at least a partial reversal in sexual activities, particularly during the autumn and mid-winter months.

In the sedentary British robin (*Erithacus rubecula*) the females establish autumn territories which are relinquished late in December or in January when pairing occurs (Lack, 1946) and the sexual organs of both sexes begin their "spring" modification (Marshall, 1952a). The female of the migratory Continental robin establishes territory and becomes aggressive after arriving in southern Italy in the autumn (Alexander, 1917). In the autumn, female European starlings sing and their beaks turn yellow. This pigmentation is a secondary sex characteristic of the male (Witschi and Miller, 1938; see Chapter XXVII). In the red-necked phalarope (*Phalaropus lobatus*) it is the brightly colored female that acquires the territory and performs the courtship display. After the eggs are laid it is the male that incubates them.

3. *Progestins*

There is now abundant evidence that progesterone or like substance occurs in birds and possibly in other submammalian classes. There is no acceptable evidence that the avian ovary (Fig. 15) develops persistent postovulatory corpora lutea (see Fell, 1924; Harrison, 1948; Matthews, 1955). Nevertheless, a progestin was demonstrated in the blood plasma of ovulating hens (Fraps *et al.*, 1948), and in nonlaying hens and cocks as well (Fraps *et al.*, 1949). The precise site of origin remains in doubt. Both the developing (Fraps, 1955) and atretic follicles (Marshall and Coombs, 1957) have been suggested.

Atretic follicles—both pre- and postovulatory—are heavily positive for cholesterol. During the incubation and parental periods greatly increased numbers of follicles become atretic and their contained cholesterol is expended, possibly in the elaboration of a progestin (see also page 192).

V. Accessory Sexual Organs

A. MALE

The accessory sexual apparatus of the male is relatively simple. On each side it consists successively of the rete testis, vasa efferentia, epididymis, and ductus (vas) deferens. The distal end of the last-named becomes seasonably hypertrophied (in passerines at least) into a highly

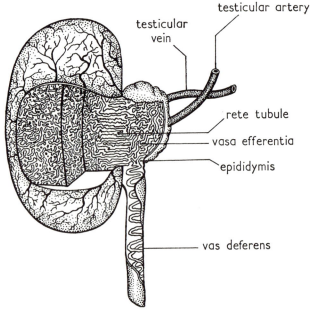

FIG. 16. Internal network of testis of domestic cock (*Gallus*) and its relationship with conducting structures. (Modified after Lake.)

convoluted seminal receptacle. This discharges through an ejaculatory duct into the urodeum and phallus. No homolog of the mammalian Cowper's gland, prostate gland, or diverticular seminal vesicle has been demonstrated.

After gaining freedom into the lumina of the seminiferous tubules, the spermatozoa pass into the tubules of the rete testis (Fig. 16). It has been mentioned previously that the avian testis is without the septa characteristic of mammals and that the convoluted tubules are anastomosed into a complicated network. At several points this network connects with the rete tubules. During the period of sexual inactivity the rete tubules are small and inconspicuously located in the tunica albuginea. With the seasonal development of sexuality they—usually between two and four in number—become progressively enlarged and may finally extend deeply into the testicular network. Bailey (1953), who has given an excellent account of the accessory organs of male fringillid birds, rarely observed spermatozoa in the rete tubules and concluded that through this area their passage is probably both rapid and periodic.

The spermatozoa are next received by the vasa efferentia. These thin tubules leave the rete tubules in the tunica albuginea and run to the epididymis. They, too, become hypertrophied during the sexual season, and there is evidence that their epithelia become secretory. Nevertheless, in the domestic cock, spermatozoa are never observed in quantity in this part of the tract.

The epididymis is a coiled tube which hypertrophies grossly in season until it becomes a prominent whitish organ (Fig. 1). It is closely adjacent to both testis and kidney. Its columnar epithelium becomes ciliated and secretory. In passerines so far carefully studied, the spermatozoa are not normally stored in the epididymides (Bailey, 1953), but, under abnormal environmental conditions, when spermatozoa are not discharged, they may contain an infarcted mass of spermatozoa (Keast and Marshall, 1954; Marshall, 1952b; and see Fig. 10).

Normally, the spermatozoa now pass into the relatively muscular ductus, or vas, deferens which runs almost directly (partly embedded in the ventral surface of the kidney in the resting condition) toward the cloaca. With the progression of the breeding season, each vas becomes convoluted and enlarged and moves free from the kidney. It remains, in passerines, relatively nonsecretory and the spermatozoa pass without delay into its terminal section, the so-called seminal vesicle (Figs. 1, 17). Both vas and "seminal vesicle" are mesonephric duct derivatives, but it is important to realize that in the adult condition the latter has nothing in common structurally with the mammalian organ of the same name. The mammalian outgrowth is purely secretory, and has never a storage function. The avian distension is (in many species) both of secretory and storage function. Although it has been conventional to refer to it in mammalian terminology, I will here call it the *seminal sac*.

During the inactive season the seminal sac is usually minute and only slightly coiled. As the sexual season progresses, it enlarges, becoming extremely convoluted and prominent. It is under androgenic control (Riddle, 1927). Like those of the testis, the sperm-filled tubules within the seminal sac can now be seen with the naked eye. Vast numbers of spermatozoa are stored. Each paired organ increases about thirtyfold by weight in the Fringillidae. The epithelium is secretory and the whole sac is surrounded by a "fibro-muscular sheath which, when contracted, is probably an important factor in evacuating the seminal vesicle during copulation" (Bailey, 1953).

According to Lake (1957) and others, the arrangement in *Gallus* is different from that in passerines. In the domestic cock Lake described a "noticeably small storage space" for spermatozoa at the distal end of the vas deferens but considers that the vas as a whole "formed the main reservoir." There was no evidence of secretion from the epithelium of the distal part of the tract.

In most, if not all, passerines the seasonal hypertrophy of the seminal sacs forces out the posterior wall of each cloaca into a nodular *cloacal protuberance* (Figs. 17, 18) which Drost (1938) has shown can be used to sex various species of passerines. Wolfson (1952), too, has shown it to be a reliable indication of reproductive capability. Wolfson asserts that in the North American swamp sparrow (*Melospiza georgiana*) it is possible to see the distended tubules through the stretched *skin* of the cloaca.

Wolfson (1952) has described a simple technique for sperm extraction from male passerines [see Burrows and Quinn (1937) in regard to domestic birds], and he has further suggested (Wolfson, 1952, 1954) for the seminal sac a thermoregulatory function comparable with that of the mammalian scrotum. It is true that some birds do not, apparently, seasonally develop cloacal protuberances; but neither do the testes descend in whales, elephants, hyraxes and some "insectivores." Wolfson (1954) has recorded a mean temperature difference of a little more than 7°F. between the main body, and the cloacal, temperatures of several finches. It may well be that the lowering of temperature of the sperm environment before ejaculation is significant. It will be recalled that Munro (1938) showed that in the domestic fowl (which does not possess distensible seminal sacs) spermatozoa removed from the testes were unable to fertilize eggs and those taken from the adjacent epididymides were effective in only 13% of the test females. On the other hand, spermatozoa taken from the lower part of the vas deferens were effective in 74% of the hens tested. There appeared to be a correlation between sperm mobility and fertilizing power. The cloacal protuberances, when present, may also facilitate intromission during copulation.

Parenthetically it should be mentioned that Cowles and Nordstrom (1946) have suggested that the abdominal air sacs may act as a cooling device in relation to the testes, but this theory has not won general acceptance.

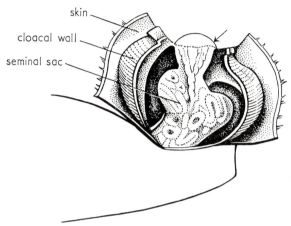

FIG. 17. Cloacal protuberance (lateral view, in dissection) of adult male passerine (*Zonotrichia albicollis*) in breeding condition. The conical area (arrowed) near the top of the cloaca, which appears to be attached to the seminal sac, is the outer surface of the proctodæum. The associated V-shaped element is a supporting structure. The urodæum, into which the seminal sac opens, is median to the distal part of the vesicle and is hidden. (Modified after Wolfson.)

FIG. 18. Cloacal protuberance (right external view) of adult male passerine (*Melospiza georgiana*) in breeding condition. The cloaca is displaced by the swollen seminal sacs; the position of the vent is indicated by surmounting tuft of feathers. (Redrawn from photographs by Wolfson.)

The most detailed studies of the actual copulatory apparatus has been made by Nishiyama (1954, 1955) and Lake (1956, 1957) in the domestic cock. Lake (1957) is of the opinion that not only the erectile ejaculatory ducts and phallus, but also adjacent specialized lymph folds and vascular bodies, are involved in sperm discharge, since these are erected together with the ejaculatory ducts during sexual excitement. Höhn (1960) has evidence that the weight of the penis of the adult mallard (*Anas platyrhynchos*) increases seasonally from 0.05% to 0.3% of the body weight. Castration in early spring prevents such enlargement.

B. FEMALE

No avian group has become viviparous, and the female accessory organs have remained simple compared with those of the mammal. Nevertheless, the development of the highly complicated, heavily yolked, cleidoic egg, an inheritance from reptilian ancestry, has involved a great differentiation and specialization of successive parts of the duct that carries the egg cells from ovary to vent and forms the receptacle in which internal fertilization occurs (Fig. 19).

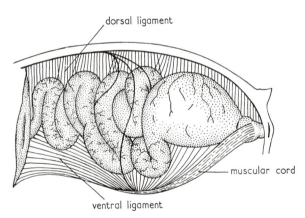

FIG. 19. Oviduct and its supporting structures in *Gallus*. In the laying hen these occupy much of the left half of the abdominal cavity. Both ligaments are thin and veil-like and folded by the convolutions of the mobile oviduct. The ventral ligament is the more muscular and terminates caudally as a "solid muscular cord which divides into bundles of fibres". These are attached to the ventral and ventrolateral aspects of the anterior part of the vagina. (Modified after Romanoff and Romanoff.)

The keen modern interest in any biological process involved in the artificial production of food for man has resulted in important advances in knowledge of the anatomy and physiology of the avian Mülleran or oviduct (cf. the lack of comparable information concerning the formation of the cleidoic egg in Reptilia).

As far as is known, the oviduct and its relationship with the ovary are singularly uniform throughout the Aves and present none of the considerable variations seen in the Mammalia. The duct is long, convoluted, internally ciliated, highly distensible, and is slung from the body wall by the dorsal ligament. The ventral ligament runs from the neighborhood of the ovary (where it is said to assist in the guidance of extruded ova into the tube) to its insertion on the vaginal wall. These two ligaments allow a considerable amount of oviducal movement and, additionally, carry important blood vessels. An open, anterior infundibulum receives the yolked exovarian eggs. By peristaltic contractions, the infundibulum starts each ovum on its journey toward the vent. This activity is pronounced only at the time of ovulation. According to Olsen and Neher (1948), fertilization normally occurs after extrusion but before the egg reaches the highly glandular magnum, the lengthy section of oviduct succeeding the infundibulum (Fig. 19). Spermatozoa remain viable in the female tract for a considerable period. Thus, in the domestic turkey hen a whole clutch of from 20 to 30 eggs (which are laid at about daily intervals) can be fertilized as the result of a single treading. In domestic fowl, fertile eggs may be laid up to 10 or 12 days after copulation, although "the percentage fertility begins to fall rapidly after the 5th to 7th day" (see Hammond, 1952).

For an understanding of the cytological changes in the oviduct (and tubal events consequent upon them) it is still necessary to consult an early paper by Richardson (1935). Brant and Nalbandov (1956) have shown that the oviduct is seasonally prepared for the completion of egg formation, and the transmission of the egg, by the synergistic operation of estrogen and progesterone (see also Lehrman and Brody, 1957). These hormones, of course, operate together also in the pregestational preparation of the mammalian uterus. Again, not only is the seasonal hypertrophy of the avian oviduct under such dual control, but the secretion of egg albumen as well. Albumen production is more rapid and prolific when the yolked egg (or a mechanical stimulus provided artificially by beads) reaches the duct.

The white albumen formed by the magnum is deposited in four layers (the chalaziferous layer innermost) on the descending ovum. The egg and its surrounding substances are now thrust posteriorly into the isthmus of the oviduct. This is less glandular; and there is evidence (see Sturkie, 1954) that both inner and outer keratinous membranes are formed by the time the egg is wholly within this part of the tract.

The egg is next received by the muscular-walled shell-gland.* This is equipped with an array of glands of dubious function. It is here that the albumen receives water and salts, and the egg becomes finally encapsulated by its porous and largely calcareous shell. The egg shell of the domestic hen is about 94% calcium carbonate, 1% magnesium carbonate, and 1% calcium phosphate, supported by a largely proteinaceous organic matrix which constitutes from 3 to 4% of the total shell.

The shell-gland does not store calcium. That needed for shell formation comes principally from ingested food, but it can also be withdrawn from deposits within the bones. The bones of some birds (e.g. pigeons) are more osseus in the female than in the male (Kyes and Potter, 1934) and there appears to be a seasonal increase in ossification (and therefore available calcium) that is correlated with the size of the Graafian follicles and therefore, probably, with the discharge of ovarian estrogen (Gardner and Pfeiffer, 1942). Bloom *et al.* (1958) have interesting data and color plates showing the differential histological state of medullary bone depending upon whether an egg of the domestic fowl is in the uterus or not.

The shell pigment, too, is added in the shell-gland. [For a wealth of detail concerning egg formation and structure see, particularly, Romanoff and Romanoff (1949).] The entrance of the muscular vagina is guarded by a powerful sphincter. From here the fully formed egg passes through an aperture (a little dorsal to the rectum) into the colaca whence it is expelled.

The typical male deferent duct and its so-called seminal vesicle (page 199) occur more or less prominently in the female of many species. Bailey (1953) reported that in fringillid finches the duct is usually bilaterally present but may be unilateral or absent altogether. The ducts enlarge during the breeding season when the epithelium of the vesicular area becomes secretory and "filled with secretory droplets and cell fragments." Callow and Parkes (1935) long ago showed that this seasonal "male" development in the female is probably under the influence of androgens (see also Chapter XXI), and Bailey (1953) has recently found that the ducts respond *only* to androgenic substances.

References

Alexander, C. J. (1917). Observations on birds singing in their winter quarters and on migration. *Brit. Birds* 11: 98–102.
Allee, W. C. (1936). Analytical studies of group behaviour in birds. *Wilson Bull.* 48: 143–151.

* The shell-gland is generally called the "uterus." It is, of course, the expanded caudal section of the oviduct and, as Richardson (1935) has suggested, is better called the shell-gland. Many people have commented on the inappropriateness of the generally used, and possibly irredeemably entrenched, expression usually employed.

Allee, W. C., and Collias, N. (1940). The influence of estradiol on the social organisation of flocks of hens. *Endocrinology* **27**: 87–94.

Allee, W. C., Collias, N., and Lutherman, C. Z. (1939). Modification of the social order in flocks of hens by the injection of testosterone propionate. *Physiol. Zoöl.* **12**: 412–440.

Aron, M., and Aron, C. (1957). "La fonction endocrine du testicule." Masson, Paris.

Asplin, F. D., and Boyland, E. (1947). The effects of pyrimidine sulphonamide derivatives upon the blood clotting system and tests of chicks and the breeding capacity of adult fowls. *Brit. J. Pharmacol.* **2**: 79–92.

Bailey, R. E. (1950). Inhibition with prolactin of light-induced gonad increase in white-crowned sparrows. *Condor* **52**: 247–251.

Bailey, R. E. (1952). The incubation patch of passerine birds. *Condor* **54**: 121–136.

Bailey, R. E. (1953). Accessory reproduction organs of male fringillis birds. Seasonal variations and response to various sex hormones. *Anat. Record* **115**: 1–20.

Bates, R. W., Lahr, E. L., and Riddle, O. (1935). The gross action of prolactin and follicle-stimulating hormone on the mature ovary and sex accessories of fowl. *Am. J. Physiol.* **111**: 361–368.

Bates, R. W., Riddle, O., and Lahr, E. L. (1937). The mechanism of the anti-gonad action of prolactin in adult pigeons. *Am. J. Physiol.* **119**: 610–614.

Beach, F. A. (1948). "Hormones and Behaviour." Hoeber, New York.

Bennet, M. A. (1940). The social hierarchy in ring doves. II. The effect of treatment with testosterone propionate. *Ecology* **21**: 148–165.

Benoit, J. (1926). Sur l'origine des cellules interstitielles de l'ovaire de la poule. *Compt. rend. soc. biol.* **94**: 873–877.

Benoit, J. (1927). Quantité de parenchyme testiculaire et quantité d'hormone élaborée. Éxiste-t-il une "sécrétion de luze" ou un "parenchyme de luxe." *Compt. rend. soc. biol.* **97**: 790–793.

Benoit, J. (1929). Le déterminisme des charactères sexuels secondaires du coq domestique. *Arch. zool. exptl. et gén.* **69**: 217–499.

Benoit, J. (1937). Facteurs externes et internes de l'activité sexuelle. II. Étude du mécanisme de la stimulation par la lumière de l'activité testiculaire chez le Canard domestique. Rôle de l'hypophyse. *Bull. biol. France et Belg.* **71**: 393–437.

Benoit, J. (1938). Rôle des yeux et de la voie nerveuse oculo-hypophysaire dans la gonadostimulation par la lumière artificielle chez le Canard domestique. *Compt. rend. soc. biol.* **129**: 231–234.

Benoit, J., and Assenmacher, I. (1951). Étude préliminaire de la vascularisation de l'appareil hypophysaire du canard domestique. *Arch. anat. microscop. et morphol. exptl.* **40**: 27–45.

Benoit, J., and Assenmacher, I. (1953). Rapport entre la stimulation sexuelle pré-hypophysaire et la neurosécrétion chez l'oiseau. *Arch. anat. microscop. et morphol. exptl.* **42**: 334–386.

Benoit, J., and Assenmacher, I. (1955). Le controle hypothalomique de l'activite préhypophysaire gonadotrophe. *J. physiol. (Paris)* **47**: 427–567.

Benoit, J., Assenmacher, I., and Brard, E. (1958). Apparition et maintien de cycles sexuels non saisonniers chez le Canard domestique placé pendant plus de trois ans à l'obscurité totale *J. physiol. (Paris)* **48**: 388–391.

Berthold, A. A. (1849). Transplantation der Hoden. *Arch. Anat. Physiol. Leipzig* pp. 42–46.

Bloom, M. A., Domm, L. V., Nalbandov, A. V., and Bloom, W. (1958). Medullary bone of laying chickens. *Am. Journ. Anat.* **102**: 411–453.

Boss, W. R. (1943). Hormonal determination of adult characters and sex behavior in herring gulls (*Larus argentatus*) *J. Exptl. Zool.* **94**: 181–209.

Boss, W. R., and Witschi, E. (1941). Male sex-hormones inducing adult characters in juvenile herring gulls (*Larus argentatus*). *Anat. Record* **81** (Suppl.): 27–28.

Boss, W. R., and Witschi, E. (1942). Hormonal determination of sex behavior in normal and castrate second year juvenile herring gulls (*Larus argentatus*). *Anat. Record* **84**: 517–518.

Brant, J. W. A., and Nalbandov, A. V. (1956). Role of sex hormones in albumen secretion by the oviduct of chickens. *Poultry Sci.* **35**: 692–700.

Breneman, W. R. (1942a). Action of prolactin and estrone on weights of reproductive organs and viscera of the cockerel. *Endocrinology* **30**: 609–615.

Breneman, W. R. (1942b). Action of diethylstilbestrol in the chick. *Endocrinology* **31**: 179–186.

Breneman, W. R. (1944). The growth of the anterior lobe of the pituitary and the testes in the cockerel. *Endocrinology* **35**: 456–463.

Breneman, W. R. (1955). Reproduction in birds: the female. *Mem. Soc. Endocrinol.* **4**: 94–113.

Bullough, W. S. (1945). Endocrinological aspects of bird behaviour. *Biol. Revs.* **20**: 89–99.

Burrows, W. H., and Byerly, T. C. (1936). Studies of prolactin in the fowl pituitary. I. Broody hens compared with laying hens and males. *Proc. Soc. Exptl. Biol. Med.* **34**: 841–844.

Burrows, W. H., and Quinn, J. P. (1937). The collection of spermatozoa from the domestic fowl and turkey. *Poultry Sci.* **16**: 19–24.

Byerly, T. C., and Burrows, W. H. (1936). Studies of prolactin in the fowl pituitary. II. Effects of genetic constitution on prolactin content. *Proc. Soc. Exptl. Biol. Med.* **34**: 844–846.

Callow, R. K., and Parkes, A. S. (1935). Growth and maintenance of the fowl's comb by androsterone. *Biochem. J.* **29**: 1414–1423.

Ceni, C. (1927). Die endokrinen Faktoren der Mutterliebe und die psychische Feminierung von Männchen. *Schweiz Arch. Neurol Psychiat.* **21**: 131–142.

Chappelier, A. (1913). Persistence et développement des organes génitaux droits chez les femelles adultes des oiseaux. *Bull. Sci. France et Belg.* **47**: 361–376.

Cole, L. J. (1933). The relation of light periodicity to the reproductive cycle, migration and distribution of the mourning dove (*Zenaidura macroura carolinensis*). *Auk* **50**: 284–296.

Collias, N. (1944). Aggressive behaviour among vertebrate animals. *Physiol. Zoöl.* **17**: 83–123.

Collias, N. (1946). Some experiments on broody behaviour in fowl and pigeon. *Anat. Record* **96** (Suppl.): 572.

Collias, N. (1950). Hormones and behaviour with special reference to birds and the mechanisms of hormone action. *Symposium on Steroid Hormones* **1950**. Ed. by Edgar S. Gordon, pp. 227–329.

Comar, C. L., and Driggers, J. C. (1949). Secretion of radioactive calcium in the hen's egg. *Science* **109**: 282.

Common, R. H. (1938). Observations on the mineral metabolism of pullets. *J. Agr. Sci.* **28**: 347–366.

Common, R. H., Bolton, W., and Rutledge, W. A. (1948). The influence of gonadal hormones on the composition of the blood and liver of the domestic fowl. *J. Endocrinol.* **5**: 263–273.

Coombs, C. J. F., and Marshall, A. J. (1956). The effects of hypophysectomy on the internal testis rhythm in birds and mammals. *J. Endrocrinolgy* **13**: 107–111.

Cowles, R. B., and Nordstrom, A. (1946). A possible avian analogue to the scrotum. *Science* **104**: 586–587.

Craig, W. (1909). The expression of emotion in the pigeons. I. The blond ring-dove (*Turtur risorius*). *J. Comp. Neurol.* **19**: 29–82.

Crew, E. A. (1923). Studies in Intersexuality, II. Sex reversal in the Fowl. *Proc. Roy. Soc.* **B95**: 256–278.

Dantchakoff, V. (1937a). Effets du testostéron-propionate sur les ébauches sexuelles de l'oiseau. *Compt. rend. soc. biol.* **124**: 235–238.

Dantchakoff, V. (1937b). Sur la faculté des tissus induits par l'hormone male, d'édifier de nouvelles structures chez l'embryon de cobaye femelle. *Compt. rend. soc. biol.* **124**: 516–518.

Dantchakoff, V., and Kinderis, A. (1937). Sur la croissance de la crète embryonnaire à la suite de l'action de l'hormone mâle. *Compt. rend. soc. biol.* **124**: 308–311.

Das, B. C., and Nalbandov, A. V. (1955). Responses of ovaries of immature chickens to avian and mammalian gonadotropins. *Endocrinology* **57**: 705–710.

Davis, D. E., and Domm, L. V. (1941). The sexual behavior of hormonally treated domestic fowl. *Proc. Soc. Exptl. Biol. Med.* **48**: 667–669.

Davis, D. E., and Domm, L. V. (1943). The influence of hormones on the sexual behavior of the fowl. *In* "Essays in Biology". Univ. California Press, Berkeley, California.

Dodd, J. M. (1955). The hormones of sex and reproduction and their effects in fish and lower chordates. *Mem. Soc. Endocrinol.* **4**: 166–185.

Domm, L. V. (1929). Spermatogenesis following early ovariotomy in the brown leghorn fowl. *Proc. Soc. Exptl. Biol. Med.* **26**: 338–341.

Domm, L. V., and Juhn, M. (1927). Compensatory hypertrophy of the testes in Brown Leghorns. *Biol. Bull.* **552**: 458–473.

Domm, L. V., and van Dyke, H. B. (1932). Precocious development of sexual characters in the fowl by daily injections of hebin. 1. The male, *Proc. Soc. Exptl. Biol. Med.* **30**: 349–350.

Domm, L. V., and Davis, D. E., and Blivaiss, B. B. (1942). Observations on the sexual behaviour of hormonally treated brown leghorn fowl. *Anat. Record* **84**: 481–482.

Driggers, J. C., and Comar, C. L. (1949). The secretion of radioactive calcium (Ca^{45}) in the hen's egg. *Poultry Sci.* **28**: 420–424.

Drost, R. (1938). Geschlechtsbestimmung lebender Vögel nach der Form der Kloaken-gegend. *Vogelzug* **9**: 102–105.

Emmens, C. W. (1938). Maximum growth of capon. *J. Physiol.* (*London*) **93**: 413–415.

Entenman, C., Lorenz, F. W., and Chaikoff, I. L. (1940). The endocrine control of lipid metabolism in the bird. III: Effects of crystalline sex hormones on blood lipids of birds. *J. Biol. Chem.* **134**: 495–504.

Faber, F. (1826). "Veber das Leben der hochnondischen Vögel." Leipzig, xvi+324 pp.

Fell, H. B. (1923). Histological studies on the gonads of the fowl. I. The histological basis of sex reversal. *Brit. J. Exptl. Biol.* **1**: 97–130.

Fell, H. B. (1924). Histological studies on the gonads of the fowl. 2. The histogenesis of the so-called "luteal" cells of the ovary. *Brit. J. Exptl. Biol.* **1**: 293–312.

Fleischmann, W., and Fried, I. A. (1945). Studies on the mechanism of the hyper-cholesterolemia and hypercalcemia induced by estrogen in immature chicks. *Endocrinology* **36**: 406–415.

Forbes, T. R. (1947). The crowing hen: early observations on spontaneous sex reversal in birds. *Yale J. Biol. and Med.* **19**: 955–970.

Fraps, R. M. (1955). The varying effects of sex hormones in birds. *Mem. Soc. Endocrinol.* **4**: 205–218.

Fraps, R. M., Hooker, C. W., and Forbes, T. R. (1948). Progesterone in blood plasma of the ovulating hen. *Science* **108**: 86–87.

Fraps, R. M., Hooker, C. W., and Forbes, T. R. (1949). Progesterone in blood plasma of cocks and non-ovulating hens. *Science* **109**: 493.

Fraps, R. M., Olsen, M. W., and Marsden, S. J. (1951). Augmentation by pregnant mares' serum of body weight response of male turkeys to testosterone propionate. *Proc. Soc. Exptl. Biol. Med.* **77**: 356–358.

Gardner, W. U., and Pfeiffer, C. A. (1942). Influence of estrogens and androgens on the skeletal system. *Physiol. Revs.* **23**: 139–165.

Goodale, H. D. (1916). Note on the behavior of capons when brooding chicks. *J. Animal Behavior* **6**: 319–324.

Goodale, H. D. (1918). Internal factors influencing egg production in the Rhode Island red breed of domestic fowl. *Am. Naturalist* **52**: 209–232.

Goodrich, E. S. (1930). "The Structure and Development of Vertebrates." Macmillan, London.

Grassé, P., ed. (1950). "Traité de Zoologie." Masson, Paris.

Green, J. D., and Harris, G. W. (1947). The neurovascular link between the neurohypophysis and adenohypophysis. *J. Endocrinol.* **5**: 136–146.

Greenwood, D. W., and Blyth, J. S. S. (1932). Reversal of the secondary sexual characters in the fowl. A castrated brown leghorn male which assumed female characters. *J. Genet.* **26**: 119–213.

Greenwood, D. W., and Blyth, J. S. S. (1938). The influence of testis on sexual plumage in the domestic fowl. *J. Genet.* **36**: 501–508.

Hammond, J. (1952). Fertility. *In* F. H. A. Marshall's "The Physiology of Reproduction" (A. S. Parkes, ed.), Vol. 2A, Longmans, Green, London and New York.

Hamilton, J. B., and Golden, W. R. C. (1939). Responses of the female to male hormone substances. *Endocrinology* **25**: 737–748.

Harris, G. W. (1948). Neural control of the pituitary gland. *Physiol. Revs.* **28**: 139–179.

Harrison, R. J. (1948). The development and fate of the corpus luteum in the vertebrate series. *Biol. Revs. Soc.* **23**: 296–331.

Hill, R. T., and Parkes, A. S. (1934). Hypophysectomy of birds. I: Technique, with a note on results. *Proc. Roy. Soc.* **B115**: 402–409.

Hoar, W. S. (1957). The gonads and reproduction. *In* "The Physiology of fishes." Vol. I. pp. 287–322. Academic Press Inc., New York.

Höhn, E. O. (1960). Seasonal changes in the mallard's penis and their hormonal control. *Proc. Zool. Soc. Lond.* (in press).

Hooker, C. W., and Forbes, T. R. (1947). A bioassay for minute amounts of progesterone *Endocrinology* **41**: 158–169.

Huston, T. M., and Nalbandov, A. V. (1953). Neurohumoral control of the pituitary in the fowl. *Endocrinology* **52**: 149–156.

Hutt, F. B. (1929). Sex dimorphism and variability in the appendicular skeleton of the Leghorn fowl. *Poultry Sci.* **8**: 202–218.

Hutt, F. B. (1949). "Genetics of the Fowl." McGraw-Hill, New York.

Juhn, M., and Gustavson, R. G. (1930). The production of female genital subsidiary characters and plumage sex characters by injection of human placental hormone in fowls. *J. Exptl. Zool.* **56**: 31–61.

Juhn, M., Gustavson, R. G., and Gallagher, T. F. (1932). The factor of age with reference to reactivity to sex hormones in fowl. *J. Exptl. Zool.* **64**: 133–185.

Jungck, E. C., Heller, G., and Nelson, W. O. (1947). Regulation of pituitary gonado-trophic secretion. Inhibition by estrogen or inactivation by ovaries. *Proc. Soc. Exptl. Biol. Med.* **65**: 148–152.

Keast, J. A., and Marshall, A. J. (1954). The influence of drought and rainfall on reproduction in Australian desert birds. *Proc. Zool. Soc. London* **124**: 493–499.

Kirschbaum, A., Pfeiffer, C. A., Van Heuverswyn, J., and Gardner, W. U. (1939). Studies in gonad-hypophysial relationship and cyclic changes in the English sparrow (*Passer domesticus* L.). *Anat. Record* **75**: 249–263.

Kleinholtz, L. H., and Rahn, H. (1940). The distribution of intermedin. A new bio-logical method of assay and results of tests under normal and experimental conditions. *Anat. Record* **76**: 157–172.

Kornfield, W., and Nalbandov, D. V. (1954). Endocrine influences on the development of the rudimentary gonad of fowl. *Endocrinology* **55**: 751–761.

Kumaran, J. D. S., and Turner, C. W. (1949). The endocrinology of spermatogenesis in birds. I: Effect of estrogen and androgen. *Poultry Sci.* **28**: 593–602.

Kyes, P., and Potter, T. S. (1934). Physiological marrow ossification in Female pigeons. *Anat. Record* **60**: 377–379.

Lack, D. (1946). "The Life of the Robin," (rev. ed.). Witherby, London.

Lake, P. E. (1956). A retarding factor in the problem of fowl semen storage. *Proc. 3rd Intern. Congr. Animal Reproduction, Cambridge, Engl. Sect. 3*, pp. 104–106.

Lake, P. E. (1957). The male reproductive tract of the fowl. *J. Anat.* **91**: 116–129.

Lange, B. (1928). Die Brutflecke der Vögel und die fur sie wichtigen Hauteigentüm-lichkeiten. *Gegenbaur morphol. Jahrb.* **59**: 610–712.

Leatham, J. H., and Wolf, R. C. (1955). The varying effects of sex hormones in mammals. *Mem. Soc. Endocrinol.* **4**: 220–233.

Lehrman, D. S. (1955). The physiological basis of parental feeding behaviour in the ring dove (*Streptopelia risoria*). *Behaviour* **7**: 241–286.

Lehrman, D. S. (1959). Hormonal responses to external stimuli in birds. *Ibis*, 478–496.

Lehrman, D. S., and Brody, P. (1957). *Proc. Soc. Exptl. Biol. Med.* **95**: 373–375.

Leonard, S. L. (1937). Luteinizing hormone in bird hypophyses. *Proc. Soc. Exptl. Biol. Med.* **37**: 566–568.

Leonard, S. L. (1939). Induction of singing in female canaries by injection of male hormone. *Proc. Soc. Exptl. Biol. Med.* **41**: 229–230.

Leopold, A. S. (1944). The nature of hereditable wildness in turkeys. *Condor* **46**: 133–197.

Lofts, B., and Marshall, A. J. (1956). The effects of prolactin administration on the internal rhythm of reproduction in male birds. *J. Endocrinol.* **13**: 101–106.

Lofts, B., and Marshall, A. J. (1958). An investigation of the refractory period of repro-duction of birds by means of exogenous prolactin and follicle stimulating hormone. *J. Endocrinol.* **17**: 91–98.

Lofts, B., and Marshall, A. J. (1959). The post-nuptial occurrence of progestins in the seminiferous tubules of birds. *J. Endocrinol.* **19**: 16–21.

Lorenz, F. W. (1938). Effects of estrin on blood lipids of the immature fowl. *J. Biol. Chem.* **126**: 763–769.

Lyons, W. R., and Page, E. (1935). Detection of mamotropin in the urine of lactating woman. *Proc. Soc. Exptl. Biol. Med.* **32**: 1049–1050.

McDonald, M. R., and Riddle, O. (1945). The effect of reproduction and estrogen administration on the partition of calcium phosphorus, and nitrogen in pigeon plasma. *J. Biol. Chem.* **159**: 445–464.

Marshall, A. J. (1949). On the function of the interstitium of the testis: The sexual cycle of a wild bird (*Fulmarus glacialis* L.). *Quart. J. Microscop. Sci.* **90**: 265–280.

Marshall, A. J. (1952a). The interstitial cycle in relation to autumn and winter sexual behaviour in birds. *Proc. Zool. Soc. London* **121**: 727–740.

Marshall, A. J. (1952b). Display and sexual cycle in the Spotted Bowerbird (*Chlamydera maculata*) (Gould). *Proc. Zool. Soc. London* **122**: 239–252.

Marshall, A. J. (1954). "Bower-birds: their Displays and Breeding Cycles." Clarendon Press, London and New York.

Marshall, A. J. (1955). Reproduction in birds: the male. *Mem. Soc. Endocrinol.* **4**: 75–89.

Marshall, A. J., and Coombs, C. J. F. (1957). The interaction of environmental internal and behavioural factors in the rook (*Corvus f. frugilegus*) Linnaeus. *Proc. Zool. Soc. London* **128**: 545–589.

Marshall, A. J., and Serventy, D. L. (1956a). The breeding cycle of the short-tailed shearwater *Puffinus tenuirostris* (Temminck) in relation to trans-equatorial migration and its environment. *Proc. Zool. Soc. London* **127**: 489–510.

Marshall, A. J., and Serventy, D. L. (1956b). A case of inter-sexuality in *Gymnorhina dorsalis*. *Emu* **56**: 207–210.

Marshall, A. J., and Serventy, D. L. (1957). On the post-nuptial rehabilitation of the avian testis tunic. *Emu* **57**: 59–63.

Marshall, A. J., and Serventy, D. L. (1959). Internal rhythm and trans-equatorial migration in the short-tailed shearwater. *Nature* **184**: 1704–1705.

Marshall, F. H. A. (1936). Sexual periodicity and the causes which determine it. *Phil. Trans. Roy. Soc. London* **B226**: 423–456.

Masure, R. H., and Allee, W. C. (1934). Flock organization of the shell-parakeet, *Melopsittacus undulatus* Shaw. *Ecology* **15**: 388–398.

Matthews, L. H. (1955). The evolution of viviparity in vertebrates. *Mem. Soc. Endocrinol.* **4**: 129–144.

Meites, J., and Turner, C. W. (1947). Effect of sex hormones on pituitary lactogen and crop glands of common pigeons. *Proc. Soc. Exptl. Biol. Med.* **64**: 465–468.

Munro, S. S. (1938). The effect of dilution and density on the fertilizing capacity of fowl sperm suspensions. *Can. J. Research* **16**: 281–297.

Nalbandov, A. V. (1945). A study of the effect of prolactin on broodiness and on cock testes. *Endocrinology* **36**: 251–258.

Nalbandov, A. V., and Baum, G. J. (1948). The use of stilboestrol inhibited-males as test animals for gonadotrophic hormones. *Endocrinology* **43**: 371–379.

Nalbandov, A., Meyer, R. K., and McShan, W. H. (1951). The role of a third gonadotrophic hormone in the mechanism of androgen secretion in chicken testes. *Anat. Record* **110**: 475–494.

Needham, J. (1950). "Biochemistry and Morphogenesis." *Cambridge Univ. Press*, London and New York.

Nishiyama, H. (1954). Studies on the reproductive physiology of the cock. V. The influence of androgens in the accessory organs of the phallus. *Proc. 10th World's Poultry Congr. A.*, 88–90.

Nishiyama, H. (1955). Studies on the accessory reproductive organs in the cock. *J. Fac. Agr. Kyushu Univ.* **10**: 277–305.

Noble, G. K., and Wurm, M. (1938). Effect of testosterone proprionate on the black-crowned night heron. *Anat. Record* **72**: (Suppl.): 60.

Noble, G. K., and Wurm, M. (1940a). The effect of testosterone propionate on the black-crowned night heron. *Endocrinology* **26**: 837–850.

Noble, G. K., and Wurm, M. (1940b). The effect of hormones on the breeding of the laughing gull. *Anat. Record* **78** (Suppl.): 50–51.

Noble, G. K., and Zitrin, A. (1942). Induction of mating behaviour in male and female chicks following injections of sex hormones. *Endocrinology* **30**: 327–334.

Nonidez, J. (1925). Studies on the gonads of the fowl. IV. The intertubular tissue of the testis in normal and hen-feathered cocks. *Am. J. Anat.* **34**: 359–425.

Oksche, A., Laws, D. F., Kamemoto, F. I and Farner, D. S. (1959). The hypothalamo-hypophysial neurosecretory system of the white-crowned sparrow *Zonotrichia leucophrys gambelli. Zeitschr. Zell.* **51**, 1–42.

Olsen, M. W., and Neher, B. H. (1948). The site of fertilization in the domestic fowl. *J. Exptl. Zool.* **109**: 355–366.

Oslund, R. (1928). Seasonal modifications in testes of vertebrates. *Quart. Rev. Biol.* **3**: 254–270.

Parkes, A. S., and Marshall, A. J. (1960). The reproductive hormones in birds. *In* F. H. A. Marshall's "Physiology of Reproduction" (A. S. Parkes, ed.). Longmans, Green, London.

Patel, S. (1936). The physiology of the formation of "pigeon's milk." *Physiol. Zoöl.* **9**: 129–152.

Payne, F. (1943). The cytology of the anterior pituitary of broody fowls. *Anat. Record* **86**: 1–13.

Payne, F. (1944). Pituitary changes in aging capons. *Anat. Record* **89**: 563.

Payne, F. (1946). The cellular picture in the anterior pituitary of normal fowls from embryo to old age. *Anat. Record* **96**: 77–91.

Pfeiffer, C. A., and Gardner, W. U. (1938). Skeletal changes and blood serum calcium level in pigeons receiving estrogens. *Endocrinology* **23**: 485–491.

Pfeiffer, C. A., and Kirschbaum, A. (1943). Relation of interstitial cell hyperplasia to secretion of male hormone in the sparrow. *Anat. Record* **85**: 211–227.

Pickford, G. E., and Atz, J. W. (1957). "The physiology of the pituitary gland in fishes." New York Zoological Society, New York.

Rahn, H., and Painter, B. T. (1941). The comparative histology of the bird pituitary. *Anat. Record* **79**: 297–311.

Richardson, K. C. (1935). The secretory phenomena in the oviduct of the fowl, including the process of shell formation examined by the micro-incineration technique. *Phil. Trans. Roy. Soc. London* **B225**: 149–195.

Riddle, O. (1924). A case of complete sex-reversal in the adult pigeon. *Am. Naturalist* **58**: 176–181.

Riddle, O. (1927). The cyclical growth of the vesicula seminalis in birds is hormone controlled. *Anat. Record* **37**: 1–11.

Riddle, O. (1935). Aspects and implications of the hormonal control of the maternal instinct. *Proc. Am. Phil. Soc.* **75**: 521–525.

Riddle, O. (1947). Endocrines and constitutions in doves and pigeons. *Carnegie Inst. Wash. Publ. No.* **572**.

Riddle, O., and Bates, R. W. (1933). Concerning anterior pituitary hormones. *Endocrinology* **17**: 689–698.

Riddle, O., and Bates, R. W. (1939). The preparation, assay, and actions of lactogenic hormones. *In* "Sex and Internal Secretions" (E. Allan, C. Danforth, and E. Doisy, eds.), 2nd ed., pp. 1088–1117. Williams & Wilkins, Baltimore, Maryland.

Riddle, O., and Lahr, E. L. (1944). On broodiness of Ring Doves following implants of certain steroid hormones. *Endocrinology* **35**: 255–260.

Riddle, O., and McDonald, M. R. (1945). The partition of plasma calcium and inorganic phosphorus in estrogen-treated normal and parathyroidectomized birds. *Endocrinology* **36**: 48–52.

Riddle, O., Bates, R. W., and Dykshorn, S. W. (1932). A new hormone of the anterior pituitary. *Proc. Soc. Exptl. Biol. Med.* **29**: 1211–1212.

Riddle, O., Bates, R. W., and Dykshorn, S. W. (1933). The preparation, identification and assay of prolactin—a hormone of the anterior pituitary. *Am. J. Physiol.* **105**: 191–216.

Riddle, O., Bates, R. W., and Lahr, E. L. (1935). Prolactin induces broodiness in the fowl. *Am. J. Physiol.* **111**: 352–360.

Riddle, O., Rauch, V. M., and Smith, G. C. (1945). Action of estrogen on plasma calcium and endoseal bone formation in parathyroidectomized pigeons. *Endocrinology* **36**: 41–47.

Romanoff, A. L., and Romanoff, A. J. (1949). "The Avian Egg." Wiley, New York.

Salomonsen, F. (1939). Moults and sequences of plumages in the rock ptarmigan (*Lagopus mutus*). *Vidensk. Medd. Dansk Naturhist. Foren.* **103**: 1–491.

Schildmacher, H., and Steubing, L. (1952). Untersuchungen zur hormonalen Regulierung des Fettwerdens der Zugvögel im Frühjahr. *Biol. Zentr.* **71**: 272–282.

Schjelderup-Ebbe, T. (1935). Social behavior in birds. *In* "A Handbook of Social Psychology" (C. Murchison, ed.). Clark Univ. Press, Worcester, Massachusetts.

Schooley, J. P. (1939). Technique for hypophysectomy in pigeons. *Endocrinology* **25**: 373–378.

Schooley, J. P., and Riddle, O. (1938). The morphological basis of pituitary function in pigeons. *Am. J. Anat.* **62**: 314–350.

Schooley, J. P., Riddle, O., and Bates, R. W. (1941). Replacement therapy in hypophysectomised juvenile pigeons. *Am. J. Anat.* **69**: 123–154.

Serventy, D. L., and Marshall, A. J. (1956). Factors influencing testis coloration in birds. *Emu* **56**: 219–221.

Shirley, Jr., H. V., and Nalbandov, A. V. (1956). Effects of transecting hypophysial stalks in laying hens. *Endocrinology* **58**: 694–700.

Shoemaker, H. H. (1939a). Social hierarchy in flocks of the canary. *Auk* **56**: 381–406.

Shoemaker, H. H. (1939b). Effect of testosterone propionate on behaviour of the female canary. *Proc. Soc. Exptl. Biol. Med.* **41**: 299–302.

Siller, W. G. (1956). A Sertoli cell tumour causing feminization in a brown leghorn capon. *J. Endocrinol.* **14**: 197–203.

Skutch, A. F. (1957). The incubation patterns of birds. *Ibis* **99**: 69–93.

Sluiter, J. W., and van Oordt, G. J. (1947). Experimental data on the function of the interstitium of the gonads: experiments with cockerels. *Quart. J. Microscop. Sci.* **88**: 135–150.

Sluiter, J. W., and van Oordt, G. J. (1949). The influence of a gonadotrophin on the seasonal changes in the testis and deferent duct of the Chaffinch (*Fringilla cœlebs*). *Quart. J. Microscop. Sci.* **90**: 1–11.

Sturkie, P. D. (1954). "Avian Physiology." Baillière, Tindall & Cox, London.

Taber, E. (1949). The source and effects of androgen in the male chick treated with gonadotrophins. *Am. J. Anat.* **85**: 231–263.

Taber, E. (1951). Androgen secretion in the fowl. *Endocrinology* **48**: 6–16.

Taibel, A. (1928). Risveglio artificiale di instinti tipicanente femminili nei maschi di taluni uccelli. *Atti soc. nat. e mat. Modena* **59**: 93.

Teilum, G. (1950). Oestrogen production by Sertoli cells in the etiology of benign senile hypertrophy of the human prostrate. Testicular "Lipoid cell ratio" and oestrogen-androgen quotient in human male. *Acta endocrinol.* Copenhagen **4**: 43–61.

Thayer, R. H., Jaap, R. G., and Penquite, R. (1945). Fattening chickens by feeding estrogens. *Poultry Sci.* **24**: 483–495.

Turner, C. W. (1948). Oral effectiveness of androgens in fowls. *Poultry Sci.* **27**: 789–792.

Watson, J. B. (1908). The behaviour of noddy and zooty terns. *Publs. Carnegie Inst.* **103**: 189–255.

White, W. W. (1941). Bird of first brood of swallow assisting to feed second brood. *Brit. Birds* **34**: 179–184.

Wilckins, L., and Fleischmann, W. (1946). The influence of various androgenic steroids on nitrogen balance and growth. *J. Clin. Endocrinol.* **6**: 383–401.

Williamson, K. (1941). First brood of swallow assisting to feed second brood. *Brit. Birds* **34**: 221–222.

Wingstrand, K. G. (1951). "The Structure and Development of the Avian Pituitary." Gleerup, *Lund*.

Witschi, E. (1935). Seasonal sex characters in birds and their hormonal control. *Wilson Bull.* **47**: 177–188.

Witschi, E. (1937). Comparative physiology of the vertebrate hypophysis (anterior and intermediate lobes). *Cold Spring Harbor Symposia Quant. Biol.* **5**: 180–190.

Witschi, E., and Miller, R. A. (1938). Ambisexuality in the female starling. *J. Exptl. Zool.* **79**: 475–487.

Wolfson, A. (1952). The cloacal protuberance. *Bird Banding* **23**: 159–165.

Wolfson, A. (1954). Sperm storage at lower-than-body temperature outside the body cavity in some passerine birds. *Science* **120**: 68–71.

Yasuda, M. (1953). Cytological studies of the anterior pituitary in the broody fowl. *Proc. Japan Acad.* **29**: 586–593.

Zitrin, A. (1942). Induction of male copulatory behaviour in a hen following administration of male hormone. *Endocrinology* **31**: 690.

Chapter XIX

Energy Metabolism, Thermoregulation and Body Temperature[1]

JAMES R. KING AND DONALD S. FARNER

I. Introduction

The chemical energy which animals obtain in food from their environment is expended in a variety of energy-requiring functions. A large fraction is used for the *mechanical work* effected by skeletal, cardiac,

[1] The preparation of this manuscript was supported in part by a grant from the National Science Foundation (No. GS 1799).

and smooth muscle. Smaller amounts are used in the work of *active transport* in the maintenance of the concentrations of cell constituents and body fluids, and in the *chemical work* of synthesis of new body constituents. An inevitable consequence of these transformations of energy under the conditions in which life exists is the liberation of heat in accordance with the second law of thermodynamics.[2] Animals produce heat as a consequence of the inefficiency with which chemical energy is transformed into useful work in the processes of metabolism. For an organism in which there is no change in body temperature, constitution, or mass (i.e. no change of state) it can be shown that:

$$H = Q + W$$

where H = energy metabolized during a given period, Q = the heat liberated from the organism during this period, and W = the quantity of work performed by the animal on its environment during this period. It is evident from this relationship that all the chemical energy ingested will be dissipated as heat if no external work is performed and if there is no change of state. This fundamental statement is emphasized here because it is only under such conditions that a determination of heat production is a true measurement of the metabolic rate of an animal. If there is a significant change of state during the period of measurement an additional term, S, must be introduced to balance the equation:

$$H \pm S = Q + W$$

This *storage term* will be either positive or negative depending upon whether the organism is decreasing or increasing in heat content or mass.

Birds and mammals, to their considerable advantage, have acquired mechanisms which within limits permit the control of the rate at which heat is produced (rate of *thermogenesis*) and the rate at which it is dissipated from the body (rate of *thermolysis*). In most species, the velocities of these opposing processes are so accurately adjusted that a very stable body temperature is maintained even in the face of highly variable internal and external conditions. This stability of internal body temperature is called *homoiothermy*, and metabolically distinguishes birds and mammals from their "cold-blooded" ancestors, the *poikilotherms*.

The heat and energy exchanges which accompany metabolic processes are often designated as "energy metabolism." In this chapter, however, we are interested primarily in the energy exchanges between birds and their environments, rather than the details of energy-yielding reactions. This is a topic which might better be called avian bioenergetics. It

---

[2] For a review of the thermodynamics of living systems the reader is referred to Bray and White (1957), Bladergroen (1955), or Blum (1950).

comprises an important contribution to our understanding of the manner in which the lives of birds are influenced by their trophic and thermal environments.

II. Energy Categories and Calorimetry

A. THE PARTITION OF ENERGY INCOME

The energy ingested as food by an animal is called the *gross energy*. The partition of this income as it passes through the animal is shown in the following diagram:

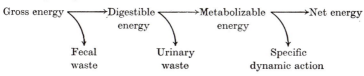

The fraction which is absorbed from the gut is called the *digestible energy*. A portion of this is excreted from the kidney as nitrogenous waste (largely uric acid), leaving the *metabolizable energy* available to the bird. Depending upon the species of bird, the composition of the ration, and the environmental conditions, this fraction amounts to about 70–90% of the gross energy (Kendeigh, 1949; Seibert, 1949; Albritton, 1954; Davis, 1955; King, unpublished). A variable fraction of the metabolizable energy appears immediately as heat and is described as the *specific dynamic action* (S.D.A.), or *calorigenic effect*, or *heat increment* of the ration. It is believed to result from the exothermic reactions of intermediary metabolism in the interconversion, transportation, and storage of food molecules; thus it may be regarded as the energy cost of assimilation. The fraction of the metabolizable energy appearing as S.D.A. is directly proportional to the plane of nutrition, and depends also upon the previous nutrition of the animal and upon the composition of the diet. Protein exhibits the greatest calorigenic effect, which has been measured as 15–18% above the basal energy expenditure in the domestic fowl (Barott *et al.*, 1938), but may be as high as 40% in mammals. Fats and carbohydrates exhibit lesser calorigenic effects. For animals in a thermoneutral environment (see Section IV, B) the S.D.A. represents entirely "waste" heat. With decreasing ambient temperature, however, the heat production of the S.D.A. may be used in maintaining body temperature thus sparing metabolizable energy.

The difference between the metabolizable energy and the S.D.A. is the *net energy* and includes the energy available to the animal for growth and maintenance, including special seasonal functions such as molting and the production of eggs, for performing external work, and for storage as fat and glycogen.

B. The Measurement of Energy Exchange

To be valid as measurements of the metabolic intensity of an organism, calorimetric determinations must be made during a period in which there is no change in the energy content of the organism. In other words, the initial and final states of the organism should be the same, or, if not the same, appropriate corrections should be applied. Variations in energy content may arise from changes in body temperature, constitution, and mass. The body temperature of most birds (with some notable exceptions; see Section IX) is sufficiently constant that this source of variation can be ignored except in the most critical determinations of the "basal" metabolism. Variation in body mass and body constituents (chiefly water, fat, and glycogen, but also protein) may be neglected in short-term determinations, but this variation becomes increasingly important as a source of error as the duration of the determination is increased. For instance, many species of migratory birds accumulate much depot fat during the migratory season. A long-term measurement of energy intake during such a period of accumulation would include calories stored as fat; the metabolic rate of the bird would accordingly appear to be greater than it actually was (if appropriate corrections were not applied).

1. Direct Calorimetry

Theoretically, the most accurate method for the determination of metabolic intensity is to measure directly the heat liberated from the subject under appropriate standard conditions. This can be done by a variety of techniques (see Kleiber, 1950a), but in general these require relatively elaborate instrumentation. Direct calorimetry has been employed rather rarely in investigations of birds (domestic turkey: Lefévre, 1903; domestic goose: Benedict and Lee, 1937; domestic goose and duck: Hári, 1917; Hári and Kriwuscha, 1918; domestic fowl: Deighton and Hutchinson, 1940; Barott and Pringle, 1941, 1946). Indirect calorimetry, because of its relative simplicity and presumably satisfactory accuracy, has been the method of choice.

2. Indirect Calorimetry

The indirect technique most commonly employed entails measurement of the respiratory exchange of oxygen and carbon dioxide ("respiratory metabolism"), which is proportional to heat production under specified conditions. This method is especially suited to relatively short-term measurements of heat production. Body balance techniques are less frequently employed but are preferable for long-term studies of animals under normal cage conditions. These techniques involve measurement of material input, output, and storage in the body. Heat production is computed from established caloric equivalents of the material exchange (see Swift and French, 1954, p. 88ff.).

a. *Respiratory metabolism.* Relationships have been established between heat production, the consumption of oxygen, and the production of carbon dioxide which permit the estimation of heat production from the measured respiratory exchange. There is not space here to elaborate on the theory underlying this technique (for which see Lusk, 1928; Clark, 1952). In brief, it depends upon the established metabolic "constants" shown in Table I. It is evident that, with certain exceptions

TABLE I

SUMMARY OF FACTORS FOR USE IN INDIRECT CALORIMETRY IN BIRDS

Substance	Metabolizable energy (kcal./gm.)	Thermal quotient (kcal./l. O_2)	Respiratory quotient
Carbohydrate	4.2	5.047	1.00
Protein[a]	4.2	4.75	0.73
Fat	9.5	4.686	0.71

[a] According to King (1957).

which will be discussed below, the respiratory quotient (R.Q.) of a mixed diet will lie between 0.71 and 1.00, and that the caloric equivalent of the measured oxygen consumption will lie between 5.047 and 4.686 kcal. per liter. In precise measurements, the oxygen consumption, carbon dioxide production, and urinary nitrogen excretion are measured simultaneously. The latter determination is required in order to assess the contribution of protein oxidation to the total heat production. One gram of urinary nitrogen is equivalent to 26.6 kcal. of metabolizable energy, 5.59 liters of oxygen, and 4.11 liters of carbon dioxide (approximate values from data of King, 1957). The oxygen and carbon dioxide exchange attributable to protein oxidation is subtracted from the measured total respiratory exchange. The remainder originates in the oxidation of fat and carbohydrate; the ratio, volumes CO_2: volumes O_2, then yields the *nonprotein* R.Q. This ratio is characteristic of one, and only one, mixture of fat and carbohydrate, whose heat of combustion can readily be computed. The thermal equivalent of the observed oxygen consumption can be calculated from the equation: kcal./liter of O_2 = 3.815 + 1.232 R.Q. (where R.Q. = the *nonprotein* ratio), or obtained from tabular values (Lusk, 1928). The heat production computed by use of this thermal equivalent is added to that determined for the protein oxidation to obtain the total heat production. In practice, the determination of urinary nitrogen is almost uniformly omitted in investigations of birds because of the technical difficulty of quantitatively collecting urine. It is customary to compute the total heat production on the basis of the over-all R.Q. It can be shown that the error incurred through the use of this simplification is negligible in fasting animals (Brody, 1945, p. 311).

Variation in the R.Q. beyond the combustion values shown in Table I can result from metabolic interconversions, such as lipogenesis and gluconeogenesis, and from various other causes (Cathcart and Markowitz, 1927; Richardson, 1929). Values of the R.Q. of up to 1.49 have been observed in force-fed geese (Benedict and Lee, 1937) and up to about 1.18 in certain passerines (Merkel, 1958) which were synthesizing fat. It has been found that the thermal equivalent of oxygen consumption in such cases is the same as at an R.Q. of unity (Benedict and Lee, 1937). At the other end of the scale, R.Q.'s below 0.71 have been observed in many species of normal, fasting birds (Mellen and Hill, 1955; King, 1957). The cause of this "abnormal" (compared with mammals) R.Q. of fasting is unknown, nor is it known what thermal equivalent of oxygen consumption should be employed in calorimetric determinations involving R.Q.'s below 0.71. For this reason it has been suggested that indirect calorimetry is not a valid technique for birds (Henry et al., 1934). Such criticisms, however, appear to be grossly overemphasized (Benedict, 1938; King, 1957).

b. Energy balance studies. In their simplest form, which will be the only one considered here, balance studies involve the measurement of gross energy input and excretory energy output. The method requires quantitative feeding and collection of excreta. The energy content of food and excreta is determined by oxygen bomb calorimetry (see Kleiber, 1950a). The difference between energy input and energy output is the metabolizable energy available to the bird for maintenance, work, and storage (minus the S.D.A.). This method has recently been applied to the study of the bioenergetics of wild birds by Kendeigh (1949), Seibert (1949), Davis (1955), Odum and Major (1956), King and Farner (1956), and Rautenberg (1957).

A relatively new technique of indirect calorimetry deserves special note because potentially it is applicable to free-living birds and may offer a long-sought method for removing energy studies from the laboratory to the field. This technique involves the indirect measurement of carbon dioxide output by determination of the turnover rate of injected isotopic water, D_2O^{18} (Lifson et al., 1955; McClintock and Lifson, 1958), and requires only the analysis of initial and final blood samples.

III. Standard Metabolic Rate and Body Weight

A. STANDARD METABOLIC RATE

The term "standard metabolic rate" (Krogh, 1916) refers to the heat production per unit of time as measured under conditions selected to provide a valid basis for making comparisons among individuals and species. Standard metabolism is also commonly called "basal metabolism," but because of the clinical implications of this term we prefer to avoid it in the present discussion. The basic objective in the selection of standard experimental conditions is to minimize extrinsic influences on the metabolism of the organism so that the only major variable involved is the inherent metabolic intensity. Because of the lability of metabolic processes this objective can be attained only by the most rigorous techniques and attention to detail. For homoiotherms, the attainment of standard conditions requires that the animal be in a postabsorptive condition (i.e. not digesting or absorbing food), that it be in thermoneutral surroundings, and that it be as completely as possible at muscular and psychical rest. Benedict (1938) notes additional factors, such as ovulation, time of day (see Section V), molting (see Section VI), which influence the heat production and which accordingly must be recognized and controlled in comparative investigations. In addition, it is evident that the ambient temperature to which the animals are adapted (see Section IV, D.) may affect the standard metabolic rate if it is more than 15–20° below the standard (thermoneutral) temperature of the determination.

Data on the standard metabolic rate of sixty species of birds are assembled in Table II. Only those data which were obtained under standard or quasi-standard conditions have been included, with a few exceptions as noted in the table. It should be clearly understood that the averages presented for the various species are not of uniform statistical reliability. However, because of the paucity of data on avian metabolism, except in the case of domestic species, it appears desirable to survey the scales of size and phylogeny as widely as possible. Those persons familiar with the literature of avian metabolism will realize that a large quantity of data from early investigations (prior to about 1925) has been excluded. With a few exceptions, the older investigations (especially those concerned with small birds) are of only historical interest because of the lack of standardized experimental conditions. The results of these investigations have been summarized by Kestner and Plaut (1924), Benedict and Fox (1927), and Groebbels (1932). Some otherwise very valuable data from recent investigations (de Bont, 1944; Winkel, 1951) are also omitted from consideration because the

TABLE II

STANDARD METABOLIC RATE IN SOME AVIAN SPECIES

Species	Body weight kg.	Determination made at night (N) or day (D)	Kcal./kg./24 hr.	Kcal./24 hr.	Reference
Casuariiformes:					
Casuarius bennetti	17.6	N	29.3	516	Benedict and Fox, 1927
Pelecaniformes:					
Pelecanus occidentalis	3.51	N	75.2	264	Benedict and Fox, 1927
Pelecanus conspicillatus	5.09	N	73.5	374	Benedict and Fox, 1927
Ciconiiformes:					
Ardea herodias	1.87	N	68.4	128	Benedict and Fox, 1927
Botaurus lentiginosus	0.60	N	93	56	Benedict and Fox, 1927
Jabiru mycteria	5.47	N	49.7	272	Benedict and Fox, 1927
Leptoptilos javanicus	5.71	N	53.8	307	Benedict and Fox, 1927
Guara alba	0.94	D	90	85	Benedict and Fox, 1927
Phoenicopterus antiquorum	3.04	N	70.7	215	Benedict and Fox, 1927
Anseriformes:					
Chauna chavaria	2.62	N	54.2	142	Benedict and Fox, 1927
Cygnus buccinator	8.88	N	47.1	418	Benedict and Fox, 1927
Branta bernicla					
Summer	1.130	D	96.02	108.5	Irving et al., 1955
Winter[a]	1.168	D	80.0	93.4	Irving et al., 1955
Aix sponsa	0.485	N	134	65	Herzog, 1930
Domestic goose, ♂	6.31	N	42.3	267	Herzog, 1930
Domestic goose, ♀	5.46	N	50.4	275	Herzog, 1930
Domestic goose	5.0	N	56	280	Benedict and Lee, 1937
Domestic goose	3.3	?	66	219	Giaja, 1931
Domestic duck	1.87	D	84.0	157	Giaja and Males, 1928

Falconiformes:					
Vultur gryphus	10.32	N	34.0	351	Benedict and Fox, 1927
Aquila chrysaëtos	3.0	D	34	102	Giaja and Males, 1928
Geranoaëtus melanoleucus	2.86	N	37.1	106	Benedict and Fox, 1927
Gypaëtus barbatus	5.07	N	45	228	Benedict and Fox, 1927
Falco tinnunculus	0.108	D	157	17.0	Giaja and Males, 1928
Galliformes:					
Crax alberti	2.80	N	48.6	136	Benedict and Fox, 1927
Penelope purpurescens	2.04	N	55	112	Benedict and Fox, 1927
Coturnix coturnix	0.097	D	235	23	Giaja and Males, 1928
Domestic fowl, ♂♂	2.270	N	70.79	160.7	Herzog, 1930
Domestic fowl, ♀♀	1.742	N	57.81	100.7	Herzog, 1930
Domestic fowl, ♀♀	2.0	N	50	101	Benedict, 1938
Domestic fowl, ♂♂	2.0	N	47	94	Benedict, 1938
Domestic fowl, ♀♀	2.00	N	68.6	137	Barott and Pringle, 1941
Domestic fowl, ♀♀	2.430	?	67.7	164.2	Barott and Pringle, 1946
Domestic fowl, ♀♀	2.71	N	45.8	124	Winchester, 1940
Domestic fowl, ♀♀	2.00	D	57.6	115	Dukes, 1937
Domestic turkey	3.7	?	50	184	Giaja, 1931
Gruiformes:					
Grus canadensis	3.89	D	43.2	168	Benedict and Fox, 1927
Anthropoïdes paradisea	4.03	N	55	220	Benedict and Fox, 1927
Charadriiformes:					
Larus hyperboreusa	1.60	D	190	304	Scholander et al., 1950a
Gabianus pacificus	1.21	D	105	127	Benedict and Fox, 1927
Catharacta skua	0.97	D	101	98	Benedict and Fox, 1927
Columbiformes:					
Columba palumbus	0.150	N	113	17.0	Benedict, 1938
Zenaidura macroura, ♀♀	0.126	N	118	14.9	Riddle et al., 1932
Zenaidura macroura, ♂♂	0.121	N	127	15.4	Riddle et al., 1932
Streptopelia decaocto	0.155	D	118	18.3	Gelineo, 1955

TABLE II—(*continued*)

Species	Body weight kg.	Determination made at night (N) or day (D)	Kcal./kg./24 hr.	Kcal./24 hr.	Reference
Streptopelia decaocto	0.152	D	143	21.8	Giaja and Males, 1928
Domestic pigeon	0.372	N	95.4	35.5	Herzog, 1930
Domestic pigeon	0.311	N	105.9	32.9	Burckard *et al.*, 1933
Domestic pigeon	0.300	N	100	30	Benedict, 1938
Domestic pigeon	0.266	D	126	33.7	Gelineo, 1955
Strigiformes:					
Strix aluco	0.520	N	83	43	Herzog, 1930
Bubo virginianus	1.45	D	74.5	108	Benedict and Fox, 1927
Caprimulgiformes:					
Nyctidromus albicollis	43.0 gm.	D	178	7.65	Scholander *et al.*, 1950a
Apodiformes:					
Calypte anna[b]	4.07	D	1410	5.83	Pearson, 1950
Selasphorus sasin[b]	3.53	D	1601	5.67	Pearson, 1950
Passeriformes:					
Pipra mentalis[b]	12	D	533	6.5	Scholander *et al.*, 1950b
Perisoreus canadensis[a]	64.5	D	310	20	Scholander *et al.*, 1950b
Corvus corax[a]	850	D	108	92	Scholander *et al.*, 1950b
Corvus caurinus					
Summer	282	D	260	73.2	Irving *et al.*, 1955
Winter[a]	306	D	316	96.7	Irving *et al.*, 1955
Parus major	18.5	N	451	8.36	Steen, 1958
Troglodytes aëdon	10.8	D	589	6.36	Kendeigh, 1939
Passer domesticus, ♂♂	24.3	D	449	10.90	Quirring and Bade, 1943
Passer domesticus, ♀♀	23.0	D	408	9.38	Quirring and Bade, 1943
Passer domesticus	26.0	D	360	9.36	Gelineo, 1955
Passer domesticus	26.0	D	450	11.7	Kendeigh, 1944

Passer domesticus	26.0	N	270	7.02	Kendeigh, 1944
Passer domesticus	25.0	N	278	6.94	Miller, 1939
Passer domesticus					
Spring	23.5	?	468	11.0	Fonberg, 1932
Winter	22.4	?	424	9.50	Fonberg, 1932
Passer domesticus	27.3	N	312	8.51	Steen, 1958
Passer montanus	22.0	N	387	8.52	Steen, 1958
Vidua paradisea	10.5	N	384	4.03	Terroine and Trautmann, 1927
Richmondena cardinalis	40.0	D	305	12.2	Dawson, 1958
Fringilla montifringilla	24.8	N	384	9.50	Steen, 1958
Chloris chloris	31.1	N	359	11.2	Steen, 1958
Chloris chloris	24.5	D	453	11.1	Gelineo, 1955
Carduelis spinus	13	D	446	5.8	Gelineo, 1955
Carduelis cannabina	15.5	D	472	7.31	Gelineo, 1955
Carduelis flammea	11.2	N	518	5.82	Steen, 1958
Pipilo aberti	46.8	D	321	15.04	Dawson, 1954
Pipilo fuscus	43.7	D	314	13.7	Dawson, 1954
Zonotrichia leucophrys	26.4	N	324	8.55	King, unpublished
Plectrophenax nivalis[a]	41.8	D	273	11.4	Scholander et al., 1950b
Emberiza citrinella	26.4	N	354	9.35	Wallgren, 1954
Emberiza hortulana	22.0	N	395	8.69	Wallgren, 1954

[a] Adapted to low ambient temperature.

[b] At rest, but not necessarily in thermoneutral range or postabsorptive condition.

determinations of heat production were made at 10–18°C. Although it is possible to correct these data to the thermoneutral range, the interspecific differences in lower critical temperature and temperature coefficient (see Table III) result in a low order of reliability for the corrected data. Many of the data of Benedict and Fox (1933) are questionable because of the long periods of fasting to which the small birds were subjected.

TABLE III

THERMONEUTRAL RANGE AND TEMPERATURE COEFFICIENT
SELECTED SPECIES

Species	Body weight	Thermoneutral range (°C.)	Temperature coefficient	Investigators
Domestic turkey	—	20–28	—	Brody, 1945
Domestic goose	5.0 kg.	17–28	3.5	Benedict, 1938
Domestic goose	—	18–25	—	Brody, 1945
Domestic fowl	2.43 kg.	18–26	1.5	Barott and Pringle, 1946
Domestic fowl	—	16–28	—	Brody, 1945
Domestic pigeon	300 gm.	29–30	4.2	Terroine and Trautmann, 1927
Domestic pigeon	270 gm.	30–36	2.7–3.4	Gelineo, 1955
Domestic pigeon	—	14–?	3.6	Steen, 1957
Domestic pigeon	—	—	3.8	Streicher et al., 1950
Troglodytes aëdon	10.8 gm.	?–38	4.2	Kendeigh, 1939
Vidua paradisea	10.5 gm.	34–38	5.6	Terroine and Trautmann, 1927
Richmondena cardinalis Winter	40.0 gm.	18–33	3.7	Dawson, 1954
Summer	40.0 gm.	24–33	—	Dawson, 1954
Chloris chloris	27.0 gm.	34–35	—	Gelineo, 1955
Carduelis spinus	13.0 gm.	33–36	—	Gelineo, 1955
Pipilo aberti	46.8 gm.	25–35	ca. 3.8	Dawson, 1954
Pipilo fuscus	43.7 gm.	23–33	ca. 1.8	Dawson, 1954
Zonotrichia leucophrys	26.4 gm.	28–32	4.2	King, unpublished
Emberiza citrinella	26.4 gm.	25–33	3.3	Wallgren, 1954
Emberiza hortulana	22.0 gm.	32–38	4.3	Wallgren, 1954

In assembling the data given in Table II it often has been necessary to recalculate values which were originally expressed on the basis of unit surface area (e.g. Gelineo, 1955) and to compute heat production from given oxygen consumption. In the latter case, if the R.Q. was not given, it was assumed that the thermal equivalent of oxygen consumption was 4.8 kcal. per liter. The labor which this conversion of data has entailed prompts us to recommend, as Kleiber (1947, p. 515) has, that the minimum requirements for the publication of data on metabolic rates should include the body weight of the organisms and the total metabolic rate or the metabolic rate per unit body weight.

Obsolete scientific names, when detected, have been corrected to conform with current usage [e.g. *Turtur risorius* of Gelineo (1955) corrected to *Streptopelia decaocto*].

B. STANDARD METABOLISM IN RELATION TO BODY WEIGHT

It is well established that the metabolic intensity of vertebrates is inversely proportional to body mass. Large vertebrates produce less heat per unit mass than do small ones (Kleiber, 1947; Zeuthen, 1947, 1953; Hemmingsen, 1950). This relationship is complicated by the fact that it is exponential, rather than linear:

$$M \propto W^n = k\,W^n \tag{1}$$

where M is metabolic rate in kilocalories per day, and W is the body weight in kilograms. Because the metabolic intensity decreases with increasing body weight, the value of the exponent n will be less than 1. This indicates that a twofold increase in body weight, for instance, will be accompanied by less than a doubling of metabolic intensity. The empirical limits of n, considering all groups of organisms, are about 0.66 and 1.0 (Zeuthen, 1953), but approach the lower value for interspecific comparisons of vertebrates. These values conform reasonably well with the theoretical limits (0.66–1.16) derived by dimensional reasoning (see Günther and Guerra, 1955). The latter authors suggest that 0.736 represents a mean value of the exponent for most weight-dependent functions.

The physiological significance of the exponent has been the subject of argument for many years, but it is still uncertain. Although the heuristic value of these arguments has been important, it seems doubtful that they will ever be resolved. The so-called "surface law" occupied a prominent place for several decades and requires special mention here because of its curious persistence in the modern literature on avian energy metabolism. In its original form, this "law" postulated that because heat production must be proportional to heat loss in a homoiotherm, it must also be proportional to the surface area through which this loss may occur. Because the surface area of a regular solid is proportional to the two-thirds power of its volume and mass, then the heat production must also be proportional to the two-thirds power of mass, or $W^{0.667}$. Certain of the early data appeared to verify this generalization. However, as adequate comparative data accumulated, it became apparent that the standard heat production followed the three-fourths power of body weight more closely than the two-thirds power (i.e. the surface area). This discovery stimulated critical reappraisal of the surface law and engendered many theoretical objections to certain aspects of it. It is beyond our purpose to consider these in detail here. They have been ably reviewed by Kleiber (1947) and are also considered by Krogh (1916), Benedict (1938), Brody (1945), Zeuthen (1947, 1953), Hemmingsen (1950), and Precht *et al.* (1955). It is in general evident that heat loss from the surface of the body depends upon the properties of the "shell" (see Section VII, A). Area is only *one* of these properties.

Rearrangement of Eq. (1) yields:

$$M/W^n = k \tag{2}$$

This form of the relationship indicates that W^n can be regarded as a "unit of metabolic body size" (Kleiber, 1947) which makes possible a direct interspecific comparison of metabolic intensity irrespective of body mass; i.e. in theory, the metabolic rate per kg.^{n} will be the same for all animals *if* body mass is the only effective variable. This is of course similar to the expression of the metabolic rate on the basis of unit surface area, or $W^{0.667}$, except that the exponent is empirically derived and does not necessarily convey theoretical implications.

Because it is mathematically inconvenient to deal with fractional powers, Eq. (1) is usually subjected to logarithmic transformation:

$$\log M = \log k + n \log W \tag{3}$$

It is evident that Eq. (3) is in the familiar linear form conventionally expressed as $y = b + mx$. If the assumption that body mass is the only effective variable is valid, a graph of log M as a function of log W will yield a straight line of slope n; log k is equivalent to the y-intercept of the line, and thus fixes the absolute metabolic level. The postulate of linearity appears to hold true for mammals (Brody, 1945; Kleiber, 1947) and for many other groups of organisms (Hemmingsen, 1950; Zeuthen, 1953; von Bertalanffy, 1957).

We agree with Kleiber (1950b) that the theoretical significance of regression equations in physiology is frequently obscure, but the definite importance of such equations in assisting the *formulation of questions* regarding functional relationships appears sufficient to justify their computation. The empirical utility of these equations in predicting the metabolic rate from known body weight is also apparent. We will accordingly examine the quantitative aspects of the relationship of standard metabolism to body mass in homoiotherms generally, and in birds especially.

On the basis of impeccable data, Kleiber (1947) has shown for mammals ranging in body weight from mice to elephants, that the regression of metabolic rate on body weight follows the equation:

$$\log M = \log 69 + 0.756 \log W \pm 0.05 \qquad (4)$$

The variance (± 0.05) indicates the standard error for the estimation of $\log M$ from $\log W$. Brody's (1945) equation for mammals does not differ significantly from Eq. (4). The similar relationship (Brody and Proctor, 1932) for birds is not so firmly based, although it appears to have been widely accepted:

$$\log M = \log 89 + 0.64 \log W \qquad (5)$$

Because complete data are not given by Brody and Proctor it is not possible to examine the statistical significance of the difference between Eq. (4) and Eq. (5). The avian equation appears to be sufficiently different, however, to invite inquiry into the basis of the difference and, indeed, the validity of the equation. On theoretical grounds there seems to be no reason to believe *a priori* that the relationship of metabolic rate and body weight should be very different in the homoiotherm classes. It may be worthy of note also that the lines of Eqs. (4) and (5) cross at about 8 kg., implying that above this body weight birds exhibit a lesser metabolic intensity than mammals. Near the upper limit of avian body weight (about 140 kg.) the Brody-Proctor equation indicates that the metabolic intensity of birds under standard conditions is less than three-quarters that of mammals of equivalent body weight. Although no data exist for birds this large, we find it difficult to believe that such a large difference in standard metabolic rate would exist.

From an empirical viewpoint, also, the data available to Brody and Proctor were not entirely satisfactory. The major criticism here is that the metabolic rates for small birds were measured during the daytime, whereas those for large birds were obtained at night. In view of the magnitude of the diurnal cycle of metabolic rate (see Section V), in which maximum values are attained during the daylight hours, it is predictable that these data would yield a line with a slope lower than the true slope and a y-intercept ($\log k$) higher than the true intercept. Because of this uncertainty about the reliability of the Brody-Proctor equation, we have reanalyzed the available data for birds. The values used in the analysis were rigorously selected from the standard metabolic rates given in Table II. They were restricted to data obtained at night from birds adapted to ambient temperatures not more than about 15° below the lower critical temperature. The averages for all of the species below about 2 kg. in body weight are based upon samples consisting of several individuals, but for data on larger birds we are dependent to a large extent upon Benedict and Fox (1927), who in most cases studied only one individual of each species. The dispersion of the selected data for twenty-eight species is shown in Fig. 1. Inspection of these data reveals that a good linear correlation exists between the logarithms of body weight and metabolic rate above about 0.125 kg. The regression line drawn to fit *this range* of the data (in Fig. 1, the solid line fitted to the solid dots) was computed by the least-squares method of Feldstein and Hirsch (1935; cf. Brody, 1945); it follows the equation:

$$\log M = \log 74.3 + 0.744 \log W \pm 0.074 \qquad (6)$$

Equation (6) is statistically indistinguishable from Kleiber's Eq. (4) for mammals (comparison in upper left in Fig. 1), and raises the question

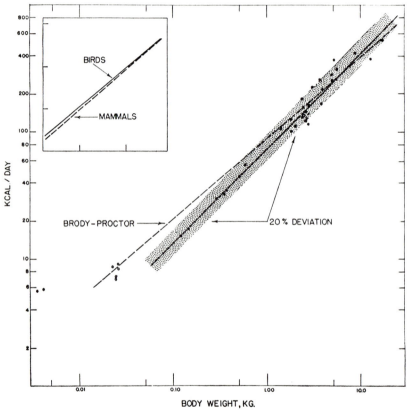

Fig. 1. Standard metabolism in relation to body weight. Full line with shaded area showing 20% deviation = line of Eq. (6) (see text) for birds weighing more than 0.1 kg. Brody-Proctor line represents Eq. (5). Lines of Eq. (4) and Eq. (6) are compared in box at upper left. Points at extreme left indicate minimum metabolic rate from humming-birds (Pearson, 1950), but are not strictly standard values and are included only to indicate the approximate metabolic level of a very small bird.

whether the relationship in birds is really different from that in mammals, at least at body weights greater than about 0.1 kg. It is obvious, however, that Eq. (6) does not adequately describe the metabolic intensity of the smaller birds, shown as open circles in Fig. 1. If these data are included in the computation of the regression line, then a relationship similar to the Brody-Proctor Eq. (5) is obtained:

$$\log M = \log 80.1 + 0.659 \log W \pm 0.076 \tag{7}$$

The "fit" of this line to the points in the center of the graph is not so satisfactory visually as the line of Eq. (6), and it likewise involves a slightly greater standard error of estimate. However, because of the paucity of the data it is not possible at present to formulate a rigorous physiological decision (as distinguished from a statistical decision) as to which of the equations best represents the metabolic intensity of birds. Data are needed particularly in the ranges of body weight between 0.03 kg. and 1.0 kg., and above 10 kg.

We do not exclude the possibility that the relationship is actually curvilinear in the lower range of body weight and may thus include the smaller species of birds without affecting the apparent linear correlation for the large birds. To account for this it is necessary to postulate that some variable in addition to body mass becomes effective in birds (but not mammals) with decreasing body weight. Until sufficient data are available to test the hypothesis that the regression is curvilinear in the lower range of body weight, however, it is pointless to indulge in extensive speculation as to what this variable might be. In any event, the regression analysis has fulfilled its heuristic role in identifying certain pertinent questions concerning comparative bioenergetics in the homoiotherm classes. For purely practical considerations, it is evident that Eq. (6) permits a more accurate prediction of the metabolic intensity of birds weighing more than about 0.1 kg. than does the Brody-Proctor Eq. (5).

IV. Energy Metabolism and Ambient Temperature

A. Theoretical Considerations

The existence of a stable body temperature in homoiotherms depends upon the maintenance of a balance between heat production and heat loss. The rate of heat loss from the surface of the body is proportional to the difference between surface temperature and the ambient temperature. It is therefore evident that the intensity of metabolism in a given individual must be influenced in a fundamental way by variation in ambient temperature, or, more properly, variation in the temperature gradient. Although the analogy between simple physical systems and living organisms is not perfect, we may nevertheless conveniently explore the basic relationships through reference to Newton's equation for the cooling of an object which has been heated to a temperature in excess of that of its surroundings:

$$Q = k\,(T_s - T_a) \tag{8}$$

where Q = rate of heat loss by conduction, convection, and radiation, k = a proportionality constant, T_s = surface temperature, and T_a = ambient temperature. For convenience, the temperature gradient, $T_s - T_a$, may be abbreviated as $\triangle T$.

Equation (8) predicts that if a homoiotherm is thermally similar to a simple physical system the rate of heat loss (and accordingly the rate of heat production) will be a linear function of the thermal gradient, as

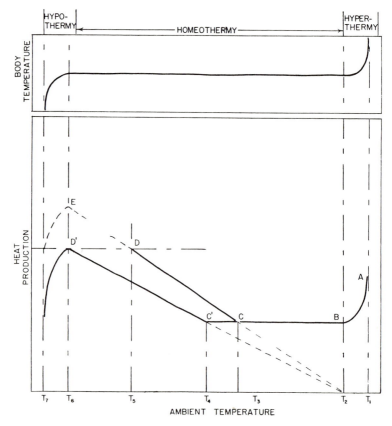

Fig. 2. Thermal relationships in homoiotherms based on Newton's law of cooling (see text). Modified from Hart (1957).

shown by the lines sloping to the left in Fig. 2. It also predicts that heat loss will be zero when $T_s = T_a$. The cooling lines accordingly intersect the abscissa at the temperature of the system under consideration, which will be the body temperature for a living system (for the present we will assume that surface temperature and deep body temperature are the same; the actual differences are fully discussed in Section VII, A). For application to the thermal relationships of a bird, Eq. (8) becomes more meaningful if modified as follows:

$$Q_p = Q_l = k' \, C \triangle T + Q_e \tag{9}$$

where, if body temperature does not change, Q_p = rate of heat production, Q_l = rate of heat loss by radiation, conduction, and convection, Q_e = rate of heat loss by the evaporation of liquid from the surfaces of the body (not entirely independent of the temperature gradient, but very nearly so), C = conductance of the insulating shell, and k' = a constant.

Unlike an object heated by an external source and cooling to the ambient temperature, an organism is a thermal system in which heat is continuously generated internally at a minimum rate which is determined by the requirements of the maintenance metabolism. There is accordingly a minimum heat production and heat loss, which is shown as the horizontal line BCC' in Fig. 2. It is evident from this graph that there is a span of ambient temperature within which the heat loss (and therefore the heat production) is independent of change in the ambient temperature. Within this thermoneutral range (T_2 to T_3–T_4) the conductance of the insulating shell must increase in proportion to decrease in the temperature gradient in order to fulfill the requirements of Eq. (9), which can be rearranged to emphasize this fundamental point:

$$\frac{Q_p - Q_e}{C \triangle T} = k' \tag{10}$$

or, because Q_e is essentially constant below T_2,

$$\frac{Q_p}{C \triangle T} = k'' \tag{11}$$

The variation of the conductance regulates the heat loss from the body and is termed *physical thermoregulation*, the special mechanisms of which are extensively discussed below (Section VII, C). As the thermal gradient increases within the thermoneutral zone the conductance is adjusted accordingly and approaches a minimum which is attained at the lower critical temperature, T_3 or T_4 in Fig. 2. Two levels of the minimum are shown in order to illustrate the result of variation in the effectiveness of insulation. The slope of the line varies inversely with the efficiency of insulation, and directly with the conductance. Below the lower critical temperature (described as the *critical gradient* by Scholander *et al.*, 1950c) it is apparent that heat loss can be balanced only by increased heat production, which must be augmented in proportion to the increase in thermal gradient. The maintenance of normal body temperature by increased metabolic intensity within this range is called *chemical thermoregulation*. There is of course an upper limit to the capacity of this thermoregulatory process, as shown at T_6 in Fig. 2. When the thermal gradient becomes so great that heat loss can no longer be balanced by heat production, the organism becomes hypothermic, metabolic intensity declines in accordance with the van't Hoff relationship, and death will eventually result at the lower lethal temperature, T_7.

Beyond the upper limit of the thermoneutral zone the metabolic intensity also increases. As the thermal gradient becomes smaller within the thermoneutral zone the conductance of the shell is proportionately increased toward a maximum by appropriate thermoregulatory mechanisms. When $\triangle T = 0$ (at T_2), however, the dissipation of heat from the body by radiation, conduction, and convection is also zero (i.e. in Eq. 9, $k'C\triangle T = 0$), and the evaporation of liquid from the surface of the body provides the only route for the excretion of heat. The point $\triangle T = 0$ in theory defines the *upper critical temperature* (T_2), above which the metabolic rate increases with increasing ambient temperature. This increase results initially from enhanced cardiopulmonary activity and "panting" by which the animal facilitates the evaporation of liquid from the pulmonary surfaces. Because this route of heat dissipation can accommodate, at a maximum, only about 50% of the minimal heat production it is inevitable that the body temperature must increase. As the body temperature rises the metabolic intensity will increase proportionately in conformance with the van't Hoff principle. This in turn augments the hyperthermia and, unless the ambient temperature decreases, leads rapidly to heat death at the upper lethal temperature, T_1.

The characteristics of the model system just discussed provide an essential physical basis for the further consideration of avian bioenergetics. The thermal exchanges of many species of birds conform rather closely with theoretical predictions, but other species exhibit various degrees of departure, usually small, from the Newtonian model. Examples of both types are found in the data of Scholander *et al.* (1950a, b), Enger (1957), and Steen (1958).

B.   THERMONEUTRALITY

The thermoneutral zone is delimited by upper and lower critical temperatures. The position of these on the thermometric scale, and accordingly the total span of the zone, depends fundamentally upon the physiological limits of the conductance of the insulative shell and the efficiency of evaporative heat loss but is influenced also by the size of the animal, the plane of nutrition, relative humidity, wind velocity, and perhaps other factors. It should be pointed out that there is no rigorous empirical definition of the thermoneutral zone. A graph of data on metabolic rate versus ambient temperature commonly shows a hyperboloid function in which, properly, only a single thermoneutral point can be distinguished. In practice, the positions at which the critical temperatures are fixed will depend upon the manner in which curves are fitted to the empirical data and upon what a given investigator regards as a significant deviation from the minimum metabolic rate. In many cases the inflections are sufficiently distinct that there is very little uncertainty regarding the positions of the critical temperatures. In other cases a relatively wide span of uncertainty exists. In view of this situation, interspecific comparisons must be undertaken very cautiously. The reality and ecological significance of small differences in the critical temperatures should be submitted to the closest scrutiny. Selected data on the critical temperatures are given in Table III.

1. Effect of the Plane of Nutrition

The relationships of heat production, plane of nutrition (i.e. level of energy intake), and ambient temperature are shown in Fig. 3. The heat production at three planes of nutrition is shown by the thick lines, and energy intake by the broken line. The calorigenic effect (S.D.A.) of the maintenance ration is designated as C_m. This ration corresponds approximately to the "existence energy" of Kendeigh (1949). The calorigenic effect of ad libitum feeding is assumed to be a constant fraction of the gross energy intake above maintenance, and is designated as C_p.

A consideration of Fig. 3 shows that the lower critical temperature is progressively decreased at higher levels of energy intake, three of which are shown. This extension of the thermoneutral range depends upon the "waste heat" of the calorigenic effect of the ration. This effect spares energy which would be required, at a lower plane of nutrition, for chemical thermoregulation. The ecological implications of this in relation to the food supply of animals and their survival in cold weather are obvious.

It is assumed that at ambient temperatures which produce hyper-thermy the homoiotherm tends to become aphagic and the plane of nutrition reverts to a submaintenance or fasting level. The upper critical temperature is thus assumed to be determined by the fasting heat production.

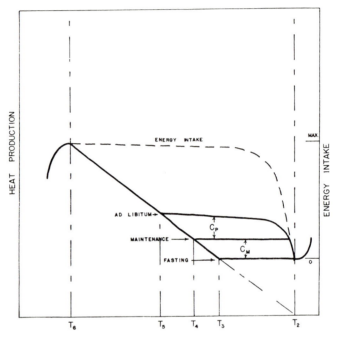

Fig. 3. Relationship of heat production (heavy lines) and energy intake (broken line) in homoiotherms. Modified from Kleiber and Dougherty (1934).

2. Effect of Relative Humidity

As ambient temperature increases from medium to very high values the evaporation of water from the pulmonary surfaces becomes a pro-gressively more important mechanism for the excretion of heat and main-tenance of normal body temperature. If the relative humidity of the ambient air is also high, the excretion of heat by this route is retarded, resulting in a decrease of the upper critical temperature and an accelera-tion in the development of hyperthermy. In *Emberiza hortulana,* for example, Wallgren (1954) found that the upper critical temperature was 33° at 95% relative humidity, but 38° at relative humidities of about 50% or less. Kendeigh (1934, showed that the survival time of *Passer domesticus* at high ambient temperatures was reduced when relative humidity was also high. Salt (1952) offers similar data which relate humidity, metabolic rate, heat stress, and ecological distribution in three species of *Carpodacus*. Hutchinson (1954) has shown that the evaporative heat loss in domestic fowl at cloacal temperatures of 40° to 44° is about 50% to 70% lower in a "moist" climate (28 mm. Hg absolute humidity) than in a "dry" climate (5 mm. Hg).

C. TEMPERATURE COEFFICIENT

Below the lower critical temperature the heat production increases with decreasing ambient temperature in accordance with the demands of chemical thermoregulation. The rate of increase in heat production is called the temperature coefficient. It is conveniently expressed as a percentage of the standard metabolic rate per degree centigrade reduction in ambient temperature (i.e. a temperature coefficient of 3.5 indicates that the metabolic rate increases 3.5% of the standard or minimal rate per degree centigrade below the lower critical temperature). Some representative temperature coefficients are given in Table III. These assume that heat production is a linear function of ambient temperature. It is well known, however, that this relationship is often curvilinear, especially in the region of the critical temperature. Accordingly, the temperature coefficient must be regarded as an average value for a given range of temperature.

It is frequently stated (e.g. Brody, 1945, p. 286) that, other things being equal, the temperature coefficient is inversely related to body size. There may indeed be a general tendency in this direction, but additional data are needed to demonstrate it with certainty. The data given in Table III reveal no striking relationship of the temperature coefficient and body weight. On the contrary, it appears that there are significant differences between closely related species which have practically the same body weight. We agree emphatically with Bartholomew (1958, p. 91) that small physiological differences between closely related forms are not necessarily adaptive, but it may be seen in Table III that some of the differences are not small and confer a significant thermoregulatory advantage which may be correlated with the comparative distribution and behavior of the species in question. It can readily be estimated, for example, from data in Tables II and III, that in order to maintain a normal body temperature when the ambient temperature is 0°, the ortolan bunting (*Emberiza hortulana*) must produce about 45% more heat per unit of body weight than the yellow bunting (*E. citrinella*). The latter species overwinters in Scandinavia, but the ortolan bunting migrates southward in the autumn (Wallgren, 1954). Scholander *et al.*

(1950a, b) show that three species of tropical birds have distinctly higher temperature coefficients and higher critical temperatures than do three species of arctic birds. These investigators consider body insulation to be the major difference in this apparent climatic adaptation. The investigations of Dawson (1954) on two species of *Pipilo*, while related to heat tolerance rather than cold tolerance, are also noteworthy for providing a physiological rationale for differences in habitat distribution.

D. Acclimatization and Heat Production

The survival of birds in their natural habitat during periods of climatic stress depends upon a complex interplay of behavioral and physiological adaptations. Adaptive changes in the mechanisms of thermoregulation comprise *acclimatization*. As a working hypothesis we assume that acclimatization is a homeostatic process directed toward the maintenance of body temperature within normal limits at a minimal caloric cost to the animal. Some of the possible mechanisms of acclimatization are illustrated in Fig. 2. We may conveniently distinguish between *insulative acclimatization* and *metabolic acclimatization*, with the understanding that these processes may occur concurrently. Because the adaptations of birds to heat stress have received very little experimental attention we will confine our discussion mainly to acclimatization to cold. In Fig. 2, it is evident that an increase in insulation would change the slope of the cooling line from CDE to C'D', with a consequent decrease in the temperature coefficient and a reduction of the critical temperature from T_3 to T_4. Metabolic adaptation to low ambient temperature may involve increase in the level of the resting metabolism (not shown in Fig. 2), resulting in a decrease in the lower critical temperature, but not necessarily affecting the temperature coefficient, or may involve an increase in the maximum metabolic rate (the broken line DE) with a resultant downward shift of the lethal temperature.

Studies of thermoregulatory properties in relation to seasonal change in climate have taken the form of (1) investigation of the annual variation in the bioenergetics of animals exposed to "normal" climatic conditions, but usually in captivity, and (2) investigation of animals exposed to artificial thermal environments in the laboratory. As Hart (1957) suggests, it is perhaps preferable to use the term *temperature conditioning* in reference to experimentally produced adaptations to different ambient temperatures. This distinguishes the process from *acclimatization*, or climate-induced changes, in which factors in addition to temperature may be operating. As will be shown, there is reason to believe that the results of temperature conditioning and acclimatization are not entirely the same.

1. *Temperature Conditioning*

The data of Gelineo (1955) indicate that adaptation to progressively lower constant air temperatures by the domestic pigeon, ring dove, and seven species of passerines results in (1) an increase in the standard metabolic rate, (2) a slight downward shift in the thermoneutral zone, and (3) in most species an extension of the limits of cold tolerance, as indicated by resistance to hypothermia and cold death. An apparent increase in the temperature coefficient may have been the result actually of the development of hypothermy at low experimental temperatures by the warm-adapted birds, as Hart (1957) explains. In these nine species, the shift of standard metabolic rate, which requires from 1 to 4 weeks between stable levels, is of the order of 20–40%, when individuals adapted to thermoneutral temperatures are compared with the same individuals adapted to 0–10°. Similar results have been reported by Miller (1939) for *Passer domesticus* in which exposure to constant ambient temperatures of $-2°$ to 3° for 2 weeks increased the mean standard metabolic rate by 18% over that of controls held at room temperature. Exposure to $-8°$ to $-2°$ for 4 days increased the metabolic rate by 16% over that of controls. In the domestic pigeon (Dontcheff and Kayser, 1934), the standard metabolism of birds adapted to 2–4° was 11% higher than that of the same birds conditioned to 26–29°. Steen (1957) reports similar results for the pigeon. Wallgren (1954) found in *Emberiza citrinella*, exposed to experimental air temperatures increasing from 22.5° by monthly increments of 2.5°, that the standard metabolism declined by 14% after 3 weeks at 27.5°; in *Emberiza hortulana* a decrease amounting to 18% occurred after 3 weeks at 32.5°. However, in other groups which were similarly treated but were exposed to 10–14° for 8 hours each day there was essentially no change in standard metabolism. This suggests that the conditioning process is suppressed by variable ambient temperature.

2. *Climate-induced Changes*

The basic questions regarding thermoregulatory acclimatization by birds include the following: (1) Does the caloric cost of thermoregulation increase significantly during the cold season? (2) If there is an increase, by what physiological and behavioral mechanisms do birds minimize it or compensate for it? (3) To what degree do the limits of tolerance vary during the annual cycle?

The few data which are available are in many respects contradictory and do not provide clear-cut answers to these questions. We will briefly survey the data, however, in order to emphasize the areas where investigation is especially needed. The question of climate-induced changes in the bioenergetics of homoiotherms in general is thoroughly reviewed by Hart (1957).

In order to discover whether or not birds are required to live at a higher metabolic intensity during the cold season, much effort has been directed toward the study of standard metabolic rate at different seasons. The results of temperature-conditioning experiments have suggested that a temperature-dependent seasonal cycle of standard metabolic rate would occur under natural conditions. The data of Miller (1939) for *Passer domesticus* captured shortly before the determination of standard metabolic rate appear to support this prediction. Although the mean ambient temperatures are unfortunately not included in the monthly summaries of the data, there is clearly a seasonal cycle of standard metabolic rate in which the maximum occurs in the cold season and the minimum in the hot season. The winter increase in standard metabolic rate above the summer minimum was 59% in males and 97% in females. Similarly, two of three domestic pigeons confined out of doors by Dontcheff and Kayser (1934) showed an inverse correlation of standard metabolic rate and ambient temperature. The change was small, however, and perhaps of questionable significance. Irving *et al.* (1955) demonstrated an increase of 18% in the resting metabolic rate of *Corvus caurinus* confined out of doors; in *Branta bernicla*, on the other hand, they found a winter *decrease* of about 16% in the resting metabolism. The mean values for late spring and summer provide the basis for the percentage comparison.

In contrast with the results of the investigations just described, Wallgren (1954) has shown in *Emberiza citrinella* confined out of doors that there is no significant seasonal variation in standard metabolism in correlation with ambient temperature. He does not believe that temperature conditioning of the type demonstrated by Gelineo (1955) and others occurs in free-living birds. The data of Dawson (1958) for *Richmondena cardinalis* lead to the same conclusion. The data of Rautenberg (1957) on *Fringilla montifringilla* and *Passer domesticus* confined for 18 months under nearly normal climatic conditions do not reveal any consistent relationship of resting metabolism and ambient temperature. The highest values for the resting metabolic rate were obtained during the summer. The disparity between these findings and those of Miller (1939) cited above may originate from the fact that Miller used birds which had been in captivity for only a few hours. Although the captive birds studied by Wallgren, Dawson, Rautenberg, Irving, and Dontcheff and Kayser were exposed to the weather out of doors, the unknown variables associated with captivity cannot be ignored. At present there are not sufficient data to determine conclusively whether or not a temperature-dependent cycle of standard metabolic rate occurs in free-living birds.

In conclusion, it is pertinent to consider some theoretical implications pertaining to "adaptive" variation in standard metabolic rate, since these cast some doubt on the ecological advantage of such variation. On the basis of Newton's law of cooling (see Fig. 2) and the assumption that a small bird has a lower critical temperature at 30° and a temperature coefficient equal to 4% of the standard metabolic rate per degree reduction in ambient temperature, it can be shown that a *doubling* of the standard metabolic rate will reduce the lower critical temperature to only 5°. Below this rather moderate temperature the bird must pay the same caloric fee for chemical thermoregulation whether or not there has been an "adaptive" increase in standard metabolism. More significantly, at any temperature above the critical temperature the "adapted" bird must expend *more* energy in resting metabolism than the "non-adapted" bird. Qualitatively, the same comparative situation prevails even if the efficiency of the insulation increases during the cold season.

It thus appears that there is no adaptive advantage associated with increase of the standard metabolic rate during the cold season. On the contrary, the potential benefit of reduction of the critical temperature is nullified by the increased caloric cost of the resting metabolism. Furthermore, the "adapted" bird with a higher resting energy expenditure is not able to store as large a fraction of the daily energy intake than the "nonadapted" bird. Because the survival of small birds during cold nights depends in part upon the magnitude of energy reserves accumulated during the daily period of feeding (Kendeigh, 1934), the "adapted" bird is placed at still another caloric disadvantage. On these grounds we are led to agree with Scholander *et al.* (1950a, b), Irving *et al.* (1955), and Hart (1957), who conclude from the experimental evidence that seasonal variation in standard metabolic rate is of minor significance in thermoregulatory acclimatization.

The investigation of seasonal change in the temperature coefficient and the lower lethal temperature is of more significance than the standard metabolism in assessing acclimatization to thermal stress. For *Passer domesticus*, Kendeigh (1934, 1949), Seibert (1949), and Davis (1955) have clearly demonstrated the existence of differences in the cold resistance of summer-adapted and winter-adapted captive individuals. Summer-adapted birds were able to maintain energy balance only above 0°, whereas winter-adapted birds were able to maintain a

s

balance down to about $-30°$. The acclimatization appears to have been in part insulative and in part metabolic. The weight of the winter plumage is about 30% greater than that of the summer plumage in *Passer domesticus* (Kendeigh, 1934), and the summer-adapted birds were able to sustain a maximum energy intake of only 23 kcal. per day, compared with a maximum intake of 32 kcal. per day in the winter-adapted birds.

For captive *Branta bernicla* exposed to the weather in the arctic, Irving *et al.* (1955) did not detect any differences in the temperature coefficient or survival of summer-adapted and winter-adapted birds at experimental temperatures down to $-40°$. The critical temperature was $+6°$ in both seasons. *Corvus caurinus* exhibited the same seasonal constancy, except that summer-adapted birds did not survive an ambient temperature of $-40°$, whereas winter-adapted birds were able to do so. In contrast, Riddle *et al.* (1934) found a distinctly higher temperature coefficient in summer-adapted tippler pigeons than in winter-adapted individuals. With regard to seasonal adaptation to heat stress, Weiss and Borbely (1957) have demonstrated in the domestic fowl that summer-adapted birds survived exposure to 40.6° longer than winter-adapted birds.

Additional mechanisms for conserving heat and prolonging survival during periods of cold stress include behavioral adaptations, such as the huddling described by Löhrl (1955), and *in extremis*, adaptive hypothermia. The latter mechanism is described by Steen (1958) for six species of passerines which were captured near Oslo in the winter and were studied within a few hours after capture. In response to experimental temperatures down to $-25°$ the newly captured birds exhibited body temperatures as low as 30° and appeared torpid (cf. Section IX below). It is of interest that these same species conditioned to $-10°$ in captivity did not exhibit significant hypothermia even at the lowest experimental air temperatures. This again emphasizes the extreme caution which must be employed in interpreting the mechanisms of acclimatization on the basis of temperature-conditioning experiments.

E. ENERGY INTAKE AND AMBIENT TEMPERATURE

The available data (cf. Kendeigh, 1949; Seibert, 1949; Davis, 1955) tend to indicate that, within the range of tolerance, the metabolizable energy intake of passerine birds is a linear function of ambient temperature. On a theoretical basis, Steen (1957) shows an inflection at about 13° ("critical temperature") in the curve of food intake versus ambient temperature in the domestic pigeon, giving a zone of thermoneutrality with respect to food intake. However, the data per se do not demonstrate an inflection and can equally well be fitted by a continuous straight line.

Table IV summarizes the data on metabolizable energy intake as a function of ambient temperature. The data for *Zonotrichia albicollis*, *Passer domesticus*, and *Junco hyemalis* have been compiled from Kendeigh (1949), Seibert (1949), and Davis (1955) and were obtained under comparable experimental conditions, with the birds confined to very small cages (22 × 23 × 11 cm.). The *Zonotrichia leucophrys* (King, unpublished) were held in larger cages (23 × 36 × 28 cm.). The relationship of metabolizable energy intake and ambient temperature is most compactly expressed in the form of a linear regression (column 4). In some cases, the original equation has been transformed to conform

TABLE IV

METABOLIZABLE ENERGY INTAKE AS A FUNCTION OF
AMBIENT TEMPERATURE IN SOME CAPTIVE BIRDS

Species	Photo-period (hr./day)	Approx. Body Wt. (gm.)	Regression, (kcal./gm./day) equals	Temperature coefficient
Zonotrichia leucophrys	9	26.5	$0.83-0.011\ T$	2.2
Zonotrichia albicollis	10	24.0	$0.79-0.0062\ T$	1.1
Zonotrichia albicollis	15	24.0	$0.93-0.0076\ T$	1.1
Junco hyemalis	10	19.0	$0.91-0.0083\ T$	1.3
Junco hyemalis	15	19.0	$1.08-0.013\ T$	2.0
Passer domesticus	10	24.0	$0.98-0.0108\ T$	1.6[a]
Passer domesticus	15	24.0	$0.99-0.0046\ T$	0.5[a]
Passer domesticus	10–15[b]	25.5	$1.02-0.0127\ T$	2.0[c]

[a] Winter-adapted birds (Kendeigh, 1949; Seibert, 1949).
[b] No significant difference between photoperiods.
[c] Summer-adapted birds (Davis, 1955).

with a standard expression. The first term of the regression gives the metabolizable energy intake (as kilocalories per gram per day) at 0°C.; T is the ambient temperature in degrees centigrade, and the coefficient of T denotes the slope of the regression line. The temperature coefficient indicates the percentage increase in metabolizable energy intake per degree centigrade decrease in ambient temperature below 30°C., expressed as a percentage of the value at 30°C.

Other fragmentary data are also available on the food intake or gross energy intake of avian species (Larguier de Bancels, 1902; Lapicque, 1911; Lapicque and Lapicque, 1909a, b; Rörig, 1905), but these will not be considered here.

V. Diurnal Variation in Energy Metabolism

The standard heat production undergoes a daily cycle in which the minimum values occur at night (except in nocturnal species, in which the cycle is presumably reversed). In certain cases (e.g. Burckard *et al.*, 1933) the mean metabolic rates for arbitrary periods (1100–1500 versus 1800–2200) are compared; in other cases the minimums of nocturnal and diurnal determinations are compared. Because it has not been possible to standardize the data for the various species, it is suggested that original sources be consulted when critical interpretations must be made. However, the data in their original form are

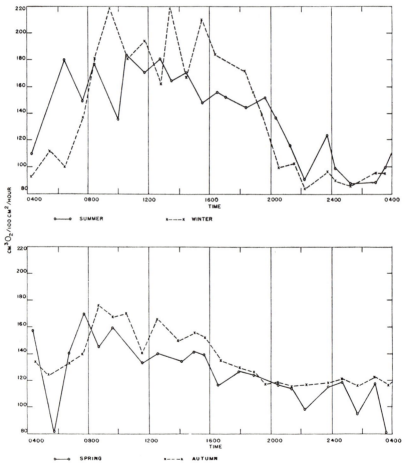

Fig. 4. Diurnal variation in resting metabolic rate of captive *Sylvia communis* in different seasons. From data of Merkel (1958).

indicative of the magnitude of daily variation in the standard metabolic rate. In the following examples we have expressed the difference between nighttime and daytime values as a percentage of the daytime value. On this basis, the nocturnal heat production in the domestic fowl has been found to be 18–30% less than the daytime value (Bacq, 1929; Benedict *et al.*, 1932; Barott and Pringle, 1941). In pigeons the nocturnal decline amounts to 15–30% (Benedict and Riddle, 1929; Burckard *et al.*, 1933; Hiebel and Reys, 1951). In small passerine birds the difference is usually greater. Thus, in *Passer domesticus* it may

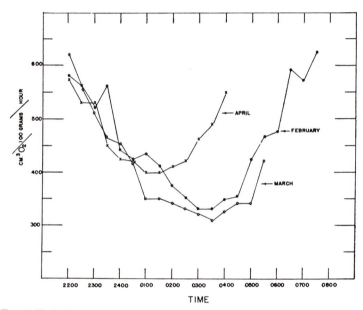

Fig. 5. Variation in nocturnal resting metabolic rate in *Fringilla montifringilla* during late winter and spring. From data of Rautenberg (1957).

amount to 32–37% (Rautenberg, 1957), 40% (Kendeigh, 1944), and 5–49% (Fill, 1942); in *Fringilla montifringilla* Rautenberg found a nocturnal decline of 27–49% at different times of the late winter and spring in individuals exposed to natural temperature and photoperiod. Fill (1942), for *Chloris chloris* and *Parus major* exposed to artificial photoperiods, reported reductions in nocturnal heat production amounting to 22–68%.

A secondary seasonal cycle of resting metabolism has also been found in those species of birds which have been studied in this respect. In captive *Sylvia communis* and *Erithacus rubecula* exposed to natural photoperiods at room temperature, Merkel (1958) shows that the magnitude of the 24-hour variation is greatest in summer and winter and least in spring and fall. The seasonal variation for *Sylvia communis* is shown in Fig. 4. The reduction of diurnal variation in spring and autumn is associated with conspicuously higher nocturnal values and generally diminished daytime values. The nocturnal increase is clearly associated with the increased motor activity of *Zugunruhe* which characterizes the migratory periods. As Merkel notes, the nocturnal metabolic rates measured during these periods cannot be regarded as reliable resting values. This situation deserves special emphasis because of its obvious effect on the design of investigations of the metabolism of migratory birds.

Another component of seasonal variation in the diurnal metabolic cycle is the shift in time and duration of the minimum nocturnal metabolism. This is demonstrated in Fig. 5 by the data of Rautenberg (1957) for captive *Fringilla montifringilla* exposed to natural temperature and photoperiod.

The basis for the diurnal rhythm of metabolism appears to reside mainly in variation in muscular tonus associated with the maintenance of posture. Hiebel and Reys (1951) were able to eliminate the daily rhythm or to reduce its amplitude markedly in domestic pigeons by transection of the lumbar and brachial plexi. Burckard *et al.* (1933) abolished the rhythm in pigeons by surgical blinding and subsequent isolation from auditory stimuli. Ablation of the cerebral hemispheres reduced the magnitude of the daily variation but did not abolish it. The rhythm can easily be reversed, even in normal pigeons, by inversion of the daily photoperiod (cf. Fill, 1942).

VI. Energy Metabolism and Molt

The standard metabolic rate increases during the molt and, according to Wallgren (1954), exhibits a higher degree of individual variability than at other times of the annual cycle. Koch and de Bont (1944) studied the progress of photically induced molt and alteration of metabolic rate in a single *Fringilla coelebs*. They found that the period of maximum metabolic rate (about 25% above the nonmolting level) occurred during the regeneration of the flight feathers, at least a month in advance of the molt of contour feathers. During postnuptial molt in *Emberiza citrinella*, the standard metabolic rate of adults was found to increase about 14%; there was no detectable change in the metabolic rate of juveniles. The increase during molt in *Emberiza hortulana* was about 26% for adults and about 10% for juveniles (Wallgren, 1954). In domestic fowl, Perek and Sulman (1945) observed an increase of about 45% in the standard metabolic rate during the autumn molt, as compared with values for the periods of spring and autumn egg laying.

It is commonly suggested (e.g. Sturkie, 1954, p. 363) that the increase in heat production which is observed during the molt is a compensation for increased heat loss during this period of presumably reduced plumage insulation. The results obtained by Koch and de Bont (1944), while admittedly limited, do not conform with this hypothesis. The initial increase in the resting metabolic rate was associated with the ecdysis and regeneration of the rectrices, which cannot have a significant insulative role. The molt of the contour feathers occurred during a period when the resting metabolism was returning to the premolt level. The increased flow of blood to the growing feather papillae may significantly increase the heat conductance of the body surface even during the molt of the flight feathers, but this has never been investigated. On the other hand, the well-known association of molt and increased thyroid activity and, especially, the ability of certain thyroid-active preparations to induce molt (see Maqsood, 1952) suggest that molt and increased metabolic rate are not necessarily associated in a cause-and-effect relationship, but may have a common basis in thyroid function.

Very little information is available on the relationship of molt and energy intake. Davis (1955) did not detect any significant alteration of metabolizable energy intake during molt in *Passer domesticus* confined on several different constant temperatures and photoperiods. There was, however, an increase in the variability of the data, as observed by Wallgren (1954) for the standard metabolism. Gerhartz (1914) reported that the metabolizable energy intake increased from 85.1 kcal. per kilogram per day to 98.1 kcal. per kilogram per day during molt in the domestic hen. His data, however, are few, and the significance of the difference (5.2%) is open to question.

Actually, it is not surprising that a significantly increased energy income is not detected during molt. If it is assumed, for example, that the plumage is completely regenerated during the postnuptial molt, then an average adult *Passer domesticus* must produce about 1.7 gm. of keratin during this process (see Kendeigh, 1934, p. 335). The heat of combustion of keratin is about 5.5 kcal. per gram (Roth and Scheel, 1923). The heat of formation from metabolic precursors will be somewhat less, but for the present approximation will be assumed to be the same. This means that an average house sparrow will produce about 9.4 kcal. of new feathers during the postnuptial molt. If the gross energetic efficiency of this process is conservatively estimated to be 10%, then the average house sparrow must expend about 94 kcal. in producing its winter plumage. This does not include the indeterminate added heat loss resulting from defective insulation during the molt. If it is further assumed that postnuptial molt occupies 60 days in captive birds, then the mean increased energy requirement due to molt will be about 1.6 kcal. per day. Naturally, the actual daily value will vary above and below this average as the intensity of endysis varies. The mean "existence" energy for free-living house sparrows is about 21 kcal. per bird per day during the postnuptial molt (Davis, 1955). The mean increase in energy intake, assuming no change in other energy-demanding functions, must thus be only about 7.6%.

VII. Thermoregulation

A. GENERAL CONSIDERATIONS

In designating adult birds as homoiothermal, it must be emphasized that the state of homoiothermy is one in which only the deep body temperatures are held within relatively narrow limits of fluctuation. From the aspect of evolution it seems patent that homoiothermy, despite its caloric cost to the organism, confers an eminent advantage in assuring a stable temperature for the activity of the central nervous system and the skeletal musculature. It seems certain that the evolution of flight in an environment of cold or variable temperature would have been impossible without prior or concurrent development of homoiothermy.

The evolution of homoiothermy has involved the development of an elaborate system of feed-back controls of the rates of thermogenesis and thermolysis.[3] In a consideration of thermoregulation it is convenient and useful to conceive of the body of the bird as consisting of two hypothetical concentric parts. The inner part, consisting of the central nervous system, visceral organs, and a variable amount of the skeletal musculature, may be designated as the *core*. It is the part in which most of the thermogenesis occurs; it is also the part in which fluctuations in temperature are minimized and in which the true advantages of homoiothermy are realized. The outer part is designated as the *shell*, and consists of the feathers and other integumentary structures, skin, and a subcutaneous layer of varying depth (including a subcutaneous

---

[3] For more detailed and exact discussions of the physical aspects of heat movement and its control in animals, the reader is referred to the monographs of Giaja (1938a, b), Thauer (1939), Burton and Edholm (1955), and particularly Precht *et al.* (1955). The monograph of Hutchinson (1954) is a good general review with emphasis on domestic birds.

layer of fat in many species, and a variable amount of skeletal musculature). The important characteristic of the outer part of the shell is its
low, but controllable, thermal conductance which makes it effectively
a layer of variable insulation. The efficiency of this insulation varies in
different parts of the shell as a function both of the structure of the
layer and its curvature (and hence also of body size). The structure and
arrangement of the feathers provide an extremely high insulating value
to the feathered surfaces (Gerhartz, 1914; Benedict *et al.*, 1932;
Prenglowitz, 1933; Deighton and Hutchinson, 1940; Hutchinson, 1954),
and control of the arrangement of the feathers is therefore an important
thermoregulatory mechanism (Baldwin and Kendeigh, 1932; Kendeigh,
1939; Hutchinson, 1954). The unfeathered portions of the leg (including

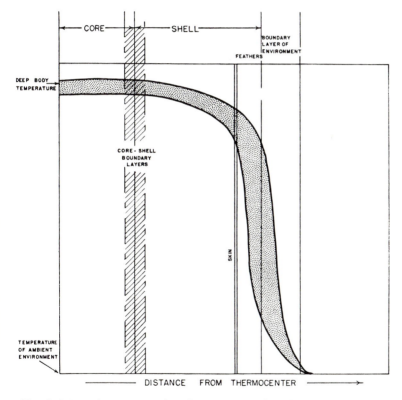

Fig. 6. Schematic representation of the thermogradient between the region of highest
temperature (thermocenter) and the ambient temperature; shaded area represents the
relative range of temperature. Based on data from Kallir (1930); Bartholomew and
Dawson (1954); Irving and Krog (1955); Steen and Enger (1957); and others.

the foot) and at least the distal parts of the wing ordinarily belong entirely to the shell. They are of particular importance in thermoregulation (Scholander *et al.*, 1950c; Scholander, 1955; Bartholomew and Cade, 1957). From a functional aspect in thermoregulation, the unfeathered parts of the leg may be regarded as controllable heat conduits of primary importance in heat dissipation.

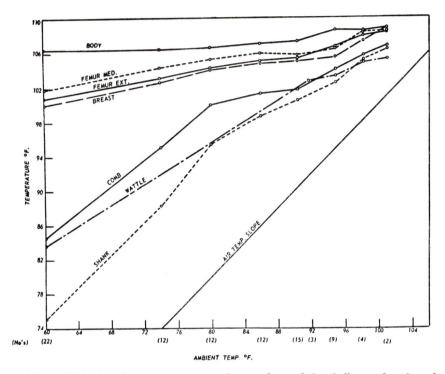

Fig. 7. Variation of temperature on various surfaces of the shell as a function of environmental temperature. From Wilson *et al.* (1952).

It is in the shell that much of the control of thermolysis is effected, although there is a partially controllable loss more directly from the core via the respiratory system. A schematic representation of the relationships between core and shell, and the relative magnitudes of temperature fluctuations therein, is given in Fig. 6. It must be emphasized that, although the shell-core concept is a most useful one, there is, of course, no precise delineation between the two. Obviously the fractions of the body properly referable to core and shell are functions of the heat load at the specific time.[4] It is evident that the maintenance of an adjustable thermogradient in the shell is indispensable in homoiothermy and that regulation of this gradient involves some of the principal thermoregulatory mechanisms.

At a given time the temperatures of different parts of the shell may vary extensively (Kallir, 1930; Wilson *et al.*, 1952). An idea of a typical gradient through the shell may be obtained from the data of Steen and Enger (1957) in pigeons. At an environmental temperature of $+20°C.$, pectoral-muscle temperature was about 40.9°; temperature under the skin, 39.4°; and on the surface of the skin (beneath the feathers), 36.3°. At $-22°$ these temperatures were, respectively, about 42.5°, about 40°, and about 35°. In *Zenaidura macroura*, Bartholomew and Dawson (1954a) found at $+25°$ ambient temperature a pectoral-muscle temperature of about 41°, and skin temperature (on surface, beneath feathers) of about 39.5°; at $+1°$ these temperatures were 41° and 35°, respectively. Figure 7 (from Wilson *et al.*, 1952) illustrates the variation of temperature on various surfaces of the shell as a function of environmental temperature.

B. The Origin, Movement, and Loss of Heat

The general relationships of heat production, heat loss, and ambient temperature have been described previously (Section IV). In general terms, it is evident that the maintenance of a steady state with regard to the heat content of the body depends upon a relatively complex system of checks and balances which control the production, transportation, and dissipation of heat. The principal, and usually the only significant, source of heat is that resulting from metabolic processes (see Section I). Only rarely and temporarily is there a direct uptake of heat per se from the environment (Table V, Fig. 13). The second law of thermodynamics requires that all components of a system tend toward a uniform temperature. The consequence of this tendency is of course a spontaneous movement of heat from places of higher temperature to places of lower temperature, or from the core toward the shell. If, as is usually the case, the bird is in an environment of lower temperature than that of the body, there will be a continuous, but variable and adjustable, loss of heat to the environment. Within the body, heat moves principally by *conduction* (important primarily over short distances) and by *convection* (principally by transport in the blood, and therefore important over greater distances). From the surfaces of the

---

[4] For a very useful critique of the shell-core concept, the reader is referred to Aschoff and Wever (1958).

TABLE V

Résumé of Thermoregulatory Processes in Birds

Basic process	Regulatory process	
	Physiological	Behavioral
Chemical		
Metabolic thermogenesis	Muscle tonus; shivering; metabolic rate in visceral organs	Active movements; food intake and consequent specific dynamic action
Heat exchange via body surface (1) Heat uptake (radiation, conduction) (2) Heat loss (radiation, conduction, convection) (3) Evaporative heat loss	(1) — (2) Vasomotor control, especially in extremities; control of feather position (3) —	(1) Adjustment of location, position, and geometric (2) configuration of body; spacing of individuals (3) Bathing
Physical		
Heat loss via respiratory system (1) Convection, conduction, radiation (2) Evaporation	(1) Ventilation rate, panting, vasomotor (2) control	—
Control of environmental temperature and humidity	—	Migration, spacing of individuals; use of nests, burrows, caves, etc; bathing

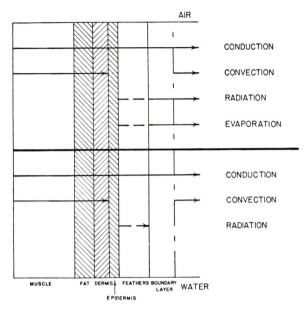

F<small>IG</small>. 8. Schematic representation of the processes of heat loss via the external body surfaces in contact with air (above) and with water (below). From Precht *et al.* (1955).

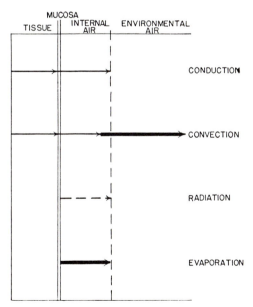

F<small>IG</small>. 9. Schematic representation of the processes of heat loss via the respiratory surfaces.

body, including the pulmonary surfaces, heat may be dissipated to the environment by *radiation, convection, conduction,* and *evaporation.* The relative importance of these thermolytic processes is shown in Figs. 8 and 9.

C. THE MECHANISMS OF THERMOREGULATION

The mechanisms of thermoregulation in birds are complex and incompletely known. The basic mechanisms and the general scheme of their integration are outlined in Table V and Fig. 10. As has been shown

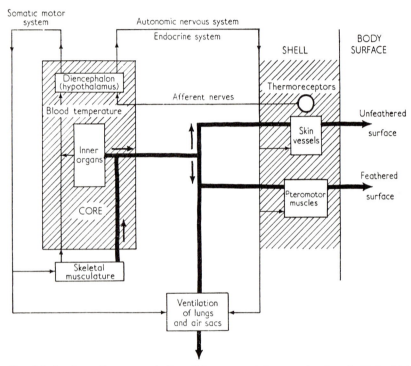

FIG. 10. A schematic representation of thermoregulatory mechanisms in birds. Light lines show regulatory relationships; heavy lines show heat flow. Modified from Precht *et al.* (1955).

previously (Section IV, B.) there is in each species a range of ambient temperature, the zone of thermoneutrality, within which the metabolic rate is minimal in the resting bird, and within which any changes in ambient temperature have minimal effect on the metabolic rate. In this thermoneutral zone almost all thermoregulation is therefore by *physical mechanisms* consisting, in effect, of adjustments of the insulation properties of the shell which require only small expenditures of energy.

When the ambient temperature decreases below the lower critical temperature, thermoregulatory adjustment becomes almost exclusively *chemical*, i.e. by alteration of the rate of thermogenesis.

1. *Physical Thermoregulation*

The *physical mechanisms* in thermoregulation are those which alter the rate of heat loss by the physical processes of conduction, radiation, convection, and evaporation. They may involve adjustments in the shell or at the respiratory surfaces, or they may involve behavioral mechanisms such as huddling, use of burrows, "sitting" on feet and legs, bathing, etc. Since birds do not have sweat glands, the heat loss by evaporation from the body surface is probably relatively slight and only indirectly controllable through alteration of the arrangement of the feathers. Consequently, heat loss occurs from the body surface primarily by heat transfer (radiation, conduction, and convection). Since the rates of loss by these three processes are functionally related to the surface temperature, control of heat loss should depend primarily on the control of skin temperature and of the insulating properties of the surface layer. With respect to the feathered surfaces, it seems well established (Kallir, 1930; Irving and Krog, 1955; Bartholomew and Dawson, 1954a; Steen and Enger, 1957) that the temperature of the skin beneath the feathers is usually above 35°C. and only rarely below 30°. It follows then that vasomotor control in the skin in feathered parts of the body is relatively unimportant compared with that of alteration of insulation by change in arrangement of the feathers (Baldwin and Kendeigh, 1932; Kendeigh, 1939; Deighton and Hutchinson, 1940; Hutchinson, 1954). Quite the opposite is the case with the unfeathered portions of the legs and feet and probably with other unfeathered areas. Since these lack effective insulation, vasomotor control is of paramount importance in adjustment of heat loss by controlling the thermogradient between the surface and the environment (Scholander *et al.*, 1950c; Irving and Krog, 1955; Bartholomew and Dawson, 1954b; Bartholomew and Cade, 1957; Wilson *et al.*, 1952). Kallir (1930) made the important observation that the temperature of the feet of *Gallinula chloropus* was reduced markedly when the feet were inserted in cold water whereas a long period in cold water reduced skin temperature only slightly, thus clearly contrasting the thermoregulatory mechanisms of the feathered and unfeathered surfaces. Irving and Krog (1955) have demonstrated in the leg of *Larus glaucescens* that there is, in addition to reduced blood flow at very low environmental temperatures, some sort of vascular heat exchange in the shank so that blood flowing into the unfeathered part of the leg has a very low temperature, thus reducing heat loss (Fig. 11). The steep gradient along the length of the feathered shank is presumably the result of exchange of heat between arterial and venous blood. According to Hyrtl (1863), however, gulls and anseriform species lack rete-type vascular heat exchangers in their legs, so that the heat exchange suggested above must be attained in some other way. Tarsal arteriovenous retia occur, however, in wading

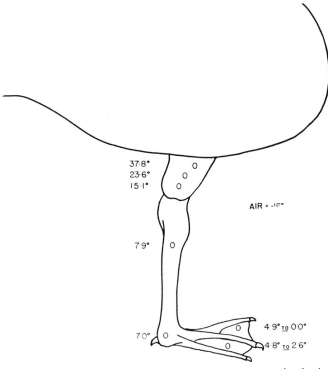

FIG. 11. Topographical distribution of superficial temperature in the leg of a gull (*Larus glaucescens*). From Irving and Krog (1955).

birds like cranes, herons, flamingos (Hyrtl, 1863, 1864), and also in some long-legged land birds such as kiwis, rheas, and ostriches (Hyrtl 1864). As is the case also in mammals, it appears that the development of these retia for heat exchange has been more important in species living in warm environments, i.e. species in which general body insulation is poorer (Scholander, 1955). Apparently most, if not all, penguins have brachial arterial retia (Jullien, 1868; Filhol, 1883a, b; Watson, 1883; Müller, 1908) suggestive of heat-exchange systems (Scholander, 1955) although corresponding venous retia are lacking. It should be noted also that a common method for reducing heat loss from the feathered parts of the legs is to "sit" on them, thus surrounding them, at least in part, with an insulating cover of feathers. In the domestic fowl, for example, the heat loss while standing is 40–50% greater than that during sitting (Deighton and Hutchinson, 1940). A similar type of mechanism is that of tucking the head beneath the wing. In the domestic fowl this reduces heat dissipation by about 12% (Deighton and Hutchinson, 1940). As mentioned above, the unfeathered parts of the legs, and to a lesser extent, other unfeathered surfaces, doubtless represent the principal routes of heat loss, particularly in species which are insulated for low environmental temperatures. Consequently the mechanisms which control this loss are of prominent importance in thermoregulation. It must be re-emphasized that these thermoregulatory mechanisms of the shell are important mainly within the thermoneutral zone; as environmental temperature drops below the lower critical temperature (Fig. 2), chemical thermoregulatory mechanisms become more, if not exclusively, important.

The second major avenue of heat loss is the respiratory heat loss (Fig. 9). In resting birds at temperatures below the upper critical temperature, heat loss by evaporation is probably relatively constant since it is a function of the amount of surface and the difference in water vapor pressure between the evaporating surface (saturation vapor pressure) and the circulating air. The latter, of course, is in turn a function of the volume-rate of ventilation. In more rapid ventilation during exercise, such as flight, heat loss via this route is doubtless increased, although experimental confirmation of this appears to be lacking. As environmental temperature approaches and exceeds the upper critical temperature, heat loss by evaporation from respiratory surfaces becomes relatively more important and is finally the sole method of heat loss. In this range panting (also gular fluttering) begins. Panting provides a marked increase in exchange of air over moist surfaces, primarily over the nonrespiratory surfaces of the respiratory system, i.e. the mouth cavity, pharynx, bronchi (and possibly air sacs). By restriction of this hyperventilation to nonrespiratory surfaces of the system the disturbing effects of hyperventilation on carbon dioxide of the blood and the possible development of alkalosis are avoided. Panting has been carefully studied by von Saalfeld (1936) in the domestic pigeon. He found that with artificial warming of the body there is first an increased rate of normal ventilation movements; when the ventilation rate reaches about 60 per minute, panting begins; at this time the body temperature is about 42–43°. With the development of panting the tidal volume is reduced to about one-third of the normal tidal volume,

T

but the ventilation rate (panting rate) increases to about 500 per minute so that the minute volume becomes three times as great as the resting minute volume. Panting is evidently controlled by a separate and distinct center in the anterodorsal part of the diencephalon. With the destruction of this center, ventilation is controlled only by the medullary respiratory center and panting is not possible. The panting center can be stimulated directly by heat. When cooled experimentally, panting is prevented even when temperature is well above the panting level. Panting is unaffected by vagotomy in the pigeon, but is abolished by this operation in the chicken (Hiestand and Randall, 1942). Strong stimulation of the respiratory center inhibits panting; similarly, stimulation of the central end of the sectioned vagus inhibits panting. The tidal volume in panting can be increased with high concentrations (6%) of CO_2 in the inhaled air. In experiments with the domestic fowl, Randall (1943) was able to show that elevation of skin temperature without elevation of head temperature fails to cause panting, thus indicating that panting is not stimulated reflexively via dermal thermoreceptors, but rather depends upon a central thermoregulatory center which is sensitive to elevated temperature; this confirms the observations of von Saalfeld (1936). Obviously the efficiency of panting as a thermoregulatory mechanism is a function of the vapor pressure of the inhaled air. This is a matter of substantial importance in comparison of thermoregulation in hot humid and hot arid environments. Table VI gives body temperatures at which panting begins in several species. Although panting is an important and effective mechanism in thermoregulation, it is of limited value alone, at least in passerine species, since as environmental temperature approaches body temperature only one-fourth to one-half of the surplus heat can be dissipated by evaporation alone. In many species, it is supplemented by a tolerance of a temporary hyperthermia as great as 4°. This hyperthermia then increases dissipation of heat by increasing the gradient between the bird and the environment. Equally important in hot environments are behavioral thermoregulatory measures (Table V) in which the bird seeks a cooler place and reduces activity during the hot part of the day. Bathing during the hot part of the day (Bartholomew et al., 1953; Dawson, 1954; Hutchinson, 1954) is also a behavioral thermoregulatory mechanism.

A possible role of the air sacs in cooling has been suggested by Viktorow (1909) and Kendeigh and Baldwin (1928). More recently Zeuthen (1942) has suggested that they may be of importance in the dissipation of heat during flight; he suggests that a higher rate of ventilation can be maintained than is required for respiration by

TABLE VI

Body Temperature at Which Panting Begins: Selected Species

Species	Body temperature at which panting begins (°C.)	Observed rates	Investigators
Domestic duck	41.6	—	Robinson and Lee (1946)
Lophortyx californicus	43.5	—	Bartholomew and Dawson (1958)
Domestic turkey	41.0	—	Robinson and Lee (1946)
Domestic fowl	42–43	—	Randall (1943); Wilson (1948)
Zenaidura macroura	42.6	—	Bartholomew and Dawson (1954a)
Domestic pigeon	42–43	>600	von Saalfeld (1936)
Melopsittacus undulatus: Adult	43.1	ca. 200	Böni (1942)
Young	41–42	200–300	Böni (1942)

contraction of the parabronchial muscles, thus preventing hyperventilation of the air capillaries and excessive loss of carbon dioxide. This is an aspect of thermoregulation which deserves further investigation.

2. *Chemical Thermoregulation*

As the ambient temperature decreases toward the lower limit of the thermoneutral zone the capacity of the mechanisms of physical thermoregulation to conserve heat approaches a maximum. With additional reduction in ambient temperature, thermoregulatory adjustment in the resting bird is accomplished almost exclusively by augmenting the rate of thermogenesis. For a variable temperature interval below the lower critical temperature chemothermoregulation is effected simply by increased muscle tonus (see, for example, Steen and Enger, 1957) and, presumably, increased metabolic intensity in the internal organs. However, a further decrease can be compensated only by further increased activity of skeletal muscle (shivering or voluntary body movements) and food procurement.

In birds at rest, metabolic rates as much as three times the thermoneutral rate can be sustained for considerable periods of time. The rate of heat production can be increased still further by voluntary activity of the skeletal musculature. This has been measured only rarely in birds. Deighton and Hutchinson (1940) showed for the domestic fowl that the metabolic rate was 40–45% greater in the standing position than in the sitting position. In the hummingbird *Calypte anna*, Pearson (1950) found that the oxygen consumption during hovering flight was about six times the rate of consumption at rest. In mammals, as a generalization, it may be shown that the metabolic rate of moderate activity, such as walking, is about double the minimum metabolic rate. The maximum, sustained metabolic intensity in strenuous work is ten to twenty times the minimum rate. It is reasonable to assume that these comparative values would apply also to birds.

Closely associated with increased body movement as a chemothermoregulatory device is the procurement of food. Not only is there a thermal increment incident to the exercise involved, but there is also the subsequent *specific dynamic action* of food (see Section II). This has been measured as 15–18% above the minimum metabolic rate in the domestic fowl (Barott *et al.*, 1938) and of the order of 20–30% above the minimum rate in the domestic pigeon (Groebbels, 1928). It is not entirely certain that all this heat can be used in maintaining body temperature; there appear to be distinct species differences in this respect (see Hart, 1957, p. 146) which require additional investigation.

Shivering in adult birds as a chemothermoregulatory mechanism appears to be basically a reserve function which comes into play primarily when other mechanisms of heat production are inadequate. In young birds, however, shivering may be of more immediate importance until the time that the feathers are well developed. The development of thermoregulation in *Troglodytes aëdon* at 18° is closely associated with the development of muscle tremors; however, once the feathers are developed muscle tremors are no longer involved in thermoregulation at this temperature (Odum, 1942). Randall (1943) found in the chicks of the domestic fowl that the ability to maintain normal body temperature at an ambient temperature of 20° developed at about the same time as the ability to shiver. His experiments indicate quite clearly that shivering can be elicited reflexively via thermoreceptors in the skin or centrally by reduction in blood temperature without alteration of skin temperature.

When the ambient temperature increases above the upper limit of thermoneutrality, there is also an increase in the metabolic rate (see Section IV, A). This superficially anomalous phenomenon means simply that the elimination of heat under such circumstances involves a marked increase in the use of energy in the acceleration of pulmonary ventilation and cardiovascular activity. Obviously, such facilitation of heat loss is effective only as long as the increased thermogenesis incident to it is equaled or exceeded by the increased thermolysis.

D. The Integration of the Mechanisms of Thermoregulation

Although the general thermoregulatory scheme in birds is now fairly well known from an empirical functional aspect, little is known of the basic nature of the regulatory pathways and the regulatory centers. The older experiments of Rogers (1919, 1920, 1923, 1924a, b, 1928), Rogers and Lackey (1923), and Rogers and Wheat (1921) indicated that temperature regulation was completely dependent upon diencephalic centers (probably hypothalamic). The investigations of Kayser (1929a, b) are in general confirmatory although they indicate that there is some residual thermoregulation following destruction of the diencephalic centers. Some of Rogers' data (1919, p. 280) suggest the same effect, but the techniques of the time were crude and interpretation is equivocal. Randall's (1943) investigations with the domestic fowl show that shivering may be caused reflexively by stimulation of cutaneous cold receptors or centrally by decreased body temperature. Panting apparently is elicited by increase in diencephalic temperature (von Saalfeld, 1936) and cannot be stimulated reflexively through skin receptors (Randall, 1943). Kayser (1929) found that pigeons with transected spinal cords still displayed increased metabolic rates when subjected to cold environments. This also suggests the presence of a central heat-sensitive thermoregulatory center. Bilaterally vagotomized pigeons are unable to maintain body temperature at ambient temperatures below 35° (Fazio, 1943; Cascio, 1948) and fail to increase metabolic rate as body temperature declines. Figure 10 represents schematically the probable relationships involved among the thermoregulatory mechanisms.

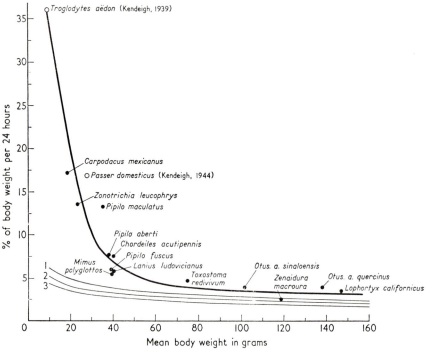

FIG. 12. Respiratory water loss as a function of body weight (indicated by the heavy line). The three lower curves indicate the theoretical relation between body weight and metabolic water produced by birds in a basal condition utilizing exclusively carbohydrates (curve *1*), fats (curve *2*), or proteins (curve *3*). From Bartholomew and Dawson (1953).

E. WATER RELATIONSHIPS IN THERMOREGULATION

Evaporative cooling provides essentially the only route for the dissipation of heat from the body when the ambient temperature approaches and exceeds the skin temperature. The fraction of the minimal, resting heat production which is lost by this route is shown for some representative species in Table VII. More extensive data on evaporative cooling as a function of ambient temperature or within the thermoneutral zone may be found in Dontcheff and Kayser (1933), Kayser (1939), Barott and Pringle (1941), Dawson (1954, 1958), Wallgren (1954), and Medway and Kare (1957). Some idea of the relative respiratory water output necessary to maintain evaporative cooling in

TABLE VII
EVAPORATIVE COOLING AT HIGH AMBIENT TEMPERATURE IN SOME
REPRESENTATIVE SPECIES OF BIRDS[a]

Species	Ambient Temperature (°C.)	% Resting heat production lost via respiratory evaporation	% Relative humidity
Domestic Pigeon	36.5	43.3	?
Troglodytes aëdon	40	50.4	?
Passer domesticus	40	39.7	>18
Richmondena cardinalis	40	39	<40
Pipilo fuscus	36	30.5	32–42
Pipilo fuscus	40	27.6	32–42
Pipilo aberti	36	44.6	32–42
Pipilo aberti	40	35.9	32–42
Emberiza citrinella	30	42.9	?
Emberiza citrinella	32.5	38.1	?
Emberiza hortulana	35	40.6	?
Emberiza hortulana	38	39.8	?
Emberiza hortulana	40	39.2	?

[a] From data of Kayser (1939), Kendeigh (1939, 1944), Dawson (1954, 1958) and Wallgren (1954).

various species may be obtained from Fig. 12 (from Bartholomew and Dawson, 1953). In the natural habitat of the species shown, the rate of water loss will often be greater than under the experimental conditions (25°, 30–60% relative humidity). Excretory water loss also must be considered. It may be seen that the rate of water loss for all species exceeds the production of metabolic water; the water deficit is especially pronounced for birds weighing less than about 40 gm. The survival of birds in hot, dry climates evidently depends upon the availability of surface water, or alternatively, succulent food (Bartholomew and Cade, 1956), the ability to tolerate a considerable hyperthermia (Dawson, 1954; Bartholomew and Dawson, 1958), and perhaps unknown behavioral adaptations.

F. THE ONTOGENY OF THERMOREGULATION

It has long been known (Edwards, 1839; Pembrey, 1895; Pembrey el al., 1895) that the altricial species whose young are hatched relatively naked do not develop good thermoregulation until a considerable time after hatching, whereas the young of precocial species, hatched with a good covering of down, develop good thermoregulation much earlier. Indeed in the latter group homoiothermy and hence some degree of thermoregulation apparently develops before hatching (Romanoff,

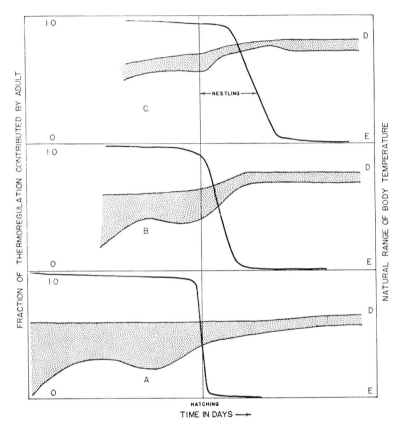

Fig. 13. Schematic representation of the ontogenetic history of homoiothermy in hypothetical procellariiform (*A*), galliform (*B*), and passerine (*C*) species. In each case the single line indicates the approximate fraction (1 to 0) of the thermoregulation of the developing embryo or hatched young contributed by the adults. The shaded areas represent the normal range of body temperatures of embryos or young. It should be emphasized that the lower tolerance limits are usually much lower than the lower limits of natural temperature shown here. In the case of the hypothetical procellariiform species (*A*), it should be emphasized that the range for the eggs is more potential than real since eggs are rarely left unincubated for more than a very brief period. However, temperatures with this range can and do occur with subsequent development of the eggs (Matthews, 1954). The scale for body temperature is linear between environmental temperature (*E*) and deep adult body temperature (*D*).

1941). Actually, as more information has accumulated, it has become apparent that the classic concepts of the altricial and precocious species represent the extremes of the entire range of the periods after hatching required for the development of effective thermoregulation. Thus the young of *Puffinus tenuirostris* maintain adult or near-adult body temperatures by the end of the first day of hatching (Farner and Serventy, 1959) and the young of *Somateria mollissima* have good thermoregulation within 2 to 7 hours after hatching (Rolnik, 1948). On the other hand, young passerine species may not develop completely effective thermoregulation until the end, or after the end, of the nestling period (Baldwin and Kendeigh, 1932; Böni, 1942). In reality the recognition of the categories of altricial and precocious species has tended to obscure the fundamentally important principle that young birds from relatively early embryonic stages develop under essentially homoiothermal conditions (see, for example, the data of Gardner, 1930; Stoner, 1937, 1939; Baldwin and Kendeigh, 1932, Barth, 1949a, b; Irving and Krog, 1956; Huggins, 1941; Holstein, 1942, 1944, 1950; Koch and Steinke, 1944; Westerskov, 1956; Dawson and Evans, 1957; Farner, 1958). In reality then, from the beginning of incubation, there is a gradual change in the thermoregulatory contributions of the adults and the young (or embryos) to the homoiothermy of the eggs or young. The changes in the ratios of these contributions to heat content and thermoregulation as functions of time from the beginning of incubation are obviously nonlinear and specifically variable. Figure 13 presents schematically the probable relationship of the egg (developing embryo) and young in three different orders. The extreme adaptation in this respect is found in the megapodes in which the adults place vegetation in the egg mounds; the decay of this vegetation provides heat for maintenance of the homoiothermal temperature and necessary conditions for incubation; in *Leipoa ocellata* solar radiation may serve as a supplemental source of heat (Frith, 1956). The homoiothermy in the developing embryo and young thus maintained jointly is by no means as perfect as that maintained by adult birds. The incubation and brooding habits of adults (Kendeigh, 1952) indicate that it may be interrupted regularly. It is therefore essential that the embryos and young up to a certain age have the ability to withstand periods of hypothermia in which the embryos or young behave essentially as poikilotherms. This ability of embryos and/or young has been noted, for example, in *Phasianus colchicus* (Ryser and Morrison, 1954; Westerskov, 1956), *Lagopus lagopus* (Barth, 1951), domestic fowl (Kaestner, 1895; Randall, 1943), *Coturnix coturnix* (Böni, 1942), *Apus apus* (Koskimies, 1950), *Jynx torquatus* (Böni, 1942), *Melopsittacus undulatus* (Böni, 1942), and *Troglodytes aëdon* (Baldwin and Kendeigh, 1932). An examination of the extensive compilation of Kendeigh (1952) on attentive behavior suggests that this ability must be extremely general. It should not be assumed that thermoregulation has necessarily reached its complete development when the young become independent of the adults. With increasing age there is generally a decreasing tolerance to hypothermia (Baldwin and Kendeigh, 1932; Randall, 1943). The functional basis of the ontogeny of thermoregulation is still a relatively uninvestigated field. The existing information consists primarily of correlations between other ontogenetic developments and empirical thermoregulatory performance. The following have been suggested (Kendeigh and Baldwin, 1928; Baldwin and Kendeigh, 1932; Böni, 1942) as the principal ontogenetic developments which contribute to the development of thermoregulation: (1) the decrease in surface-volume ratio in the growing young, thus decreasing the thermolytic surface per gram of thermogenic tissue; (2) improvement of insulation of the shell by the development of feathers; (3) increase in rate of thermogenesis; (4) possibly the development and beginning of function of the air sacs; (5) the development of nervous and hormonal control mechanisms, including, certainly, the development of a central temperature-sensitive regulatory center (presumably hypothalamic).

G. Evolutionary Aspects of Thermoregulation

The evolutionary adaptation of an avian species to a new environment with a different temperature range theoretically could be accomplished by adjustment of any one or any combination of the following: (1) body temperature, (2) metabolic rate, (3) control of dissipation of heat. A perusal of the available information (see in particular, Eklund, 1942; Wetmore, 1921; Udvardy, 1953, Irving and Krog, 1954; Scholander, 1955) can lead only to the conclusion that body temperature, despite a certain degree of lability, is generally nonadaptive and that the relatively small specific differences are to be explained in other ways. It is true that some species can tolerate a hyperthermia resulting from a temporary increment in heat content (Dawson, 1954; Bartholomew and Dawson, 1958; Kendeigh, 1944). The adaptation here is more properly one of tolerance to the temporary hyperthermia rather than a real adaptation in body temperature. A further interesting adaptation is that of the temporary hypothermia which can occur in some of the swifts, hummingbirds, and goatsuckers (see Section IX). This also may be considered as an adaptive tolerance to a temporary hypothermia as an energy-conserving device during a period in which energy intake is insufficient to meet thermoregulatory requirements.

In general it appears that the evolution of thermoregulation has been such that the thermoneutral range overlaps a large portion of the common range of environmental temperatures, thus permitting the bird to control body temperature ordinarily at rest primarily by physical mechanisms (Scholander, 1955). This means that in increased activity the primary thermoregulatory problem is that of increased rate of heat dissipation. It means that the chemothermoregulatory mechanisms may be regarded more as emergency mechanisms which compensate for extremely low environmental temperatures. Basically then, adaptation to a particular range of temperatures requires adjustment of the thermoneutral zone to the appropriate range. Since body temperature remains constant, this means that the product of resting metabolic rate and rate of heat dissipation (or conductance of the shell) must be adjusted to the level required by the environment. However, within fairly restricted limits, metabolic rate is a function of body size and is similar for tropical and arctic species of the same body size; it follows then that the evolutionary adaptation must be attained primarily by adjustment of heat dissipation and hence of the insulative properties of the shell (Scholander et al., 1950b; Scholander, 1955). The contribution of specific behavioral adaptations to thermoregulation is essentially unknown, but at least in some cold-tolerant species appears to be too prominent to ignore (see, for instance, Löhrl, 1955).

It is not within the province of this chapter to present a detailed commentary on the much-discussed Bergmann's and Allen's "rules." The cases for and against them have been argued by Rensch (1936, 1938, 1939) and Reinig (1938, 1939), respectively (see also, Mayr, 1942, 1956). It is sufficient here to observe first that neither of the rules appears to hold really generally for most species with extensive latitudinal (and hence temperature) distributions. Furthermore, the relatively slight differences in the size of the body and the lengths of the appendages are quite trivial with respect to the adjustment of heat dissipation (Hutchinson, 1954; Scholander, 1955, 1958). This is not meant to argue for the invalidity of the "rules" in species in which such clines do clearly occur, for it is quite plausible that these clines may have developed because of the slight energy-conserving advantages conferred by these differences. It must be emphasized, however, that the magnitude of the changes of bodily dimension necessary to provide the adequate adjustment of heat dissipation, or even any appreciable fraction thereof, far exceeds the genetic potential of any species. Unquestionably, adaptations to hotter or colder environments have occurred primarily by adaptation of the insulation and thermoregulatory mechanisms of the shell.

With regard to the thermoregulatory problems of the young of arctic species as compared with tropical species, the few data that are available indicate that there has been little if any adaptation in the time required for the development of effective thermoregulation by the nestlings (Rolnik, 1948; Barth, 1951; Bartholomew and Dawson, 1952, 1954b). Although it might appear superficially that an early onset of thermoregulatory ability would be of considerable advantage in the development of the young of arctic species, it must be remembered that this ability commits its possessor to an elevated energy expenditure whenever it is exposed to low ambient temperature (see Rolnik, 1948).

VIII. Body Temperature

A. GENERAL CONSIDERATIONS

A sufficient quantity of information has been accumulated now to indicate that, although the range of normal adult deep body temperatures among the entire class is only of the order of six or seven degrees, there are certainly well-established species differences, the functional bases of which remain obscure. A comparison of body temperatures among species is difficult because of differences among individual birds of the same species, the lability of temperature within the individual (Baldwin and Kendeigh, 1932; Bartholomew and Dawson, 1954a, 1958; Dawson, 1954; Bartholomew and Cade, 1957; Udvardy, 1953), diurnal variations (Hildén and Stenbäck, 1916; Simpson and Galbraith, 1905; Baldwin and Kendeigh, 1932; Bartholomew and Dawson, 1954a, 1958; Dawson, 1954; Irving, 1955; Farner et al., 1956), variations at different sites within the bird (Kallir, 1930; Steen and Enger, 1957), and methods of measurement (Baldwin and Kendeigh, 1932; Bernard et al., 1944; Udvardy, 1953; Bartholomew and Dawson, 1958; Irving and Krog, 1954). Among the common methods of measuring deep body temperatures are: (1) use of thermometer in cloaca or proventriculus with appropriate care in handling of the bird to reduce "handling artifact" to a minimum, (2) use of thermometer in cloaca or proventriculus immediately after shooting, (3) use of temporarily inserted thermocouples in proventriculus or cloaca, and (4) use of indwelling thermocouples implanted in pectoral muscles (Bartholomew and Dawson, 1954a) or subdermally (Williams, 1958). The last is doubtless the most useful and reliable, although the nature of the method places a severe restriction on the conditions under which it can be used. Useful information can be obtained by all these methods, although the innate characteristics of each, including procedures of the individual investigators, make it necessary to effect comparisons with caution.

B. Comparison of Deep Body Temperatures

Because of the lability in body temperature, particularly in active birds, the best basis for comparison is doubtless through the use of *standard deep body temperatures*. These should be measured in the cloaca, proventriculus, or pectoral muscles of the bird in darkness, in the thermoneutral temperature range, with the bird in postabsorptive state, and preferably at night (except for truly nocturnal species); the measurements should be made with minimum disturbance to the bird. Actually, few data obtained on this basis are available. Those compiled in Table VIII, in most instances, only approach conformance with these criteria; those from the investigations of Bartholomew and Dawson are taken from their continuous records using thermocouples in the pectoral muscles and are doubtless the closest to standard deep body temperature. A series of standard temperatures taken with mercury thermometers for single individuals of twenty-one species by Benedict and Fox (1927) range from 39.2° for *Casuarius bennetti* to 41.2° for *Gabianus pacificus* and thus conform quite well with those compiled in Table VIII. Of equal interest, but more difficult to study comparatively, is the *deep body temperature of normal active* (but not flying) *birds*. Obviously, because of the differences in levels of activity and the greater lability of temperature under such conditions, meaningful comparisons are still more difficult. Table IX contains data selected as widely as possible among the orders of birds. Data are included only when at least several individuals of the species have been measured and when the precautions and techniques are explicitly stated and appear to be adequate.

C. Diurnal Variation in Body Temperature

The deep body temperature of most species appears to have a rather pronounced daily cycle, with the higher temperature occurring during the active part of the day and the lower during the inactive part. This phenomenon has been known since the investigations of Chossat (1843). Figures 14 (from Bartholomew and Dawson, 1954a) and 15 (from Farner *et al.*, 1956) illustrate this phenomenon for a diurnal species (*Zenaidura macroura*) and a nocturnal species (*Apteryx australis*). The order of magnitude between the temperature of the active period and the temperature during the inactive period is 1–4°, being at least in part an inverse function of body size (Table X). The daily temperature cycle has an obvious endogenous component, probably associated in some way with the endogenous component of the daily activity cycle (see for example, Aschoff, 1953, 1955, 1957), since it can be shifted in

TABLE VIII

Adult Body Temperatures under Standard or Quasi-standard Conditions: Selected Species

Species	Site	Ambient temperature (°C.)	Body temperature (°C.)	Investigators
Galliformes:				
Lophortyx californicus	Pectoral muscles	24–26	ca. 39.5	Bartholomew and Dawson, 1958
Lophortyx gambelii	Pectoral muscles	24–26	ca. 39.5	Bartholomew and Dawson, 1958
Procellariiformes:				
Oceanodroma leucorhoa	Cloaca	13–16	39.1	Folk, 1949, 1951
Columbiformes:				
Zenaidura macroura	Pectoral muscles	23	39.5	Bartholomew and Dawson, 1954
Falconiformes:				
Falco sparvarius	Pectoral muscles	20–22	39.2–40.0	Bartholomew and Cade, 1957
Accipiter nisus	Cloaca	ca. 20	40.4	Udvardy, 1953
Charadriiformes:				
Calidris alpina	Proventriculus	ca. 20	39.8	Udvardy, 1953
Calidris ferruginea	Proventriculus	ca. 20	40.2	Udvardy, 1953
Philomachus pugnax	Proventriculus	ca. 20	40.3	Udvardy, 1953
Philomachus pugnax	Cloaca	ca. 20	38.7	Udvardy, 1953
Charadrius hiaticula	Proventriculus	ca. 20	39.9	Udvardy, 1953
Charadrius hiaticula	Cloaca	ca. 20	38.3	Udvardy, 1953
Passeriformes:				
Troglodytes aëdon, ♂♂	Proventriculus	ca. 20	40.2	Baldwin and Kendeigh, 1932
Troglodytes aëdon, ♀♀	Proventriculus	ca. 20	40.6	Baldwin and Kendeigh, 1932
Troglodytes troglodytes	Proventriculus	ca. 20	39.7	Udvardy, 1953
Spizella passerina	Proventriculus	ca. 20	40.5	Baldwin and Kendeigh, 1932
Pipilo aberti	Pectoral muscles	23	ca. 39.5	Dawson, 1954

Pipilo fuscus	Pectoral muscles	23	ca. 39.5	Dawson, 1954
Emberiza citrinella	Proventriculus	ca. 20	40.5	Udvardy, 1953
Emberiza citrinella	Cloaca	ca. 20	39.2	Udvardy, 1953
Anthus spinoletta	Proventriculus	ca. 20	40.5	Udvardy, 1953
Anthus spinoletta	Cloaca	ca. 20	39.9	Udvardy, 1953
Motacilla alba	Proventriculus	ca. 20	40.6	Udvardy, 1953
Phylloscopus trochilus	Proventriculus	ca. 20	40.4	Udvardy, 1953
Muscicapa striata	Proventriculus	ca. 20	40.9	Udvardy, 1953
Phoenicurus phoenicurus	Proventriculus	ca. 20	41.0	Udvardy, 1953
Erithacus rubecula	Proventriculus	ca. 20	40.6	Udvardy, 1953
Sturnus vulgaris	Proventriculus	ca. 20	41.5	Udvardy, 1953
Parus cinctus	Proventriculus	0–14	40.6	Udvardy, 1955

TABLE IX

Deep Body Temperature of Active Nonflying Adult Birds: Selected Species

Species	Number of individuals	Body temperature (°C.)	Site	Method[a]	Investigators
Apterygiformes:					
Apteryx australis	7	39.0	Cloaca	II	Farner et al., 1956
Podicepidiformes:					
Podiceps caspicus	6	40.2	Cloaca	I	Wetmore, 1921
Sphenisciformes:					
Megadyptes antipodes	13	37.8	Cloaca	II	Farner, 1958
Pygoscelis adeliae	23	37.9	Cloaca	II	Eklund, 1942
Pygoscelis papua	33	38.1	Cloaca	II	Farner, unpublished
Aptenodytes patagonica	28	37.7	Cloaca	II	Farner, unpublished
Procellariiformes:					
Pachyptila turtur	28	39.9	Cloaca	II	Farner, 1956
Puffinus tenuirostris	37	40.9	Cloaca	II	Farner and Serventy, 1959
Diomedea exulans	11	39.6	Cloaca	II	Eydoux and Souleyet, 1838
Pelecaniformes:					
Pelecanus occidentalis	6	40.3	Cloaca	I	Wetmore, 1921
Phalacrocorax auritus	6	40.1	Cloaca	I	Wetmore, 1921
Phalacrocorax carbo	12	39.8	Cloaca	I	Simpson, 1912a
Phalacrocorax aristotelis	49	40.4	Cloaca	I	Simpson, 1912a
Morus bassanus	7	41.7	Cloaca	I	Simpson, 1912a
Morus bassanus	7	41.0	Cloaca	V	Bernard et al., 1944
Ciconiiformes:					
Egretta candidissima	13	40.2	Cloaca	I	Wetmore, 1921
Anseriformes:					
Domestic duck	110	42.1	Cloaca	II	Martins, 1856

	n		Site		Reference
Domestic duck	—	41.5–42.5	Cloaca	II	Löer, 1909a, b; 1910
Anas platyrhynchos	11	41.2	Cloaca	I	Wetmore, 1921
Anas carolinensis	27	41.2	Cloaca	I	Wetmore, 1921
Anas cyanoptera	12	41.7	Cloaca	I	Wetmore, 1921
Anas acuta	11	41.3	Cloaca	I	Wetmore, 1921
Anas penelope	18	41.5	Cloaca	II	Martins, 1856
Aythya affinis	10	41.3	Cloaca	I	Wetmore, 1921
Domestic goose	40	40.8	Cloaca	II	Löer, 1909a, b; 1910
Domestic goose	97	41.3	Cloaca	II	Martins, 1856
Branta canadensis	11	41.1	Cloaca	V	Bernard et al., 1944
Falconiformes:					
Accipiter nisus	22	41.2	Cloaca	III	Udvardy, 1953
Falco sparverius	10	40.5	Proventriculus	IV	Bartholomew and Cade, 1957
Galliformes:					
Phasianus colchicus	7	41.9	Cloaca	II	Westerskov, 1956
Phasianus colchicus	40	42.6	Cloaca	II	Löer, 1909a, b; 1910
Domestic turkey	40	41.2	Cloaca	II	Löer, 1909a, b; 1910
Domestic fowl	29	41.0	Cloaca	II	Yeates et al., 1941
Domestic fowl	114	41.5–42.2	Cloaca	II	Simpson, 1912b
Lagopus lagopus	53	41.3–42.0	Cloaca	I	Irving and Krog, 1954
Lagopus leucurus	13	41.5	Cloaca	I	Irving and Krog, 1954
Lophortyx gambelii	7	40.0–41.5	Pectoral muscle	IV	Bartholomew and Dawson, 1958
Lophortyx californicus	10	40.0–41.5	Pectoral muscle	IV	Bartholomew and Dawson, 1958
Charadriiformes:					
Charadrius vociferus	10	41.7	Proventriculus	I	Wetmore, 1921
Totanus melanoleucus	10	41.5	Cloaca	I	Wetmore, 1921
Catoptrophorus semipalmatus	17	41.4	Cloaca	I	Wetmore, 1921
Limosa fedoa	31	40.7	Cloaca	I	Wetmore, 1921
Ereunetes mauri	25	41.8	Proventriculus	I	Wetmore, 1921
Limnodromus griseus	19	40.9	Cloaca	I	Wetmore, 1921
Recurvirostra americana	26	41.5	Cloaca	I	Wetmore, 1921

U

TABLE IX—(continued)

Species	Number of individuals	Body temperature (°C.)	Site	Method[a]	Investigators
Lobipes lobatus	26	41.8	Proventriculus	I	Wetmore, 1921
Catharacta skua	30	41.2	Cloaca	II	Eklund, 1942
Larus dominicanus	16	40.9	Cloaca	II	Eklund, 1942
Larus glaucescens	7	41.7	Cloaca	II	Irving and Krog, 1954
Larus glaucus	12	40.7	Cloaca	II	Martins, 1856
Larus argentatus	10	42.3	Cloaca	II	Martins, 1856
Larus pipixcan	7	40.9	Cloaca	I	Wetmore, 1921
Rissa tridactyla	16	41.5	Cloaca	I	Simpson, 1912a
Sterna forsteri	8	41.4	Cloaca	I	Wetmore, 1921
Hydrochelidon nigra	10	41.6	Cloaca	I	Wetmore, 1921
Cepphus grylle	24	40.4	Cloaca	I	Simpson, 1912a
Columbiformes:					
Zenaidura macroura	13	42.7	Cloaca	I	Wetmore, 1921
Zenaidura macroura	7	42.5	Pectoral muscle	IV	Bartholomew and Dawson, 1954
Zenaida asiatica	15	42.5	Cloaca	I	Wetmore, 1921
Domestic pigeon	20	42.2	Cloaca	I	Chossat, 1843
Strigiformes:					
Asio flammeus	7	41.2	Cloaca	II	Irving and Krog, 1954
Bubo virginianus	8	40.8	Cloaca	V	Bernard *et al.*, 1944
Piciformes:					
Dendrocopos pubescens	9	41.9	Proventriculus	I	Wetmore, 1921
Passeriformes:					
Empidonax flaviventris	10	42.3	Proventriculus	I	Wetmore, 1921
Empidonax trailli	10	42.3	Proventriculus	I	Wetmore, 1921
Eremophila alpestris	9	43.0	Proventriculus	I	Wetmore, 1921
Riparia riparia	660	41.4	Proventriculus	II	Stoner, 1937

Pica pica	18	41.8	Proventriculus	I	Wetmore, 1921
Parus carolinensis	12	42.3	Proventriculus	I	Wetmore, 1921
Parus cinctus	6	41.5	Proventriculus	III	Udvardy, 1955
Telmatodytes palustris	10	41.6	Proventriculus	I	Wetmore, 1921
Mimus polyglottos	6	42.7	Proventriculus	I	Wetmore, 1921
Turdus migratorius	9	43.2	Proventriculus	I	Wetmore, 1921
Passer domesticus	108	43.5	Proventriculus	V	Bernard *et al.*, 1944
Junco hyemalis	37	43.0	Proventriculus	V	Bernard *et al.*, 1944
Junco hyemalis	11	42.6	Proventriculus	I	Wetmore, 1921
Richmondena cardinalis	9	42.9	Proventriculus	I	Wetmore, 1921
Richmondena cardinalis	—	41.0–42.5	Cloaca	II	Dawson, 1958
Pipilo aberti	20	42.0	Pectoral muscle	IV	Dawson, 1954
Pipilo fuscus	17	41.7	Pectoral muscle	IV	Dawson, 1954

[a] Methods of obtaining data: I Measured with mercury thermometer immediately after shooting. II Measured with mercury thermometer immediately after capture; struggling held to a minimum. III Measured with temporarily inserted thermocouple immediately after capture. IV Measured with an indwelling thermocouple. V Measured with mercury thermometer after holding in dark for 30-45 minutes after capture.

phase, but only slightly, if at all, in frequency (Simpson and Galbraith, 1905; Hildén and Stenbäck, 1916; Aschoff, 1955). In addition, its magnitude is functionally related to environmental temperature since it is suppressed by elevated and constant environmental temperatures (Wilson, 1948; Bartholomew and Dawson, 1954a; Dawson, 1954).

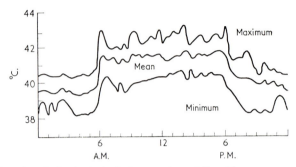

FIG. 14. Diurnal variation in the body temperature of *Zenaidura macroura*, as measured by an indwelling thermocouple in the pectoral musculature. Lights on 6 A.M. to 6 P.M. From Bartholomew and Dawson (1954a).

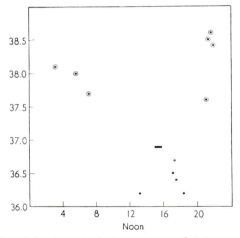

FIG. 15. Diurnal variation in the body temperatures of *Apteryx australis*, as measured in the cloaca by a mercury thermometer. From Farner *et al.* (1956).

IX. Temporary Hypothermia

Although temporary hypothermia may occur repeatedly in young birds before the development of adequate thermoregulation, its occurrence in adult birds represents an adaptive specialization apparently

TABLE X
DIURNAL CYCLES IN BODY TEMPERATURE: SELECTED SPECIES

Species	Activity habit	Deep body temperature (°C.)			Investigators
		Active part of day	Inactive part of day	Difference	
Apteryx australis	Nocturnal	38.2–39.9	36.4–37.2	0.7–2.3	Farner *et al.*, 1956
Domestic duck	Diurnal	42.2	41.3	0.9	Simpson and Galbraith, 1905
Branta nigricans	Diurnal	42.3	41.0	1.3	Irving, 1955
Philacta canagica	Diurnal	43.2	41.0	2.2	Irving, 1955
Domestic goose	Diurnal	41.4	39.9	1.5	Simpson and Galbraith, 1905
Lophortyx gambelii	Diurnal	40.0–41.5	—	ca. 1.5	Bartholomew and Dawson, 1958
Lophortyx californicus	Diurnal	40.0–41.5	—	ca. 1.5	Bartholomew and Dawson, 1958
Domestic fowl	Diurnal	41.7–43.0	40.3–40.6	1.1–2.4	Fronda, 1921
Domestic turkey	Diurnal	41.5	40.6	0.9	Fronda, 1921
Guinea fowl	Diurnal	42.4	40.6	1.8	Fronda, 1921
Phasianus colchicus	Diurnal	43.3	41.8	1.5	Fronda, 1921
Falco sparverius	Diurnal	40.2–41.4	39.0–40.0	ca. 1.0	Bartholomew and Cade, 1957
Falco tinnunculus	Diurnal	—	—	2.1	Simpson and Galbraith, 1905
Asio flammeus	Diurnal	—	—	2.2	Irving, 1955
Zenaidura macroura	Diurnal	42.5	39.5	3.0	Bartholomew and Dawson, 1954
Domestic pigeon	Diurnal	42.2	41.5	0.7	Chossat, 1843
Domestic pigeon	Diurnal	43.3	41.2	2.1	Fronda, 1921
Domestic pigeon	Diurnal	—	—	1.0–2.1	Hildén and Stenbäck, 1916
Turdus merula	Diurnal	42.7	38.5	4.2	Simpson and Galbraith, 1905
Sturnus vulgaris	Diurnal	—	—	3.3	Simpson and Galbraith, 1905
Richmondena cardinalis	Diurnal	41.0–42.5	38.5–40.0	2.0–3.0	Dawson, 1958
Pipilo aberti	Diurnal	42.0	39.2	2.8	Dawson, 1954
Pipilo fuscus	Diurnal	41.7	39.5	2.2	Dawson, 1954

characteristic of a restricted number of groups. Reports of hypothermia in birds have appeared persistently in the scientific and popular literature for nearly four centuries (McAtee, 1947) although it is difficult to assess the reliability and significance of many of the accounts. Although the phenomenon has been attributed to a large variety of species, significantly, most of the accounts concern swallows, swifts, goatsuckers, and hummingbirds (McAtee, 1947; Huxley *et al.*, 1939; Pearson, 1950, 1953; Bartholomew *et al.*, 1957). With the exception of the hummingbirds, these are completely dependent on flying insects as a source of food, a source which can be temporarily eliminated by inclement weather.

Temporary hypothermia ("torpidity" or "hibernation") has been observed sufficiently frequently so that it can be regarded as a normal phenomenon in *Phalaenoptilus nuttalli* and possibly also in *Chordeiles acutipennis* (Jaeger, 1948, 1949; Thorburg, 1953; Marshall, 1955; Stebbins, 1957; Bartholomew *et al.*, 1957; Farner, unpublished). The hypothermia in *Phalaenoptilus nuttalli* can be quite extreme; deep body temperatures of the order of 5–10° have been recorded (Marshall, 1955; Bartholomew *et al.*, 1957; Howell and Bartholomew, 1959). Duration of the hypothermia apparently is usually of the order of a few hours to half a day. The value of temporary hypothermia as an energy-saving device is illustrated well by investigations of Bartholomew *et al.* (1957), who found that a torpid poorwill with a body temperature of 5° had a metabolic rate which was only about 3% its rate at normal body temperature. The immediate cause of the development of hypothermia is not apparent, although in some instances it is associated with a depletion of energy reserves as indicated by low body weight. Arousal rates are rapid.

Among the hummingbirds, temporary hypothermia has been observed in *Calypte anna* (Pearson, 1950; Bartholomew *et al.*, 1957), *Selasphorus sasin* (Pearson, 1950), and *Oreotrochilus estella* (Pearson, 1953); it is possibly widespread in this group. Bartholomew *et al.* (1957) have concluded that "The onset of torpidity . . . is rapid and presumably nightly except in advanced nestlings and incubating females . . ." The rapid arousal rates (about 1–1.5° per minute) are apparently advantageous by reducing exposure time to diurnal predators to a minimum. The value of the phenomenon in energy conservation has been emphasized by Pearson (1950, 1953, 1954).

Among swifts the occurrence and value of temporary hypothermia has been well established by the investigations of Koskimies (1948, 1950) on *Apus apus* in Finland. During inclement weather when the aerial plankton is impoverished, most of the swifts move away from the area of inclement weather. However, incubating birds and young birds may enter a state of hypothermia which may last for a few days. The development of hypothermia is associated with a depletion of energy reserves as indicated by loss in body weight.

In experiments with *Aëronautes saxatalis*, Bartholomew *et al.* (1957) were able to obtain hypothermia by maintaining the swifts under a variety of conditions resulting in a depletion of energy reserves. Temperatures during hypothermia were variable, but generally of the order of 20–25°. Arousal was at the rate of about 0.4° per minute.

According to Cowles (Bartholomew *et al.*, 1957) temporary hypothermia may also develop in *Colius striatus*, thus giving support to the reports (McAtee, 1947) of the occurrence of this phenomenon among the colies.

Still remaining for careful investigation is the matter of temporary hypothermia in swallows. There are sufficient anecdotal accounts in the literature (McAtee, 1947) to suggest that this may be a fruitful field for research.

References

Albritton, E. C. (ed.) (1954). "Standard Values in Nutrition and Metabolism." Saunders, Philadelphia, Pennsylvania.

Aschoff, J. (1953) Aktivitätsperiodik bei Gimpeln unter natürlichen und künstlichen Belichtungsverhältnissen. *Z. vergleich. Physiol.* **35**: 159–166.

Aschoff, J. (1955). Exogene und endogene Komponente der 24 Stunden-Periodik bei Tier und Mensch. *Naturwissenschaften* **42**: 569–575.

Aschoff, J. (1957). Aktivitätsmuster der Tagesperiodik. *Naturwissenschaften* **44**: 361–367.

Aschoff, J., and Wever, R. (1958). Kern und Schale im Wärmehaushalt der Menschen. *Naturwissenschaften* **45**: 477–485.

Bacq, Z. M. (1929). Sur l'existence d'un rythme nycthéméral de métabolisme chez le coq. *Ann. physiol. physicochim. biol.* **5**: 497–511.

Baldwin, S. P., and Kendeigh, S. C. (1932). Physiology of the temperature of birds. *Sci. Publ. Cleveland Museum Nat. Hist.* **3**: 1–196.

Barott, H. G., and Pringle, E. M. (1941). Energy and gaseous metabolism of the hen as affected by temperature. *J. Nutrition* **22**: 273–286.

Barott, H. G., and Pringle, E. M. (1946). Energy and gaseous metabolism of the chicken from hatch to maturity as affected by temperature. *J. Nutrition* **31**: 35–50.

Barott, H. G., Fritz, J. C., and Pringle, E. M. (1938). Heat production and gaseous metabolism of young male chickens. *J. Nutrition* **15**: 145–167.

Barth, E. K. (1949a). Redetemperaturer og rugevaner. *Naturen* **1949**: 81–95.

Barth, E. K. (1949b). Kroppstemperatur hos fugler og pattedyr. *Fauna o. flora* **1949**: 163–177.

Barth, E. K. (1951). Kroppstemperatur hos måkeunger. *Nytt Mag. Naturv.* **88**: 213–245.

Bartholomew, G. A. (1958). The role of physiology in the distribution of terrestrial vertebrates. *Publ. Am. Assoc. Advance. Sci. No.* **51**: 81–95.

Bartholomew, G. A., and Cade, T. J. (1956). Water consumption of House Finches. *Condor* **58**: 406–412.

Bartholomew, G. A., and Cade, T. J. (1957). The body temperature of the American Kestrel, *Falco sparvarius*. *Wilson Bull.* **69**: 149–154.

Bartholomew, G. A., and Dawson, W. R. (1952). Body temperatures in nestling Western Gulls. *Condor* **54**: 58–60.

Bartholomew, G. A., and Dawson, W. R. (1953). Respiratory water loss in some birds of southwestern United States. *Physiol. Zoöl.* **26**: 162–166.

Bartholomew, G. A., and Dawson, W. R. (1954a). Body temperature and water requirements of the Mourning Dove, *Zenaidura macroura marginella*. *Ecology* **35**: 181–187.

Bartholomew, G. A., and Dawson, W. R. (1954b). Temperature regulation in young pelicans, herons, and gulls. *Ecology* **35**: 466–472.

Bartholomew, G. A., and Dawson, W. R. (1958). Body temperatures in California and Gambel's Quail. *Auk* **75**: 150–156.

Bartholomew, G. A., Dawson, W. R., and O'Neill, E. J. (1953). A field study of temperature regulation in young White Pelicans, *Pelecanus erythrorhynchos*. *Ecology* **34**: 554–560.

Bartholomew, G. A., Howell, T. R., and Cade, T. J. (1957). Torpidity in the White-throated Swift, Anna Hummingbird, and the Poorwill. *Condor* **59**: 145–155.

Benedict, F. G. (1938). Vital energetics: a study in comparative basal metabolism. *Carnegie Inst. Wash. Publ. No.* **503**.

Benedict, F. G., and Fox, E. L. (1927). The gaseous metabolism of large wild birds under aviary life. *Proc. Am. Phil. Soc.* **66**: 511–534.

Benedict, F. G., and Fox, E. L. (1933). Der Grundumsatz von kleinen Vögeln (Spatzen, Kanarienvögeln, und Sittichen). *Arch. ges. Physiol. Pflüger's* **232**: 357–388.

Benedict, F. G., and Lee, R. C. (1937). Lipogenesis in the animal body, with special reference to the physiology of the goose. *Carnegie Inst. Wash. Publ. No.* **489**.

Benedict, F. G., and Riddle, O. (1929). The measurement of the basal heat production of pigeons. II. Physiological technique. *J. Nutrition* **1**: 497–536.

Benedict, F. G., Landauer, W., and Fox, E. L. (1932). The physiology of normal and frizzle fowl, with special reference to basal metabolism. *Univ. Conn. Storrs Agr. Expt. Sta. Bull. No.* **177**: 15–101.

Bernard, R., Cayouette, R., and Brassard, J. A. (1944). Mesure de la température normale des oiseaux au moyen de thermomètres à mercure. *Rev. can. biol.* **3**: 251–277.

Bladergroen, W. (1955). "Einführung in die Energetik und Kinetik biologischer Vorgänge." Wepf, Basel.

Blum, H. F. (1950), "Time's Arrow and Evolution." Princeton Univ. Press, Princeton, New Jersey.

Böni, A. (1942). Ueber die Entwicklung der Temperaturregulation bei verschiedenen Nesthockern. *Arch. Suisses ornithol.* **2**: 1–56.

Bray, H. G., and White, K. (1957). "Kinetics and Thermodynamics in Biochemistry." Academic Press, New York.

Brody, S. (1945). "Bioenergetics and Growth." Reinhold, New York.

Brody, S., and Proctor, R. C. (1932). Growth and development, with special reference to domestic animals. XXIII. Relation between basal metabolism and mature body weight in different species of mammals and birds. *Missouri Univ. Agr. Expt. Sta. Research Bull. No.* **166**: 89–101.

Burckard, E., Dontcheff, L., and Kayser, C. (1933). Le rythme nycthéméral chez le pigeon. *Ann. physiol. physicochim. biol.* **9**: 303–368.

Burton, A. C., and Edholm, O. G. (1955). "Man in a Cold Environment." Edward Arnold, London.

Cascio, G. (1948). Temperatura limite del colombo vagatomizzato. *Boll. Soc. Ital. Sper.*, **24**: 565–567.

Cathcart, E. P., and Markowitz, J. (1927). The influence of various sugars on the respiratory quotient. A contribution to the significance of the R.Q. *J. Physiol. (London)* **63**: 309–324.

Chossat, C. (1843). Recherches expérimentales sur l'inanition. *Ann. sci. nat. Sér. II Zool.* **20**: 54–81.

Clark, W. M. (1952). "Topics in Physical Chemistry," 2nd ed. Williams & Wilkins, Baltimore, Maryland.

Davis, E. A., Jr. (1955). Seasonal changes in the energy balance of the English Sparrow. *Auk* **72**: 385–411.

Dawson, W. R. (1954). Temperature regulation and water requirements of the Brown and Abert Towhees, *Pipilo fuscus* and *Pipilo aberti*. *Univ. Calif. (Berkeley) Publs. Zoöl.* **59**: 81–124.

Dawson, W. R. (1958). Relation of oxygen consumption and evaporative water loss to temperature in the Cardinal. *Physiol. Zoöl.* **31**: 37–48.

Dawson, W. R., and Evans, F. C. (1957). Relation of growth and development to temperature regulation in nestling Field and Chipping sparrows. *Physiol. Zoöl.* **30**: 315–327.

de Bont, A. F. (1944). Métabolisme de repos de quelques espèces d'oiseaux, *Ann. Soc. zool. Belg.* **75**: 75–80.

Deighton, T., and Hutchinson, J. C. D. (1940). Studies on the metabolism of the fowls. II. The effect of activity on metabolism. *J. Agr. Sci.* **30**: 141–157.

Dontcheff, L., and Kayser, C. (1933). Régulation thermique et mouvements d'eau chez le pigeon. *Compt. rend. soc. biol.* **113**: 1074–1076.

Dontcheff, L., and Kayser, C. (1934). Le rythme saisonnier de métabolisme de base chez le pigeon en fonction de la température moyenne de milieu. *Ann. physiol. physicochim. biol.* **10**: 285–300.

Dukes, H. H. (1937). Studies on the energy metabolism of the hen. *J. Nutrition* **14**: 341–354.

Edwards, W. F. (1839). Animal Heat. *In* "Todd's Cyclopedia of Anatomy and Physiology," Vol. 2, 648–684.

Eklund, C. R. (1942). Body temperatures of antarctic birds. *Auk* **59**: 544–548.

Enger, P. S. (1957). Heat regulation and metabolism in some tropical mammals and birds. *Acta Physiol. Scand.* **40**: 161–166.

Etchécopar, R. D., and Prévost, J. (1954). Données oologiques sur l'avifaune de Terre Adélie. *Oiseau* **24**: 227–247.

Eydoux, F., and Souleyet (1838). Sur la température de l'homme et des oiseaux. *Compt. rend. acad. sci.* **6**: 456–458.

Farner, D. S. (1956). Body temperature of the Fairy Prion (*Pachyptila turtur*) in flight and at rest. *J. Appl. Physiol.* **8**: 546–548.

Farner, D. S. (1958). Incubation and body temperatures in the Yellow-eyed Penguin. *Auk* **75**: 249–262.

Farner, D. S., Chivers, N., and Riney, T. (1956). The body temperature of North Island Kiwis. *Emu* **56**: 199–206.

Farner, D. S., and Serventy, D. L. (1959). Body temperature and thermoregulation in the Slender-billed Shearwater. *Condor* **61**: 426–433.

Fazio, F. (1943). Azioni dei vaghi sugli scambi gassosi. *Arch. Fisiol.* **43**: 326–340.

Feldstein, M, J., and Hirsch, A. H. (1935). The calculation of relative growth constants. *Am. Naturalist* **69**: 610–613.

Filhol, H. (1883a). De la disposition de l'artère humérale de *Pygoscelis antarcticus*. *Bull. soc. philomath. Paris* [7] **7**: 17–18.

Filhol, H. (1883b). De la disposition de l'artère humérale chez le *Spheniscus demersus*. *Bull. soc. philomath. Paris* [7] **7**: 92–93.

Fill, W. (1942). Der Einfluss des Lichtes auf Stoffwechsel und Geschlechtsreife bei Warmblütern. *Z. wiss. Zool.* **155**: 343–395.

Folk, G. E. (1949). Body temperature of Leach's Petrel. *Anat. Record* **105**: 590.

Folk, G. E. (1951). Observations on the body temperature of Leach's Petrel. *Anat. Record* **111**: 541–542.

Fonberg, A. (1932). Sezonowe zmiany u intenoywności przemiany gazowej u wróbli. *Sprawozdania Posiedzeń Towarz. Nauk. Warszaw. Wydziat IV* **25**: 59–67.

Frith, H. J. (1956). Temperature regulation in the nesting mounds of the Mallee-fowl *Leipoa ocellata* Gould. *Australia Commonwealth Sci. Ind. Research Organization* **1**: 70–95.

Fronda, F. M. (1921). A comparative study of the body temperature of the different species and some representative breeds of poultry. *Poultry Sci.* **1**: 16–22.

Gardner, L. L. (1930). On the body temperatures of nestling altricial birds. *Auk* **47**: 367–379.

Gelineo, S. (1955). Température d'adaptation et production de chaleur chez les oiseaux de petite taille. *Arch. sci. physiol.* **9**: 225–243.

Gerhartz, H. (1914). Untersuchungen über die Energieumsetzungen des Haushuhns. *Landwirtsch. Jahrb.* **46**: 797–814.

Giaja, A. (1931). Contribution à la thermorégulation des oiseaux. *Ann. physiol. physicochim. biol.* **7**: 12–80.

Giaja, J. (1938a). L'Homéothermie *Actualités sci. et ind.* **576**.

Giaja, J. (1938b). La Thermorégulation *Actualités sci. et ind.* **577**.

Giaja, J., and Males, B. (1928). Sur la valeur du métabolisme de base de quelques animaux en fonction le leur surface. *Ann. physiol. physicochim. biol.* **4**: 875–904.

Groebbels, F. (1928). Fortgesetzte Untersuchungen über den Stoffwechsel der Vögel und das Stoffwechselproblem im allgemeinen. *Arch. ges. Physiol. Pflüger's* **218**: 99–114.

Groebbels, F. (1932). "Der Vogel," Vol. I. Gebrüder Borntraeger, Berlin.

Günther, B., and Guerra, E. (1955). Biological similarities. *Acta Physiol. Latinoam.* **5**: 169–186.

Hári, P. (1917). Beiträge zum Stoff- und Energieumsatz der Vögel. *Biochem. Z.* **78**: 313–348.

Hári, P., and Kriwuscha, A. (1918). Weitere Beiträge zum Stoff- und Energieumsatz der Vögel. *Biochem. Z.* **88**: 345–362.

Hart, J. S. (1957). Climatic and temperature induced changes in the energetics of homeotherms. *Rev. can. biol.* **16**: 133–174.

Hemmingsen, A. M. (1950). The relation of standard (basal) energy metabolism to total fresh weight of living organisms. *Rept. Steno Hosp. (Copenhagen)* **4**: 7–58.

Henry, K. M., Magee, H. E., and Reid, E. (1934). Some effects of fasting on the composition of the blood and respiratory exchange in fowls. *J. Exptl. Biol.* **11**: 58–72.

Herzog, D. (1930). Untersuchungen über den Grundumsatz der Vögel. *Wiss. Arch. Landwirtsch. Abt. B Arch. Tierernähr. u. Tierzucht* **3**: 610–626.

Hiebel, G., and Reys, P. (1951). Le rythme nycthéméral de la calorification et de l'activité. Étude faite sur le pigeon et le rat blanc. *Compt. rend. soc. biol.* **145**: 1224–1227.

Hiestand, W. A., and Randall, W. C. (1942). Influence of proprioceptive vagal afferents on panting and accessory panting movements in mammals and birds. *Am. J. Physiol.* **138**: 12–15.

Hildén, A., and Stenbäck, K. S. (1916). Zur Kenntniss der Tageschwankungen der Körpertemperatur bei den Vögeln. *Skand. Arch. Physiol.* **34**: 382–413.

Holstein, V. (1942) "Duehøgen." Hirschsprungs Forlag, Copenhagen.

Holstein, V. (1944). "Hvepsevaagen, *Pernis apivorus apivorus.*" Hirschsprungs Forlag, Copenhagen.

Holstein, V. (1950). "Spurvehøgen, *Accipiter nisus nisus* (L.)." Hirschsprungs Forlag, Copenhagen.

Howell, T. R., and Bartholomew, G. A. (1959). Further experiments on torpidity in the Poor-will. *Condor* **61**: 180–185.

Huggins, R. (1941). Egg temperatures of wild birds under natural conditions. *Ecology* **22**: 148–157.

Hutchinson, J. C. D. (1954). Heat regulation in birds. *In* "Progress in the Physiology of Farm Animals" (J. Hammond, ed.), Vol. 1, pp. 299–362. Butterworths, London.

Huxley, J. S., Webb, C. S., and Best, A. T. (1939). Temporary poikilothermy in birds. *Nature* **143**: 683–684.

Hyrtl, J. (1863). Neue Wundernetze und Geflechte bei Vögeln und Säugethieren. *Sitzber. Akad. Wiss. Wien Abt. III* **48**: 6–7.

Hyrtl, J. (1864). Neue Wundernetze und Geflechte bei Vögeln und Säugethieren. *Denkschr. Akad. Wiss. Wien* **22**: 113–152.

Irving, L. (1955). Nocturnal decline in the temperature of birds in cold weather. *Condor* **57**: 362–365.

Irving, L., and Krog, J. (1954). Body temperatures of arctic and subarctic birds and mammals. *J. Appl. Physiol.* **6**: 667–680.

Irving, L., and Krog, J. (1955). Skin temperature in the arctic as a regulator of heat. *J. Appl. Physiol.* **7**: 354–363.

Irving, L., and Krog, J. (1956). Temperature during the development of birds in arctic nests. *Physiol. Zoöl.* **29**: 195–205.

Irving, L., Krog, H., and Monson, M. (1955). The metabolism of some Alaskan animals in winter and summer. *Physiol. Zoöl.* **28**: 173–185.

Jaeger, E. C. (1948). Does the Poor-will "hibernate"? *Condor* **50**: 45–46.

Jaeger, E. C. (1949). Further observations on the hibernation of the Poor-will. *Condor* **51**: 105–109.

Jullien, J. (1868). Note sur l'appareil circulatoire de l'*Aptenodytes patagonica. Bull. soc. philomath. Paris* [7] **2**: 151–156.

Kaestner, S. (1895). Über künstliche Kälteruhe von Hühnereiern im Verlauf der Bebrütung. *Arch. Anat. Physiol. (Anat. Abt.)* **1895**: 319–338.

Kallir, E. (1930). Temperaturtopographie einiger Vögel. Experimentelle Untersuchungen. *Z. vergleich. Physiol.* **13**: 231–248.

Kayser, C. (1929a). Régulation thermique après section médulliare dorsale chez le pigeon. *Compt. rend. soc. biol.* **100**: 286–288.

Kayser, C. (1929b). Contribution à l'étude du mécanisme nerveaux de la régulation thermique. *Ann. physiol. physicochim. biol.* **15**: 131–223.

Kayser, C. (1939). Échanges respiratoires des hibernants réveillés. *Ann. physiol. physicochim. biol.* **15**: 1087–1219.

Kendeigh, S. C. (1934). The role of environment in the life of birds. *Ecol. Monographs* **4**: 299–417.

Kendeigh, S. C. (1939). The relation of metabolism to the development of temperature regulation in birds. *J. Exptl. Zool.* **82**: 419–438.

Kendeigh, S. C. (1944). Effect of air temperature on the rate of energy metabolism in the English Sparrow. *J. Exptl. Zool.* **96**: 1–16.

Kendeigh, S. C. (1949). Effect of temperature and season on the energy resources of the English Sparrow. *Auk* **66**: 113–127.

Kendeigh, S. C. (1952). Parental care and its evolution in birds. *Illinois Biol. Monographs No.* **22**.

Kendeigh, S. C., and Baldwin, S. P. (1928). Development of temperature control in nestling House Wrens. *Am. Naturalist* **62**: 249–278.

Kestner, O., and Plaut, R. (1924). Physiologie des Stoffwechsels. *In* "Handbuch der vergleichenden Physiologie" (H. Winterstein, ed.), Vol. II, pp. 1036–1065. Fischer, Jena.

King, J. R. (1957). Comments on the theory of indirect calorimetry as applied to birds. *Northwest Sci.* **31**: 155–169.

King, J. R., and Farner, D. S. (1956). Bioenergetic basis of light-induced fat deposition in the White-crowned Sparrow. *Proc. Soc. Exptl. Biol. Med.* **93**: 354–359.

Kleiber, M. (1947). Body size and metabolic rate. *Physiol. Revs.* **27**: 511–541.

Kleiber, M. (1950a). Calorimetric measurements. *In* "Biophysical Research Methods" (F. M. Uber, ed.), pp. 175–209. Interscience, New York.

Kleiber, M. (1950b). Physiological meaning of regression equations. *J. Appl. Physiol.* **2**: 417–423.

Kleiber, M., and Dougherty, J. E. (1934). The influence of environmental temperature on the utilization of food energy in baby chicks. *J. Gen. Physiol.* **17**: 701–726.

Koch, A., and Steinke, L. (1944). Temperatur- und Feuchtigkeitsmessungen im Brutnest von Gänsen, Puten und Hühnern. *Beitr. zur Fortpflanzungsbiol. Vögel* **20**: 41–45.

Koch, H. J., and de Bont, A. F. (1944). Influence de la mue sur l'intensité de métabolisme chez le pinson, *Fringilla coelebs coelebs* L. *Ann. Soc. zool. Belg.* **75**: 81–86.

Koskimies, J. (1948). On temperature regulation and metabolism in the swift, *Micropus a. apus* L., during fasting. *Experientia* **4**: 274–276.

Koskimies, J. (1950). The life of the swift, *Micropus apus* (L.) in relation to the weather. *Ann. Acad. Sci. Fennicae Ser. A. IV.* **15**: 1–151.

Krogh, A. (1916). "The Respiratory Exchange of Animals and Man." Longmans, Green, London.

Lapicque, L. (1911). Sur la nutrition des petits oiseaux. *Bull. museum hist. nat.* (Paris). **17**: 2–7.

Lapicque, L., and Lapicque, M. (1909a). Consommations alimentaires d'oiseaux de grandeurs diverses en fonction de la température extérieure. *Compt. rend. soc. biol.* **66**: 289–292.

Lapicque, L., and Lapicque, M. (1909b). Consommations alimentaires des petits oiseaux aux températures élevées. *Compt. rend. soc. biol.* **67**: 337–339.

Larguier des Bancels, M. J. (1902). De l'influence de la température extérieure sur la ration d'entretien chez l'oiseau. *Compt. rend. soc. biol.* **54**: 162–164.

Lefévre, J. (1903). Introduction critique à l'étude expérimentale de rayonnement aux diverses températures. *J. physiol. (Paris)* **5**: 783–794.

Lifson, N., Gordon, G. B., and McClintock, R. (1955). Measurement of total carbon dioxide production by means of D_2O^{18}. *J. Appl. Physiol.* **7**: 704–710.

Löer, F. (1909a). Über den Einfluss des Alters auf die Körperwärme bei Gänsen und Enten. *Arch. ges. Physiol. Pflüger's* **128**: 555–560.

Löer, F. (1909b). Vergleichende physiologische Untersuchungen über die normale Rektaltemperatur, Atem- und Pulsfrequenz der Vögel, unter besonder Berücksichtigung unseres Hausgeflügels. Inaugural Dissertation, Universität Bern, R. Schoetz, Berlin.

Löer, F. (1910). Untersuchungen über den Sexualeinfluss auf die Bluttemperatur der Vögel. *Arch. ges. Physiol. Pflüger's* **133**: 287–290.

Löhrl, H. (1955). Schlafengewöhnheiten der Baumlaüfer (*Certhia brachydactyla, C. familiaris*) und andere Kleinvögel in kalten Winternächten. *Vogelwarte* **18**: 71–77.

Lusk, G. (1928). "Elements of the Science of Nutrition." Saunders, Philadelphia, Pennsylvania.

McAtee, W. L. (1947). Torpidity in birds. *Am. Midland Naturalist* **38**: 191–206.

McClintock, R., and Lifson, N. (1958). Determination of the total carbon dioxide output of rats by the D_2O^{18} method. *Am. J. Physiol.* **192**: 76–78.

Maqsood, M. (1952). Thyroid functions in relation to reproduction of mammals and birds. *Biol. Revs. Cambridge Phil. Soc.* **27**: 281–319.

Marshall, J. T. (1955). Hibernation in captive goatsuckers. *Condor* **57**: 129–134.

Martins, C. (1856). Sur la température moyenne des oiseaux palmipèdes du nord de l'Europe. *Compt. rend. acad. sci.* **42**: 515–518.

Matthews, G. V. T. (1954). Some aspects of incubation in the Manx Shearwater, *Procellaria puffinus*, with particular reference to chilling resistance in the embryo. *Ibis* **96**: 432–440.

Mayr, E. (1942). "Systematics and the Origin of Species." Columbia Univ. Press, New York.

Mayr, E. (1956). Geographical character gradients and climatic adaptation. *Evolution* **10**: 105–108.

Medway, W., and Kare, M. R. (1957). Water metabolism of the domestic fowl from hatching to maturity. *Am. J. Physiol.* **190**: 139–141.

Mellen, W. J,, and Hill, F. W. (1955). Studies of the avian respiratory quotient. *Poultry Sci.* **34**: 1085–1089.

Merkel, F. W. (1958). Untersuchungen über tages- und jahresperiodische Änderungen im Energiehaushalt gekäfigter Zugvögel. *Z. vergleich. Physiol.* **41**: 154–178.

Miller, D. S. (1939). A study of the physiology of the sparrow thyroid. *J. Exptl. Zool.* **80**: 259–281.

Müller, E. (1908). Beiträge zur Morphologie des Gefässsystems. III. Zur Kenntnis der Flügelarterien der Pinguine. *Anat. Hefte* **35**: 553–648.

Odum, E. P. (1942). Muscle tremors and the development of temperature regulation in birds. *Am. J. Physiol.* **136**: 618–622.

Odum, E. P., and Major, J. C. (1956). The effect of diet on photoperiod-induced lipid deposition in the White-throated Sparrow, *Condor* **58**: 222–228.

Pearson, O. P. (1950). The metabolism of hummingbirds. *Condor* **52**: 145–152.

Pearson, O. P. (1953). Use of caves by hummingbirds and other species at high altitudes in Peru. *Condor* **55**: 17–20.

Pearson, O. P. (1954). The daily energy requirements of a wild Anna Hummingbird. *Condor* **56**: 317–322.

Pembry, M. S. (1895). The effect of variation in external temperature upon the output of carbonic acid and the temperature of young animals. *J. Physiol. (London)* **18**: 363–379.

Pembry, M. S., Gordon, M. H., and Warren, R. (1895). On the response of the chick, before and after hatching, to change of external temperature. *J. Physiol. (London)* **17**: 331–348.

Perek, M., and Sulman, F. (1945). The basal metabolic rate in molting and laying hens. *Endocrinology* **36**: 240–243.

Precht, H., Christopherson, J., and Hensel, H. (1955). "Temperatur und Leben." Springer, Berlin.

Prenglowitz, R. (1933). Zur thermischen Isolierung bei Vögeln. *Zool. Jahrb. Abt. Syst. Ökol.* **64**: 129–148.

Prévost, J. (1955). Observations écologiques sur la Manchot Empereur (*Aptenodytes forsteri*). *Acta 11th Congr. Intern. Ornithol.* pp. 248–251.

Quirring, D. P., and Bade, P. H. (1943). Metabolism of the English Sparrow. *Growth* **7**: 309–315.

Randall, W. C. (1943). Factors influencing the temperature regulation of birds. *Am. J. Physiol.* **139**: 46–63.

Rautenberg, W. (1957). Vergleichende Untersuchungen über den Energiehaushalt des Bergfinken (*Fringilla montifringilla* L.) und des Haussperlings (*Passer domesticus* L.). *J. Ornithol.* **98**: 36–64.

Reinig, W. F. (1938). "Elimination und Selektion." Fischer, Jena.

Reinig, W. F. (1939). Besteht die Bergmannsche Regel zu Recht? *Arch. Naturges-chichte* [N.F.] **8**: 70–88.

Rensch, B. (1936). Studien über klimatische Parallelität der Merkmalsausprägung bei Vögeln und Säugern. *Arch. Naturgeschichte* [N.F.] **5**: 317–363.

Rensch, B. (1938). Bestehen die Regeln klimatischer Parallelität der Merkmalsaus-prägung von homöothermen Tieren zu Recht? *Arch. Naturgeschichte* [N.F.] **7**: 364–389.

Rensch, B. (1939). Klimatische Auslese von Grössenvarianten. *Arch. Naturgeschichte* [N.F.] **8**: 89–129.

Richardson, H. B. (1929). The respiratory quotient. *Physiol. Revs.* **9**: 61–125.

Riddle, O., Smith, G. C., and Benedict, F. G. (1932). The basal metabolism of the Mourning Dove and some of its hybrids. *Am. J. Physiol.* **101**: 260–267.

Riddle, O., Smith, G. C., and Benedict, F. G. (1934). Seasonal and temperature factors and the determination in pigeons of percentage metabolism range per degree of temperature change. *Am. J. Physiol.* **107**: 333–342.

Robinson, K. W., and Lee, D. H. K. (1946). Animal behavior and heat regulation in hot atmospheres. *Univ. Queensland Papers Dept. Physiol.* **1**(9): 1–8.

Rogers, F. T. (1919). Studies on the brain stem. I. Regulation of body temperature in the pigeon and its relation to certain cerebral lesions. *Am. J. Physiol.* **49**: 271–283.

Rogers, F. T. (1920). Studies on the brain stem. The relation of the cerebral hemispheres to arterial blood pressure and body temperature regulation. *A.M.A. Arch. Neurol. Psychiat.* **4**: 148–150.

Rogers, F. T. (1923). The relations between lesions of the brain stem, water elimination and body temperature. *Am. J. Physiol.* **66**: 284–287.

Rogers, F. T. (1924a). On hyperthermias induced by cerebral lesions and pituitary extract. *Am. J. Physiol.* **68**: 139.

Rogers, F. T. (1924b). Studies on the brain stem. On the relation of cerebral puncture hyperthermia to an associated anhydremia. *Am. J. Physiol.* **68**: 507–516.

Rogers, F. T. (1928). Studies on the brain stem. XI. The effects of artificial stimulation and of traumatization of the avian thalamus. *Am. J. Physiol.* **86**: 639–650.

Rogers, F. T., and Lackey, R. W. (1923). Studies on the brain stem. VII. The respiratory exchange and heat production after destruction of the body temperature-regulating centers of the hypothalamus. *Am. J. Physiol.* **66**: 453–460.

Rogers, F. T., and Wheat, S. D. (1921). Studies on the brain stem. V. Carbon dioxide excretion after destruction of the optic thalamus and the reflex functions of the thalamus in body temperature regulation. *Am. J. Physiol.* **57**: 218–227.

Rolnik, V. V. (1948). Razvitye tyermoryegulyatsii u nyekotorykh ptits syevyera. *Zool. Zhur.* **27**: 535–546.

Romanoff, A. L. (1941). Development of homeothermy in birds. *Science* **94**: 218–219.

Rörig, G. (1905). Studien über die wirtschaftliche Bedeutung insektfressender Vögel. *Arb. biol. Reichsanstalt Land- u. Forstwirtsch.* (*Biol. Abt. Land- u. Forstwirtsch. Gesundheits*) **4**: 1–50.

Roth, W., and Scheel, K., eds. (1923). "Physikalisch-Chemische Tabellen," 5th ed., Vol. 2, p. 1628. Springer, Berlin.

Ryser, F. A., and Morrison, P. R. (1954). Cold resistance of the young Ring-necked Pheasant. *Auk* **71**: 253–266.

Salt, G. W. (1952). The relation of metabolism to climate and distribution in three finches of the genus *Carpodacus*. *Ecol. Monographs* **22**: 121–152.

Sapin-Jaloustre, J. (1954). Quelques aspects de la vie du Manchot Adélie en Terre Adélie. *Acta 11th Congr. Intern. Ornithol.* pp. 231–240.

Scholander, P. F. (1955). Evolution of climatic adaptations in homeotherms. *Evolution* **9**: 15–26.

Scholander, P. F. (1958). Climatic rules. *Evolution* **10**: 339–340.

Scholander, P. F., Hock, R., Walters, V., Johnson, F., and Irving, L. (1950a). Heat regulation in some arctic and tropical mammals and birds. *Biol. Bull.* **99**: 237–258.

Scholander, P. F., Hock, R., Walters, V., and Irving, L. (1950b). Adaptation to cold in arctic and tropical mammals and birds in relation to body temperature, insulation, and basal metabolic rate. *Biol. Bull.* **99**: 259–271.

Scholander, P. F., Walters, V., Hock, R., and Irving, L. (1950c). Body insulation of some arctic and tropical mammals and birds. *Biol. Bull.* **99**: 225–236.

Seibert, H. C. (1949). Difference between migrant and non-migrant birds in food and water intake at various temperatures and photoperiods. *Auk* **66**: 128–153.

Simpson, S. (1912a). Observations on the body temperatures of some diving and swimming birds. *Proc. Roy. Soc. Edinburgh* **32**: 19–35.

Simpson, S. (1912b). An investigation into the effects of seasonal changes in body temperature. *Proc. Roy. Soc. Edinburgh* **32**: 110–135.

Simpson, S., and Galbraith, J. J. (1905). An investigation into the diurnal variation of the body temperature of nocturnal and other birds and a few mammals. *J. Physiol.* (*London*) **33**: 225–238.

Stebbins, R. C. (1957). A further observation on torpidity in the Poor-will. *Condor* **59**: 212.

Steen, J. (1957). Food intake and oxygen consumption in pigeons at low temperatures. *Acta Physiol. Scand.* **39**: 22–26.

Steen, J. (1958). Climatic adaptation in some small northern birds. *Ecology* **39**: 625–629.

Steen, J., and Enger, P. S. (1957). Muscular heat production in pigeons during exposure to cold. *Am. J. Physiol.* **191**: 157–158.

Stoner, D. K. (1937). Records of bird temperatures. *N. Y. State Museum Bull. Circ.* **19**, 16 pp.

Stoner, D. K. (1939). Temperature and growth studies of the Eastern Phoebe. *N.Y. State Museum Bull. Circ.* **22**, 42 pp.

Streicher, E., Hackel, D. B., and Fleischmann, W. (1950). Effects of extreme cold on the fasting pigeon, with a note on the survival of fasting ducks at −40°C. *Am. J. Physiol.* **161**: 300–306.

Sturkie, P. D. (1954). "Avian Physiology." Comstock, Ithaca, New York.

Swift, R. W., and French, C. E. (1954). "Energy Metabolism and Nutrition." Scarecrow Press, Washington D.C.

Terroine, E. F., and Trautmann, S. (1927). Influence de la température extérieure sur la production calorique des homéothermes et loi des surfaces. *Ann. physiol. physicochim. biol.* **3**: 422–457.

Thauer, R. (1939). Der Mechanismus der Wärmeregulation. *Ergeb. Physiol. u. exptl. Pharmakol.* **41**: 609–805.

Thorburg, F. (1953). Another hibernating Poor-will. *Condor* **55**: 274.

Udvardy, M. D. F. (1953). Contributions to the knowledge of the body temperature in birds. *Zool. Bidrag Uppsala* **30**: 25–42.

Udvardy, M. D. F. (1955). Body temperature of parids in the arctic winter. *Ornis Fennica* **32**: 101–107.

von Bertalanffy, L. (1957). Quantitative laws in metabolism and growth. *Quart. Rev. Biol.* **32**: 217–231.

von Saalfeld, E. (1936). Untersuchungen ueber das Hacheln bei Tauben. *Z. vergleich. Physiol.* **23**: 727–743.

Viktorow, C. (1909). Die kühlende Wirkung der Luftsäcke bei Vögeln. *Arch. ges. Physiol. Pflüger's* **126**: 300–322.

Wallgren, H. (1954). Energy metabolism of two species of the genus *Emberiza* as correlated with distribution and migration. *Acta zool. Fennica* **84**: 1–110.

Watson, M. (1883). Report on the anatomy of the Spheniscidae collected during the voyage of H.M.S. *Challenger. Zoology*, Vol. 7, pt. 18, 244 pp.

Weiss, H. S., and Borbely, E. (1957). Seasonal changes in the resistance of the hen to thermal stress. *Poultry Sci.* **36**: 1383–1384.

Westerskov, K. (1956). Incubation temperatures of the pheasant, *Phasianus colchicus. Emu* **56**: 405–420.

Wetmore, A. (1921). A study of the body temperature of birds. *Smithsonian Misc. Collections* **72** (12): 51 pp.

Williams, D. D. (1958). A histological study of the effects of subnormal temperature on the testis of the fowl. *Anat. Record* **130**: 225–242.

Wilson, W. O. (1948). Some effects of increasing environmental temperatures on pullets. *Poultry Sci.* **27**: 813–817.

Wilson, W. O., Hillerman, J. P., and Edwards, W. H. (1952). The relation of high environmental temperature to feather and skin temperatures of laying pullets. *Poultry Sci.* **31**: 843–846.

Winchester, C. F. (1940). Seasonal metabolic and endocrine rhythms in the domestic fowl. *Missouri Univ. Agr. Expt. Sta. Research Bull. No.* **315**: 56 pp.

Winkel, K. (1951). Vergleichende Untersuchungen einiger physiologischer Konstanten bei Vögeln aus verschiedenen Klimazonen. *Zool. Jahrb. Abt. Syst., Ökol. Geograph. Tiere* **80**: 256–276.

Yeates, N. T. M., Lee, D. H. K., and Hines, H. J. G. (1941). Reactions of domestic fowls to hot atmospheres. *Proc. Roy. Soc. Queensland* **53**: 105–128.

Zeuthen, E. (1942). The ventilation of the respiratory tract in birds. *Kgl. Danske Videnskab. Selskab Biol. Medd.* **17**: 1–51.

Zeuthen, E, (1947). Body size and metabolic rate in the animal kingdom. *Compt. rend. trav. lab. Carlsberg Sér. chim.* **26**: 17–161.

Zeuthen, E. (1953). Oxygen uptake as related to body size in organisms. *Quart. Rev. Biol.* **28**: 1–12.

CHAPTER XX

Flight

R. H. J. BROWN

I. Aerodynamics of Flight

Before considering the flight of birds it is necessary to understand the basic aerodynamic properties of a wing. In its movement through the air any object experiences a force which is, in most cases, a resistance to motion. The wing, however, has a shape which gives a resultant force with a large component at right angles to the direction of motion, and it is this property which makes flight possible.

When a rigid wing is subjected to a constant air stream over its surfaces, and the angle of attack (Fig. 1) is varied, it is found that at a

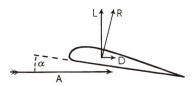

FIG. 1. The forces acting on a wing section in an air stream. The section is shown with an angle of attack to the stream. The force on the wing is represented by the resultant R, which is normally considered as being divided into a lift force L in opposition to gravity, and a drag force D in the direction of motion.

certain angle the force component at right angles to the air flow (the *lift*) is zero. If the angle of attack is now increased, the lift increases steadily until the angle reaches about 15 degrees, when it starts to fall: this fall is due to an effect known as stalling. It is important to remember that the lift of the wing is largely due to a reduction of pressure on the upper surface and that this region of low pressure can exist only when air is flowing smoothly over the surface of the wing. When too great an angle of attack occurs, the air is unable to follow the shape of the wing; the flow becomes turbulent, most of the lift vanishes, and the wing is said to stall. While the lift is increasing with angle of attack, so also the force component parallel to the air stream (*drag*) increases steadily, and for any particular type of wing there is one angle of attack

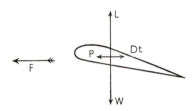

Fig. 2. Stable level-flight conditions. A section representing the whole wing is in equilibrium at any particular angle of attack when the lift L equals the weight W of the animal, and the propulsive force P equals the total drag D^t of the wings and body.

at which the ratio of lift to drag is a maximum; the wing is then working at its point of maximum efficiency.

If one considers a flying mechanism in level flight (Fig. 2) where the lift is equal to the weight, one can look at the airfoil properties in a different way. Since up to the stalling angle, and with constant speed, the lift increases with angle of attack, and also at constant angle of attack the lift increases with speed, it follows that if the lift is to remain equal to the weight, the angle of attack must increase as the speed is decreased. The speed can fall until the stalling angle is reached: at this

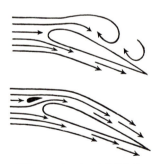

Fig. 3. Effect of wing slots. When a simple airfoil is in an air stream at too large an angle of attack (upper diagram) the air does not follow the contour of the upper surface, the wing stalls, and the lift is greatly reduced. The subsidiary airfoil (lower diagram) deflects the stream downward, and stalling occurs only at a much higher angle of attack.

point the system is at what is known as the stalling speed, which is the lowest velocity at which flight is possible with a simple fixed wing.

There are various ways in which a wing may be modified in order to enable it to work at higher angles and therefore lower speeds without stalling. By mounting a small subsidiary airfoil ahead of the wing (Fig. 3) so arranged that it directs the airflow downward over the upper surface of the wing, the smooth flow can be maintained at angles of attack higher than would otherwise be possible. This system can be further elaborated by constructing the wing in the form of a series of narrow overlapping airfoils, each stabilizing the flow over the one behind and enabling very large angles of attack to be achieved without stalling.

The properties of an airfoil are normally written in the form of non-dimensional coefficients—lift C_l and drag C_d—and are given by the expressions:

$$C_l = \frac{L}{\frac{\rho}{2} S V^2}$$

$$C_d = \frac{D}{\frac{\rho}{2} S V^2}$$

where L is the lift, D is the drag, ρ is the mass density of the air, S is the surface area of the wing, and V is the velocity. For any wing its most efficient condition arises when the ratio C_l/C_d is a maximum, and since this occurs at a particular angle of attack, there is for a given weight a particular speed of flight which requires the least power.

There are further properties of the wing which are important. Owing to its finite length and the difference in pressure on the two sides, there is an outward flow of air underneath the wing and an inward flow on the upper surface. This results in the development of wing tip vortexes which are maintained by energy from the propelling system. The effect of these vortexes is equivalent to a slight but important tilt of the air flow and a decrease in the angle of incidence; the resultant lift force on the wing being tilted backward and a component appearing as drag. This is known as induced drag and its magnitude is dependent on the lift coefficient and on the ratio of the length to the width of the wing. This ratio is known as the aspect ratio. It can be shown that the induced drag coefficient C_{di} is given by:

$$C_{di} = \frac{2}{\pi A} C_L^2$$

where A is the aspect ratio. Other factors being equal, it is therefore valuable to have a long, narrow wing if the system is required to operate at low speeds and high-lift coefficients.

The other parameter which must be mentioned is the span loading W/S^2, which is the total weight divided by the square of the wing span. This can be shown to be proportional to the induced drag, so that a low value of span loading results in a system which requires a low power to maintain flight.

II. Gliding Flight

The conditions which apply in a stable glide are shown in Fig. 4. The flight path is inclined downward, and the lift force L has an inclination ahead of the vertical. The resultant of L and the weight W can be

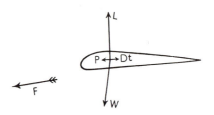

Fig. 4. Gliding. The wing moving downward and forward in a stable glide may be considered as having the lift force tilted forward. This, combined with the weight, produces a force in the direction of motion which is in equilibrium with the drag force D.

represented as a force in the direction of flight which is equal and opposite to the total drag of the animal. Clearly the higher the ratio of lift to total drag, L/D_t, the smaller the angle of glide.

When a bird is soaring, i.e. maintaining or increasing its height without flapping its wings, then it is obtaining energy from the air through which is passes. The air conditions within which this is possible may be summarized as follows: (1) wind velocity not uniform, or (2) wind direction not horizontal.

Gliding and soaring birds can be grouped in two main types, the land soarers, such as vultures, and the sea soarers.

The soaring of land birds depends primarily on the presence of thermal instability in the atmosphere, with rising bubbles of air heated by contact with the ground. These regions of rising air may not be large, the bird must be able to circle within them and will rise if the vertical component of its glide path is smaller than the rate of rise of the air. Clearly the requirements of the aerodynamic system are: (1) a low vertical component of glide path (sinking speed); (2) maneuverability. A low forward speed is no great disadvantage. Low sinking speed is achieved by having a light wing loading, therefore a large wing area; whereas maneuverability requires a fairly short wing of low inertia. The combination results in a wing of low aspect ratio, and this relatively short wing has obvious advantages for the bird landing and taking off among trees.

The sea birds are in a quite different situation. First, thermal bubbles do not develop over the sea. Second, unlike over land, the winds tend to be stronger and steadier close to the surface. In these conditions there are two types of air movement which can provide the energy for soaring flight: (1) the air streams deflected upward by obstacles such as shore line cliffs or the face of an oceanic swell; (2) the increase in velocity of the air with height which arises from the fact that the lower layers are slowed by friction with the surface. This velocity increase may be quite large up to a hundred feet or more above the sea.

It is fairly easy to see how the air that is deflected upward by an obstacle can support the animal if its vertical component is sufficiently large. The soaring on a wind gradient (dynamic soaring) is not so obvious. It can be shown, however, that bird gliding above its minimum speed against the wind at a low level can rise, with loss of ground speed; if this rise takes it into a stratum of air with higher velocity, then its air speed may not fall. This rise can continue to the top of the wind gradient. The bird can then glide downward, gaining air speed through the lower and slower strata. This cycle can be repeated. Alternatively it can turn downwind at the top of the rising phase and achieve a prolonged glide before turning into wind again, thus carrying out a kind of circling flight with a leeward drift. There is one feature common to both these soaring situations—the presence of a steady wind—and the bird must have a high gliding speed if it is to be able even to maintain its position. This requires a wing of high lift:drag ratio if the vertical component is not to be large; therefore a high aspect ratio, with low induced drag. The narrow wing with short stiff secondary feathers will probably have section suitable for high speed. The high aspect ratio will inevitably involve a large structure weight and inertia with loss of maneuverability and increased liability to damage, but we must assume that these factors are of less importance to a bird in these conditions than is the increase in aerodynamic efficiency.

It must be realized that here we have been considering the two types of gliding structure as represented by, let us say, the vulture and albatross. These are the extremes in their separate lines, and among all the birds that soar there are many which are not to be classified so easily. The difficulties may primarily be due to the fact that the degree of importance to different species of soaring efficiency in relation to other factors will vary widely. Two general points, however, do apply. The ability to glide slowly with wings of minimal length is probably a

major factor in the evolution of land soarers; while the requirement of
a small gliding angle with a wide speed range and high top speed
determine the characteristics of the sea soaring species.

III. Flapping Flight

The aerodynamics of flapping flight is very complex and as yet there
is no quantitive information on the process. This is not surprising when
we realize that we are dealing with a wing which both supports and
propels the bird, and whose shape and form of beat differ widely in
different species and even in different circumstances in the same species.
There is, however, much to be learned from a study of the shape and
movements of a particular wing and an examination of the aerodynamic forces from a purely qualitative viewpoint.

A. Take-off, Hovering, and Slow Flight

In considering flapping flight it is convenient to start with take-off
and hovering flight, that is, flight where the velocity of the air stream
relative to the body of the animal is low compared with the velocity
over the wing arising from its own flapping movements.

The simplest process is that found in the hovering hummingbird
(Fig. 5). Here the fully extended wing, which has a shoulder joint with

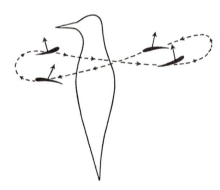

Fig. 5. Hovering flight. The hummingbird wing moves backward and forward, giving
forces on each phase whose horizontal components cancel, leaving only the vertical
components which support the animal.

great rotational freedom, is moved backward and forward in a more or
less horizontal plane, with its dorsal and ventral surfaces alternately
facing downward. It thus obtains from each phase of the beat air
reactions which are nearly vertical, and whose horizontal components

are in opposite sense and cancel, leaving only the vertical sustaining forces. Throughout such hovering flight the body axis remains vertical. By slight changes in the form of the beats and the inclination of the body the bird can move slowly forward or backward.

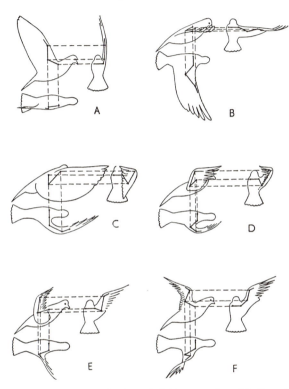

Fig. 6. Slow flight of a pigeon. A, B, and C. Downstroke with the wing at first fully extended, followed by the forward swing. Note that the forward swing involves flexure of the elbow and pronation of the manus. D. Beginning of backward flick. Note further flexure and the backward and upward rotation of the humerus. E. Further development of the flick: continued rotation of the humerus and supination of the hand. F. Completion of the upstroke: extension of the wing will bring it back to the position shown in diagram A. Redrawn from the *Journal of Experimental Biology* by permission of the Company of Biologists.

The next type of movement to be considered is found in many small passerines. Starting with the wings extended dorsally they move downward and forward toward the ventral side. Since in slow flight the body axis is nearly always vertical, the plane of the movement has only a slight downward inclination, and for most of the downstroke the movement is horizontal. This phase must produce a force on the body which is mainly vertical, with possibly a slight forward component at the beginning and a backward force at the end. This phase is then followed by the upstroke which takes the following form. The wings, which are extended ventrally and are nearly parallel, start to flex and to rotate back in a dorsal direction. The flexion of wrist and elbow proceed until the furled wing passes back over the side of the body and is then extended before the next downstroke. During this recovery phase little external work must be done, but probably the wing produces a small forward force balancing the horizontal component of the downstroke.

The next clearly defined type of movement is seen in many birds as large as and larger than a pigeon. Its characteristic feature is a propulsive upstroke. The downstroke is similar to those previously described (Fig. 6); the wings start fully extended and almost or actually in contact dorsally. They then move along a curved path which is at first vertically downward and ends with a horizontal forward movement, so that the wings come together with their ventral surfaces facing each other in front of the body. This phase provides lift, but it is clear that a propulsive force can be developed only during the vertical movement. In fact, there is no evidence in photographic records of any acceleration during the downstroke of the pigeon. The upstroke is very much more complex. Starting with the wings extended ventrally and with their surfaces nearly vertical, the first movement is a flexion of wrist and elbow and a backward rotation of the humerus. As a result the wrist, with the orientation of the distal skeletal structures and the primary feathers unaltered, approaches the shoulder joint; then follows a very rapid rotation of the retracted wing at the shoulder and an extension of the arm. This produces a backward flick of the primary feather group. The feathers are separated by the aerodynamic forces on their dorsal surfaces, and each acts as a single airfoil and develops a large upward and forward force. It is the combined effect of these forces arising from the backward movement of the primary feathers which provides almost all the propulsion in slow flight. The development of large forces can be deduced from the bending of the feathers, and the propulsive effect is evident from the acceleration seen in motion picture records.

It is possible to remove all the secondary feathers from the wing of a pigeon without greatly impairing the slow flight; this confirms the impression that the inner part of the wing must move too slowly through the air to produce a useful reaction. On the other hand, even partial removal of the primary feathers makes take-off and slow flight difficult or impossible, though the pigeon can still fly if thrown forward.

This type of movement does not occur in the large species, probably because the inertia of the wings is too great, except as a momentary phase lasting perhaps for only one or two wingbeats. In the swan, for example, and certainly in many other large birds, this slow flight is not possible and the animals cannot take off without either running forward or else facing a sufficiently strong wind.

B. Fast Flight

Here the picture is much less complex. For the hummingbird there is no reliable information, but it is probable that there is no great change in the pattern of wing movement relative to the animal; as the forward speed increases the body axis assumes a horizontal position due to slight changes in the plane of the wingbeat, and the mean aerodynamic force

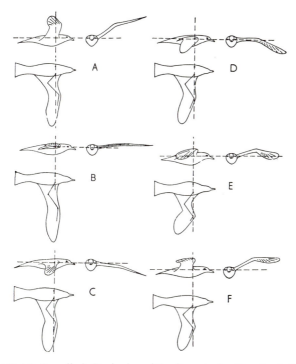

Fig. 7. Fast flight of a gull. A. Beginning of the downstroke: the wing is fully extended and is moving at right angles to the long axis of the body. B. Middle of the downstroke: the wing tip shows slight twisting to give a forward force. C. End of the downstroke: the wing is still fully extended and is lifting over its whole length. D. Beginning of the upstroke: flexure at the wrist and slight retraction; increase of the angle of attack of the arm portion to compensate for loss of tip lift. E. Middle of upstroke: the primaries are folded over each other and are unstressed; slight further retraction of wrist and increased angle of attack. F. End of upstroke: the wing is extending and the primaries are swinging forward again for the next downstroke. Redrawn from the *Journal of Experimental Biology* by permission of the Company of Biologists.

TABLE I

Analysis of Slow Flight

	Hovering birds	Passerine	Intermediate (pigeon)
	Downstroke		
Wing tip:			
Angle of attack	Positive	Positive	Positive
Angle to direction of flight	Positive	Negative then positive	Positive
Function	Lift	Lift and propulsion	Lift
Inner wing:			
Angle of attack	Positive	Positive	Positive
Angle to direction of flight	Positive	Positive	Positive
Function	Lift	Lift	Lift
	Upstroke		
Wing tip:			
Angle of attack	Positive (feathers inverted)	Zero	Positive (feathers inverted)
Angle to direction of flight	—	—	—
Function	Lift and propulsion	Passive recovery	Lift and propulsion
Inner wing: no function			

TABLE II

Analysis of Fast Flight

	Downstroke
Wing tip:	
Angle of attack	Positive
Angle to direction of flight	Negative
Function	Lift and propulsion
Inner wing:	
Angle of attack	Positive
Angle to direction of flight	Positive
Function	Lift
	Upstroke
Wing tip:	
Angle of attack	Positive (area reduced)
Angle to direction of flight	Positive
Function	Small lift
Inner wing:	
Angle of attack	Positive
Angle to direction of flight	Positive
Function	Lift

is directed forward with a small upward component which balances the weight of the bird. A similar change must take place in the small passerines.

In the larger species, which can take off slowly, there are marked differences in the wing movements in fast and slow flight. In the gull, for example, as the forward speed increases the body angle approaches the horizontal and the flick on the upstroke gradually disappears. It is replaced by a flexure of the wrist (Fig. 7), without retraction of the elbow. The tip feathers are folded over each other, and the whole wing rotates about its long axis to lower the trailing edge and increase the angle of attack; this movement is combined with a relatively slow raising of the wing, which is then fully extended at the top of the stroke. The upstroke has now become a passive recovery phase whose only function is to support the bird. The downstroke, which, owing to the attitude of the animal has become almost vertical, now takes over all the propulsion and therefore has a reaction with a large forward component. In motion picture records, particularly of large birds, it is clear that acceleration occurs only during the downstroke, while there is always some reduction of velocity during the raising of the wing.

C. Summary

The functional cycle in slow flight is summarized in Table I. In the hovering type of bird the only significant change in fast flight is a loss of lift function of the wing tip during the upstroke. For all other birds the functional cycle in fast flight is summarized in Table II.

While four subdivisions of the flight (as exemplified by humming bird, passerine, pigeon and swan) pattern are clearly separable, it must be remembered that they do merge into one another, so that a particular species may use one or more types of movement under different conditions. Also the large birds, which in general cannot take off without a run, will usually show the typical flick-type upstroke when landing for perhaps no more than about ten wingbeats, but the evidence suggests that the bird is unable to maintain height. The primary function is to reduce the forward speed, by the production of a forward force on the downstroke.

IV. Wing Shape

The plan form of the wings of birds shows great variation, and an exact evaluation of the significances of the differences is possible only in a few cases.

The problem is made more complex by the fact that the shape is required to cater for various conflicting aerodynamic, structural, and environmental requirements.

The structural restrictions arise from the need to fold the wing, the skeletal structure necessary to take the stresses of flapping, and the additional strength needed to avoid damage by accident.

The environmental restrictions are fairly obvious. As was suggested in connection with gliding the very long wing is a disadvantage to a bird living among trees. Also the wing of a bird with soaring habit will develop toward a much higher aerodynamic efficiency than will the wing of a species living in thickets, whose normal flight is short but with rapid take-off and acceleration.

We have already considered the wing shape of the soaring bird, where the reasons for the different shapes seem reasonably certain, but the significance of wing shape in flapping flight is much more difficult to evaluate. The required aerodynamic shape of a wing with a large difference in air flow velocity between root and tip, as is found in fast-flapping birds, is not known. Theoretical knowledge is also lacking of the properties of a structure the size of the wing of a sparrow.

The wings of small species with up to about 30 cm. span are with few exceptions very similar in shape; they all have very low aspect ratios and little emargination. The clear exceptions are those birds whose habit is mainly aerial, such as the swift. As size increases, so the differences in shape become more marked, ranging from the narrow tapered wings of a tern with an aspect ratio of about 10, to the very short, greatly emarginated wing of a partridge with an aspect ratio of about 4. Here again is a correlation between length and open habitat. It is obvious that such arbitrary subdivisions have no real basis in nature but may enable one to see some of the factors which are operating. Some points are clear. First, a habitat free from obstacles permits a large aspect ratio with its inherent high efficiency; but aspect ratio has another effect. For a given angle of attack a long, flapping wing will have less twist per unit length along the span than a short one. Such twist, if fixed, will be a disadvantage in gliding. A pigeon's wing, which is greatly twisted, when studied in a wind tunnel, can be seen to reach its angle of maximum lift at the root long before the tip is carrying much load, and is therefore very inefficient as a fixed airfoil.

Wings with high aspect ratios may therefore meet better the contradictory requirements of gliding and flapping, but may be too fragile or clumsy in many habitats. Secondly, can we say that the small species with their low aspect ratios are in fact inefficient, and that their confined habitat precludes a better wing shape? Or is it better to suggest that such a shape in small oscillating wings may have properties yet unknown?

Finally there is a clear association, in all but the smaller birds, of low aspect ratio and extensive emargination. It is more than probable that the true explanation is that suggested by Graham (1930). He points out that a wing with deeply emarginated feathers does not need much inherent twist, since the individual feathers can flex so as to limit their angle of attack on the downstroke. A uniformly emarginated wing without twist, in contrast to the twisted wing of a pigeon, may well be more efficient in gliding. There is, however, another factor which may be of great importance. It is possible that the separated primary feathers may be acting as a multislotted airfoil. In such a structure each small airfoil is operating in the downwardly directed air stream of the one in front, in such a way that the group, while having a high drag, is able to develop large lift forces at very high angles of attack. There are two facts which are of interest here: First, it must be noted that the emarginated series, of whatever extent, is always continuous from the first primary feather backward, strongly suggesting that the slots do in fact control the air flow over the wing. Second, that those birds such as the pheasant and partridge, with high wing loading for their size and low aspect ratio, have a great development of slots. High wing loading must be associated with high air velocity over the wing if the lift is to be sufficient, and this, taken together with short wings, requires a high flapping-rate at take-off, which results in a large velocity change along the span. It is reasonable to suggest that the necessary large amount of twist might be impossible in a short, broad wing without the freedom given by emargination for the independent flexion of the primary feathers.

V. Stability and Control

The general principle which must form the basis for any consideration of this topic is that stability and maneuverability are antagonistic. In other words, a highly stable system which cannot be upset by chance disturbances always requires large forces to deflect it from its rest position, and its responses are in general slow. Conversely a maneuverable system will usually need continual supervision by a controlling mechanism; this is the normal biological condition.

In studying the conditions obtaining in bird flight, it is convenient to consider the bird's stability around three primary axes: a transverse horizontal axis, the pitching axis; a longitudinal horizontal axis, the rolling axis; and a vertical or yawing axis.

The control of pitch can be effected in two ways, by movements of the tail and also by forward or backward movements of the wing tips, thereby moving the average point of application of the lift force relative to the center of gravity of the animal. Control in the rolling and yawing axes is carried out by differential movement of the wings, and it is important to realize that a bird, unlike an airplane, has no rear fin and rudder and has therefore no inherent stability in yaw (weathercock stability). Since the development of yaw in a gliding bird would cause an increase in air speed on one side and therefore an increase in lift, its occurrence would also produce a roll. But a further complication arises from the fact that an oscillatory wing system has in fact high stability in roll.

Let us consider the simple case of a gliding gull which starts a turn. Having no rudder, the bird must start its turn by an increase in wing

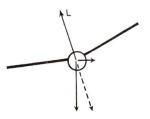

Fig. 8. Turning. A diagram of the forces arising during a stable turn. The bird is considered to be turning toward the reader's left. The total lift L has an inclination toward the center of the turning circle, so that there is a horizontal component to balance the centrifugal force. Note that the lift force must be higher than in straight flight, and therefore more power is required

drag on one side. This can be achieved by an increase in angle of attack which will increase the drag but must be coupled with a flexion of the wing to reduce its area; otherwise the lift will also rise and produce a rolling force in the opposite direction to the turn. In fact, in order that the turn shall be made without sideslip (Fig. 8), the lift must initially be reduced on the inner side to produce a roll. Once the turn has started, the outer wing will be moving at a higher speed and will augment the roll.

There are a few definite conclusions one can offer. First the aerodynamic system of the bird is essentially unstable and could not be maintained in flight without continuous minor corrections which are too small to be visible to an observer. Second, the tail is primarily concerned with control in pitch but takes on the functions of a rudder in steep turns. There is no doubt that we can associate great maneuverability with a large tail with stiff feathers. The converse is also true in that a bird with a small tail cannot, if it flies fast, make sharp turns. It must, however, be recognized that to consider the tail only as a surface which can be tilted up and down is an oversimplification. The tail of a soaring gull can be seen to be in continual movement. Upward, downward, and lateral movements can be seen, as well as several distortions, such as raising one side, or both sides, without the center. In addition to all these possible changes, the area of the tail can be altered by spreading the feathers. All these movements must have an effect on the aerodynamic system, but we can do no more than guess their significance.

VI. Theoretical Work

There has been little successful work on the quantitative analysis of bird flight, though it has interested many people for many years. Lilienthal (1911), taking the parameters of known artificial wings, calculated that the power output of a stork at about 30 miles per hour was 0.1 horsepower. This figure was reduced by Gnosspelius (1925) to 0.05 horsepower. This was reckoned to be little less than one half the maximum continuous power output of a man, and he considered that it was too high to be acceptable.

Boel (1929) approached the problem in a different way. He assumed a lift:drag ratio of 20 for a condor weighing 22 pounds, calculated the power at a velocity of 50 feet per second, and obtained a figure of 55 foot-pounds per second, or 220 pounds of body weight per horsepower. He compares this with equivalent figures for a man which give 1,240 pounds body weight per horsepower in sustained work and 308 in a brief exceptional effort.

There is yet another way to approach the problem. There seems to be general acceptance of a figure of 0.01 horsepower per pound weight of mammalian muscle. If we assume that the avian muscle does not greatly differ from this, then, knowing the weight of muscle and the total weight of the bird, we can calculate the over-all efficiency of the aerodynamic system (as lift:drag ratio) at any speed thus:

$$\text{power } (P) = \text{drag } (D) \times \text{velocity } (V)$$

or
$$D = \frac{P}{V}$$

and
$$\text{Weight } (W) = \text{lift } (L) \text{ in level flight}$$

$$\therefore \quad \frac{L}{D} = \frac{WV}{P}$$

P being given by the weight of flight muscle.

Various examples can be quoted. A pigeon weighing 0.67 pounds with a muscle weight of 0.176 pounds at 50 feet per second (34 miles per hour) give lift:drag ratio of 35, which is very high. A herring gull weighing 0.94 pounds gives an $L:D$ ratio of over 50. Now a figure as large as this is at best highly improbable. At this point we can say no more than that either the bird has a very low drag of a value unapproachable in man-made apparatus, or else its muscles are much more powerful per unit of weight than any yet measured. Certainly the flight speeds assumed are not unreasonable, and it must be remembered that the calculations assume constant-speed, level flight; if the bird is accelerating or climbing, the power requirements will rise.

There are some data on one species which resolve some of the problems. By following a gliding coragyps in a sailplane of known performance, Raspet (1950) has obtained an estimate of its performance. The figures show a maximum lift:drag ratio of about 22, which, with a bird weighing 5.1 pounds, requires 0.019 horsepower to maintain level flight. The pectoralis weight is certainly not more than one-eighth of the weight of the bird and therefore must have an output of not less than 0.03 horsepower per pound weight. This is a minimum. It was also found that the skin friction was effectively the minimum theoretically possible for a smooth, flat plate. We are left, therefore, to conclude that probably the power output is high compared with that of the mammal, and that, also, the bird has means not yet understood for controlling the airflow over its surface to produce a very low drag.

References

In this account of bird flight few authorities have been cited. This arises from the fact that it would be impossible to do more than refer repeatedly to the best-known workers in the subject. There is appended therefore a short bibliography of general works and a few references which provide starting points for further study of specific topics.

GENERAL WORKS

Aymar, G. C. (1936). "Bird Flight." London.

Lorenz, K. (1933). Beobachtetes über das Fliegen der Vögel and über die Beziehungen der Flügelund Steuerform zur Art des Fluges. *J. Ornithol.* **81**: 107–236.

Marey, E. J. (1890). "Vol des Oiseaux." Paris.

Slijper, E. J. (1950). "Die Vliegkunst in het Dierenrijk." Leiden.

Warner, L. H. (1931). Facts and theories of bird flight. *Quart. Rev. Biol.* **6**: 84–98.

FLAPPING FLIGHT

Brown, R. H. J. (1948). The flapping cycle of the pigeon. *J. Exptl. Biol.* **25**: 322–333.

Brown, R. H. J. (1951). Flapping flight. *Ibis* **93**: 333–359.

Brown, R. H. J. (1953). Wing function in relation to flight speed. *J. Exptl. Biol.* **30**: 90–103.

Graham, R. R. (1930). Safety devices in the wings of birds. *Brit. Birds* **24**: 2–21, 34–47, 58–63.

Jongbloed, J. (1937). Zur Aerodynamik des Vogelfluges. *Z. vergleich. Physiol.* **25**: 529–540.

Stolpe, M., and Zimmer, K. (1939). Der Schirrflug der Kolibris im Zeitlupenfilm. *J. Ornithol.* **87**: 136–155.

THEORETICAL AND PRACTICAL AERODYNAMICS

Boel, M. (1929). Scientific study of natural flight. *Trans. Am. Soc. Mech. Engrs.* **51**: 217–242.

Gnosspelius, O. F. (1925). Notes on bird flight. *J. Roy. Aeronaut. Soc.* **29**: 543–547.

Holst, E.v., and Kuchemann, D. (1942). Biological and aerodynamical problems in animal flight. (Translation.) *J. Roy. Aeronaut. Soc.* **46**: 39–56.

Lilienthal, G. (1911). "Bird Flight as the Basis for Aviation." London.

Raspet, G. (1950). Performance measurements of a soaring bird. *Gliding* **6**: 145–151.

Walker, G. T., Sir (1927). Flapping flight of birds. *J. Roy. Aeronaut. Soc.* **31**: 337–342.

Walker, G. T., Sir (1930). Notes on the wings of gliding birds. *J. Roy. Aeronaut. Soc.* **34**: 84–98.

Weis-Fogh, T., and Jensen, M. (1956). Biology and physics of locust flight. 1. Basic principles of insect flight. A critical review. *Phil. Trans. Roy. Soc. London* **B239**: 415–458.

W

Chapter XXI

Breeding Seasons and Migration

A. J. MARSHALL

I. Introduction

Since the epochal studies of Rowan it has become a commonplace that the neural and reproduction physiology of many vertebrates has somehow become adapted to respond to external photofluctuations. Both previous and subsequent work has shown that this response enables them to breed at the period of the year when food for the young is most plentiful, the food harvest itself being governed by the cycle of the sun and associated factors. It is a matter for regret that Rowan's great advance has tended to obscure the obvious fact that not only day length, but many and various factors are influential in the control of the breeding seasons (including migration) of vertebrate animals. It is important to realize that on this point Rowan himself was never in any doubt.

One of the most striking characteristics of animal tissue is its extreme plasticity as revealed by the adaptive responses it makes in relation to external pressures. And so it is difficult to imagine that any vertebrate, however precisely its sexual cycle was originally adapted to photofluctuations, would not fail to develop a response to other external stimuli if such were possible and *if the changing environment made it beneficial for it to do so.*

That, in fact, is what has happened in a great many species of birds (and other vertebrates) in wide areas of the tropics and outside them. It was inevitable that this should be so. If animals that populated the equatorial regions, or special areas (e.g. arid regions) often far away from the equator, did not, in fact, adopt diverse regulatory and "timing" devices they could not have survived. The stocks that did survive did so by means of natural selection. They abandoned their traditional response to photostimulation (those that already possessed such a response) and came to obey more appropriate stimuli that would ensure that their young would be produced at the period most propitious for their survival and, it follows, the survival of the species. It is today as true as ever that nature is red in tooth and claw and that the "fittest" tend to survive. But the ultimate test of "fitness" is reproductive success.

In this chapter we will not mention the routes taken by migratory birds, nor consider at length the possible origins of the phenomenon. Those interested in migration routes are advised to consult Wetmore (1930), Thomson (1945), Bourlière (1950), Lack (1959), and various regional books and journals. Works on the origins of the habit are of necessity essentially speculative (see Mayr and Meise (1930); Amadon, 1948; Mayr, 1953; Berlioz, 1950; Salomonsen, 1955; Drost, 1956; Darlington, 1957). Probably the most that can be said at present is that, after the breeding season, birds—migratory, or nomadic, and sometimes even "stationary," species—tend to disperse in varying degrees toward areas where there is a better chance of sustenance and that they likewise generally return to breed in the area, and often the specific place, in which they themselves were bred. In the case of many northern species, failure to migrate southward would mean extinction. It is significant that among certain European species the British race (exposed to a relatively benign island climate) remain "stationary," whereas the continental races regularly migrate and so escape the harsh winter vicissitudes of the Eurasian land mass.

It is almost certainly true that the migratory habit is of greater antiquity than the last glacial epochs. Nevertheless, it is probable that in many species, and in various areas, migration was developed as a need in times when the climate was very different from that obtaining there today. The occurrence of harsher winter (or otherwise unpropitious) conditions initiated migration—and made for its continuance. At the same time it is also undeniably true that the migrants of today do not generally employ as immediate stimuli to migration the conditions that make it beneficial for them to move. They cannot reproduce successfully, for example, in conditions of intense cold or inadequate food. But they usually desert their northern nuptial grounds before such conditions appear; and they depart from their contranuptial "wintering" places when the environment there is still more benign than the place to which they will fly.

II. Internal Regulation of Breeding

A. General Remarks

The partly endogenous and partly exogenous rhythm of reproduction, involving successive phases of postnuptial *regeneration* (reflected in subsequent recovery, after sudden loss, of breeding function) *acceleration* (characterized by sex hormone production and gametogenesis), and *culmination* (involving ovulation and insemination) can be considered as a sort of cogwheel which is engaged at various times by changing environmental "teeth" that are helpful, or otherwise, to reproductive success and to the existence of the species.

The internal rhythm is the primary seasonal *initiator*. As young birds mature, so does their neuroendocrine apparatus. Young budgerygahs (*Melopsittacus undulatus*) (Vaugien, 1953) and zebra finches (*Poephila castanotus*) (Marshall and Serventy, 1958) will produce bunches of spermatozoa within 60 days in almost total darkness if given adequate warmth, food, and water. These are temperate zone birds which live in dry, but *not desert*, areas. It is hoped that other workers will show us whether or not young birds of species living in a relatively lush environment (e.g. other parts of Australia, in Europe or North America) will behave in this way. Surprising results may be obtained though many, perhaps most, species probably may not so react. In the zebra finch, and numerous other species, reproduction can occur within six months of hatching.

Likewise, among adults the internal rhythm is the seasonal initiator. Until the postnuptial regeneration phase is past, the male certainly, and the female probably, is uninfluenced by the external stimuli that would cause gametogenesis at other periods of the cycle. After the spontaneous progression from regeneration to acceleration (when sex hormones are once more liberated and gametogenesis is again possible) the neuroendocrine machinery of each individual comes under the constant influence of two sets of external factors as follows:

$$accelerators \rightleftharpoons inhibitors$$

These are antagonistic. The cycle hastens, slows, or sometimes stops altogether, depending upon the factors currently presented to it by the changing environment. The more unstable the climate, the more obvious the truth of this becomes. For example, light is an accelerator of the sexual cycle of many Temperate Zone birds; cold, an inhibitor of the cycle of most species. In an unusually cold spring the effects of light are nullified, and so reproduction is delayed. Among water birds and many others a frequent inhibitor is the lack of a safe and traditional nesting site. If the seasonal appearance of such a site is delayed sufficiently long in a habitually single-brooded species, internal changes that lead to metamorphosis of the testis occur and so reproduction, as far as that particular season is concerned, is frustrated. Other accelerators are the behavioral reactions induced in each sex by their gradually changing endocrinology, including the presence of the displaying mate. Yet ovulation, even after the first egg is laid, may be inhibited by sudden cold, fear, or other traditional inhibitor.

B. Phases of the Internal Rhythm

1. *Regeneration Phase*

This comes immediately after reproduction in single-brooded species and after the final ovulation of the season in plural-brooded ones. It varies in duration between species. It is a period in which the neuro-endocrine apparatus does not respond to photostimulation, hence the use of the term "refractory period" by Bissonnette and Wadlund (1932). It is accompanied by the almost complete metamorphosis of the testes. After the seasonal exhaustion, or near exhaustion, of the inter-stitium, the Sertoli and germ cell cytoplasm is converted into a mass of cholesterol-positive lipid material which appears to give rise to pro-gestins (Marshall, 1949a, Lofts and Marshall, 1959). The same effects can be induced by the injection of prolactin (Lofts and Marshall, 1956), or by the removal of the anterior lobe of the pituitary gland (Coombs and Marshall, 1956). Automatically, and even after the removal of the hypophysis, the interstitium rhythmically regenerates and the tubule lipids disappear. The rate of disappearance varies between species. At the same time there is no suggestion that the interstitium could *secrete* in the absence of the hypophysis. While not denying that the anterior lobe may undergo a refractory phase, I used to believe that until the testis metamorphosis was concluded and the new interstitium became mature, a given male would remain unreceptive to external stimuli and sexually quiescent (Marshall, 1951a). I held this view despite the sug-gestive work of Miller (1949), who had shown that minor testis enlarge-ment occurred in golden-crowned "sparrows" (*Zonatrichia coronata*) that had been given large daily doses (50 I.U.) of pregnant mare's serum late in October and long after the initial stages of regeneration were past. However, Benoit *et al.* (1950a) and Greeley and Meyer (1953) soon provided conclusive evidence that this testis condition is a reflection of events somewhere else. Lofts and Marshall (1958) finally showed that the massive quantity of lipids formed in recently hypophysectomized pigeons can be dispersed, and spermatocytes produced, shortly after the injection of follicle-stimulating hormone equaling only about one-hundredth of Miller's dosage. We still do not know what constitutes "physiological dosage," but that is purely an academic question in the present matter.

Although the testis is thrown out of productivity during the regeneration phase, and there is evidence (Riley and Witschi, 1938) that the ovary, too, becomes "refractory," it would seem that these events are governed from elsewhere. Most workers suggest that it is the anterior pituitary that is the seat of seasonal negativity. There is no anatomical evidence that this is so, but there is both experimental and histological evidence that the adenohypophysis is at least involved. For example, the testes of Arctic nonbreeders sometimes metamorphose before they reach full spermatogenesis. This is probably due to effects, exerted by the unsatisfactory state of the environment, on the central nervous system and, it follows, on the anterior lobe, which then ceases to produce gonadotropins (Marshall, 1952a).

Among seasonal breeders in which the interstitium (unlike that of nonseasonal animals) is regenerated only once a year, the depletion of sex hormones may possibly be a factor in the male, but not, apparently, in the female (Marshall and Coombs, 1957). That interstitial or adenohypophyseal exhaustion may be involved is suggested by the experimental data of Bissonnette and Wadlund (1932).

The evidence customarily used to implicate the anterior lobe could apply equally well to the hypothalamus, or any other part of the central nervous system that periodically activates the adenohypophysis. We know that single-brooded species regularly become "refractory" after one nesting, and plural-brooded birds only after several, and this suggests that the factors controlling the onset of this regenerative period of sexual negativity are neural ones. Ultimately these may be dictated by external events including, particularly, behavioral reactions between the pair. That the nervous system is involved is further proved by numerous experiments, dating from the nineteenth century (see F. H. A. Marshall, 1936) showing that certain species will continue to lay almost indefinitely if one egg is removed from the nest daily and the neural "tactile pattern" is caused to remain incomplete.

I have variously referred to the postnuptial phase of sexual quiescence as that of "negativity," "regeneration," or "rehabilitation." It is probably this period that Wolfson (1959a, b) calls the "preparatory phase" in the migratory *Junco hyemalis*. Preferring a term that implies a return to a former condition, I will retain the expression *regeneration phase*. It suggests precisely what happens, i.e. the restoration of reproductive potential.

During the regeneration phase sexual behavior is nil, or almost so. Many normally solitary species tend to flock, often in company with other species. The postnuptial molt begins and proceeds strongly. The duration of the period in the wild bird appears to be stable within the species. As a result of photostimulation work, it can now be predicted when a given spring breeding species will end its regeneration phase, i.e. cease to be "refractory" (Kendeigh, 1941; Miller, 1951; Farner and Mewaldt, 1955a; Shank, 1959).

Apart from the experimental testing of light-susceptible species by photostimulation, the only known indication that a male has entered, or is perhaps still in, its regeneration phase is tubule metamorphosis, i.e. the continued occlusion of its seminiferous tubules by *massive* quantities of newly arisen postnuptial lipids. Unless the experimental bird is killed (or at least unilaterally castrated) and the testes examined histologically, one cannot be sure whether true metamorphosis has taken place. For this reason the reported production by photostimulation of repeated "cycles" of gonad growth and regression in a single year must not, in the absence of proof, be confused with true metamorphosis.

At the same time there is no reason to believe that the experimental production of two, or perhaps even three, true cycles, within a year is impossible (Miyazaki, 1934). The sooty tern (*Sterna fuscata*) of Ascension Island regularly breeds twice within a single calendar year (Murphy, 1936). This phenomenon of complete testis metamorphosis is common to seasonal birds of widely unrelated families irrespective of whether they exist under the almost constant day lengths of the equator, in the temperate zones, or under the 24 hour-long days of the high Arctic summer. Nevertheless, some workers (e.g. Wolfson, 1952a, 1959a, b) assert that all phases of the avian sexual cycle, including that of regeneration, are under the control of day length. In regard to the regeneration phase this conclusion is based on experimental data that support Burger's (1947, 1949) evidence that the "refractory period" of caged starlings is prematurely dissipated by reduction of day length and, theoretically therefore, by natural subjection to the short days of autumn. Wolfson reports that when certain North American fringillids are placed under repeated schedules of 16 hours of light and 8 hours of darkness they do not go into the regeneration (=preparatory) phase. However, as mentioned above, free-living Arctic birds of dozens of species of course do, in fact, do so under a far greater relative proportion of light.

Again, many "stationary" equatorial species possess distinct breeding seasons (Moreau, 1931; Baker, 1938) and nevertheless undergo a postnuptial period of regeneration. These cannot possibly receive, and do not require, shorter days to dispel it. There seems to be insufficient evidence to allow us to believe that the regeneration period of all birds is modifiable by photoperiodicity under natural conditions. Wolfson (1959a) has recently concluded that "once the preparatory [=regeneration] phase is completed the progressive [acceleration] phase probably begins automatically." This is indeed so—it is part of the internal rhythm of reproduction, a phenomenon that is generally obscured by the photostimulation of caged birds; and sometimes denied in reports dealing with the results of such work.

If, as has been argued, birds emerge rhythmically from their regeneration phase at periods characteristic of the species, it follows that the length of the period may be a powerful factor in the regulation of their reproduction date. Marshall (1951a, 1955, 1959) has explained the curious breeding cycle of the sooty tern of Ascension Island on such a premise and has extended the postulates of Rowan (1927), Moreau (1931), F. H. A. Marshall (1936, 1937), and Baker (1938) (concerning the existence and significance of an internal rhythm of reproduction) to argue that internal rhythm may "time" the prenuptial journey of northern species that "winter" on and below the equator (Marshall, 1957), provided the sexual cycle is "timed" on the northern breeding grounds (see also Curry-Lindahl, 1958, and Marshall and Williams, 1959, specifically in regard to *Motacilla flava*). The sooty tern of tropical Ascension Island breeds every 9.6 months at a latitude of 7°54′ S. (Murphy, 1936; Chapin, 1954). Here the warm ocean environment apparently provides an abundance of food all the year round and so, after each regeneration phase, it is advantageous for the succeeding acceleration phase to proceed immediately and without the customary halt imposed upon most species, including many equatorial ones, by dry season, winter, or other external factors. It is of outstanding interest that colonies of sooty terns on certain other oceanic islands do in fact pause considerably between regeneration and acceleration: they breed annually.

If we assume that late summer and autumnal interstitial rehabilitation and sexual display mark the end of the regeneration (=refractory) period the following data are of considerable interest. The testes of the starling (Bullough, 1942) collapse in May and begin to grow again late in September, probably indicating a regeneration period of about four months. Those of the mallard (*Anas platyrhynchos*) (Höhn, 1947) collapse in June and interstitial growth and display occurs late in October (regeneration period of perhaps five months). Those of the rook (*Corvus frugilegus*) metamorphose late in April, and the first signs of interstitial activity, and sexual display, are seen at the end of August, increasing markedly during September (regeneration period about four months). In each case the cycle is then halted by external inhibitors. A glance at Chapin's (1954) data for the sooty tern of Ascension Island will show that unless this species undergoes an unusually lengthy period of prenuptial behavior at sea, its regeneration (=refractory) period is longer than that of any of the land birds mentioned above.

If there exists in equatorial and transequatorial migrants a regeneration phase that is even longer, it follows that such a mechanism could constitute a primary regulation device that allows a brief period of sexual display in the contranuptial ground, the resultant achievement of social and sexual cohesion, and furthermore, the "timing" of the journey that annually brings such birds to their Scandinavian nuptial grounds in time for summer reproduction. This argument is developed in greater detail elsewhere (Marshall, 1958; Marshall and Williams, 1959). If this were true, the cycle is ultimately "timed" by the nesting and associated stimuli that operate in the northern breeding ground (Marshall, 1951a, 1955) (see page 321).

Wolfson (1959a) has recently concluded that "the progressive [=acceleration] phase proceeds spontaneously *without increases in daylength* [Wolfson's italics] and when the days are as short as the shortest days of December and remain short." He emphasizes that this conclusion is a major change from those arising out of earlier experiments in which migration was induced out of season by subjecting birds to artificial increases in day length.

From the data given previously it is clear that this conclusion is valid, but the question of how far gametogenesis will proceed remains in doubt. We have seen that despite universal sexual behavior, total gametogenesis in autumn is frustrated in the rook even when the days are still longer than at the spring period of rapid acceleration. Benoit *et al.* (1956) kept ducks in total darkness and, by means of X-ray examination at various periods, reported that the rhythm continued to wax and wane, the peaks coming at more extended intervals with the passage of time. They were, of course, unable to examine the gonads histologically. However, when Lofts and Marshall (1960) kept two groups of migratory bramblings (*Fringilla montifringilla*) under midwinter day lengths, neither had exhibited *Zugunruhe* by May 17, which is probably at least a week later than the normal period of spring migration. One group was now subjected to day lengths equaling those of mid-April, and within a week profound *Zugunruhe* occurred. The control group showed no such activity. They may have done so if given more time (see Benoit *et al.* (1956), above). However, we must remember that in the field no bird could encounter conditions that did not present some kind of stimuli on the one hand, or inhibitors on the other, after the termination of its regeneration period.

2. *Acceleration Phase*

Automatically this follows the regeneration phase: the animal has now reached a physiological condition in which its neuroendocrine apparatus is susceptible to external stimuli. Morley (1943) and Marshall (1952b) have provided numerous references that many British birds, and others elsewhere, undergo autumnal sexuality. This follows the secretion of gonadotropins which, in turn, reactivate the gonads and cause the flow of sex hormones, the sharp or gradual disappearance of the last remnants of tubule lipids, and the occasional autumn multiplication of germ cells. This phase varies enormously in its duration between species as well as in relation to the state of the environment, including the partner and the flock. In most birds the postnuptial molt ends early in this phase. It is a "progressive phase" (Burger, 1949; Wolfson, 1959a), but a burst of bad weather will halt gametogenesis and may, in fact, lead to a small degree of lipoidal degeneration in some of the newly formed germ cells. Among Arctic and desert nonbreeders, as well as birds in zoos, progression is halted by environment (Marshall, 1952a; Keast and Marshall, 1954). The acceleration phase is a period of territory selection, song, and increasingly intensive sexual activity. Certain birds develop secondary sexual characters (e.g. the assumption of beak colors and nuptial plumes). An early start of such activities (in autumn) is probably conducive to later reproductive success. At the same time, external inhibitors will temporarily halt the process late in autumn and prevent the wastage of the reproductive potential in winter.

Among many tropical species the advent of dry weather, or otherwise unfavorable external conditions, does likewise. In xerophilous (not necessarily desert) species that habitually breed upon the more or less regular advent of the wet season(s), the acceleration phase is usually under way long before the rains come. If the rain falls and changes the environment the cycle culminates. If rain does not fall the cycle is halted. If the cycle has proceeded as far as gametogenesis "regressive" changes occur in the gonads (Figs. 6–8, 10, 11, p.p. 185–6).

Among various tropical species [e.g. Ascension Island sooty terns, and certain other birds (see Miller, 1954; Marshall and Roberts, 1959)] the continuous abundance of food and the absence or relative absence of such inhibitors permits the abandonment of the more or less precisely annual cycle. Various species of *Munia* are in full spermatogenesis throughout the year at the equator at Kuching (Marshall and Harrisson, unpublished). Miller (1959) has now shown that in *Zonatrichia capensis* at 3°30′ N. "the cycles of the individual average six months in duration and two complete cycles are manifest each year." Miller interprets the six-month rhythm as "an expression of innate cyclic tendency": it is "uncoerced by small variations in photoperiod and is only incompletely controlled by the seasonal occurrence of rainfall". Rainfall (or its effects) nevertheless appears to stimulate a majority of individuals to reproductive activity in the latter part of each of the two wetter periods of the year. As greater numbers of investigators turn their attention to tropical biology, more and more animals will be found to exhibit more than one complete cycle each year. Among Temperate Zone birds whose acceleration phase began in late summer or early autumn, and was depressed or halted in winter, there is after the winter solstice a sharp renewal of sexual behaviour, accompanied by gameto-genesis. The cycle now continues under the influence of spring stimuli and inhibitors until its culmination with reproduction.

3. *Culmination Phase*

It is now that nest building is completed and insemination and ovulation occur. This phase may be considered a separate one because special *species requirement* (Marshall, 1955) of end stimulation is required before the cycle culminates in reproduction. At the end of the accelera-tion phase the testes contain massive bunches of spermatozoa. Many are free in the lumina and great numbers have already reached the seminal vesicles. The accessory sexual organs of the female have been enlarging but she has nevertheless lagged behind the male in her gametogenetic development (Marshall, 1950; 1951a, 1952b). But further special en-vironmental influences, including those of the mate and perhaps the flock, are necessary before there begins the final swift oocyte develop-ment that ends in ovulation and egg deposition through a now grossly hypertrophied oviduct.

The recent work of Lehrman (1959) has produced results of great value in this respect. But although the internal physiology may be now wholly prepared for reproduction, this phase (like that of acceleration) is highly susceptible to stimuli (e.g. those of the nest, behavioral inter-actions, etc.) and inhibitors (e.g. sudden cold, fear, or nest destruction). In many, perhaps most, species it is the end stimuli that permit nidification, insemination, and ovulation that are the ultimate "timers" of the sexual cycle There is no evidence that the photoperiod has any influence on it whatever. The period lasts until the final clutch is laid, after which individuals once more enter the phase of sexual negativity and regeneration previously described.

III. External Regulation of Breeding

A. General Remarks

This subject is one in which the amateur ornithologist can make substantial contributions. The problem can be attacked both in the field and by means of caged birds. It is notoriously difficult, however, to distinguish without experimentation the various regulatory external factors. I have found that the best field dividends are paid, so to speak, by opportunist methods in which the environment can sometimes be used as a sort of natural laboratory. This is particularly possible in areas of climatic instability such as in desert and polar regions. In particular, the determination of external factors that inhibit reproduction has produced a great deal of information during the past decade. Very considerable additions to the understanding of suspected regulators can be made by the inexpensive construction of a few cages in which a common species can be kept and by means of which conditions can be varied to reveal the combinations of factors that control the acceleration and culmination phases mentioned above. By inexpensive means the birds can be kept under any light regime that is required.

B. Specific Factors

1. Light

Rowan's (1925, 1926, 1929, 1930, 1931) experimental work will remain for all time a landmark in the literature. Many years before Rowan, however, Schäfer (1907) indicated the advantages of light as a regulator. It is the only external factor (to which a special sense is undeniably receptive) that is absolutely regular (for all "practical" purposes) in its periodicity. It may be that other thoughtful people deduced in past times that light would be an ideal regulator of animal migration; but Rowan's imagination led him to believe that perhaps, somehow, it did in fact influence vertebrates seasonally, and with great determination and ingenuity he devised and performed vital experiments in an era before the planned experiment became a widely recognized tool for attacks on ecological problems.

The supreme virtue of light as a regulator is its regularity; but likewise (a point never sufficiently emphasized) this regularity must be a force of destruction to any animal that is compelled to obey it in a habitat in which good conditions for the survival of the young did not accompany a particular phase of photoperiodicity. So it is that great numbers of species in dry (but not necessarily desert) areas and in tropical regions have abandoned (if they ever used) light as a seasonal regulator. Such species (belonging to all vertebrate classes) have, of course, developed a response to such external "timers" as are appropriate to their particular habitat. Some of these will be discussed later; here it is only necessary to add that xerophilous birds like the budgerygah (Vaugien, 1953), *Quelea quelea* (Marshall and Disney, 1956), and the zebra finch (Marshall and Serventy, 1958) have been shown experimentally to retain something of what appears to be an ancient capacity to respond to photostimulation. For this reason it is futile to use data obtained by the photostimulation of caged equatorial birds as "evidence" that they respond to light in the wild. Birds like the zebra finch (which are only meagerly influenced by light) are closely related to others that are probably regularly influenced by it. Such birds cannot be claimed to illustrate the gradual evolution of a response to light. The reverse is the case; they have largely lost such a response, and illustrate the evolution of other capacities. This is just another example of the extraordinary adaptability of animal tissue to external pressures. In this respect it will be recalled that migratory and nonmigratory races of the same fringillid species appear to have probably evolved differential responses to illumination in relation to fat deposition (Blanchard, 1941).

Rowan himself modified his original ideas and came to believe that the anterior pituitary and the "entire physiology" of the bird is concerned in migration (1946). He also postulated the "wakefulness hypothesis" that was to cause so much controversy (see Rowan, 1938, 1946; Bissonnette, 1936). It was not until recently that this hypothesis was neatly disposed of by Farner and Mewaldt (1955b); and today most people seem to be agreed that it is the seasonal appearance of a specific and appropriate day length, not merely increasing day length, that sets the avian neurohormonal machinery in motion and (once the regeneration period is past) starts the seasonal gametogenesis. It is true, however, that no photoexperimentalist has yet influenced the sexual cycle of any vertebrate with an additional light ration as small as that which must be influential in nature if, as seems probable, day length is the primary accelerating factor in most north Temperate Zone birds (cf. the data of Norris, 1958, cited below). I have previously (Marshall, 1952b) drawn attention to the case of the European robin (*Erithacus rubecula*), which begins its "spring" sexual resurgence and pairing in the foggy English Midlands early in January when the days are only 14 minutes longer than at the winter solstice and when (on January 7), the daily increase is of the order of 1.5 minutes. The days are of the same length a few weeks *before* the solstice, and yet gametogenesis does not begin. As the weather (an inhibitory factor) is no less severe in January than in December, the suggestion is that either the regeneration period lasts until early in January (when the cycle can once again be influenced by external stimuli) or, on the other hand, it is *increasing* day lengths, rather than the mere assumption of a certain photoperiod, that is influential. It could, of course, be claimed that the robin does in fact remain in its regeneration phase of sexual negativity ("refractoriness") until immediately after the solstice, but the autumnal sexual activity in which it habitually indulges does not support such a contention unless we assume that even though the interstitial cell-stimulating element of the adenohypophysis becomes active, the follicle-stimulating element does not (page 173).

Marshall and Coombs (1957) reported that the rook (*Corvus frugilegus*), too, comes spontaneously out of its regeneration phase in August. The whole population then indulges in pronounced sexual behavior at a period when, in September and October, conditions for reproduction, including the traditional food of the young, seems as good as in the spring (Lockie, 1955). Day length is much greater than during the late-winter period when the "spring" gametogenesis begins. Yet only 13.6% of the birds produce spermatozoa and ovulate, and reproduction is rare. Here again was a suggestion that if photoperiodicity is responsible for reproduction, it is increasing light and not merely day length. Again it could be asserted that although the adenohypophyseal hormone which stimulates the production of gonad hormone (and subsequently sexual behavior) is in operation, the hormone needed to bring about gametogenesis is not. This is a very dubious proposition.

It is relevant at this point to mention the recent work of Morris (1958), who has shown that in *Nomadacris septemfasciata* Serv. (Orthoptera, Acrididae) diapause is induced at about 7°S. in March when the daily decrement in light is equivalent to less than 30 seconds. This seems to be the only example yet known of an animal possessing so refined a response to changing day length.

So far there is no evidence that decrease of day lengths activates or accelerates the sexual cycle of any bird although it has been reported to be a controlling factor in a fish (Hoover and Hubbard, 1937) and mammals (Bissonnette, 1941; Yeates, 1949). Marshall and Serventy (1956) considered it possible that the prenuptial August-September migration of the short-tailed shearwater (*Puffinus tenuirostris*) from the Aleutians to its Tasmanian breeding islands might be in response to decreasing day lengths, but subsequent experimental work led them to doubt this view (Marshall and Serventy, 1959). It has been shown experimentally that the regeneration period of the male of the xerophilous dioch (*Quelea quelea*) lasts a mere six weeks (Disney, Lofts & Marshall, 1959). As yet, no autumn- or winter-breeding bird has been investigated.

Finally I come to the controversial "summation hypothesis" of Wolfson (1952a, b, 1959a, b). In the course of experiments in which the "pre-migratory physiological state was induced in winter in Juncos, White-throated sparrows, and other fringillids," a few individuals were subjected suddenly to constant long day lengths. These birds "responded sooner" than those subjected to gradually increased day lengths. Wolfson thought it possible that "the amount of light which a bird received each day, or the total amount within a given period of time, might determine the time of response." Hence, it was postulated that "summation of day-lengths or the daily dose of light, rather than increasing day-lengths as such, might be the critical environmental factor in determining the time of migration and the time of breeding." He continued: "If this were true, the constant day-lengths or decreasing day-lengths to which equatorial and transequatorial migrants are subjected might play a role in the timing of the stimulus for spring migration. Summation of day-lengths could also explain timing of breeding in the tropics."

Recently Wolfson (1959b) has claimed specifically that "the timing of spring migratory behaviour in migrants wintering on the equator, in the tropics, or in the southern hemisphere" can be explained by it since constant photoperiods of 12 hours have been shown to be effective in North American fringillids, and the duration of the photoperiod regulates the rate of response. Therefore, birds "wintering" in the equatorial region could be responding to the relatively constant day lengths of 12 hours. The birds that cross the equator and winter in the Tropical or Temperate Zone are all exposed to gradually increasing day lengths after they arrive in October or November and to gradually decreasing day lengths after the solstice (December 22). These reach a value of about 12 hours at the next equinox (March 20). Wolfson says that experimental fringillids need short days to complete their preparatory (=regeneration) phase (page 310) but "some juncos could 'prepare' on a constant twelve light – twelve dark schedule." Therefore, he believes, it is probable that the equatorial and transequatorial migrants "would be exposed to a sufficient number of twelve to thirteen hour days during their fall migration to complete their preparatory phase." Once the preparatory phase is past, "the long days of the equatorial region and the southern hemisphere, whether they are relating constant, increasing, or decreasing, would regulate the rate at which the phase proceeded" (Wolfson, 1959a).

We may sum up: There is abundant experimental evidence (see modern reviews by Farner, 1955; Wolfson, 1959a) that after the conclusion of the regeneration phase the sexual cycles of many Temperate Zone species can be accelerated by artificial exposure to specific photoperiods. There is suggestive data, but no conclusive evidence, that in nature the cycles of some species may be accelerated by incremental photoperiods during times of the year (e.g. early January in England) at which natural day lengths are insufficiently long to accelerate the cycle of captives of comparable size or, perhaps, reproductive habits. In most, but not all, photostimulation experiments an incremental element has been involved. There is yet no evidence that decreasing light affects the avian sexual cycle, and so far no autumn- or winter-breeding species has been experimentally tested to this end. In regard to equatorial breeding seasons and migration, Wolfson's summation hypothesis appears, in essence, to imply the spontaneous emergence of birds from their regeneration period after which they can be stimulated to breed or migrate by nearly constant day lengths. A more plausible hypothesis seems to be that after the automatic emergence, involving sex hormone liberation, *various* environmental factors (including particularly behavioral interactions) start the cycle anew. Thus, the behavior of yellow wagtails "wintering" at the equator begins to change some time before migration. As the first gametogenetic development occurs in both sexes a greater social cohesion becomes apparent and the birds begin to associate in pairs, no doubt as a result of the postregeneration production of sex hormones. After a further short period of almost constant day lengths the birds leave for their northern nuptial grounds, where their breeding season (and sexual cycle) is ultimately timed by the external factors that permit successful nesting and reproduction (Marshall, 1951a, 1955; Marshall and Williams, 1959).

2. *Temperature*

Before the classic experiments of Rowan, people tended to assume that reproduction in temperate zones was controlled by the rising temperature of spring (e.g. Loisel, 1900, 1901). Rowan's work so dramatically emphasized the influence of light that most people lost sight of the other factors that are extremely important. In particular, the effects of temperature were underestimated and generally denied. One of Rowan's experiments showed that photostimulated juncos sang as their gonads matured at temperatures of about 52° below zero (84° of frost). This experiment has sometimes been cited to "prove" temperature to be unimportant in the avian sexual cycle. It has been copied uncritically into at least one widely used book. Rowan himself, of

x

course, had no doubts concerning the importance of low temperatures as a breeding inhibitor *under natural conditions* (Rowan, 1938).

It is almost certain that each species is physiologically adjusted to a temperature range. If the environment is suitably warm during the acceleration and culmination periods, the birds display appropriately and development proceeds. If it is unusually cold for the period, sexual processes are retarded. Rowan (1918), ironically enough, had reported this very fact long before his classic experiments led others, but not himself, to discount the importance of temperature in reproduction. An experiment involving the examination of a series of wild birds at precisely the same time and place during two successive winters—one unusually hard and the following one markedly mild—demonstrated the inhibiting effect of cold (Marshall, 1949b). Although the severe winter and early spring weather undeniably halted gametogenesis, a subsequent unusually sharp burst of high temperature and sunshine (page 326) will allow some species nevertheless to breed at the normal time. After the next mild winter several species bred abnormally early. Kluijver (1951) has evidence suggesting that the great tit (*Parus major*) breeds later if the days below freezing point in January and February are greater in number than usual. Sudden cold inhibits ovulation.

Snow (1955) has reported that the unusually mild English weather of November and December, 1953, resulted in considerable winter egg laying. Baker and Baker (1932) and Snow (1958) have data that suggest that temperature is influential in timing the sexual cycle of the blackbird (*Turdus merula*). Von Haartman (1956) has many data that point to the same in the pied fly-catcher (*Muscicapa hypoleuca*).

An examination of the literature will no doubt reveal many other instances of the control of both acceleration and culmination phases of the sexual cycle by temperature fluctuations. Data relating to the acceleration phase are rare only because birds must be killed before the evidence is unequivocal. One study has led to the suggestion that temperature partly, yet habitually, controls breeding over an extremely wide area (Serventy and Marshall, 1957). In relatively dry areas of Western Australia that lie well within the Temperate Zone, avian reproduction is controlled not by the wide local photofluctuations, but by stimulation by rainfall and associated factors in conjunction with inhibiting effects of low temperatures.

If experiments involving temperature were carried out, a body of laboratory evidence could be obtained. It is essential to remember, however, that, as Rowan showed, photostimulation will advance spermatogenesis in the face of conditions sufficiently chill to prevent gametogenesis, nest building, and ovulation under normal conditions.

The work of Engels and Jenner (1956) reemphasizes this point. Nevertheless, they showed that after 6 weeks the testes of birds of a "warm group" under 12 hours' light were about four times as big as those of a "cold group" under the same photoperiod.

3. *Rainfall and Associated Factors*

An extensive though scattered literature indicates that rainfall, or its effects, is a powerful regulator of reproduction. The modern accounts of Moreau (1931, 1936, 1950), Baker (1938), Lack (1950a), Skutch (1950), Marshall (1951a, b, 1955) and Voous (1950) bring much old and new data together. A great deal of the information refers to tropical (not necessarily equatorial) birds, or those that live in dry areas in which a rigid adherence to any particular phase of periodicity would be disastrous: such birds breed irrespective of the cycle of the sun (see page 308). Yet it must not be thought that it is only tropical and xerophilous birds that have become independent of photoperiodicity. Serventy and Marshall (1957) have shown that over a vast area of Western Australia both aquatic and terrestrial species have escaped from such an influence. In fact, a habitational gradient occurs there so that after unseasonable rainfall the breeding of similar species is much greater in areas where the annual rainfall is only 14 inches than where the mean is 40 inches! This is a physiological aspect of drought adaptation. Species that failed to respond to rainfall stimuli would be eliminated by natural selection.

When it is claimed that birds breed in response to rainfall, there is rarely evidence that rainfall per se is responsible rather than the environmental effects that follow it. Marshall and Disney (1957), however, designed an experiment that showed that first-year diochs (*Quelea quelea*) were influenced by the green grass that grew after rainfall in tropical Tanganyika. When the experiment was repeated with *older* birds it was found that rainfall itself, or the accompanying high humidity, also appeared to exert a strong stimulus to building. That rainfall or humidity affects the neuroendocrine system was indicated by old nonbreeders which molted from one breeding plumage to another without the customary intervening period of neutral plumage. Under the stimulus of rain, green grass, and abundant food, young birds (caught while still being fed by the parents) went straight from juvenile to breeding plumage. When deprived of adequate stimuli, such juveniles went only partly into breeding dress. Then they molted into the neutral plumage which replaces the juvenile dress under normal conditions. Such birds later came into breeding plumage at the same time as did the wild population. We tend to believe that there operates in the dimorphic

Quelea a mechanism, involving the quick assumption of nuptial dress in the young, comparable with that which allows the rapid spermatogenesis in young budgerygahs (Vaugien, 1953) and zebra finches (Marshall and Serventy, 1958) in times of plenty. (See also pp. 319–20.)

4. Breeding Area

Despite statements to the contrary, there is no good evidence that migratory birds leave their contranuptial "wintering" area with inactive gonads (page 328). When migratory passerines (e.g. *Sylvia* spp.) arrive in southern England in the spring, the males are in a state of advanced gametogenesis, many possessing bunched spermatozoa. The females have enlarged oocytes. The contents of their stomachs show that they have recently paused and fed on the European continent yet, despite their advanced reproductive condition, they did not stay there and breed (Marshall, 1952c). Not until these migrants encounter the stimulus of their traditional area do they stop. Merkel (1956) has experimental data showing that in captivity the spring migratory unrest of whitethroats (*Sylvia communis*), blackcaps (*S. atricapilla*), and robins is prolonged into the summer months, and he suggests that such activity is normally terminated by stimuli from the breeding area.

5. Territory

A volume of information emphasizes how greatly sexual behavior is increased after the establishment of territory (Howard, 1929, 1935; and many other observers). Concurrently the gametogenetic cycle leaps ahead. The relative importance of the stimuli from the mate as compared with those from the territory is of course undetermined.

6. Nesting Site and Materials

The availability and acquisition of a specific nest site is an event of profound significance in the progression, and particularly the culmination, of the sexual cycle. Unavailability of a safe site (Lack, 1933) or its destruction delays or inhibits (Marshall, 1952a) ovulatory processes. Among numerous species the discovery, and even brief observation by man of the nest site will inhibit ovulation. In many Temperate Zone species the breeding season is ultimately "timed" by nest-site availability; the pair can breed only when the environment changes sufficiently to give them their traditional cover. For example, of two species existing side by side, that which breeds in the hedge or low thicket can build sooner than that which habitually nests in the cover that will develop above it at a slightly later date. Xerophilous species in particular can breed only when nest material or cover becomes adequately tall, and aquatic birds often breed in relation to water level and the fluctuating availability of suitable material (Frith and Davies, 1958).

7. Food Supply

The supreme importance of an abundant supply of suitable food for the young has been recognized for many years as an "ultimate factor" (in the terminology of Baker, 1938, 1947). Schäfer (1907), Davis (1933), Marshall (1942, 1950a, 1951b), Lack and Silva (1949), Lack (1950a, b), Thomson (1950), and subsequently others have indicated that the young of a wide variety of species are produced at the period when the environment contains a maximum of food supply. In the early 1940's Hirst found that captive satin bowerbirds (*Ptilonorhynchus violaceus*) were unable to rear young if they were not provided with suitable protein food, and during the same period Marshall (1942) found that although these birds begin their "spring" sexual resurgence during the winter months, the female does not ovulate until November and December when the environment becomes full of flying insects (Marshall, 1950, 1954). The close correlation between the actual reproduction of the Arctic snowy owl (*Nyctea scandiniaca*) and of certain skuas (*Stercorarius longicaudus* and *S. pomarinus*) and the presence of lemming is well attested (Manniche, 1910; Schaanning, 1916; Pedersen, 1930; and Løppenthin, 1932). It seems highly probable, too, that the seed-eating crossbill (*Loxia curvirostra*), which has been reported to breed in all months in at least one part of its range (Griscom, 1937), is stimulated by the cone crop.

Yet it must be emphasized that there exists as yet no experimental evidence that the seasonal appearance of any specific type of food acts as a breeding stimulus. Nevertheless, Breneman (1955) has shown that if the normal food intake of domestic fowls is reduced by 25% gonad activity almost ceases.

8. Behavioral Interactions

The Croonian Lecture of F. H. A. Marshall (1936) stands as a landmark in the literature and it summarizes the pioneer work of Huxley (1914), Howard (1929, 1935), and others in regard to the functions of sexual display. The reviews of Beach (1948), Collias (1950), Lehrman (1955, 1956, 1959) provide much detailed information about the influence of hormones on this and other aspects of reproductive behavior. At all times after the conclusion of the regeneration phase, internal secretions and environmental situations combine to evoke innate and specific display and other behavioral interactions which, given rein, evoke further endocrine activity and accelerate gametogenesis. The elimination of such stimuli by environmental changes, sudden inclement weather, death of the mate, fear, hunger, etc., will inhibit display and delay, or even prevent, reproduction. Odd pieces of evidence of these things have been reported by aviculturists for the last half-century, but little precise information is available. Polikarpova (1940), however, has interesting and relevant data on *Passer domesticus*.

9. *Miscellaneous Hypothetical Factors*

From time to time various external factors, notably the different components of light, including ultraviolet, have been suggested as breeding stimuli. Infrared, too, has been considered. Theoretically, infrared would be an ideal regulator in that it penetrates a foggy landscape (such as the English Midlands early in the year, see page 319), but Benoit and Ott (1944) and Benoit *et al.* (1950b) have evidence that ducks at least are no more susceptible to infrared than is man.

That sunshine (as distinct from temperature or day length) is an important stimulus in countries with relatively dull winter weather (e.g. Britain) has been suggested by Marshall (1951a). A burst of sunshine undoubtedly causes birds suddenly to sing and display, and this no doubt influences internal physiology.* Unfortunately it is difficult experimentally to treat separately the effect of sunshine in order to measure precisely its probable effect as a breeding accelerator. Conversely, inclement weather almost certainly can be a powerful inhibitory influence. There are numerous data indicating that both acceleration and culmination phases of the sexual cycle of widely unrelated species in highly diverse habitats (e.g. equatorial and Arctic), are retarded by the advent of disagreeable weather conditions (Marshall, 1951a, 1952a; Lack, 1956; Marshall and Roberts, 1959). It has sometimes been suggested that vitamins A or B, occurring in green food, may be stimulating factors, but confirmatory evidence has not been obtained. In fact, a study by Lehmann (1953) showed that although breeding in the bobwhite quail (*Colinus virginianus*) was associated with "lush" conditions, it did not appear that high vitamin A reserves (as revealed by liver analysis) "were necessary for awakening the breeding urge." It is doubtful if any special vitamin or amino acid component of the seasonal food supply is itself a stimulus to reproduction, however essential such

---

* Ornithological observers who went to the Canary Islands where a total eclipse of the sun occurred for a minute and three quarters on October 2, 1959, reported that although the landscape remained "rather light" the Chaffinch (*Fringilla coelebs*) was silenced for 23 minutes, the blue tit (*Parus caeruleus*) for 17 minutes, the blackbird (*Turdus merula*) for 10 minutes and certain other species for lesser periods. Robins, in full autumnal song, remained apparently unaffected. (*The Times* (London), October 3, 1959, p. 6).

may be as a dietary element for development. The stimulus is probably far less precise. Once green grass appears, or the insect harvest emerges, the vital dietary components will appear anyway.

A most intriguing theoretical possibility is suggested by the recent work of Sauer (1957). It is *perhaps* possible that nocturnal migrants, having come spontaneously into migratory unrest, may be stimulated to depart (as well as to navigate correctly) when they perceive an appropriate star pattern. If such is true, it is not illogical to think that the distinguished researches of the late Gustav Kramer on solar navigation (Chapter XXII) may lead to an explanation of migratory timing, as distinct from orientation, of day migrants. Solar and/or stellar "timing" might conceivably explain the astonishing regularity with which the short-tailed shearwater (*Puffinus tenuirostris*) leaves its Aleutian "wintering" quarters in time to arrive off the Victorian and Tasmanian coasts during the same 11 days every year (Marshall and Serventy, 1956) or even, perhaps, the relative regularity of the northward departure of yellow wagtails and other migrants from the equator.

IV. Discussion

It may be profitable, briefly, to emphasize what we do *not* know in the hope that it may provide a stimulus to future work. The truth is that we are still unaware of the precise combination of external factors that regulates the seasonal breeding of even the London sparrow, and, apart from pituitary-gonad relationships, and those involving prolactin reactions, knowledge of the internal factors relating to reproduction is equally limited.

There is an immense field for neurophysiological and cytological research in the determination of the ultimate means by which various stimuli—environmental (including behavioral and tactile) and hormonal—influence the hypothalamic centers which probably produce neurosecretory material that descends through the hypophyseal portal system and influences the anterior lobe (page 171). There is an even greater ignorance (if that is possible) about how hormones, liberated as a result of such activity, in turn operate to bring into play the innate behaviorisms essential to successful reproduction.

This uncertainty is perhaps not surprising in view of the technical difficulties involved in such studies. What is very remarkable is the continued uncertainty concerning two questions that are relatively easy to investigate, i.e. firstly, whether the period of negativity characteristic of the regeneration phase is basically neural or hypophyseal (page 311), and secondly, whether sex hormones are primarily responsible for prenuptial migration or is the assumption of some "total physiological state" required before such migration can start.

The early photostimulation work of Rowan was for some time generally believed to substantiate Jenner's (1924) long forgotten conclusions that (leaving external factors out of consideration) the gonads are primarily influential in starting migration to the breeding grounds. This traditional view has been seriously challenged in recent years. In one of the most recent reviews Aschoff (1955) says "admittedly there is no direct dependence of migration on the functional state of the gonads" (translation), and Farner (1950, 1955) considers it improbable that the gonads are a "generally essential part of the stimulator mechanism." In support of this view, Farner (1955) cited: (1) prenuptial migration of castrated birds, (2) the improbability of identical functions of hormones produced by ovaries and testes, and (3) the failure by Wolfson (1945) to provoke premigratory fat deposition with gonadotropin whereas an essentially somatropic preparation did so.

It would seem, however, that an equally good case can be made out for an opposite view: (1) Liberated castrates can be expected to migrate in company with intact fellows as a result of flock stimulation, (2) Considering the widely varying effects of testosterone and estrogen, and the fact that prenuptial migration is essentially sexual in its utility, the second reason is of dubious validity; and (3) Schildmacher and Steubing (1952) have since recorded fat deposition after injections of pregnant mare's serum, by photostimulation, and after the implantation of pellets of testosterone.

Some writers, too, have claimed that migrants arrive at their breeding grounds with "inactive" gonads. This view is probably due to the use of outmoded histological techniques. Just because a gland is still small it does not follow that it remains inactive, as careful cytological investigation readily shows. Witschi (1945) has interesting experimental evidence on this point. He says that the change of bill color from black to yellow in the common starling "heralds the start of the breeding season when testicular changes are barely observable under the microscope and the deferent ducts still remain in the eclipse condition." An equally inconspicuous hormonal discharge may stimulate migratory unrest. There is as yet no valid evidence that any prenuptial migrant has left its contranuptial locality with truly inactive gonads. There is much evidence that the reverse is true in both passerines and charadriiformes (Rowan and Batrawi, 1939; Marshall and Williams, 1959; Marshall, Robinson, and Serventy, unpublished). Further, many species exhibit undeniable sexual behavior (including pairing) before migration.

Song during passage has been recorded (Witherby *et al.*, 1943). Again, a number of species produce bunched spermatozoa before they arrive at their distant breeding grounds (Marshall, 1952c).

Migratory birds come twice a year into *Zugunruhe*, and almost restless nocturnal premigratory activity. It is generally believed that *Zugunruhe* in cage birds has the same physiological basis as in migration (Wagner, 1930, 1936; Palmgren, 1944, 1949). At the same time, considerable caution is needed since D. S. Farner (personal communication) reports that, in warm room temperatures, midwinter nocturnal activity may occur in the nonmigratory subspecies of *Zonotrichia leucophrys*.

However, because *Zugunruhe* can be accurately and quantitatively measured in spring cages, it (if used with due caution) almost certainly provides a valuable tool for laboratory studies. It is accompanied in many, but apparently not all, migratory species (Nice, 1946) by the accumulation of depot fat in specific areas. Measurement of *Zugunruhe* under various conditions by Schildmacher (1933, 1934a, b) and other authors suggested that sex hormones are the primary stimulus to the prenuptial movement and that estrogen, administered when the gonads are reduced after reproduction, will depress contranuptial migration, i.e. movement away from the breeding ground. Such experiments, however, were based on very few individuals and have been much criticized (Merkel, 1938; Thomson, 1936; van Oordt, 1949; and others).

The measurement of the nocturnal activity of photostimulated castrated migrants is an obvious way to test the recent hypothesis that sex hormones are not, in fact, directly involved. Such a study was carried out on the brambling (*Fringilla montifringilla*) by Lofts and Marshall (1960). The nocturnal movements of six castrates and six intact males were measured during exposure to different artificial day lengths. Under 14 hours of light *both* groups showed what appeared to be a highly significant increase in activity. The castrates showed an even greater restlessness than did the controls, which by now had considerably enlarged testes. Unfortunately during the final check laparotomy it was found that in one castrate a testis had become fully regenerated and secretory. Hormone-induced activity in this single, imperfectly castrated individual possibly might have influenced the total castrates in adjacent cages.

It has to be recognized, too, that even if birds are proved to exhibit *Zugunruhe* in the absence of gonads, such activity might be still an androgenic influence of the adrenal cortex. Virilism associated with cortical tumor has been recorded in the domestic fowl (McGowan, 1936). There is evidence (Koch, 1939; Kar, 1947a, b) that the adrenal cortex enlarges after gonadectomy. Kar showed that in young capons the proportion of cortical tissue rose from about 40% to 70% of the total gland and there was hypertrophy of individual cells. However, although glandular activity appeared considerable, there was in Kar's birds no indication of any comb growth that would suggest androgen secretion.

During recent years considerable attention has been paid to the possible role played in migration by the substantial subcutaneous and visceral fat deposits that are accumulated in specific areas by migrating species (see, e.g. Wolfson, 1945). McGreal and Farner (1956) have described fifteen such regions in adults of the migratory white-crowned sparrow. In this species there occurs a striking accumulation of depot fat during the 2 weeks preceding the prenuptial migration when, in wild populations, "mean lipid indices increase from about 5% to more than 20%" (King and Farner, 1956). This fat deposition is followed by the development of *Zugunruhe*. Observations such as these have helped establish the modern view that a "total physiological state" is necessary before migration can start.

The factors which stimulate this premigratory fat deposition (which may provide metabolic water as well as energy en route) have not been determined with certainty. Wolfson (1945) has shown that photostimulation leading to gonad activation is followed by fat deposition in migratory birds. Schildmacher and Steubing (1952) provided more precise information that premature fat deposition in bramblings is induced not only by photostimulation and the administration of pregnant mare's serum, but by the implantation of testosterone. They incline to the view, however, that an agent other than sex hormone is responsible for fat deposition before the postnuptial (autumn) migration. Lofts and Marshall (1957) also found that fat deposition occurred in some contranuptial migrants that had not yet developed a functional interstitium. It has never, of course, been suggested that the contranuptial *Zugunruhe* is caused by sex hormones. In fact, some have held that whereas the prenuptial journey is stimulated by sex hormones, movement away from the breeding territory is allowed essentially by their absence (see Bullough, 1945). The latter view has been criticized by Marshall and Coombs (1957) and Lofts and Marshall (1957), who showed that some migratory birds develop at least a potentially secretory interstitium before their autumn departure and may exhibit premigratory sexual behavior before the appearance of the apparently innate, neural drive toward the traditional "wintering" ground. It is of interest that Promptov (cited by Farner, 1955) showed, in an admittedly small number of scarlet grosbeaks (*Carpodacus erythrinus*), that the contranuptial *Zugunruhe* started at a specific age and not at a particular time of the year. Nobody has yet attempted to measure the nocturnal activity of hypophysectomized postbreeders in autumn. It might not be unrewarding to do the same with hypophysectomized, photostimulated spring migrants as well, since such a study would provide evidence tending to eliminate—or substantiate—the suggestion that the assumption of *Zugunruhe* and/or fat deposition is entirely neural in origin.

Spring *Zugunruhe* is a behavior pattern that is undeniably activated by photostimulation and probably by testosterone. Fat deposition, which apparently does not occur in all migratory species (Nice, 1946; Farner, 1955), can be induced by photostimulation, gonadotropins, and testosterone. Although a great deal has been written, perhaps justifiably, about "total physiological state" involving preliminary fat deposition before migration, it is only now that we are attempting to keep birds before the migration time at a dietary level insufficient for the accumulation of depot fat in order to measure the nocturnal activity of some of them after photostimulation and of others after castration as well (Lofts, Marshall and Wolfson, unpublished).

That migratory birds of both sexes of a species that normally produces heavy fat deposits are capable of apparently normal spring gonad development in the absence of such deposits has been proved by Wolfson (personal communication). Juncos were subjected to long periods of darkness interspersed with periods of light. It is probable that the relatively prolonged darkness decreased weight by reducing feeding activity. The total weight, except in very few birds, fell to a minimum that was below the normal basic weight without premigratory fat.

That the thyroid, which exhibits cyclical changes, is directly involved in migration has been suggested by various authors, but its role remains essentially speculative (Höhn, 1950; Oakeson and Lilley, 1954).

Viewing the world, rather than merely the European and North American avifauna, we may sum up:

The sexual cycle of seasonal birds is regulated by *various* external factors that ensure movement to the traditional breeding ground in time for the young to be produced at the period of optimum harvest of the food on which they are fed.

There exists in birds a partly endogenous, partly exogenous internal rhythm of reproduction involving successive phases of postnuptial *regeneration, acceleration,* and *culmination* which may be considered as a cogwheel which is engaged at various times by changing environment, and teeth ("regulators," "external stimuli," or "timers") that are helpful, or otherwise, to reproductive success and therefore to the existence of the species.

After the spontaneous progression from the regeneration phase (which seems to be stable in duration) to the acceleration phase (when sex hormones are again liberated and spasmodic postnuptial display occurs), the neuroendocrine machinery of each individual comes under the week-to-week influence of the two antagonistic sets of *accelerators* and *inhibitors*. Dependent upon its length, and upon the environment in which the species exists, the regeneration (="refractory" or "negative") phase may be an important internal timing device in many species.

Light is a particularly important postregeneration accelerator of the sexual cycle of Temperate Zone birds. Others, under natural conditions, are warmth (and probably sunshine per se), territory, adequate food, the nest site, nesting materials, and behavioral interactions. Inhibitors are cold, inclement weather, hunger, fear, and lack of appropriate nesting material and the traditional nest site. This is particularly true of the female. Paradoxically, inhibitors ultimately may be beneficial in that they sometimes prevent reproduction at unpropitious times of the year.

External *culminators* (which are often synonymous with accelerators) bring the sexual cycle to a successful conclusion. No single over-all factor (such as day length) is responsible for the timing of avian egg laying. The breeding season is kept in step with the sun essentially by the external factors that influence the female exteroceptor organs and ultimately permit nidification and ovulation on the habitual breeding ground. Of these, the most important may be appropriate nesting materials, a safe nesting site, mild weather, and an abundance of the food on which the young are traditionally fed.

The sexual cycle and timing of reproduction in Arctic and xerophilous species, equatorial and transequatorial migrants, species such as the sooty tern of Ascension Island, as well as Temperate Zone birds can be explained in broad outline in the light of the data outlined above.

ACKNOWLEDGMENTS

At odd times I have had the benefit of discussions with my friends Drs. Donald S. Farner and Albert Wolfson. They have made our meetings both helpful and stimulating and it is an incidental matter that we continue to disagree on certain fundamental aspects of the subject.

References

Amadon, D. (1948). Continental drift and bird migration. *Science*, **108**: 705–707.
Aschoff, J. (1955). Jahresperiodik der Fortpflanzung bei Warmblütern. *Studium Gen.* 8: 742–776.
Baker, I., and Baker, J. R. (1932). The breeding season of the blackbird. *Proc. Zool. Soc. London* **1932**: 661–667.
Baker, J. R. (1938). The evolution of breeding seasons. *In* "Evolution" (G. R. de Beer, ed.) pp. 161–177. Oxford Univ. Press, London and New York.

Baker, J. R. (1947). The seasons in a tropical rain-forest (New Hebrides). Part 7. Summary and general conclusions. *J. Linnean Soc. London Zool.* **41**: 248–258.

Beach, F. A. (1948). "Hormones and Behavior." Hoeber-Harper, New York.

Benoit, J., Assenmacher, I., and Brard, E. (1956). Apparition et maintien de cycles sexuels non saisonniers chez le Canard domestique placé pendant plus de trois ans à l'obscurité totale. *J. Physiol. (Paris)* **48**: 388–391.

Benoit, J., Assenmacher, I., and Walter, F. X. (1950a). Réponses du mécanisme gonado-stimulant à l'éclairement artificiel et de la préhypophyse aux castrations bilatérale et unilatérale, chez le canard domestique male, au cours de la période de régression testiculaire saisonnière. *Compt. rend. soc. biol.* **144**: 573–577.

Benoit, J., and Ott, L. (1944). External and internal factors in sexual activity. Effect of irradiation with different wavelengths on the mechanisms of photo-stimulation of the hypophysis and on testicular growth in the immature duck. *Yale J. Biol. and Med.* **17**: 27–46.

Benoit, J., Walter, F. X., and Assenmacher, I. (1950b). Nouvelles recherches 1elatives à l'action de lumière de différentes longueurs d'onde sur la gonado stimulation du canard male impubère. *Compt. rend. soc. biol.* **144**: 1206–1211.

Berlioz, J. (1950). Carreteres généraux et origines des migrations 1074–1088. *In* "Traité de Zoologie" (P. Grassé, ed.), Vol. XV—Oiseaux. Masson et Cie, Paris.

Bissonnette, T. H. (1936). Sexual photoperiodicity. *Quart. Rev. Biol.* **11**: 371–386.

Bissonnette, T. H. (1941). Experimental modification of breeding cycles in goats. *Physiol. Zoöl.* **14**: 379–383.

Bissonnette, T. H., and Wadlund, A. P. (1932). Duration of testis activity of *Sturnus vulgaris* in relation to type of illumination. *J. Exptl. Biol.* **9**: 339–350.

Blanchard, B. D. (1941). The White-crowned Sparrows (*Zonotrichia leucophrys*) of the Pacific seaboard: environment and annual cycle. *Univ. Calif. (Berkeley) Publn. Zool.* **46**: 1–18.

Boulière, F. (1950). Physiologie de migration 1089–1099. *In* "Traite de Zoologie" (P. Grassé, ed.), Vol. XV—Oiseaux. Masson et Cie, Paris.

Breneman, W. R. (1955). Reproduction in birds: the female. *Mem. Soc. Endocrinol* **4**: 94–110.

Bullough, W. S. (1942). The reproductive cycles of the British and Continental races of the Starling. *Phil. Trans. Roy. Soc. London* **B231**: 165–246.

Bullough, W. S. (1945). Endocrinological aspects of bird behaviour. *Biol. Rev.*, **20**, 88–89.

Burger, J. W. (1947). On the relation of day-length to the phases of testicular involution and inactivity of the spermatogenetic cycle of the Starling. *J. Exptl. Zool.* **105**: 259–267.

Burger, J. W. (1949). A review of experimental investigations on seasonal reproduction in birds. *Wilson Bull.* **61**: 211–230.

Chapin, J. P. (1954). The calendar of Widewake Fair. *Auk* **71**: 1–15.

Collias, N. E. (1950). Hormones and behavior with special reference to birds and the mechanism of hormone action. *In* "Steroid Hormones" (S. Gordon, ed.), pp. 277–329. Univ. Wisconsin Press, Madison, Wisconsin.

Coombs, C. J. F., and Marshall, A. J. (1956). The effects of hypophysectomy on the internal testis rhythm in birds and mammals. *J. Endocrinol.* **13**: 107–111.

Curry-Lindahl, K. (1958). Internal timer and spring migration in an equatorial migrant the Yellow wagtail (*Motacilla flava*). *Arkiv Zool.* [2] **11**: 541–557.

Darlington, P. J. (1957). "Zoogeography". Wiley, New York.

Davis, W. B. (1933). The span of the nesting season of birds in Butte Country, California, in relation to their food. *Condor* **35**: 151–154.

Disney, H. J. de S., Lofts, B., and Marshall, A. J. (1959). The duration of the *regeneration period* of the internal reproductive rhythm in a xerophilous equatorial bird, *Quelea quelea* Linn. *Nature*, **184**; 1659–1660.

Drost, J. (1956). "Les Migrations des Oiseaux." Payot, Paris.

Engels, W. L., and Jenner, C. E. (1956). The effect of temperature on testicular recrudescence in Juncos at different photoperiods. *Biol. Bull.* **110**: 129–137.

Farner, D. S. (1950). The annual stimulus for migration. *Condor* **52**: 104–122.

Farner, D. S. (1955). The annual stimulus for migration: experimental and physiological aspects. *In* "Recent Studies in Avian Biology" (A. Wolfson, ed.), pp. 198–237. Univ. Illinois Press, Urbana, Illinois.

Farner, D. S., and Mewaldt, L. R. (1955a). The natural termination of the refractory period in the White-crowned sparrow. *Condor* **57**: 112–116.

Farner, D. S., and Mewaldt, L. R. (1955b). Is increased activity or wakefulness an essential element in the mechanism of the photoperiodic responses of avian gonads? *Northwest Sci.* **29**: 53—65.

Frith, H. J., and Davies, S. J. (1958). The magpie goose. *Australian Museum Mag.* **12**: 348–351.

Greeley, F., and Meyer, R. K. (1953). Seasonal variation in testis-stimulating activity of male pheasant pituitary glands. *Auk* **70**: 350–358.

Griscom, L. (1937). A monographic study of the red crossbill. *Proc. Boston. Soc. Nat. Hist.* **41**: 77–210.

Höhn, E. O. (1947). Sexual behaviour and seasonal changes in the gonads and adrenals of the Mallard. *Proc. Zool. London* **A117**: 281–304.

Höhn, E. O. (1950). Physiology of the thyroid gland in birds: a review. *Ibis* **92**: 464–473.

Hoover, E. E., and Hubbard, H. E. (1937). Modification of the sexual cycle of trout by control of light. *Copeia* **1937**: 206–210.

Howard, H. E. (1929). "An Introduction to the Study of Bird Behaviour." Cambridge Univ. Press, London and New York.

Howard, H. E. (1935). "The Nature of a Bird's World." Cambridge Univ. Press, London and New York.

Huxley, J. S. (1914). The courtship-habits of the Great Crested Grebe (*Podiceps cristatus*); with an addition to the theory of sexual selection. *Proc. Zool. Soc. London* **1914**: 491–562.

Jenner, E. (1824). Some observations on the migrations of birds. *Phil. Trans. Roy. Soc. London* **1824**: 11–41.

Kar, A. B. (1947a). The action of male and female sex hormones on the adrenals in the fowl. *Anat. Record* **97**: 551–561.

Kar, A. B. (1947b). The adrenal cortex testicular relations in the fowl: the effect of castration and replacement therapy on the adrenal cortex. *Anat. Record* **99**: 177–197.

Keast, J. A., and Marshall, A. J. (1954). The influence of drought and rainfall on reproduction in Australian desert birds. *Proc. Zool. Soc. London* **124**: 493–499.

Kendeigh, S. C. (1941). Length of day and energy requirements for gonad development and egg-laying in birds. *Ecology* **22**: 237–248.

King, J. R., and Farner, D. S. (1956). Bioenergetic basis of light-induced fat deposition in the White-crowned Sparrow. *Proc. Soc. Exptl. Biol. Med.* **93**: 354–359.

Kluijver, H. N. (1951). The population ecology of the Great Tit, *Parus m. major*. L. *Ardea* **39**: 1–135.

Koch, E. C. (1939). *In* "Sex and Internal Secretions" (E. Allen, C. H. Danforth, and E. H. Doisy, eds.), 2nd ed., Chapter 12. Williams and Wilkins, Baltimore, Maryland.

Lack, D. (1933). Nesting conditions as a factor controlling breeding time in birds. *Proc. Zool. Soc. London* **1933**: 231–237.

Lack, D. (1950a). Breeding seasons in the Galapagos. *Ibis* **92**: 268–278.

Lack, D. (1950b). The breeding seasons of European birds. *Ibis* **92**: 288–316.

Lack, D. (1956). Further notes on the breeding biology of the swift *Apus apus*. *Ibis* **98**: 606–619.

Lack, D. (1959). Migration across the sea. *Ibis* **101**, 374–399.

Lack, D., and Silva, E. T. (1949). The weight of nestling Robins. *Ibis* **91**: 64–78.

Lehmann, V. W. (1953). Bobwhite population fluctuations and vitamin A. *Trans. 18th North Am. Wildlife Conf.* pp. 199–246.

Lehrman, D. S. (1955). The physiological basis of parental feeding behaviour in the Ring-dove (*Streptopelia risoria*). *Behaviour* **7**: 241–286.

Lehrman, D. S. (1956). On the organization of maternal behaviour and the problem of instinct. *In* "L'instinct dans le comportement des animaux et de l'homme." Masson et Cie, Paris.

Lehrman, D. S. (1959). Hormonal responses to external stimuli in birds. *Ibis* **101**, 478–496.

Lockie, J. D. (1955). The breeding and feeding of Jackdaws and Rooks, with notes on Carrion Crows and other Corvidae. *Ibis* **97**: 341–369.

Lofts, B., and Marshall, A. J. (1956). The effects of prolactin administration on the internal rhythm of reproduction in male birds. *J. Endocrinol.* **13**: 101–106.

Lofts, B., and Marshall, A. J. (1957). The interstitial and spermatogenetic tissue of autumn migrants in Southern England. *Ibis* **99**: 621–627.

Lofts, B., and Marshall, A. J. (1958). An investigation of the refractory period of reproduction in male birds by means of exogenous prolactin and follicle stimulating hormone. *J. Endocrinol.* **17**: 91–98.

Lofts, B., and Marshall, A. J. (1959). The post-nuptial occurrence of progestins in the seminiferous tubules of birds. *J. Endocrinol.* **19**: 16–21.

Lofts, B., and Marshall, A. J. (1960). The experimental regulation of *Zugunruhe* and the sexual cycle in the brambling *Fringilla montifringilla*. *Ibis*, **102**: 209–214.

Loisel, G. (1900). Études sur la Spermatogenèse chez le Moineau Domestique. *J. Anat., Paris* pp. 140–185.

Loisel, G. (1901). Études sur la Spermatogenèse chez le Moineau Domestique. *J. Anat., Paris* pp. 193–216.

Løppenthin, B. (1932). Die Vögel Nordostgrönlands zwischen 73°00′ und 75°30′ N.Br. samt Beobachtungsergebnissen von der Dänischen Godthaab-Expedition 1930. *Medd. Grønland* **91**: 1–127.

McGowan J. P. (1936). Suprarenal "virilism" in a domestic hen; its possible significance. *J. Exptl. biol.* **13**: 377–382.

McGreal R. D., and Farner, D. S. (1956). Pre-migratory fat depositions in the Gambel White-crowned Sparrow. *Northwest Sci.* **30**: 12–23.

Manniche, A. L. V. (1910). The terrestrial birds and mammals of North-east Greenland: biological observations. Danmark-Expedition til Grønlands Nordoskyst 1906–1908. *Medd. Grønland* **45**: 1–200.

Marshall, A. J. (1942). Display and bower building in bower birds. Thesis. University of Sydney.

Marshall, A. J. (1949a). On the function of the interstitium of the testis. The sexual cycle of a wild bird *Fulmarus glacialis* (L.) *Quart. J. Microscop. Sci.* **90**: 265–280.

Marshall, A. J. (1949b). Weather factors and spermatogenesis in birds. *Proc. Zool. Soc. London* **A119**: 711–716.

Marshall, A. J. (1950). The function of the bower of the Satin Bower-bird in the light of experimental modifications of the breeding cycle. *Nature* **165**: 388–392.

Marshall, A. J. (1951a). The refractory period of testis rhythm in birds and its possible bearing on breeding and migration. *Wilson Bull.* **63**: 238–261.

Marshall, A. J. (1951b). Food availability as a timing factor in the sexual cycle of birds. *Emu* **50**: 267–282.

Marshall, A. J. (1952a). Non-breeding among Arctic Birds. *Ibis* **94**: 310–333.

Marshall, A. J. (1952b). The interstitial cycle in relation to autumn and winter sexual behaviour in birds. *Proc. Zool. Soc. London* **121**: 727–740.

Marshall, A. J. (1952c). The condition of the interstitial and spermatogenetic tissue of migratory birds on arrival in England in April and May. *Proc. Zool. Soc. London* **122**: 287–295.

Marshall, A. J. (1954). "Bower Birds." Oxford Univ. Press, London and New York.

Marshall, A. J. (1955). Reproduction in birds: The male. *Mem. Soc. Endocrinol.* **4**: 75–89.

Marshall, A. J. (1958). The role of the internal rhythm of reproduction in the "timing" of avian breeding seasons, including migration. *Abstr. XII Congr. Int. Orn. Helsinki.* p. 18.

Marshall, A. J., and Coombs, C. J. F. (1957). The interaction of environmental, internal and behavioural factors in the rook *Corvus frugilegus* Linnaeus. *Proc. Zool. Soc. London* **128**: 545–589.

Marshall, A. J., and Disney, H. J. de S. (1956). Photostimulation of an equatorial bird (*Quelea quelea* Linnaeus). *Nature* **177**: 143–144.

Marshall, A. J., and Disney, H. S. de S. (1957). Experimental induction of the breeding season in a xerophilous bird. *Nature* **180**: 647.

Marshall, A. J., and Roberts, J. D. (1959). The breeding biology of equatorial vertebrates: Reproduction of cormorants (Phalacrocoracidae) at lat. 0°20' N. *Proc. Zool. Soc. London* **132**: 617–625.

Marshall, A. J., and Serventy, D. L. (1956). Breeding periodicity in the Short-tailed Shearwater (*Puffinus tenuirostris* Temminck) in relation to trans-equatorial migration and its environment. *Proc. Zool. Soc. London* **127**: 489–510.

Marshall, A. J., and Serventy, D. L. (1958). The internal rhythm of reproduction in xerophilous birds under conditions of illumination and darkness. *J. Exptl. Biol.* **35**: 666–670.

Marshall, A. J., and Serventy, D. L. (1959). The experimental demonstration of an internal rhythm of reproduction in a transequatorial migrant, the Short-tailed Shearwater, *Puffinus tenuirostris, Nature* **184**, 1704–1705.

Marshall, A. J., and Williams, M. C. (1959). The pre-nuptial migration of Yellow Wagtails (*Motacilla flava*) from latitude 0°04' N. *Proc. Zool. Soc. London* **132**: 313–320.

Marshall, F. H. A. (1936). Sexual periodicity and the causes which determine it. *Phil. Trans. Roy. Soc. London* **B226**: 423–456.

Marshall, F. H. A. (1937). On the change over in the oestrous cycle in animals after transference across the equator, with further observations on the incidence of the breeding seasons and the factors controlling sexual periodicity. *Proc. Roy. Soc.* **B122**: 413–428.

Mayr, E. (1953). On the origin of bird migration in the Pacific. *Proc. Seventh Pacific Sci. Congr.* **4**, 387–394.

Mayr, E. and Meise, W. (1930). Theoretisches zur Geschichte des Vogelzuges. *Der Vogelzug* (Berlin), **1**: 149–172.

Merkel, F. W. (1938). Zur Physiologie der Zugunruhe bei Vögeln. *Ber. Ver. Schlesischer Ornithol.* **25** (*Sonderh*): 1–72.

Merkel, F. W. (1956). Untersuchungen über tages- und jahresperiodische Aktivitätsänderungen bei gekäfigten Zugvögeln. Z. Tierpsychol. **13**: 278–301.

Miller, A. H. (1949). Potentiality for testicular recrudescence during the annual refractory period of the Golden-crowned Sparrow. Science **109**: 546.

Miller, A. H. (1951). Further evidence on the refractory period in the reproductive cycle of the golden-crowned sparrow. Auk **68**: 380–383.

Miller, A. H. (1954). Breeding cycles in a constant equatorial environment in Colombia, South America. Acta XI Congr. Intern. Ornithol. pp. 495–503.

Miller, A. H. (1959). Reproductive cycles in an equatorial sparrow. Proc. Nat. Acad. Sci. **45**: 1095–1100.

Miyazaki, H. (1934). On the relation of the daily period to the sexual maturity and to the moulting of Zosterops palpebrosa japonica. Sci. Repts Tôhuku Imp. Univ., Fourth Ser. **9**: 183–203.

Moreau, R. E. (1931). Equatorial reflections on periodism in birds. Ibis [13] **1**: 553–570.

Moreau, R. E. (1936). Breeding seasons of birds in East African evergreen forest. Proc. Zool. Soc. London **1936**: 631–653.

Moreau, R. E. (1950). The breeding seasons of African Birds. 1. Land Birds. Ibis **92**: 223–267.

Morley, A. (1943). Sexual behaviour of British Birds from October to January. Ibis **85**: 132–158.

Murphy, R. C. (1936). "Oceanic Birds of South America." Am. Mus. Nat. Hist. N.Y.

Nice, M. M. (1946). Weights of resident and winter visitant Song Sparrows in Central Ohio. Condor **48**: 41–42.

Norris, M. J. (1958). Influence of photoperiod on imaginal diapause of acridids. Nature **181**: 58.

Oakeson, (B. Blanchard), and Lilley, B. R. (1954). The thyroid cycle in migratory and resident white-crowned sparrows (Zonotrichia leucophys) Abstr. XV Int. Congr. Zool. Copenhagen Sect. **XI**: (15) 1–2.

Oordt, G. J. van (1949). "Vogeltrek," 3rd ed. E. J. Brill, Leiden.

Palmgren, P. (1944). Studien über die Tagesrhythmik gekäfigter Zugvögel. Z. Tierpsychol. **6**: 44–86.

Palmgren, P. (1949). On the diurnal rhythm of activity and rest in birds. Ibis **91**: 561–576.

Pedersen, A. (1930). Fortgesetzte Beiträge zur Kenntnis der Säugetier- und Vogelfauna der Ostküste Grönlands. Medd. Grønland **77**: 341–507.

Polikarpova, E. (1940). Influence of external factors upon the development of the sexual gland of the Sparrow. Compt. rend. acad. sci. U.R.S.S. **27**: 91–95.

Riley, G. M., and Witschi, E. (1938). Comparative effects of light stimulation and administration gonadotropic hormones on female sparrows. Endocrinology **23**: 618–624.

Rowan, W. (1918). Power of control over deposition of eggs. Brit. Birds. **12**: 42–43.

Rowan, W. (1925). Relation of light to bird migration and developmental changes. Nature **115**: 494–495.

Rowan, W. (1926). On photoperiodism, reproductive periodicity and the annual migrations of birds and certain fishes. Proc. Boston Soc. Nat. Hist. **38**: 147–189.

Rowan, W. (1927). Migration and reproductive rhythm in Birds. Nature **119**: 351–352.

Rowan, W. (1929). Experiments in bird migration. I. Manipulation of the reproductive cycle: seasonal histological changes in the gonads. Proc. Boston. Soc. Nat. Hist. **39**: 151–208.

Rowan, W. (1930). Experiments in bird migration. II. Reversed migration. Proc. Natl. Acad. Sci. U.S. **16**: 520–525.

Rowan, W. (1931). "The Riddle of Migration." Williams and Wilkins, Baltimore, Maryland.

Rowan, W. (1938). Light and seasonal reproduction in animals. *Biol. Revs.* **13**: 374–402·

Rowan, W. (1946). Experiments in bird migration. *Trans. Roy. Soc. Can.*, III **40**: 123–135.

Rowan, W., and Batrawi, A. M. (1939). Comments on the gonads of some European migrants collected in East Africa immediately before their spring departure. *Ibis* [14] **3**: 58–65.

Salomonsen, F. (1955). The evolutionary significance of bird migration. *Kgl. Danske Videnskab. Selskab Biol. Medd.* **22** (6): 3–62.

Sauer F. (1957). Die Sternenorientierung nächtlich ziehender Grasmücken (*Sylvia atricapilla, borin und curruca*). *Z. Tierspsychol.* **14**: 29–70.

Schaanning, H. T. L. (1916). Bidrag til Novaja Semljas Fauna. *Dansk. Ornithol. Foren. Tidsskr.* **10**: 145–190.

Schäfer, E. A. (1907). On the incidence of daylight as a determining factor in bird migration. *Nature* **77**: 159–163.

Schildmacher, H. (1933). Zur Physiologie des Zugtriebes, I. Versuche mit weiblichem Sexualhormon. *Vogelzug* **4**: 21–24.

Schildmacher, H. (1934a). Zur Physiologie des Zugtriebes, II. Weitere Versuche mit weiblichem Sexualhormon. *Vogelzug* **5**: 1–9.

Schildmacher, H. (1934b). Weiblicher Sexualhormon und Vogelzug **5**: 171–172.

Schildmacher, H., and Steubing, L. (1952). Untersuchungen zur hormonalen Regulierung des Fettwerdens der Zugvögel im Frühjahr. *Biol. Zentr.* **71**: 272–282.

Serventy, D. L., and Marshall, A. J. (1957). Breeding periodicity in Western Australian birds. *Emu* **57**: 99–126.

Shank, M. C. (1959). The natural termination of the refractory period in the Slate-coloured Junco and in the White-throated Sparrow. *Auk* **76**: 44–54.

Skutch, A. F. (1950). The nesting seasons of Central American birds in relation to climate and food supply. *Ibis* **92**: 185–222.

Snow, D. W. (1955). The abnormal breeding of birds in the winter of 1953–54. *Brit. Birds* **48**: 120–126.

Snow, D. W. (1958). The breeding of the blackbird *Turdus merula* at Oxford. *Ibis* **100**: 1–30.

Thomson, A. L. (1936) Recent progress in the study of bird-migration: a review of the literature, 1926–35. *Ibis* [13] **6**: 472–530.

Thomson, A. L. (1945). "Bird migration," rev. ed. H. F. and G. Witherby, London.

Thomson, A. L. (1950). Factors determining the breeding seasons of birds: an introductory review. *Ibis* **92**: 173–184.

Vaugien, L. (1953). Sur l'apparition de la maturité sexuelle des jeunes perruches ondulées males soumises à diverses conditions d'éclairement: Le développement testiculaire est plus rapide dans l'obscurité complète. *Bull. Biol. France et Belg.* **87**: 274–286.

von Haartman, L. (1956). The phenological research work organized by the Societas Scientiarum Fennica. A discussion of methods and aims. *Soc. Sci. Fenn., Årsbok* **XXXIII** B: *3*, 1–23.

Voous, K. H. (1950). The breeding seasons of birds in Indonesia. *Ibis* **92**: 279–287.

Wagner, H. O. (1930). Über Jahres- und Tagesrhythmus bei Zugvögeln. *Z. vergleich. Physiol.* **12**: 703–724.

Wagner, H. O. (1936). Über den Jahresrhythmus verschiedener Grasmücken (*Sylvia*) in Mexico. *Vogelzug* **7**: 109–112.

Wetmore, A. (1930). "The migration of Birds." Harvard Univ. Press, Cambridge, Massachusetts.

Witherby, H. F. et al. (1943). "The Handbook of British Birds." Witherby, London.

Witschi, E. (1945). Quantitative studies on the seasonal development of the deferent ducts in passerine birds. J. Exptl. Zool. **100**: 549–564.

Wolfson, A. (1945). The role of the pituitary, fat deposition, and body weight in bird migration. Condor **47**: 95–127.

Wolfson, A. (1952a). Day length, migration and breeding cycles in birds. Sci. Monthly **74**: 191–200.

Wolfson, A. (1952b). The occurrence and regulation of the refractory period in the gonadal and fat cycles of the junco. J. Exptl. Zool. **121**: 311–325.

Wolfson, A. (1959a). The role of light and darkness in the regulation of the Spring migration and reproductive cycles in birds. In "Photoperiodism and Related Phenomena in Plants and Animals" (R. B. Withrow, ed.).

Wolfson, A. (1959b). Role of light and darkness in the regulation of the refractory period in the gonadal and fat cycles of migratory birds. Physiol. Zool. **32**: 160–176.

Yeates, N. T. M. (1949). The breeding season of the sheep with particular reference to its modification by artificial means using light. J. Agr. Sci. **39**: 1–42.

Chapter XXII

Long-Distance Orientation

G. KRAMER

I. Introduction

There have been two traditional lines of approach in experimental research in bird orientation. These are: first, displacement experiments n birds bound to their nesting sites, and second, experiments on migratory birds. The first systematic experiments of the first category vere described in wild birds by Watson and Lashley in 1915, although oming pigeons had previously been the subject of experiments, or at east of theoretical discussions, ever since the beginning of the twentieth entury. The first experiments on migratory birds were those of Thienemann (1931) during 1926–1928. He retained young storks in their ome area until all the other storks had left; thus the young would not e influenced by experienced birds.

Both lines of approach have yielded substantial results. Displacement xperiments on breeding birds (homing pigeons in particular) have led articularly in the last few years to a sharper definition of problems. Experiments on free migrants displaced at right angles to their normal line of migratory flight have demonstrated the separability of purely directional flying and goal finding.

In 1949 Kramer introduced the cage method; this permitted a more direct experimental approach to the problem of bird orientation. The cage method has cleared the way for the investigation of astronomical orientation.

The present survey of the situation today (1958) has been made during a period of intense activity. No less than one-fourth of all the papers cited were published in or after 1957.

II. Field Experiments Not Directly Concerning the Mechanism of Orientation

A. FIELD EXPERIMENTS ON MIGRATORY BIRDS

Thienemann's (1931) early work led to displacement experiments which raised two precise points for clarification; first, is direction of migration inherited? and, second, does the migrating bird have a specific goal like birds homing to their nest, or does it simply fly without any specific goal in a certain direction which will normally bring it to winter quarters and, on the return trip, to the vicinity of its nesting place?

In regard to the first question, Thienemann (1931) found that young storks which had been retained in their own population area, when released, departed in directions conforming on the whole with the normal direction of storks in the wild. Storks in Central European areas usually select one of two different routes according to whether their home lies east or west of approximately 7° east longitude. Those east of this line head southeast and those west head southwest. Schüz (1950, 1951) demonstrated that young eastern storks raised in the western area displayed no difference from western storks when permitted to depart with them (presumably guided migration). Young transplanted eastern storks, retained until all the free birds had departed so that they could not be influenced by them, headed in directions not altogether parallel with that of normal eastern storks, but noticeably more to the east than western birds (Schüz, 1949, 1951). This would indicate inherited reasons for directional differences specific to population.

The question of whether migratory flight is governed by goal orientation or directional flying has been the subject of a whole series of displacement experiments during migration [European starling *Sturnus vulgaris* (Krätzig and Schüz, 1936; Perdeck, 1954, 1957); hooded crow *Corvus cornis* (Rüppell, 1944); American crow *Corvus brachyrhynchos* (Rowan, 1946); European sparrow hawk *Accipiter nisus* (Drost, 1939)].

In all of the tests at least the bulk of the birds of the same year flew parallel to the normal migratory route. Old birds displayed a stronger tendency to "home" towards the normal distribution area of their population. Many of the displaced old birds (sparrow hawk, starling) flew goal-oriented to their population's winter quarters in the same season.

A series of releases in Switzerland (Basel, Zürich, Geneva) of migrating starlings captured in Holland (Perdeck, 1954, 1957) yielded particularly clear-cut results. The pattern of recoveries of young starlings released indicated a direction of resumed flight of roughly 235° (if uninfluenced by old birds). These recoveries were made during the same migratory season in which the birds were displaced. This direction checked very satisfactorily with that of broad-front migration of starlings in Holland, but differed slightly from the departing direction of starlings native of the host country. This would tend to confirm the directional differences specific to population noted in storks. In later years the young transplanted starlings returned faithfully to the winter quarters to which they had previously gone as a result of their displacement and their inherent directional tendency. When the birds flew north again, however, they returned in typical cases to nest in their native area.

New migratory patterns, therefore, may result from displacements. Thus Baltic starlings wintered in Central France or Spain instead of on the coast of the English Channel or in England. The route followed by such starlings (with "artificial winter quarters") is probably "dog-legged," the part between the nesting area and the coast of Belgium coinciding with the route of normal starlings.

The pattern of recoveries of old starlings displaced in the same manner showed a marked difference from that of the young transplanted starlings, in that the old starlings returned to winter quarters typical of their population (average direction from the release place approximately 300°).

From the standpoint of orientation research, the following may be concluded:

1. Purely directional orientation does exist, but it has only been established with reasonable certainty in the case of birds that were unacquainted with their "goal," i.e. their winter quarters. Directional tendency appears to be inherited.

2. Field tests have shown equally clearly that goal orientation does exist in migratory flight. In the case of autumn migration, it was usually demonstrated in birds that had previous personal knowledge of their winter quarters.

B. The Question of the Bird's Settlement on a Living Area

Settlement on a living area is a question closely bound to that of direction orientation and goal orientation. Until proof to the contrary is forthcoming it can be assumed that the physical factors serving as orientation clues are identical with those with which the bird is "imprinted" at its home site.

As mentioned above, evidence thus far indicates that migratory birds, at least of certain species, will return as long as they live to the same winter quarters they have once acquired. Loyalty to nesting area is such a common phenomenon that there is no need to give detailed references. Evidence thus far indicates that it is personal experience which causes a bird to return to the same nesting area, as well as to the same winter quarters (see above). This is true at any rate within the limits of the distribution area of the species. Birds hatched in an area other than where the eggs were laid have consistently displayed loyalty to the site where they themselves were hatched. Also, transplantation after hatching has proved to produce settlement in young precocial birds [several species of ducks; reviewed by Hochbaum (1955, pp. 211–212, 235–236)] as well as in altricial species [white storks (Schüz, 1943, 1952, p. 164) and flycatchers (see below)].

Russian researchers (cited by Mauersberger, 1957) have conducted transplanting experiments on young pied flycatchers (*Muscicapa hypoleuca*). Attempts to settle young birds in uncolonized areas before they were completely fledged were consistently successful. The homing results in Table I check with those of birds not transplanted. Löhrl (1957) has investigated the more specific question of the sensitive period during which the birds adopt their home. In his experiments even those birds that were not transferred until the approach of their juvenile molt (28 to 35 days after they were fledged) and thus only two weeks before starting migration, permanently adopted their new home. Those transferred in a completely molted condition however failed to return either to their new home or to their original one. Löhrl's data actually pertain to three different localities, namely, the one in which the eggs were hatched, the one in which the birds were raised, and, thirdly, the one where they were released. The locality in which the birds were raised may be considered equivalent, for the present purpose, to their native home.

As is shown in Table II, attempts to resettle adult flycatchers can be successful if they are taken to their new home at the beginning of the nesting season. In such a case the urge to breed apparently overcomes the homing impulse. These experiments however are so recent that we

TABLE I

SPRING RETURNS OF THE FLYCATCHERS (*Muscicapa hypoleuca* Pall. and *M. albicollis* Temm.) DISPLACED AT JUVENILE STAGES

Species	Source	Year of Displacement	Distance and direction of displacement	Number displaced	Stage at displacement (days after fledging)	Recoveries	
						At place of origin	At host place
M. hypoleuca	Schtscherbakow[a]	1953	30 miles south	200		—	11
	Schtscherbakow[a]	1954	30 miles south	208	Before or shortly after fledging	—	19
	Poliwanow[a]	1953	250 miles south	963		—	58 (64?)
M. albicollis	Löhrl[b]	1955	56 miles south	98	11–16 days	—	10+
	Löhrl[b]	1956		44	28–35 days, molting	—	4+
	Löhrl[b]	1956		48	42 days, past molt; migration imminent	—	—

[a] Quoted from Mauersberger (1957).
[b] Informally submitted at the *5th Intern. Ethol. Congr.* The author has kindly given permission to quote these data.

TABLE II

RETURNS OF PIED FLYCATCHERS (*Muscicapa hypoleuca* Pall.)
DISPLACED AT THE ADULT STAGE

Source	Year of displacement	Distance and direction of displacement	Number displaced	Reproductive stage at displacement	Recoveries	
					At place of origin	At host place
Treus and Uspenskij	1953 and 1954	620 miles south	308	Beginning of breeding	14 (6 same spring)	26 (all same spring)
Poliwanow	1953	250 miles south	148	End of breeding	24 (spring, 1954)	—

Quoted from Mauersberger (1957)

do not as yet know whether the birds have permanently adopted their new home.

Homing pigeons are easy to transplant when they are just fledged. Later on transplantation is more difficult, but it can be facilitated by mating the birds to natives of the new locality. There are cases, however, in which pigeons thought to be permanently settled in their new homes have in time returned to their old ones. A female pigeon allowed free flight for nine months at her new home (where she raised a family) finally departed and appeared 30 hours later at her old loft over 300 miles to the northeast (Kramer, 1953a). Thausiez (1910) reports another case of a resettled bird which ultimately returned to its original home.

Male ducks normally display a tendency to follow females from different birth areas and eventually adopt these areas as their own. Resettlement has hence become normal as a consequence of the accelerated pair formation that takes place in the common winter quarters.

III. An Established Mechanism of Diurnal Direction Finding: Sun Orientation

It has long been known that even caged birds will display spontaneous migratory activity. Kramer demonstrated, at first with nocturnal migrants [red-backed shrike *Lanius collurio* (Kramer, 1949); warblers *Sylvia* (Kramer, 1950a)] and, later on, with the starling *Sturnus vulgaris* (Kramer, 1950b, 1951) that migratory activity is oriented when conditions are appropriate. In the above-cited experiments the test bird was placed in a round cage, 2 feet in diameter, that permitted its movements to be registered statistically by observation from below. In the most favorable cases the birds display "fluttering" activity. Flying at a standstill was observed on the circular perch with the axis of the body pointed in a direction which, in the case of the warblers and the starling, displayed a definite trend conforming to the direction of migration in the wild.

The experiments conducted on the starling were the first to permit successful analysis. When the sky was completely overcast, migratory activity was diffuse. When the direction of the sunlight was changed by reflecting it with mirrors the bird shifted its direction accordingly; it was thus demonstrated that use is made of the sun in orientation.

As the directional tendency of the starling under observation remained constant for hours at a time, there was from the very beginning indication of its ability to allow for the changing position of the moving sun. This was brought out even more clearly by special tests.

Instead of migratory activity, training in a specific direction can be used for manifestation of direction finding. Starlings trained at a definite time of day, and then tested at another time (when the sun was at a considerably different angle) displayed a directional tendency that did not conform to constant angle sun orientation, but corresponded roughly to the compass bearings taken from the position of the sun in relation to the time of day. The errors displayed were characteristic of the individual. Some birds apparently overestimated, and others underestimated the angular speed of the sun. An attempt to train a starling by feeding it always in the actual direction of the sun was only partially successful (Kramer, 1952).

"Artificial sun" experiments confirmed the existence of a computing mechanism, although the choices made showed less reliability than behavior in natural sunlight. During these experiments, great care was taken at first to make the elevation of the artificial sun conform to that of the natural sun. It became evident, however, that it made no difference to the bird how high or low was the sun. The starlings apparently evaluated only the sun azimuth (Kramer, 1953a).

The physiological mechanism which is the basis of sun orientation was further analyzed by Hoffmann (1954) from the point of view of the bird's sense of time or "internal clock." By artificial regulation of the cycle of light and darkness, the estimation of time by starlings was either set forward, or set back, 6 hours. Their choice of direction changed accordingly by 90°. In the first case the change was counter clockwise, in the second case clockwise.

The starlings whose estimation of time had been phase-shifted by 6 hours were used for a further and more effective test of the role played by the elevation of the sun in the sky. If a starling whose "clock" has been set forward 6 hours is shown the sun at 3 P.M. by its time (that is to say 9 A.M. sun time) it will find the elevation of the sun normal, for the sun is at the same elevation at 9 A.M. as at 3 P.M. By varying the time of testing, Hoffmann was able to show the starlings the sun at an elevation appearing normal to them or conversely at an elevation that they would not expect. In these tests, too, the elevation of the sun made no difference to the birds' orientation responses. Obviously they were interested only in the azimuth position of the sun.

Several other species were tested by U. von Saint-Paul who found a sun orientation ability in the meadow lark *Sturnella magna* (1956), the barred warbler *Sylvia nisoria* and the red-backed shrike *Lanius collurio* (1953). The discovery of a sun orientation mechanism in warblers and shrikes is particularly interesting in view of the fact that their migration is exclusively nocturnal.

IV. Homing Orientation

A. Can Directed Homing without Known Landmarks be Questioned?

To answer this question there is little use in reviewing the impressive series of homing experiments made since Watson and Lashley conducted their first tests in 1915. For the sake of brevity we shall limit our discussion mainly to results obtained with the homing pigeon which has been the subject of the most intensive investigation (see reviews on homing in Schüz, 1952; Matthews, 1955).

It is doubtful whether homing pigeons can be considered fully representative of wild birds (if "wild birds" can be considered a homogeneous plural), but if the pigeon's talents differ, they are less rather than greater. At any rate, the homing pigeon lends itself so well to experimental study that it is reasonable to take it as a model at the present stage of research.

Figure 1, taken from Pratt and Wallraff (1958), gives new results of experiments on four colonies of consanguineous pigeons exclusively bred from Wilhelmshaven stock. None of the pigeons used in the experiments had ever been taken farther than 59 miles from its home loft. Sixteen of the northern group, and 75 of the southern loft (Freiburg), had never been taken farther than 22 miles. Ten northern pigeons and eleven southern pigeons were virgin flyers. The three criteria used in evaluating homing ability, namely, direction of departure as established by field-glass observation (not reported in Fig. 1), recoveries on the way, and actual homing success, all demonstrate oriented flight.

Two-direction experiments in the United States have not yielded such clear-cut results as the one cited above. In some cases the North American experiments revealed no directional tendency whatsoever (Kramer et al., 1957). This does not answer the question of goal orientation in a negative manner, however: it only complicates it. Regional and directional differences in orientation accuracy will be discussed below in this chapter (see page 354).

Another method by which goal orientation can be very emphatically shown consists in the release and tracing of pigeons raised in an aviary. One bird returned over 200 miles to its aviary in $2\frac{1}{2}$ days (Kramer and von St. Paul, 1954). Fifteen out of 88 birds released came back from over 100 miles (Kramer, 1958). The reports of birds en route showed that they pointed predominantly toward home. A more detailed description of this field of investigation will be given in the next section (page 353).

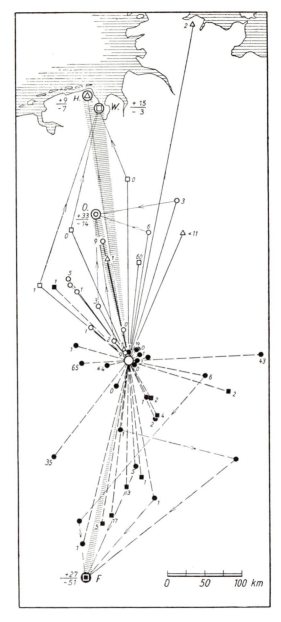

Fig. 1. Map showing release place (center) and four home sites of pigeons liberated on three different days in 1955 and 1957. Home sites to the north: $H.$=Hohenkirchen; $W.$=Wilhemshaven; $O.$=Osnabrück. Home site to the south: $F.$=Freiburg. Small symbols represent locations where pigeons were recovered on their way. North symbols

The two-direction experiments as well as the aviary method are particularly suitable for the quick and thorough demonstration of the existence of primary goal-finding ability. Many researchers were of the opinion, however, that neither the Wilhelmshaven (Kramer and co-workers) nor the English (Matthews) experiments were necessary to establish "primary" goal orientation. Rüppell's investigation (Rüppell, 1935, 1936, 1937, 1944; Rüppell and Schüz, 1948) of song birds, for instance, had hardly left any doubt on the subject, quite apart from the possibility that the successful individuals were familiar with the landscape over a wide range. That, however, is extremely unlikely since the birds homed from directions with which they could hardly have been familiar from migratory experience. Rüppell's experiments offer the criterion of recoveries of birds on the way, as well as actual homing success. Three starlings were killed en route in locations only slightly off the beeline course (Fig. 2).

Conservative authors have a tendency to question true goal finding in a particular group or species as long as it has not yet been demonstrated in that group or species. The Heinroths (1941), while convinced that wild birds do in fact possess the faculty in question, denied its existence in pigeons. They based this assumption on negative evidence obtained from their own experiments. Wilkinson (1952), while admitting that homing pigeons are endowed with true home-finding ability, has submitted mathematical deductions to show that there are no stringent reasons for attributing the same faculty to wild birds. Meanwhile, Heinroth's negative assertion has become obsolete; Wilkinson's approach may survive as an estimable piece of academic discussion. Its conclusions provide a challenge for us to produce more stringent evidence in the case of wild species, and this has already been done in part (Matthews, 1952, 1953). Yet at the present, very initial, stage of our understanding of such phenomena, it must be stated that, however difficult it may be to furnish solid evidence in *favor* of true goal finding, it is much more difficult to prove its absence if, in even one instance, it has been proved to occur.

(open) are differentiated as to home lofts: triangles=Hohenkirchen; squares=Wilhelmshaven; circles=Osnabrück. Within symbols pertaining to Freiburg, (full) squares refer to 1955, circles to 1957 releases. Fractions near home sites specify numbers of pigeons homed (plus sign) as against those lost (minus sign). Symbols of first recoveries are accompanied by numbers telling how many days after release the birds were found. After Pratt and Wallraff (1958).

The pattern of departures of birds released for homing has been a subject of repeated study. Until Matthews' experiments, however, departure diagrams failed to demonstrate in wild birds a tendency toward the goal, or even, in fact, a positive correlation between direction of departure and homing success (Griffin, 1943). Except for homing

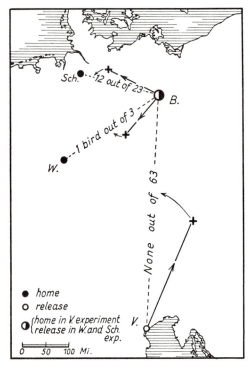

FIG. 2. Map showing displacement stretches of starlings. Each cross indicates a location where a starling was found dead. On the beeline courses the number of birds returned out of the total released is given. After Rüppell (1937).

pigeons, it was not until the experiments of Matthews on gulls *Larus* and shearwaters *Puffinus* that statistically oriented departures were demonstrated.

This summary has no historical pretentions. In the field of biology there is hardly another subject in which opinions have differed so greatly as on the question of homing orientation. The divergence of views expressed has been to a great degree a reflection of the divergent interests of those who have approached the problem, e.g. ornithologists, pigeon fanciers, experimental zoologists and physiologists, physicists, psychologists, and parapsychologists. It is surprising how little appreciated have been early experiments on homing pigeons such as those conducted by Thausiez (1910). As early as 1926, Thomson wrote (see page 13 of reference) that "the performances of relatively untrained birds, and of birds flown in directions other than that of training, require further investigation."

B. Experiments with Aviary Pigeons

The ability to home of pigeons raised and confined for life in aviaries first emerged through the impressive distribution of recoveries provided by a series of birds released 200 miles to the south. Nine out of eighteen birds were reported on, and all of them had made headway towards home. One bird actually homed in $2\frac{1}{2}$ days (Kramer and von St. Paul, 1954).

This result was important because it proved that scanning over a wide range is not necessary to acquaint the bird with its home site. Moreover, a new experimental tool was made available: space in an aviary is limited enough to allow variations of the environmental conditions that might prevent pigeons from getting the knowledge of the characters of their home site which are used for orientation.

An impairment of orientation was indeed obtained by placing an aviary in a large crater that was deep enough to preclude caged birds from viewing the horizon, even from the highest point they could reach. None out of 91 pigeons succeeded in returning from a distance of 100 miles. Only 12 out of 26 recovered birds got closer to home, whereas 14 were found farther away. This corresponds to random distribution. Random scatter was found also in pigeons raised in an aviary surrounded by a wooden palisade slightly higher than the top of the cage. Again none out of 28 birds returned. Only 2 of the 9 recovered had made progress toward home; the rest were found at distances greater than the beeline track. A regular gradation was shown by controls from open aviaries: of 88, 15 actually homed and 31 were reported; 24 of those reported managed to get closer to their home, and 7 were found farther away (Kramer, 1958).

While it is difficult to prove that the crater and palisade birds were completely deprived of clues to recognize their home, the statistical analysis nevertheless demonstrates a clear-cut difference in orientation ability between pigeons raised in open, and those raised in shielded aviaries. This difference is shown even without including the 15 birds that reached home; it seems to indicate that a tendency toward the goal

z

is already present at early stages of the travel. This conclusion is further supported by observations of the initial flight directions which indicated a more pronounced homeward tendency of the open-aviary birds. (This difference is not demonstrated by conventional standards, however: $p = 0.07$.) Therefore, landscape recognition may be excluded (even on the present results alone) particularly when it is considered that one of the two open aviaries gave only a very limited outlook in all directions (120 meters to 2.5 km.). The tentative conclusion must be that a view of part of the sky, of some little elevation above the horizon, is indispensable for the acquisition of knowledge of the home site. Further analysis is required to show whether the birds need the full panorama or only certain sectors of this narrow one.

The above results should be considered in connection with some of the subsequent sections. The small significance of landmark recognition is emphasized by the direction effect (see below); by our experiences with short-distance homing (page 355); and finally, by redirection obtained by the shifted "clock" (page 357). In particular, the fact that occlusion of a narrow sky zone prevents the home contact is also a contribution to our later discussion of sun navigation. Indeed, the lower parts of the sun's path are not accessible to birds in completely shielded cages. However, at least in midsummer, one of our palisades allows a view, through a northward gap, of the full sun path. All 15 recoveries so far made still show random distribution (unpublished data). We do not yet know what effect is produced by a gap to the south.

C. Is Long-Distance Homing Based on Sun Navigation?

After the discovery of a sun-azimuth orientation mechanism it was only a step further to offer bicoordinate navigation by the sun as the explanation for goal orientation. (The term "navigation" is henceforth used only for bicoordinate navigation.) The dependence of initial orientation on visibility of the sun, which Matthews was the first to emphasize, points to this explanation. The homing pigeon results cited below, however, fail to give support to any sort of astronomical navigation.

1. Directional and Regional Differences

In the Wilhelmshaven area, as well as in North Carolina (Kramer et al., 1956, 1958), pigeons do not home equally well from all directions. The "good" and the "poor" directions are not the same in the two areas. Direction effect was evident in tests over even the longest distances (Wilhelmshaven: 105 miles; Durham, North Carolina: 128 miles). Again, the direction of departure, the pattern of recoveries and actual homing results of the two-direction release reported in Fig. 1 clearly indicate a more accurate orientation while flying north than while flying south. All the pigeons used in this experiment were consanguineous.

Orientation does not appear to be as good in the American testing area as in Germany (Kramer et al., 1957), but so far no exchange of stock has been made to verify this phenomenon.

2. Quickness of Initial Orientation

True sun navigation requires not instantaneous, but protracted observation of the sun. Kramer (1953b) demonstrated that pigeons actually denied the possibility of observing the sun's path were quickly oriented (within a minute or less) even if they were released at a time when the elevation of the sun was the same as at the home site. Thanks to the improved method of observation of departures worked out by Pratt and Thouless (1955), it can be positively stated that, in many areas at least, pigeons not exposed to the sun until release nevertheless display the same directional tendency 20 seconds after their release as they do when they disappear from sight 2 to 4 minutes later (see also Kramer, 1957).

The study of homing over short distances is extremely important in connection with the question of the role of the sun. Since this chapter is relatively complex it will be treated under a new heading.

D. SHORT-DISTANCE ORIENTATION

At first glance it seems sensible to assume that birds homing from short distances, say, up to 35 miles, are guided by familiar landmarks. Such reasoning is conservative in that it makes use of a known sensory organ, but it is also anthropomorphic because in going beyond the purely optical qualities of the eye it takes for granted high faculties of configurative vision and correction of perspective distortion thus far only known to exist in man. The facts cited below indicate that the so-called short-distance orientation is at least partially based on other than visual orientation:

(a) Homing is affected by an overcast sky in a similar manner over short distances as over long ones. Even if the loft area is visible to the naked human eye, both initial orientation and homing success are hindered by a high overcast [minimum distance thus far: 7.5 miles; (Kramer, 1957)].

(b) Direction effect is noticeable down to a distance of 5 miles (Kramer et al., 1958). It is difficult to understand how visual recognition of landmarks or of a landscape complex could be consistently easier from one direction than from another. A particularly significant example of direction effect is the fact that the majority of pigeons released from one location $15\frac{1}{2}$ miles east of Wilhelmshaven fly off in the opposite direction without any known physiographic reason for doing so (Wallraff, unpublished).

(c) Homing ability is greatly impaired in winter even at short distances. Wallraff (1957) has recently demonstrated a distinct correlation to temperature. It is not known whether the cold affects the pigeon itself or the physical basis of the orienting mechanism. The bird's reproductive state, which might be suspected to play a part by controlling the homing impulse, is not significant: artificial stimulation of the breeding activity of part of the test birds did not increase homing success. Any suggestion that cold weather acts by changing landscape features has been excluded because some of the birds had not seen the test area except in winter conditions (Kramer and von St. Paul, 1956). At any rate it cannot be assumed that cold affects their capacity to understand topography.

(d) Departure patterns and homing success vary from day to day in a manner that cannot be explained in terms of any conventionally recorded weather factor (Wallraff, unpublished).

The demonstration of the participation of an unknown mechanism in short-distance orientation provides indirect evidence against sun navigation. Until proof of the contrary is obtained, it can be assumed that the orienting mechanism used in homing over short distances is used over long distances as well.

The consideration of short-distance orientation leads to a discussion of experimental results on birds whose internal rhythm has been phase-shifted.

E. The Map-and-Compass Concept and the Effect of the Shifted "Clock"; Further Discussion of Orientation by Topographic Clues

All conjectures on the mechanism of homing orientation must take into account the paradox of initial orientation being lessened, or even abolished, by an overcast sky on the one hand, and the existence of substantial evidence disproving sun navigation on the other, at least within the range of distances so far considered. This situation led to the assumption that the entire performance of homing orientation is achieved in two independent steps (Kramer, 1953). The first would consist of establishing the geographic position of the release site relative to the home site, including the "theoretical" homing direction.

The latter is an immediate deduction from the first: both, therefore, are considered as one step and are called the "map" constituent. The second step would consist of ascertaining the deduced homing direction in the field. This, in the analogous human performance, is usually done by means of a compass; it is therefore called the "compass" step. As the bird is known to use the sun for direction finding, lack of initial orientation with overcast skies would be sufficiently explained in the framework of this concept. Since position finding—as conceived in the two-step concept—is unaffected by the sun, the only step that the seemingly disoriented birds are unable to perform is the "compass" step. Repeated determination of position, however, should produce the homing direction in the field by triangulation. Therefore, birds released under overcast sky should not be lost, but merely hindered in getting their initial orientation quickly. This, of course, would also produce poorer homing. This is exactly what is observed.

The map-and-compass concept cannot properly be called a hypothesis for the same reason that nobody would care to call the old belief in a "sense of site" or "sense of position" a hypothesis. Nevertheless an organization of the problem is attained with the help of the two-step formulation. For instance it may be concluded that in a number of "effects" described above—such as direction effect, winter effect, and day-to-day variations—it must be the map constituent that is affected.

The two-step concept suggested also an experimental approach which starts from our knowledge that shifting the physiological rhythm (in other words, resetting the internal clock) produces predictable alterations of direction finding. If in goal orientation the sun gives only bearings, a shifted clock should produce the same alterations as in direction finding: clock shifted forward, counter clockwise; backward, clockwise. This expectation was already tentatively confirmed in one of a small number of long-distance releases made by K. and A. Rawson (1953, unpublished). Since then Schmidt-Koenig (1958) has demonstrated, by comparing with controls, the behavior of a large series of pigeons whose phase had been shifted 6 hours forward (Fig. 3). The result was an average deviation of 66° counter clockwise in the vanishing directions, and a corresponding deviation in the extended flight route, as indicated by the pattern of recoveries and reduced homing success. Shifting effect was observed down to the shortest release made, 5.5 miles, although it was very weak at that distance. These results, beyond supporting the map-and-compass concept, cast interesting light on short-distance orientation by showing that pigeons can be thrown off course within easy sight of their home area. In addition, Schmidt-Koenig used largely the same two classes of pigeons throughout a long series of releases, each time alternating their role as test or control birds, thus minimising the importance of landmark recognition.

Visual landmark orientation, even at short distances, it has now become obvious, plays a subordinate role in several instances. Neither would high overcast and low temperatures be expected to have such an

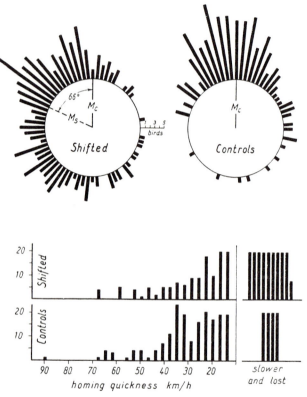

FIG. 3. Upper part: Frequency distribution of departure directions of pigeons whose "internal clock" was set forward six hours, and of controls treated the same way except that the artificial day-night cycle was in phase with the astronomical one. Lower part: Histograms showing the homing success of both groups. After Schmidt-Koenig (1958).

obvious bearing upon home finding, nor could the direction effect at short distances exist, or at least be evident, if there existed effective ability to utilize topographic features. Indirect evidence for another unknown orientation mechanism has been provided above; however, the existence of such a mechanism is *directly* demonstrated by re-orientation enforced by a shifted rhythm. The same experiment discounts the importance of landmarks in two different ways: indirectly, by stressing the role of other, unknown clues; and directly, by showing that the birds reject topography instead of yielding to it.

Nevertheless, evidence for topographic orientation in homing pigeons is not altogether negative. Griffin (1952a) was successful in predicting flight directions after his assumption that the pigeons would take to misleading shorelines similar to familiar ones. Pratt (1957) observed that pigeons whose loft site was in a settled area were attracted, shortly after being released elsewhere, by the outskirts of another town. It must therefore be concluded that the ability to pilot by topographic properties is not absent, but rather inefficient, being based on general features and dominated normally by other means of orientation. This is particularly so if good clues of the other sort are available. There are, in fact, solid grounds for admitting regional differences in this regard (see page 354).

Simple landmark recognition in wild species has been demonstrated by Lashley (see Watson and Lashley, 1915) in terns within the close range of their nesting site. Laven (1949) analyzed the importance of proximate landmarks for nest finding in the ring-necked plover. Signs at a distance of 75 cm. or less lead to an accurate localization of the nest site. As the distance of available landmarks increases, the accuracy of nest finding drops rapidly. If a tent at a distance of 30 meters was left as the closest landmark available, searching activity spread over a range of 15–20 meters. (The total width of the beach used as a biotope was only 20–30 meters.) In the herring gull, Goethe (1937) found the recognition of the nesting site to be somewhat more complex. Lorenz' (1927) first tame jackdaw appeared to be unfamiliar with territory beyond a distance of 200 meters from its home cage, at least in its first autumn, although it made much more distant excursions in company with its master and with other corvids. Lorenz himself thinks that, in this particular case, the home range was abnormally small. Nevertheless, this example further tends to make us revise the generally accepted view of the large size of the "target" that the homing bird must hit with the help of a mechanism other than that based on landmarks. The target size suggested by Griffin (1952) in his analysis of exploration (greatest diameter of target is equal to half the distance of displacement, or is even greater) is considerably too large for pigeons and probably also for wild birds.

Recent experiments by Gould (1959) on box turtles (*Terrapene carolina*) revealed an orientation faculty independent of visual landmarks (distances tested: 0.28 to 5.6 miles). When the sun was visible, the turtles steered toward their living area. When the sun was occluded by clouds, they walked at random, their behavior thus agreeing perfectly with the map-and-compass concept. Box turtles may well be better subjects than homing pigeons for investigating certain aspects of bird orientation. In view of the common origin of birds and reptiles, it may be tentatively assumed that they are endowed with the same basic means of orientation.

F. Other Attempts to Explain Goal Finding.
A Final Consideration of Astronomical Navigation

Redirection obtained by a shifted clock makes it clear that homing cannot be achieved by direct sensory contact. The same experimental result also disposes of the hypothesis that birds retrace their journey. In a more general way it may be said that all evidence pointing to the map-and-compass concept (i.e. to separating direction finding from a previously obtained determination of position), militates against a suggestion of direct perception of the home, or of the retracing of the route of transportation. Several experimenters, furthermore, subjected their birds during transportation to influences tending to confuse or exclude impressions that might be used in tracing their paths. No difference whatsoever was observed as a result of such measures. It is not within the scope of this short survey to review all the explanations of position finding suggested thus far (see review by Matthews, 1955), but two recent theories, said by their proponents to be substantiated by factual evidence, should not be passed over.

Yeagley (1947, 1951) maintains that birds, pigeons in particular, use a two-coordinate system of navigation based on two geophysical fields, namely, the Coriolis field and the vertical component of the geomagnetic field. As the axes of these two fields diverge, their isolines intersect at a rather obtuse angle. Yeagley's hypothesis raised intense criticism, summarized in Matthews' book (1955). One of Yeagley's tests, the magnetic wing experiment, was repeated by several workers with negative results. Yeagley's theory was even more easily disproved because his own factual evidence did not withstand critical examination.

Matthews' hypothesis (1955) of homing orientation is a particular variant of the sun navigation hypothesis. Its distinguishing feature consists of the very short time given the bird for the procedure of measuring and comparing sun arcs, i.e. only 2 to 3 minutes, instead of the much longer period of time required by human methods. The sun-arc hypothesis, as originally formulated, is subject to a number of theoretical doubts, but one can reformulate it to make it theoretically sound. However, this reformulation would increase the prerequisites concerning the bird's faculties very considerably, mainly, because the sun's path, to be measured by the bird in respect to the horizon, is a sinusoidal curve rather than a circle. This circumstance makes it much more difficult for the bird to extrapolate the curve of the sun's path (Kramer, 1957).

Since any explanation of such a seemingly miraculous phenomenon as homing orientation is bound to sound incredible, the theoretical aspect of the sun-arc hypothesis should not arouse undue scepticism. A matter of greater consequence is that the whole bulk of evidence against sun navigation in general is equally valid against Matthews' variant.

In addition, important elements of Matthews' method of demonstration are open to criticism (Kramer, 1957). It was also impossible to reproduce in Wilhelmshaven (Kramer, 1957) and Cambridge (Hoffmann, 1958) Matthews' result in relation to what was believed to be one of the principal supports of the sun-arc hypothesis, namely the sun-occlusion experiment.

Although it is held that Matthews' hypothesis has been disproved, bicoordinate sun navigation in general cannot be ruled out as a method in goal finding. So far there is no evidence in its favour. The effect of a screened sun cannot be adduced as such evidence in view of the short distances at which it is observed. What remains is a general doubt that sun navigation could be at work at very long distances (which are not considered in the experiments so far conducted) and, perhaps, in species (e.g. sea birds) other than the homing pigeon. Shearwaters in particular are known to home over enormous distances (Matthews, 1953).

Similar doubts are admissible with regard to navigation by stars, by which more accurate information could be gained than by the sun (see below). We do not know if nocturnal migrants home in daytime, or by night, when displaced from their nest, nor can it be excluded that birds have a better ability to detect stars in daylight than has man. Such considerations do not weaken the conclusion that there exists a method of position finding independent of astronomical navigation.

We are not yet able to make any trustworthy statement about even the sensory modality responsible for goal orientation. The conjecture that vision is responsible is scarcely more than a mere generalization taken from other analysed mechanisms of orientation. Hochbaum (1955, pp. 64–72) released 81 hooded birds of various species without observing an active choice of any particular direction. These and other observations on the behavior of blindfolded birds are probably of small importance: it is obvious that the general disturbance caused by blindfolding might well suppress the more refined functions involved.

There is in at least one species a "distance" orientation mechanism that is not based upon vision. Griffin (1953) proved that the oilbird (*Steatornis caripensis*) uses echo location in finding its way about the completely dark caves where it spends the daylight hours and in which it nests. The oilbird emits clicking sounds in bursts separated by short intervals. Each click is of very short duration—about 1 millisecond— and consists of only a few sound waves with a frequency around 7000 cycles per second. Birds with ears experimentally plugged were unable to avoid collisions with the walls of a dark room, but flew with safety after removal of the plugs. It is possible that the oilbird uses sound orientation not only in the caves, but also during the nocturnal excursions outside. Nevertheless, in the context of a discussion on goal-finding ability in the traditional sense, a decisive role of echolocation can be excluded even if it were present in other bird species. While this orientation method constitutes a highly specialized device in a cave-dwelling animal, its range is necessarily limited to a multiple of about 10 meters at the most. In view of the higher frequencies used by bats, it is supposed that the effective range of their echo location considerably exceeds the conjectural figure suggested above for the oilbird's range.

V. Nocturnal Orientation

F. and L. Sauer's (1955) round-cage experiments on warblers (*Sylvia*) amplified Kramer's (1950) findings. The Sauers observed clear-cut directional tendencies in spring and autumn. Their observations further indicated that birds pay very close attention to details of the sky. The occurrence of a shooting star, for instance, was consistently followed by a temporary disturbance in the directional tendency of their migratory activity. Tests conducted under the artificial sky of a planetarium clearly demonstrated that the Blackcap (*Sylvia atricapilla*), the Garden warbler (*S. borin*), and the Lesser Whitethroat (*S. curruca*) used the stars to orientate themselves (cf. comprehensive paper by F. Sauer, 1957). Directional tendencies under artificial skies that imitate the local skies of a given season and time of day were clear-cut during both seasons of migration.

It is particularly remarkable that even individuals that had never before seen the nocturnal sky (one *S. atricapilla*, one *S. borin*) were oriented from the very beginning. On the basis of the evidence available, it is difficult to avoid the conclusion that the entire faculty of night orientation is inherited.

When the Lesser Whitethroat (*Sylvia curruca*), was shown skies longitudinally different from the local sky, it usually responded to such gross changes by altering its direction tendencies. In a series of tests involving longitudinal displacements to the east amounting to as much as 60°, the bird clearly altered its course accordingly by heading in a westerly direction. This indicates true bicoordinate navigation. Such a correction was not observed in the case of changes simulating westward displacements, however. When the same bird was shown skies corresponding to increasingly lower latitudes, it gradually shifted its course from SE to due S in a manner corresponding to the natural migratory route.

In evaluating the reactions of the birds to simulated changes of position, two circumstances of these planetarium tests must be taken into account: (1) The artificial sky stood still and its time adjustment was consistently retarded corresponding to westerly displacements of as much as 15° longitude or, in a few cases, even more. (2) The test cage had to be placed excentrically in the planetarium, the center of the room being occupied by the projector. In most cases the cage was placed south of center. As the dome was only 6 meters in diameter, parallactic distortion was unavoidable. Even the displacement of the bird as it moved about the cage must have caused parallactic "leaps." The total effect of these unavoidable technical shortcomings may have been such that the navigating performance displayed by the birds was far from their best. For instance, the frequent lag in time may well have produced hardening against westward displacement.

The evidence adduced by Sauer is on the whole so convincing, and refers to such a central point of the orientation complex, that it should be considered in detail in this context even if some minor conflicts have emerged. The first has already been mentioned: the Lesser Whitethroat did not correct for feigned westward displacements, although it did so for eastward displacements. Another difficulty is caused by the evidence for true bicoordinate navigation on the one hand, and the fact that clear-cut spring orientation was observed both under artificial and natural skies although these corresponded to the approximate breeding area. A third conflict will be mentioned, and tentatively explained, on page 368.

It has not been determined yet what celestial features are the principal orienting clues for the bird, but all evidence indicates that it is not a pattern of general brightness. The blanketing of limited areas of the sky by opaque clouds causes no disorientation. It does, however, cause changes of direction. These are probably attempts to avoid the overcast areas. If the sky is slightly overcast to the extent that it is probably impossible for the bird to observe the course of the Milky Way, but not so overcast as to obscure the major stars, the bird does not become disoriented even though it is less accurate in maintaining its course. In all tests, the sky zone lower than about 35° above the horizon was not shown. The clues used are probably of a configurative nature, the bird recognizing and evaluating geometrical correlations of stars and, very likely, distinguishing between constellations.

If this supposition is true, it excludes the simple way of dealing with the azimuth change as demonstrated in sun orientation, because the progression in azimuth of circumpolar stars and stars low on the horizon is considerably different. If this difference is allowed for by the bird, it signifies virtually the introduction of a second coordinate, which by itself would bring star orientation close to true navigation.

In contrast to use of the sun, if bearings are taken from constellations, position finding is fundamentally possible without direct observation of

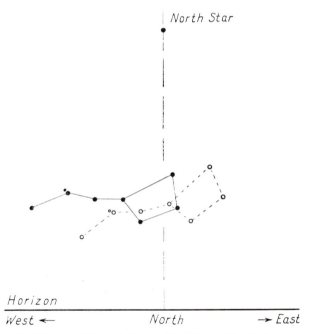

FIG. 4. The Big Dipper half hour before and half hour after its lower culmination.

their motion in the sky, providing the time of day and time of year are known. Figure 4 shows the position of the Big Dipper half an hour before and after its lower culmination. Despite the fact that the center of gravity of the constellation is at the same height above the horizon in both cases, the two-dimensional extent of the constellation yields criteria not available by observation of individual celestial bodies. In a similar case, observation of the sun would yield an ambiguous result even if only longitude were taken as a variable. If the latitude is also a variable, ambiguity is considerably increased. Observation of a constellation, on the other hand, leads to only one interpretation if only the longitude is unknown. If the latitude is unknown, too, even then more extensive relationships between constellations and/or stars would lead to an unambiguous interpretation.

VI. Facts of Visible Migration versus Experimental Evidence

Since a great deal of daylight migration of small birds proceeds out of the reach of the naked human eye it is difficult to decide how migration frequencies with clear sky and high overcast compare quantitatively. In any case migration with overcast skies is normal. Hence, a question to be answered is how orientation is achieved under such circumstances. There are two possibilities: (1) The birds use auxiliary clues temporarily to maintain their course. (2) They make use of fundamentally different means of orientation.

Indication that the first alternative may be the solution is found in the directional perseverance observed by Kramer (1951) in experiments on the starling. In these experiments such observed perseverance can be explained partly by visual criteria inside a stationary pavilion and partly by kinesthetic criteria. Observation of the direction of flight of migrating starlings made by L. Tinbergen and co-workers (1954, 1956) revealed gradual increase of directional scatter on successive cloudy days, but, when the sun shone again for 2 hours on one afternoon, the starlings were next morning sharply oriented, despite the fact that the sun was again hidden. This would indicate that the starlings, while resting during the afternoon, made use of the sun to reset their compass adjustment in relation to landmarks so that again they had bearings to go by the next morning, even if the sun did not shine. Observation of chaffinches also revealed increasing deviation of direction during three successive days without sun (Mook et al., 1957).

The foregoing does not prove that use is not also made of other means of orientation. Perdeck (1957) demonstrated by the round-cage method that a starling caught on the autumn passage displayed satisfactory precision in its southwest tendency as long as the sun was visible. When the sky became overcast, the bird was disoriented at first, but managed to get its bearings again when the sky remained overcast for a period of several days. Field observation of migrating birds over hilly ground under a heavy blanket of haze in the early morning revealed orientation that is difficult to attribute to persistent guidance by visual clues (Sutter, 1957). Here it may also be mentioned that

Precht and co-workers (1956) have obtained indicative evidence that gulls displaced from their nesting colony strive toward their home site, despite their being prevented from viewing either their surroundings or the sun. These tests, which were made in a round cage, need confirmation.

Thus, on the whole, it may be said that the findings obtained on diurnal migrants by means of widely different methods agree satisfactorily as far as classification has been obtained at all. It is safe to say that birds steer by the sun outside as well as inside the laboratory. On the other hand, observations on caged migrant birds, as well as results with homing pigeons, coupled with field observations, all converge to indicate that there exist means of orientation still unknown to us.

The same cannot be said for nocturnal orientation. It has long been known that drifting plays a role in night migration. This has been determined by indirect observation (location of resting birds) as well as by the direct method (moon observation; Lowery, 1951). Field observers have gone so far as to conclude that tail-wind orientation is an essential part of night orientation (Lowery), or that flight direction by night is regularly affected by wind drift and requires "redetermination" in daytime (Nisbet, 1957). It should be noted, however, that well-directed night migration regardless of wind direction has been directly observed by Bullis (1954) in Lowery's general observation area. Dinnendahl (1954), by analyzing trapping results of Vogelwarte Heligoland, tested the possible correlation between wind direction and migration over the North Sea on 241 nights: no correlation was observed. It was previously ascertained that off-shore winds did not favor the passage over Heligoland, a fact in itself arguing against drift effects.

Since it may now be considered proved that birds orientate themselves by means of the stars, it can no longer be assumed that drift has a positive function in night migration. As it is certain that nocturnal migrants often cannot see the ground (for instance, when flying over water) correction for drift can at most be approximate. Without reference to the ground, wind direction can be judged only by variations in wind speed. At the higher altitudes, however, the winds are very steady. This concerns drift displacements of a smaller scale, where control of position by star navigation cannot be efficient. The hazard of gross drifting displacements is particularly great when a high overcast cuts off a view of the sky while the birds are flying over water, where they cannot interrupt their flight, nor can receive information by star navigation. Thus it seems likely that drifting occurs more frequently at night than during the day. It is, however, probably only an unimportant and easily remedied disadvantage of a principle of orientation, the advantages of which far outweigh its defects. One is even tempted to think that it is this possibility of achieving orientation by stars which has helped to make many day-loving species change to nocturnal migration.

It is at present a matter of individual conjecture whether or not night orientation has been completely explained by the important discovery of star navigation. Since there are marked gaps in our knowledge about diurnal orientation, it seems wise to conclude that similar, if not identical, gaps occur in our knowledge about nocturnal orientation as well.

There are good reasons for ascribing a high degree of habitual constancy in the maintenance of migrating routes, particularly by birds that migrate in family flocks [mainly geese and cranes (see Hochbaum, 1955)]. Such habits probably do not replace innate elements in choosing the migratory direction, but they have a compensating effect upon the progress of wandering. Since fresh-water ponds suitable for feeding and resting are scarce enough even in primeval conditions, waterfowl particularly need fixed routes for their journeys. Since waterfowl are more amenable to experimental treatment than most other birds, it should be possible to subject geese (e.g. *Branta canadensis*) to field experiments similar to those made with storks and crows (see page 342). Even if it were proved that the movements of geese are chains of sub-goals until the final wintering quarter is reached it should nevertheless be remembered that this would not decide anything about the mechanism of orientation used.

This leads to a consideration of the phenomenon of "hooked" or angled migration routes. As an example, the route of starlings originating from the Baltic area may be chosen. Their general direction in the fall is W to SSW, as appears from the results obtained by Rossitten and Texel bands. When the birds approach the coast of the English Channel, at least certain populations must definitely change their directional tendency, otherwise they would not reach England and Ireland. As quoted above (page 343), Perdeck transferred such starlings to the south just before they turned to the north. After they were released these birds did not show the "hook" but went on SSW (only birds of the year behave in this manner). These results may possibly suggest that the shift takes place only in a given stimulus situation and would thus confirm suggestions made by Schüz (1951, p. 266).

VII. Birds and Bees

Flights of the magnitude of several miles are routine for honey-gathering bees. Their ability to find their way depends on impressions received either by social contact with fellow bees, or by personal acquisition of knowledge of the route. As far as it is yet known, a bee when displaced in a shielded box can fly home oriented only if it is released within the range of familiar landmarks. Otherwise homing is attributable to diligent search and chance.

Birds and bees thus differ in that the latter have no "primary" home-finding ability. They also differ with regard to sensory physiology. Whereas the sun-orienting ability of birds is inactivated when the sun and its surrounding glow are hidden, bees have a highly specialized auxiliary mechanism that permits them to locate the sun even if only small portions of blue sky are visible. Bees perceive the planes of oscillation of polarized light that form a characteristic pattern around the sun (von Frisch, 1956). Birds have no power to do so (Kramer, 1953a; Sauer, 1957).

Lindauer (1957) has demonstrated that bees from India can orient themselves by the sun in Munich, provided they are given time to become familiar with the path of the sun in that part of the world. Lindauer has shown, too, that Bavarian bees, unexposed to the sun until gathering maturity (after 4 weeks of imaginal life) were unable to allow for the sun's motion. Indeed, they still failed to do so after 4 days' experience. Six weeks later, however, they were able to do so. Hoffmann's (1953) experiences, on the contrary, tend to indicate that estimation of azimuth speed and direction of motion of the sun is endogenously fixed and probably innate. Sauer's experiences with warblers, which gave well-directed orientation responses when exposed to the starry sky for the first time in their life, further add to the evidence in favor of a tightly fixed framework for the use of celestial geometry in navigation. A contradiction seems to exist between this result of Sauer, and another well-proved fact, that the "home" is established during the individual's life, mainly at a determinate period (see page 343). It may well be that the two facts refer to different ranges. A wider range specific to species or races, including all steps along the migrating route plus the wintering area, may be represented by inherited ability to respond to astronomical clues, while the attachment to a more narrowly circumscribed area is acquired.

The differential observations made on bees indicate that additional experiments on birds are highly desirable in order that more light may be thrown on this further radical difference in the nature of orienting mechanisms of bees and birds.

References

Bullis, H. R. (1954). Trans-gulf migration, Spring 1952. *Auk* **71**: 298–305.

Dinnendahl, L. (1954). Nächtlicher Zug und Windrichtung auf Helgoland. *Vogelwarte* **17**: 188–194.

Drost, R. (1939). Über den Einfluss von Verfrachtungen zur Herbstzugzeit auf den Sperber, *Accipiter nisus* (L.). *Proc. 9th Intern. Ornithol. Congr. Rouen 1938* pp. 503–521.

Frisch, K. von (1956). The "language" and the orientation of the bees. *Proc. Am. Phil. Soc.* **100**: 515–519.

Goethe, F. (1937). Beobachtungen und Untersuchungen zur Biologie der Silbermöwe (*Larus a. argentatus Pontopp.*) auf der Vogelinsel Memmertsand. *J. Ornithol.* **85**: 1–119.

Gould, E. (1957). Orientation in box turtles, *Terrapene c. carolina* (L.). *Biol. Bull.* **112**: 336–348.

Griffin, D. R. (1943). Homing experiments with Herring Gulls (*Larus argentatus*) and Common Terns (*Sterna hirundo*). *Bird Banding* **14**: 7–33.

Griffin, D. R. (1952a). Airplane observations of homing pigeons. *Bull. Museum Comp. Anat.* **107**: 411–440.

Griffin, D. R. (1952b). Bird navigation. *Biol. Revs. Cambridge Phil. Soc.* **27**: 359–393.

Griffin, D. R. (1953). Acoustic orientation in the Oil Bird, *Steatornis. Proc. Natl. Acad. Sc. U. S.* **39**: 884–893.

Heinroth, O., and Heinroth, K. (1941). Das Heimfindevermögen der Brieftauben. *J. Ornithol.* **89**: 213–256.

Hochbaum, H. A. (1955). "Travels and Traditions of Waterfowl." *St. Paul, Minnesota.*

Hoffmann, K. (1953). Die Einrechnung der Sonnenwanderung bei der Richtungsweisung des sonnenlos aufgezogenen Stars. *Naturwissenschaften* **40**: 148.

Hoffmann, K. (1954). Versuche zu der im Richtungsfinden der Vögel enthaltenen Zeitschätzung. *Z. Tierpsychol.* **11**: 453–475.

Hoffmann, K. (1958). Repetition of an experiment on bird orientation. *Nature* **181**: 1435–1437.

Kramer, G. (1949). Über Richtungstendenzen bei der nächtlichen Zugunruhe gekäfigter Vögel. *In* "Ornithologie als Biologische Wissenschaft" (E. Mayr and E. Schüz, eds.) pp. 269–283. C. Winter, Heidelberg.

Kramer, G. (1950a). Orientierte Zugaktivität gekäfigter Singvögel. *Naturwissenschaften* **37**: 188.

Kramer, G. (1950b). Weitere Analyse der Faktoren, welche die Zugaktivität des gekäfigten Vogels orientieren. *Naturwissenschaften* **37**: 377–378.

Kramer, G. (1951). Eine neue Methode zur Erforschung der Zugorientierung und die bisher damit erzielten Ergebnisse. *Proc. 10th Intern. Ornithol. Congr. Upsala,* pp. 269–280.

Kramer, G. (1952). Experiments on bird orientation. *Ibis* **94**: 265–285.

Kramer, G. (1953a). Die Sonnenorientierung der Vögel. *Verhandl. deutsch. zool. Ges. Freiburg 1952*: 72–84.

Kramer, G. (1953b). Wird die Sonnenhöhe bei der Heimfindeorientierung verwertet? *J. Ornithol.* **94**: 201–219.

Kramer, G. (1957). Experiments on bird orientation and their interpretation. *Ibis* **99**: 196–227.

Kramer, G. (1958). Über die Heimfindeleistung unter Sichtbegrenzung aufgewachsener Brieftauben. *Verhandl. deutsch. zool. Ges. Frankfurt 1958*: 168–176.

Kramer, G., Pratt, J. G., and von St. Paul, U. (1958). Neue Untersuchungen über den "Richtungseffekt." *J. Ornithol.* **99**: 178–191.

Kramer, G., and von St. Paul, U. (1954). Das Heimkehrvermögen gekäfigter Brieftauben. *Ornithol. Beobachter* **51**: 3–12.

Kramer, G., and von St. Paul, U. (1956). Weitere Erfahrungen über den "Wintereffekt" beim Heimfindevermögen von Brieftauben. *J. Ornithol.* **97**: 353–370.

Kramer, G., Pratt, J. G., and von St. Paul, U. (1956). Directional differences in pigeon homing. *Science* **123**: 329–330.

Kramer, G., Pratt, J. G., and von St. Paul, U. (1957). Two-direction experiments with homing pigeons and their bearing on the problem of goal orientation. *Am. Naturalist* **91**: 37–48.

Krätzig, H., and Schüz, E. (1936). Ergebnis der Versetzung ostbaltischer Stare ins Binnenland. *Vogelzug* **7**: 163–175.

Laven, H. (1949). Vögel als Augentiere. *In* "Ornithologie als Biologische Wissenschaft" (E. Mayr and E. Schüz, eds.), pp. 147–152. C. Winter, Heidelberg.

Lindauer, M. (1957). Sonnenorientierung der Bienen unter der Äquatorsonne und zur Nachtzeit. *Naturwissenschaften* **44**: 1–6.

Löhrl. H. (1957). Zur Frage des Zeitpunktes einer Prägung auf die Heimatregion beim Halsbandschnäpper (Ficedula albicollis). *In litteros.*

Lorenz, K. (1927). Beobachtungen an Dohlen. *J. Ornithol.* **75**: 511–519.

Lowery, G. H. (1951). A quantitative study of the nocturnal migration of birds. *Publs. Museum Natl. Hist. Univ. Kansas* **3**: 361–472.

Matthews, G. V. T. (1952). An investigation of homing ability in two species of gulls. *Ibis* **94**: 243–264.

Matthews, G. V. T. (1953). Navigation in the Manx Shearwater. *J. Exptl. Biol.* **30**: 370–396.

Matthews, G. V. T. (1955). "Bird navigation." Cambridge Univ. Press, London and New York.

Mauersberger, G. (1957). Umsiedlungsversuche am Trauerschnäpper (Muscicapa hypoleuca), durchgeführt in der Sowjetunion. *J. Ornithol.* **98**: 445–447.

Mook, J. H., Rooth, J., and Zijlstra, J. J. (1957). Stichting Vogeltrekstation Texel 1956: De Vogeltrekwaarnemingen op de Noord-Veluwe. *Limosa* **30**: 76–83.

Nisbet, I. C. T. (1957). Passerine migration in South Scandinavia in the autumn of 1954. *Ibis* **99**: 228.

Perdeck, A. C. (1954). Jaarverslag 1953. *Jversl. Vogeltrekst. Texel* **1953**: 3–13.

Perdeck A. C. (1957). Stichting Vogeltrekstation Texel Jaarverslag over 1956. *Limosa* **30**: 62–75.

Pratt, J. G. (1957). Research on animal orientation, with emphasis on the phenomenon of homing in pigeons. *Annual Progress Report* **1956**, Nr. 160/244.

Pratt, J. G., and Thouless, R. (1955). Homing orientation in pigeons in relation to opportunity to observe the sun before release. *J. Exptl. Biol.* **32**: 140–157.

Pratt, J. G., and Wallraff, H. G. (1958). Zwei-Richtungsversuche mit Brieftauben: Langstreckenflüge auf der Nord-Süd-Achse in Westdeutschland. *Z. Tierpsychol.* **15**: 332–339.

Precht, H., and co-workers (1956). Einige Versuche zum Heimfindevermogen von Vögeln. *J. Ornithol.* **97**: 377–383.

Rowan, W. (1946). Experiments in bird migration. *Trans. Roy. Soc. Can. V* [3] **40**: 123–135.

Rüppell, W. (1935). Heimfindeversuche mit Staren 1934. *J. Ornithol.* **83**: 462–524.

Rüppell, W. (1936). Heimfindeversuche mit Staren und Schwalben 1935. *J. Ornithol.* **84**: 180–198.

Rüppell, W. (1937). Heimfindeversuche mit Staren, Rauchschwalben, Wendehälsen, Rotrückenwürgern und Habichten 1936. *J. Ornithol.* **85**: 120–135.

Rüppell, W. (1944). Versuche über das Heimfinden ziehender Nebelkrähen nach Verfrachtung. *J. Ornithol.* **92**: 106–132.

Rüppell, W., and Schüz, E. (1948). Ergebnisse der Verfrachtung von Nebelkrähen während des Wegzugs. *Vogelwarte* **15**: 30–36.

Saint-Paul, U. von (1953). Nachweis der Sonnenorientierung bei nächtlich ziehenden Vögeln. *Behaviour* **6**: 1–7.

Saint-Paul, U. von (1956). Compass directional training of western meadowlarks (*Sturnella neglecta*). *Auk* **73**: 203–210.

Sauer, F., and Sauer, L. (1955). Zur Frage der nächtlichen Zugorientierung von Grasmücken. *Rev. suisse Zool.* **62**: 250–259.

Sauer, F. (1957). Die Sternenorientierung nächtlich ziehender Grasmücken. *Z. Tierpsychol.* **14**: 29–70.

Schmidt-Koenig, K. (1958). Der Einfluss experimentell veränderter Zeitschätzung auf das Heimfindevermögen bei Brieftauben. *Naturwissenschaften* **45**: 47.

Schüz, E. (1943). Versuche über die Bindung des weissen Storchs an seinen Aufzuchtort. *Vogelzug* **14**: 137–141.

Schüz, E. (1949). Die Spätauflassung ostpreussischer Jungstörche in Westdeutschland 1933. *Vogelwarte* **15**: 63–78.

Schüz, E. (1950). Früh-Auflassung ostpreussischer Jungstörche in Westdeutschland durch die Vogelwarte Rossitten 1933–1936. *Bonn. Zool. Beitr.* **1**: 239–253.

Schüz, E. (1951). Überblick über die Orientierungsversuche der Vogelwarte Rossitten (jetzt: Vogelwarte Radolfzell). *Proc. 10th Intern. Ornithol. Congr. Upsala* pp. 249–268.

Schüz, E. (1952). "Vom Vogelzug." P. Schöps, Frankfurt-Main.

Sutter, E. (1957). Radar als Hilfsmittel der Vogelzugforschung. *Ornithol. Beobachter* **54**: 70–96.

Thauziès, M. A. (1910). L'oriéntation lointaine. *Proc. 6th Congr. Intern. Psychol. Geneve 1909* pp. 263–280.

Thienemann, J. (1931). "Vom Vogelzug in Rossitten." J. Neumann, Neudamm.

Thomson, A. L. (1926). "Problems of Bird Migration." H. F. and G. Witherby, London.

Tinbergen, L., and Zijlstra, J. J. (1954). De veldwaarnemingen: een schakel die ontbrak. *Jversl. Vogeltrekst. Texel. 1953*: 14–22.

Tinbergen, L. (1956). Field observations of migration and their significance for the problems of migration. *Ardea* **44**: 231.

Wallraff, H. G. (1957). Korrelation zwischen Heimfindevermögen von Brieftauben und Temperatur. *Naturwissenschaften* **44**: 568–569.

Watson, J. B., and Lashley, K. S. (1915). Homing and related activities of birds. *Papers Tortugas Lab.* **7**: 5–83.

Wilkinson, D. H. (1952). The random element in bird "navigation." *J. Exptl. Biol.* **29**: 532–560.

Yeagley, H. L. (1947). A preliminary study of a physical basis of bird navigation. *J. Appl. Phys.* **18**: 1035–1063.

Yeagley, H. L. (1951). A preliminary study of a physical basis of bird navigation. II. *J. Appl. Phys.* **22**: 746–760.

CHAPTER XXIII

Behavior

R. A. HINDE

I. Introduction

Birds evolved from diapsid stock, the earliest known specimens having been found in Jurassic rocks. Like many other aspects of their anatomy, the brain structure provides evidence of their reptilian affinities: the large striatal regions and the pallial areas are similar in many respects to those of modern lizards, and very different from those of mammals. Partly because plasticity of behavior is often held to be characteristic of the mammalian line, and partly because their brain structure suggests an accentuation of trends to be seen in lizards, the behavior of birds is often contrasted with that of mammals as "rigid," "stereotyped," or "almost entirely instinctive." Such generalizations are overstatements. Although every species of bird has a large repertoire of more or less stereotyped responses, so has every mammal. The feeding behavior of the horse is no more plastic than that of the great tit, and species-characteristic responses play their part in the sexual behavior of the rat just as they do in that of the chaffinch. In fact, birds' capabilities for learning are comparable in many respects with those of most mammals.

This marked learning ability, coupled with the large repertoire of striking and thus easily recognizable "instinctive" patterns possessed by each species, render birds a particularly interesting group for the study of behavior. Progress in this work has been facilitated by the similarities between their sensory capacities and those of man. Further, birds are numerous and widespread, and many species make excellent laboratory animals. They have undergone a marked adaptive radiation, so that many types of life history and many variations on behavioral themes are found within the group—and their aesthetic appeal has ensured that the necessary foundation of a broad knowledge of their natural history has been securely laid.

In view of these facts, it is not surprising that the literature on bird behavior already fills many thousand scientific papers and innumerable volumes. A number of excellent reviews of parts of this field are already available. The earlier work is discussed by Maier and Schneirla (1935) and by Warden et al. (1936). Nice (1943) has placed her own classic work on the song sparrow (*Melospiza melodia*) against a comprehensive analysis of observations on other species, and Armstrong (1947) has summarized much of the literature on reproductive behavior. More recently, Tinbergen (1951) has set out some principles underlying the "instinctive" behavior of birds, and Thorpe (1956) has reviewed the literature on avian learning.

It is thus unnecessary, as well as impracticable, to attempt a broad survey of the study of bird behavior here. Rather attention has been concentrated on some of the more recent work in this field, many aspects of natural history on the one hand and physiology on the other being omitted. Further, many of the more controversial issues have been bypassed. Since bird behavior has been studied by physiologists and zoologists, psychologists and naturalists, systematists and ecologists, and each group has introduced its quota of new concepts, theoretical approaches are legion (e.g. Emlen, 1955). These often seem to conflict, but many of the controversies to which they have given rise are merely a reflection of the differing interests of those who espouse them. No attempt is made here to give a detailed exposition of any particular framework of theoretical ideas, though this chapter is based on the type of approach worked out by Lorenz (1935, 1937, 1950) and Tinbergen (1951), which has led to great advances in the study of behavior in recent years.

II. The Analysis of Bird Behavior

A. Stereotyped Patterns

Comparative study reveals that many motor patterns used by birds are characteristic of the species. The precise way in which the wings are moved during flight or the tail is flicked before take-off, the manner in which food is caught, the postures used by the male in courting the female, the call notes and song, are usually similar in all members of a given species, but may differ between even closely related ones (Lorenz, 1935, 1950).

A concept useful in the analysis of these species-characteristic movements is the "fixed action pattern." This refers to movements which may themselves be quite complicated, involving the use of many different effectors and muscle groups, and consisting of a temporal pattern of muscular contractions, but which cannot be analyzed into successive responses depending on qualitatively different external stimuli: they are therefore not chain reactions. They form useful units into which much instinctive behavior can be analyzed and, being conspicuous and easily recognizable, form a convenient starting point for analysis (Lorenz, 1935, 1950; Tinbergen, 1942, 1951). Fixed action patterns can be identified in every aspect of a bird's life—the begging of the young, courtship and threat postures, sleeping, hunting, and so on. While some are characteristic of the species, others are to be found throughout a genus, family, or higher systematic category; they are thus useful to the systematist, and indeed it was for this reason that attention was first focused on them (e.g. Lorenz, 1950).

Sometimes fixed action patterns are performed without specific orientation toward the external environment. More usually, however, they are directed spatially with reference to external objects. This orientation may depend on the same stimuli and muscle groupings as the fixed action pattern itself, so that the two are inseparable. Sometimes, however, the "orientation component" depends on different stimuli. For instance, many ground-nesting birds retrieve an egg which has rolled out of the nest by placing their beak beyond it and drawing it back toward their breast, simultaneously making lateral balancing movements to prevent the egg rolling out to one side. These balancing movements cease if the egg is replaced by a cylinder or removed altogether, but the sagittal movement usually continues. Here, then, the latter can be regarded as the fixed action pattern and the former as an orientation or taxis component which is continuously under the influence of environmental stimuli (Lorenz and Tinbergen, 1938). Often the addition of an orientation component implies a considerable degree of variability in the pattern of muscular contraction—a detailed description of all the occasions on which a male great tit struck its rival would reveal enormous variability.[1] However, whenever the fixed action pattern depends on stimuli or on muscle groupings that differ from the orientation stimuli or groupings, it can be studied separately.

B. Appetitive and Consummatory Behavior

It is sometimes convenient to divide the behavior of a species into "appetitive" and "consummatory" components (Sherrington, 1906; Craig, 1918). According to this, the more variable earlier phases in a behavior sequence, such as patrolling the territory or "looking for" food, are classed as appetitive, while the final stereotyped act which brings the sequence to an end, such as striking the rival or swallowing, is termed consummatory. This distinction is useful in the early stages of analysis, though it rests on several heterogeneous and uncorrelated characters (e.g. place in behavior sequence, degree of rigidity, effect of performance on motivation of whole sequence). It is therefore only a classificatory device for use at an early stage of analysis, and does not imply distinct types of underlying mechanisms. In practice, appetitive and consummatory behavior differ only in degree, and many behavior patterns have characteristics of both categories.

Appetitive behavior is usually labeled in terms of the behavior to which it leads—food seeking, fighting, sleeping, etc. Three characteristics may assist in its identification—(1) the motor pattern(s), (2) the orientation component, and (3) the stimuli to which the animal is particularly responsive while showing the behavior. Thus a feeding great tit may hop (motor pattern) under a beech tree (orientation component), "looking for" (to use a convenient shorthand) beech mast. A nesting great tit may hop under the trees looking for moss. Often the motor pattern is a locomotor one, but sometimes the movement is entirely one of orientation. The responsiveness to stimuli is the most difficult characteristic to investigate, and yet often the most interesting: it is the changes in responsiveness that mark off the different phases of appetitive behavior. Since it is always a relative matter (thus passerines are nearly always responsive to a flying hawk, whatever else they are doing; or a bird may snatch up a particle of food while looking for nest material), the labeling of appetitive behavior is often neither easy nor precise.

For behavior which can more conveniently be characterized as consummatory, it is usually also possible to describe the motor pattern and

[1] This of course does not mean infinite complexity in the underlying mechanism, since only three dimensions of space are involved.

the orientation, though some patterns lack a distinct orientation component. Often it is also possible to identify "consummatory stimuli" (e.g. "food in stomach") which are responsible for the subsequent fall in motivation and may be compared with the "stimuli to which the bird is particularly responsive" when showing appetitive behavior.

C.   Sign Stimuli and Releasers

Much avian behavior can be evoked by relatively simple stimulus situations. For instance Lack (1939), investigating the behavior of robins (*Erithacus rubecula*), found that stuffed adult robins placed in the territory were nearly always attacked or threatened, while stuffed juvenile robins, which resemble the adult but lack the red breast, were

Fig. 1. Threat display of robin (*Erithacus rubecula*). Redrawn from Lack (1939). Redrawn from "The Ornithologists' Guide," by permission of the British Ornithologists' Union.

ignored. Further, a bunch of red breast feathers was threatened more readily than a complete stuffed juvenile: the red breast is thus more effective in eliciting attack than all other characteristics together (Fig. 1).

Similarly Tinbergen and Perdeck (1950) investigated the stimuli eliciting the begging response of young herring gulls (*Larus argentatus*) with cardboard models. The adult of this species has a red spot near the tip of its beak, and the experiments showed that "the object that releases the pecking . . . is characterized for the chick by (1) movement, (2) shape (elongate, not too short, thin), (3) lowness, (4) downward pointing position, (5) nearness, and (6) the bill-patch, which must be (a) red, and (b) differing, by contrast, from the ground colour of the bill" (Tinbergen, 1951). Head shape and color had no influence on the response. Similar investigations concerning stimuli of many sensory modalities have been reviewed by Tinbergen (1948, 1951). In each case some aspects of the total stimulus situation are more effective in eliciting a particular response than others. In other words, the animal responds selectively and appropriately to the stimuli it receives.

In practice, selection takes place in stages. In the first instance, the sense organs themselves are more responsive to changes in some types of physical variable than to others, and the properties of the perceptual mechanisms ensure that some stimulus configurations are responded to more readily than others: for instance, circles are more conspicuous than other closed shapes to most vertebrates. In these cases stimuli or configurations of stimuli which are especially conspicuous have this property for all types of behavior.

In other cases of selective responsiveness, however, the stimulus character in question is effective in eliciting one type of behavior only. Such responsiveness may be characteristic of the species and independent of any previous experience of the particular stimulus situation, but not explicable in terms of properties of the sense organs or perception. Thus, a male chaffinch in breeding condition may make a hovering copulatory approach to a female stuffed in the soliciting posture, but take little notice of one stuffed in a perching position.

These species-characteristic stimulus-response connections are, however, much modified by individual experience. Indeed, it is a necessary working assumption that every time a bird responds to a stimulus, learning occurs which modifies the responsiveness on future occasions. The extent of this learning varies with numerous factors including the age of the bird and the response involved (page 387).

Of course after learning, as well as in purely "instinctive" behavior, it is found that some parts of the total stimulus situation are more important than others. However, where the stimulus-response connections are not formed by learning, the more essential elements are the same for all members of the species. When learning has occurred, on the other hand, individuals may come to respond to different aspects of the naturally occurring stimulus situation.

Those characteristics of the stimulus situation which are especially important in eliciting responses are termed "sign stimuli" (Russell, 1943). Many responses depend initially on relatively few sign stimuli, but these are often themselves complex and have configurational as well as purely quantitative characteristics. The stimuli which elicit instinctive responses in nature are not necessarily the optimal ones. Thus, in his experiments with young herring gulls, Tinbergen found that a long thin red rod with three white rings near the end, which thereby displayed in an exaggerated form just those characters which are important in eliciting begging (see above), was more effective than a real herring gull's head.

We can distinguish three immediate effects of external stimuli. First, they may elicit a response or lower its threshold—as the alarm call of many passerines elicits flying to cover. Second, they may inhibit a response or raise its threshold—as the presence of the female often reduces the song of male passerines. Finally, they may direct a response —thus, flying to cover is directed by the nearest bush, the alarm call having no directional effect (Marler, 1956). The stimuli which direct a response are often identical with those which elicit it, but this is not always so.

Both appetitive and consummatory behavior may depend on sign stimuli. In a chain of behavior, each phase is elicited by a different set of sign stimuli, and must be studied separately. Even when one object evokes a number of responses, the characteristics of the object which are important may be different for each response. Thus, generalizations, for instance, about the stimuli eliciting sexual behavior in a species obscure the independence of the different phases. Conversely, a deduction from the study of one phase of a functional chain about the whole is equally misleading. Allen's (1934) conclusion, drawn from the observation that "a stuffed grouse, a grouse skin or a dead grouse" all elicit copulatory behavior, that male ruffed grouse (*Bonasa umbellus*) do not distinguish between the sexes, is unwarranted. The facts merely show that the copulatory response of the male is released by stimuli presented by all these objects (Tinbergen, 1951).

Where a fixed action pattern is normally elicited by a number of sign stimuli, absence of any of them results in a decrease in the intensity of the response, but not in a change in its nature. The reduction in the intensity of the response depends on the extent of the deficiency in the stimulus situation, but not on which sign stimuli are absent (heterogeneous summation, Seitz, 1940).

Sign stimuli play an essential role in all aspects of bird behavior. When used in social communication between individuals, natural selection can operate not only on the responding individual's sensitivity to the given stimulus, but also on the individual giving the signal, making the latter more effective. Selection can thus result in the elaboration of special postures, colors, or calls for social communication. Many of the conspicuous colors, displays, and calls of birds are of this type: they are known as "social releasers" (Lorenz, 1935, 1950; Tinbergen 1948, 1952; Daanje, 1950).

D. INTERNAL FACTORS INFLUENCING BEHAVIOR

The threshold of every response varies with time. Such changes in responsiveness must be due to factors inside the animal. It is convenient to divide these into two groups: some can be described as learning and will be discussed later; while the rest, which can be grouped for present purposes as motivational factors, can be considered under the following headings:

(1) *Hormones.* Although much of the work on the effects of hormones on bird behavior refers to the domestic chicken, a considerable volume of data on other species is now accumulating. Recent summaries have been given by Beach (1948), Sturkie (1954), Marshall (1954), and Lehrman (in press), and further review is unnecessary here. In general, the effects of hormone treatment are broadly similar to those obtained with mammals. This conclusion is often accepted as a matter of course, but it *is* remarkable that the same hormone will induce male sexual behavior in rats and finches, and another maternal behavior in guinea pigs and doves, even though the common ancestor probably lived in the Carboniferous, and in the last case, at least, the actual mechanisms involved are quite different.

Lehrman's (1955) work on the effect of prolactin on parental behavior in the ring dove (*Streptopelia risoria*) requires special mention, as it shows that hormones affecting behavior do not necessarily affect the central nervous system directly. Prolactin leads to feeding of the young primarily because it causes enlargement of the crop. If the crop region is anesthetized, injections of prolactin do not induce parental behavior in naïve birds.

(2) *Nutritional factors.* These can be regarded as mostly of a pathological nature, absence of the appropriate food constituents producing behavioral abnormalities (Biester and Schwarte, 1952). At least some ability to select diet according to nutritional factors is present (references in Wood-Gush, 1955).

(3) *Diurnal changes.* Most activities show some sort of diurnal rhythm. The factors controlling these rhythms are little known, but they are undoubtedly complex and involve interactions between different response mechanisms (Palmgren, 1949).

(4) *Internal sensory stimuli.* The effects of internal sensory stimuli on the behavior of birds have been little studied, but it seems likely that they play as important a role as in mammals—for instance, in the control of hunger (e.g. Rogers, 1926 and references cited). Lehrman (1955) has demonstrated their importance in the parental behavior of the ring dove.

(5) *"Consummatory stimuli."* This term refers to stimuli which cause a response to cease, even though the eliciting factors are still present. For instance, a great tit separated from its mate will show appetitive behavior until it finds her again but will then resume feeding near her: the appetitive behavior is inhibited by her proximity. This category, of course, overlaps with the preceding one, and it is likely that cessation

or waning of some responses is due to a series of consummatory factors, some external and some internal, each of which is effective for a different period (e.g. nest building, feeding).

(6) *Other internal factors.* In general there is a relation between the stimulus necessary to elicit a response and the time since the response was last given. Sometimes such changes in responsiveness are partially explicable in terms of changes in internal sensory stimuli, but there are also changes of short duration, the origin of which cannot (yet) be

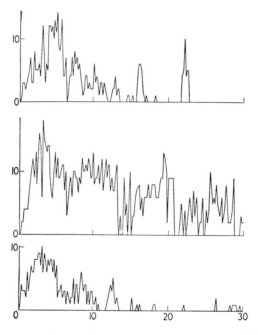

Fig. 2. The waning of the mobbing responses of chaffinches (*Fringilla coelebs*) to stuffed owls. Ordinate = number of calls per 10-second interval. Abscissa = time since start of presentation, in minutes. (From Hinde, 1954.)

traced in this way. Thus, the intensity of a response to a stimulus which is continuously present changes from moment to moment in a complex way. Figure 2 shows the number of calls given by chaffinches in successive 10-second periods while mobbing a stuffed owl. There is an initial warming-up phase, followed by a slow waning, but superimposed on these are shorter-term fluctuations in response strength. It thus seems that each response, or each moment of responding, must be associated with complex internal changes which affect subsequent behavior. These internal changes cannot be studied directly, but can be classified according to whether they produce long-term or short-term effects on behavior, the extent to which they are specific to the stimulus, whether they increase or decrease the response strength, and so on (Prechtl, 1953; Hinde, 1954; Schleidt, 1952).

(7) Finally, the performance of one type of behavior influences the threshold of others. Such relations are often, but not always, inhibitory: the animal tends not to do two things at the same time. Other types of relations between activities can be described in Sherringtonian terms (reciprocal inhibition, successive induction, etc.); but these have so far been little explored in birds.

The internal factors governing behavior are thus complex. For some purposes it is convenient to refer to those influencing a group of behavior types as "motivation," "drive," or "tendency," for instance during the initial analysis of complex types of behavior (e.g. courtship, see page 399). For more detailed analysis, however, "drive" must be measured in terms of quantifiable variables. Since (1) the internal factors influencing behavior are complex, (2) the external factors often involve relational properties which cannot easily be reduced to numerical terms, and (3) the various possible measures of response strength are often not highly correlated, quantification on a single scale is not possible and the concept becomes of less value.

The behavior given at any moment depends on both external stimuli and internal state. If the internal factors are strong, a response may be given to an external stimulus situation that at other times would be grossly inadequate. Sometimes, indeed, an animal will show a pattern of instinctive behavior with no change in the external stimulus situation. For instance, Lorenz (1937) described how a starling (*Sturnus vulgaris*) repeatedly went through all the actions of hunting insect prey without any apparent external stimulus. When patterns of this type are shown in the virtual absence of an external stimulus, they are called "vacuum activities" (*Leerlaufreaktionen*).

E. Ambivalent Behavior

For most of the time, factors for more than one type of behavior are present. For example, there may be conflicting tendencies to feed and fly with the flock, and during the breeding season each member of a pair has conflicting tendencies to attack, flee from, and behave sexually toward, its mate. It is often impossible to do more than one thing at a time, and such ambivalence may have various outcomes.

(1) *Inhibition of all but one response.* Sometimes only one of the alternative patterns is shown, the others being suppressed completely.

Thus the appearance of a flying predator causes passerines to flee to cover, and an immediate suppression of all other behavior.

(2) *Alternation*. The bird may alternate between the two alternatives: a fighting bird, with conflicting tendencies to attack and flee from its rival, may edge a little toward him, and then away again, and so on repeatedly. A bird which is uneasy while it is feeding will take a few beakfuls and then look round for predators, and then feed again.

(3) *Intention movements*. Sometimes the bird will make a series of incomplete movements expressing one or other or both of the conflicting tendencies. Thus, a half-tame moorhen (*Gallinula chloropus*) offered food may make incipient pecks toward it, and even swallowing movements, even though it does not dare to approach near enough to take any (see also Daanje, 1950).

(4) *Compromise behavior*. Sometimes a response is given which resembles responses depending on both the incompatible tendencies. Thus the tail-flicking of a hungry bird which does not approach a food dish because of a frightening object there, expresses both hunger (flying to dish) and fear (flying away) (Andrew, 1956).

(5) *Ambivalent posturing*. Sometimes the bird adopts a posture which simultaneously expresses both tendencies. Many threat and courtship postures are of this type, the various components (e.g. wing raising, tail spreading) of the posture expressing one or other of the conflicting tendencies (e.g. Tinbergen, 1952; Hinde, 1952, 1953; Moynihan, 1955).

(6) *Redirection activities*. Here the motor pattern of one of the conflicting tendencies is shown, but is oriented to another object. Thus the male black-headed gull (*Larus ridibundus*) with a female on his territory often redirects on to other birds the aggressiveness which she elicits (Moynihan, 1955).

(7) *Displacement activities*. Sometimes a bird under the influence of two or more conflicting tendencies shows an apparently irrelevant type of behavior: for instance, fighting great tits may suddenly break off the attack and peck vigorously at buds, and courting ducks may preen their wing feathers (Lorenz, 1941). Such cases are labeled "displacement activities" (Tinbergen, 1940, 1952; Kortlandt, 1940). This is undoubtedly a heterogeneous category, and little is yet known about their causation. In some cases, however, external stimuli for the irrelevant activity were already present. This is the case with the great tit example quoted above, which thus also has characters of a redirection activity (Moynihan, 1955). Similarly, Räber (1948) showed that when a turkey (*Meleagris* sp.) had conflicting tendencies to attack and flee, the appearance of displacement feeding or drinking depended in the availability of food or water. Internal causal factors for the irrelevant behavior also may

already be present. For instance, the initial posture of the thwarted animal may produce proprioceptive stimuli already associated with the irrelevant activity (Tinbergen, 1952).

In addition to such factors, three suggestions concerning the mechanisms of displacement activities have been advanced:

(a) Some may be due to autonomic activity aroused as a consequence of fear-provoking stimuli or other aspects of the external situation. Thus during sexual chases male buntings show behavior similar to that used in cooling—presumably a consequence of autonomic activity originally initiated by fear of the female (Andrew, 1956; Morris, 1956).

(b) The occurrence of displacement preening in incubating terns (*Sterna* spp.) has been ascribed to inhibitory relations between the mechanisms controlling escape behavior and incubation, and between incubation and preening. When incubating is partially inhibited by escape, its inhibitory effect on preening is reduced and preening appears (van Iersel and Bol, 1958).

(c) In some cases displacement behavior may be due to a general lowering of response thresholds, possibly mediated by the reticular system or its functional equivalent (Hinde, 1956a).

These, however, are only hints at the causal bases of a few examples of apparently irrelevant behavior, and much work remains to be done in this field.

(8) *Regression.* Sometimes intense conflict seems to result in regression to a more juvenile phase. This is well known in mammals but has been little studied in birds (but see Holzapfel, 1949). Neurosis, likewise, cannot be discussed here.

As we shall see later, some of these modes of behavior have become elaborated in evolution for a signal function. Most threat and courtship displays have been evolved from intention movements, redirection activities, or displacement activities.

F. INTEGRATION OF PARTIAL PATTERNS

The types of behavior shown by any species can be classified into functional groups: nest building, sexual behavior, feeding, and so on. The means by which discrete activities are integrated to produce functional sequences must now be considered.

The simplest way is the chain response—each response brings the animal into the stimulus situation releasing the next one. Most chains of appetitive behavior-consummatory behavior are of this type. During each phase of the appetitive behavior the bird is particularly sensitive to the stimulus situation which elicits the next phase and, apparently, the perception of the stimuli eliciting one phase can act as a reinforcement for the learning of the behavior performed in the preceding one.

In addition to this chaining together of behavior types by stimuli specific to each successive link, the members of a behavior sequence usually also share common causal factors. Perhaps because it is more economical in terms of nervous mechanisms, functionally related activities are thus often also causally related: thus in many birds male sex hormone influences song, territorial behavior, and all male sexual activities. This sharing of common causal factors is thus a second method by which functional integration is brought about.

When, in a chain response, the stimuli for the next phase are encountered, the preceding type of appetitive behavior ceases. Thus there must be an inhibitory effect consequent directly or indirectly upon the perception of the new stimuli. Often this inhibitory effect affects not only the immediately preceding activity, but also a number of other functionally related types of activity. Thus, in the cormorant (*Phalacrocorax carbo*) the possession of a nest has an inhibitory effect on all other nesting activities, even though the causal factors for nest building (hormones, twigs, etc.) are still present (Kortlandt, 1940).

Lehrman (1953, see page 406) has already demonstrated that behavior sequences may be built up as a result of learning, and the importance of this is not limited to cases where conventional rewards are present. Thus the stimuli for one phase of appetitive behavior serve as a reinforcement for the behavior in the preceding phase, as well as inhibiting it. There is, indeed, growing evidence from mammals that the eliciting stimuli for any phase in a behavior sequence can act as a reinforcement for behavior in the preceding phase, and the same is true at least for nest building in birds (Hinde, 1958; see also Wolfe and Kaplon, 1941). The building of a complete nest, however, seems to be reinforced more strongly than the mere performance of the component patterns in the sequence, and this may play a major part in the functional integration of the latter. Indeed, Thorpe (1956) has suggested that a "directiveness" of this kind must play an essential part not only in nest building but in all types of instinctive behavior.

These four principles—chain responses, common causal factors, inhibitory relations, and the reinforcing effect of stimulus situations which release functionally later responses—play a major part in the integration of discrete activities into functional wholes. It is not possible here to consider the further complexities involved in this problem.[1]

---

[1] See Kortlandt (1955) for a discussion of these problems from a rather different viewpoint.

G. The Ontogeny of Behavior

Every character of behavior depends on both heredity and environment. Much argument, however, has centered round the extent to which learning is necessary for the development of specific responses. Certainly the fact that a response is characteristic of all members of a species is no evidence that learning does not enter into its ontogeny. For instance, tits (*Parus* spp.) use the foot for holding large food objects, but chaffinches (*Fringilla coelebs*) do not. Observation shows that learning enters into the development of the behavior in tits. We can thus say that tits are innately different from chaffinches in using the foot in feeding, even though learning is essential for the development of the behavior.

On the other hand some responses appear, completely integrated, when the appropriate stimulus is first presented, even with birds which have been reared in isolation from others. This of course does not imply that individual learning plays no part in the development of the constituent parts of the pattern, but it does mean that the total behavior appears as an integrated whole in the absence of example, practice, or reward. To give but a few examples: Chaffinches reared in isolation give the same courtship and threat postures to the same stimuli as normal birds. Great tits reared by hand crouch to a high-pitched whistle just as they would to the alarm call of their parents. Canaries, reared without nest material, will go through all the movements of nest building in an empty pan. Further, when given material for the first time, they will carry it to the nest pan almost immediately (see also Heinroth, 1924–33; Sauer, 1954, 1956). Observations of this type show, then, that each individual has the potentiality of developing certain motor patterns which are characteristic of the species, and that these will appear the first time the appropriate stimulus is presented.

The ability of birds with grossly abnormal beaks to feed themselves shows that the feeding patterns are more labile than appears at first sight. With such labile patterns the direction of learning is normally controlled by structural or other species-characteristic features so that the normal movement nearly always develops.

The extent to which learning enters into the development of the constituents of such patterns is often controversial, and few cases have been analyzed in detail. Grohmann (1938) has shown that improvement in flying ability during a certain period of development is due to maturation and not practice, and it seems likely that maturation plays an important role in many simple activities. However, conflicting views are held on the development of the pecking response in chicks: Kuo

(1932) traces even the first simple head movements of the newly hatched chick to similar movements induced, possibly by breathing, before hatching, but other authors consider that he overestimates the role of learning. Maier and Schneirla (1935), Lehrman (1953), and others have emphasized the importance of learning in the building up of complex patterns.

Space does not permit a complete summary of the evidence on these problems here, but in general it may be said that although many complex behavior traits appear on the first presentation of the appropriate stimulus in a completely integrated form, showing that both the motor pattern and the stimulus-response relation is independent of example or previous practice, the latter particularly is subject to subsequent modification by learning. This is considered in the next section.

H. The Modifiability of Behavior

Among birds, the species-characteristic behavior patterns can be molded by individual experience to an extent greater than in any other group except mammals. Indeed, this learning ability is essential for many aspects of avian economy—their active, wide-ranging life and complex social behavior are possible only by virtue of the modifiability of their behavior. Furthermore, through these faculties they are able actively to explore their environment, and their curiosity enables them both to exploit its resources more fully and to avoid its dangers more successfully.

The literature on learning in birds has recently been thoroughly reviewed by Thorpe (1956), who has classified the types of learning which they show into various categories. This section largely depends on his work. The physiological changes underlying learning are, however, unknown, and the number of distinct mechanisms is still uncertain. Here it will be convenient to consider in succession the various aspects of the stimulus-response sequence which learning may affect.

1. *The Eliciting Stimuli*

Although instinctive responses often appear on the first occasion that the appropriate stimulus is presented, there are many cases in which the eliciting stimuli are wholly or partially learned. Thus Craig (1912) showed that young doves, which had never drunk before, showed no tendency to drink at the sight or sound of water: only the presence of water inside the mouth elicits the reflex of swallowing. The first drink probably results from the bird "accidentally" pecking at a drop or pool of water: subsequently the bird learns very rapidly the characteristics of the container or other surroundings of the water and later still, presumably, the characteristics of water itself.

Even when a response is elicitable by appropriate sign stimuli on the first occasion they are presented, the range of objects eliciting the response is at first very large, and is reduced later by learning [see James's (1892) "Law of inhibition of instincts by habits"].

A simple type of modification to the eliciting stimuli consists of "habituation"—a learning not to respond: this is discussed later. Another is produced by classic conditioning techniques. The response proper to one stimulus is linked to a second stimulus when the two are applied in overlapping sequence. It is, however, an artificially isolated part of the learning process, for the animal's free activity must be curtailed during the experiment, and only a small part of the total response is studied. While there have been a number of studies of conditioning in birds, and the conditioning technique has been valuable for investigating sensory capacities, it is not possible to consider it further here.

More important from a biological point of view is "trial-and-error" learning. By this is meant "the development of an association, as the result of reinforcement during appetitive behavior, between a stimulus or situation and an independent motor action as an item in that behaviour when both stimulus and motor action precede the reinforcement and the motor action is not the inevitable inherited response to the reinforcement" (Thorpe, 1956). In other words, it concerns the adjustment of the appetitive motor behavior to the changing environment. Thorpe suggests that under natural conditions trial-and-error learning usually consists of classic conditioning and instrumental or motor conditioning.

In the laboratory, trial-and-error learning has been studied with puzzle boxes and mazes. In the former the bird must learn how to open the door of a box in order to reach a reward. The method by which the door is opened has no obvious connection with the door, and the first solution comes by chance. After that, however, the birds fairly rapidly learn to concentrate their attempts in a particular place, and later on to open the door (Porter, 1906, 1910). In mazes (Diebschlag, 1940) the performance of pigeons is in some ways comparable to that of mammals, but it soon becomes rather stereotyped and thus, having learned one maze, they change only slowly to another.

Under more natural conditions, we have already seen the importance of trial-and-error learning in the drinking of doves. It has also been studied in copulation (Craig, 1914), the nest building of cormorants (Kortlandt, 1940) and canaries, and many other contexts. Even the pecking of chicks is subject to modification by trial-and-error learning:

the improvement which occurs about 30 hours after hatching is due to an increase in the skill with which the grain is seized and swallowed (Moseley, 1925).

The narrowing of the range of objects capable of eliciting a response has been studied especially in the following responses of the young of some nidifugous species, where it is known as "imprinting." In these species there is only a very vague inherited recognition of the characteristics of the parent, the details being learned in early life. Thus the greylag gosling (*Anser anser*) responds to the first relatively large moving object which it sees by following it and behaving toward it as though it were its parent. The object's characteristics are learned rapidly and, once this has occurred, other objects are ignored (Heinroth, 1911). Similarly, newly hatched domestic chicks will follow a wide variety of moving objects: normally the chick responds to the call of the hen, and this ensures that the object which it follows and learns to treat as its mother is the right one, but the visual characteristics of the mother are learned (Spalding, 1873). Similar studies have been made with a number of other species (references in Thorpe, 1956; Jaynes, 1956).

Lorenz (1935) suggested that imprinting is a special type of learning on the basis of four characteristics:

(a) The learning occurs rapidly, and is limited to a definite and brief part of the life cycle.

(b) It is irreversible—once the young bird has learned to follow one object, it will not subsequently ignore this and follow others.

(c) Young birds imprinted on a foster parent may later, when they are adult, court similar individuals and not members of their own species. Thus the learning occurs before some of the behavior, to which the imprinted pattern will ultimately become linked, is established.

(d) It involves the learning of supra-individual characteristics: the imprinted gosling will later court any individual from the foster parent's species, and not only the particular individual which brought it up.

Although the uniqueness of imprinting can no longer be maintained (Fabricius, 1951; and many later writers), imprinting of the following response is a clear example of learning with no conventional reward, and its study raises many important problems. Further, learning which resembles in many respects the imprinting of the following response occurs in many other contexts. The sign stimuli which elicit such diverse types of behavior as feeding, nest site selection and pairing behavior become restricted by learning in just the same way as those which elicit following in nidifugous species.

Limitations of space forbid further examples of modification to eliciting stimuli, but their importance cannot be overemphasized. Even when the bird has some nonlearned recognition of the objects appropriate to its instinctive responses, this can at most be a general recognition of a class of objects. Individual characteristics of mates, rivals, young, nest site, territory, food sources, and so on are always learned and, of course, given the avian type of life history, this capacity for learning is essential for survival.

Further, it is not only the association between motor pattern and external stimuli which is learned, for in some cases the relation to internal motivational state must also be established by experience. Lehrman (1956) has stressed the importance of this, and the pecking of young passerines, which first appears only when the bird is not hungry, is probably an example.

2. *The Orienting Stimuli*

The importance of modifications to the orienting stimuli again cannot be overestimated. Practically every type of appetitive behavior is subject to modification in this way, and it is unnecessary to enumerate instances. The most remarkable are concerned with the homing abilities of birds. This implies not only the ability to fly on a given course, but also to navigate—i.e. to fix present position and fly the correct course for home. The literature on bird navigation has been reviewed several times recently (Griffin, 1952; Matthews, 1955; Thorpe, 1956; Kramer, 1957).

3. *The Motor Pattern*

Modifications to the motor patterns of appetitive behavior have already been mentioned briefly under trial-and-error learning, of which instrumental conditioning often forms an essential part.

Many of the fixed action patterns used in locomotion, preparing food, nest building, fighting, courting, and so on, however, seem to be modifiable only in intensity or in relation to the eliciting or orienting stimuli. We have already seen (page 386) that this does not necessarily mean that learning plays no part in their ontogeny. Quite complicated stereotyped movements can be taught birds by a training technique in which movements approximating to the desired one are reinforced. Later, such movements will appear "spontaneously" when the same internal state occurs (Grindley, 1932; Skinner, 1948).

There is one group of motor patterns which are often subject to extensive modification as the result of experience, namely, those involved in the production of vocal utterances. Thus, while in some species the song is rigid and unmodifiable, in others it is largely learned during the individual's lifetime. The bullfinch (*Pyrrhula pyrrhula*), for instance, can be taught to add whole new tunes to its repertoire, whereas the song of the great tit is almost unmodifiable. The chaffinch (*Fringilla coelebs*) provides an interesting intermediate condition. The song normally consists of three phrases. There is a restricted basis, consisting in an ability to produce a song of about the right length, composed of a crescendo series of notes of decreasing frequency concluded by a single note of relatively high pitch: this is not dependent on learning. All further details are acquired by individual learning, but the instinctive basis is sufficiently selective to ensure that the bird does not normally acquire notes from individuals of other species. There is evidence that some of the further details are learned in the first few weeks of life, before the bird is able to sing itself, while the finer details are learned during a period in its first spring (Thorpe, 1956).

McDougall (1936) pointed out that vocal utterances are the only actions which are received by the animal's own sense organs in the same way as if they had been performed by another individual, as well as by proprioceptive and other channels. The difficulty which birds have in imitating other types of motor pattern may be related to their inability to see themselves perform.

4. *The Consummatory Stimuli*

These are the stimuli which, when perceived, cause a decrease in the tendency to perform the preceding behavior (page 380). So far little is known about the possibilities of modifying the consummatory stimuli—chiefly because of the difficulty of distinguishing between modifications to the consummatory stimuli and modifications to the eliciting stimuli of the next phase. But imprinting of the following response, for instance, must involve something of this sort. Most nidifugous birds have a special type of appetitive behavior which they show when they lose contact with their parents, whose proximity normally provides the consummatory stimulus situation. The learning of parental characteristics involved in imprinting involves modifications to these consummatory stimuli as well as to the eliciting and orienting stimuli of the following response. The mechanism may, of course, be the same in both cases.

5. *Changes in Responsiveness to Constant Stimulus*

If a constant stimulus is presented either continuously or on a number of occasions, the strength of the response gradually changes. The processes involved are undoubtedly complex, and may occur at many different stages between receptor and effector processes. They can be classified in terms of (a) their degree of permanence, and (b) the extent of their specificity to the stimulus situation. Temporary changes of this sort have already been considered: relatively permanent ones with some degree of specificity to the stimulus situation can be classified as learning. The process leading to a stimulus-specific decrement in responsiveness as a result of successive or continuous presentation is known as "habituation." For example, Rouse (1905) found that pigeons continued to respond to some sounds, such as the calls of other birds, but became habituated to "meaningless" sounds even when these were as loud as pistol shots. In nature, of course, birds rapidly become habituated to trains, aircraft, and gunfire.

However, habituation even to actual predators may occur. If an owl (stuffed or living) is shown to a chaffinch on successive days, the "mobbing" response of the latter generally wanes. The processes involved in this waning are complicated, for habituation to an "owl-in-the-circumstances-of-the-experiment" also involves some degree of habituation to other "predators-in-the-circumstances-of-the-experiment." Furthermore, the reduction in the responsiveness seems to be the resultant of several processes, some leading to a decrease in responsiveness (habituation) and others to an increase (conditioning). The importance of "the-circumstances-of-the-experiment" suggest that this habituation is not just a simple dropping out of a response to a stimulus but is inseparable from associative learning.

Of course, habituation does not operate only in responses to danger stimuli, but plays a role in every sphere of the bird's life—feeding, sexual behavior, nest building, and so on.

This brief sketch of learning in birds does little justice to their capabilities. Two further examples, one from the field and one from the laboratory, may be cited in conclusion. The nutcracker (*Nucifraga caryocatactes*) stores hazelnuts during the autumn and relies on them for food in winter and spring. Although the caches may be hidden under half a meter of snow, the birds are remarkably adept at finding them again, over 80% of diggings being successful (Swanberg, 1951).

Finally, experiments on the "number concept" suggest that birds are little inferior to mammals in their ability to count. Koehler (1943) has investigated two types of counting ability. The first is the ability to compare groups of units presented simultaneously by means of seen numbers of those units only. In a typical experiment of this type the bird is taught to discriminate between 2, 3, 4, 5, and 6 black spots on the lids of small boxes, the "key" for its choice being a group of one of these numbers of objects lying in front. The second is the ability to estimate numbers of incidents following each other, and thus to keep in mind numbers presented successively in time, independently of rhythms or other clues. Thus, birds were taught to open boxes placed in a row until a certain number of baits had been secured, and then to stop, the distribution of baits among the boxes being varied between experiments. In each case the limit attainable is about 5 or 6. Insofar as it is possible to perform comparable experiments in which counting named numbers is eliminated, the limit achieved by man is comparable to that attained by birds.

III. Bird Behavior Illustrated by Functional Groups of Activities

Birds have undergone an adaptive radiation which in recent geological time has been rivaled by no other vertebrates except the teleosts. The diversity of their ways of life and the small proportion of species which have been studied in any detail makes any attempt to catalogue or review the behavior of birds out of the question. Therefore only a few functional aspects of bird behavior are considered here, and these very briefly. The aim is to provide, not a review, but some indication of the diversity of behavior within the group, of how the principles discussed in the previous section find application to these varied facets of the bird's life, and in some cases to consider some functional and evolutionary aspects of the behavior under discussion.

A. FLOCKING

Most birds are gregarious for at least part of the year. Flocking is more common outside the breeding season, many species which defend large breeding territories becoming gregarious for the rest of the year. On the other hand, some sea birds nest colonially but are solitary at other times, and some species (e.g. some weavers) are always gregarious (see Emlen, 1952).

Although most birds flock by preference with conspecific individuals, mixed flocks are common. In such cases the sign stimuli which elicit flocking can apparently be quite unspecific, another bird of about the same size being sufficient to induce the response. However many species have evolved social signals—call notes, conspicuous rump and wing markings, and so on—which function in flock integration. Often these are quite similar in unrelated species—presumably by convergence, for the color patterns are often such as make the movements of taking flight conspicuous, and the call notes have characteristics which make them easily locatable and are audible over a distance not greatly exceeding that necessary for this function (Marler, 1957b).

When a member of a gregarious species becomes separated from its flock it shows a special type of appetitive behavior. In the great tit, for instance, this consists of hopping through the bushes, peering around (presumably looking for flock companions), and giving the flocking calls frequently. When it rejoins the flock, it resumes feeding quietly. Flocking behavior thus has several types of appetitive behavior— looking for the flock, flying in company, etc.—but no consummatory act, the appetitive behavior ceasing when other individuals are close (Hinde, 1952).

Among birds which flock closely there is usually a strong tendency for "social facilitation"—that is, the performance of a particular pattern of behavior by one member of the flock increases the likelihood that other individuals will behave similarly. In some species this is so marked that one individual which has been fed to satiation will start to feed again when it sees other individuals feeding (Katz and Révész, 1921), while an individual which is hungry will not feed for a while when placed with satiated individuals (Lorenz, 1935). No doubt this plays an important part in flock integration.

Flocks may be so closely integrated that the birds fly only a few inches apart and twist and turn synchronously, or they may be merely loose aggregations. The degree of flock integration depends on two groups of factors: those promoting integration, such as the various sign stimuli and appetitive behavior considered above, and opposing disruptive factors. Amongst the latter are the food-seeking movements of individuals which, in many species, would tend to produce a random dispersal if not guided by the social patterns. There are also, however, factors tending to produce overdispersal—that is, to space the birds out more than randomly—in particular the aggressive and individual-distance behavior of the birds composing the flock. The nature of the flock is thus the result of these conflicting tendencies (Emlen, 1952; Hinde, 1952).

Ultimately, the structure of the flock is a compromise between the conflicting advantages of gregarious and solitary life. Among the former are the decreased susceptibility to attack by predators enjoyed by birds in a flock, and increased efficiency in the exploitation of food sources—by a process known as "local enhancement" the attention of the other members of a flock may be called to a new food source discovered by one individual. On the other hand, too great a proximity to other individuals involves too great a risk of food robbery. Clearly the balance between these factors will be determined by many other aspects of the species biology, such as predation pressure and the nature and availability of food. The few species which are never gregarious—

some raptors, some birds which hold territory throughout the year—
probably remain solitary because their feeding habits necessitate it
(Lack, 1954).

B. FEEDING

The feeding habits of birds are so diverse, and the structural and
behavioral adaptations so numerous, that only a few points can be
mentioned here.

Each species has a number of motor patterns used in feeding. As we
have seen, learning may enter into the development of these patterns,
even though they are species-characteristic (page 386). Such patterns
are usually conservative in evolution, being similar in closely related
species: in only relatively few cases where there has been marked
divergence in the type of prey taken do related species use markedly
different motor patterns (contrast, for example, *Recurvirostra avosetta*
with other waders).

In accordance with Gause's principle (1934), however, there is usually
little competition between species over food (Lack, 1954). Thus the
sign stimuli eliciting or guiding the behavior differ more than the motor
patterns themselves. In some cases it is primarily the eliciting stimuli
which differ—thus different species of finch eat seeds of different sizes.
In other cases the type of food taken is similar (although not necessarily the same), but the place where it is found differs between species
—thus when food is scarce the various *Parus* species feed in different
places in the trees (Hartley, 1953; Gibb, 1954).

However, although there are characteristic species differences in
feeding behavior, it is not very clear how these differences arise, for
learning plays a large part in the development of feeding behavior in
the individual. Even in domestic chicks, where the first "pecking
movements . . . are inborn in the sense that the central nervous, proprioceptive and visual co-ordinations which render them possible are
virtually fully organized and perfected at the moment of the first
peck" (Thorpe, 1956), learning occurs at every peck and influences the
course of subsequent feeding behavior. It seems likely that specific
preferences are not wholly inherited directly, but depend partly on
learning whose course is influenced by the specific structural characteristics. The development of feeding preferences may thus be quite
complex even in more or less monophagous species, and must be even
more so in polyphagous ones. It may be more than coincidence that
many polyphagous species also have a reputation for intelligence (e.g.
Corvidae, Paridae).

Furthermore, although few physiological experiments on feeding in birds comparable with the work on mammals have been carried out, it is clear that the motivational basis of feeding behavior is far from simple. Thus the motivation of hunting may be to some degree independent of that of feeding. For instance, a little owl (*Athene noctua*) which has been satiated with food may go through all the actions of catching and killing mice even though no mice are present (Thorpe, 1948). Blue tits (*Parus caeruleus*) often learn to invade houses, employing the motor patterns which they normally use in feeding in tearing down wallpaper, etc., even though there is no food there and no shortage of food elsewhere.

C. Predators

Nearly all species are markedly susceptible to predation. Among the adaptations promoting safety from predators can be mentioned:

(1) *The development of a cryptic coloration.* Sometimes this is extraordinarily effective: the females of many ground-nesting birds cannot be detected from a distance of a few yards (Cott, 1940).

(2) *The use of postures which enhance the value of the cryptic coloration.* Thus most ground-nesting birds remain very still when a predator approaches, and some frogmouths (*Podargus*) which nest on the branches of trees adopt a posture which makes them seem like a broken-off stump (Cott, 1940).

(3) *Instinctive responses to stimuli likely to indicate danger.* These are of two types: First, responses to loud noises, quickly moving objects, unusual objects in a familiar environment, and so on. These are subject to rapid habituation if not reinforced by further stimuli indicative of danger. Second, each species has responses to stimuli indicative of particular predators—owls, hawks, snakes and so on (Thorpe, 1956). Just how specific these responses actually are is uncertain: certainly it is possible to combine characters of an owl and a mammal to produce a composite object which is very effective at evoking a response. Such responses to specific predators are probably less liable to habituation than the general responses mentioned earlier, though even here habituation does occur (see page 388).

Many species have two or more distinct responses to predators. In passerines, flying predators produce an immediate dash to cover and crouching, while mammalian or perched avian predators induce mobbing—a form of ambivalent behavior compounded from fleeing, investigatory, and aggressive behavior. Actual attacks on predators by small birds are rare, but larger species, like the bittern (*Botaurus stellaria*), may fight vigorously in defense of their nest.

(4) *Exploratory behavior*. Any bird, finding itself in a new environment, will actively explore it. This exploratory behavior undoubtedly helps to protect birds from predators, as well as to exploit the area's resources. Furthermore, "curiosity" is shown toward strange objects, especially those having some, but not many, of the characters of a predator; and also to a real predator by young birds, whose predator-responses have not yet matured (Hinde, 1954).

(5) *Warning calls*. Gregarious species have a system of warning calls which increase the safety of individuals in the flock.

(6) *Distraction display*. Many species have a special display which appears to function by directing a predator away from the nest or young on to themselves. They achieve this by simulating another easily available type of prey—a sick or injured bird, a rodent, etc. Such displays apparently depend on conflicting tendencies to attack and to flee from the predator, and sometimes also to incubate or brood the young. The resultant behavior has been elaborated in evolution in accordance with its display function (Armstrong, 1949; Simmons, 1952).

D. Fighting and Territory

While in a flock, most birds attempt to maintain a space around themselves (the "individual distance") free from other birds, by threatening, attacking, or fleeing from other individuals which approach (Hediger, 1950; Conder, 1949). The primary functions of this individual distance are probably increased immunity from food-robbing by other birds, or adequate room for sudden take-off, according to the species. Its extent varies between species and, within species, according to the occasion: sometimes it is zero (e.g. many estrilids).

Sometimes the area defended is not that round the bird, but round some object or situation which is important for survival or reproduction, such as a mate, song post, nest site, or territory. Such territorial behavior occurs in many other groups (e.g. fish, reptiles, mammals), but it has been studied particularly in birds. Avian territories are defended mainly during the breeding season, but in some species at other times as well. Territory size varies from several square miles (some birds of prey) to the distance the sitting bird can peck (many cliff-nesting species). It is absent apparently only in the emperor penguin (*Aptenodytes forsteri*), where the advantages of close huddling as a protection from the cold winds more than compensate for the lack of territorial seclusion (Stonehouse, 1953). The biological significance of territory has been much discussed; in most species its prime function probably lies in the formation and maintenance of the sexual bond between the pair: a food value is unlikely except in relatively few cases (reviews by Hinde, 1956b; Tinbergen, 1957).

The external stimulus for aggression is normally certain stimuli from a fellow member of the species (see, e.g. page 377; Marler, 1955–1956). Sometimes it is elicited by members of other species—for instance if they approach the nest—and by predators. It ceases on the disappearance of the eliciting stimuli: there are no consummatory stimuli distinct from the absence of the eliciting ones (contrast feeding). It has been shown for a number of species that male sex hormone increases aggressiveness (Shoemaker, 1939), but little is known about the effects of other aspects of the internal state. Marler (1955–1956) and Andrew (1957b) have shown that a period of food deprivation does not affect the threshold for aggression of chaffinches and buntings (*Emberiza* spp.) at a feeding place; the internal state may, however, be important in giving significance to an external object which is the immediate cause of the fight. Thus, a great tit in reproductive mood will attack a male who, though 100 yards distant, is intruding on his territory, but tolerate him 10 yards away across the boundary. Two minutes later the same territory owner may, while feeding, ignore an intruder 3 feet from him inside the territory.

Fig. 3. Head-up threat display of great tit (*Parus major*). Redrawn from "The Ornithologists' Guide," by permission of the British Ornithologists' Union.

A territory owner normally attacks conspecific individuals on his territory, but flees from his neighbors if he is trespassing on their territory. The boundary is the line along which the tendencies to attack and to flee are more or less in balance in each of the two rivals. During a skirmish, each combatant is in an ambivalent condition, with tendencies to attack and flee from the rival. The precise nature of the behavior or threat posture shown depends on the nature of the balance. These threat postures are social signals—they serve to intimidate the rival (Figs. 1 and 3) (Tinbergen, 1939, 1952, 1953; Hinde, 1952, 1953).

FIG. 4. Submissive posture of great tit. Redrawn from "The Ornithologists' Guide," by permission of the British Ornithologists' Union.

In addition to threat postures, submissive and appeasement postures play an important part in fighting. These serve to indicate "nonaggressiveness" and thus to reduce the aggressiveness of a dominant rival. They are given primarily in situations where a tendency to flee is in conflict with some other incompatible tendency. Many of them have evolved from intention movements of fleeing, or displacement activities, and depend for their effect on the nonpresentation of stimuli for aggression to the rival (e.g. compare Figs. 3 and 4).

E. Pair Formation and Courtship

Birds may be monogamous or polygamous, polyandrous or promiscuous. The pair bond may last for life or for the duration of a mating attempt. With such diversity, few generalizations about sex relations can be given here: a recent review has been given by Armstrong (1947). There are, however, some principles about the mechanisms involved which have now been established for a number of groups and are probably widely applicable.

Each individual carries characters which may elicit attacking, fleeing, and/or sexual behavior in other individuals. Thus, whereas during fights the rivals have two conflicting tendencies (page 382), during courtship the mates have three. The nature of the courtship display shown at any time depends on the strengths and relative strengths of these three tendencies: as the tendencies change through the season, so do the courtship displays.

The courtship of some cardueline and fringilline finches can be used to illustrate this (Figs. 5 and 6). The first response of the male in pair formation is an aggressive one given to all other members of the species which approach. At this stage the male may already be established on a territory (chaffinch) or the birds may still be in flocks. If

FIG. 5. A. Head-forward threat posture of bullfinch (*Pyrrhula pyrrhula*). A posture of this type is widespread among passerines. The body is oriented toward the rival. B. Courtship posture of canary. The body is oriented obliquely to the female. C. Courtship posture of chaffinch (*Fringilla coelebs*). The body is oriented laterally to the female. D. Courtship posture of bullfinch. The body is oriented laterally to the female. E. Soliciting posture of female chaffinch. F. Precopulatory posture of male chaffinch. (Redrawn from Hinde, 1955).

the newcomer is a male or nonreceptive female, it may behave aggressively or flee. If it is a receptive female, she may adopt a submissive posture and show a passive resistance to the male's attack. After a while the male begins to behave sexually. As his sexual tendency increases, his tendency to attack the female decreases; she exploits this and becomes dominant to him. Correlated with this change, the head-forward threat posture used by the male becomes gradually replaced by courtship postures. These differ from the threat postures primarily by an increasingly oblique or lateral orientation of the body toward the

A   B

C

FIG. 6. Courtship feeding of bullfinches; the female is on the left. B. and C. Billing ceremonies, derived from courtship feeding, in hawfinch (*Coccothraustes coccothraustes*). (Redrawn from Hinde, 1955.)

female, and an increasingly upright position of the body and neck. At this stage his tendency to attack the female may be relatively weak, but full sexual behavior is prevented by his tendency to flee. Eventually, sexual factors predominate, and copulation attempts occur.

This account is, of course, highly schematic, and there are great variations between species even among these finches. Thus, in the chaffinch the male's change-over from aggressive to courtship display is usually almost immediate, while in many carduelines the male's aggressiveness is much more persistent. In many species "courtship feeding" occurs—that is, the male feeds the female who begs like a young bird: in the chaffinch this is absent. Furthermore, there are of course great interspecies differences in the displays.

Nevertheless, it is probable that the courtship of most birds consists of variations on this theme; there is always an interplay between tendencies to attack, flee from, and behave sexually toward the mate. Many of the variations are correlated with the degree of sexual dimorphism—the more dissimilar the sexes are in color, the more rapidly "sex recognition" occurs and also the more different are the displays of male and female. But in each species the evolution of the courtship pattern has been influenced by many other aspects of the life history: the degree of gregariousness, territorial behavior, the nature of the habitat, availability of food, sex ratio, and so on.

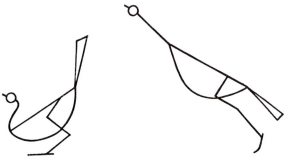

Fig. 7. The two phases of a take-off leap. The various components of these play a prominent part in many display postures (see Figs. 1 and 3). Redrawn after Daanje 1950; Reproduced from "The Ornithologists' Guide," by permission of the British Ornithologists' Union.

Threat and courtship displays have been elaborated in evolution from the various types of behavior which appear in conflict situations—primarily intention movements, redirection activities, and displacement activities (page 382). The intention movements are often those of locomotion (Fig. 5), but incipient movements of striking, copulating, etc., also occur. The displacement activities (i.e. apparently functionally irrelevant activities) are extremely diverse. Among the commonest are various types of feather raising or lowering (page 383) and various preening and cleaning movements.

These movements have changed in evolution, becoming more effective for their signal function. The changes involved consist largely of absolute and relative threshold changes in the various components of the movement (Daanje, 1950). These result in changes in the relations between the components, so that, for instance, the withdrawal of the head in the first phase of a take-off leap may be associated with the depressed tail of the second (Fig. 7). Further, they may result in a decrease in the variability of the movement such that the same response is given to a larger range of eliciting factors (Morris, 1957). It has been suggested that in some cases the movement may become emancipated from the causal factors which originally controlled it, so that it is now evoked by quite different ones (Lorenz, 1951). This seems to be the case, for instance, in courtship feeding: often a female will beg for food from her mate when she has just been feeding herself, and even when she is carrying food in her beak. However, as yet too little is known about the possible existence of causal factors common to the original and display contexts for the generality of the principle of emancipation to be assessed (Tinbergen, 1939, 1948, 1952; Moynihan, 1955; Morris, 1957).

Fig. 8. Various display postures showing the correlation between movement and conspicuous structure. Modified after Tinbergen (1951).

Among cardueline finches many of the components of the display postures are associated with one or other of the conflicting tendencies—wing raising with attacking and crest raising with fleeing, for instance. The relationship between the display components and tendencies are similar in a wide range of species and interspecies hybrids.

As well as changes in the display movements, conspicuous structures have been developed which make the movements more striking. Since, within groups of closely related species, the same display posture may exhibit diverse structural characters, it would seem that the movement is the more primitive and that the structural features were evolved later to make it more conspicuous. Nevertheless, there has probably usually been a parallel elaboration of both movement and structure (Fig. 8).

All these changes are to be understood as adaptations to the signal functions of the displays. These functions of courtship displays are of four main types (Tinbergen, 1954):

(1) *Synchronization of the behavior of the sexes.* This may be long-term, involving, for instance, hormonal changes; or short-term, synchronizing the mating activities of the pair.

(2) *Orientation.* Some displays have primarily a guiding function—for instance the nest site display of the great tit and many other hole-nesting species, and the song of many passerines.

(3) *The suppression of nonsexual responses.* Thus "submissive" postures help to suppress the aggressiveness of the male.

(4) *Maintenance of reproductive isolation.* Thus sympatric closely related species always differ markedly in display, color and/or song (Huxley, 1942).

In summary, then, we see that an increased understanding of the nature of bird display has been reached by a realization of the ubiquity of ambivalence in the underlying motivation and of the importance of sign stimuli in social communication.

F. Nest Site and Nest

Although a few species (e.g. guillemot) build no nest, most birds lay their eggs in a more or less elaborate one. The form of these nests is extremely diverse, and the technique of building often complex.

The nest site is apparently recognized by a relatively small number of sign stimuli; in some (e.g. hole-nesting) species these may be partially visual, but usually tactile senses seem to be primary (Craig, 1918).

Nest building depends in the first instance on a number of species-characteristic motor patterns and instinctively recognized stimulus situations. Even simple nests, however, pose a real problem to the ethologist. Surely behavior of great complexity must be required for their construction? Thorpe (1956), following an earlier description by Tinbergen, has listed the distinct movements or combinations of movements in the nest building of the long-tailed tit (*Aegithalos caudatus*), and shown that responsiveness to at least eighteen distinct stimulus situations is necessary.

Similarly, in canaries, the building of the nest involves not only a number of stereotyped motor patterns, but also responsiveness to many stimulus situations. Although the motor patterns of nest building and much of the appropriate responsiveness to stimuli appear in naive individuals who have had no previous opportunity of manipulating grass or other materials, learning plays an important role in the building of the nest. This is revealed by experiments in which birds are deprived of material throughout the whole of their first nesting cycle. Abnormal habits develop which may persist in later cycles when material is available. Thus, under these adverse conditions, habits are learned which at least permit the carrying out of the stereotyped motor patterns of nest building, although under natural conditions only that behavior which also contributes to the finished nest becomes fixed. Further complications are introduced by the fact that the changes in behavior required for the completion of the nest are not solely the result of the changing stimuli from the partially completed nest. For instance, the change from grass (used for the outside of the cup) to feathers (used for lining) is partially internally controlled, probably by a hormonal change altering the sensitivity of the ventral epithelium to stimuli from the nest-cup (Hinde, 1958). A detailed account of the nest building of the cormorant (*Phalacrocorax carbo*) has been given by Kortlandt (1940) and suggests similar conclusions.

G. Parental Behavior

Birds can be divided into two groups: nidicolous species, in which the young are completely helpless on hatching and entirely dependent on the parents for food and protection; and nidifugous species, which leave the nest almost at once and feed themselves, although they still depend on their parents for protection. Some groups (e.g. Laridae) are intermediate.

Parental behavior involves several functional groups of behavior patterns, including those of incubating the eggs and brooding the young, removing egg shells and feces, protecting the young from predators with warning calls (page 406), and distraction displays (page 397), as well as feeding them. Where both parents play a part, their duties often bring them into close proximity, with the consequent tendencies to attack, flee from, and behave sexually toward each other (page 382): complicated ceremonies (e.g. nest-relief ceremonies) have been evolved which apparently smooth parental relations. Further, when the young begin to resemble the adults, they also may evoke aggressive behavior in their parents, and their behavior becomes modified by the adoption of a submissive posture which alleviates this (Tinbergen, 1953): also the juvenile usually lacks those features which are especially significant in aggressive behavior in the adults.

Detailed studies of incubation and feeding behavior have been made by Kendeigh (1952). While the primitive condition seems to have been for both sexes to share parental responsibilities, there has been an evolutionary trend in most orders for the female to take the major share; in a few orders, however, the reverse is the case.

The stimuli eliciting begging by the young have been investigated in thrushes (Tinbergen and Kuenen, 1939) and in the herring gull (Tinbergen, 1953). The importance of sign stimuli in feeding is demonstrated by the occurrence of conspicuous colors in the gape, beak, or head of the parent or young in nearly all species.

The following response of nidifugous species has been investigated in studies of imprinting (page 389; Lorenz, 1935; Fabricius, 1951; Fabricius and Boyd, 1954; Hinde, et al., 1956; Ramsay and Hess, 1954; Jaynes, 1956) and it is clear that young birds will learn to follow a moving object without any conventional reward. In nature this is of course only one of the ways in which the young learn to recognize their parents, and many different factors contribute to the parent/young relationship. These include the provision of warmth, food, etc. by the parents and also the various greeting ceremonies which serve a primarily communicatory function and may be comparable to the human smile.

Although a number of studies have been made on the sign stimuli involved in parental behavior, and a certain amount is known about its hormonal basis (Beach, 1948), little is yet known about the integration of the part patterns into a functional whole. A valuable leader is provided by Lehrman's work on the ring dove where he demonstrates that prolactin elicits feeding behavior in a nonbreeding adult only if it has had previous experience of feeding squabs. Apparently prolactin acts primarily by causing engorgement of the crop and suppressing sexual behavior. In naive parents the regurgitation response is given first to tactual stimulation of the breast by the squab's head, but quickly becomes conditioned to auditory and visual stimulation from the young.

H. VOICE

Vocal utterances have an important role in social communication. All species have a number of calls which function as sign stimuli and elicit responses in other members of the species. Most conspicuous among these are the songs of the oscines and other devices which function as a proclamation of territorial ownership. In many species which defend large territories, the male establishes the territory before pair formation and his song subsequently attracts females and repels males. The role of learning in the development of song has already been considered (page 390).

The most extensive study of the other calls of any one species is that given by Marler (1956) for the chaffinch (see also Andrew, 1957a). The vocabulary of the adults comprises "a flight call, a social call, an injury call, an aggressive call, three escape calls, subsong and song and three courtship calls." There are also nestling and fledgling begging calls. Some of these, especially the courtship calls, occur during ambivalence, but many of them occur when there is no sign of conflict. (Those which occur in conflict situations are more variable than the others, and intermediates occur.)

The form of the calls varies with their function: in particular, those which do not convey information about position (the alarm calls) share certain characteristics (long duration, no sudden changes in pitch, beginning and end gradual). Social calls, which must be easily locatable, have the opposite characteristics. Among other factors ultimately governing the forms of the calls is the need for distinctiveness from the calls of other sympatric species. This is especially the case with song. With the "see" alarm call, on the other hand, which serves in interspecific communication, there is a selective value in convergence on a common type.

ACKNOWLEDGEMENT

I am grateful to Dr P. Narler for reading the manuscript and for discussion of a number of points.

References

Allen, A. A. (1934). Sex rhythms in the Ruffed Grouse (*Bonasa umbellus* L.) and other birds. *Auk* **51**: 180–199.

Andrew, R. J. (1956). Some remarks on behaviour in conflict situations with special reference to *Emberiza* spp. *Brit. J. Animal Behaviour* **4**: 41–45.

Andrew, R. J. (1957a). A comparative study of the calls of *Emberiza* spp. *Ibis* **99**: 27–43.

Andrew, R. J. (1957b). Influence of hunger on aggressive behaviour in certain buntings of the genus *Emberiza*. *Physiol. Zool.* **30**: 177–186.

Armstrong, E. A. (1947). "Bird Display and Behaviour." Lindsay Drummond, London.

Armstrong, E. A. (1949). Diversionary display. *Ibis.* **91**: 88–97, 179–188.

Beach, F. A. (1948). "Hormones and Behavior." Hoeber, New York.

Biester, H. E., and Schwarte, L. H. (1952). "Diseases of Poultry." Iowa State College Press, Ames, Iowa.

Conder, P. (1949). Individual distance. *Ibis* **91**: 649–656.

Cott, H. B. (1940). "Adaptive Colouration in Animals." Methuen, London.

Craig, W. (1912). Observations on doves learning to drink. *J. Animal Behavior* **2**: 273–279.

Craig, W. (1914). Male doves reared in isolation. *J. Animal Behavior* **4**: 121–133.

Craig, W. (1918). Appetites and aversions as constituents of instincts. *Biol. Bull.* **34**: 91–107.

Daanje, A. (1950). On the locomotory movements of birds and the intention movements derived from them. *Behaviour* **3**: 48–98.

Diebschlag, E. (1940). Über den Lernvorgang bei der Haustaube. *Z. vergleich. Physiol.* **28**: 67–104.

Emlen, J. T. (1952). Flocking behaviour in birds. *Auk.* **69**: 160–171.

Emlen, J. T. (1955). The study of behavior in birds. *In* "Recent Studies in Avian Biology," (A. Wolfson, ed.), p. Univ. Illinois Press, Urbana, Illinois.

Fabricius, E. (1951). Zur Ethologie junger Anatiden. *Acta Zool. Fennica* **68**: 1–178.

Fabricius, E., and Boyd, H. (1954). Experiments on the following reactions of ducklings. *Wildfowl Trust Ann. Rept.* **1952–1953**: 84–89.

Gause, G. F. (1934). "The Struggle for Existence." Baltimore, Maryland.

Gibb, J. (1954). Feeding ecology of tits. *Ibis* **96**: 513–543.

Griffin, D. R. (1952). Bird Navigation. *Biol. Revs. Cambridge Phil. Soc.* 359–400.

Grindley, G. C. (1932). The formation of a simple habit in guineapigs. *Brit. J. Psychol.* **23**: 127–147.

Grohmann. J. (1938). Modification oder Funktionsregung? Ein Beitrag zur Klärung der wechselseitigen Beziehungen zwischen Instinkthandlung und Erfahrung. *Z. Tierpsychol.* **2**: 132–144.

Hartley, P. H. T. (1953). An ecological study of the feeding habits of the English titmice. *J. Animal Ecol.* **22**: 261–288.

Hediger, H. (1950). "Wild Animals in Captivity." Butterworth, London.

Heinroth, O. (1911). Beitrage zur Biologie, namentlich Ethologie und Physiologie der Anatiden. *Verhandl. 5th Intern. Ornithol. Kongr.* pp. 589–702.

Heinroth, O., and Heinroth, M. (1924–33). "Die Vögel Mittel europas." Berlin.

Hinde, R. A. (1952). The behaviour of the Great Tit (*Parus major*) and some other related species. *Behaviour, Supplement No.* **2**: 1–201.

Hinde, R. A. (1953). The conflict between drives in the courtship and copulation of the Chaffinch. *Behaviour* **5**: 1–31.

Hinde, R. A. (1954). Factors governing the changes in strength of a partially inborn response, as shown by the mobbing behaviour of the Chaffinch. *Proc. Roy. Soc.* **B, 142**: 306–331, 331–358.

Hinde, R. A. (1955). A comparative study of the behaviour of certain finches. *Ibis* **97**: 706–745; **98**: 1–23.

Hinde, R. A. (1956a). Ethological models and the concept of drive. *Brit. J. Phil. Sci.* **6**: 321–331.

Hinde, R. A. (1956b). The biological significance of the territories of birds. *Ibis* **98**: 340–369.

Hinde, R. A. (1958). The nest-building behaviour of domesticated canaries. *Proc. Zool. Soc. London* **131**: 1–48.

Hinde, R. A., Thorpe, W. H., and Vince, M. A. (1956). The following response of young moorhens and coots. *Behaviour* **9**: 214–242.

Holzapfel, M. (1949). Die Beziehung zwischen den Trieben junger und erwachsener Tiere. *Schweiz. Z. Psychol.* **8**: 32–60.

Huxley, J. S. (1942). "Evolution: The Modern Synthesis." Allen and Unwin, London.

van Iersel, J. J. A., and Bol, A. C. (1958). Preening of two tern species. *Behaviour* **13**: 1–88.

James, W. (1892). "Textbook of Psychology." Macmillan, London.

Jaynes, J. (1956). Imprinting: the interaction of learned and innate behaviour. *J. Comp. and Physiol. Psychol.* **49**: 201–206.

Katz, D., and Révész, G. (1921). Experimentelle Studien zur vergleichenden Psychologie (Versuche mit Hühnern). *Z. angew. Psychol.* **18**: 307–330.

Kendeigh, S. C. (1952). "Parental Care and its Evolution in Birds." Univ. Illinois Press, Urbana, Illinois.

Koehler, O. (1943). "Zahl"-versuche an einem Kohlraben und Vergleichsversuche an Menschen. *Z. Tierpsychol.* **5**: 575–712.

Kortlandt, A. (1940). Eine Übersicht der angeborenen Verhaltungsweisen des Mitteleuropäischen Kormorans (*Phalacrocorax carbo sinensis*), ihre Funktion, ontogenetische Entwicklung und phylogenetische Herkunft. *Arch. néerl. zool.* **4**: 401–442.

Kortlandt, A. (1955). Aspects and prospects of the concept of instinct. *Arch. néerl. zool.* **11**: 155–284.

Kramer, G. (1957). Experiments on bird orientation and their interpretation. *Ibis* **99**: 196–227.

Kuo, Z. Y. (1932). Ontogeny of embryonic behaviour in Aves. IV. The influence of prenatal behaviour on post-natal life. *J. Comp. Psychol.* **14**: 109–121.

Lack, D. (1939). The behaviour of the Robin. *Proc. Zool. Soc. London* (A) **109**: 169–178.

Lack, D. (1954). "The Natural Regulation of Animal Numbers." Oxford Univ. Press, London and New York.

Lehrman, D. S. (1953). A critique of Konrad Lorenz's theory of instinctive behaviour. *Quart. Rev. Biol.* **28**: 337–363.

Lehrman, D. S. (1955). The physiological basis of parental feeding behaviour in the Ring Dove (*Streptopelia risoria*). *Behaviour* **7**: 241–286.

Lehrman, D. S. (1956). On the organization of maternal behaviour and the problem of instinct. Foundation Singer-Polignac. *In* "L'instinct dans le comportement des animaux et de l'homme." Masson, Paris.

Lorenz, K. (1935). Der Kumpan in der Umwelt des Vögels. *J. Ornithol.* **83**: 137–214, 289–413.

Lorenz, K. (1937). Über den Begriff der Instinkthandlung. *Folia Biotheoretica* **2**: 17–50.

Lorenz, K. (1941). Vergleichende Bewegungstudien an Anatinen. *J. Ornithol.* **89**: 194–294.

Lorenz, K. (1950). The comparative method of studying innate behaviour patterns. *Symposia Soc. Exptl. Biol.* **4**: 221–268.

Lorenz, K. (1951). Über die Entstehung auslösender "Zeremonien." *Vogelwarte* **16**: 9–12.

Lorenz, K., and Tinbergen, N. (1938). Taxis und Instinkthandlung in der Eirollbewegung der Graugans. I. *Z. Tierpsychol.* **2**: 1–29.

McDougall, W. (1936). "An Outline of Psychology." Methuen, London.

Maier, N. R. F., and Schneirla, T. C. (1935). "Principles of Animal Psychology." McGraw Hill, London and New York.

Marler, P. (1955–1956). Studies of fighting in Chaffinches. *Brit. J. Animal Behaviour* **3**: 111–117, 137–146; **4**: 23–30.

Marler, P. (1956). The voice of the Chaffinch and its function as a language. *Ibis* **98**: 231–261.

Marler, P. (1957a). The behaviour of the Chaffinch. *Behaviour Supplement No.* **5**: 1–184.

Marler, P. (1957b). Specific distinctiveness in the communication signals of birds. *Behaviour* **11**: 13–39.

Marshall, A. J. (1954). "Bower-Birds." Oxford Univ. Press, London and New York.

Matthews, G. V. T. (1955). "Bird Navigation." Cambridge Univ. Press, London and New York.

Morris, D. (1954). The reproductive behaviour of the Zebra Finch (*Poephila guttata*) with special reference to pseudofemale behaviour and displacement activities. *Behaviour* **6**: 271–322.

Morris, D. (1956). The feather postures of birds and the problem of the origin of social signals. *Behaviour* **9**: 75–113.

Morris, D. (1957). Typical intensity and its relation to the problem of ritualisation. *Behaviour* **11**: 1–12.

Moseley, D. (1925). The accuracy of the pecking response in chicks. *J. Comp. Psychol.* **5**: 75–97.

Moynihan, M. (1955). Some aspects of reproductive behaviour in the Black-headed Gull (*Larus ridibundus* L.) and related species. *Behaviour Supplement No.* **4**: 1–201.

Nice, M. (1943). Studies in the life history of the song sparrow. II. *Trans. Linnean Soc. N.Y.* **6**: 1–328.

Palmgren, P. (1949). On the diurnal rhythm of activity and rest in birds. *Ibis* **91**: 561–576.

Porter, J. P. (1906). Further study of the English Sparrow and other birds. *Am. J. Psychol.* **17**: 248–271.

Porter, J. P. (1910). Intelligence and imitation in birds: a criterion of imitation. *Am. J. Psychol.* **21**: 1–71.

Prechtl, H. F. R. (1953). Zur Physiologie der angeborenen auslösenden Mechanismen. *Behaviour* **5**: 32–50.

Räber, H. (1948). Analyse des Balzverhaltens eines domestizierten Truthahns (*Meleagris*) *Behaviour* **1**: 237–266.

Ramsay, A. O., and Hess, E. H. (1954). A laboratory approach to the study of imprinting. *Wilson Bull.* **66**: 196–206.

Rogers, F. T. (1926). Contribution to the physiology of the stomach. *Am. J. Physiol.* **44**: 555.

Rouse, J. E. (1905). Respiration and emotion in pigeons. *J. Comp. Neurol.* **15**: 494–513

Russell, E. S. (1943). Perceptual and sensory signs in instinctive behaviour. *Proc. Linnean Soc. London* **154**: 195–216.

Sauer, F. (1954). Die Entwicklung der Lautäusserungen vom Ei abschalldichtgehaltener Dorngrasmücken (*Sylvia c. communis* L.) im Vergleich mit später isolierten und mit wildlebenden Artgenossen. *Z. Tierpsychol.* **11**: 10–93.

Sauer, F. (1956). Über das Verhalten junger Gartengrasmücken *Sylvia borin. J. Ornithol.* **97**: 156–187.

Schleidt, M. (1952). Untersuchungen über die Auslösung des Kollerns beim Truthahn (*Meleagris gallapagos*). *Z. Tierpsychol.* **11**: 417–435.

Seitz, A. (1940). Die Paarbilding bei einigen Cichliden. *Z. Tierpsychol.* **4**: 40–84; (1941) **5**: 74–101.

Sherrington, C. S. (1906). "The Integrative Action of the Nervous System." Yale Univ. Press.

Shoemaker, H. H. (1939). Effect of testosterone propionate on behaviour of the female canary. *Proc. Soc. Exptl. Biol. Med.* **41**: 299–302.

Simmons, K. E. L. (1952). The nature of the predator-reactions of breeding birds. *Behaviour* **4**: 161–172.

Skinner, B. F. (1948). Superstition in the pigeon. *J. Exptl. Biol.* **38**: 168–172.

Spalding, D. (1873). Instinct, with original observations on young animals. Reprinted (1954). *Brit. J. Animal Behaviour* **2**: 2–11.

Stonehouse, B. (1953). The Emperor Penguin. I. *Falkland Islands Dependencies Survey Sci. Rept. 6* London.

Sturkie, P. D. (1954). "Avian Physiology." Comstock, Ithaca, New York.

Swanberg, P. O. (1951). Food storage, territory and song in the Thick-billed Nutcracker. *Proc. 10th Intern. Congr. Ornithol. Upsala* pp. 545–554.

Thorpe, W. H. (1948). The modern concept of instinctive behaviour. *Bull. Animal Behaviour* **7**: 2–12.

Thorpe, W. H. (1956). "Learning and Instinct in Animals." Methuen, London.

Tinbergen, N. (1939). The behaviour of the Snow Bunting in spring. *Trans. Linnean Soc. N.Y.* **5**: 1–91.

Tinbergen, N. (1940). Die Überspringbewegung. *Z. Tierpsychol.* **4**: 1–40.

Tinbergen, N. (1942). An objectivistic study of the innate behaviour of animals. *Bibliotheca Biotheoretica* **1**: 39–98.

Tinbergen, N. (1948). Social releasers and the experimental method required for their study. *Wilson Bull.* **60**: 6–52.

Tinbergen, N. (1951). "The Study of Instinct." Oxford Univ. Press, London and New York.

Tinbergen, N. (1952). Derived activities: their causation, biological significance, origin and emancipation during evolution. *Quart. Rev. Biol.* **27**: 1–32.

Tinbergen, N. (1953). "The Herring Gull's World." Collins, London.

Tinbergen, N. (1954). The origin and evolution of courtship and threat display. *In* "Evolution as a Process" (A. C. Hardy, J. S. Huxley, and E. B. Ford, eds.), London.

Tinbergen, N. (1957). The functions of territory. *Bird Study* **4**: 14–28.

Tinbergen, N., and Kuenen, D. J. (1939). Über die auslösende und die richtunggebende Reizsituation der Sperrbewegung von jungen Drosseln. *Z. Tierpsychol.* **3**: 37–60.

Tinbergen, N., and Perdeck, A. C. (1950). On the stimulus situation releasing the begging response in the newly-hatched Herring Gull chick (*Larus argentus* Pont.). *Behaviour* **3**: 1–38.

Warden, C. J., Jenkins, T. N., and Warner, L. H. (1936). "Comparative Psychology." Ronald Press, New York.

Wolfe, J. B., and Kaplon, M. (1941). Effect of amount of reward and consummative activity on learning in chickens. *J. Comp. Psychol.* **31**: 353–361.

Wood-Gush, D. G. M. (1955). The behaviour of the domestic chicken. *Brit. J. Animal Behaviour* **3**: 81–110.

CHAPTER XXIV

Bird Populations

JOHN A. GIBB

I. Introduction

The study of animal populations is a comparatively recent branch of biology, and research has followed three main lines: observations on natural populations in the field; studies of populations kept under controlled conditions in the laboratory; and mathematical and logical argument. Field observations on natural populations of birds have been especially rewarding, principally because birds can be watched and counted more easily than most other animals. On the other hand, populations of birds cannot be kept in the laboratory; and because greater precision is obtainable in the laboratory than in the field, theoretical work on animal populations has been strongly influenced by laboratory work—notably with insects (e.g. Nicholson, 1933; Park, 1948; but cf. Capildeo and Haldane, 1954). One of the most promising lines of research on bird populations is to compare and contrast what happens in the field with the theoretical predictions derived from simplified laboratory experiments involving other animals.

Since the study of animal populations is essentially concerned with their numbers, the first task in the field must be to devise methods of measuring the population: on the accuracy of these measurements all else depends. Other measurements will be concerned with rates of reproduction and mortality, with age and sex ratios, migration and dispersal; and with all those elements of the environment which may affect the lives and deaths of the animals.

In writing briefly over so wide a field, it is impossible to give more than a thumbnail sketch of what is known. For a more detailed discussion of the topics raised in this chapter, the reader is referred to Lack's comprehensive review in his "The Natural Regulation of Animal Numbers" (1954a). Much of the material and inspiration for this chapter have come from Lack's book, and the extent of the present writer's debt will be obvious to those already familiar with it. It is, however, some measure of the speed of advance in this field that more than half the references quoted in this chapter are post-Lack (1954a), which covered literature on birds up to the end of 1952.

In this short chapter it may seem that some species receive more than their fair share of the space; this is partly because they happen to be those that have been studied in greatest detail, but also because it has seemed more useful to present a fuller picture of a few species than to spread the load more evenly, but disjointedly, over many.

II. The Measurement of Bird Populations

A. Ways and Means

Populations of birds may be variously expressed according to the purposes for which they have been measured. It is essential clearly to define the objects of the investigation before embarking on measurements in the field; as Morris (1955) rightly remarked about work on insect populations, so also with birds: "Any program initiated on the vague impulse of learning something about insect numbers is unlikely to be productive."

Since adult birds of one species do not vary much in size, it is generally most convenient and meaningful to measure bird populations in terms of the numbers living on a defined area. Even when for special purposes bird populations are expressed in terms of their biomass (Thiele, 1958;

Turček, 1956, 1957), or of their mineral content (Grimshaw *et al.*, 1958), the single bird normally remains the basic unit of measurement. Populations can sometimes also be broken down into age groups or sexes.

Population measurements fall into two distinct categories: censuses, which aim at obtaining an absolute measure of the whole or a defined part of the population; and population indexes, which aim at giving only a relative measure of the abundance of, say, one species in different habitats or of different species in the same habitat. The word "census" should not be used loosely to apply to all types of population measurement.

There is no easy or straightforward way of counting bird populations over extensive blocks of country, and various indirect methods have been used differing with what is practicable in the field. The numerous methods of estimating populations of gallinaceous birds in North America have been reviewed by Hickey (1955): they range from road counts to aerial censuses, from quadrat inventories to fecal counts.

Censuses of birds have been most successfully taken in the breeding season when the birds are "anchored" to their nests. It is sometimes sufficient to count only the number of males heard calling in spring, or the number of occupied nests; and provided that it is not then assumed that every male has a mate or only one mate, or that there is a pair of birds to each nest found and that every bird is paired and has a nest, such short cuts are useful and justified. It is often instructive to compare counts of the same species in the same area made in different ways.

A method of estimating animal populations that has been used successfully with insects and small mammals, but which has been rather neglected by ornithologists [cf. Glading *et al.* (1945) for bobwhite quail (*Colinus virginianus*)], is that of releasing a known number of captured and marked individuals into the population and then recording the proportion of marked to unmarked individuals present. It has to be assumed that the marked individuals will become completely reabsorbed into the population after their release; that marked and unmarked individuals can be recorded subsequently with equal ease; and that there has been no mortality, immigration, or emigration between release and the count of marked and unmarked individuals. If this is so, the unmarked population can be calculated from the equation $x = yx'/y'$ where $x =$ the unmarked population to be measured, $y =$ the number of animals marked and released, $x' =$ the number of unmarked, and $y' =$ the number of marked animals observed afterward. Refinements of this method allow for known mortality and movement (Bailey, 1951, 1952). Since some individual birds become "trap-shy" and others "trap-happy," it is generally useless to rely on retrapped birds for measuring the proportion of marked to unmarked birds in the population; but if the birds are marked with colored leg bands (rings) or in some other distinctive way, the proportions of marked to unmarked birds can sometimes be observed in the field. Failure to secure random sampling will, of course, result in serious errors in estimating the size of the population.

Because it is often difficult to take any kind of census of birds in the field, other useful but less informative indexes of population size have been used; most of these are based on the frequency with which the birds or their traces (e.g. tracks, droppings, old nests) are encountered by the observer. Attempts have been made to relate the frequency of such encounters to the absolute density of the birds (cf. Nordberg, 1948; Yapp, 1956), but this is always a risky procedure.

The abundance of species of one community is sometimes expressed by an order of dominance, giving the percentage of the total bird population contributed by each species. This method is, however, probably of less value to ornithologists than to the botanists from whom it has been borrowed; for reliable orders of dominance cannot be made without complete censuses or accurate relative counts of all the species concerned, and the raw data are usually much more telling than any order of dominance derived from them.

B. Selected Estimates

World-wide censuses of bird populations have naturally been confined to comparatively few rare or exceedingly local species whose exact distribution is known. Thus, in North America, only 28 whooping cranes (*Grus americana*) were thought to be alive in 1956, despite elaborate efforts to protect them. In 1955, about 22 néné or Hawaiian geese (*Branta sandvicensis*) survived in the wild; plus some 48 in captivity in Hawaii or Britain, where stocks are being built up. Probably not more than about 100 takahe (*Notornis mantelli*), until 1948 thought extinct for 50 years, survive in the Murchison Range of the South Island, New Zealand. The California condor (*Gymnogyps californicus*) was down to between 50 and 100 birds in 1953. Recently, a total of 432 singing males of Kirtland's warbler (*Dendroica kirtlandii*) were counted in the jack pine barrens of Michigan, its only known breeding ground; while in the last 40 years only one specimen has been seen on their wintering grounds in the Bahama Islands, where they were formerly quite common. These and many other similar cases have been ably assembled by Greenway (1958); who also makes the points that birds, like other animals, are most commonly brought to the brink of extinction through loss of suitable habitat, and that highly specialized species are the least adaptable to changed conditions.

Among flourishing species, Fisher and Vevers (1943–1944, 1951) using aerial photography estimated that all the colonies of the North Atlantic gannet (*Sula bassana*) amounted to approximately 83,000 nests in 1939. Of these, about 70,000 were on the eastern seaboard, where a repeat census in 1949 gave a total of about 82,000 nests.

The approximate average density of birds in different habitats ranges from less than 10 to more than 300 birds per 10 acres in Britain (Fisher, 1946), and similar densities have been recorded in North America and elsewhere (Udvardy, 1957); but in general the habitats in which birds live are so varied that relatively small sample counts will not be of much value in assessing total populations of large areas, as discussed by Nicholson (1959) reviewing Merikallio's (1958) estimates of total bird populations in Finland.

III. Longevity, Mortality, and Sex Ratio

Senility is a phenomenon virtually confined to civilized man and to some of his domestic animals. The life span of captive birds is commonly much greater than their expectation of life in the wild: thus a captive chaffinch (*Fringilla coelebs*) attained the ripe old age of 29 years (Moltoni, 1947), and an eagle owl (*Bubo bubo*) 68 years (Bourlière, 1946). Nevertheless, some remarkably aged wild birds are on record. The oldest of 22 oyster catchers (*Haematopus ostralegus*) of known age was 27 years old and their average age was $13\frac{1}{2}$ years (Jungfer, 1954; cf. Drost and Hartmann, 1949); a common tern (*Sterna hirundo*) was recovered where it had been banded as an adult 23 years earlier (Austin, 1953); and a swift (*Apus apus*) was still breeding in 1956 in the Swiss colony where it had been banded 17 years before (Weitnauer, 1956).

Farner (1955) has recently examined methods of calculating the average annual adult mortality[1] of wild birds from banding data. The recorded extremes are 72% for blue tits (*Parus caeruleus*) in Britain (Snow, 1956), and a mere 3% (approximately) for royal albatrosses (*Diomedia epomophora*) breeding in New Zealand; at this rate adult royal albatrosses must have an average expectation of further life of around 36 years (Richdale, 1952, quoted in Lack, 1954a)—which would compare favorably with that of modern man. The average annual mortality among small passerine birds and ducks ranges from about

---

[1] Average annual mortality can be expressed as average expectation of life by using the formula $\dfrac{2-m}{2m}$, where m = per cent annual mortality.

40 to 60%; that of gallinaceous birds, waders, and gulls, 20 to 40%; and of swifts, 20% (Lack, 1954a; Hickey, 1955). Richdale (1957) estimated that only 10% of adult yellow-eyed penguins (*Megadyptes antipodes*) die each year; and Boyd (1956), 26% of adult pink-footed geese (*Anser brachyrhynchus*). The average annual adult mortality of most species of wild birds seems to remain more or less constant for each successive year of the bird's life (references in Lack, 1954a; Farner, 1955; Richdale, 1957); though the survival of oyster catchers may continue to improve with age over a long period (Drost and Hartmann, 1949).

In a stable population the birth rate must equal the death rate. It will be shown that the reproductive rate of birds varies from one part of their range to another; it follows that the death rate should vary correspondingly. Snow (1956) compared the proportions of adult to first-year blue tits from different parts of their range in museum collections; from this he demonstrated that the members of the Spanish and Canary Islands populations, whose clutch size is about half that in Britain, were in fact about twice as likely as British birds to survive from one breeding season to the next (cf. Lack and Schifferli, 1948).

TABLE I

THE SEX RATIO OF YOUNG CALIFORNIA QUAILS (*Lophortyx californica*)
IN CENTRAL OTAGO, NEW ZEALAND[a]

Age group	1955 and 1956 combined	
(weeks)	Number in sample[b]	% Males
6–9	50	28
10–13	172	36
14–17	190	54
18+	42	57
Adults	299	64

[a] After Williams (1957).
[b] The birds were sampled by trapping.

With few exceptions, the sex ratio of birds is approximately 1:1 at hatching, though males slightly outnumber females in many adult populations (Mayr, 1939). This implies that more females than males die each year, perhaps from special hazards in breeding. Table I shows that in the California quail (*Lophortyx californica*) in Central Otago, New Zealand, males formed less than one third of the approximately 10-week-old juvenile population, but about two thirds of the adult population (Williams, 1957). Excessive hunting pressure on turkey (*Meleagris gallopavo*) gobblers in one year resulted in a sex ratio of one male to twenty-one females (Walker, 1949, quoted in Hickey, 1955).

Males of many species are a little larger than the females and dominate them in the social hierarchy; this could give them some advantage over females in intraspecific competition, for instance for food. Likewise, Kluyver (1957) has shown that in winter male great tits tend to get safer roost-sites, for which there is often acute intraspecific competition, than do the females; and that this probably enhances their chances of survival. Significantly, female sparrow hawks (*Accipiter nisus*) and goshawks (*A. gentilis*) are larger than the males and outnumber them.

IV. Rates of Reproduction and Juvenile Mortality

A. REPRODUCTIVE RATE AS A PRODUCT OF NATURAL SELECTION

Lack (summarized 1954a) has championed the view that the reproductive rate of birds and probably also of other animals is a product of natural selection and is not, as has sometimes been supposed, somehow adjusted to the normal mortality of the species. Natural selection must favor those individuals which produce the most offspring that survive to maturity. Hence the age at which birds first breed, their breeding seasons, the number of broods reared per pair each year, and the number of eggs laid per clutch will generally correspond to whatever leads to the greatest number of young being reared to maturity. Though Lack's hypothesis, in effect that birds rear as many young as they can, has been challenged from time to time, for example by Skutch (1949) and Wagner (1957) for tropical birds and by Wynne-Edwards (1955) for sea birds, it is supported by an impressive bulk of evidence.

B. AGE OF FIRST BREEDING

Most small passerine birds first breed at the end of their first year; other, generally larger, birds not until they are 2 or more years old, and royal albatrosses not until they are at least 8 years old (Richdale, 1952). The relation between size and age of first breeding is by no means consistent, however, for among those species that breed when 1 year old are most ducks and gallinaceous birds, while among those not breeding until their second year are the swifts (*Apus* spp.) (Lack, 1954a).

C. BREEDING SEASONS AND THE NUMBER OF BROODS PER SEASON

The breeding seasons of birds are discussed fully in Chapter XXI (Vol. II), so it is necessary only to suggest here why birds breed when they do. In general, the breeding seasons of birds "are adapted to the environmental cycle in such a way as to secure that the maximum supply of appropriate food will be available when the young are hatched and for a sufficient time after they are first on the wing. The evidence on this point seems . . . overwhelming" (Thomson, 1950).

As a rule, birds have a single, more or less well-defined breeding season each year. A few species, notably those living in those parts of the Tropics with two rainy seasons, have two breeding seasons, and "there is in fact reason to believe that at least in some species the individuals breed twice" (Thomson, 1950). Other exceptional species breed at irregular intervals corresponding with unpredictable changes in their food supply (e.g. Marshall, 1949). The wideawake tern (*Sterna fuscata*) is the only bird known to breed at regular intervals of less than 12 months: in the huge colony on Ascension Island in the Atlantic the birds breed together regularly every $9\frac{1}{2}$ months (Chapin, 1946), though on the Seychelles the same species has a normal annual cycle (Moreau, 1950)[1]. Individual royal albatrosses breed only in alternate years because they take longer than 12 months to rear their single young (Richdale, 1951); and for the same reason king penguins (*Aptenodytes patagonica*) rear only two chicks, one at a time, every three years (Stonehouse, 1956).

Although most birds have a single restricted breeding season, many individuals succeed in rearing two or three or more broods in a season. Species are not consistent in this matter: in broad-leaved woods for instance, only about 7 per cent of the great tits (*Parus major*) rear second broods in England, compared with about 36% in the Netherlands (Lack, 1955; Kluijver, 1951); while in Malaya they normally rear two, and often three broods in a season (Cairns, 1956).

D. Clutch Size

While each species has its own characteristic clutch size, the average clutch size of most birds varies in different parts of the species' range, from one habitat to another, from one year to another, from one week to another in the same locality, with the age of the individual, and between individuals of the same age in the community. Though the clutch size of birds is presumably controlled genetically, it is not fixed

---

[1] A British Ornithologists' Union Centenary Expedition to Ascension Island, under Dr. Bernard Stonehouse, recently completed an 18-months study of the ecology and behaviour of the wideawake terns and other sea-birds there. Full findings have yet to be published (April 1959); but early reports from the island suggest that other species besides the wideawakes may also breed "at intervals which are neither annual nor simple fractions of a year" (Stonehouse, 1958).

for many species and many of the observed variations are probably adapted to the environment (Lack, 1956a).

Purely individual variation in clutch size within one population suggests that no one size of clutch is always the most productive. Sometimes more young may survive from unusually small, and at other times from unusually large, clutches than from those of the average size; but over a period of years more young will survive from average-sized than from smaller or larger clutches. Thus in Britain, swifts usually lay clutches of two or three eggs, and exceptionally of one or four eggs. In fine summers, when insect food is plentiful, the broods of three young are each more productive than those of two young; but in wet summers, when food is scarce, more young are reared from each brood starting with two young than from each of those starting with three or more young; and in very bad summers actually more from broods starting with one young than from those starting with two. On the average, however, the most frequent clutch size is the most productive; while genotypes resulting in clutches of above or below average size are preserved in the population because they are favored occasionally (Lack, 1956a). A similar situation prevails among other species of birds investigated—in starlings (*Sturnus vulgaris*), English robins (*Erithacus rubecula*), and great tits, for instance (references in Lack, 1954a; Lack *et al.*, 1957).

A small minority of birds, the so-called determinate layers, lay a set number of eggs per clutch. These are invariably species which lay small clutches: thus petrels and shearwaters (Procellariidae) all lay a single egg; most pigeons (Columbidae), two eggs; and most waders (Charadriidae), consistently either three or four eggs. Petrels and shearwaters rely on a notoriously precarious food supply and often have to travel vast distances from their breeding stations to get it (Lockley, 1953); the single chick grows slowly, stays in the nest for a long period, and may have to fast for several days on end. If there were two chicks per brood instead of one, the survival of both would be jeopardized and probably fewer, not more, young would be reared.

The number of eggs laid per clutch is not, or is rarely, limited physiologically, for more eggs are formed than are laid, and unlaid eggs are resorbed. Moreover, if eggs are removed from an incomplete clutch, some birds will make up the full complement—though others will not (Davis, 1955; Snow, 1958). Nor does the clutch size of most birds correspond to the greatest number of eggs that the bird can incubate: for it has been repeatedly demonstrated that the number of eggs in the clutch does not affect the proportion that hatch (references in Lack, 1954a).

On the other hand, the clutch size of birds often corresponds broadly with the greatest number of young that the parents can rear, and in particular with the number they can feed. This is most clearly apparent among nidicolous birds whose young are entirely dependent upon their parents for several weeks after hatching. It is much less apparent why those nidifugous birds whose young are more or less independent after hatching should not lay more eggs and rear more young than they do; further observations are needed to answer this point for most of such species. In the megapodes, which lay one egg every few days in the laying season and whose young hatch at corresponding intervals and are completely independent of their parents immediately upon hatching, the number of eggs laid may be determined primarily by the length of the breeding season (Frith, 1956). The number of eggs laid by parasitic birds, such as certain cuckoos (*Cuculiidae*) and the cowbird (*Molothrus spp.*), whose young are wholly reared by foster parents, could be limited by the number of suitable nests in which to lay. E. P. Chance (Witherby *et al.*, 1938–1941), for instance, induced a European cuckoo (*Cuculus canorus*) to lay twenty-five eggs in one season, about five times the normal complement, by securing for it a succession of meadow pipits' (*Anthus pratensis*) nests at the right stage for laying.

In connection with the importance of food for the young in determining clutch size, it is significant, as Lack (1954a) points out, that European cuckoos which are much larger than their hosts, lay but a single egg in each of their hosts' nests, and that the young cuckoo ejects all its nestmates as soon as it hatches, so receiving the undivided attention of its foster parents; whereas female great spotted cuckoos (*Clamator glandarius*), which are about the same size as their corvid hosts, merely remove one of the hosts' eggs when laying their own, and the young cuckoo grows up with the young of its host.

The correspondence between the clutch size of nidicolous birds and the amount of food available for their young is conspicuous in those predators, notably buzzards (*Buteo* spp.) and owls (Strigidae), which feed upon voles (*Microtus* spp.). These birds lay much larger clutches and rear much larger families during vole plagues than at other times. Again, Swanberg (quoted in Lack, 1954a) induced wild nutcrackers (*Nucifraga caryocatactes*) to lay especially large clutches by providing them with an additional supply of hazelnuts.

If the clutch size of many birds is really limited by the capacity of the parents to look after, and particularly to feed, their young, it should be found that the chances of survival are less good for a young bird from a large, than from a small family. The relevant mortality could occur before or after the young have left the nest, or at both stages.

Moreau (1947), working with nine different species of birds in Tanganyika, established that "the more young in the nest the more frequent the parents' visits, but not in proportion to the increase in the number of young; so that on the average a solitary nestling gets more food than a member of a pair or of a trio." This has since been confirmed in a wide variety of birds (references in Lack, 1954a) that includes the house wren (*Troglodytes aedon*) in North America (Kendeigh, 1952) and the great tit in Britain (Gibb, 1955)—both studied by means of mechanical recorders at their nests. The nestling great tits were also weighed, and it was found that those in the larger broods were in fact lighter than those in the smaller broods, especially in summers when their food was least abundant (Gibb, 1950 and unpublished). But whereas the young swifts referred to earlier in this section died in the nest, the young great tits rarely did so; and there was little difference in the proportion of the young that fledged from broods of different sizes. Instead, young great tits from the large broods are apparently handicapped after leaving the nest; Table II indicates that their chances of reaching maturity are less good than are those of the young from smaller broods (Lack *et al.*, 1957, and Lack, 1958; see also Lockie, 1955, for corvids).

TABLE II

Survival of Young Great Tits (*Parus major*) and Blue Tits (*P. caeruleus*) according to Brood Size, in a Mixed Broad-leaved Wood in Britain[a]

Number of young per brood	Number of young banded	% Recovered alive more than 3 months later
Great tit		
3–10	1337	6.9
11–13	317	2.2
Blue tit		
3–10	699	5.0
11–13	619	3.1

[a]After Lack *et al.* (1957).

Lack (1947–1948) brought together much evidence that European birds tend, with few exceptions, to lay larger clutches in the northern and eastern parts than in the southern and western parts of their range. He attributed the north-south trend to the longer day length in the north than in the south, which would enable birds to bring more food to their nests each day and so to rear more young.

However obvious it may seem that much of the variation in the clutch size of birds is governed ultimately by the number of young that

the parents can rear, the proximate factors involved are largely unknown.

E. Breeding Success

Nice (1957), reviewing published data, concluded that on the average
about 46% of eggs laid by nidicolous birds in open nests, and about
66% of those laid in nests in holes, develop into young that leave the
nest successfully. Mrs Nice points out that the difference between open
and hole-nesting species is actually greater than this suggests because
hole-nesting birds stay in their nests longer and leave at a more advanced stage of development than do open-nesters: thus the daily loss
of eggs or young from nests in holes is only about 1%, compared with
about 2% from open nests. These data were derived exclusively from
studies in the North Temperate zone; nesting losses may be heavier in
the Tropics.

The breeding success of nidifugous birds cannot be exactly equated
with that of nidicolous birds; but evidently they suffer heavier losses of
eggs than is usual even among open-nesting nidicolous species. In the
Phasianinae on the average about 36%, and in the Tetraoninae 51%,
of the nests survive to hatching (Hickey, 1955).

Probably most losses of eggs and nestlings among small birds are
due to predation by birds and mammals, or to inclement weather. In
certain years in Britain, weasels (*Mustela nivalis*) have destroyed more
than half the nests of tits (*Parus* spp.) in nest boxes in broad-leaved
woods and pine plantations (Lack, 1958). Foxes accounted for 89%
of the losses of eggs of ruffed grouse (*Bonasa umbellus*) in North America;
while two species of birds of prey (Accipitres) accounted for most of the
losses of their young, which amounted to 63% of those hatched
(Bump *et al.*, 1947).

Although young passerine birds rarely die from starvation while in
the nest, young birds of prey often do: indeed birds of prey usually lay
more eggs and hatch more young than they are likely to be able to
rear. Unlike most passerine birds, birds of prey commonly start incubating as soon as the first egg of the clutch has been laid, with the result
that the brood hatches over a period of several days. The youngest and
weakest nestlings survive only if food is unusually plentiful. This
system appears to be an adaptation by birds of prey to cope with an
unpredictable food supply.

Lockley (Fisher and Lockley, 1954) once found "hundreds" of young
puffins (*Fratercula arctica*) dying from excessive bloodsucking by the
red mite (*Dermanyssus gallinae*), in the Channel Islands. Bloodsucking
larvae of calliphorid flies also occasionally kill nestling birds, but

seldom cause heavy mortality (Owen, 1954; but cf. Neff, 1945). Bendell (1955), however, found that parasitism of the chicks of blue grouse (*Dendragapus fuliginosus*) by helminths was an important mortality factor.

F. Juvenile Mortality

In every species so far investigated juvenile birds suffer a heavier mortality than the adults [references in Lack (1954a); see also Lack and Arn (1953), Schmidt and Hantge (1954), and Boyd (1956) for the alpine swift (*Apus melba*), Whinchat (*Saxicola rubetra*), and pink-footed goose, respectively]. From about 20 to 50% of the young of gallinaceous birds die in their first two months after hatching (Hickey, 1955). Young birds may be especially vulnerable just after they have become independent of their parents: thus Southern *et al.* (1954) found that almost all fledgling tawny owls (*Strix aluco*) survived while they were being fed by their parents—for about two months after leaving the nest—but that many died shortly afterward. The young owls suddenly became independent after a long period of complete dependence upon their parents for food, whereas the young of most birds achieve their independence gradually.

Emlen (1940) found that first-year birds represented about 70% of the total population of California quail in October, after the breeding season, about 60% by December, and about 50% from April to June of the next breeding season. Juvenile tits suffer a heavier mortality than the adults until they are about 6 months old (Snow, 1956); and, at the other extreme, yellow-eyed penguins for their first two or three years of life, though especially in the first year (Richdale, 1957).

In a rapidly expanding population both adults and young have a better chance of survival than in a stable population. The collared turtledove (*Streptopelia decaocto*), which has spread 1200 miles westward across Europe in the last twenty-five years, is an example (see also Fig. 3): in a two-year study in West Germany, 60% and 46% of the young reared were still alive and in the same neighborhood in the following breeding season (Hofstetter, 1954). Since each pair raised on the average five young in a season, many more must have died had the population been stable.

V. Changes in Bird Populations

A. Associated with Changes in Geographical Range and Habitat

The mobility of birds is their most impressive characteristic; and this allows them to move quickly into and out of temporarily favorable habitats and to even out local irregularities in their population density. Substantial increases in bird populations are often accompanied not only by an increased density in the preferred habitats, but also by the occupation of marginal habitats, which may or may not involve an extension of their geographical range. The spread of the fulmar (*Fulmarus glacialis*) round the coasts of Britain (Fisher, 1952) and of the collared turtledove across Europe (Fisher, 1953) are both examples of a simultaneous increase in population and extension of range; while Schorger (1942) reported that in early Wisconsin the turkey was periodically wiped out along the northern borders of its range, but systematically recolonized the state from better parts of its range in Illinois to the south. Since even annual changes in bird populations are frequently accompanied by concomitant changes in geographical range or habitat, any measure of bird populations based solely on their population density in one locality is likely to be incomplete.

Deliberate introductions by man, notably in the second half of the last and early in the present century, have led to some of the most spectacular explosions on record in the ranges and populations of birds, as of other animals (see Elton, 1958, for examples).

B. Restricted Fluctuations

The populations of most birds seem to fluctuate irregularly within rather narrow limits from year to year. Thus Kluijver and others (Kluijver, 1951) counted the great tits breeding in nest boxes in a Dutch pine forest from 1912 to 1943 (Fig. 1); as the habitat improved over the period, the average density of the great tits increased, but their numbers also fluctuated irregularly from year to year. A high population in one year was often followed by a low population in the next, and vice versa. The number of great tits present in one breeding season bore no relation to the number of young reared in the previous season. With their high reproductive capacity great tits are able to recover from ordinary setbacks in a single breeding season.

Populations of herons (*Ardea cinerea*) and white storks (*Ciconia ciconia*) in Britain and Europe, respectively, fluctuate irregularly within narrower limits than the great tits (references in Lack, 1954a,b). Figure 2 shows that herons are much reduced by such severe winters as that of 1946–1947, and unlike the tits may take up to four years to recover their former density. The factors affecting the numbers of storks are unknown, but they too take two or more years to recover from major setbacks. Both species have a much lower reproductive rate than have the tits.

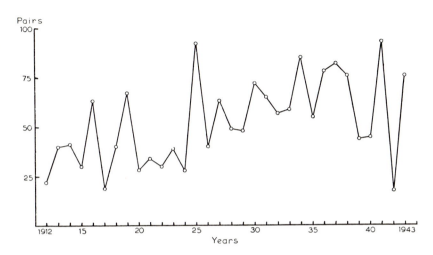

FIG. 1. The number of pairs of great tits (*Parus major*) breeding in 129 ha. (approximately 320 acres) of pine and mixed woodland in the Netherlands, from 1912 to 1943. The population slowly increased as the habitat became more favorable. After Kluijver (1951).

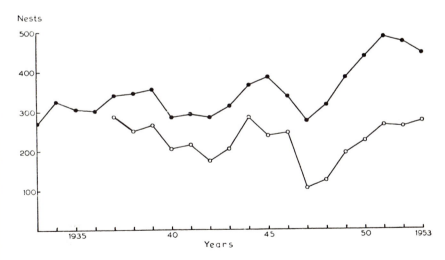

FIG. 2. The number of occupied nests of the European heron (*Ardea cinerea*) in two regions in Britain, (a) the Thames drainage area (upper graph, blacked-in circles) and (b) Cheshire and South Lancashire (lower graph, open circles); counted by members of the British Trust for Ornithology. After Lack (1954b).

C. "Invasion" Species

The so-called "irruption" or "invasion" birds comprise a small group of species largely coming from high latitudes in Europe, Asia, and America, but including, for instance, the rose-colored starling (*Sturnus roseus*) of southeastern Europe and southern Asia.

Svärdson (1957) made the following distinctions between "invasion" and ordinary migratory species. Food shortage is acknowledged to be the ultimate factor inducing the migration of both groups; but whereas the migration of ordinary migrants is adapted to a regular seasonal shortage, that of "invasion" species is adapted to irregular annual variations in the food supply. Consequently, ordinary migrant birds are undeterred by a local or unseasonable abundance of food, which would delay "invasion" species until it was exhausted. Again, the breeding ranges of ordinary migrant birds are fairly constant from year to year, but "invasion" species settle to breed wherever they happen to find enough food. The breeding populations of most birds are therefore more or less evenly distributed over their range and constant from year to year; while those of "invasion" species are aggregated locally and vary markedly from year to year. Finally, the routes taken by ordinary migrants are similar from year to year (and typically north to south), but those of "invasion" species are less predictable (and commonly east to west in Europe and Asia).

The crossbill (*Loxia curvirostra*) is an outstanding "invasion" species; with others of its group it is a food specialist—on the seeds of spruce (*Picea*) in northern Europe. The crops of spruce cones are notoriously unreliable, and the birds move around from district to district in search of them. Thus Reinikainen (1937) found that the density of crossbills breeding in one district in Finland was closely correlated with the size of the cone crop over an eleven-year period.

Siivonen (1941) observed that waxwings (*Bombycilla garrulus*), another typical "invasion" species, emigrated from northern to central Europe in any winter when the crop of berries, their main food, failed; but that the really large-scale invasions began earlier in the autumn than the lesser movements, and before the birds could assess the size of the coming crop of berries. These big invasions coincided with especially high populations of the birds following a successful breeding season. Thus the frequent small movements began as a direct response to food shortage; while the large invasions, triggered off by abnormally high populations of birds, were apparently in anticipation of food shortage—due not to a failure of the crop of berries but simply to the large numbers of birds among which the crop must be shared. Anticipatory behavior of this kind is of course a frequent product of natural selection.

D. Cycles

We have just seen that the fluctuations in the numbers of certain species normally living in high latitudes are often of greater amplitude than is common in temperate regions. The populations of a few other species of birds also from high latitudes not only fluctuate widely, but do so—or seem to do so—at more or less regular intervals of time; moreover, the fluctuations of several different species of mammals and birds are seemingly synchronized with each other.

In the conifer forests of North America the numbers of the varying hare (*Lepus americanus*) and of its predator the lynx (*Lynx canadensis*) reach a peak about every ten years and then "crash"; in the Arctic tundra of northern Europe, lemmings (*Dicrostonyx groenlandicus* and *Lemnus lemnus*), and, between the tundra and the conifers, voles (*Microtus* spp.), reach peaks in numbers about every four years. In each case, the fluctuations in the numbers of the bird and mammal predators on the hares, lemmings and voles have a similar periodicity. In addition, too, the numbers of gallinaceous birds living in the same regions seem to be synchronized with the numbers of the lemmings or voles. Thus in North America, peaks in the numbers of ruffed grouse seem linked with the ten-year cycle of the varying hare; and in Norway, the willow grouse (*Lagopus lagopus*) with the four-year cycle of the lemmings (Elton and Nicholson, 1942; references in Lack, 1954a and in Hickey, 1955).

A symposium number of the *Journal of Wildlife Management* (January, 1954) revealed wide differences of opinion concerning cycles in animal numbers. Statisticians have difficulty in distinguishing cyclic from purely random changes in numbers (cf. Palmgren, 1949; Andrewartha and Birch, 1954); while biologists are at a loss to account for their underlying causes. Bump *et al.* (1947), for instance, examined no less than twelve different "explanations." Svärdson (1957) produced evidence that in southern Sweden winters with abundant crops of spruce seed recur every third or fourth year and suggested that this might account for the cyclic fluctuation of those birds and mammals which largely depend on the seeds for food. Fortunately, whatever the underlying causes in the cyclic changes in the numbers of the hares, lemmings, and voles, it is generally agreed that the numbers of their predators, notably the arctic fox (*Alopex lagopus*) and snowy owl (*Nyctea scandiaca*), respond to the abundance of the prey species (references in Lack, 1954a).

The connection between the cyclic changes in the numbers of hares, lemmings, and voles, and of their predators, with those of the game birds in the same region is less apparent. Leopold (1933) observed that the predators turned to prey upon the game birds when their main food of small mammals was exhausted. As the predators are most numerous when the numbers of their chief prey "crash," and as the game birds are in any case normally much less numerous than the mammal prey, the predators might reasonably have a pronounced effect on the numbers of the game birds, which could serve only as a temporary buffer between the predators and starvation (Lack, 1954a; Hickey, 1955). Hoffmann (1958) has pointed out, however, that populations of grouse sometimes decline *ahead* of the drop in the population of the predators' usual mammal prey. Chitty (1952), Williams (1954) and others have suggested that weather must play an important part in achieving synchrony between the cycles of different animals living in the same region; but this, too, has yet to be demonstrated (e.g. Moran, 1954).

In a theoretical situation involving one species of predator and one species of prey, where the numbers of the one depend on those of the other, the resulting changes in the populations of each will tend to oscillate regularly with time (Gause, 1934; Nicholson and Bailey, 1935). As the numbers of the prey increase, so also will those of the predator— until the predators become so numerous that they cause a decline in the numbers of the prey, and so in turn also of themselves. There will, however, be a time lag between the oscillations of the prey and those of the predator. This is the so-called Lotka-Volterra type of oscillation, involving what Varley (1947) termed "delayed density-dependent" mortality. No certain examples have been described from among birds, though some of Errington's (1945) census figures for bobwhite quail in Wisconsin are suggestive, as discussed by Lack (1954a). Some cyclic changes in bird populations could be explained in this way; but present evidence is inconclusive.

VI. The Natural Regulation of Bird Populations

A. THE STABILITY OF BIRD POPULATIONS

Notwithstanding the considerable annual fluctuations in bird populations that have been recorded in almost every species investigated, it is their comparative stability over long periods that is their most remarkable attribute. As Lack (1954a) remarked of animal populations generally, "compared with the theoretical possibilities of geometric increase, even the huge fluctuations of certain insect pests are tiny ripples."

The existence of a real control on the size of most bird populations is well illustrated by contrasting the restricted population changes described in the previous section with what can happen to an almost uncontrolled population. This is still best exemplified by Einarsen's (1945) well-quoted census figures for a population of pheasants (*Phasianus colchicus*) on Protection Island (about 400 acres) in Oregon, given in Fig. 3. Two cocks and six hens, with a couple of tom cats as predators, were liberated in 1937; and the population was then counted every

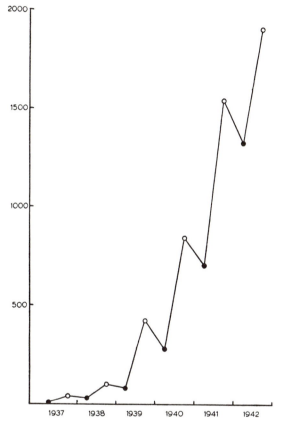

FIG. 3. The number of pheasants (*Phasianus colchicus*) on Protection Island, Oregon; counted each spring (blacked-in circles) and fall (open circles) for six years after the liberation of two cocks and six hens in 1937. After Einarsen (1945).

spring and fall for the next six years. The phenomenal increase in the population over this period followed a typical sigmoid growth curve. World War II unfortunately put a stop to this delightful experiment.

If the numbers of any animal are to be effectively controlled in nature, it is reasonable to suppose that the control "should act more severely against an average individual when the density of animals is high, and less severely when the density is low"; moreover, "any factor having the necessary property for the control of populations must be some form of competition" (quotations from Nicholson, 1933). Although Nicholson's views have found wide acceptance among students of animal populations, they have been disputed from time to time (e.g. Andrewartha and Birch, 1954); and it must be admitted that theory has outpaced fact in this field. If Nicholson is correct, however, then either the mortality of animal must vary with, or its reproductive rate inversely with, its density.

While the adverse effects of high density have rightly received greater prominence, Allee (in Allee *et al.*, 1949) has illustrated, with many examples from birds and other animals, the widespread phenomenon that very small populations are also commonly unfavorable for survival and growth.

B. Density-dependent Reproduction

Lack (1954a) assembled a number of references indicating a reduced fecundity at high densities in animals generally; but in birds this has been demonstrated only in the genus *Parus*, the tits. Kluijver (1951) was first to show that great tits in Dutch pine forests laid slightly fewer eggs per clutch, and that a smaller proportion of them tried to rear second broods, when their numbers were high than when they were low; and similar results have now been obtained for great tits, blue tits, and coal tits (*Parus ater*) in Britain (Lack, 1958). The differences are, however, too small to contribute significantly to the natural control of the tit populations (Kluijver, 1951; Lack, 1952).

From numerous studies of gallinaceous birds, Hickey (1955) concluded that: "In general, the percentage of summer gain is inversely proportional to the density in spring." But this was more probably due to density-dependent mortality among the young than to a density-dependent fecundity of the adults. On the other hand, Jenkins (1957) believes that in the partridge (*Perdix perdix*) "juvenile survival rates vary according to the amount of mutual disturbance among the adults before the breeding season, suggesting an adverse effect on their reproductive powers which is passed on to their young and favours their early death" (cf. Chitty, 1957).

Snowy owls and some other birds of prey lay their largest clutches and rear most young in years when their prey are most plentiful. Since the owls are also most numerous when and where their food abounds, their fecundity is greatest when their density is highest (i.e. the opposite of what was found for the tits); but there is no reason to think that a high density of owls per se induces large clutches.

Though there is no good evidence of a density-dependent fecundity except in tits, the reproductive rate of a species could vary inversely with the size (if not with the density) of the whole population if more birds dispersed into poorer habitats when their numbers were high than when they were low (cf. Kluyver and Tinbergen, 1953; Hamerstrom and Hamerstrom, 1955; MacArthur, 1958); and if those that so dispersed reared fewer young than those left in the richer habitats. Such dispersal could be accelerated by the birds' territorial behavior. Unfortunately, the field observations necessary to test this possibility have yet to be made.

Apart from this, it is unlikely that comparatively small differences in the reproductive rate of birds will be important in the natural control of populations. Neither Kluijver (1951) for great tits, nor Schüz (1940) for storks, found any correlation between the number of young reared and the number surviving to breed. Although Bendell (1955) thought that parasitism of the chicks of blue grouse by helminths was "a major cause of their population stability," the effective density-dependent mortality regulating bird populations seems normally to occur after the young have become independent of their parents.

C. DENSITY-DEPENDENT MORTALITY

Lacking substantial density-dependent variations in the reproductive rates of birds, it might be supposed that their rates of mortality would be obviously density-dependent; whereas in fact such mortality has been demonstrated only in the bobwhite quails studied by Errington (1945) in Wisconsin. Lack (1954a) interpreted Errington's population data for fourteen years as showing that the more quail at the end of the breeding season, the higher their percentage mortality before the following November.

Most but not all forms of mortality will operate in a density-dependent way, and Nicholson (1933) stressed the important element of competition in density-dependent mortality. Disease, predation, and starvation are probably the most likely causes of mortality which birds may compete to avoid. The relative importance of each is extremely difficult to judge because the effects of one cannot usually be disentangled from those of the others. Rudebeck (1950–1951), for instance, recorded that birds captured by peregrines [duck hawks (*Falco peregrinus*)] and sparrow hawks include a disproportionate number of abnormal individuals: although predation was the immediate, disease or starvation may have been the ultimate, cause of death.

EE

1. *Disease*

The report of Lovat (1912) on strongylosis in red grouse (*Lagopus scoticus*) remains a classic and is the only recorded instance in which the mortality resulting from disease has been shown to be density-dependent. Lack (1954a) has pointed out, however, that food shortage rather than strongylosis may have been the ultimate cause of death.

Other evidence of disease in wild birds is mostly fragmentary; it has been usefully reviewed by Herman (1955). More is known of the incidence of ectoparasites among birds than of other forms of disease, probably because they are more amenable to field study. Comparatively simple methods have been devised for collecting ectoparasites from live birds (Williamson, 1954). Rothschild and Clay (1952) have written an excellent account of the varied relationships of fleas and Mallophaga with birds. Miles and Stoker (1948) and Surrey-Dane *et al.* (1953) reported a virus epizootic among adult Manx shearwaters (*Puffinus puffinus*); psittacosis is known to have killed large numbers of fulmars in Iceland in the 1930's, "but there is no evidence that it has made any serious difference to the actual fulmar population" (Miles and Shrivastav, 1951); and there are many other scattered references, especially in the literature on game birds.

Lack (1954a) concluded, perhaps rightly, that disease is most commonly a secondary rather than a primary cause of death among wild birds; nevertheless we should heed McDiarmid (1956), who, after stating that tuberculosis and aspergillosis seemed to be the most prevalent diseases among wild birds, complained that "the ecologist is . . . too often inclined to . . . attribute mortality and fluctuations in populations to such factors as availability of food, weather conditions and predation."

2. *Predation*

To review adequately the effects of man's predation on birds and his subsequent efforts at conservation and management would demand a volume unto itself. Man has to be considered as one of many density-dependent causes of mortality among birds. Predation by man may reduce the intensity of other causes of mortality, so that the population is not necessarily depleted by his activities: Hickey (1955), for instance, concluded that hunting "does not appear to exert a generally depressive effect on most galliform populations in America." Those concerned with the conservation of wildfowl may feel differently, however. The reader is referred to Cott's (1953) comprehensive account of man's exploitation of wild birds for their eggs for another aspect of this problem.

The impact of predators other than man on bird populations has been measured only for one or two species. Bump *et al.* (1947) calculated that 80% of the mortality of adult and yearling ruffed grouse was caused by predators (notably by owls, hawks, and foxes). Since half the population of grouse died each year, the predators were evidently taking around 40% of all the adults and yearlings—a remarkably high proportion. On the other hand, the virtual elimination of predators from certain American preserves has not resulted in a permanent increase in the density of gallinaceous birds (references in Hickey, 1955).

In the Netherlands, Tinbergen (1946) estimated (a) the proportion of the populations of several species of song-birds eaten by sparrow hawks in the month of May, and (b) the proportion of the total mortality of each of these species that the hawks' predation represented. His estimates include the following species of prey: chaffinch (a) 3%, (b) 30%; house sparrow (*Passer domesticus*) (a) 8%, (b) 79%; great tit (a) 6%, (b) 44%; coal tit (a) 2%, (b) 15%. These data are valuable chiefly because they are unique.

See also Section V, D (Cycles) for further observations on predation of birds.

3. *Starvation*

Lack (1954a) has argued convincingly that starvation is probably the most widespread density-dependent cause of death among wild birds. This need not imply that more birds die from starvation than from other causes; nor even that mortality from starvation is always density-dependent. For mortality from starvation to be density-dependent there must be intraspecific competition for a limited food supply. It is a commonplace that birds are generally most numerous where their food is most plentiful, and there is good evidence that many birds die of starvation; but it is extraordinarily difficult to prove or disprove intraspecific competition for food, and relevant observations are consequently scarce.

The reality of competition for food *between* species has been amply demonstrated. Thus the hypothesis developed by Gause (1934), that no two species of animals with identical requirements can survive together in the same habitat, has been widely confirmed among birds. Gause's hypothesis has been variously interpreted and misinterpreted, and perhaps too glibly accepted at times—as discussed generally by Macfadyen (1957), and with reference to the New World warblers (*Dendroica* spp.) by MacArthur (1958). As a rule, each species of one community occupies a distinct niche in that community, in which it excels above all other species. In the rich avifauna of Tropical Africa,

Moreau (1948) could detect little or no interspecific competition: virtually all the species occurring in the same habitat differed from each other in habit, particularly in their feeding habits. Again, in English broad-leaved woodland, five members of the genus *Parus* live side by side: superficially alike and with similar ethology (Hinde, 1952), while in winter all may be found foraging in the same flock, yet the food and feeding habits of each species are recognizably distinct (Hartley, 1953; Gibb, 1954; Betts, 1955). Even when two or more species feed together on the same food they may still evade competition: thus, in Britain two waders (*Arenaria interpres* and *Calidris maritima*) and a passerine (*Anthus spinoletta*) habitually feed together on the small periwinkle (*Littorina neritoides*) in winter; but each species selects periwinkles of a different size (Gibb, 1956a).

It is often difficult to know exactly what to look for when seeking to detect intraspecific competition for food among birds in the field. If birds fight for food and die from starvation, it is reasonable enough to suggest that they are competing and that their mortality will probably be density-dependent. In Britain, tits as well as corvids fight for food, especially in winter when they are most likely to be short of it (Hinde, 1952; Gibb, 1954; Lockie, 1956). But competition for food is usually more subtle than this. Birds are equally competing whenever the presence of one individual reduced the feeding efficiency of another: the first bird may already have eaten an item of food that the second bird would otherwise have found, or its presence may merely distract or deter the other bird.

Apart from distractions involving the behavior of the birds, we may surmise that competition for food will not be severe unless the birds are together destroying a reasonably substantial proportion of the available supply, or are occupying all or most of the available feeding places. Measurements of the impact of birds on their stocks of food are therefore extremely relevant in assessing competition.

Tinbergen's (1946) observations, mentioned earlier, suggested that sparrow hawks killed over 8% of the total population of house sparrows in May alone. As sparrow hawks kill sparrows throughout the year, they must destroy a substantial part of the sparrow population and so may compete for the available supply.

Southern (quoted in Lack, 1954a) estimated that tawny owls accounted for between a quarter and a half of all the deaths of two species of voles occurring in a whole year, in a mixed broad-leaved wood in Britain. Many of the owls were thought to have died of starvation; and as they must have competed for the voles, which were a staple food in their diet, their mortality may well have been density-dependent.

In English pine plantations the density of insectivorous birds, notably tits, varies from year to year with the abundance of their food in winter. Quantitative measurements both of the bird and of the insect populations show that in some winters the tits indeed eat a very substantial part of their total stock of food; and regularly eat more than 50% of the stock of certain desirable items in their diet, such as the larvae of the eucosmid moth *Ernarmonia conicolana* (Heyl.) (Fig. 4), for which intraspecific competition must be intense (Gibb, 1958, and in press).

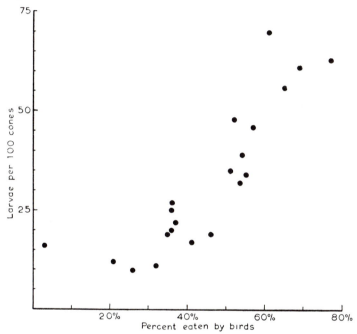

Fig. 4. The percentage of larvae of the eucosmid moth *Ernarmonia conicolana* (Heyl.) eaten by blue and coal tits (*Parus caeruleus* and *P. ater*) in the winter of 1955–1956. Each plot in the figure represents a different locality in Thetford Chase, East Anglia. The larvae spend the winter in the cones of Scots pines (*Pinus sylvestris*). Note that the more numerous the larvae, the larger the proportion eaten by the tits. After Gibb (1958).

Little has been published concerning the impact of bird predation on vegetable foods; and where this has been done the results have been more often measured in economic than in biological terms (cf. Hartley, 1954). Even without precise measurements, however, it is obvious that in Britain thrushes (*Turdus* spp.) often completely strip the crops of certain berries and that many of them die of starvation. With such competition their mortality is likely to be strongly density-dependent.

The foregoing examples emphasize the reality of competition for food in the lives of many birds. Though the evidence must still be regarded as inconclusive, it does suggest that most bird populations may be ultimately controlled by food shortage rather than by other causes of density-dependent mortality.

VII. The Territorial Behavior of Birds as a Possible Regulating Mechanism

Whatever the most important causes of density-dependent mortality among birds, there is clearly strong survival value for them to limit the densities of their populations. Birds, in common with most other organisms, do not become unduly crowded together—as individuals, colonies, or flocks—nor are they distributed entirely at random; instead, they are often "over-dispersed" (in the sense used by Hinde, 1956). It is instructive to consider how birds achieve this state of overdispersion.

A. In the Breeding Season

Howard (1920) believed that the territorial behavior of birds prevented overcrowding, chiefly in the breeding season. This has been disputed, but the weight of evidence still seems to support Howard's belief (e.g. Hinde, 1956; Tinbergen, 1957). Territorial and nonterritorial birds are alike distributed approximately in accordance with the abundance of their food supply. This and the fact that English robins, which are territorial, sometimes do succeed in settling in an area in the face of opposition, led Lack (1954a) to believe "that in both territorial and colonial species, dispersion is primarily due to the avoidance of occupied or crowded ground by potential settlers, not to the aggressive behaviour of those in occupation."

But consider a bird looking for somewhere to settle in spring, which will be guided by natural selection to whatever place offers the best prospects for breeding. In sampling the available ground it will tend to favor rich habitats but to avoid crowded ones: hence, as Kluyver and Tinbergen (1953) pointed out, its final decision will result from a compromise between these two normally conflicting ideals. If however the decision rests solely with the intending settler, then the birds should eventually become distributed so that the prospects for breeding are similar in every accessible habitat: the intrinsic richness of one habitat would be countered by its dense population, and the poorness of another by its sparse population. But the prospects for breeding are emphatically not similar in different habitats. Thus great and blue tits,

which are typically species of broad-leaved woodland, are conspicuously
unsuccessful when they attempt to breed in English pine plantations:
their nestlings often die of starvation in the pines but rarely do so
in broad-leaved woods (Lack, 1955, 1958), and those young that do
leave the nests in the pines are so underweight that they can have
little chance of surviving (Gibb, unpublished). Here is a clear indication that birds do not always settle where the prospects for breeding
are best, but are often compelled, presumably by the aggressive

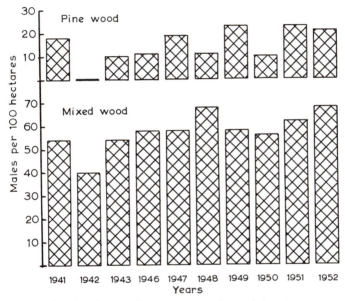

FIG. 5. The density of male great tits (*Parus major*) in adjoining pine and mixed broad-
leaved woods in the Hoge Veluwe, Netherlands; the pine woods were much more extensive than the mixed woods. Note that the population changes were proportionately
much greater in the rather poor pine woods than in the richer mixed woods. After
Kluyver and Tinbergen (1953).

territorial behavior of those already occupying the richer habitats, to
resort to less favorable sites. This is understandable since it is as much
to the advantage of established birds to keep out newcomers as it is
to the advantage of would-be settlers to avoid crowded places; indeed,
we may incline to agree with Tinbergen (1957) that "both attack and
escape are involved, further that a certain balanced proportion of the
strengths of these two opposite tendencies is essential, and has been
selected for."

Further evidence of the action of territorial behavior is provided by
Kluyver and Tinbergen's (1953) observations in two separate localities,

each consisting of a rich broad-leaved wood and poorer pine plantations. The number of great and blue tits in the rich habitat remained relatively steady from year to year, while their density in the adjacent pines fluctuated markedly (Fig. 5) (cf. also Hamerstrom and Hamerstrom, 1955). Huxley (1934) likened the territories of birds to rubber disks whose area is compressible, but only with increasing pressure as their area diminishes. These observations suggest that there is a size below which the territories are hardly further compressible. The average territory size for each species is presumably a product of natural selection and may be at least partly dictated by the normal resources of the environment.

B. At Other Seasons

Tinbergen (1957) discerned that the advantages of territorial behavior are of two kinds, resulting (1) from attachment to a familiar site, and (2) from the exclusion of others of the same species; and that either can occur without the other. Many of the suggested advantages of territorial behavior under either heading could apply with as great force in winter as in the breeding season: familiarity with one area may be important in finding food (Southern, 1954), shelter from the weather, and cover from predators; and limitation of density may enable each bird to secure enough of these resources and may impede the spread of disease organisms.

The significance of territorial behavior in winter has been much neglected (e.g. Hinde, 1956), though its recurrence in autumn is a commonplace of observation among many species of birds (Morley, 1943). Indeed, it can be argued with some justification that many birds maintain territories for just so long as their economy permits. If the individuals or pairs cannot defend territories in winter as in spring, they may still be faithful to one area, and so retain the advantages of living in a familiar area, while foregoing those resulting from the exclusion of others of the same species from that area.

Except perhaps in the Tropics, most birds have two seasons of special stress, namely the breeding season and the winter, when they are so busy searching for food that they have little time for other activities (Gibb, 1954, 1956a). They must therefore secure suitable breeding or winter quarters well in advance of these crucial periods; hence it is no argument against the value of territories that active territorial defense is relaxed at the height of these seasons (Tinbergen, 1957).

Some species or some individuals can keep to the same territory throughout the year; other species or individuals spend the winter in the same district in which they bred or were reared, but have to forage over an area too extensive to defend, but which usually includes the former territory; while yet other species or individuals must forage over such an extensive area in winter that the former territory seems to be of no consequence to them. Every gradation is shown within the genus *Parus*, from the strictly sedentary plain tits (*P. inornatus*) of North America, which keep to the same territories all the year, to the blue tits of Continental Europe, which are long-distance migrants and are territorial only in the breeding season (references in Gibb, 1956b; Dixon, 1956). A few species contrive to combine territorial behavior out of the breeding season with extensive foraging: thus desert chats (*Oenanthe* spp.) set up temporary territories, in which they feed and from which they exclude their congeners, wherever they happen to be while on migration (Hartley, 1949; Simmons, 1951; cf. Pitelka, 1942).

C. Conclusion

Territorial behavior displayed in spring and autumn may effectively restrict the population density of some species during the ensuing periods of stress. Although territorial behavior is most evident in spring in anticipation of the breeding season, autumn territorial behavior in anticipation of the winter could have as great survival value for some species. If territories are not perfectly compressible and if territorial behavior really limits the density especially in rich habitats, then a proportion of the population will presumably be forced into less suitable habitats, where they will be able to rear fewer young and will have less good chances of survival than those in the rich habitats. Moreover, since the proportion of the population forced into the poorer habitats will probably be greater the higher the population, the resulting mortality will be density-dependent and could therefore contribute substantially to the stability of the population.

References

Allee, W. C., Emerson, A. E., Park, O., Park, T., and Schmidt, K. P. (1949). "Principles of Animal Ecology," chapter 23. Saunders, Philadelphia and London.

Andrewartha, H. G., and Birch, L. C. (1954). "The Distribution and Abundance of Animals." Univ. Chicago Press, Chicago, Illinois.

Austin, O. L. (1953). A Common Tern at least 23 years old. *Bird-Banding* **24**: 20.

Bailey, N. T. J. (1951). On estimating the size of mobile populations from recapture data. *Biometrika* **38**: 293–306.

Bailey, N. T. J. (1952). Improvements in the interpretation of recapture data. *J. Animal Ecol.* **21**: 120–127.

Bendell, J. F. (1955). Disease as a control of a population of Blue Grouse *Dendragapus obscurus fuliginosus* (Ridgway). *Can. J. Zool.* **33**: 195–223.

Betts, M. M. (1955). The food of titmice in oak woodland. *J. Animal Ecol.* **24**: 282–323.

Bourlière, F. (1946). Longévité moyenne et longévité maximum chez les vertébrés. *Années Biologiques* **22**: 249–270.

Boyd, H. (1956). Statistics of the British population of the Pink-footed Goose. *J. Animal Ecol.* **25**: 253–273.

Bump, G., Darrow, R. W., Edminster, F. C., and Crissey, W. F. (1947). "The Ruffed Grouse. Life History, Propagation, Management." N.Y. State Conservation Dept., Albany, New York.

Cairns, J. (1956). The Malayan Great Tit. *J. Bombay Nat. Hist. Soc.* **53**: 367–373.

Capildeo, R., and Haldane, J. B. S. (1954). The mathematics of bird population growth and decline. *J. Animal Ecol.* **23**: 215–223.

Chapin, J. P. (1946). Wideawake Fair invaded. *Nat. Hist.* **1946**: 313–319.

Chitty, D. (1952). Mortality among voles (*Microtus agrestis*) at Lake Vyrnwy, Montgomeryshire in 1936–9. *Phil. Trans.* (B) **236**: 505–552.

Chitty, D. (1957). Self-regulation of numbers through changes in viability. *Cold Spring Harbor Symposia on Quantitative Biology* **22**: 277–280.

Cott, H. B. (1953–1954). The exploitation of wild birds for their eggs. *Ibis* **95**: 409–449, 643–675; **96**: 129–149.

Davis, D. E. (1955). Determinate laying in Barn Swallows and Black-billed Magpies. *Condor* **57**: 81–87.

Dixon, K. L. (1956). Territoriality and survival in the Plain Titmouse. *Condor* **58**: 169–182.

Drost, R., and Hartmann, G. (1949). Hohes Alter einer Population des Austernfischers *Haematopus o. ostralegus* L. *Vogelwarte* **2**: 102–104.

Einarsen, A. S. (1945). Some factors affecting Ring-necked Pheasant population density. *Murrelet* **26**: 39–44.

Elton, C., and Nicholson, M. (1942). The ten-year cycle in numbers of the Lynx in Canada. *J. Animal Ecol.* **11**: 215–244.

Elton, C. S. (1958). "The ecology of invasions by animals and plants." Methuen, London.

Emlen, J. T. (1940). Sex and age ratios in survival of the California Quail. *J. Wildlife Management* **4**: 92–99.

Errington, P. L. (1945). Some contributions of a fifteen-year local study of the Northern Bobwhite to a knowledge of population phenomena. *Ecol. Monographs* **15**: 1–34.

Farner, D. S. (1955). Birdbanding in the study of population dynamics. *In* "Recent Studies in Avian Biology" (A. Wolfson, ed.), pp. 397–449. Univ. Illinois Press, Urbana, Illinois.

Fisher, J. (1946). "Watching Birds." Penguin Books, Harmondsworth, Middlesex, and New York.

Fisher, J. (1952). A history of the Fulmar *Fulmarus* and its population problems. *Ibis* **94**: 334–354.

Fisher, J. (1953). The Collared Turtle Dove in Europe. *Brit. Birds* **46**: 153–181.

Fisher, J., and Lockley, R. M. (1954). "Sea Birds." Collins, London.

Fisher, J., and Vevers, H. G. (1943–1944). The breeding distribution, history and population of the North Atlantic gannet (*Sula bassana*). *J. Animal Ecol.* **12**: 173–213; **13**:49–62.

Fisher, J., and Vevers, H. G. (1951). The present population of the North Atlantic gannet (*Sula bassana*). *Proc. 10th Intern. Ornithol. Congr. Uppsala* 1950 pp. 463–467.

Frith, H. J. (1956). Breeding habits in the family Megapodiidae. *Ibis* **98**: 620–640.

Gause, G. F. (1934). "The Struggle for Existence." Williams & Wilkins, Baltimore, Maryland.

Gibb, J. (1950). The breeding biology of the Great and Blue Titmice. *Ibis* **92**: 507–539.

Gibb, J. (1954). Feeding ecology of tits, with notes on Treecreeper and Goldcrest. *Ibis* **96**: 513–543.

Gibb, J. (1955). Feeding rates of Great Tits. *Brit. Birds* **48**: 49–58.

Gibb, J. (1956a). Food, feeding habits and territory of the Rock Pipit *Anthus spinoletta*. *Ibis* **98**: 506–530.

Gibb, J. (1956b). Territory in the genus *Parus*. *Ibis* **98**: 420–429.

Gibb, J. A. (1958). Predation by tits and squirrels on the eucosmid *Ernarmonia conicolana* (Heyl.). *J. Animal Ecol.* **27**: 375–396.

Gibb, J. A. (in press). Populations of tits and Goldcrests and their food supply in pine plantations. *Ibis*.

Glading, B., Selleck, D. M., and Ross, F. T. (1945). Valley Quail under private management at the Dune Lakes club. *Calif. Fish & Game* **31**: 166–183.

Greenway, J. C. (1958). "Extinct and Vanishing Birds of the World." Special Publication No. 13, American Committee for International Wild Life Protection, New York.

Grimshaw, H. M., Ovington, J. D., Betts, M. M., and Gibb, J. A. (1958). The mineral content of birds and insects in plantations of *Pinus sylvestris* L. *Oikos* **9**: 26–34.

Hamerstrom, F., and Hamerstrom, F. (1955). Population density and behaviour in Wisconsin Prairie Chickens (*Tympanuchus cupido pinnatus*). *Proc. 11th Intern. Ornithol. Congr. Basel* 1954 pp. 459–466.

Hartley, P. H. T. (1949). The biology of the Mourning Chat in winter quarters. *Ibis* **91**: 393–413.

Hartley, P. H. T. (1953). An ecological study of the feeding habits of English titmice. *J. Animal Ecol.* **22**: 261–288.

Hartley, P. H. T. (1954). Wild fruits in the diet of British thrushes. A study in the ecology of closely allied species. *Brit. Birds* **47**: 97–107.

Herman, C. M. (1955). Diseases of birds. *In* "Recent Studies in Avian Biology" (A. Wolfson, ed.), pp. 450–467. Univ. Illinois Press, Urbana, Illinois.

Hickey, J. J. (1955). Some American population research in gallinaceous birds. *In* "Recent Studies in Avian Biology" (A. Wolfson, ed.), pp. 326–396. Univ. Illinois Press, Urbana, Illinois.

Hinde, R. A. (1952). The behaviour of the Great Tit (*Parus major*) and some other related species. *Behaviour Suppl.* **2**: 1–201.

Hinde, R. A. (1956). The biological significance of the territories of birds. *Ibis* **98**:340–369.

Hoffmann, R. S. (1958). The role of predators in "cyclic" declines of grouse populations. *J. Wildlife Management* **22**: 317–319.

Hofstetter, F. B. (1954). Untersuchungen an einer Population der Türkentaube. *J. Ornithol.* **95**: 348–410.

Howard, H. E. (1920). "Territory in Bird Life." Murray, London.

Huxley, J. S. (1934). A natural experiment on the territorial instinct. *Brit. Birds* **27**: 270–277.

Jenkins, D. (1957). Chick survival in a Partridge population. *Animal Health* **7**: 6–10.

Jungfer, W. (1954). Ueber Paartreue, Nestplatztreue und Alter der Austernfischer (*Haematopus o. ostralegus*) auf Mellum. *Vogelwarte* **17**: 6–15.

Kendeigh, S. C. (1952). Parental care and its evolution in birds. *Illinois Biol. Monographs* **22**: 1–356.

Kluijver, H. N. (1951). The population ecology of the Great Tit, *Parus m. major* L. *Ardea* **39**: 1–135.

Kluyver, H. N., and Tinbergen, L. (1953). Territory and the regulation of density in titmice. *Arch. néerl. zool.* **10**: 265–289.

Kluyver, H. N. (1957). Roosting habits, sexual dominance and survival in the Great Tit. *Cold Spring Harbor Symposia on Quantitative Biology* **22**: 281–285.

Lack, D. (1947–1948). The significance of clutch-size. *Ibis* **89**: 302–352; **90**: 25–45.

Lack, D. (1952). Reproduction rate and population density in the Great Tit: Kluijver's study. *Ibis* **94**: 167–173.

Lack, D. (1954a). "The Natural Regulation of Animal Numbers." Oxford Univ. Press, London and New York.

Lack, D. (1954b). The stability of the Heron population. *Brit. Birds* **47**: 111–119.

Lack, D. (1955). British Tits (*Parus* spp.) in nesting boxes. *Ardea* **43**: 50–84.

Lack, D. (1956a). Variations in the reproductive rate of birds. *Proc. Roy. Soc.* **B145**: 329–333.

Lack, D. (1956b). "Swifts in a Tower." Methuen, London.

Lack, D. (1958). A quantitative breeding study of British tits. *Ardea* **46**: 91–124.

Lack. D., and Arn, H. (1953). Die mittlere Lebensdauer des Alpenseglers. *Ornithol. Beobachter* **50**: 133–137.

Lack, D., Gibb, J., and Owen, D. F. (1957). Survival in relation to brood-size in tits. *Proc. Zool. Soc. London* **128**: 313–326.

Lack, D., and Schifferli, A. (1948). Die Lebensdauer des Stares. *Ornithol. Beobachter* **45**: 107–114.

Leopold, A. (1933). "Game Management." Scribner, New York.

Lockie. J. D. (1955). The breeding and feeding of Jackdaws and Rooks, with notes on Carrion Crows and other Corvidae. *Ibis* **97**: 341–369.

Lockie, J. D. (1956). Winter fighting in feeding flocks of Rooks, Jackdaws and Carrion Crows. *Bird Study* **3**: 180–190.

Lockley, R. M. (1953). On the movements of the Manx Shearwater at sea during the breeding season. *Brit. Birds* **46**: *Suppl.* 1–48.

Lovat, Lord (1912). Moor management. *In* "The Grouse in Health and in Disease" (A. S. Leslie, ed.), pp. 321–342. Smith and Elder, London.

MacArthur, R. H. (1958). Population ecology of some warblers of northeastern coniferous forests. *Ecology* **39**: 599–619.

McDiarmid, A. (1956). Some diseases of free-living wild birds in Britain. *Bull. Brit. Ornithol. Club* **76**: 145–150.

Macfadyen, A. (1957). "Animal Ecology, aims and methods." Pitman, London.

Marshall, A. J. (1949). Weather factors and spermatogenesis in birds. *Proc. Zool. Soc. London* **119**: 711–716.

Mayr, E. (1939). The sex ratio in wild birds. *Am. Naturalist* **73**: 156–179.

Merikallio, E. (1958). Finnish birds. Their distribution and numbers. *Fauna Fennica* **5**: 1–181.

Miles, J. A. R., and Shrivastav, J. B. (1951). Ornithosis in certain sea-birds. *J. Animal Ecol.* **20**: 195–200.

Miles, J. A. R., and Stoker, M. G. P. (1948). Puffinosis, a virus epizootic of the Manx Shearwater (*Puffinus p. puffinus*). *Nature* **161**: 1016–1017.

Moltoni, E. (1947). Fringuello vissuto in schiavitu per ben 29 anni. *Riv. ital. ornithol.* **17**: 139.

Moran, P. A. P. (1954). The statistical analysis of game-bird records. II. *J. Animal Ecol.* **23**: 35–37.

Moreau, R. E. (1947). Relations between number in brood, feeding-rate and nestling period in nine species of birds in Tanganyika Territory. *J. Animal Ecol.* **16**: 205–209.

Moreau, R. E. (1948). Ecological isolation in a rich tropical avifauna. *J. Animal Ecol.* **17**: 113–126.

Moreau, R. E. (1950). The breeding seasons of African birds. *Ibis* **92**: 223–267, 419–433.

Morley, A. (1943). Sexual behaviour in British birds from October to January. *Ibis* **85**: 132–158.

Morris, R. F. (1955). The development of sampling techniques for forest insect defoliators, with particular reference to the spruce budworm. *Can. J. Zool.* **33**: 225–294.

Neff, J. A. (1945). Maggot infestation of nestling Mourning Doves. *Condor* **47**: 73–76.

Nice, M. M. (1957). Nesting success in altricial birds. *Auk* **74**: 305–321.

Nicholson, A. J. (1933). The balance of animal populations. *J. Animal Ecol.* **2**: 132–178.

Nicholson, A. J., and Bailey, V. A. (1935). The balance of animal populations. *Proc. Zool. Soc. London* **1935**: 551–598.

Nicholson, E. M. (1959). Bird numbers in Finland: a bold effort towards estimating a nation's avifauna. *Brit. Birds* **52**: 22–30.

Nordberg, S. (1948). Ein Vergleich zwischen Probeflächenmethode und Linientaxierungsmethode bei quantitativen Aufnahmen des Vogelbestandes. *Ornis Fennica* **24**: 87–92.

Owen, D. F. (1954). Protocalliphora in birds nests. *Brit. Birds* **47**: 236–243.

Palmgren, P. (1949). Some remarks on the short-term fluctuations in the numbers of northern birds and mammals. *Oikos* **1**: 114–121.

Park, T. (1948). Experimental studies of interspecies competition. 1. Competition between populations of the flour beetles, *Tribolium confusum* Duval and *Tribolium castaneum* Herbst. *Ecol. Monographs* **18**: 265–307.

Pitelka, F. A. (1942). Territoriality and related problems in North American hummingbirds. *Condor* **44**: 189–204.

Reinikainen, A. (1937). The irregular migrations of the Crossbill, *Loxia c. curvirostra*, and their relation to the cone-crop of the conifers. *Ornis Fennica* **14**: 55–64.

Richdale, L. E. (1951). "Sexual Behaviour in Penguins." Kansas Univ. Press, Lawrence, Kansas.

Richdale, L. E. (1952). Post-egg period in albatrosses. *Biological Monographs* **4**: 1–166 (private publication by the author, Dunedin, New Zealand).

Richdale, L. E. (1957). "A Population Study of Penguins." Oxford Univ. Press London and New York.

Rothschild, M., and Clay, T. (1952). "Fleas, Flukes, and Cuckoos. A Study of Bird Parasites." Collins, London.

Rudebeck, G. (1950–1951). The choice of prey and modes of hunting of predatory birds with special reference to their selective effect. *Oikos* **2**: 65–88; **3**: 200–231.

Schmidt, K., and Hantge, E. (1954). Studien an einer farbig beringten Population des Braunkehlchens (*Saxicola rubetra*). *J. Ornithol.* **95**: 130–173.

Schorger, A. W. (1942). The Wild Turkey in Wisconsin. *Wilson Bull.* **54**: 173–182.

Schüz, E. (1940). Bewegungen im Bestand des weissen Storches seit 1934. *Ornithol. Monatsber.* **48**: 1–14.

Siivonen, L. (1941). Über die Kausalzusammenhänge der Wanderungen beim Seidenschwanz *Bombycilla g. garrulus* (L.). *Ann. Zool. Soc. Zool.-Botan. Fennicae Vanamo* **8**: 1–38.

Simmons, K. E. L. (1951). Interspecific territorialism. *Ibis* **93**: 407–413.

Skutch, A. F. (1949). Do tropical birds rear as many young as they can nourish? *Ibis* **91**: 430–455.

Snow, D. W. (1956). The annual mortality of the Blue Tit in different parts of its range. *Brit. Birds* **49**: 174–177.

Snow, D. W. (1958). The breeding of the Blackbird *Turdus merula* at Oxford. *Ibis* **100**: 1–30.

Southern, H. N. (1954). Tawny Owls and their prey. *Ibis* **96**: 384–410.

Southern, H. N., Vaughan, R., and Muir, R. C. (1954). The behaviour of young Tawny Owls after fledging. *Bird Study* **1**: 101–110.

Stonehouse, B. (1956). The King Penguin of South Georgia. *Nature* **178**: 1424–1426.

Stonehouse, B. (1958). Letter from Ascension Island dated 15 July 1958. *Ibis* **100**: 643–645.

Surrey-Dane, D., Miles, J. A. R., and Stoker, M. G. P. (1953). A disease of Manx Shearwaters: further observations in the field. *J. Animal Ecol.* **22**: 123–133.

Svärdson, G. (1957). The "invasion" type of bird migration. *Brit. Birds* **50**: 314–343.

Thiele, H. (1958). Die Vogelbestände zweier Waldtypen des Bergischen Landes. *Waldhygiene* **2**: 201–223.

Thomson, A. L. (1950). Factors determining the breeding season of birds: an introductory review. *Ibis* **92**: 173–182.

Tinbergen, L. (1946). De Sperwer als roofvijand van Zangvogels. *Ardea* **34**: 1–213.

Tinbergen, N. (1957). The functions of territory. *Bird Study* **4**: 14–27.

Turček, F. J. (1956). On the bird population of the spruce forest community in Slovakia. *Ibis* **98**: 24–33.

Turček, F. J. (1957). The bird succession in the conifer plantations on mat-grass land in Slovakia (CSR). *Ibis* **99**: 587–593.

Udvardy, M. D. F. (1957). An evaluation of quantitative studies in birds. *Cold Spring Harbor Symposia on Quantitative Biology* **22**: 301–311.

Varley, G. C. (1947). The natural control of population balance in the Knapweed Gallfly (*Orophora jaceana*). *J. Animal Ecol.* **16**: 139–187.

Wagner, H. O. (1957). Variation in clutch size at different latitudes. *Auk* **74**: 243–250.

Walker, E. A. (1949). Factors influencing Wild Turkey. *Texas Game Fish and Oyster Comm. FA Rept. Ser. No.* **4**: 1–20.

Weitnauer, E. (1956). Ein siebzehnjähriger Mauersegler. *Ornithol. Beobachter* **53**: 94.

Williams, G. R. (1954). Population fluctuations in some Northern Hemisphere game birds (*Tetraonidae*). *J. Animal Ecol.* **23**: 1–34.

Williams, G. R. (1957). Changes in the sex ratio occurring with age in young California Quail in Central Otago, New Zealand. *Bird-Banding* **28**: 145–150.

Williamson, K. (1954). The Fair Isle apparatus for collecting bird ectoparasites. *Brit. Birds* **47**: 234–235.

Witherby, H. F., Jourdain, F. C. R., Ticehurst, N. F., and Tucker, B. W. (1938–1941). "The Handbook of British Birds." Witherby, London.

Wynne-Edwards, V. C. (1955). Low reproductive rates in birds, especially sea-birds. *Proc. 11th Intern. Ornithol. Congr. Basel* 1954 pp. 540–547.

Yapp, W. B. (1956). The theory of line transects. *Bird Study* **3**: 93–104.

Author Index

A

Adams, J. L., 100, *112*
Albertin, R. H., 102, *113*
Albritton, E. C., 217, *279*
Alexander, C. J., 197, *204*
Allee, W. C., 190, 196, *204, 205, 210*, 432, *441*
Allen, A. A., 379, *407*
Amadon, D., 308, *332*
Amerlinck, A., 49, *54*
Andrew, R. J., 383, 384, 398, 407, *407*
Andrewartha, H. G., 429, 432, *441*
Andrews, F. N., 107, *114*
Armstrong, E. A., 374, 397, 399, *407*
Arn, H., 425, *444*
Arnsdorf, R. E., 129, *164*
Aron, C., 187, *205*
Aron, M., 187, *205*
Aschoff, J., 251, 269, 276, *279*, 328, *332*
Asmundson, V. S., 115, *164*
Asplin, F. D., 170, *205*
Assenmacher, I., 91, 102, *112*, 171, 173, *205*, 310, 314, 326, *333*
Atz, J. W., 171, *211*
Austin, O. L., 417, *441*
Aymar, G. C., *304*

B

Bacq, Z. M., 245, *279*
Bade, P. H., 224, *286*
Bailey, N. T. J., 415, *441*
Bailey, R. E., 94, *112*, 179, 180, 181, 199, 200, 204, *205*
Bailey, V. A., 430, *445*
Bajandurow, B. J., 47, *48*
Baker, I., 322, *332*
Baker, J. R., 116, *166*, 312, 313, 322, 323, 325, *332*
Baldwin, S. P., 249, 255, 258, 265, 266, 268, 270, *279, 284*
Barth, E. K., 265, 268, *279*
Bartholomew, G. A., 237, 249, 250, 251, 255, 258, 259, 262, 263, 266, 268, 269, 270, 274, 276, 277, 278, 279, *279, 283*
Barott, H. G., 217, 218, 223, 226, 245, 260, 263, *279*

Bates, R. W., 178, 179, 181, *205, 211, 212*
Bath, W., 41, *48*
Batrawi, A. M., 328, *338*
Bauer, K. F., 37, *48*
Baum, G. J., 176, *210*
Beach, F. A., 189, *205*, 325, *333*, 380, 406, *407*
Bendell, J. F., 425, 433, *442*
Benedict, F. G., 218, 220, 221, 222, 223, 224, 226, 228, 229, 242, 245, 249, 269, *280, 286*
Benjamins, C. E., 53, *54*
Bennet, M. A., 191, *205*
Benoit, J., 91, 102, 109, 112, *112*, 129, 139, 156, *164*, 171, 173, 174, 176, 188, 195, *205*, 310, 314, 326, *333*
Berlioz, J., 308, *333*
Bernard, R., 268, 273, 274, 275, *280*
Berthold, A. A., 187, *205*
Best, A. T., 278, *283*
Betts, M. M., 415, 436, *442, 443*
Biester, H. E., 380, *407*
Birch, L. C., 429, 432, *441*
Bissonnette, T. H., 310, 311, 318, 319, *333*
Bladergroen, W., 216, *280*
Blanchard, B. D., 318, 331, *333, 337*
Blest, A. D., 67, *68*
Blivaiss, B. B., 157, *164*, 190, *207*
Bloom, M. A., 204, *205*
Bloom, W., 204, *205*
Blum, H. F., 216, *280*
Blyth, J. S. S., 157, *165*, 192, *208*
Boeke, J., 37, 38, *48*
Boel, M., 303, *305*
Böni, A., 259, 265, 266, *280*
Bol, A. C., 384, *408*
Bolton, W., 197, *206*
Borbely, F., 242, *288*
Boss, W. R., 102, *112*, 132, 133, 135, 145, 149, *164*, 189, *206*
Botezat, E., 38, 39, 41, *48*
Boulière, F., 307, *333*, 417, *442*
Boyd, H., 406, *408*, 418, 425, *442*
Boyland, E., 170, *205*
Brant, J. W. A., 203, *206*
Brard, E., 173, *205*, 314, *333*
Brassard, J. A., 268, 273, 274, 275, *280*

447

Subject Index

A

Adaptation, radiative, 34
Adrenals, 88, 89, 93, *102*, 329
Attack, eye inhibition, 67

B

Beaks, bills, 2, 21, 89, 99, 107, 141, 195, 197, 315, 328, 406
Blood system
  arteries, 88
  blood calcium, 108, 109, 197
  blood phosphorus, 197
  blood pressure, 95, 106
  brood patch, 94, 180
  heart, 30, 88, 106
  red cell number, 98
  veins, 88
Behavior, 373
  alternation, 383
  ambivalent, 382, 399, 404, 407
  appetitive, 376, 391, 394
  brooding, 90, 94, 173, 178, 179, 181, 190, 196
  chain response, 384, 385
  common causal factors, 385
  compromise, 383
  conditioning, 388, 392
  consummatory behavior, 376
  consummatory stimuli, 380, 381
  copulation, 90, 190, 401
  counting, 392
  courtship, 90, 179, 181, 190, 325, 399 *et seq.*, 499
  displacement, 383, 402
  distraction display, 397
  diurnal changes, 380
  eliciting stimuli, 387, 395, 398, 406
  exploratory, 397
  external stimuli, 382, 398
  feeding, 386, 395
  fighting, 67, 189, 397, 398, 399
  fixed-action pattern, 375
  flocking, 312, 393
  functional aspects, 393
  habituation, 392, 396

hormones, 90, 98, 179, 181, 189, 190, 196, 312, 325, 328–330, 380, 398, 405, 406
imprinting, 389, 391, 406
incubation, 405, 406
inhibition, 382, 385
integration of partial patterns, 384, 406
intention movements, 383, 402
internal factors, 379, 398
internal sensory stimuli, 380
learning, 378, 385, 386, 387, 390, 391, 392, 405
mazes, 388
mobbing, 381, 382, 396
motor patterns, 376, 387, 390, 391, 395, 404
nesting, 90, 190, 196, 404
nutritional factors, 380
ontogeny, 386
orientation component, 375, 376
orienting stimuli, 390
pair formation 399 *et seq.*
parental, 405
predators, 396, 398
puzzle boxes, 388
reciprocal inhibition, 382
redirection activities, 383, 402
regression, 384
reinforcing effect of stimulus situations, 385
releasers, 377
selective responsiveness, 378
sign stimuli, 377, 389, 394, 395, 404, 406
social facilitation, 394
species—characteristic movements, 375, 386, 387, 404
stereotyped patterns, 375
successive induction, 382
territorialism, 90, 190, 197, 324, 397, 406, 438
voice, 190, 406
warning calls, 397
Brain, 1
  alar plate, 15, 19

459